DEATH NOTE

Black Edition
II

Story by Tsugumi Ohba   Art by Takeshi Obata

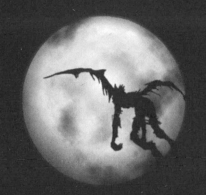

Original Graphic Novel Edition
Volume 3

Original Graphic Novel Edition
Volume 4

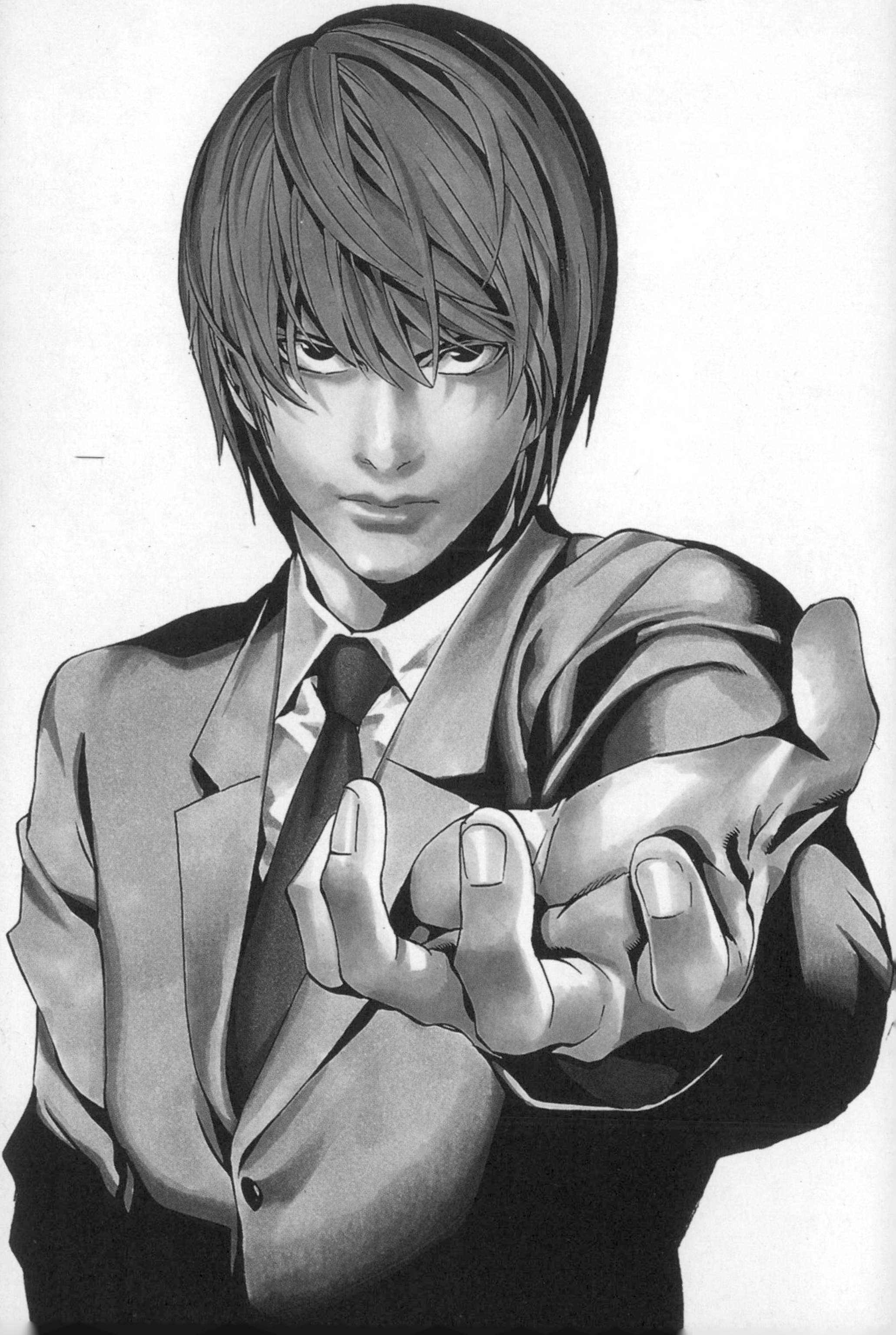

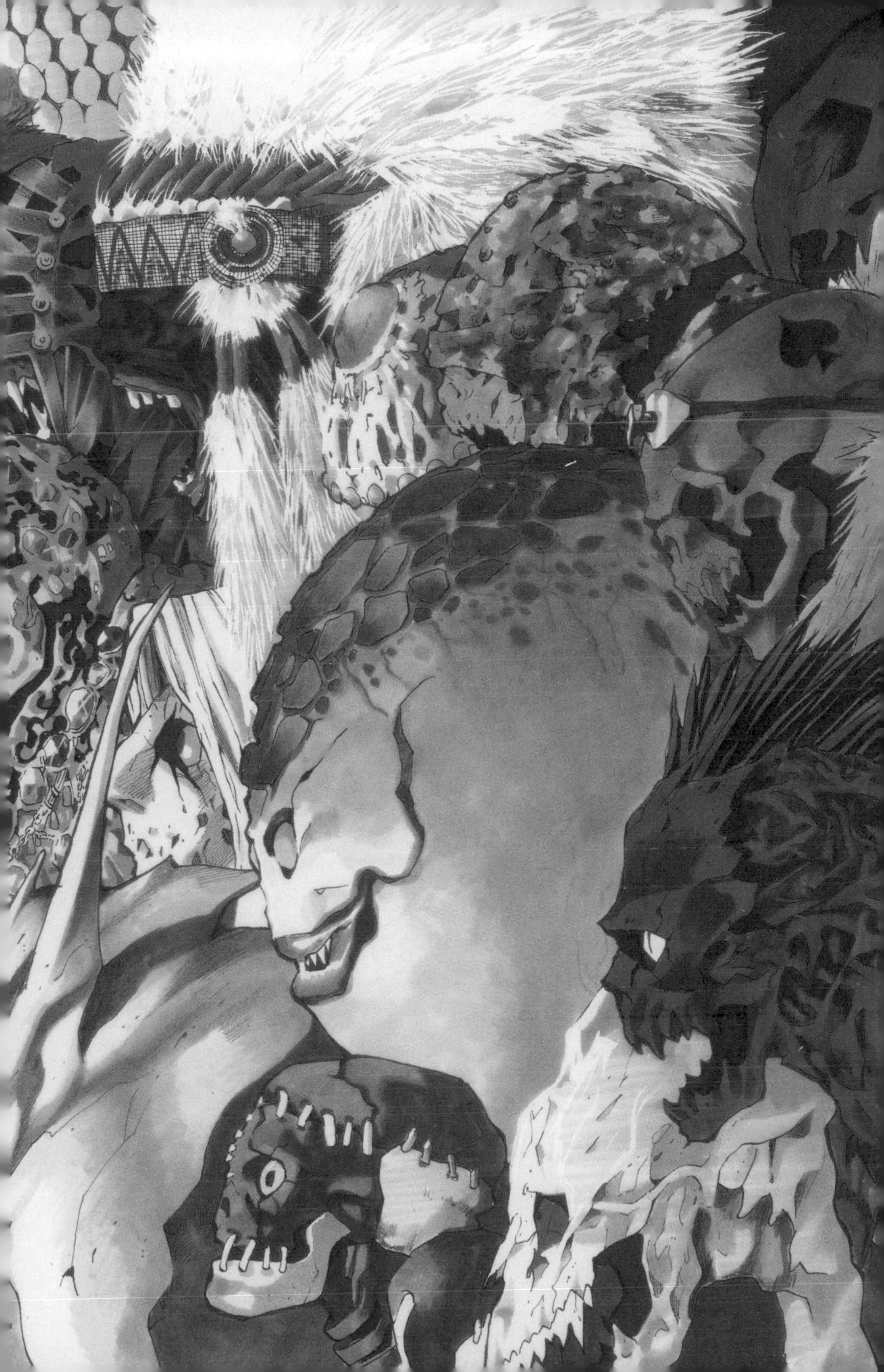

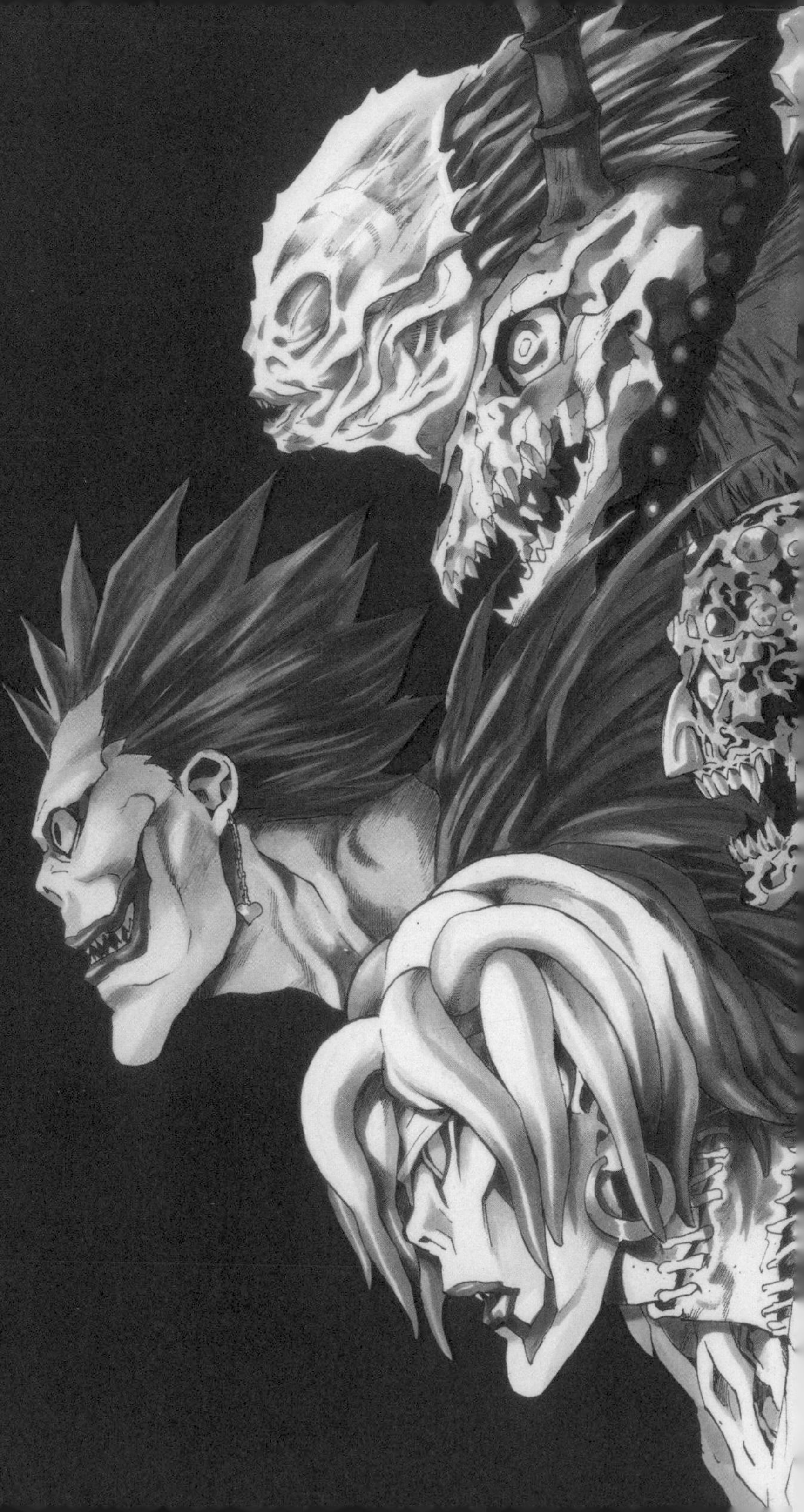

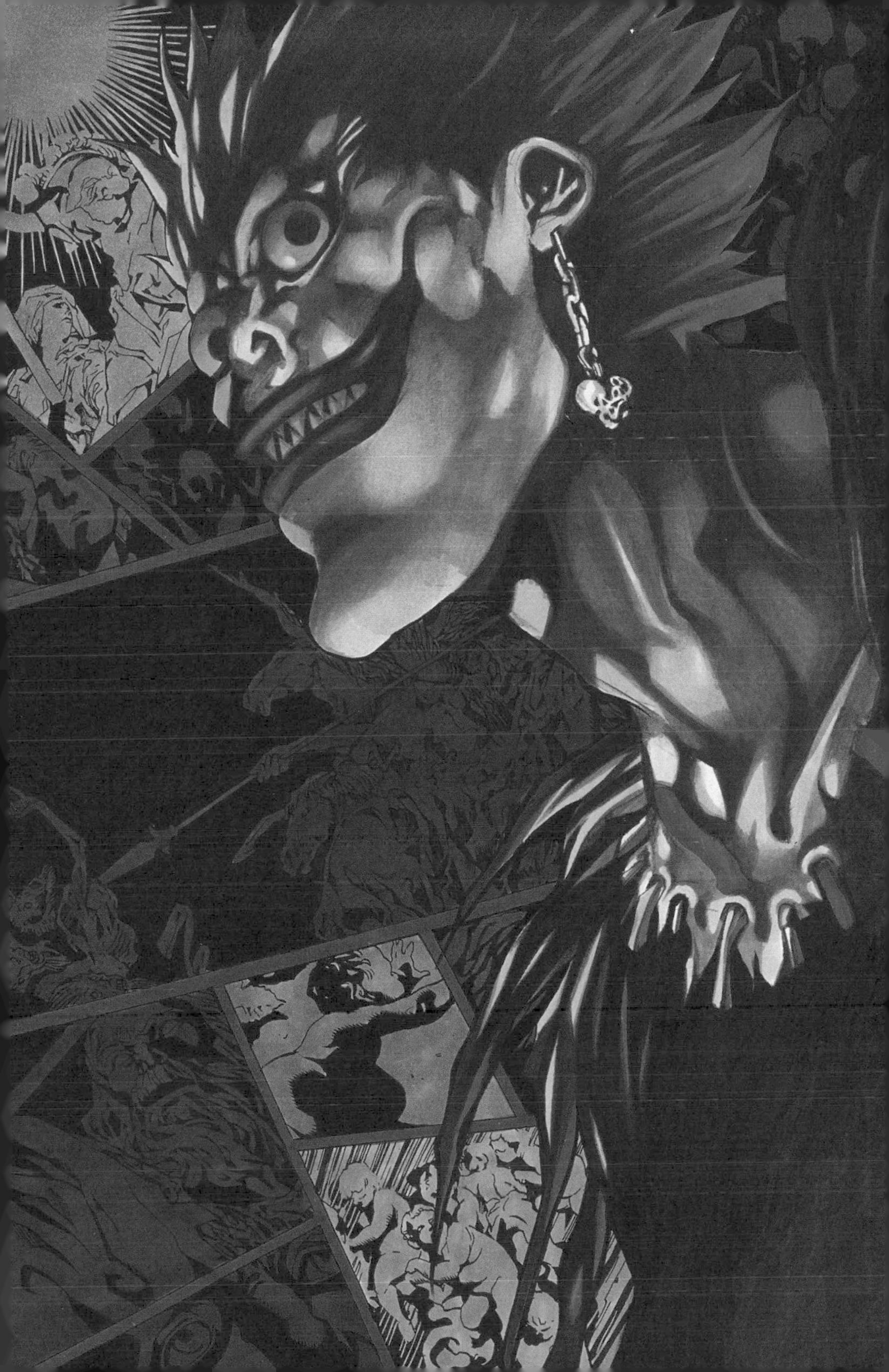

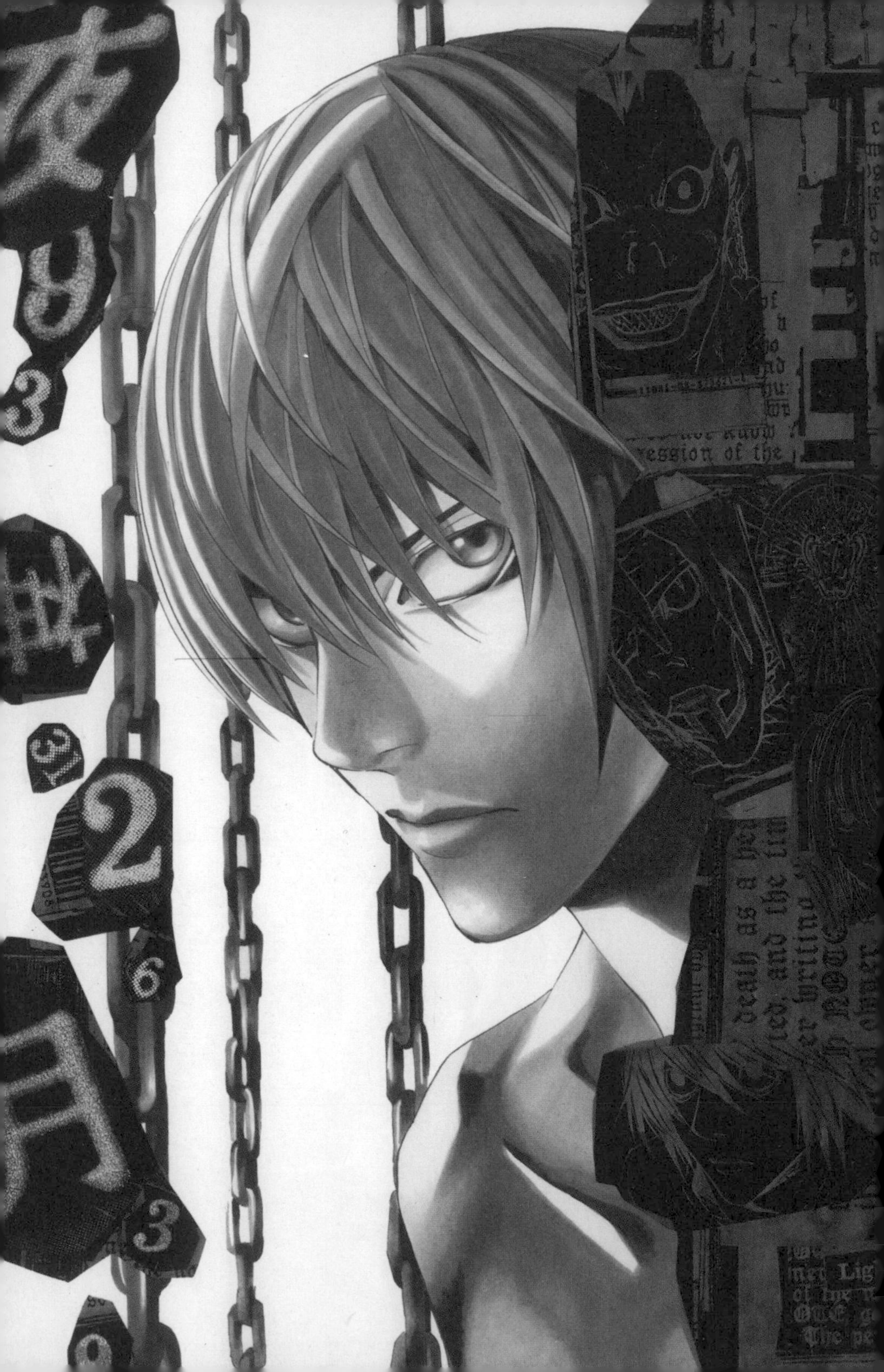

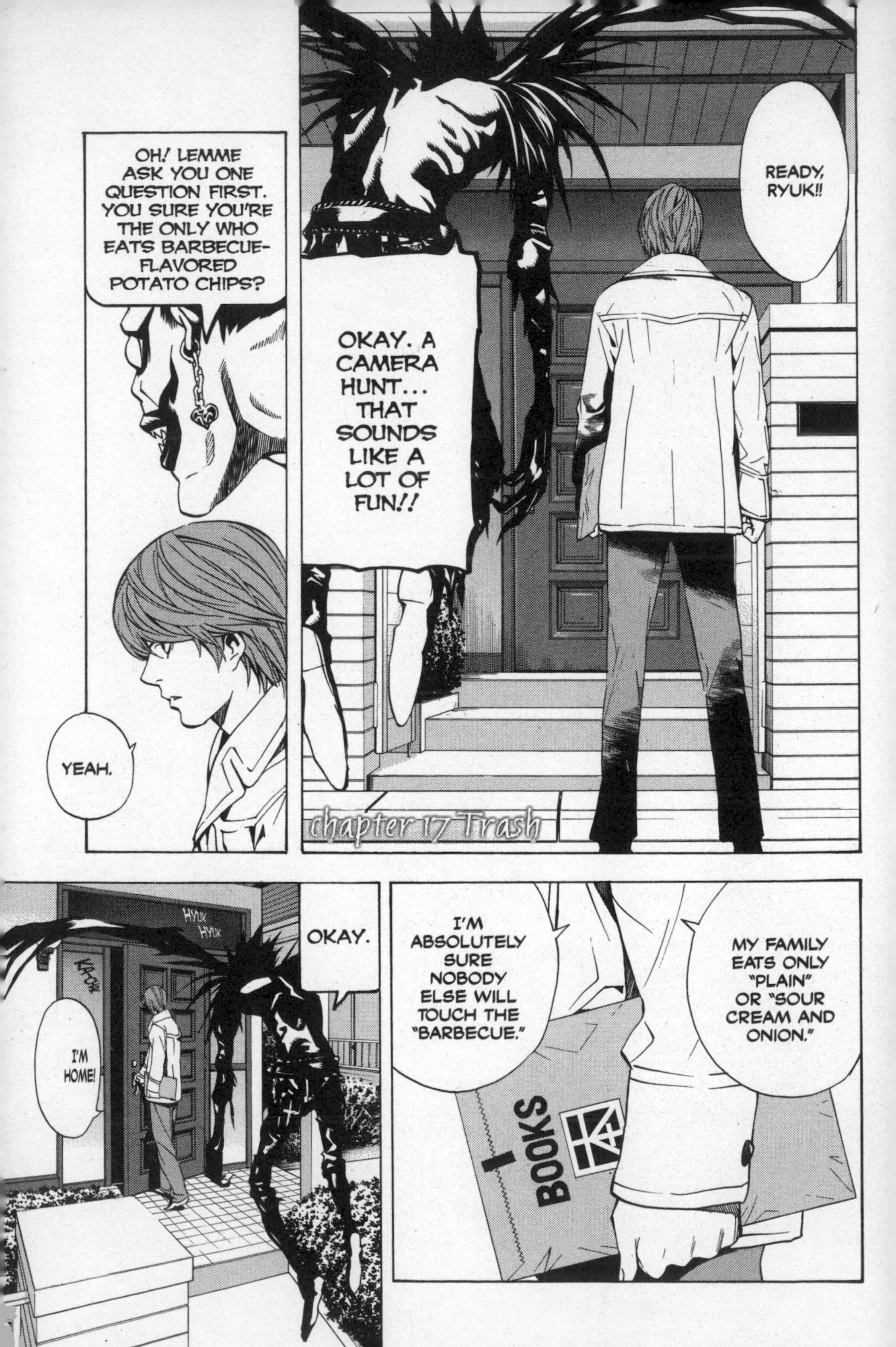
READY, RYUK!!
OKAY. A CAMERA HUNT... THAT SOUNDS LIKE A LOT OF FUN!!
chapter 17 Trash
OH! LEMME ASK YOU ONE QUESTION FIRST. YOU SURE YOU'RE THE ONLY WHO EATS BARBECUE-FLAVORED POTATO CHIPS?
YEAH.
MY FAMILY EATS ONLY "PLAIN" OR "SOUR CREAM AND ONION."
I'M ABSOLUTELY SURE NOBODY ELSE WILL TOUCH THE "BARBECUE."
BOOKS
OKAY.
HYUK HYUK
I'M HOME!

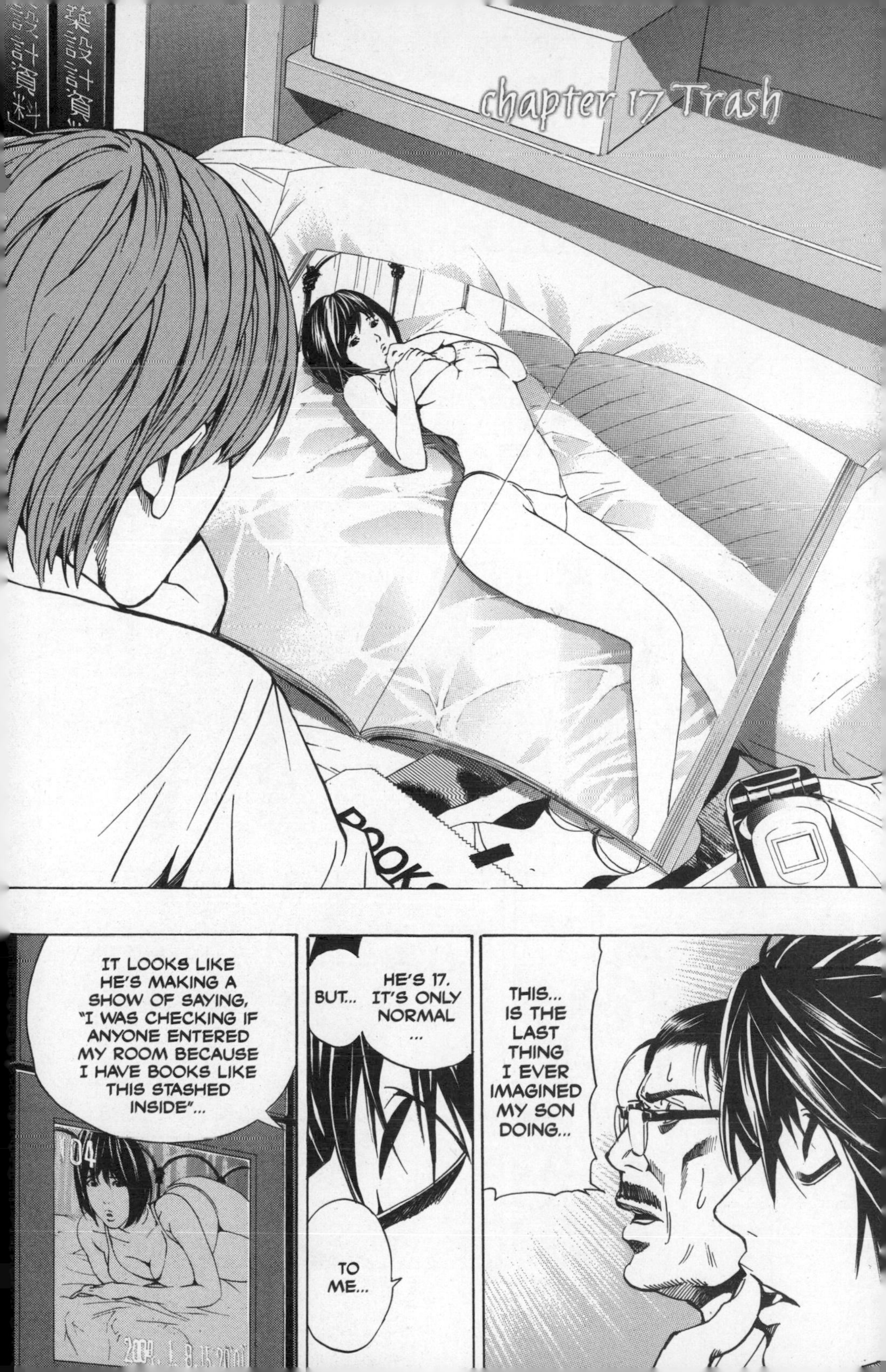
chapter 17 Trash
THIS... IS THE LAST THING I EVER IMAGINED MY SON DOING...
HE'S 17. IT'S ONLY NORMAL ...
BUT...
TO ME...
IT LOOKS LIKE HE'S MAKING A SHOW OF SAYING, "I WAS CHECKING IF ANYONE ENTERED MY ROOM BECAUSE I HAVE BOOKS LIKE THIS STASHED INSIDE"...

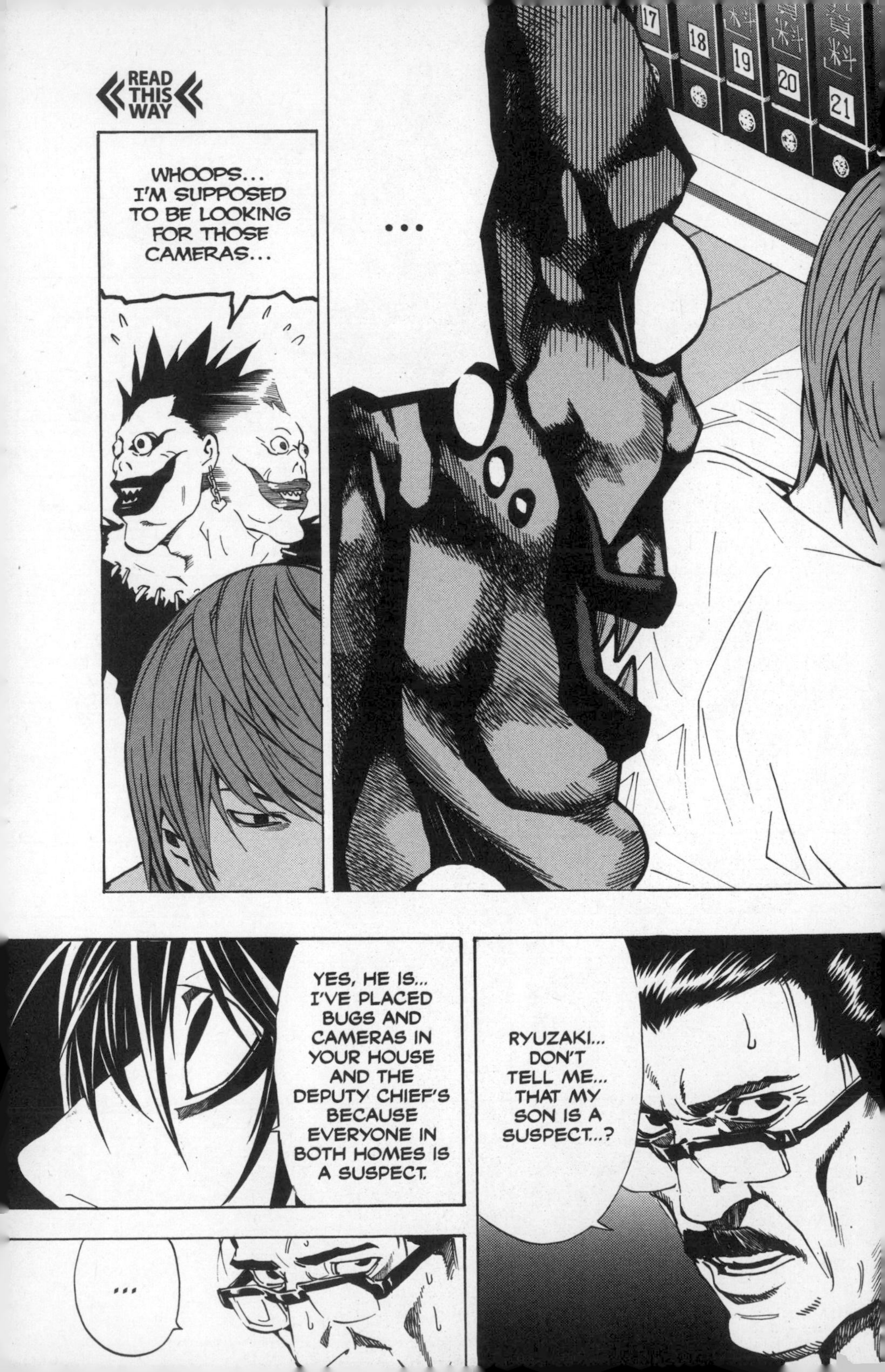
READ THIS WAY
...
WHOOPS... I'M SUPPOSED TO BE LOOKING FOR THOSE CAMERAS...
RYUZAKI... DON'T TELL ME... THAT MY SON IS A SUSPECT...?
YES, HE IS... I'VE PLACED BUGS AND CAMERAS IN YOUR HOUSE AND THE DEPUTY CHIEF'S BECAUSE EVERYONE IN BOTH HOMES IS A SUSPECT.
...

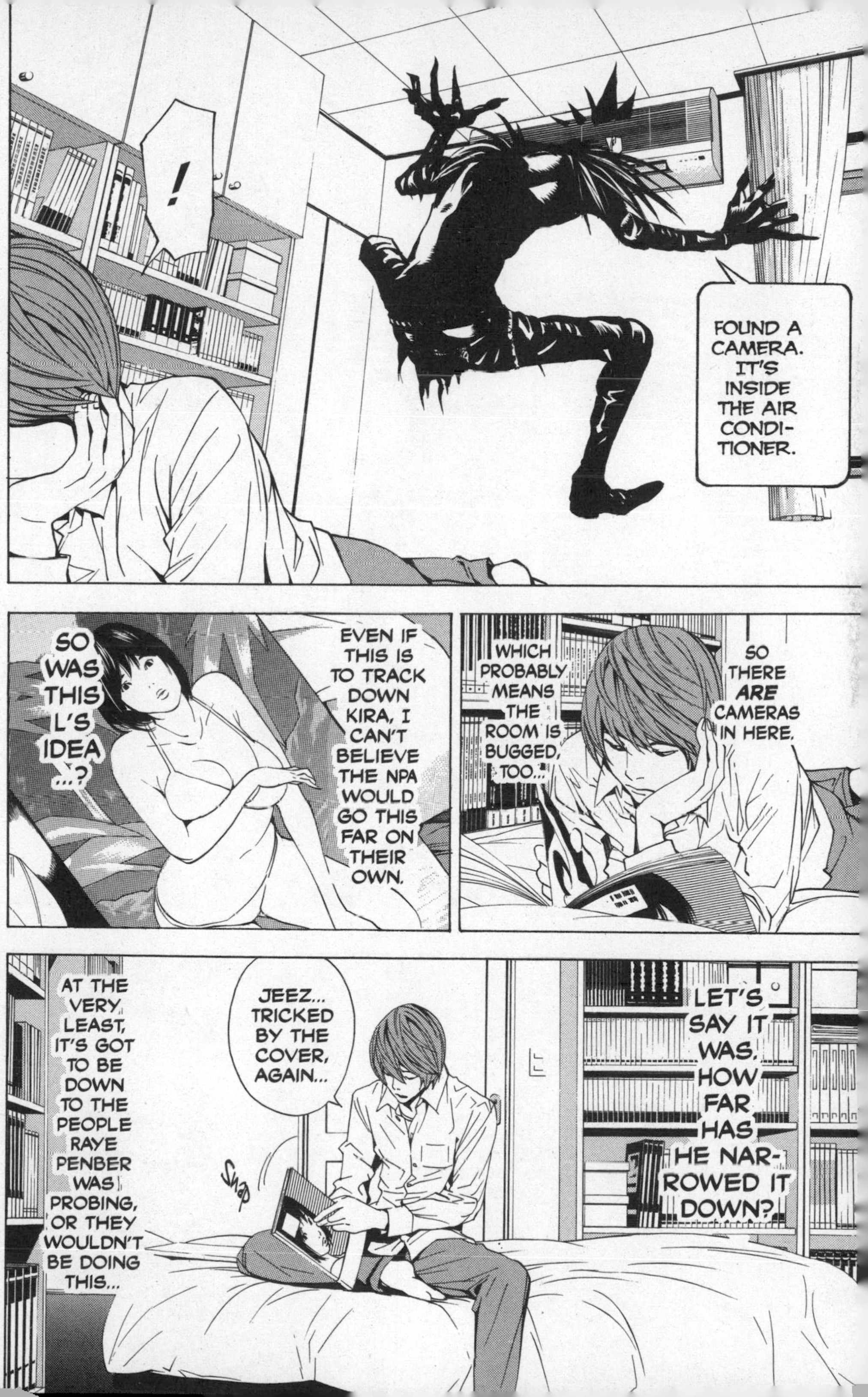
FOUND A CAMERA. IT'S INSIDE THE AIR CONDI-TIONER.
!
SO THERE *ARE* CAMERAS IN HERE.
WHICH PROBABLY MEANS THE ROOM IS BUGGED, TOO...
EVEN IF THIS IS TO TRACK DOWN KIRA, I CAN'T BELIEVE THE NPA WOULD GO THIS FAR ON THEIR OWN.
SO WAS THIS L'S IDEA ...?
LET'S SAY IT WAS. HOW FAR HAS HE NAR-ROWED IT DOWN?
JEEZ... TRICKED BY THE COVER, AGAIN...
Snap
AT THE VERY LEAST, IT'S GOT TO BE DOWN TO THE PEOPLE RAYE PENBER WAS PROBING, OR THEY WOULDN'T BE DOING THIS...

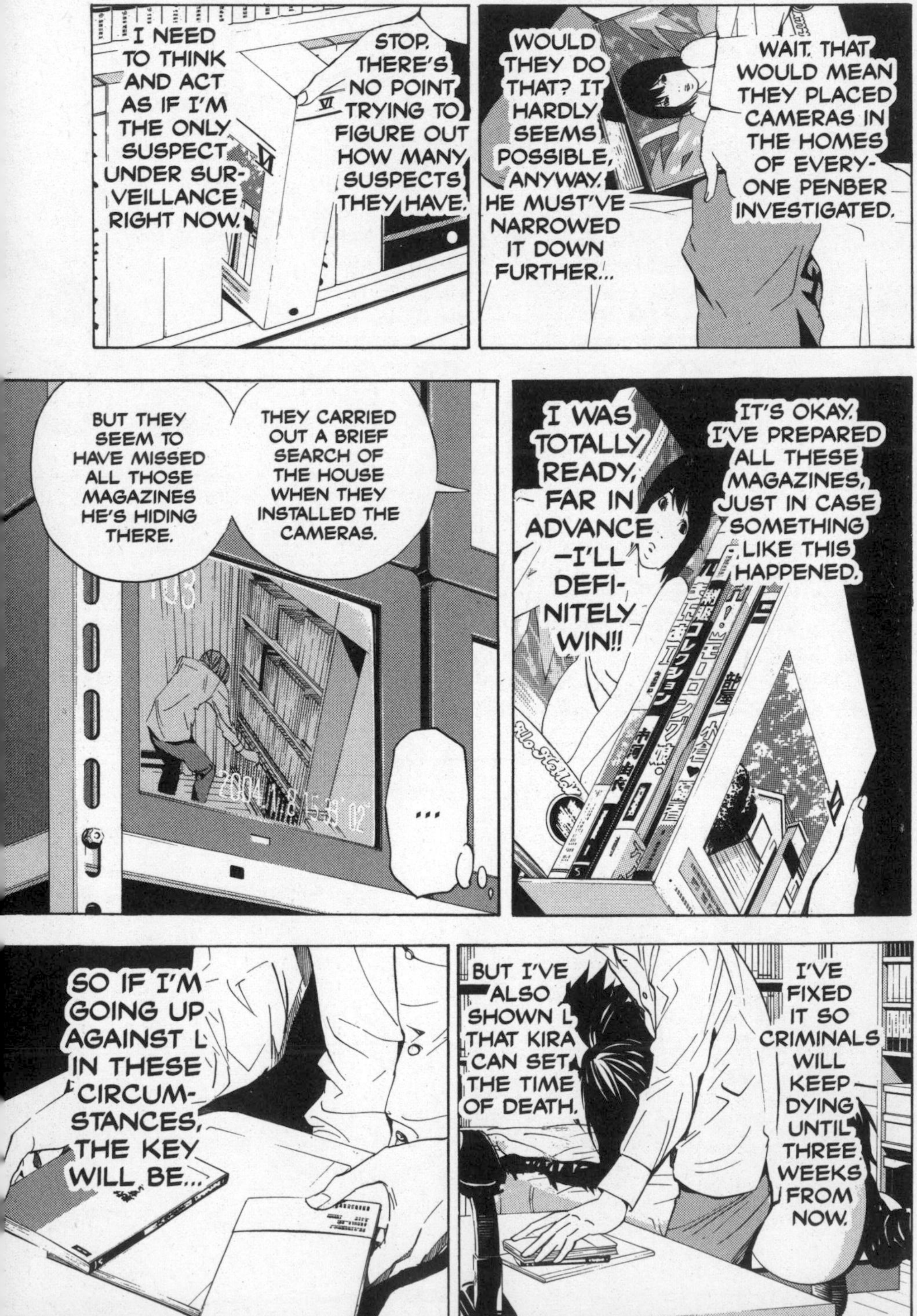
WAIT. THAT WOULD MEAN THEY PLACED CAMERAS IN THE HOMES OF EVERY-ONE PENBER INVESTIGATED.
WOULD THEY DO THAT? IT HARDLY SEEMS POSSIBLE, ANYWAY. HE MUST'VE NARROWED IT DOWN FURTHER...
STOP. THERE'S NO POINT TRYING TO FIGURE OUT HOW MANY SUSPECTS THEY HAVE.
I NEED TO THINK AND ACT AS IF I'M THE ONLY SUSPECT UNDER SUR-VEILLANCE RIGHT NOW.
IT'S OKAY. I'VE PREPARED ALL THESE MAGAZINES, JUST IN CASE SOMETHING LIKE THIS HAPPENED.
I WAS TOTALLY READY, FAR IN ADVANCE —I'LL DEFI-NITELY WIN!!
THEY CARRIED OUT A BRIEF SEARCH OF THE HOUSE WHEN THEY INSTALLED THE CAMERAS.
BUT THEY SEEM TO HAVE MISSED ALL THOSE MAGAZINES HE'S HIDING THERE.
...
I'VE FIXED IT SO CRIMINALS WILL KEEP DYING UNTIL THREE WEEKS FROM NOW.
BUT I'VE ALSO SHOWN L THAT KIRA CAN SET THE TIME OF DEATH.
SO IF I'M GOING UP AGAINST L IN THESE CIRCUM-STANCES, THE KEY WILL BE...

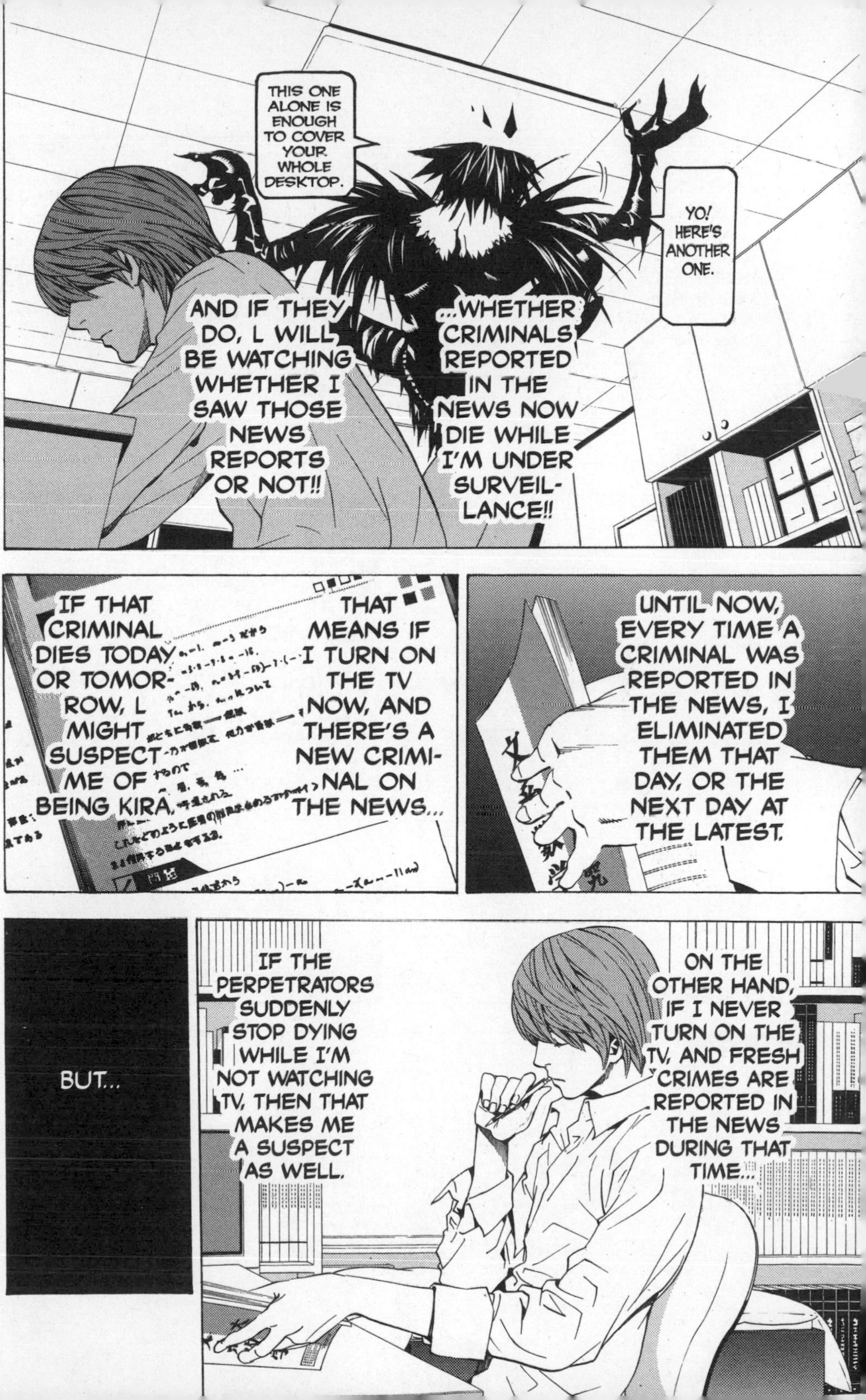
YO! HERE'S ANOTHER ONE.
THIS ONE ALONE IS ENOUGH TO COVER YOUR WHOLE DESKTOP.
...WHETHER CRIMINALS REPORTED IN THE NEWS NOW DIE WHILE I'M UNDER SURVEIL-LANCE!!
AND IF THEY DO, L WILL BE WATCHING WHETHER I SAW THOSE NEWS REPORTS OR NOT!!
UNTIL NOW, EVERY TIME A CRIMINAL WAS REPORTED IN THE NEWS, I ELIMINATED THEM THAT DAY, OR THE NEXT DAY AT THE LATEST.
THAT MEANS IF I TURN ON THE TV NOW, AND THERE'S A NEW CRIMI-NAL ON THE NEWS...
IF THAT CRIMINAL DIES TODAY OR TOMOR-ROW, L MIGHT SUSPECT ME OF BEING KIRA.
ON THE OTHER HAND, IF I NEVER TURN ON THE TV, AND FRESH CRIMES ARE REPORTED IN THE NEWS DURING THAT TIME...
IF THE PERPETRATORS SUDDENLY STOP DYING WHILE I'M NOT WATCHING TV, THEN THAT MAKES ME A SUSPECT AS WELL.
BUT...

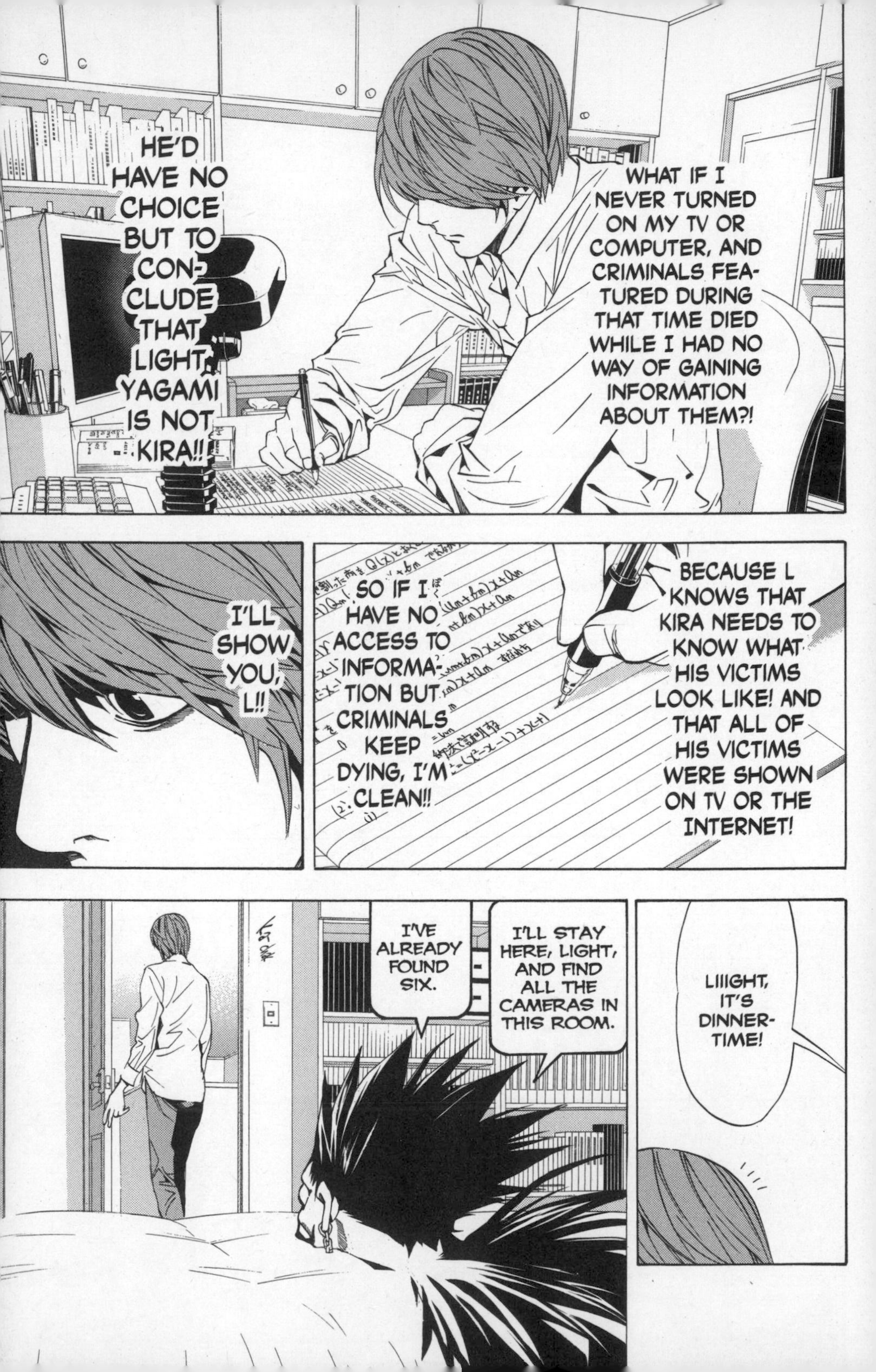
WHAT IF I NEVER TURNED ON MY TV OR COMPUTER, AND CRIMINALS FEATURED DURING THAT TIME DIED WHILE I HAD NO WAY OF GAINING INFORMATION ABOUT THEM?!
HE'D HAVE NO CHOICE BUT TO CONCLUDE THAT LIGHT YAGAMI IS NOT KIRA!!
BECAUSE L KNOWS THAT KIRA NEEDS TO KNOW WHAT HIS VICTIMS LOOK LIKE! AND THAT ALL OF HIS VICTIMS WERE SHOWN ON TV OR THE INTERNET!
SO IF I HAVE NO ACCESS TO INFORMATION BUT CRIMINALS KEEP DYING, I'M CLEAN!!
I'LL SHOW YOU, L!!
LIIIGHT, IT'S DINNER-TIME!
I'LL STAY HERE, LIGHT, AND FIND ALL THE CAMERAS IN THIS ROOM.
I'VE ALREADY FOUND SIX.

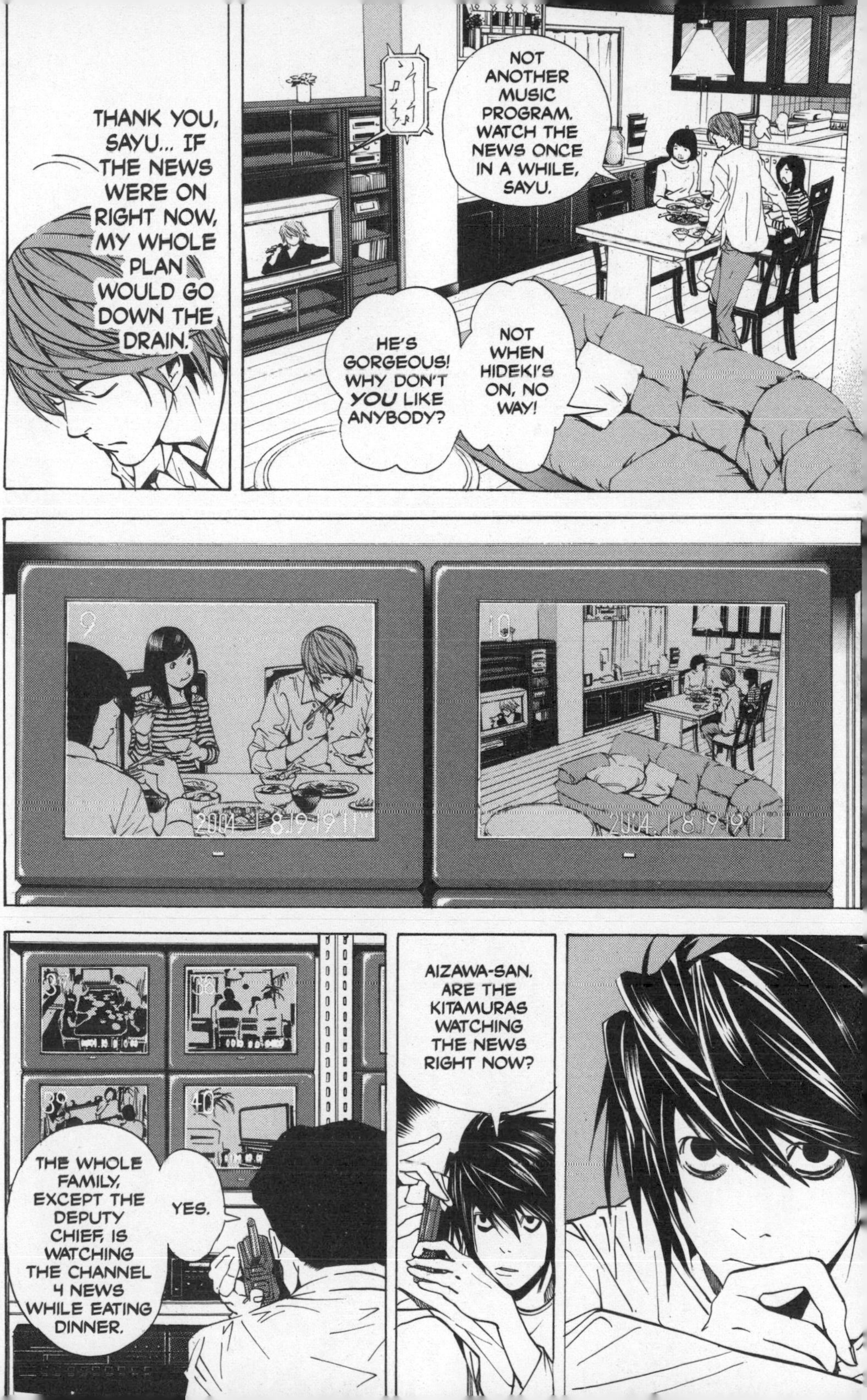
NOT ANOTHER MUSIC PROGRAM. WATCH THE NEWS ONCE IN A WHILE, SAYU.
NOT WHEN HIDEKI'S ON, NO WAY!
HE'S GORGEOUS! WHY DON'T *YOU* LIKE ANYBODY?
THANK YOU, SAYU... IF THE NEWS WERE ON RIGHT NOW, MY WHOLE PLAN WOULD GO DOWN THE DRAIN.
AIZAWA-SAN. ARE THE KITAMURAS WATCHING THE NEWS RIGHT NOW?
YES.
THE WHOLE FAMILY, EXCEPT THE DEPUTY CHIEF, IS WATCHING THE CHANNEL 4 NEWS WHILE EATING DINNER.

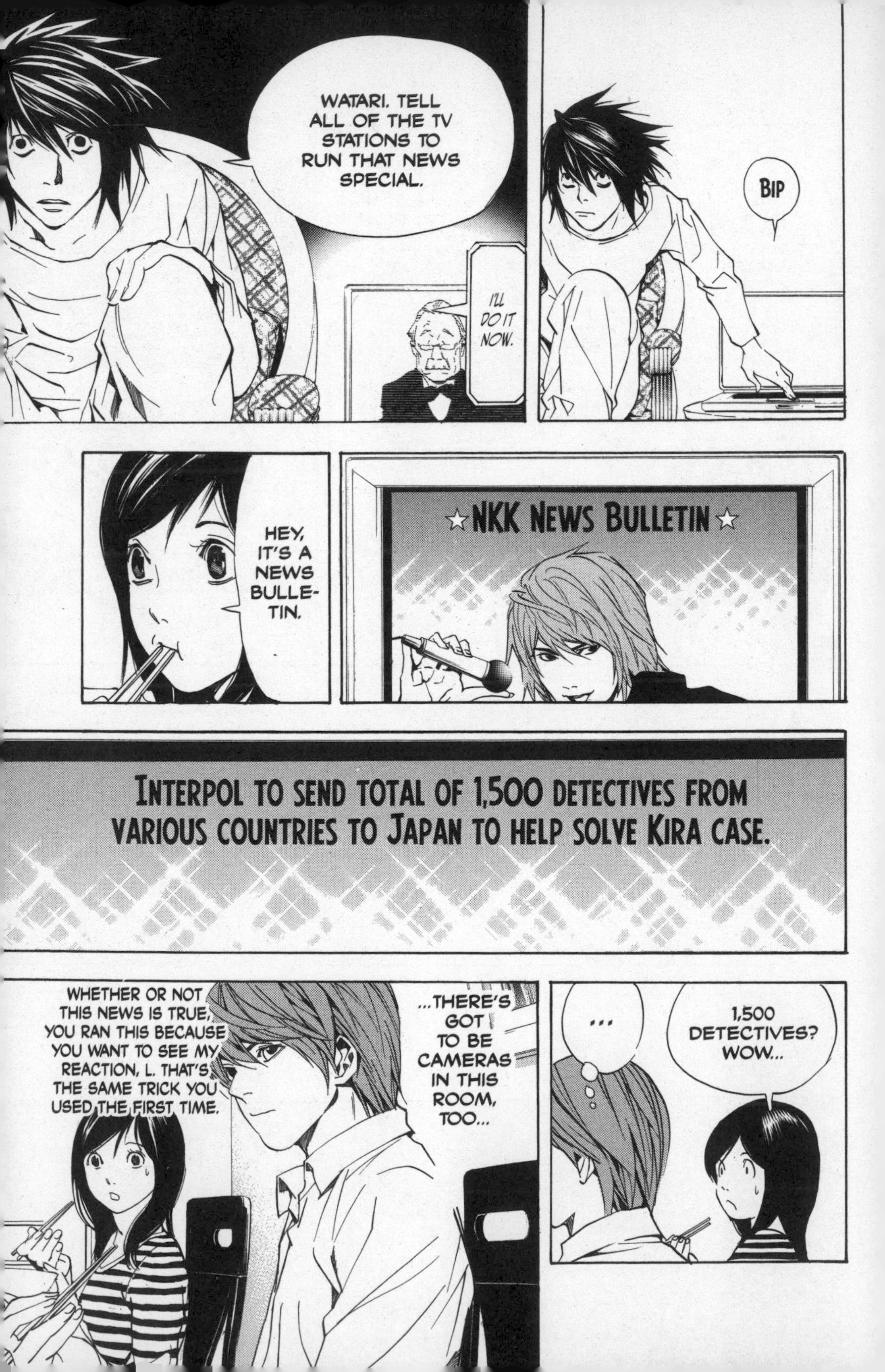
BIP
WATARI. TELL ALL OF THE TV STATIONS TO RUN THAT NEWS SPECIAL.
I'LL DO IT NOW.
★NKK NEWS BULLETIN★
HEY, IT'S A NEWS BULLE-TIN.
INTERPOL TO SEND TOTAL OF 1,500 DETECTIVES FROM VARIOUS COUNTRIES TO JAPAN TO HELP SOLVE KIRA CASE.
1,500 DETECTIVES? WOW...
...
WHETHER OR NOT THIS NEWS IS TRUE, YOU RAN THIS BECAUSE YOU WANT TO SEE MY REACTION, L. THAT'S THE SAME TRICK YOU USED THE FIRST TIME.
...THERE'S GOT TO BE CAMERAS IN THIS ROOM, TOO...

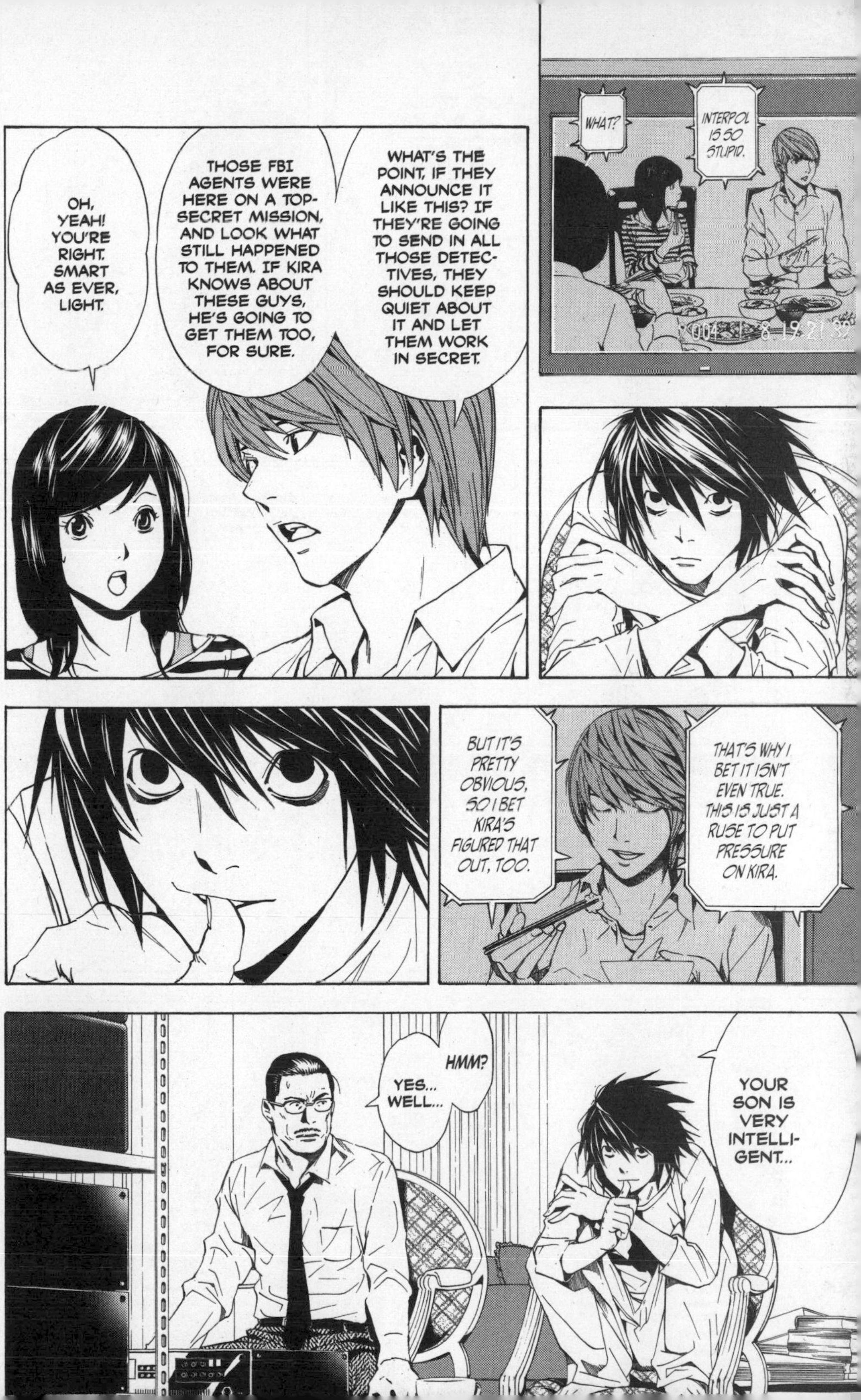
INTERPOL IS SO STUPID.
WHAT?
2004 8.19 21:32
WHAT'S THE POINT, IF THEY ANNOUNCE IT LIKE THIS? IF THEY'RE GOING TO SEND IN ALL THOSE DETECTIVES, THEY SHOULD KEEP QUIET ABOUT IT AND LET THEM WORK IN SECRET.
THOSE FBI AGENTS WERE HERE ON A TOP-SECRET MISSION, AND LOOK WHAT STILL HAPPENED TO THEM. IF KIRA KNOWS ABOUT THESE GUYS, HE'S GOING TO GET THEM TOO, FOR SURE.
OH, YEAH! YOU'RE RIGHT. SMART AS EVER, LIGHT.
THAT'S WHY I BET IT ISN'T EVEN TRUE. THIS IS JUST A RUSE TO PUT PRESSURE ON KIRA.
BUT IT'S PRETTY OBVIOUS, SO I BET KIRA'S FIGURED THAT OUT, TOO.
YOUR SON IS VERY INTELLIGENT...
HMM?
YES... WELL...

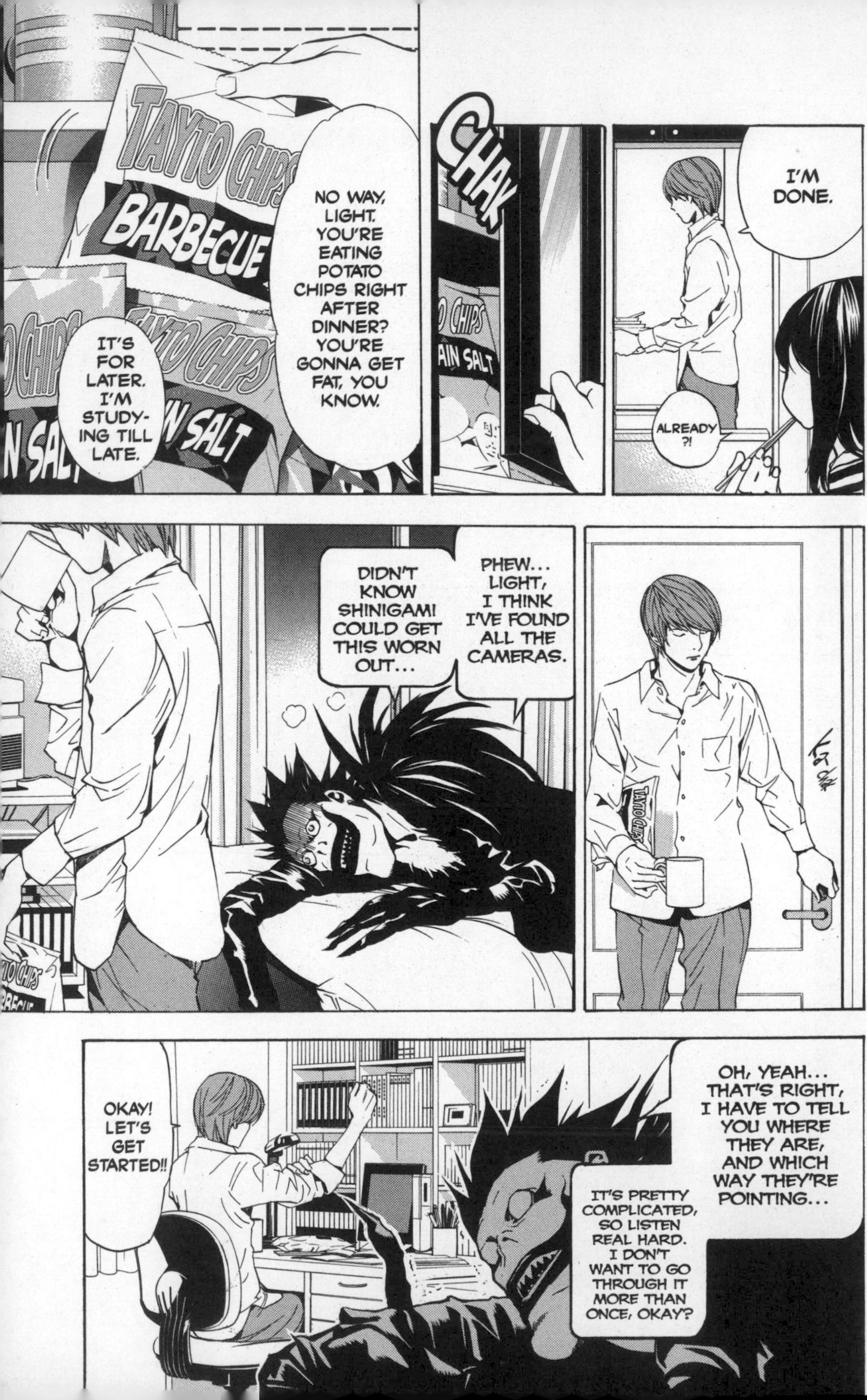
I'M DONE.
ALREADY?!
CHAK
NO WAY, LIGHT. YOU'RE EATING POTATO CHIPS RIGHT AFTER DINNER? YOU'RE GONNA GET FAT, YOU KNOW.
TAYTO CHIPS
BARBECUE
IT'S FOR LATER. I'M STUDYING TILL LATE.
PHEW... LIGHT, I THINK I'VE FOUND ALL THE CAMERAS.
DIDN'T KNOW SHINIGAMI COULD GET THIS WORN OUT...
OH, YEAH... THAT'S RIGHT, I HAVE TO TELL YOU WHERE THEY ARE, AND WHICH WAY THEY'RE POINTING...
IT'S PRETTY COMPLICATED, SO LISTEN REAL HARD. I DON'T WANT TO GO THROUGH IT MORE THAN ONCE, OKAY?
OKAY! LET'S GET STARTED!!

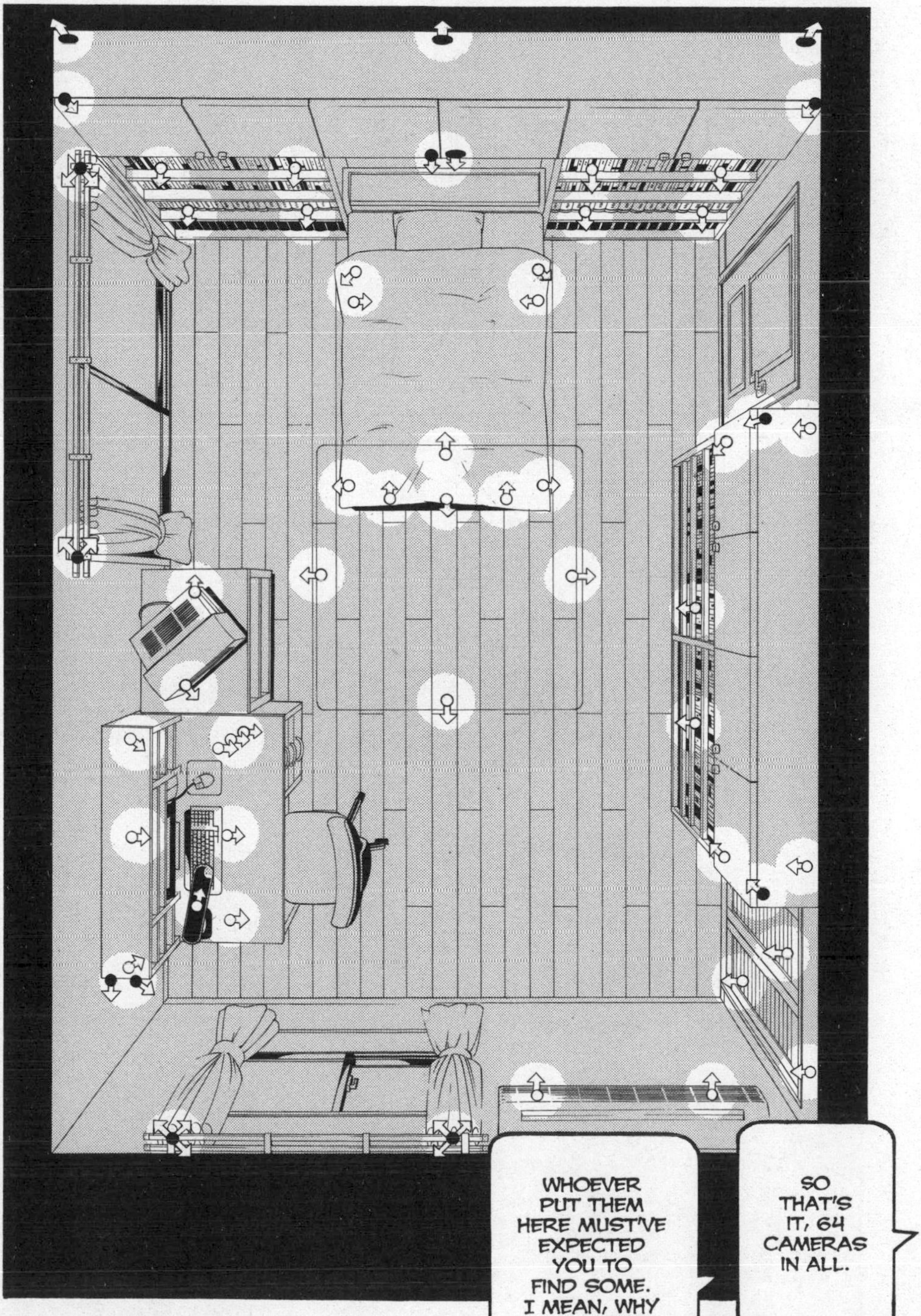
SO THAT'S IT, 64 CAMERAS IN ALL.
WHOEVER PUT THEM HERE MUST'VE EXPECTED YOU TO FIND SOME. I MEAN, WHY ELSE PUT SO MANY?

READ THIS WAY

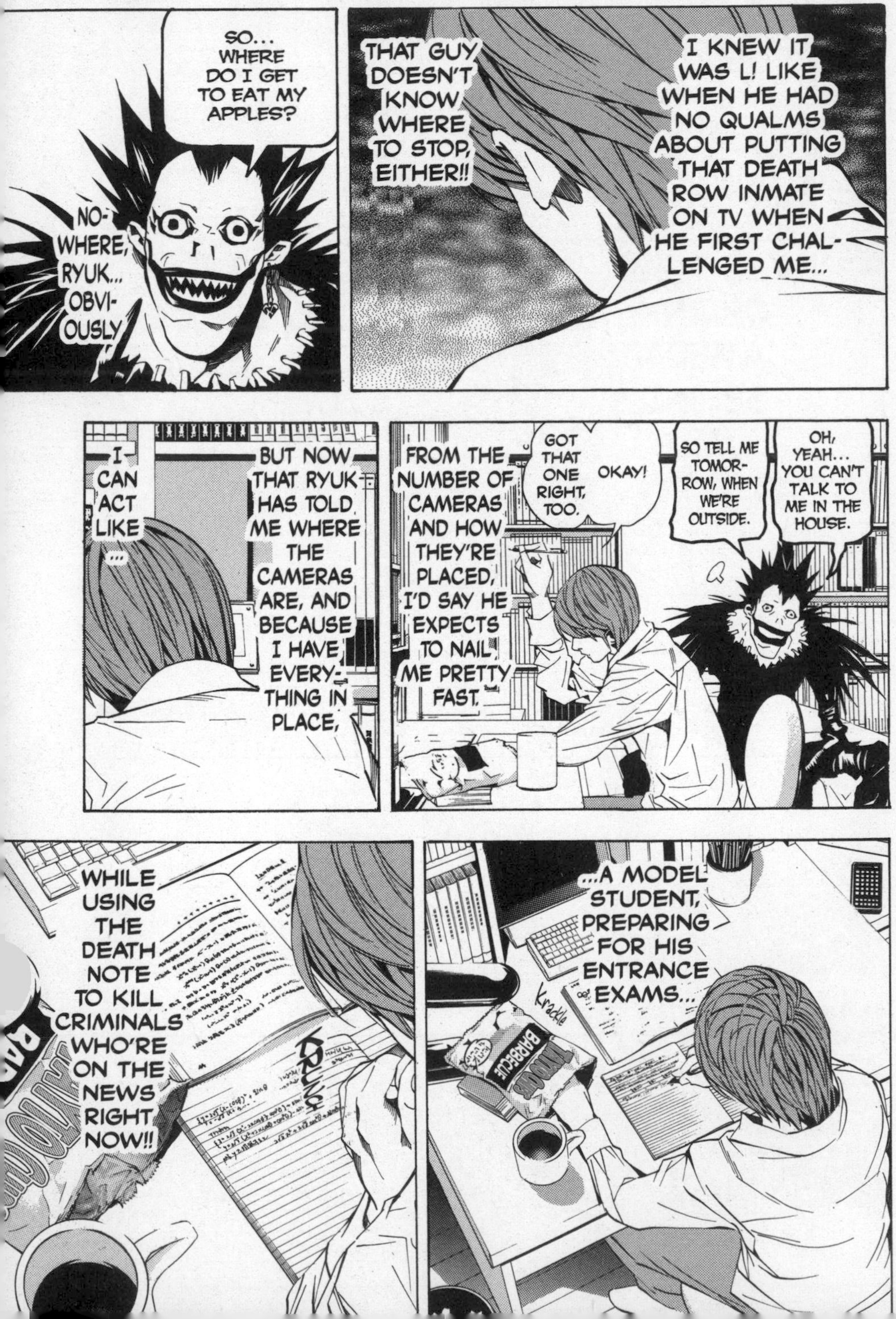

I KNEW IT WAS L! LIKE WHEN HE HAD NO QUALMS ABOUT PUTTING THAT DEATH ROW INMATE ON TV WHEN HE FIRST CHALLENGED ME...
THAT GUY DOESN'T KNOW WHERE TO STOP, EITHER!!
SO... WHERE DO I GET TO EAT MY APPLES?
NOWHERE, RYUK... OBVIOUSLY
OH, YEAH... YOU CAN'T TALK TO ME IN THE HOUSE.
SO TELL ME TOMORROW, WHEN WE'RE OUTSIDE.
OKAY!
GOT THAT ONE RIGHT, TOO.
FROM THE NUMBER OF CAMERAS AND HOW THEY'RE PLACED, I'D SAY HE EXPECTS TO NAIL ME PRETTY FAST.
BUT NOW THAT RYUK HAS TOLD ME WHERE THE CAMERAS ARE, AND BECAUSE I HAVE EVERYTHING IN PLACE,
I CAN ACT LIKE...
...A MODEL STUDENT, PREPARING FOR HIS ENTRANCE EXAMS...
Krackle
BARBECUE
WHILE USING THE DEATH NOTE TO KILL CRIMINALS WHO'RE ON THE NEWS RIGHT NOW!!
KRUNCH

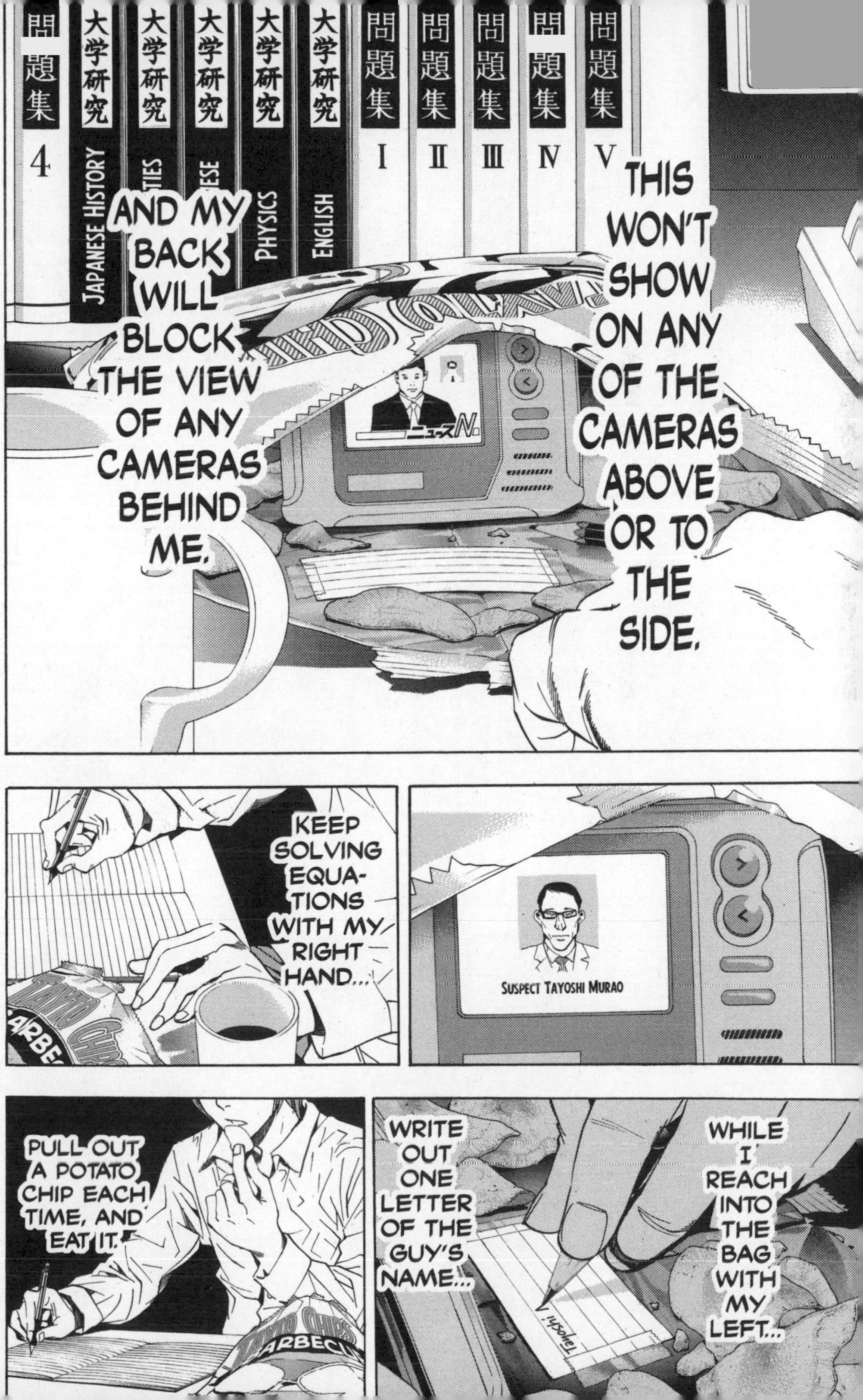

問題集 V
問題集 IV
問題集 III
問題集 II
問題集 I
大学研究 ENGLISH
大学研究 PHYSICS
大学研究 JAPANESE HISTORY
問題集 4
THIS WON'T SHOW ON ANY OF THE CAMERAS ABOVE OR TO THE SIDE.
AND MY BACK WILL BLOCK THE VIEW OF ANY CAMERAS BEHIND ME.
ニュースN.
SUSPECT TAYOSHI MURAO
KEEP SOLVING EQUA-TIONS WITH MY RIGHT HAND...
WHILE I REACH INTO THE BAG WITH MY LEFT...
WRITE OUT ONE LETTER OF THE GUY'S NAME...
Tayoshi
PULL OUT A POTATO CHIP EACH TIME, AND EAT IT.

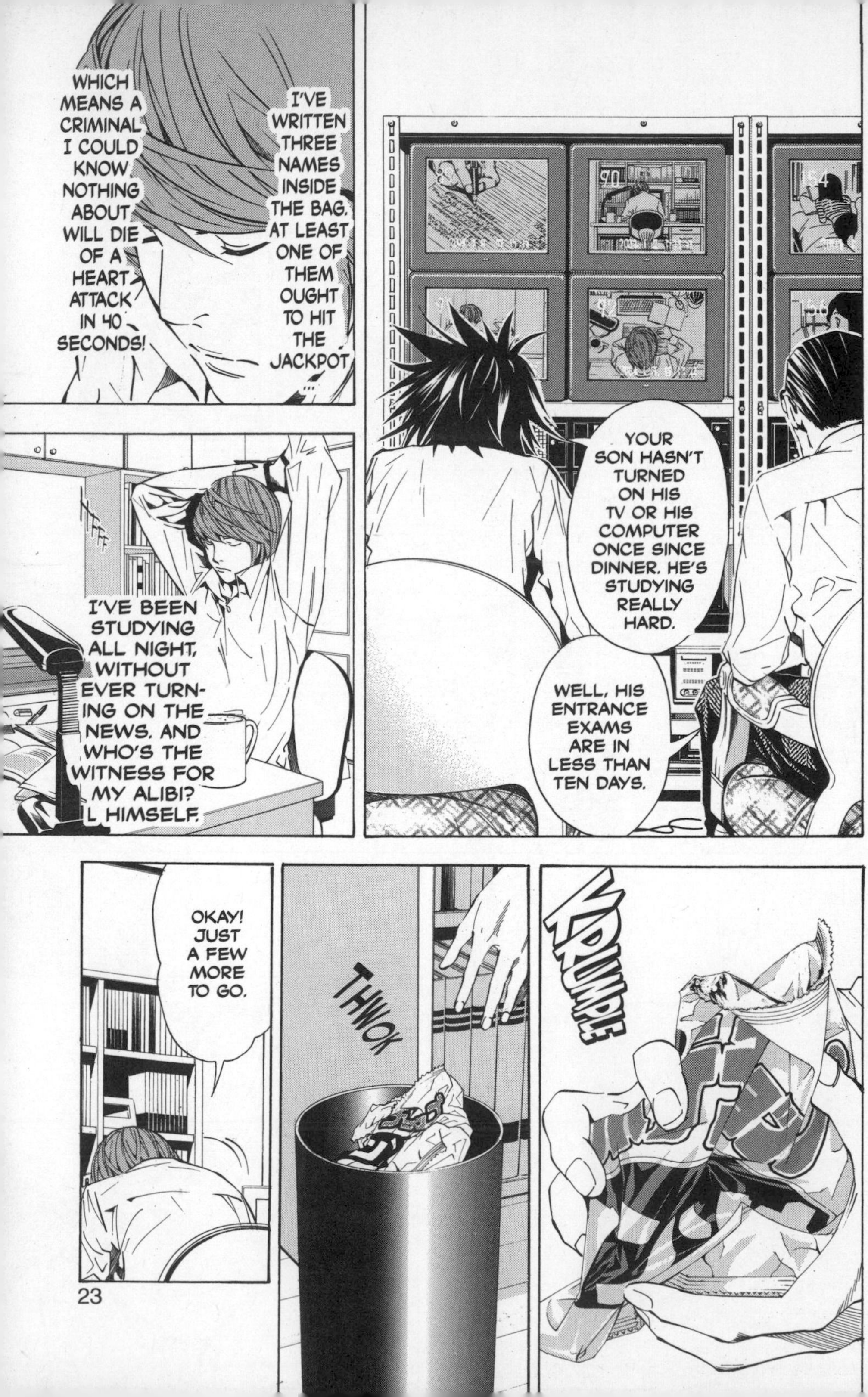
YOUR SON HASN'T TURNED ON HIS TV OR HIS COMPUTER ONCE SINCE DINNER. HE'S STUDYING REALLY HARD.
WELL, HIS ENTRANCE EXAMS ARE IN LESS THAN TEN DAYS.
I'VE WRITTEN THREE NAMES INSIDE THE BAG. AT LEAST ONE OF THEM OUGHT TO HIT THE JACKPOT...
WHICH MEANS A CRIMINAL I COULD KNOW NOTHING ABOUT WILL DIE OF A HEART ATTACK IN 40 SECONDS!
HFFF
I'VE BEEN STUDYING ALL NIGHT, WITHOUT EVER TURNING ON THE NEWS. AND WHO'S THE WITNESS FOR MY ALIBI? L HIMSELF.
KRUMPLE
THWOK
OKAY! JUST A FEW MORE TO GO.

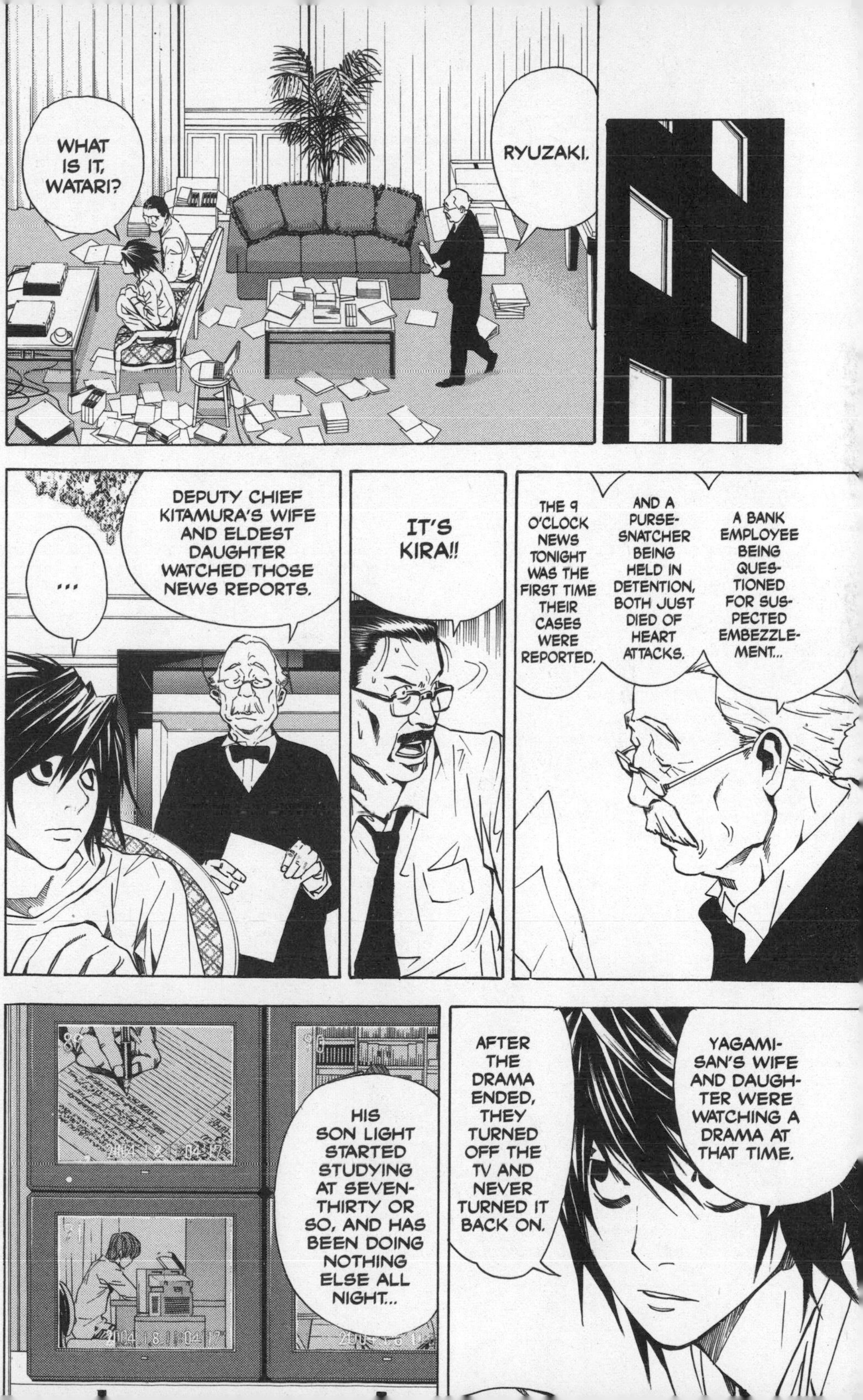
RYUZAKI.
WHAT IS IT, WATARI?
A BANK EMPLOYEE BEING QUESTIONED FOR SUSPECTED EMBEZZLEMENT...
AND A PURSE-SNATCHER BEING HELD IN DETENTION, BOTH JUST DIED OF HEART ATTACKS.
THE 9 O'CLOCK NEWS TONIGHT WAS THE FIRST TIME THEIR CASES WERE REPORTED.
IT'S KIRA!!
DEPUTY CHIEF KITAMURA'S WIFE AND ELDEST DAUGHTER WATCHED THOSE NEWS REPORTS.
...
YAGAMI-SAN'S WIFE AND DAUGHTER WERE WATCHING A DRAMA AT THAT TIME.
AFTER THE DRAMA ENDED, THEY TURNED OFF THE TV AND NEVER TURNED IT BACK ON.
HIS SON LIGHT STARTED STUDYING AT SEVEN-THIRTY OR SO, AND HAS BEEN DOING NOTHING ELSE ALL NIGHT...

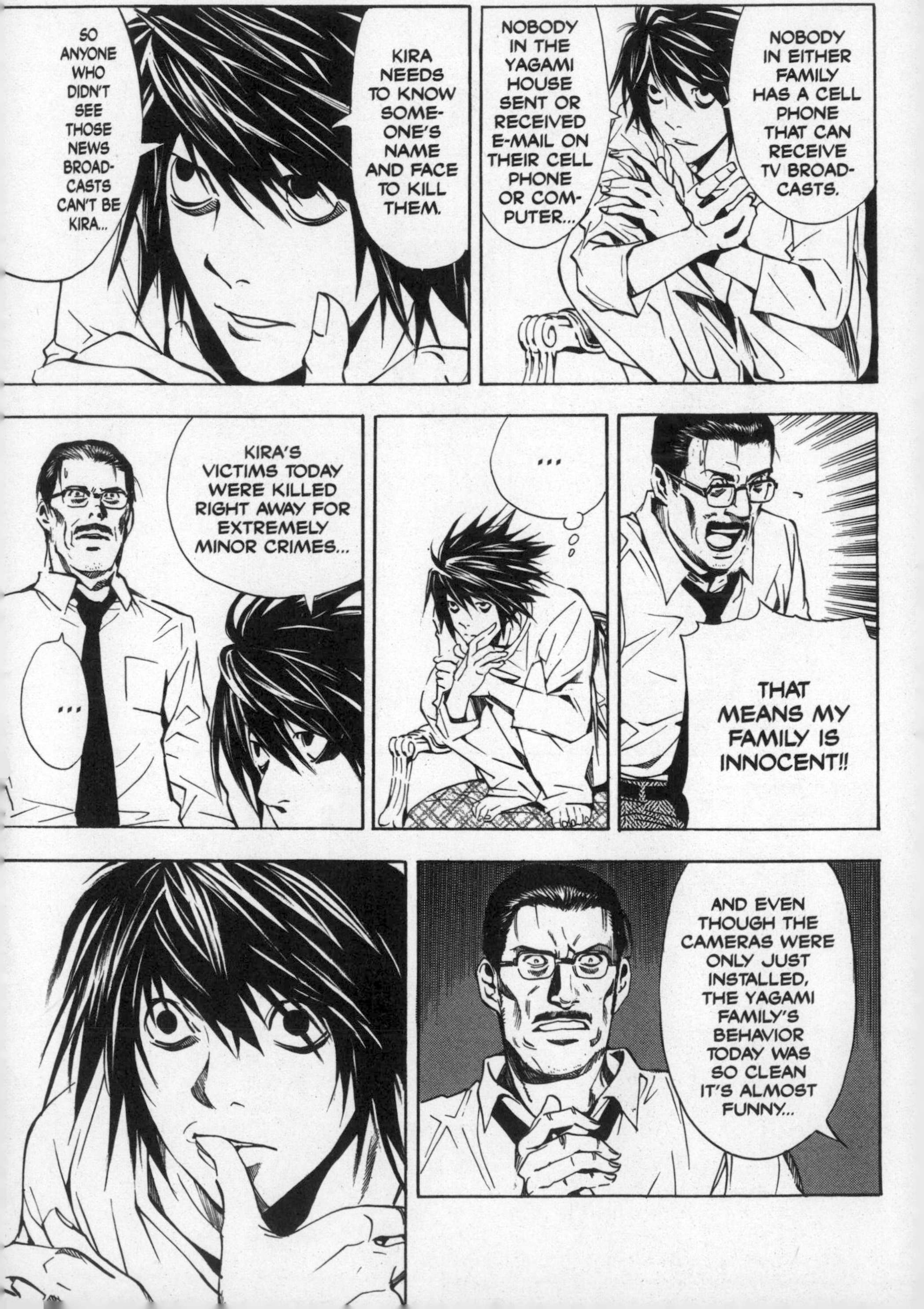
NOBODY IN EITHER FAMILY HAS A CELL PHONE THAT CAN RECEIVE TV BROADCASTS.
NOBODY IN THE YAGAMI HOUSE SENT OR RECEIVED E-MAIL ON THEIR CELL PHONE OR COMPUTER...
KIRA NEEDS TO KNOW SOMEONE'S NAME AND FACE TO KILL THEM.
SO ANYONE WHO DIDN'T SEE THOSE NEWS BROADCASTS CAN'T BE KIRA...
THAT MEANS MY FAMILY IS INNOCENT!!
...
KIRA'S VICTIMS TODAY WERE KILLED RIGHT AWAY FOR EXTREMELY MINOR CRIMES...
...
AND EVEN THOUGH THE CAMERAS WERE ONLY JUST INSTALLED, THE YAGAMI FAMILY'S BEHAVIOR TODAY WAS SO CLEAN IT'S ALMOST FUNNY...

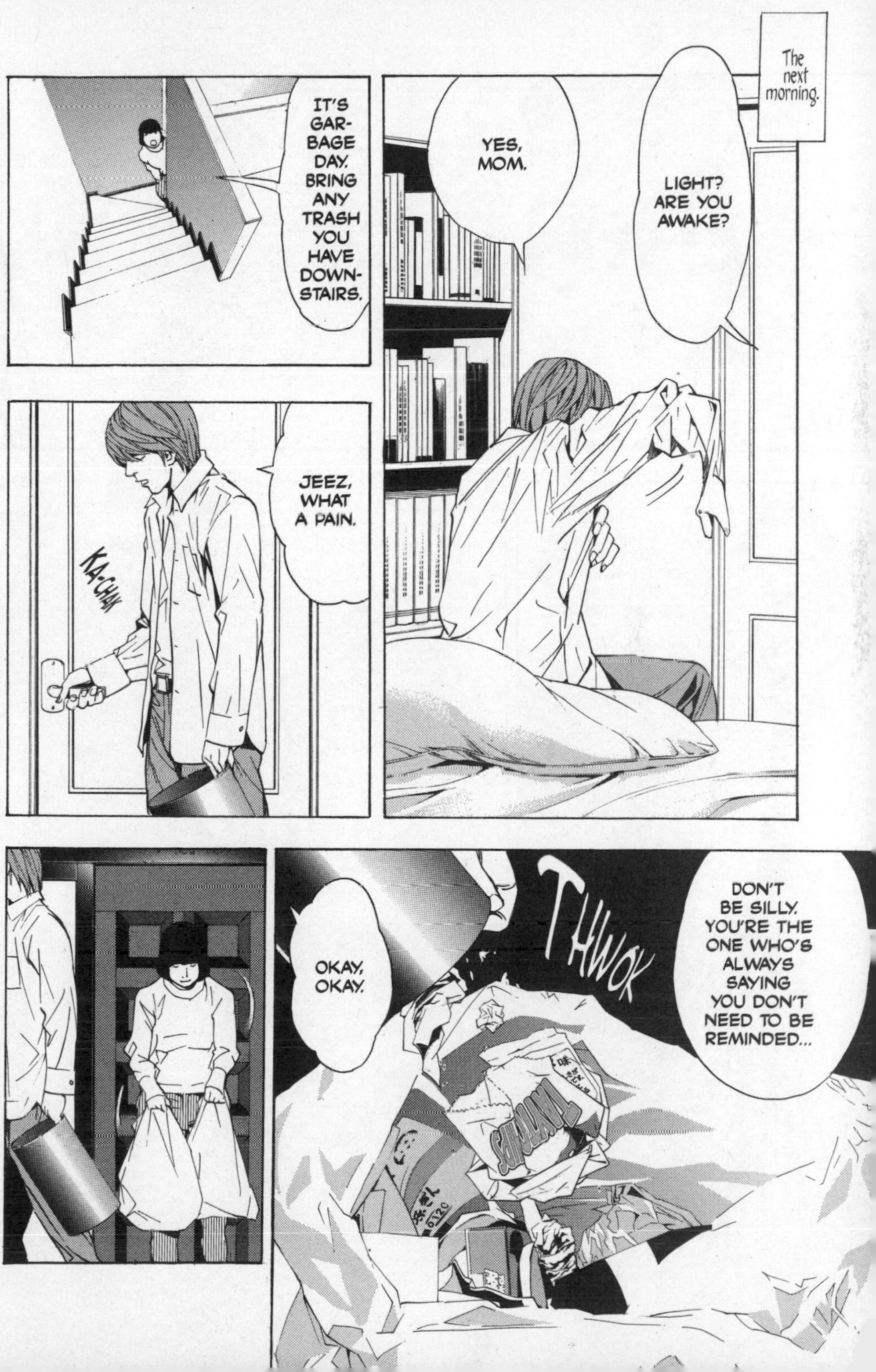
The next morning.
LIGHT? ARE YOU AWAKE?
YES, MOM.
IT'S GARBAGE DAY. BRING ANY TRASH YOU HAVE DOWNSTAIRS.
JEEZ, WHAT A PAIN.
KA-CHAK
DON'T BE SILLY. YOU'RE THE ONE WHO'S ALWAYS SAYING YOU DON'T NEED TO BE REMINDED...
THWOK
OKAY, OKAY.

READ THIS WAY

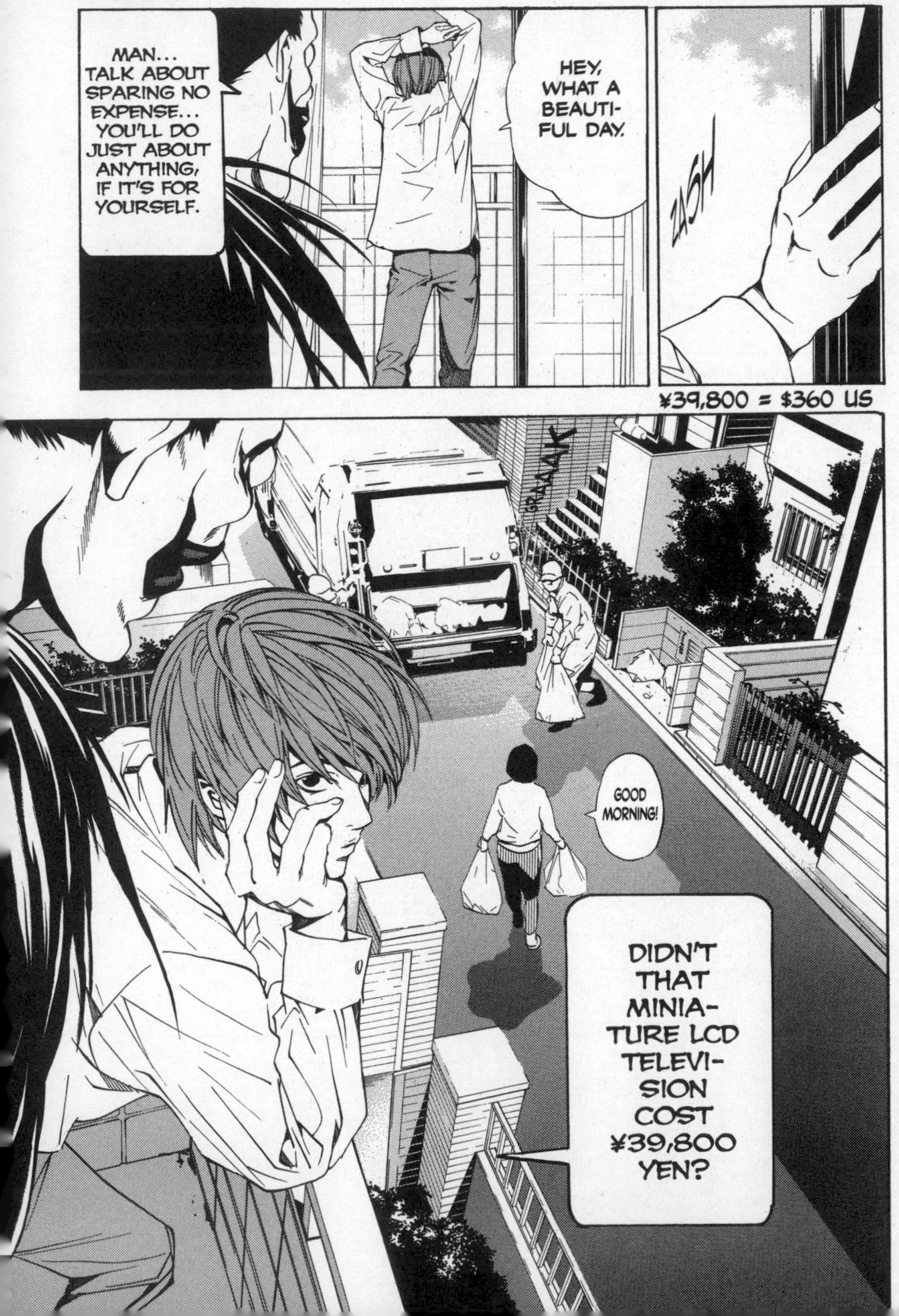
ZASH
HEY, WHAT A BEAUTI-FUL DAY.
MAN... TALK ABOUT SPARING NO EXPENSE... YOU'LL DO JUST ABOUT ANYTHING, IF IT'S FOR YOURSELF.
¥39,800 = $360 US
GRAAAK
GOOD MORNING!
DIDN'T THAT MINIA-TURE LCD TELEVI-SION COST ¥39,800 YEN?

DEATH NOTE
How to use it

XI

- Even after the individual's name, the time of death, and death condition on the DEATH NOTE were filled out, the time and condition of death can be altered as many times as you want, as long as it is changed within 6 minutes and 40 seconds from the time it was filled in. But, of course, this is only possible before the victim dies.

  デスノートに名前、死の時刻、死の状況を書いた後でも、6分40秒以内であれば、死の時刻、死の状況は何度でも変更できる。しかし、もちろん6分40秒以内であっても、変更が可能なのは死んでしまう前である。

- Whenever you want to change anything written on the DEATH NOTE within 6 minutes and 40 seconds after you wrote, you must first rule out the characters you want to erase with two straight lines.

  デスノートに書いた内容を6分40秒以内で変更する場合、まず直したい部分の文字の上に二本の棒線を引く。

- As you see above, the time and condition of death can be changed, but once the victim's name has been written, the individual's death can never be avoided.

  時間や死の状況は上記のように変更可能であるが、名前を書かれた人間の死は、どんな手段をもっても取り消せない。

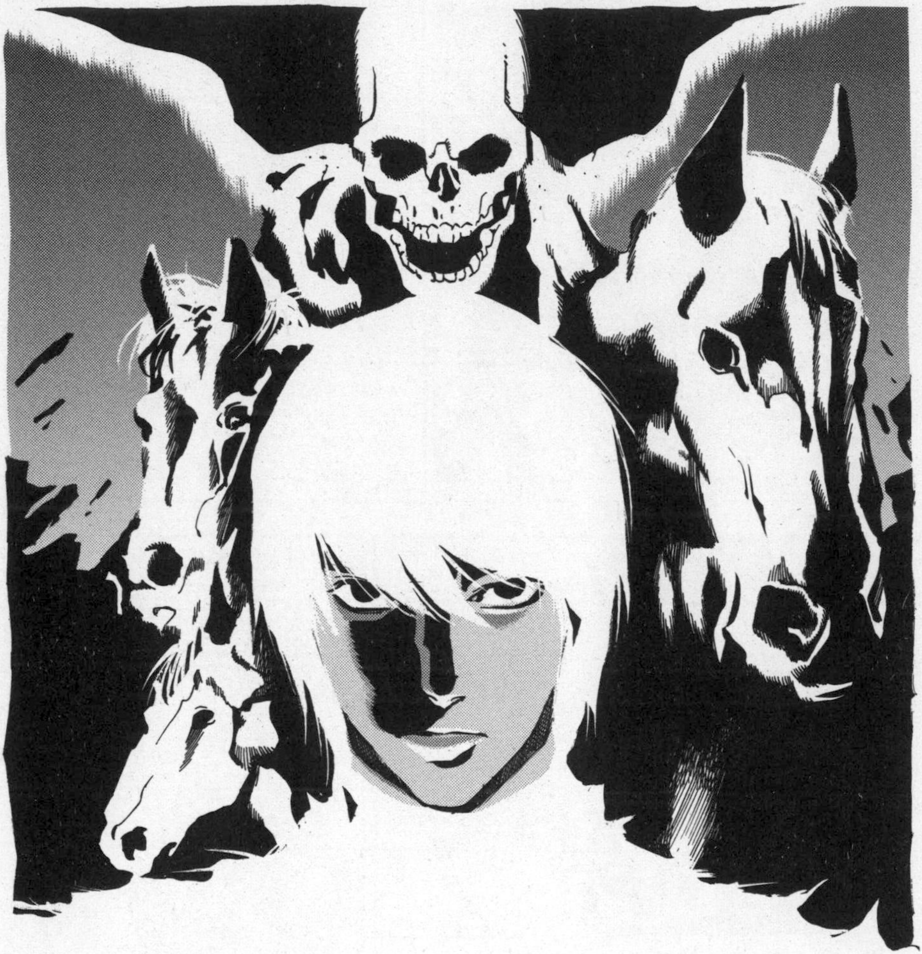

chapter 18 Gaze

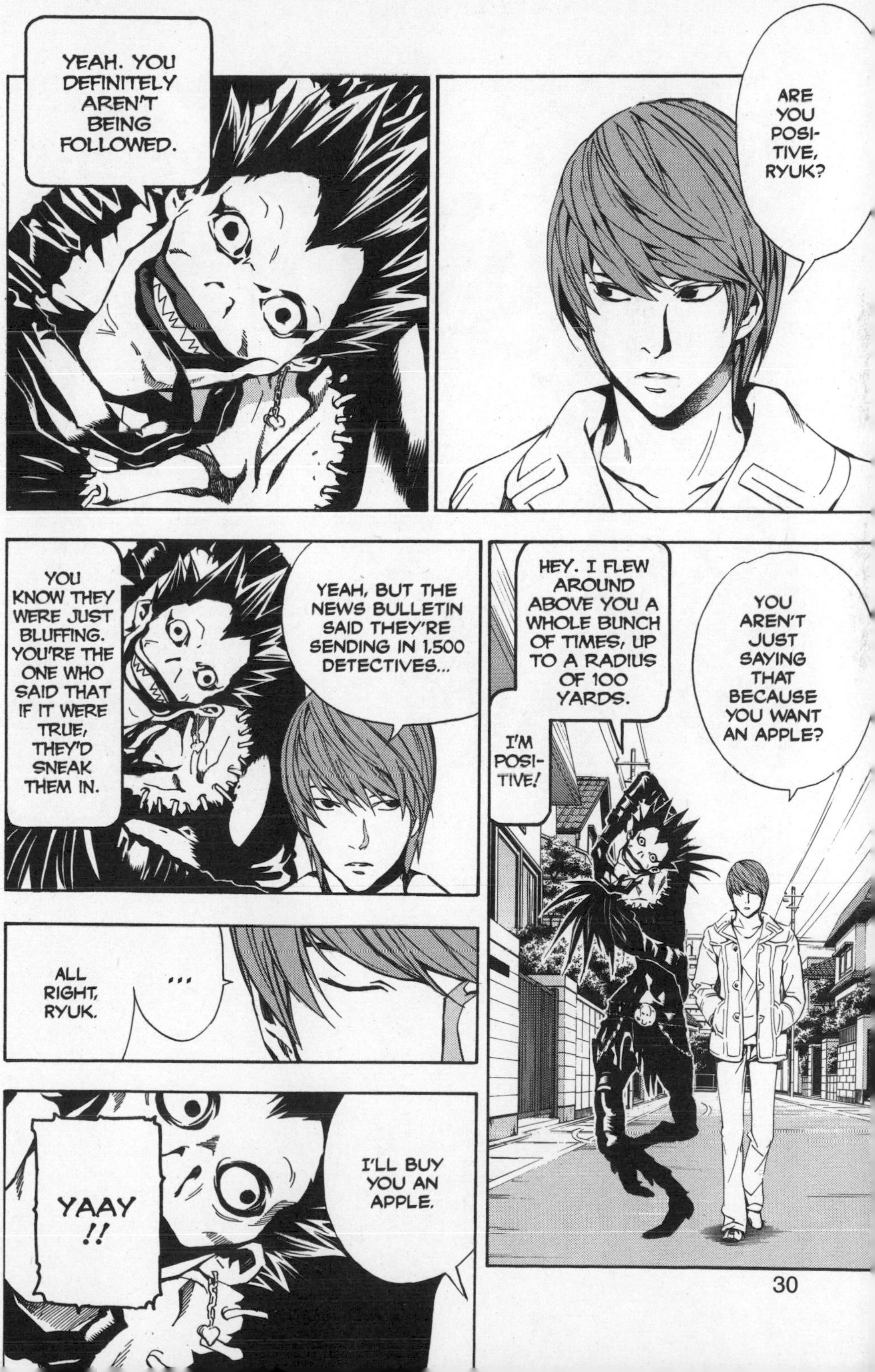
ARE YOU POSITIVE, RYUK?
YEAH. YOU DEFINITELY AREN'T BEING FOLLOWED.
YOU AREN'T JUST SAYING THAT BECAUSE YOU WANT AN APPLE?
HEY. I FLEW AROUND ABOVE YOU A WHOLE BUNCH OF TIMES, UP TO A RADIUS OF 100 YARDS.
I'M POSITIVE!
YEAH, BUT THE NEWS BULLETIN SAID THEY'RE SENDING IN 1,500 DETECTIVES...
YOU KNOW THEY WERE JUST BLUFFING. YOU'RE THE ONE WHO SAID THAT IF IT WERE TRUE, THEY'D SNEAK THEM IN.
...
ALL RIGHT, RYUK.
I'LL BUY YOU AN APPLE.
YAAY!!

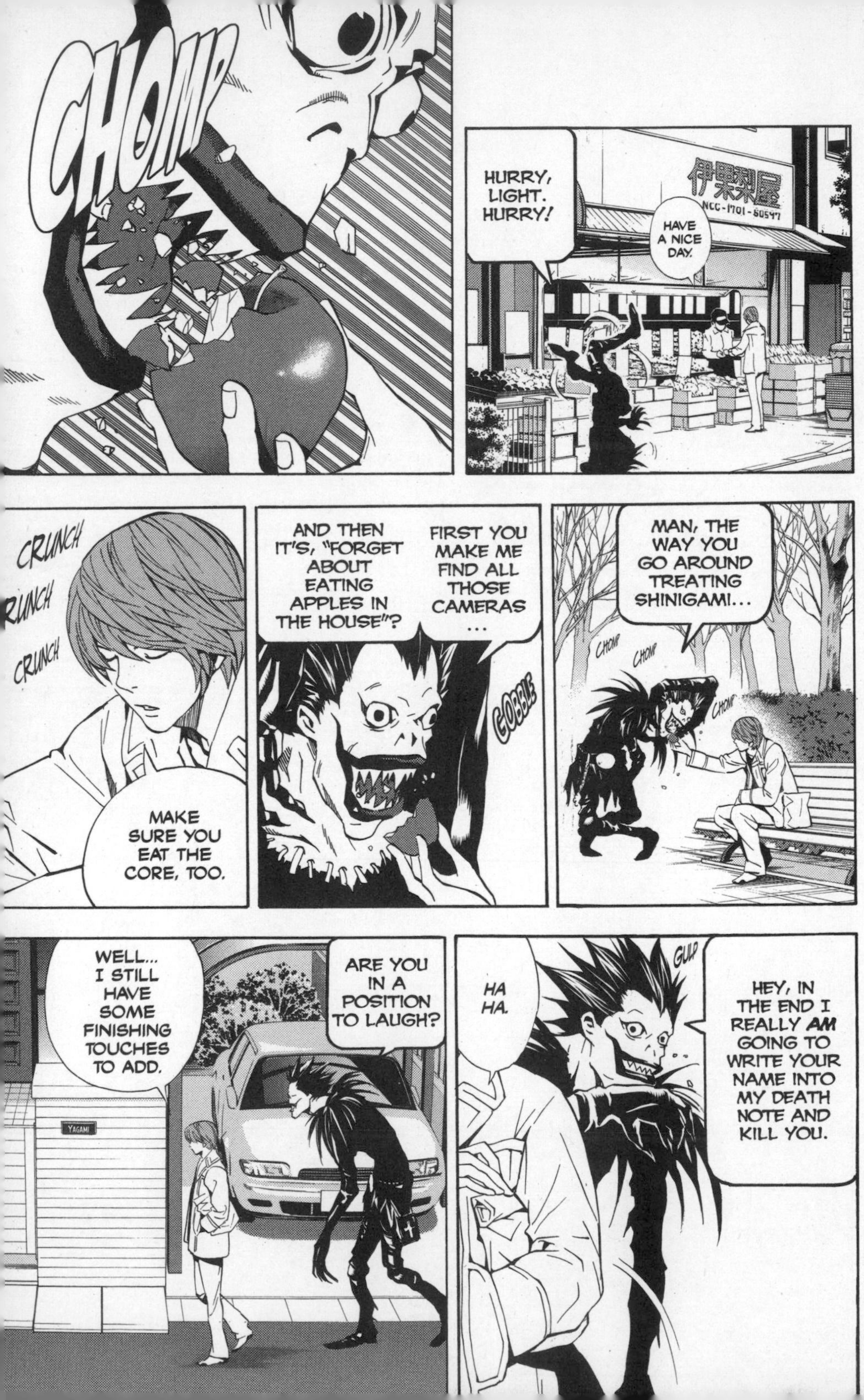
伊果梨屋
NCC-1701-80547
HAVE A NICE DAY.
HURRY, LIGHT. HURRY!
CHOMP
MAN, THE WAY YOU GO AROUND TREATING SHINIGAMI...
CHOMP
CHOMP
CHOMP
FIRST YOU MAKE ME FIND ALL THOSE CAMERAS ...
AND THEN IT'S, "FORGET ABOUT EATING APPLES IN THE HOUSE"?
GOBBLE
CRUNCH
CRUNCH
CRUNCH
MAKE SURE YOU EAT THE CORE, TOO.
GULP
HEY, IN THE END I REALLY ***AM*** GOING TO WRITE YOUR NAME INTO MY DEATH NOTE AND KILL YOU.
HA HA.
ARE YOU IN A POSITION TO LAUGH?
WELL... I STILL HAVE SOME FINISHING TOUCHES TO ADD.
YAGAMI

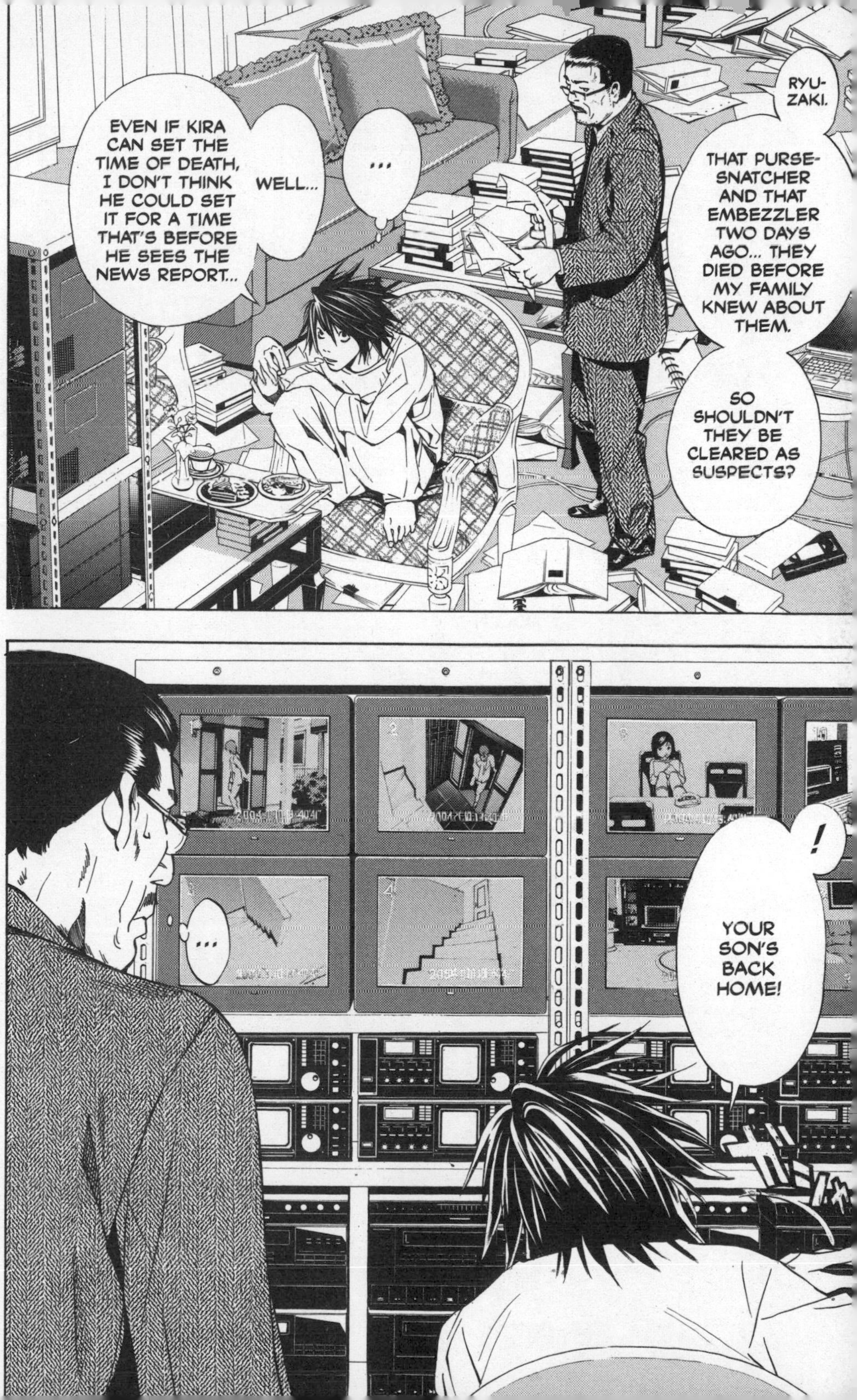
RYU-ZAKI.
THAT PURSE-SNATCHER AND THAT EMBEZZLER TWO DAYS AGO... THEY DIED BEFORE MY FAMILY KNEW ABOUT THEM.
SO SHOULDN'T THEY BE CLEARED AS SUSPECTS?
...
WELL...
EVEN IF KIRA CAN SET THE TIME OF DEATH, I DON'T THINK HE COULD SET IT FOR A TIME THAT'S BEFORE HE SEES THE NEWS REPORT...
!
YOUR SON'S BACK HOME!
...

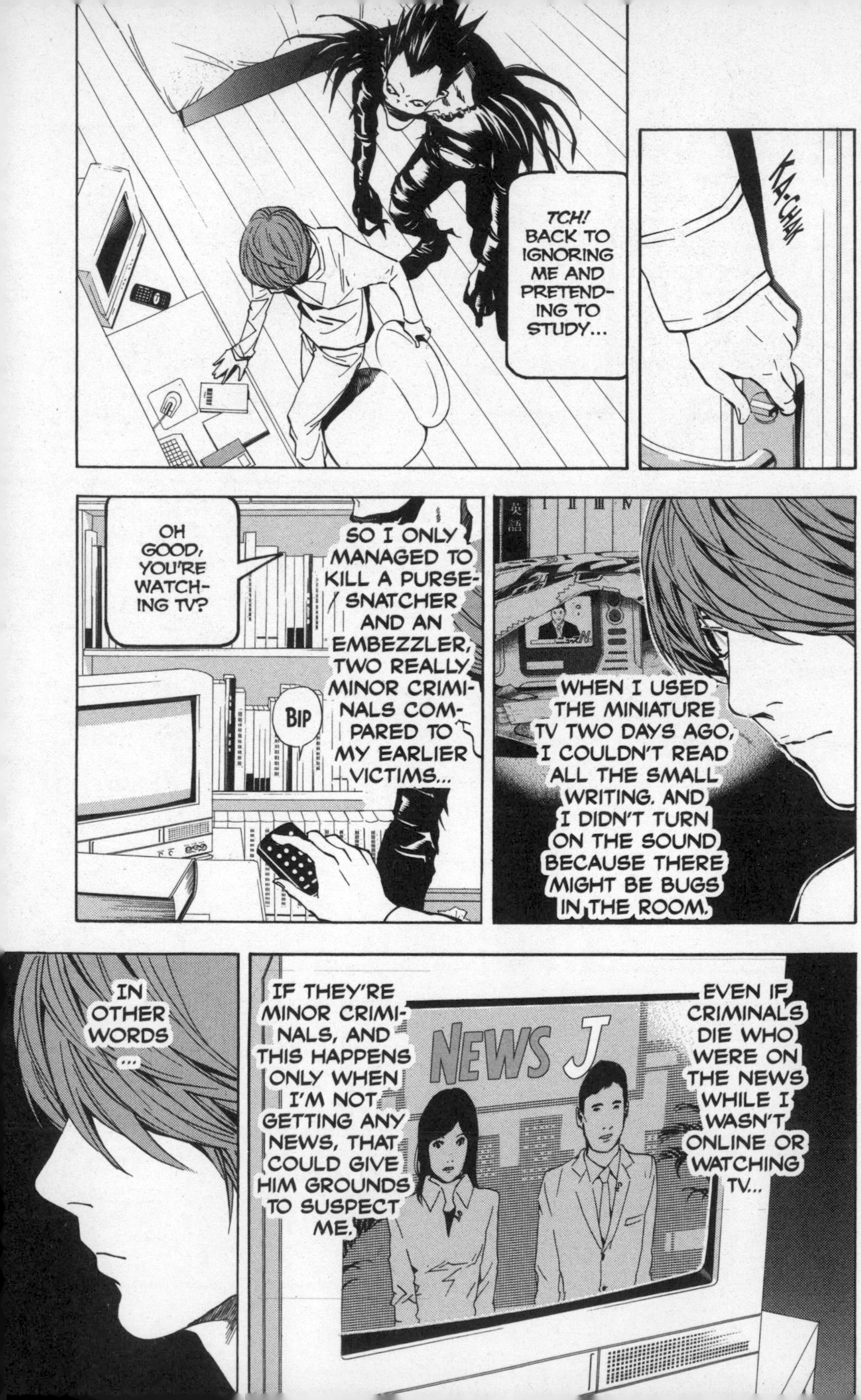
KA-CHAK
TCH! BACK TO IGNORING ME AND PRETENDING TO STUDY...
WHEN I USED THE MINIATURE TV TWO DAYS AGO, I COULDN'T READ ALL THE SMALL WRITING. AND I DIDN'T TURN ON THE SOUND BECAUSE THERE MIGHT BE BUGS IN THE ROOM.
SO I ONLY MANAGED TO KILL A PURSE-SNATCHER AND AN EMBEZZLER, TWO REALLY MINOR CRIMINALS COMPARED TO MY EARLIER VICTIMS...
OH GOOD, YOU'RE WATCHING TV?
BIP
EVEN IF CRIMINALS DIE WHO WERE ON THE NEWS WHILE I WASN'T ONLINE OR WATCHING TV...
IF THEY'RE MINOR CRIMINALS, AND THIS HAPPENS ONLY WHEN I'M NOT GETTING ANY NEWS, THAT COULD GIVE HIM GROUNDS TO SUSPECT ME.
NEWS J
IN OTHER WORDS ...

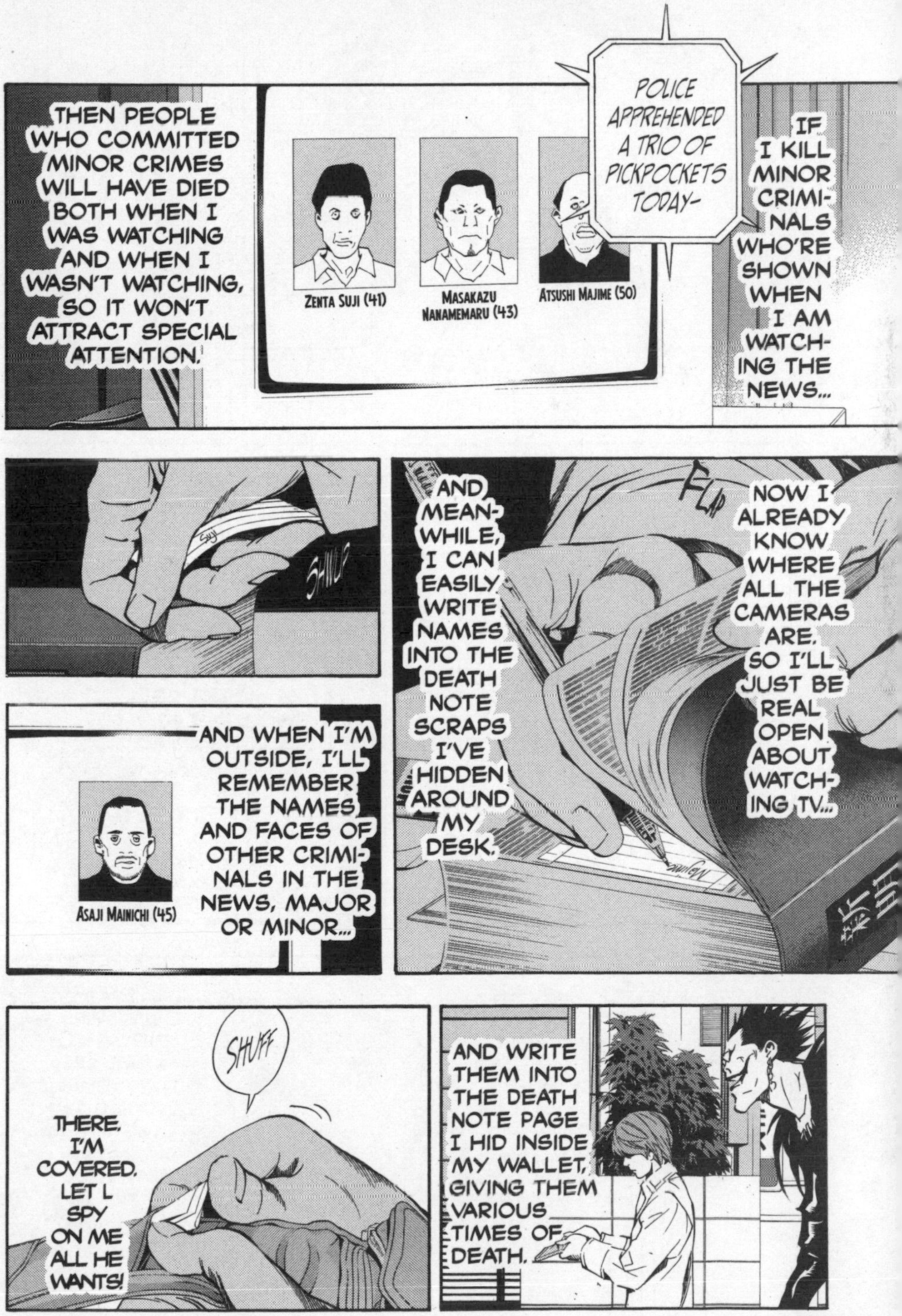
POLICE APPREHENDED A TRIO OF PICKPOCKETS TODAY-
IF I KILL MINOR CRIMINALS WHO'RE SHOWN WHEN I AM WATCHING THE NEWS...
Atsushi Majime (50)
Masakazu Nanamemaru (43)
Zenta Suji (41)
THEN PEOPLE WHO COMMITTED MINOR CRIMES WILL HAVE DIED BOTH WHEN I WAS WATCHING AND WHEN I WASN'T WATCHING, SO IT WON'T ATTRACT SPECIAL ATTENTION.
NOW I ALREADY KNOW WHERE ALL THE CAMERAS ARE. SO I'LL JUST BE REAL OPEN ABOUT WATCHING TV...
FLAP
AND MEANWHILE, I CAN EASILY WRITE NAMES INTO THE DEATH NOTE SCRAPS I'VE HIDDEN AROUND MY DESK.
SHWUP
AND WHEN I'M OUTSIDE, I'LL REMEMBER THE NAMES AND FACES OF OTHER CRIMINALS IN THE NEWS, MAJOR OR MINOR...
Asaji Mainichi (45)
AND WRITE THEM INTO THE DEATH NOTE PAGE I HID INSIDE MY WALLET, GIVING THEM VARIOUS TIMES OF DEATH.
SHUFF
THERE. I'M COVERED. LET L SPY ON ME ALL HE WANTS!

READ THIS WAY

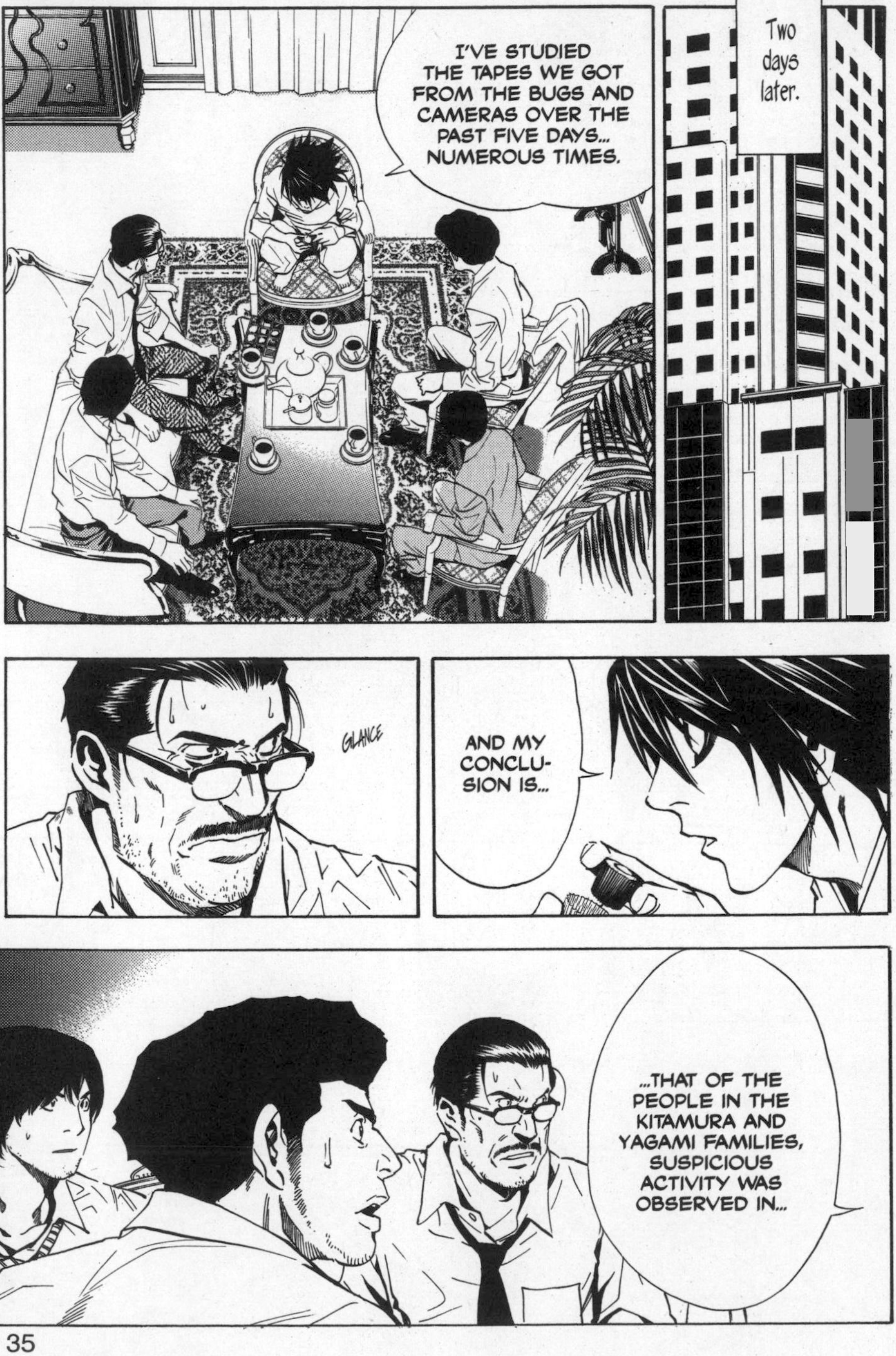

Two days later.
I'VE STUDIED THE TAPES WE GOT FROM THE BUGS AND CAMERAS OVER THE PAST FIVE DAYS... NUMEROUS TIMES.
AND MY CONCLU- SION IS...
GLANCE
...THAT OF THE PEOPLE IN THE KITAMURA AND YAGAMI FAMILIES, SUSPICIOUS ACTIVITY WAS OBSERVED IN...

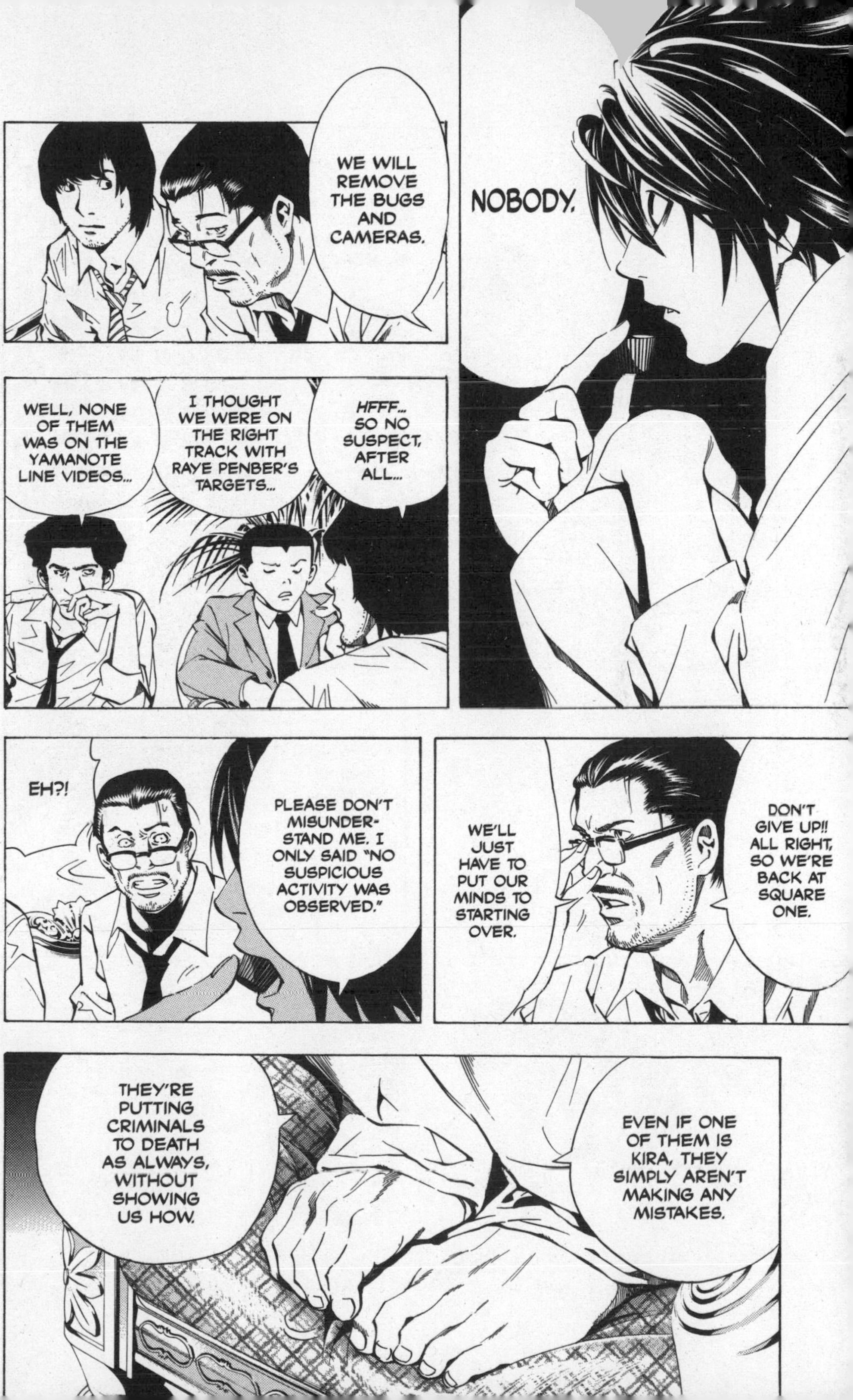
NOBODY.
WE WILL REMOVE THE BUGS AND CAMERAS.
HFFF... SO NO SUSPECT, AFTER ALL...
I THOUGHT WE WERE ON THE RIGHT TRACK WITH RAYE PENBER'S TARGETS...
WELL, NONE OF THEM WAS ON THE YAMANOTE LINE VIDEOS...
DON'T GIVE UP!! ALL RIGHT, SO WE'RE BACK AT SQUARE ONE.
WE'LL JUST HAVE TO PUT OUR MINDS TO STARTING OVER.
PLEASE DON'T MISUNDER-STAND ME. I ONLY SAID "NO SUSPICIOUS ACTIVITY WAS OBSERVED."
EH?!
EVEN IF ONE OF THEM IS KIRA, THEY SIMPLY AREN'T MAKING ANY MISTAKES.
THEY'RE PUTTING CRIMINALS TO DEATH AS ALWAYS, WITHOUT SHOWING US HOW.

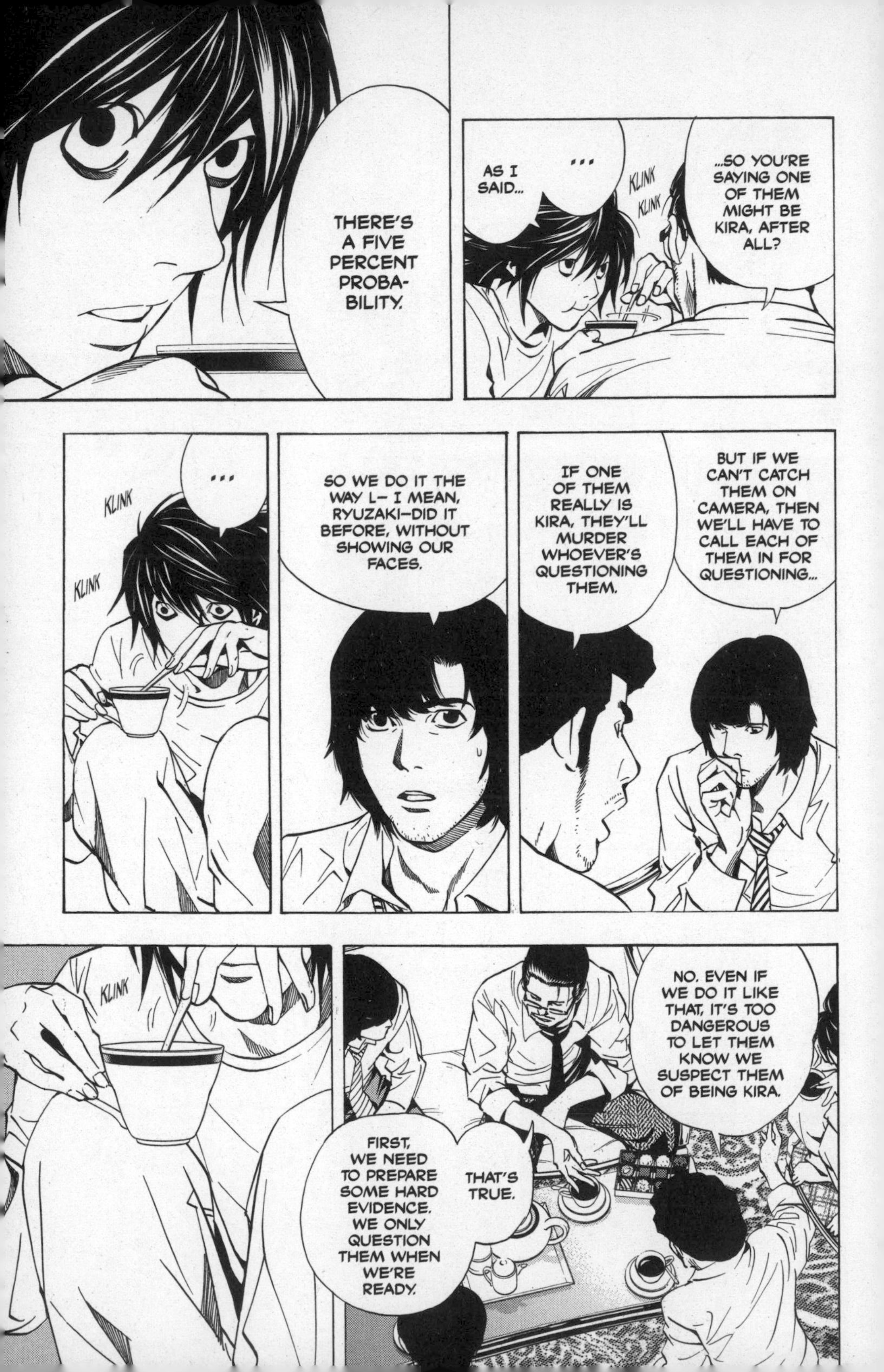
...SO YOU'RE SAYING ONE OF THEM MIGHT BE KIRA, AFTER ALL?
KLINK
KLINK
...
AS I SAID...
THERE'S A FIVE PERCENT PROBA-BILITY.
BUT IF WE CAN'T CATCH THEM ON CAMERA, THEN WE'LL HAVE TO CALL EACH OF THEM IN FOR QUESTIONING...
IF ONE OF THEM REALLY IS KIRA, THEY'LL MURDER WHOEVER'S QUESTIONING THEM.
SO WE DO IT THE WAY L— I MEAN, RYUZAKI—DID IT BEFORE, WITHOUT SHOWING OUR FACES.
...
KLINK
KLINK
NO. EVEN IF WE DO IT LIKE THAT, IT'S TOO DANGEROUS TO LET THEM KNOW WE SUSPECT THEM OF BEING KIRA.
THAT'S TRUE.
FIRST, WE NEED TO PREPARE SOME HARD EVIDENCE. WE ONLY QUESTION THEM WHEN WE'RE READY.
KLINK

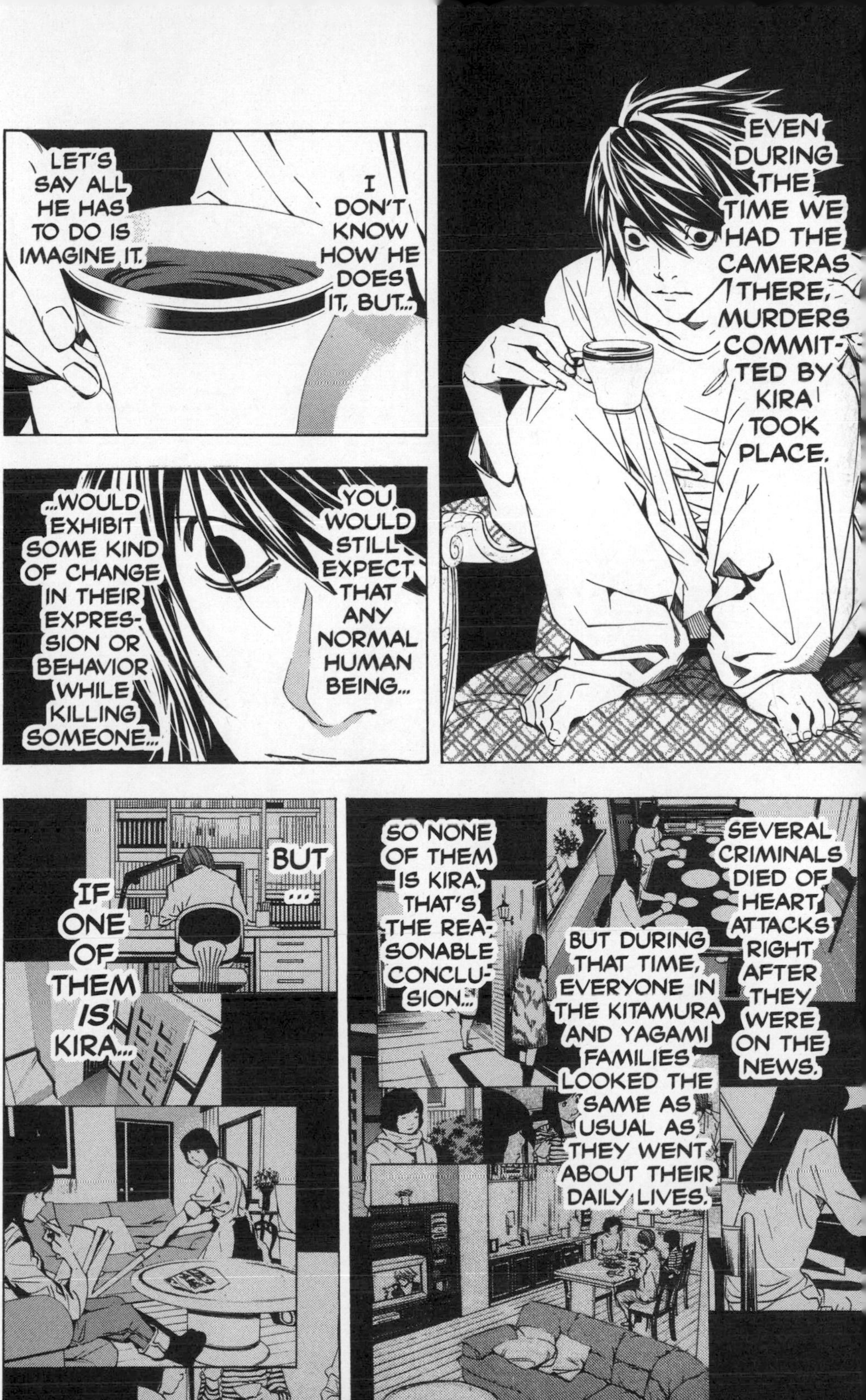
EVEN DURING THE TIME WE HAD THE CAMERAS THERE, MURDERS COMMITTED BY KIRA TOOK PLACE.
I DON'T KNOW HOW HE DOES IT, BUT...
LET'S SAY ALL HE HAS TO DO IS IMAGINE IT.
YOU WOULD STILL EXPECT THAT ANY NORMAL HUMAN BEING...
...WOULD EXHIBIT SOME KIND OF CHANGE IN THEIR EXPRESSION OR BEHAVIOR WHILE KILLING SOMEONE...
SEVERAL CRIMINALS DIED OF HEART ATTACKS RIGHT AFTER THEY WERE ON THE NEWS.
BUT DURING THAT TIME, EVERYONE IN THE KITAMURA AND YAGAMI FAMILIES LOOKED THE SAME AS USUAL AS THEY WENT ABOUT THEIR DAILY LIVES.
SO NONE OF THEM IS KIRA, THAT'S THE REASONABLE CONCLUSION...
BUT ...
IF ONE OF THEM IS KIRA...

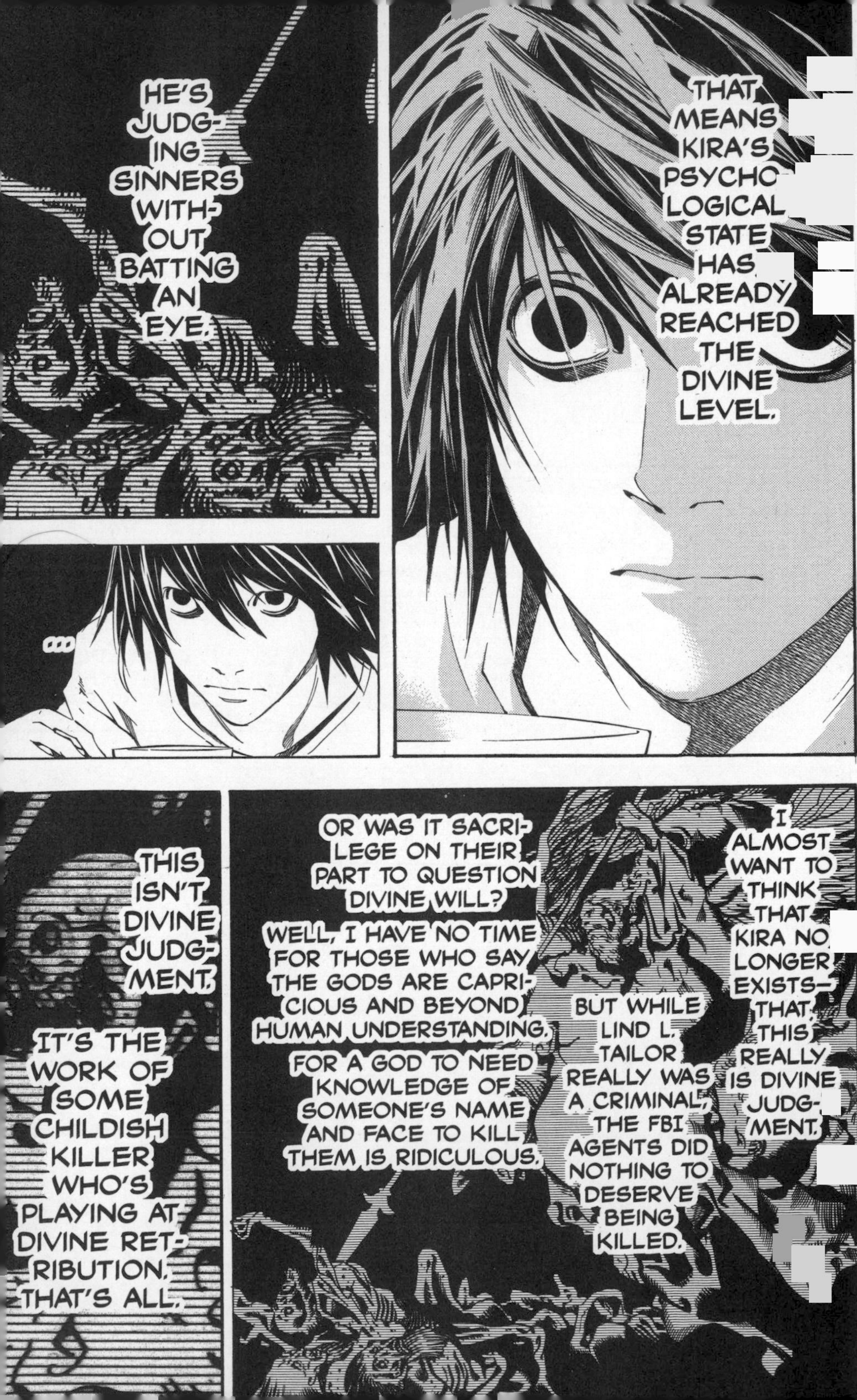
THAT MEANS KIRA'S PSYCHOLOGICAL STATE HAS ALREADY REACHED THE DIVINE LEVEL.
HE'S JUDGING SINNERS WITHOUT BATTING AN EYE.
...
I ALMOST WANT TO THINK THAT KIRA NO LONGER EXISTS—THAT THIS REALLY IS DIVINE JUDGMENT.
BUT WHILE LIND L. TAILOR REALLY WAS A CRIMINAL, THE FBI AGENTS DID NOTHING TO DESERVE BEING KILLED.
OR WAS IT SACRILEGE ON THEIR PART TO QUESTION DIVINE WILL?
WELL, I HAVE NO TIME FOR THOSE WHO SAY THE GODS ARE CAPRICIOUS AND BEYOND HUMAN UNDERSTANDING.
FOR A GOD TO NEED KNOWLEDGE OF SOMEONE'S NAME AND FACE TO KILL THEM IS RIDICULOUS.
THIS ISN'T DIVINE JUDGMENT.
IT'S THE WORK OF SOME CHILDISH KILLER WHO'S PLAYING AT DIVINE RETRIBUTION, THAT'S ALL.

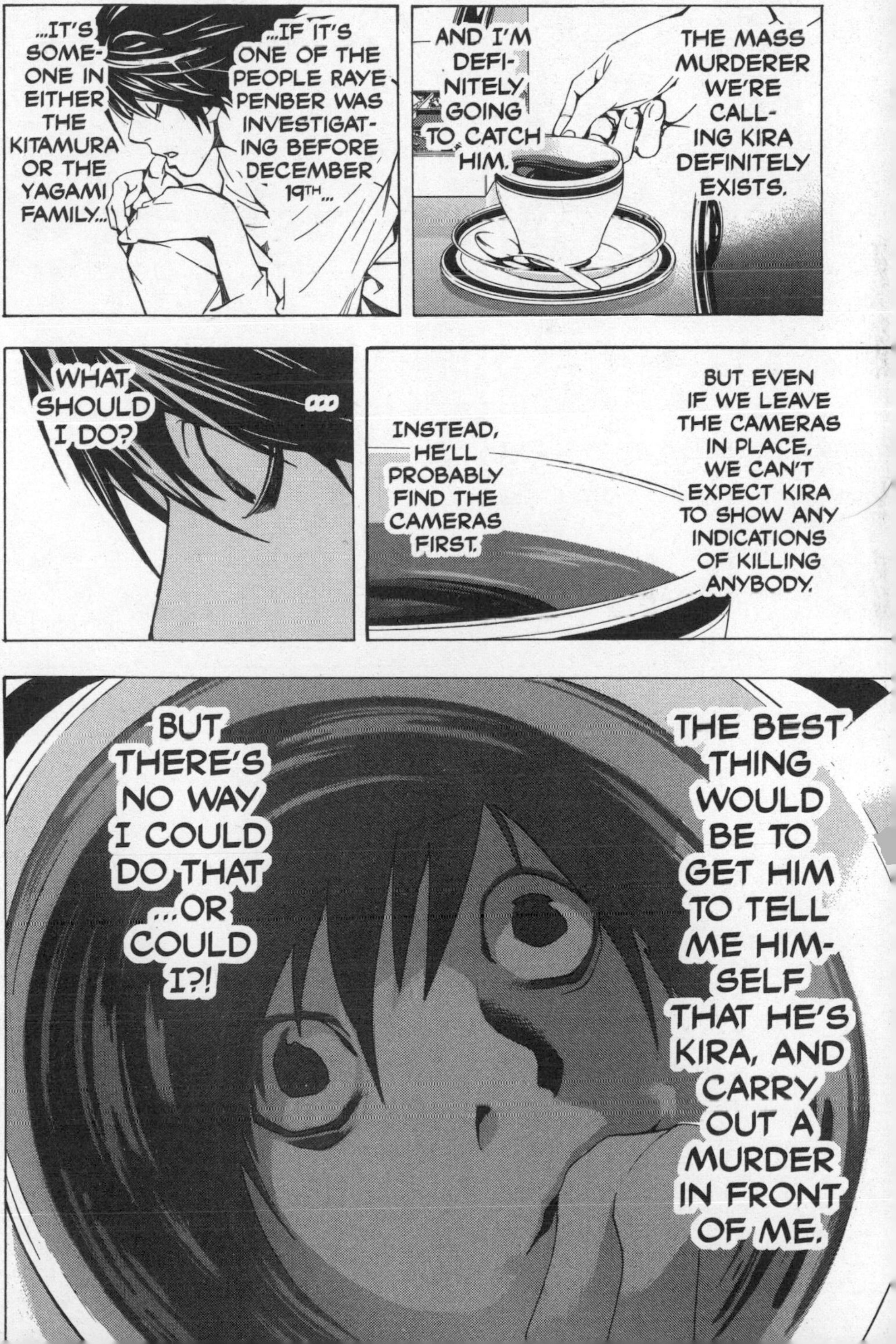
THE MASS MURDERER WE'RE CALLING KIRA DEFINITELY EXISTS.
AND I'M DEFINITELY GOING TO CATCH HIM.
...IF IT'S ONE OF THE PEOPLE RAYE PENBER WAS INVESTIGATING BEFORE DECEMBER 19TH...
...IT'S SOMEONE IN EITHER THE KITAMURA OR THE YAGAMI FAMILY...
BUT EVEN IF WE LEAVE THE CAMERAS IN PLACE, WE CAN'T EXPECT KIRA TO SHOW ANY INDICATIONS OF KILLING ANYBODY.
INSTEAD, HE'LL PROBABLY FIND THE CAMERAS FIRST.
...
WHAT SHOULD I DO?
THE BEST THING WOULD BE TO GET HIM TO TELL ME HIMSELF THAT HE'S KIRA, AND CARRY OUT A MURDER IN FRONT OF ME.
BUT THERE'S NO WAY I COULD DO THAT ...OR COULD I?!

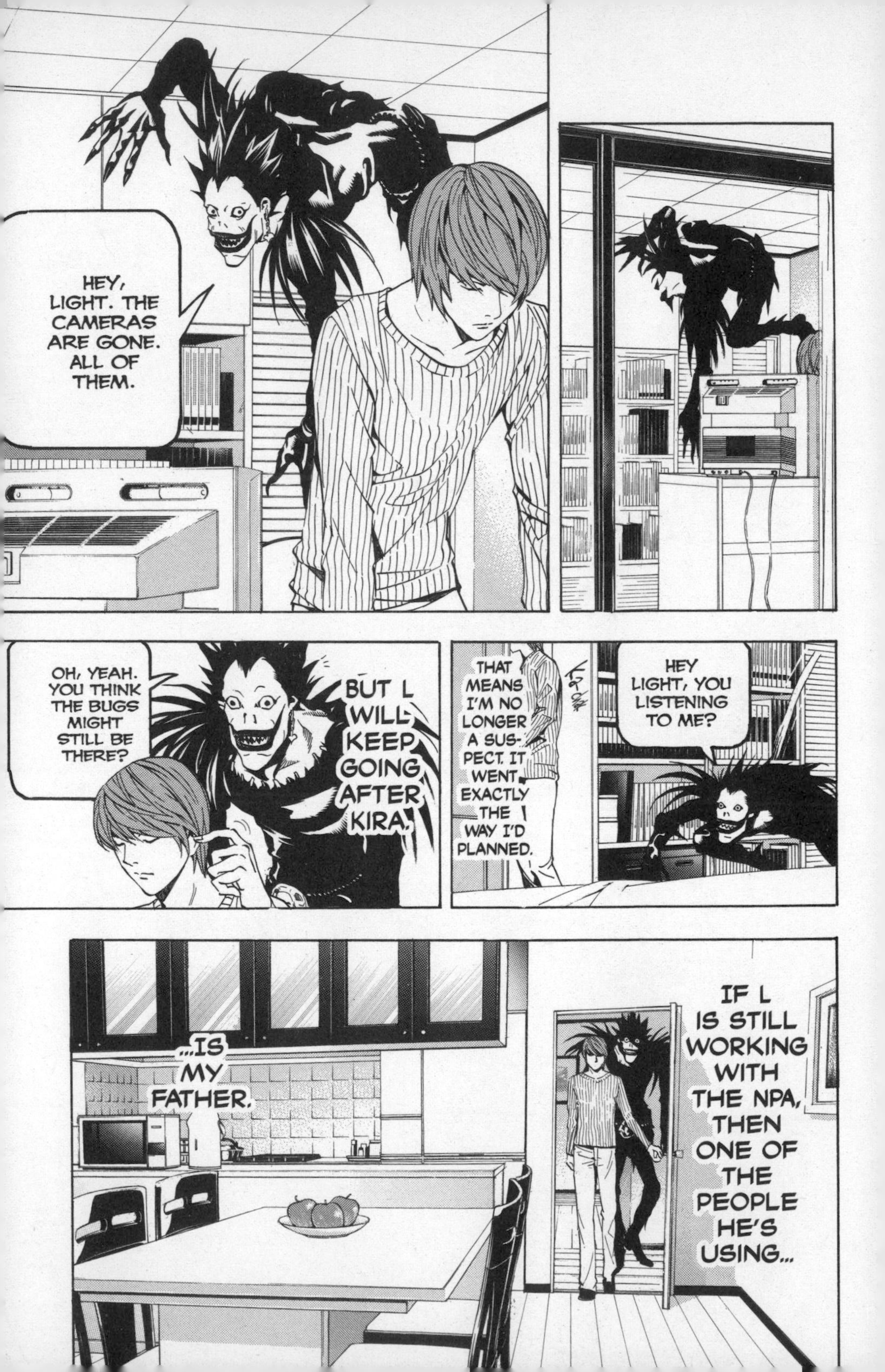
HEY, LIGHT. THE CAMERAS ARE GONE. ALL OF THEM.
HEY LIGHT, YOU LISTENING TO ME?
THAT MEANS I'M NO LONGER A SUSPECT. IT WENT EXACTLY THE WAY I'D PLANNED.
OH, YEAH. YOU THINK THE BUGS MIGHT STILL BE THERE?
BUT L WILL KEEP GOING AFTER KIRA.
IF L IS STILL WORKING WITH THE NPA, THEN ONE OF THE PEOPLE HE'S USING...
...IS MY FATHER.

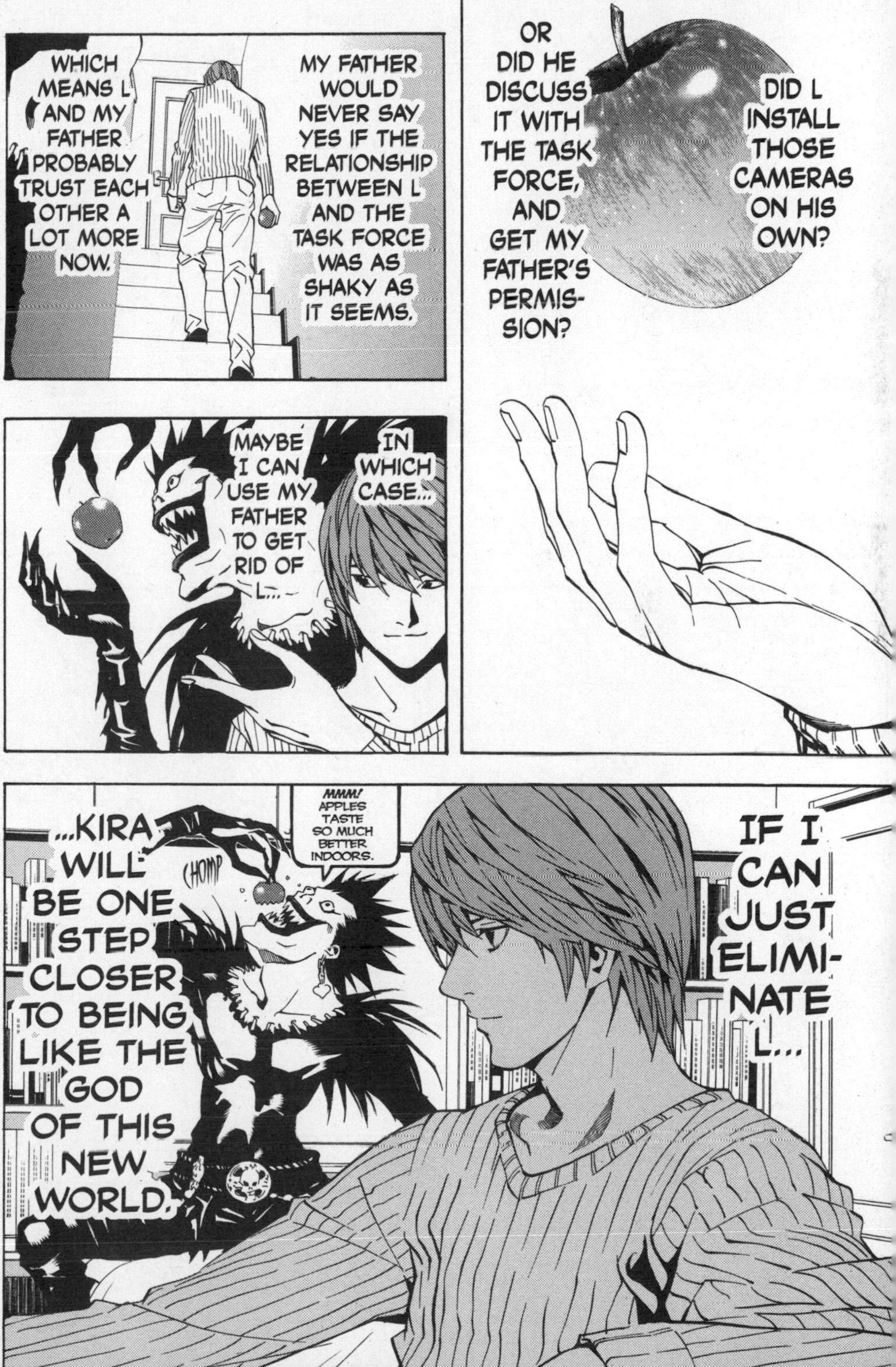
DID L INSTALL THOSE CAMERAS ON HIS OWN?
OR DID HE DISCUSS IT WITH THE TASK FORCE, AND GET MY FATHER'S PERMIS-SION?
MY FATHER WOULD NEVER SAY YES IF THE RELATIONSHIP BETWEEN L AND THE TASK FORCE WAS AS SHAKY AS IT SEEMS.
WHICH MEANS L AND MY FATHER PROBABLY TRUST EACH OTHER A LOT MORE NOW.
IN WHICH CASE...
MAYBE I CAN USE MY FATHER TO GET RID OF L...
IF I CAN JUST ELIMI-NATE L...
MMM! APPLES TASTE SO MUCH BETTER INDOORS.
CHOMP
...KIRA WILL BE ONE STEP CLOSER TO BEING LIKE THE GOD OF THIS NEW WORLD.

READ THIS WAY

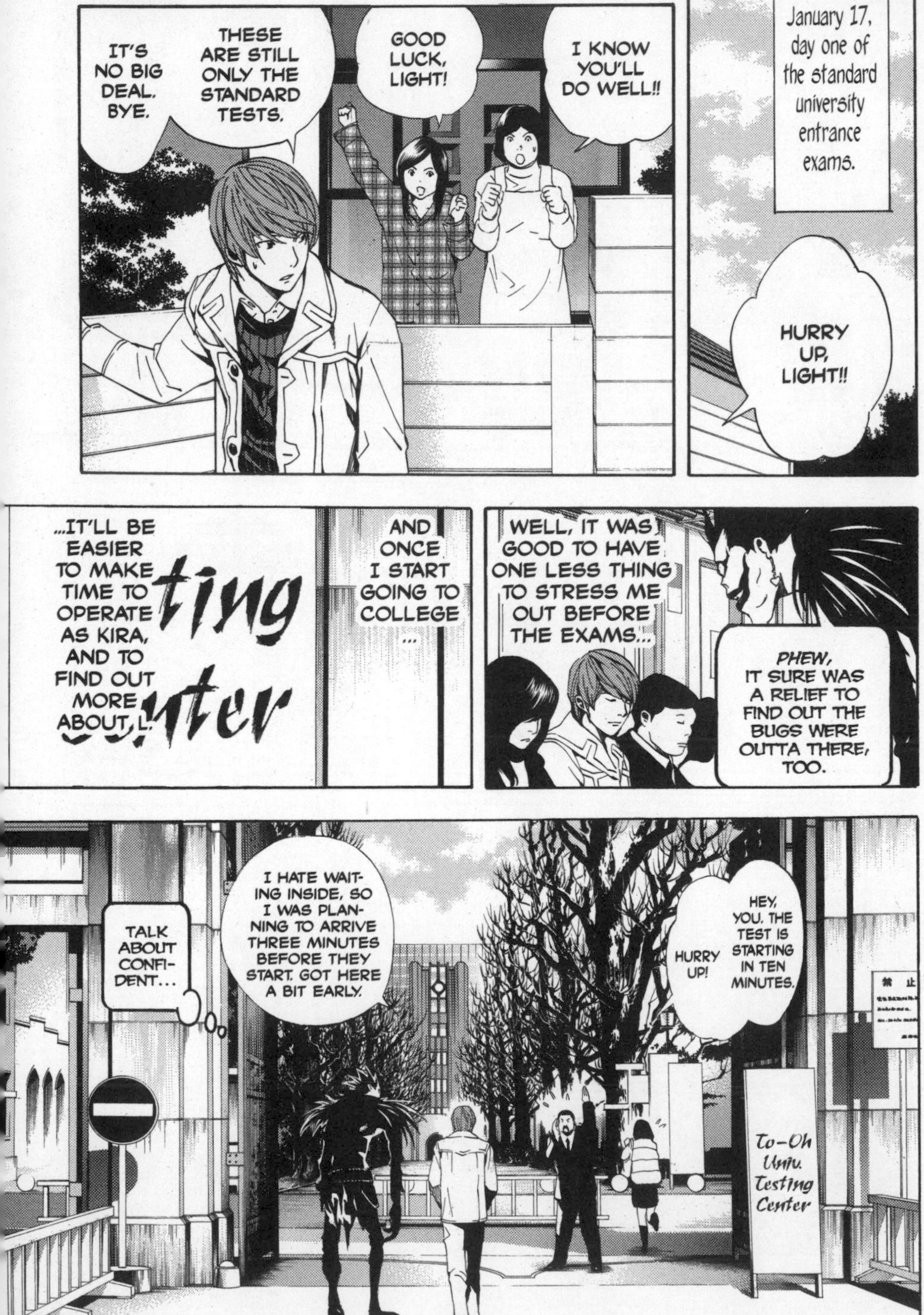
January 17, day one of the standard university entrance exams.
HURRY UP, LIGHT!!
I KNOW YOU'LL DO WELL!!
GOOD LUCK, LIGHT!
THESE ARE STILL ONLY THE STANDARD TESTS.
IT'S NO BIG DEAL. BYE.
WELL, IT WAS GOOD TO HAVE ONE LESS THING TO STRESS ME OUT BEFORE THE EXAMS...
PHEW, IT SURE WAS A RELIEF TO FIND OUT THE BUGS WERE OUTTA THERE, TOO.
AND ONCE I START GOING TO COLLEGE...
...IT'LL BE EASIER TO MAKE TIME TO OPERATE AS KIRA, AND TO FIND OUT MORE ABOUT L.
HEY, YOU. THE TEST IS STARTING IN TEN MINUTES.
HURRY UP!
To-Oh Univ. Testing Center
I HATE WAITING INSIDE, SO I WAS PLANNING TO ARRIVE THREE MINUTES BEFORE THEY START. GOT HERE A BIT EARLY.
TALK ABOUT CONFIDENT...

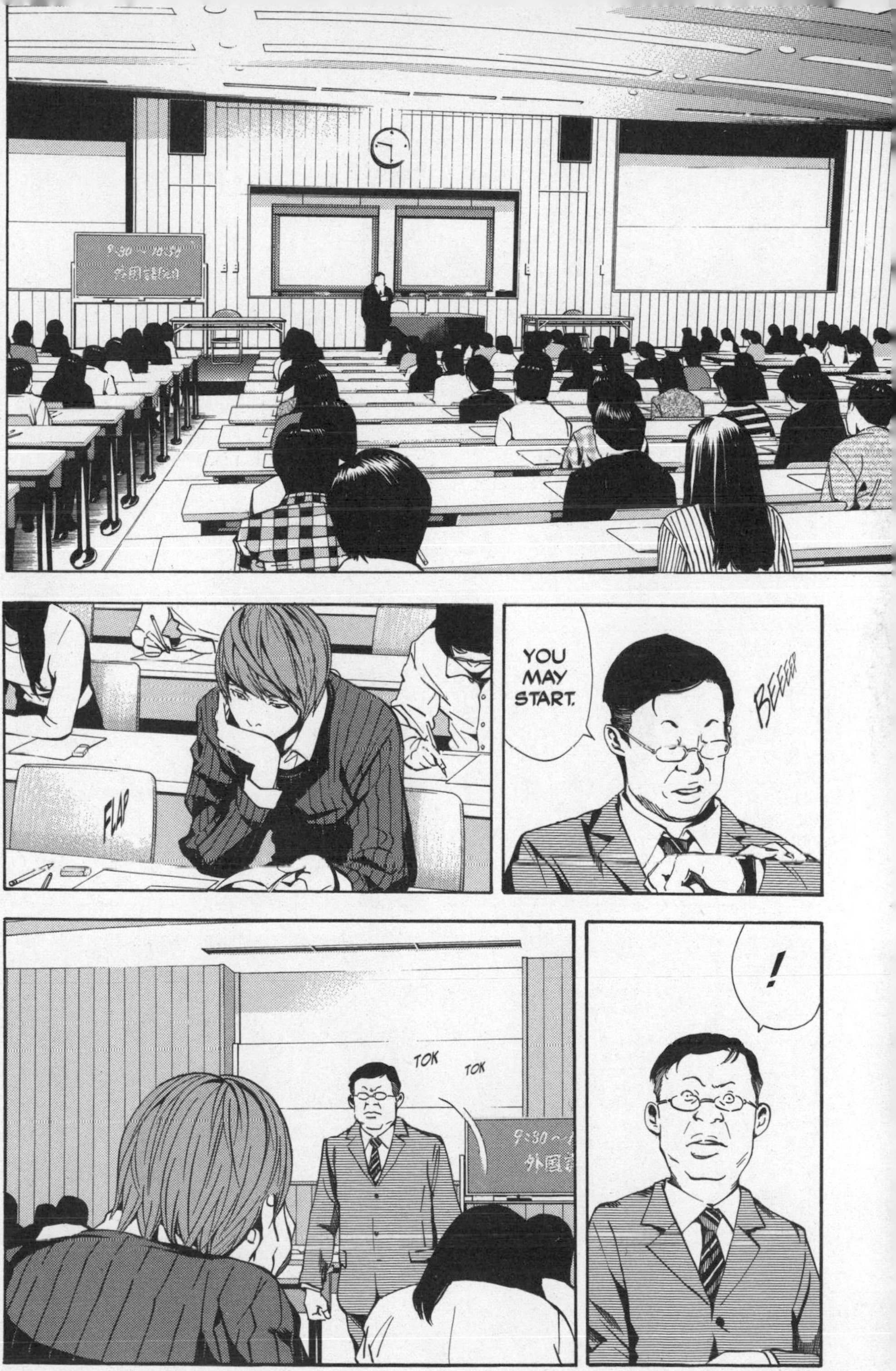

YOU MAY START.
BEEEP
FLAP
!
TOK
TOK

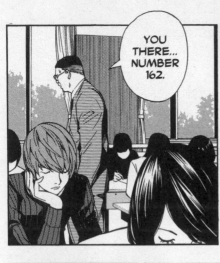

YOU THERE... NUMBER 162.

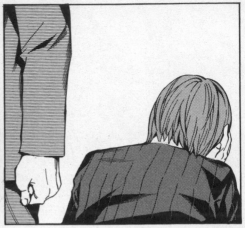

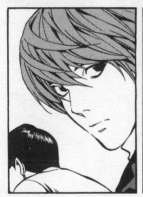

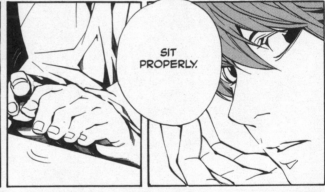

SIT PROPERLY.

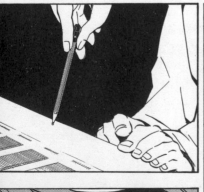

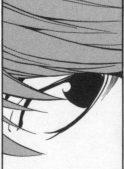

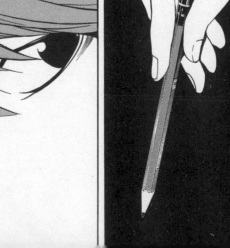

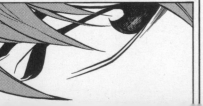

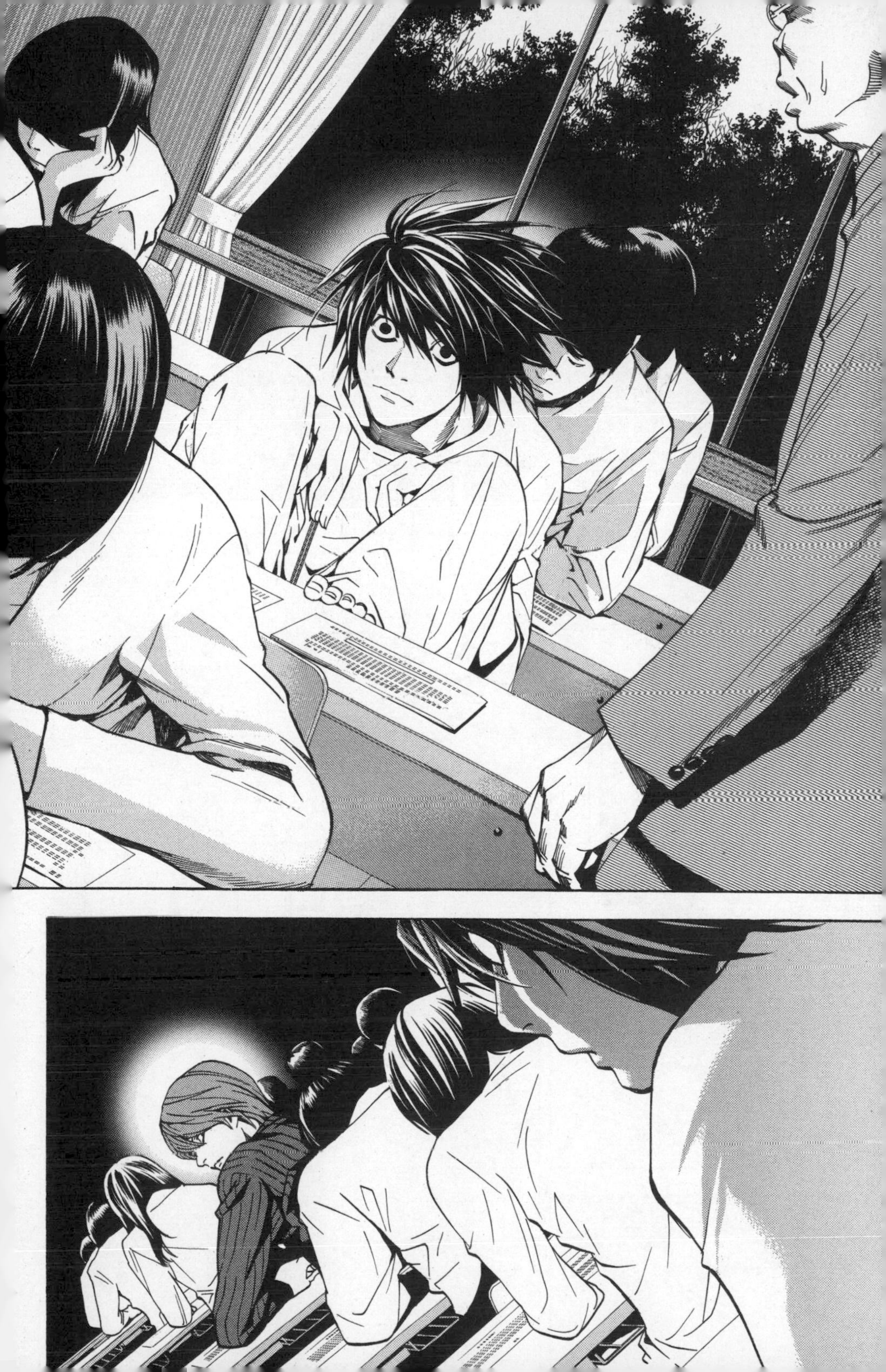

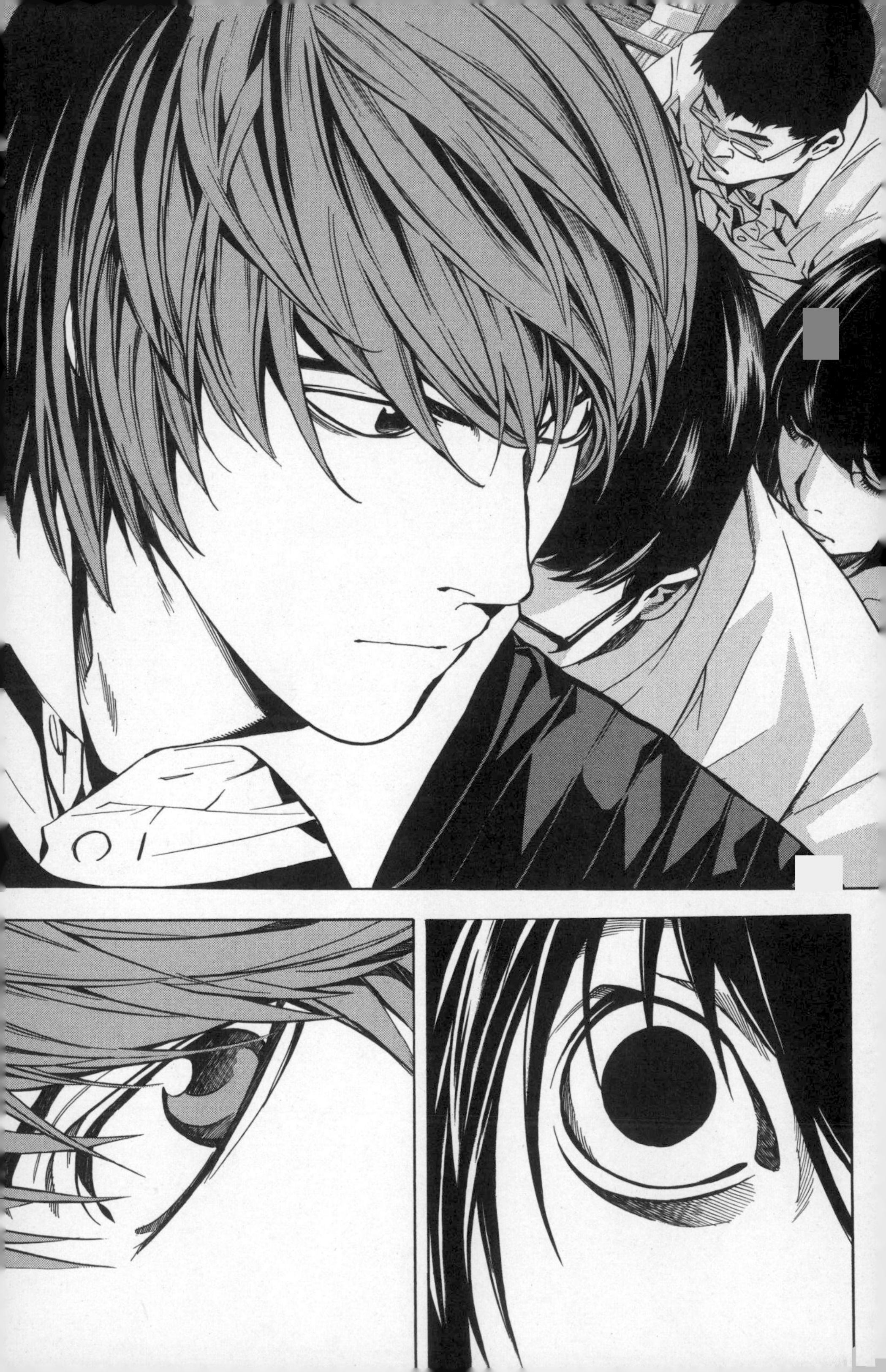

chapter 19 Humiliation

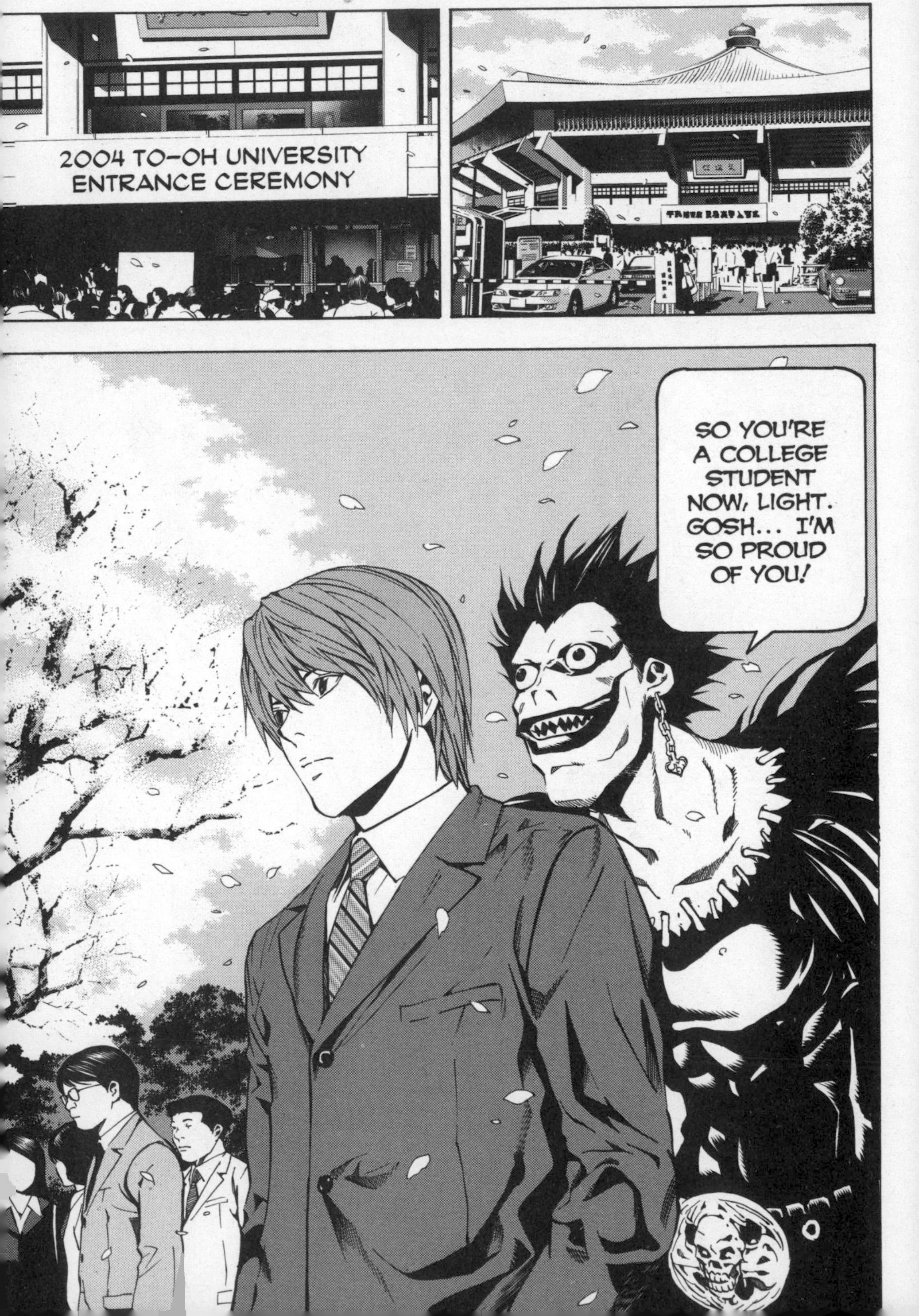
2004 TO-OH UNIVERSITY
ENTRANCE CEREMONY
SO YOU'RE A COLLEGE STUDENT NOW, LIGHT. GOSH... I'M SO PROUD OF YOU!

chapter 19 Humiliation

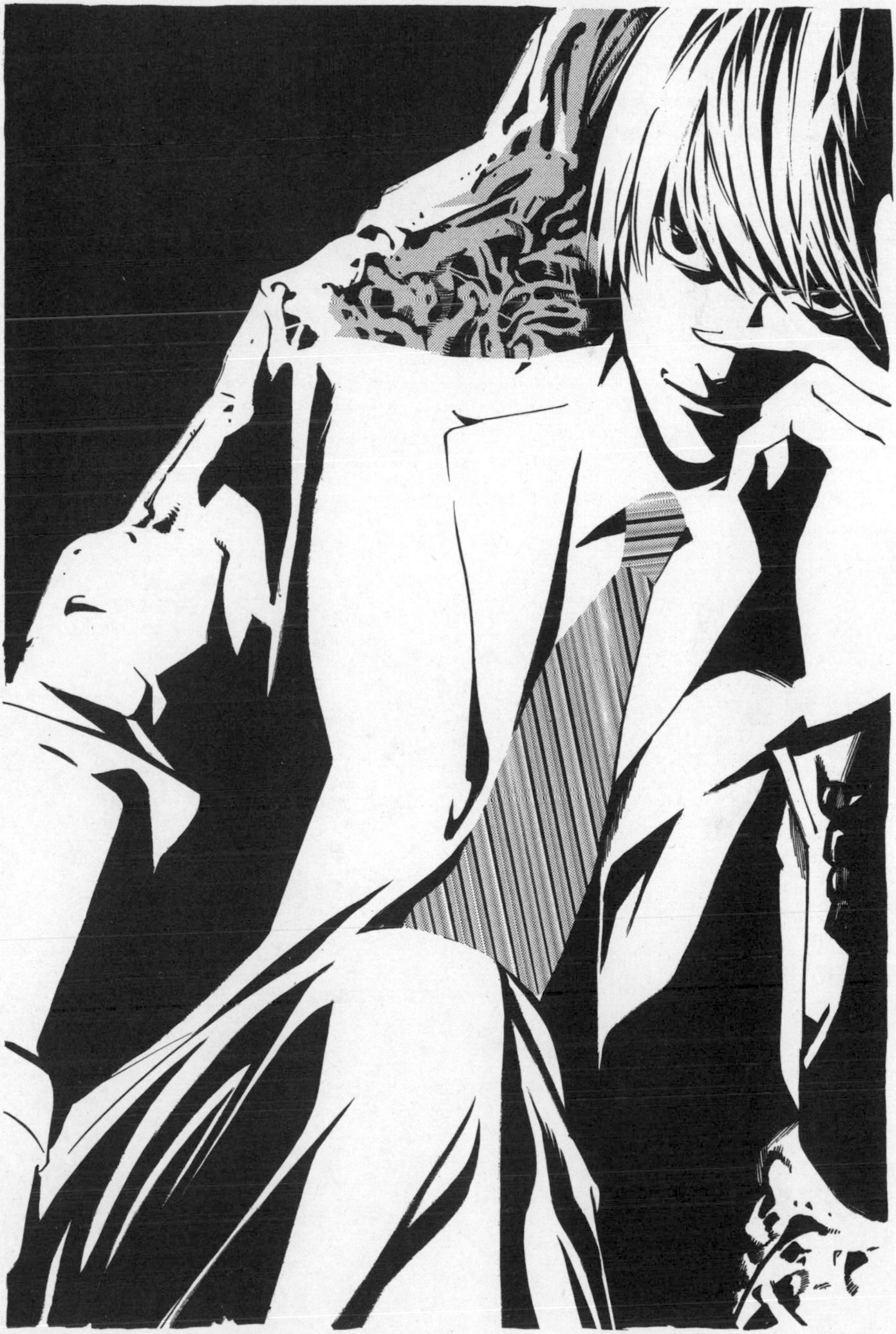

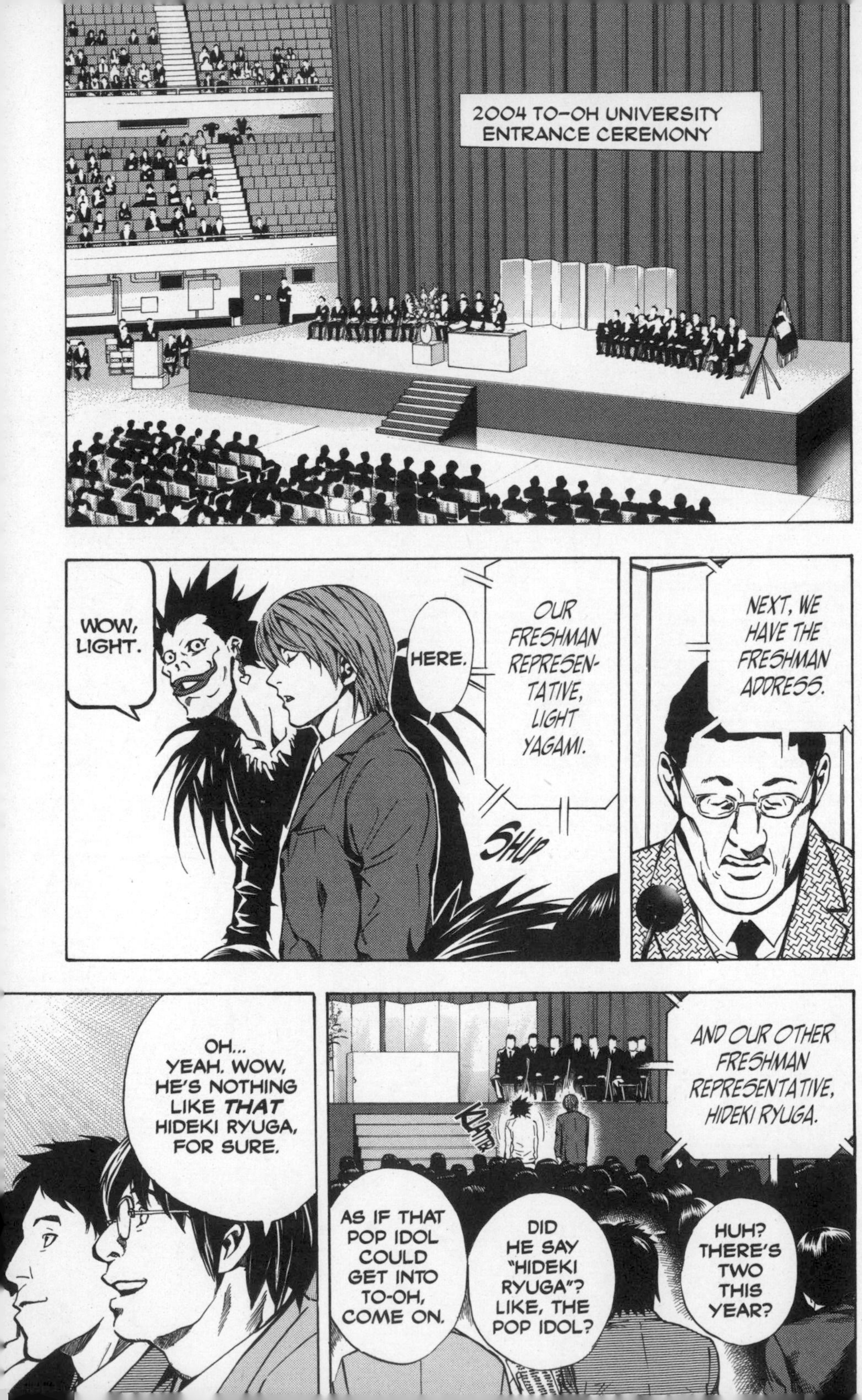
2004 TO-OH UNIVERSITY ENTRANCE CEREMONY
NEXT, WE HAVE THE FRESHMAN ADDRESS.
OUR FRESHMAN REPRESENTATIVE, LIGHT YAGAMI.
HERE.
WOW, LIGHT.
SHUP
AND OUR OTHER FRESHMAN REPRESENTATIVE, HIDEKI RYUGA.
HUH? THERE'S TWO THIS YEAR?
DID HE SAY "HIDEKI RYUGA"? LIKE, THE POP IDOL?
AS IF THAT POP IDOL COULD GET INTO TO-OH, COME ON.
OH... YEAH. WOW, HE'S NOTHING LIKE *THAT* HIDEKI RYUGA, FOR SURE.

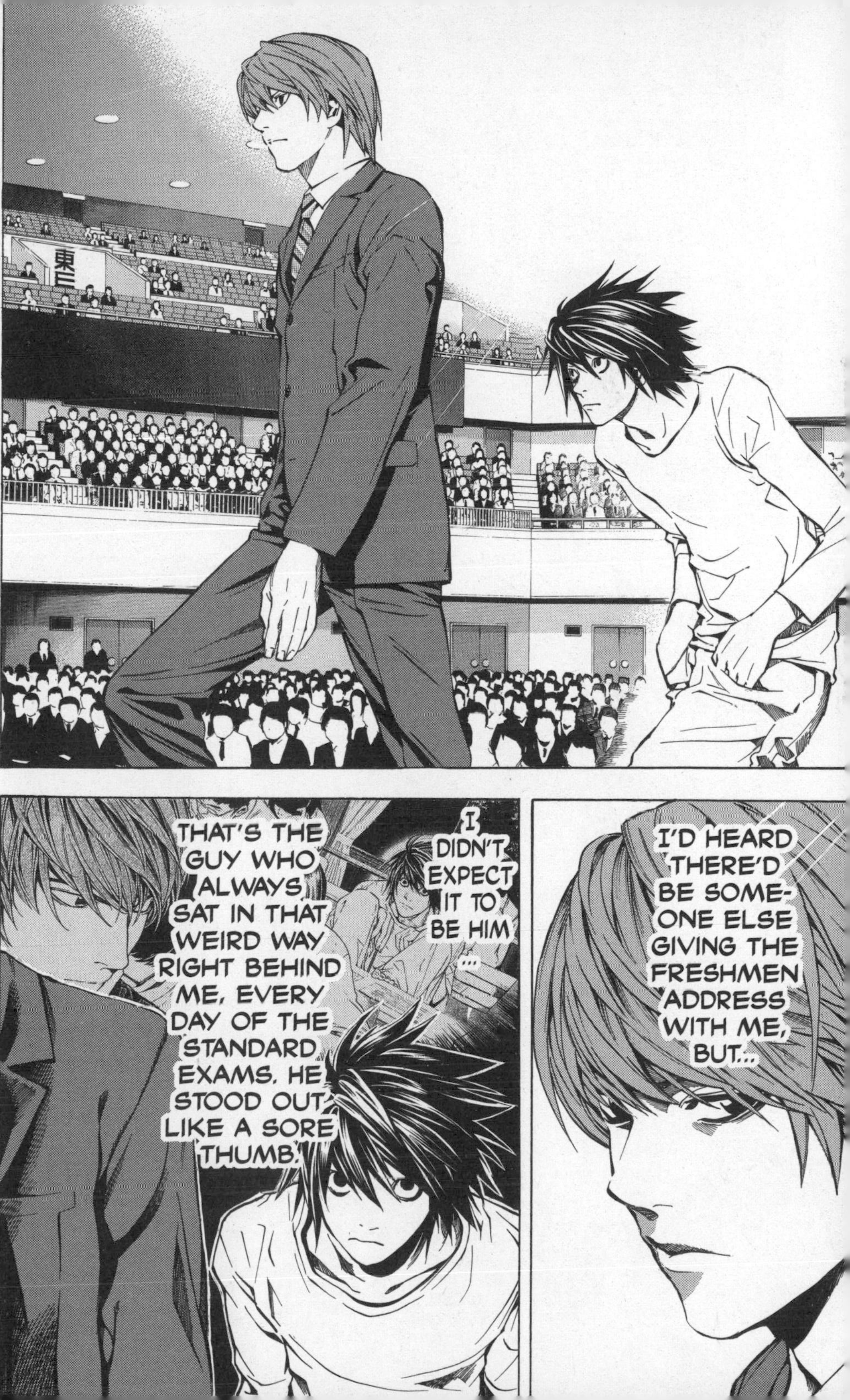
I'D HEARD THERE'D BE SOME-ONE ELSE GIVING THE FRESHMEN ADDRESS WITH ME, BUT...
I DIDN'T EXPECT IT TO BE HIM...
THAT'S THE GUY WHO ALWAYS SAT IN THAT WEIRD WAY RIGHT BEHIND ME, EVERY DAY OF THE STANDARD EXAMS. HE STOOD OUT LIKE A SORE THUMB.

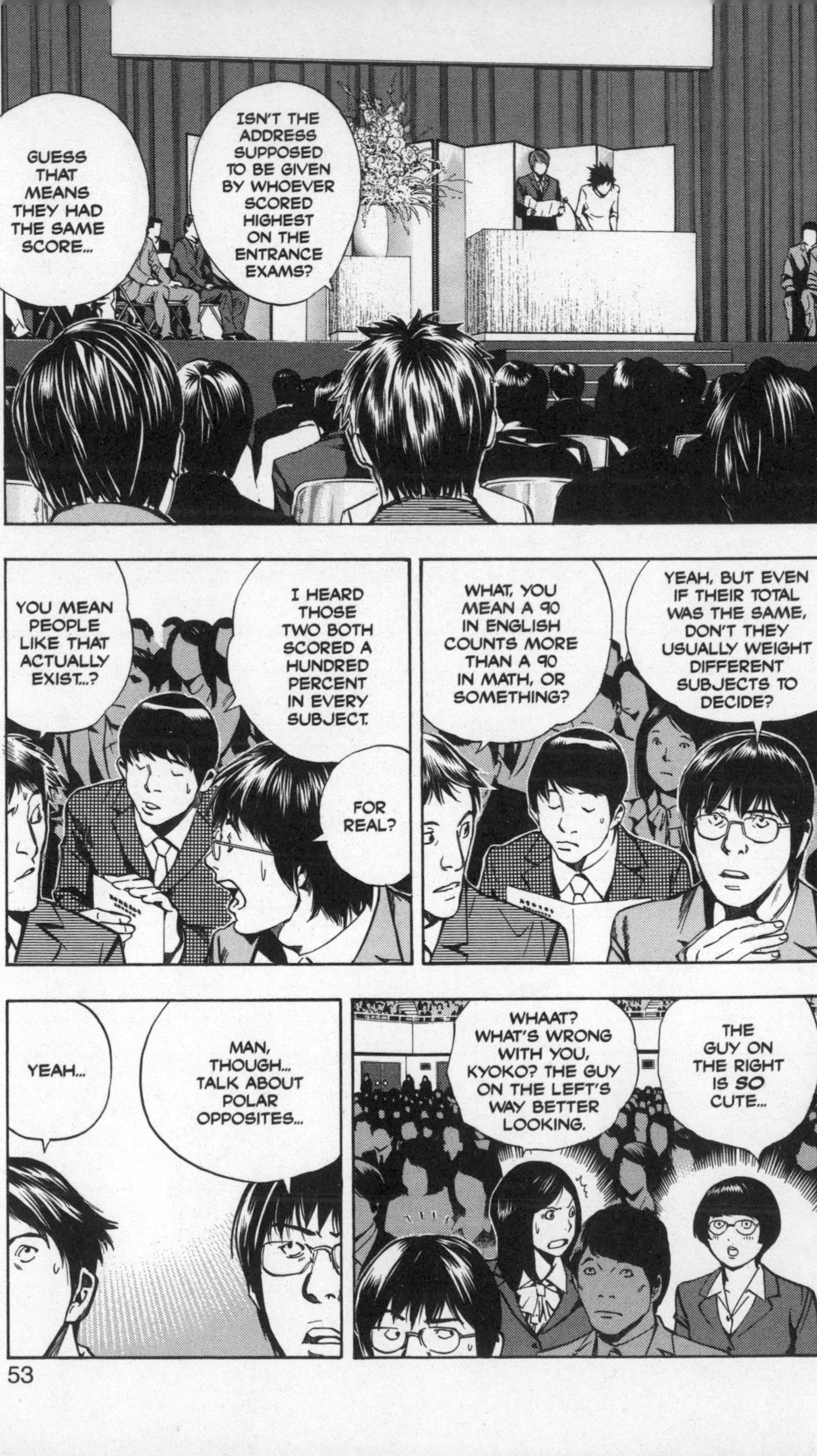

ISN'T THE ADDRESS SUPPOSED TO BE GIVEN BY WHOEVER SCORED HIGHEST ON THE ENTRANCE EXAMS?
GUESS THAT MEANS THEY HAD THE SAME SCORE...
YEAH, BUT EVEN IF THEIR TOTAL WAS THE SAME, DON'T THEY USUALLY WEIGHT DIFFERENT SUBJECTS TO DECIDE?
WHAT, YOU MEAN A 90 IN ENGLISH COUNTS MORE THAN A 90 IN MATH, OR SOMETHING?
I HEARD THOSE TWO BOTH SCORED A HUNDRED PERCENT IN EVERY SUBJECT.
FOR REAL?
YOU MEAN PEOPLE LIKE THAT ACTUALLY EXIST...?
THE GUY ON THE RIGHT IS SO CUTE...
WHAAT? WHAT'S WRONG WITH YOU, KYOKO? THE GUY ON THE LEFT'S WAY BETTER LOOKING.
MAN, THOUGH... TALK ABOUT POLAR OPPOSITES...
YEAH...

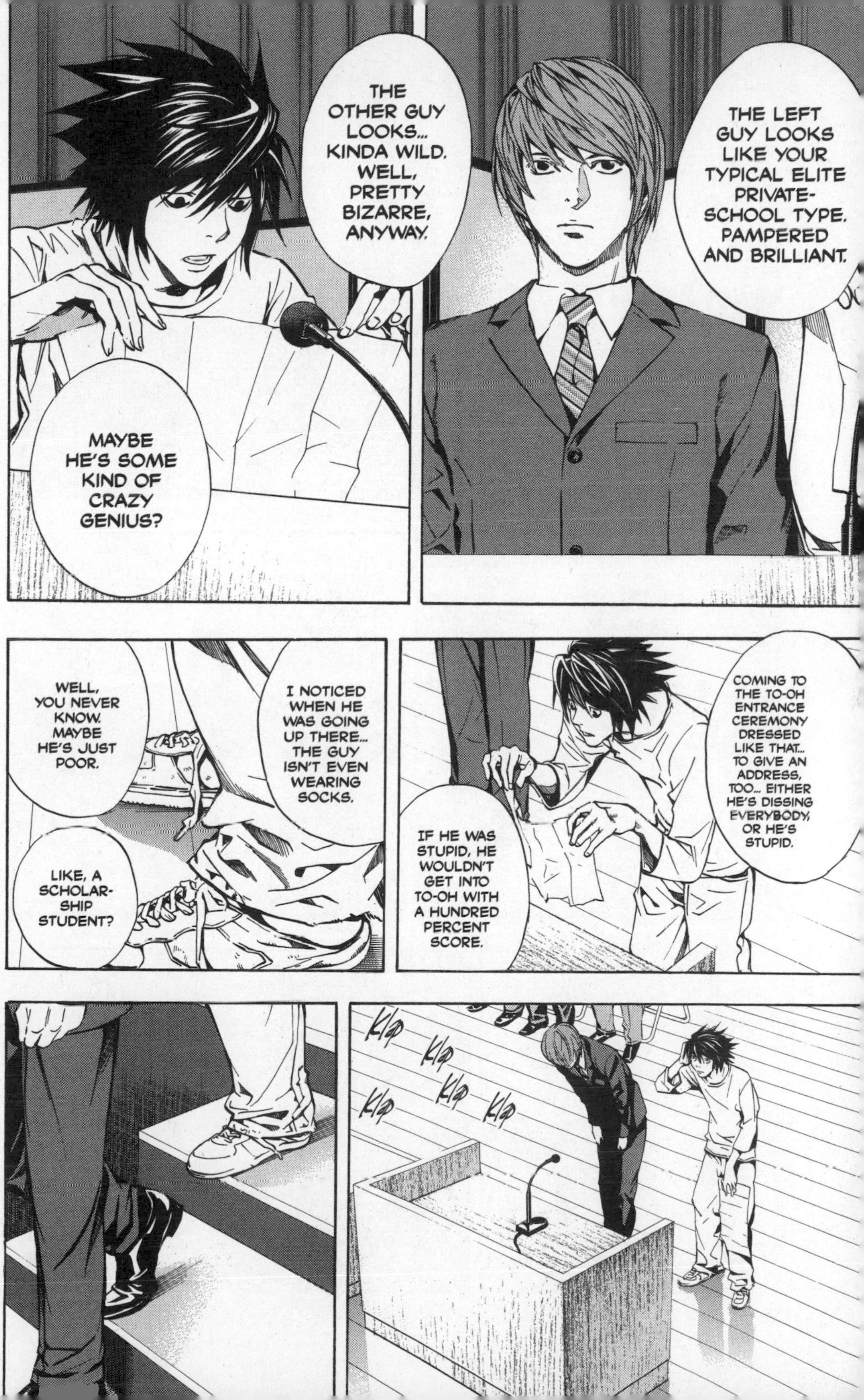
THE LEFT GUY LOOKS LIKE YOUR TYPICAL ELITE PRIVATE-SCHOOL TYPE. PAMPERED AND BRILLIANT.
THE OTHER GUY LOOKS... KINDA WILD. WELL, PRETTY BIZARRE, ANYWAY.
MAYBE HE'S SOME KIND OF CRAZY GENIUS?
COMING TO THE TO-OH ENTRANCE CEREMONY DRESSED LIKE THAT... TO GIVE AN ADDRESS, TOO... EITHER HE'S DISSING EVERYBODY, OR HE'S STUPID.
IF HE WAS STUPID, HE WOULDN'T GET INTO TO-OH WITH A HUNDRED PERCENT SCORE.
I NOTICED WHEN HE WAS GOING UP THERE... THE GUY ISN'T EVEN WEARING SOCKS.
WELL, YOU NEVER KNOW. MAYBE HE'S JUST POOR.
LIKE, A SCHOLAR-SHIP STUDENT?
KLAP
KLAP
KLAP
KLAP
KLAP
KLAP

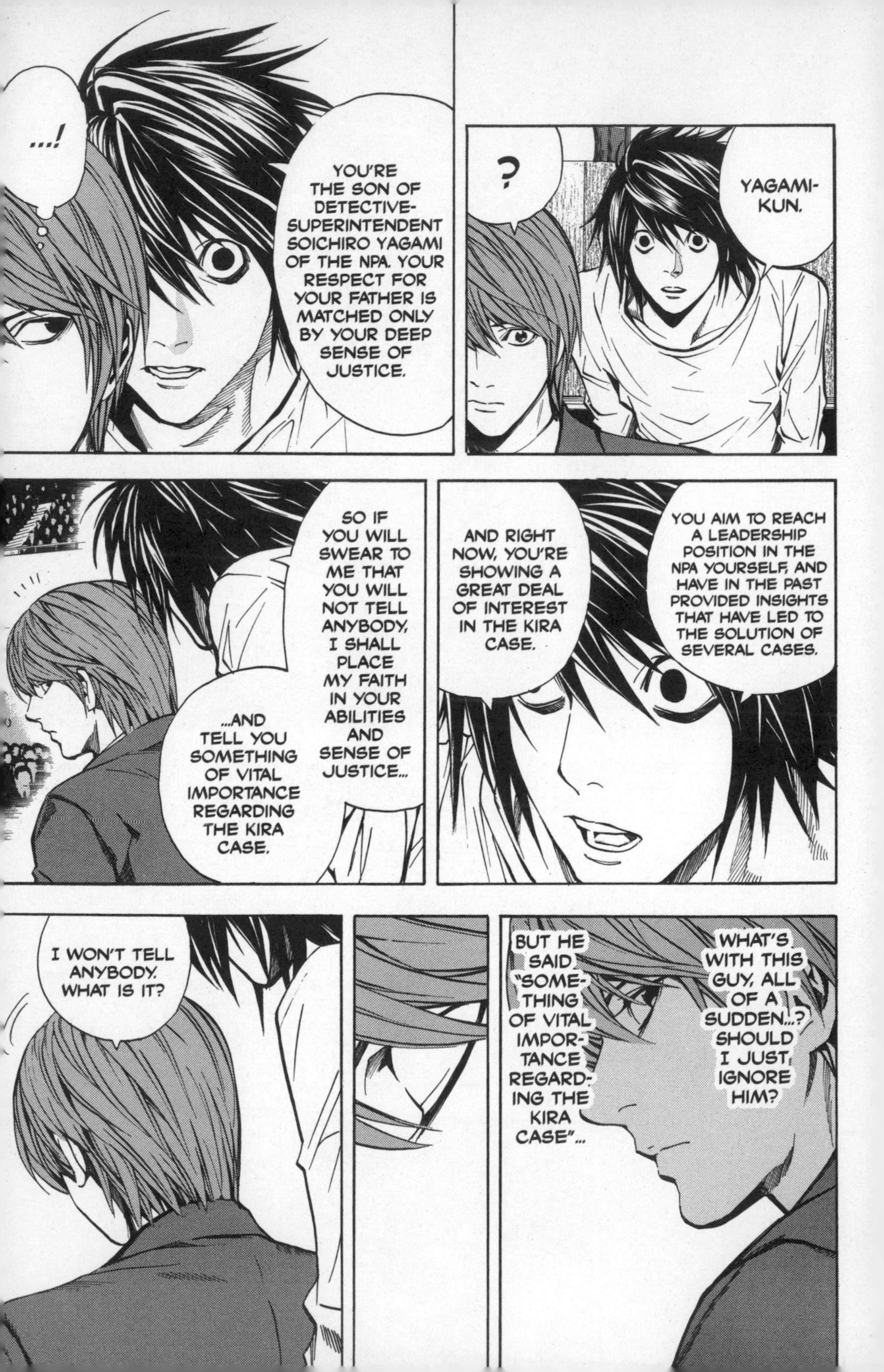
YAGAMI-KUN.
?
YOU'RE THE SON OF DETECTIVE-SUPERINTENDENT SOICHIRO YAGAMI OF THE NPA. YOUR RESPECT FOR YOUR FATHER IS MATCHED ONLY BY YOUR DEEP SENSE OF JUSTICE.
...!
YOU AIM TO REACH A LEADERSHIP POSITION IN THE NPA YOURSELF, AND HAVE IN THE PAST PROVIDED INSIGHTS THAT HAVE LED TO THE SOLUTION OF SEVERAL CASES.
AND RIGHT NOW, YOU'RE SHOWING A GREAT DEAL OF INTEREST IN THE KIRA CASE.
SO IF YOU WILL SWEAR TO ME THAT YOU WILL NOT TELL ANYBODY, I SHALL PLACE MY FAITH IN YOUR ABILITIES AND SENSE OF JUSTICE...
...AND TELL YOU SOMETHING OF VITAL IMPORTANCE REGARDING THE KIRA CASE.
WHAT'S WITH THIS GUY, ALL OF A SUDDEN...? SHOULD I JUST IGNORE HIM?
BUT HE SAID "SOME-THING OF VITAL IMPOR-TANCE REGARD-ING THE KIRA CASE"...
I WON'T TELL ANYBODY. WHAT IS IT?

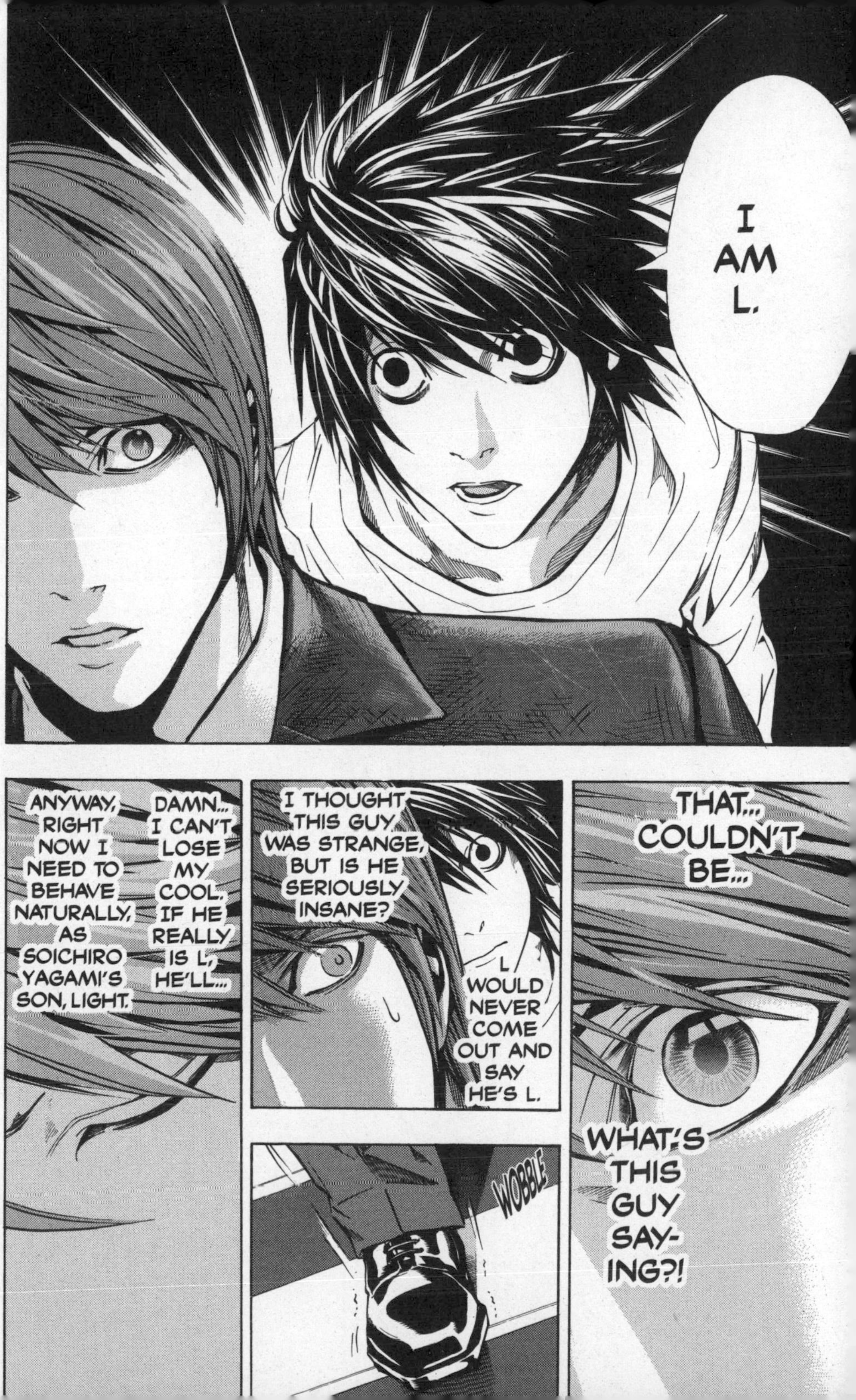
I AM L.
THAT... COULDN'T BE...
WHAT'S THIS GUY SAYING?!
I THOUGHT THIS GUY WAS STRANGE, BUT IS HE SERIOUSLY INSANE?
L WOULD NEVER COME OUT AND SAY HE'S L.
WOBBLE
DAMN... I CAN'T LOSE MY COOL. IF HE REALLY IS L, HE'LL...
ANYWAY, RIGHT NOW I NEED TO BEHAVE NATURALLY, AS SOICHIRO YAGAMI'S SON, LIGHT.

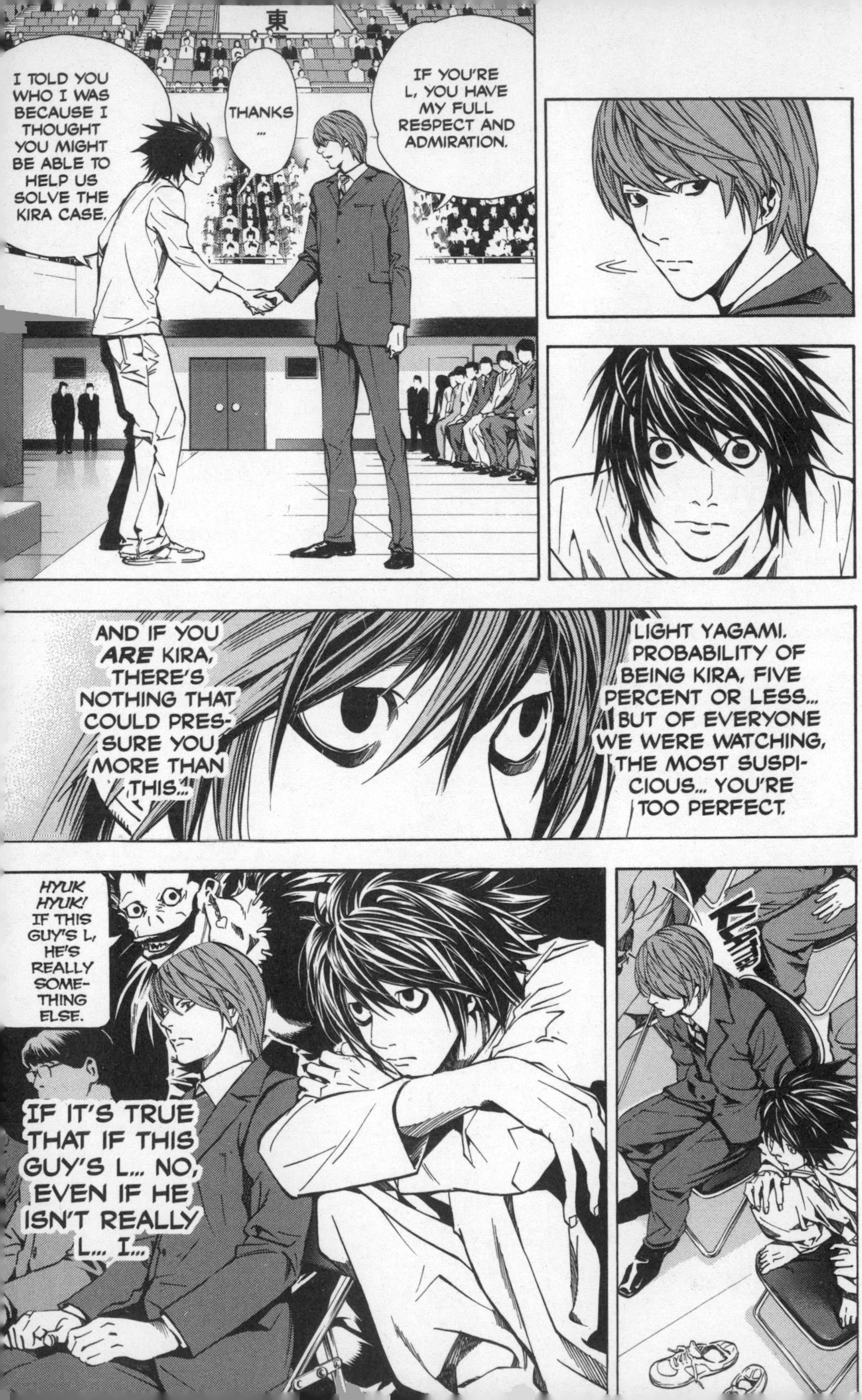
IF YOU'RE L, YOU HAVE MY FULL RESPECT AND ADMIRATION.
THANKS ...
I TOLD YOU WHO I WAS BECAUSE I THOUGHT YOU MIGHT BE ABLE TO HELP US SOLVE THE KIRA CASE.
LIGHT YAGAMI. PROBABILITY OF BEING KIRA, FIVE PERCENT OR LESS... BUT OF EVERYONE WE WERE WATCHING, THE MOST SUSPICIOUS... YOU'RE TOO PERFECT.
AND IF YOU *ARE* KIRA, THERE'S NOTHING THAT COULD PRESSURE YOU MORE THAN THIS...
HYUK HYUK! IF THIS GUY'S L, HE'S REALLY SOMETHING ELSE.
IF IT'S TRUE THAT IF THIS GUY'S L... NO, EVEN IF HE ISN'T REALLY L... I...

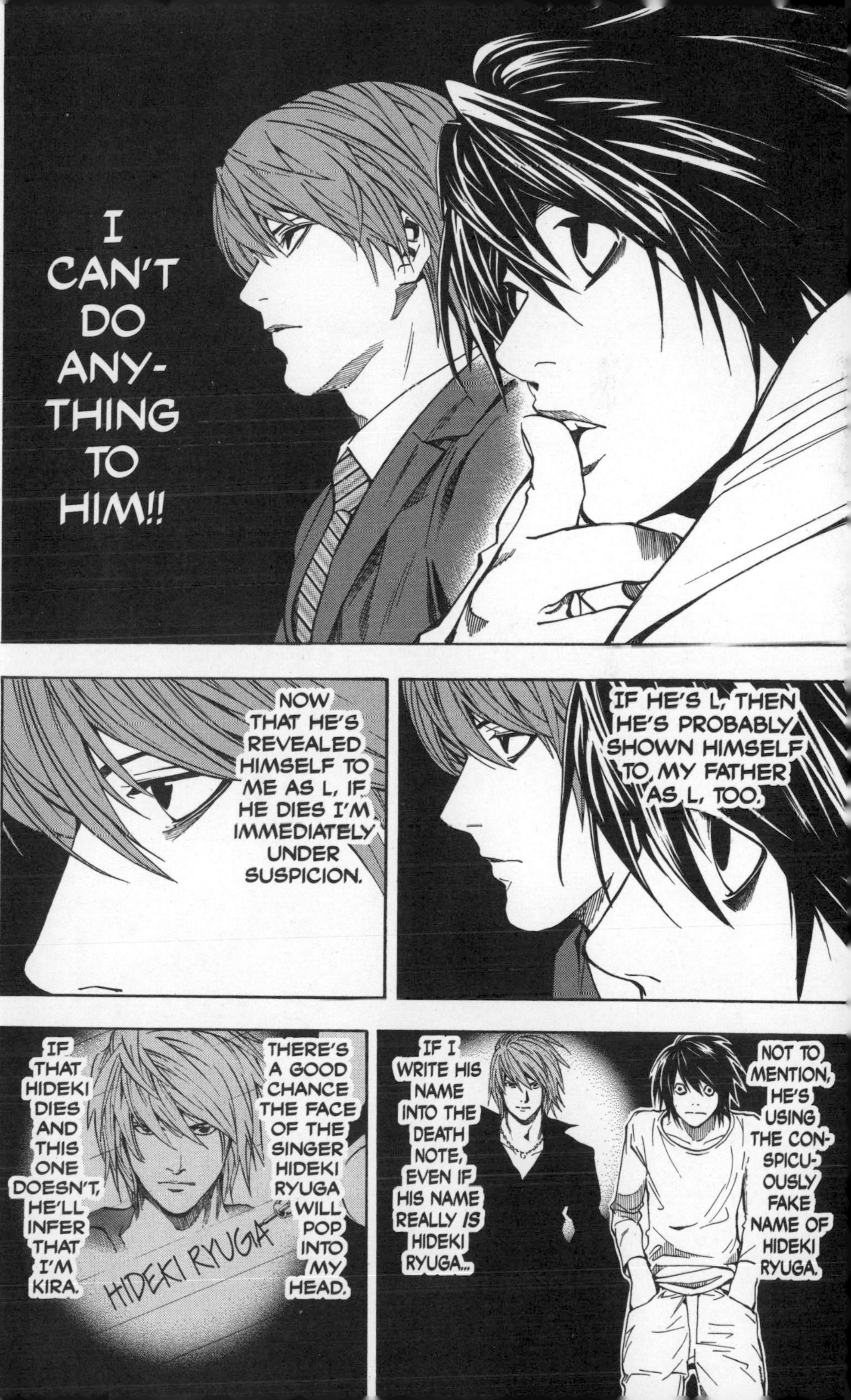
I CAN'T DO ANYTHING TO HIM!!
IF HE'S L, THEN HE'S PROBABLY SHOWN HIMSELF TO MY FATHER AS L, TOO.
NOW THAT HE'S REVEALED HIMSELF TO ME AS L, IF HE DIES I'M IMMEDIATELY UNDER SUSPICION.
NOT TO MENTION, HE'S USING THE CONSPICUOUSLY FAKE NAME OF HIDEKI RYUGA.
IF I WRITE HIS NAME INTO THE DEATH NOTE, EVEN IF HIS NAME REALLY *IS* HIDEKI RYUGA...
THERE'S A GOOD CHANCE THE FACE OF THE SINGER HIDEKI RYUGA WILL POP INTO MY HEAD.
HIDEKI RYUGA
IF THAT HIDEKI DIES AND THIS ONE DOESN'T, HE'LL INFER THAT I'M KIRA.

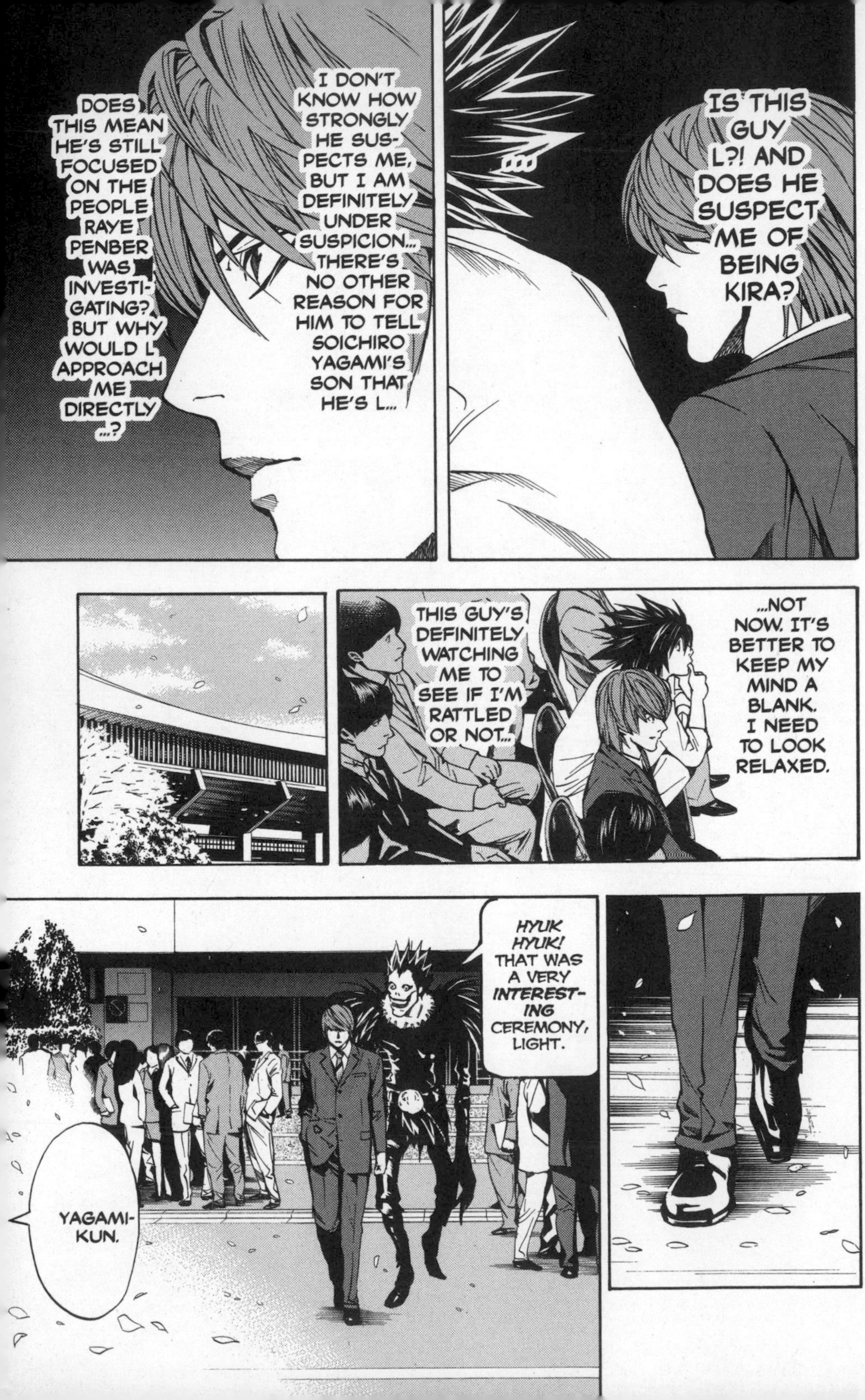
IS THIS GUY L?! AND DOES HE SUSPECT ME OF BEING KIRA?
...
I DON'T KNOW HOW STRONGLY HE SUS-PECTS ME, BUT I AM DEFINITELY UNDER SUSPICION... THERE'S NO OTHER REASON FOR HIM TO TELL SOICHIRO YAGAMI'S SON THAT HE'S L...
DOES THIS MEAN HE'S STILL FOCUSED ON THE PEOPLE RAYE PENBER WAS INVESTI-GATING? BUT WHY WOULD L APPROACH ME DIRECTLY ...?
...NOT NOW. IT'S BETTER TO KEEP MY MIND A BLANK. I NEED TO LOOK RELAXED.
THIS GUY'S DEFINITELY WATCHING ME TO SEE IF I'M RATTLED OR NOT...
HYUK HYUK! THAT WAS A VERY *INTEREST-ING* CEREMONY, LIGHT.
YAGAMI-KUN.

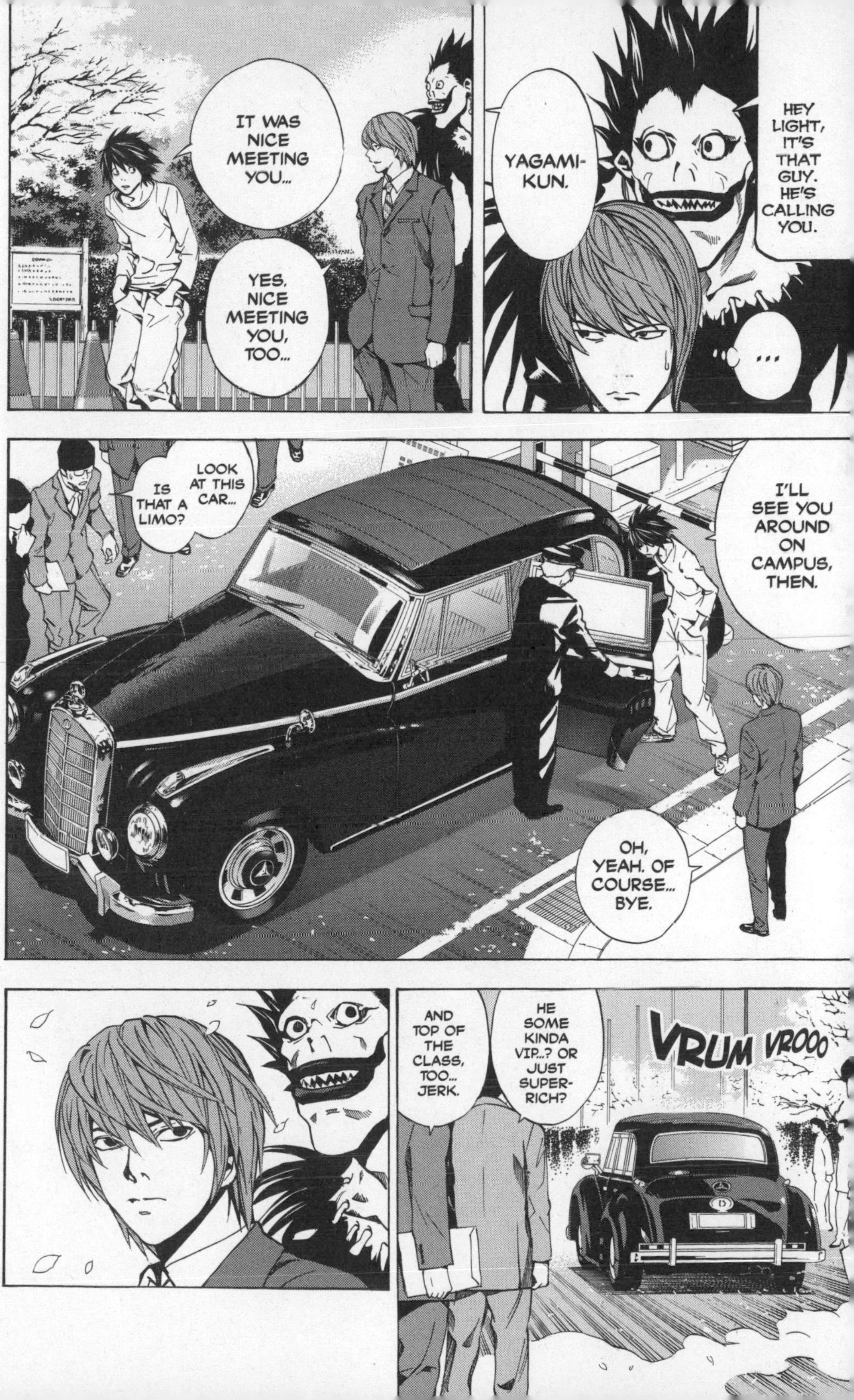
YAGAMI-KUN.
HEY LIGHT, IT'S THAT GUY. HE'S CALLING YOU.
...
IT WAS NICE MEETING YOU...
YES. NICE MEETING YOU, TOO...
I'LL SEE YOU AROUND ON CAMPUS, THEN.
OH, YEAH. OF COURSE... BYE.
LOOK AT THIS CAR...
IS THAT A LIMO?
VRUM VROOO
HE SOME KINDA VIP...? OR JUST SUPER-RICH?
AND TOP OF THE CLASS, TOO... JERK.

READ THIS WAY

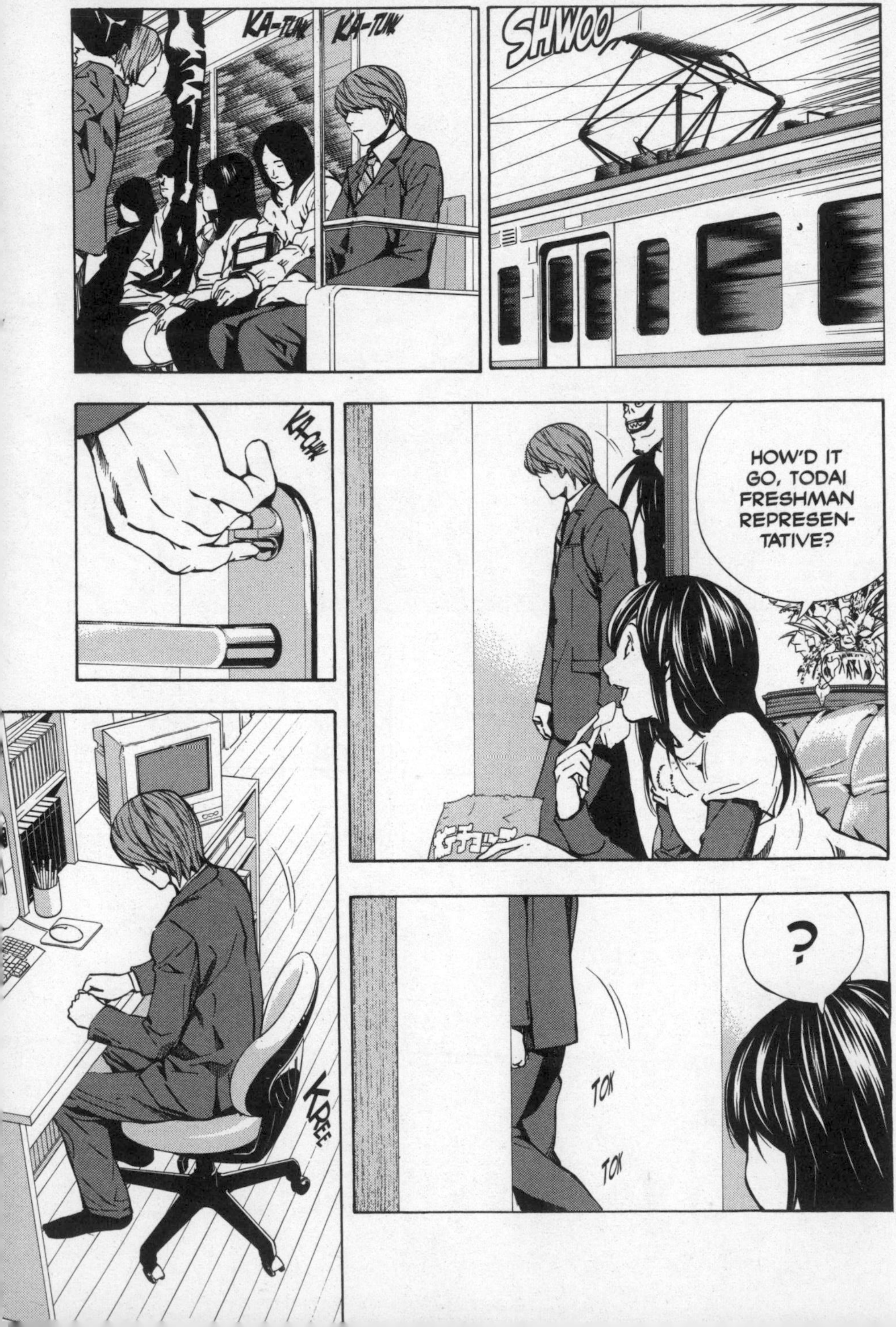
SHWOO
KA-TUNK
KA-TUNK
HOW'D IT GO, TODAI FRESHMAN REPRESEN-TATIVE?
?
TOK
TOK
KA-CHAK
KREE

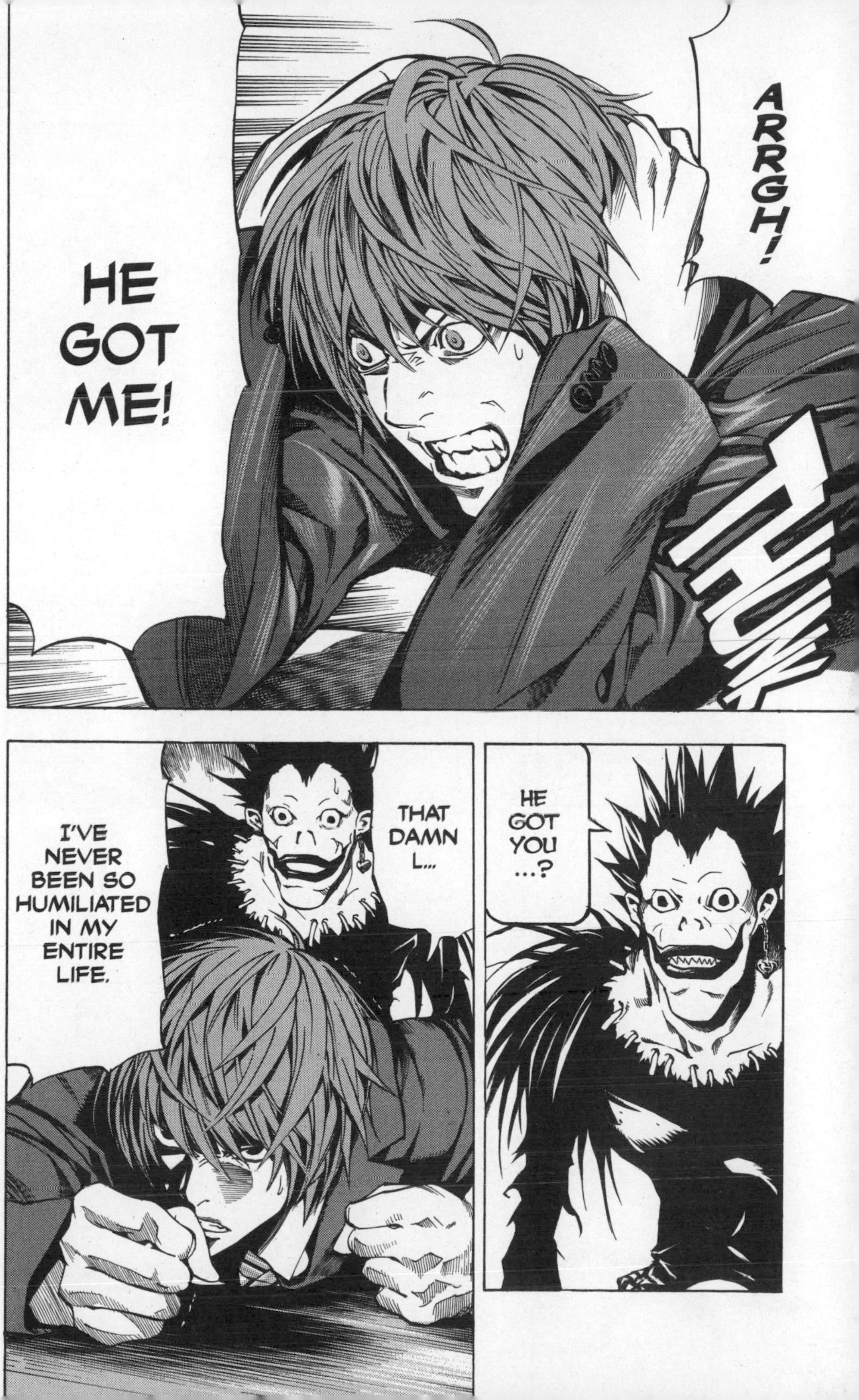
ARRGH!
THUNK
HE GOT ME!
HE GOT YOU ...?
THAT DAMN L...
I'VE NEVER BEEN SO HUMILIATED IN MY ENTIRE LIFE.

READ THIS WAY

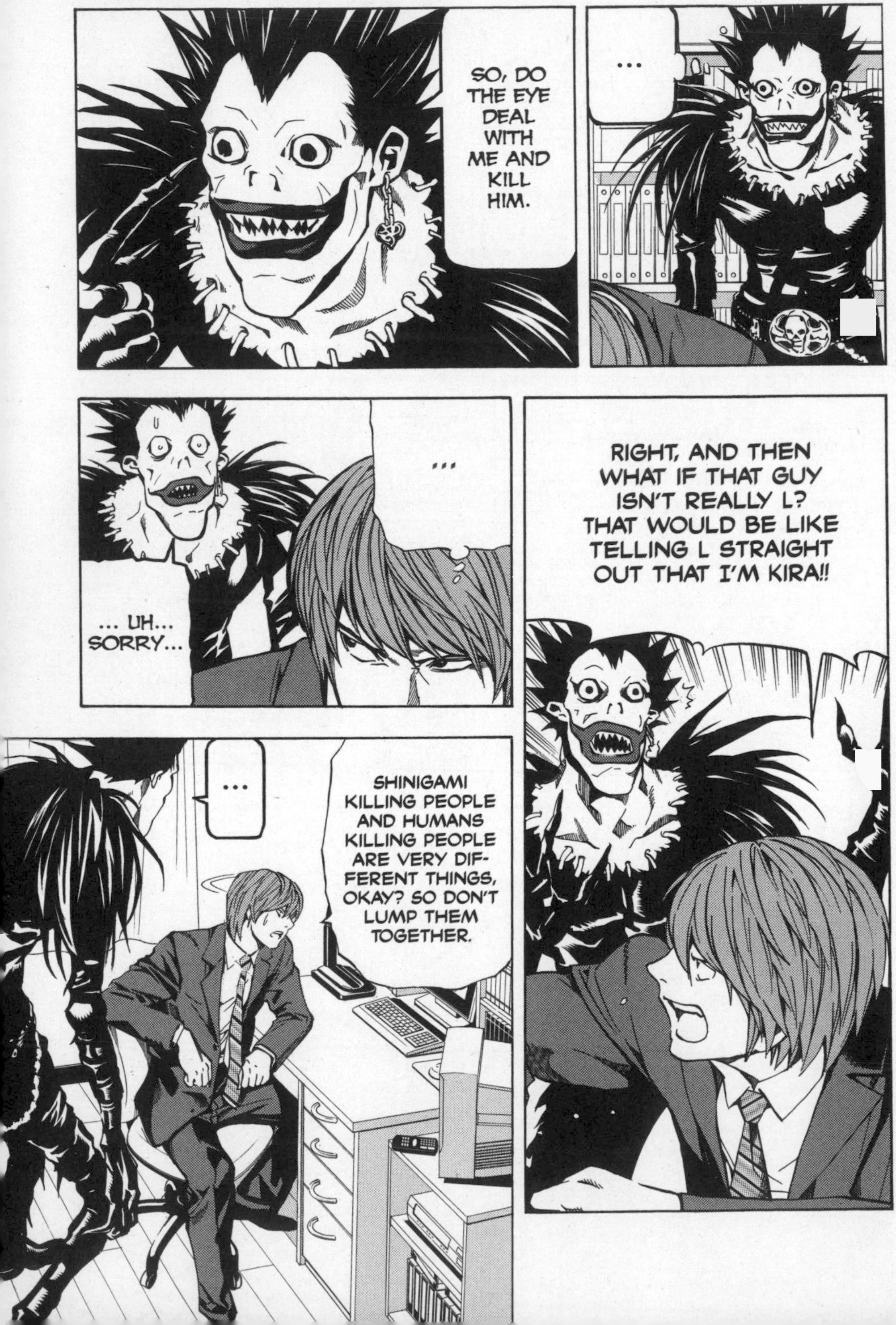
...
SO, DO THE EYE DEAL WITH ME AND KILL HIM.
RIGHT, AND THEN WHAT IF THAT GUY ISN'T REALLY L? THAT WOULD BE LIKE TELLING L STRAIGHT OUT THAT I'M KIRA!!
...
... UH... SORRY...
SHINIGAMI KILLING PEOPLE AND HUMANS KILLING PEOPLE ARE VERY DIF-FERENT THINGS, OKAY? SO DON'T LUMP THEM TOGETHER.
...

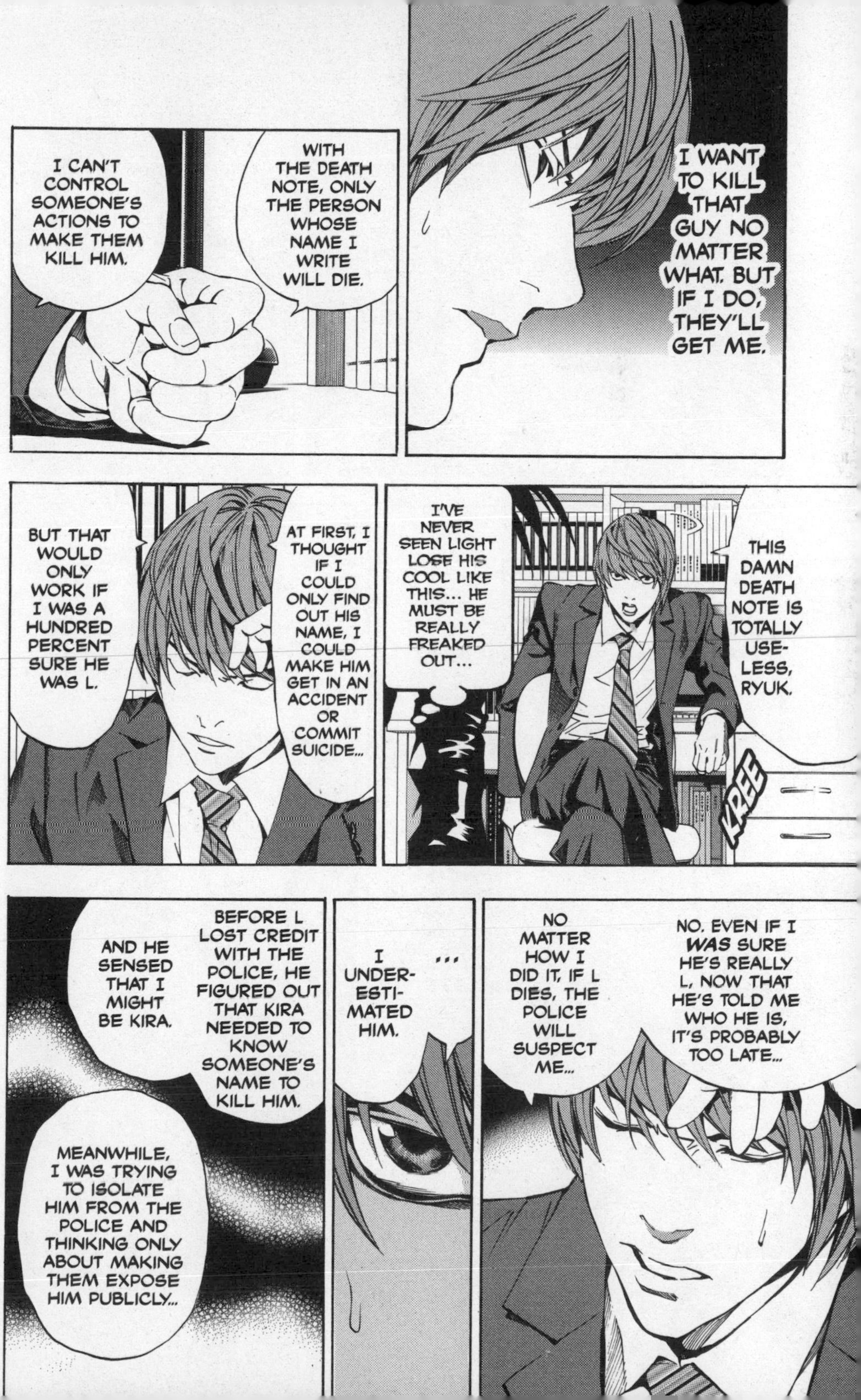
I WANT TO KILL THAT GUY NO MATTER WHAT. BUT IF I DO, THEY'LL GET ME.
WITH THE DEATH NOTE, ONLY THE PERSON WHOSE NAME I WRITE WILL DIE.
I CAN'T CONTROL SOMEONE'S ACTIONS TO MAKE THEM KILL HIM.
THIS DAMN DEATH NOTE IS TOTALLY USE-LESS, RYUK.
I'VE NEVER SEEN LIGHT LOSE HIS COOL LIKE THIS... HE MUST BE REALLY FREAKED OUT...
KREE
AT FIRST, I THOUGHT IF I COULD ONLY FIND OUT HIS NAME, I COULD MAKE HIM GET IN AN ACCIDENT OR COMMIT SUICIDE...
BUT THAT WOULD ONLY WORK IF I WAS A HUNDRED PERCENT SURE HE WAS L.
NO. EVEN IF I *WAS* SURE HE'S REALLY L, NOW THAT HE'S TOLD ME WHO HE IS, IT'S PROBABLY TOO LATE...
NO MATTER HOW I DID IT, IF L DIES, THE POLICE WILL SUSPECT ME...
...
I UNDER-ESTI-MATED HIM.
BEFORE L LOST CREDIT WITH THE POLICE, HE FIGURED OUT THAT KIRA NEEDED TO KNOW SOMEONE'S NAME TO KILL HIM.
AND HE SENSED THAT I MIGHT BE KIRA.
MEANWHILE, I WAS TRYING TO ISOLATE HIM FROM THE POLICE AND THINKING ONLY ABOUT MAKING THEM EXPOSE HIM PUBLICLY...

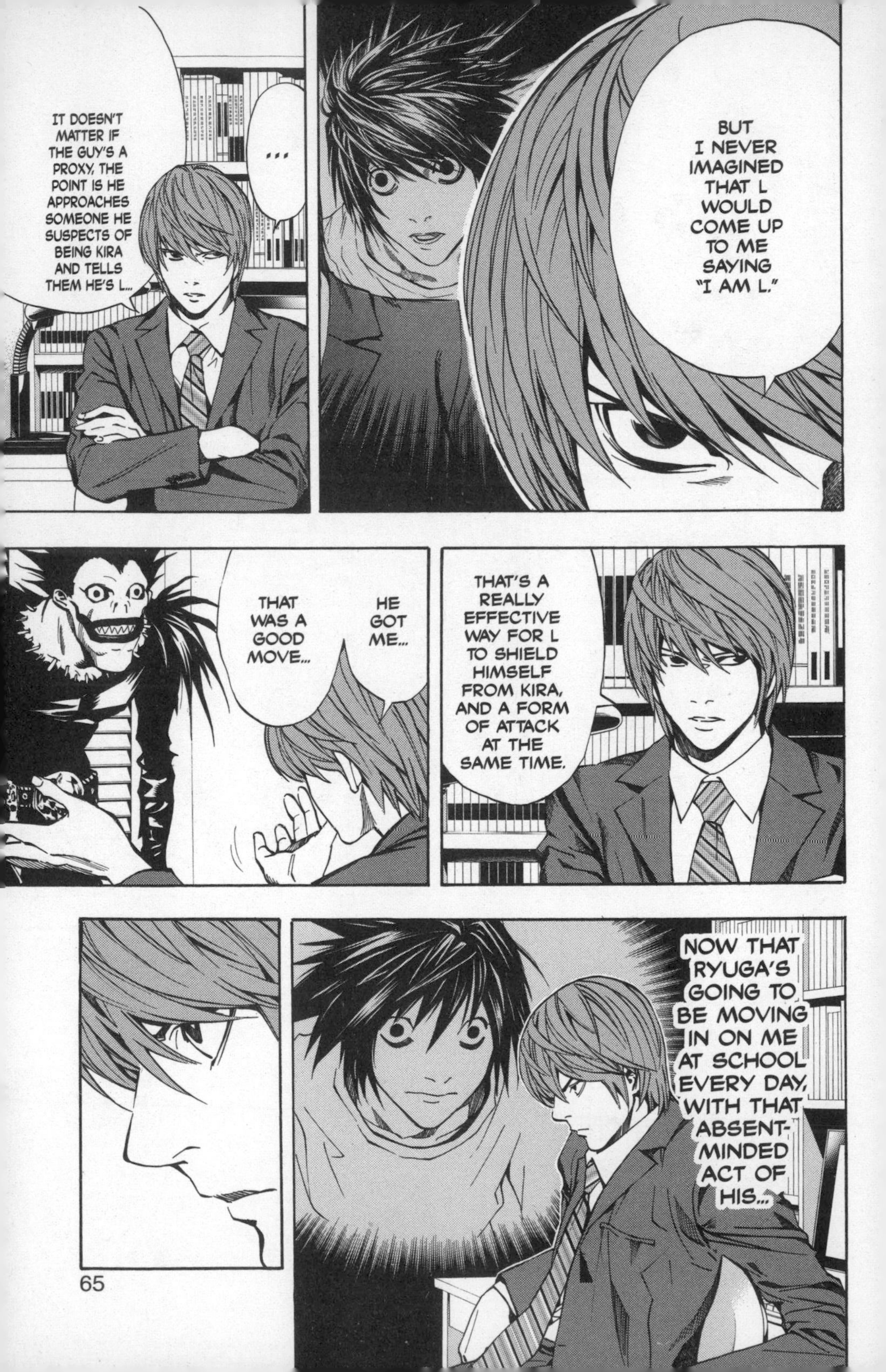
BUT I NEVER IMAGINED THAT L WOULD COME UP TO ME SAYING "I AM L."
IT DOESN'T MATTER IF THE GUY'S A PROXY, THE POINT IS HE APPROACHES SOMEONE HE SUSPECTS OF BEING KIRA AND TELLS THEM HE'S L...
...
THAT'S A REALLY EFFECTIVE WAY FOR L TO SHIELD HIMSELF FROM KIRA, AND A FORM OF ATTACK AT THE SAME TIME.
HE GOT ME...
THAT WAS A GOOD MOVE...
NOW THAT RYUGA'S GOING TO BE MOVING IN ON ME AT SCHOOL EVERY DAY, WITH THAT ABSENT-MINDED ACT OF HIS...

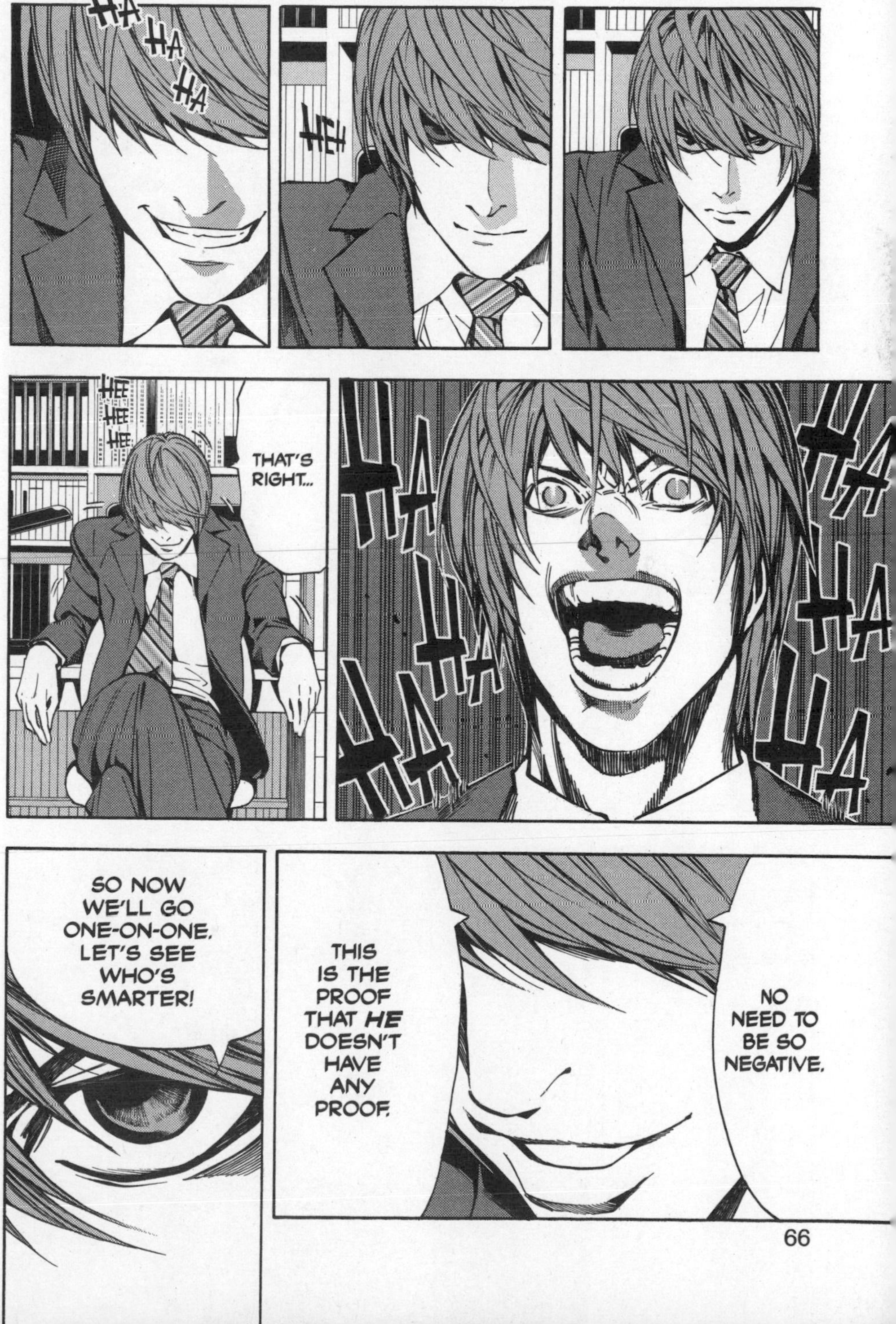
HEH
HA HA HA
HA HA HA HA HA
HA HA HA HA HA
HEE HEE HEE
THAT'S RIGHT...
NO NEED TO BE SO NEGATIVE.
THIS IS THE PROOF THAT *HE* DOESN'T HAVE ANY PROOF.
SO NOW WE'LL GO ONE-ON-ONE. LET'S SEE WHO'S SMARTER!

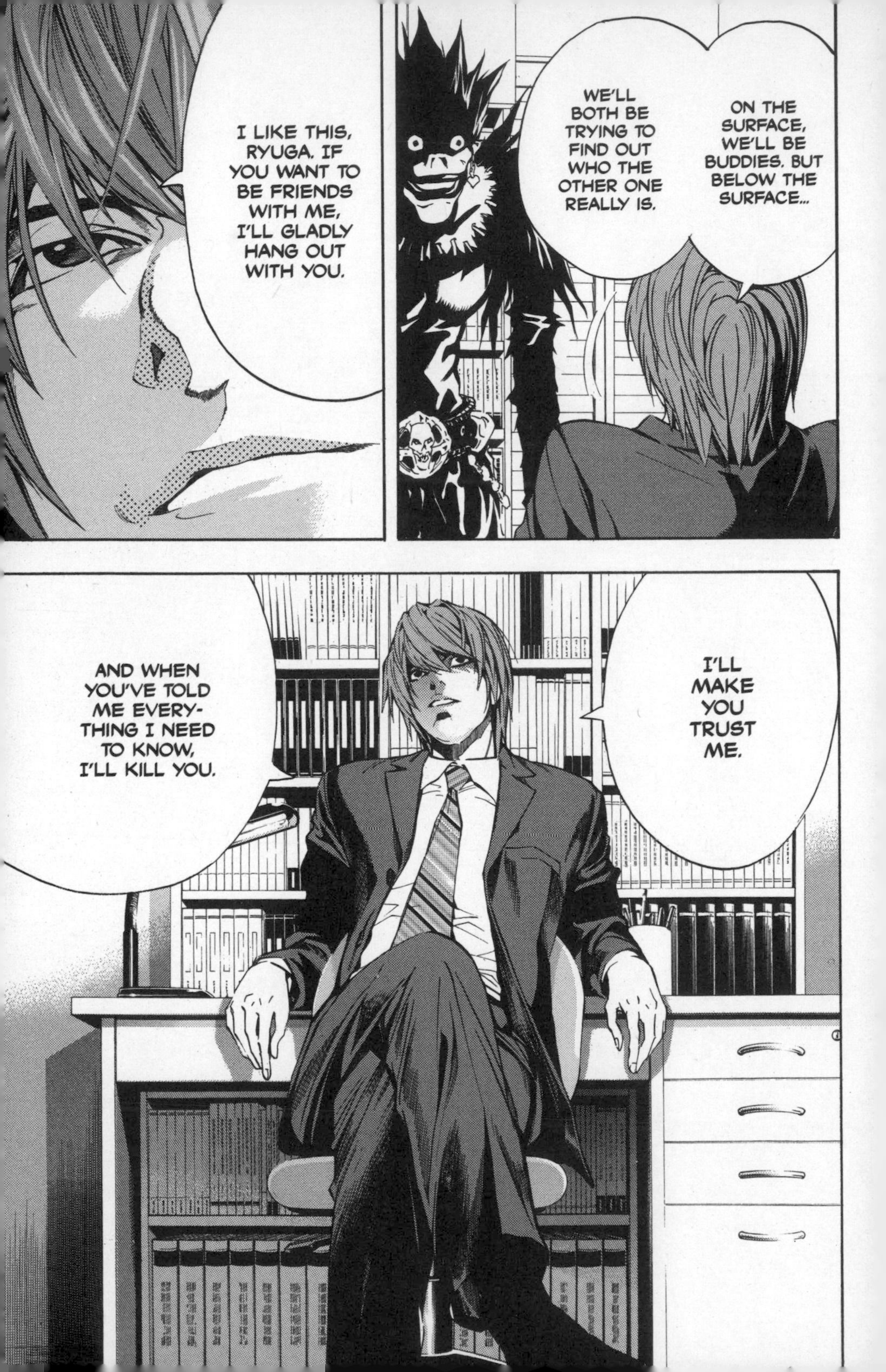
ON THE SURFACE, WE'LL BE BUDDIES. BUT BELOW THE SURFACE...
WE'LL BOTH BE TRYING TO FIND OUT WHO THE OTHER ONE REALLY IS.
I LIKE THIS, RYUGA. IF YOU WANT TO BE FRIENDS WITH ME, I'LL GLADLY HANG OUT WITH YOU.
I'LL MAKE YOU TRUST ME.
AND WHEN YOU'VE TOLD ME EVERY-THING I NEED TO KNOW, I'LL KILL YOU.

DEA♱H NO♱E
HOW to USE It

XII

- If you lose the DEA♱H NO♱E or have it stolen, you will lose its ownership unless you retrieve it within 490 days.

  デスノートを紛失および盗まれた場合、
  ４９０日以内に再び手にしないと、所有権を失う。

- If you have traded the eye power of a god of death, you will lose the eye power as well as the memory of the DEA♱H NO♱E, once you lose its ownership.
  At the same time, the remaining half of your life will not be restored.

  死神の目の取引をした者は、所有権を失うと
  ノートの記憶と共に目の能力を失う。
  その際、半分になった余命は元には戻らない。

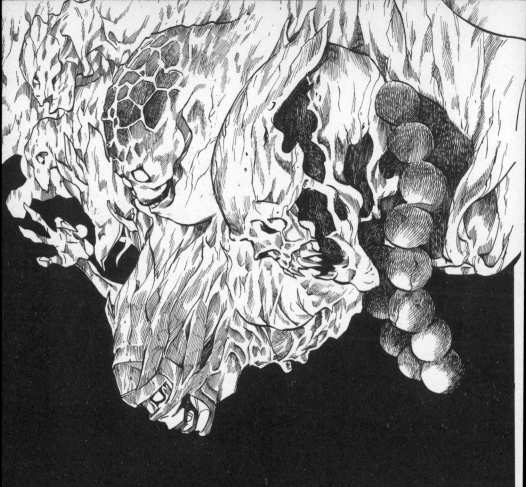

chapter 20 First Move

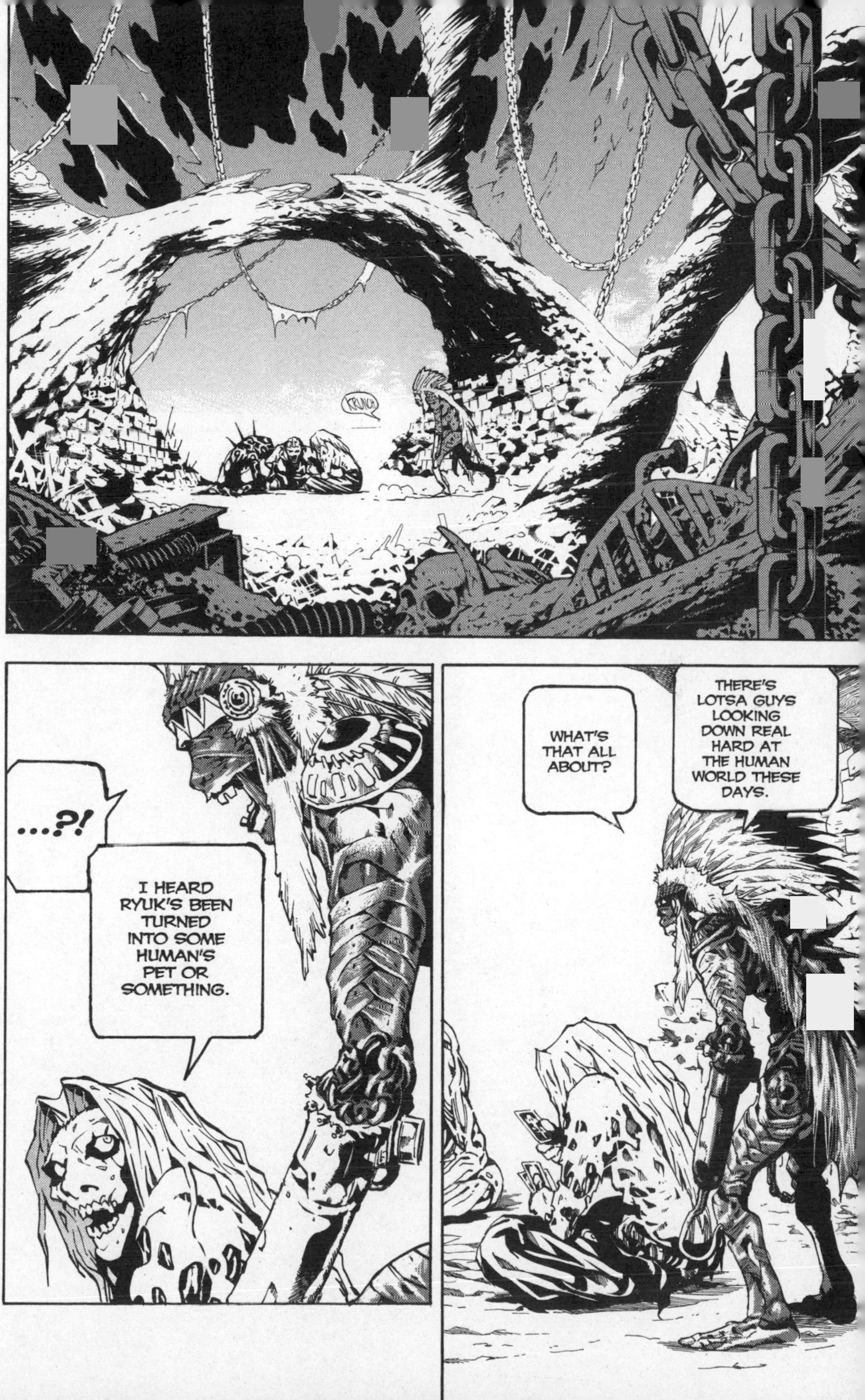
KRUNCH
THERE'S LOTSA GUYS LOOKING DOWN REAL HARD AT THE HUMAN WORLD THESE DAYS.
WHAT'S THAT ALL ABOUT?
I HEARD RYUK'S BEEN TURNED INTO SOME HUMAN'S PET OR SOMETHING.
...?!

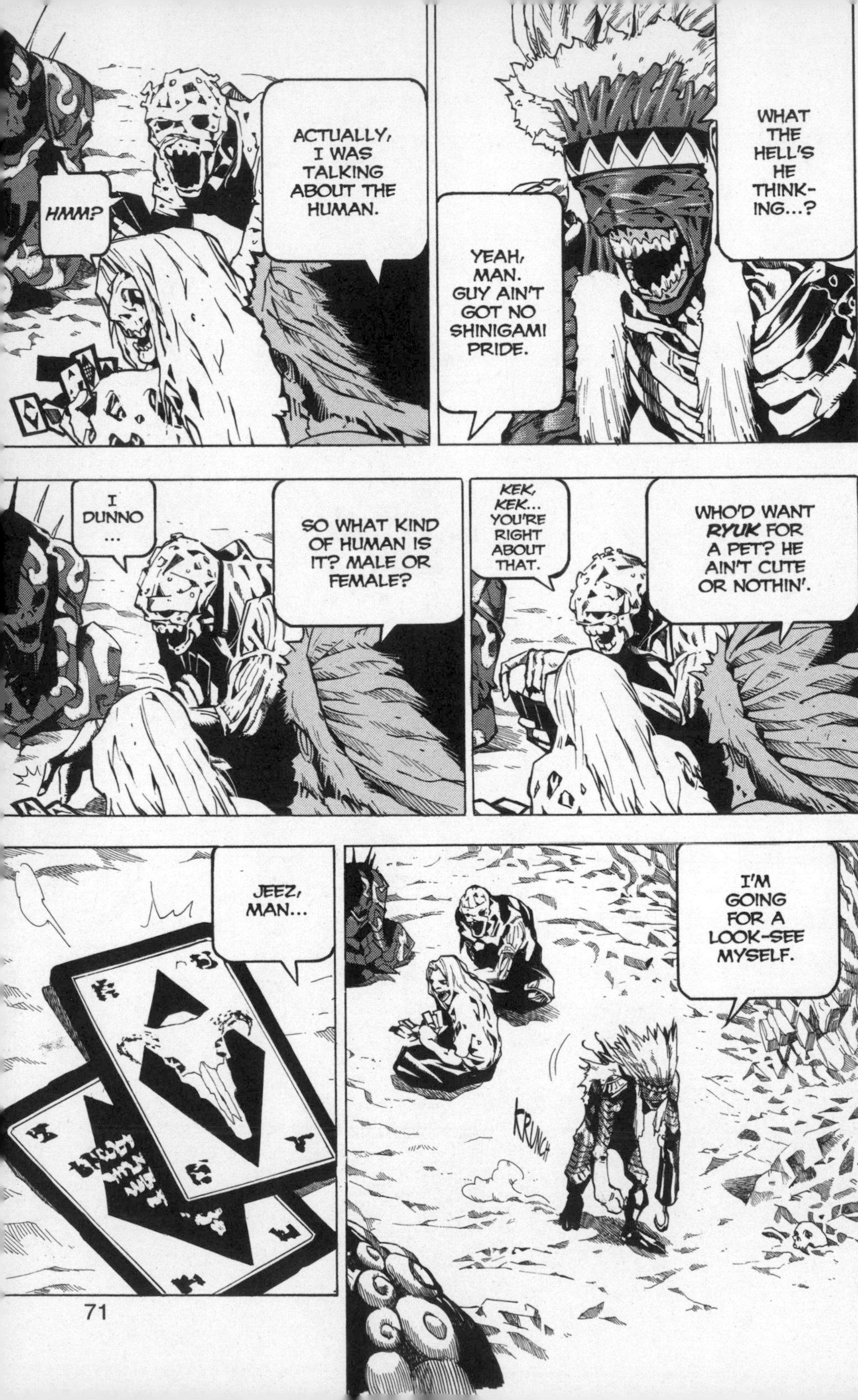
WHAT THE HELL'S HE THINKING...?
YEAH, MAN. GUY AIN'T GOT NO SHINIGAMI PRIDE.
ACTUALLY, I WAS TALKING ABOUT THE HUMAN.
HMM?
WHO'D WANT ***RYUK*** FOR A PET? HE AIN'T CUTE OR NOTHIN'.
KEK, KEK... YOU'RE RIGHT ABOUT THAT.
SO WHAT KIND OF HUMAN IS IT? MALE OR FEMALE?
I DUNNO ...
I'M GOING FOR A LOOK-SEE MYSELF.
KRUNCH
JEEZ, MAN...

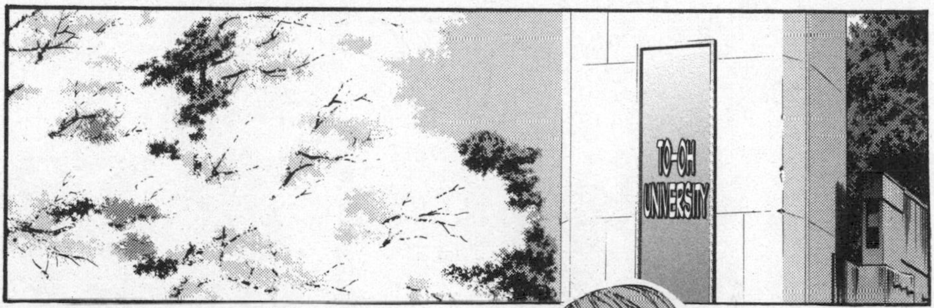
TO-OH
UNIVERSITY
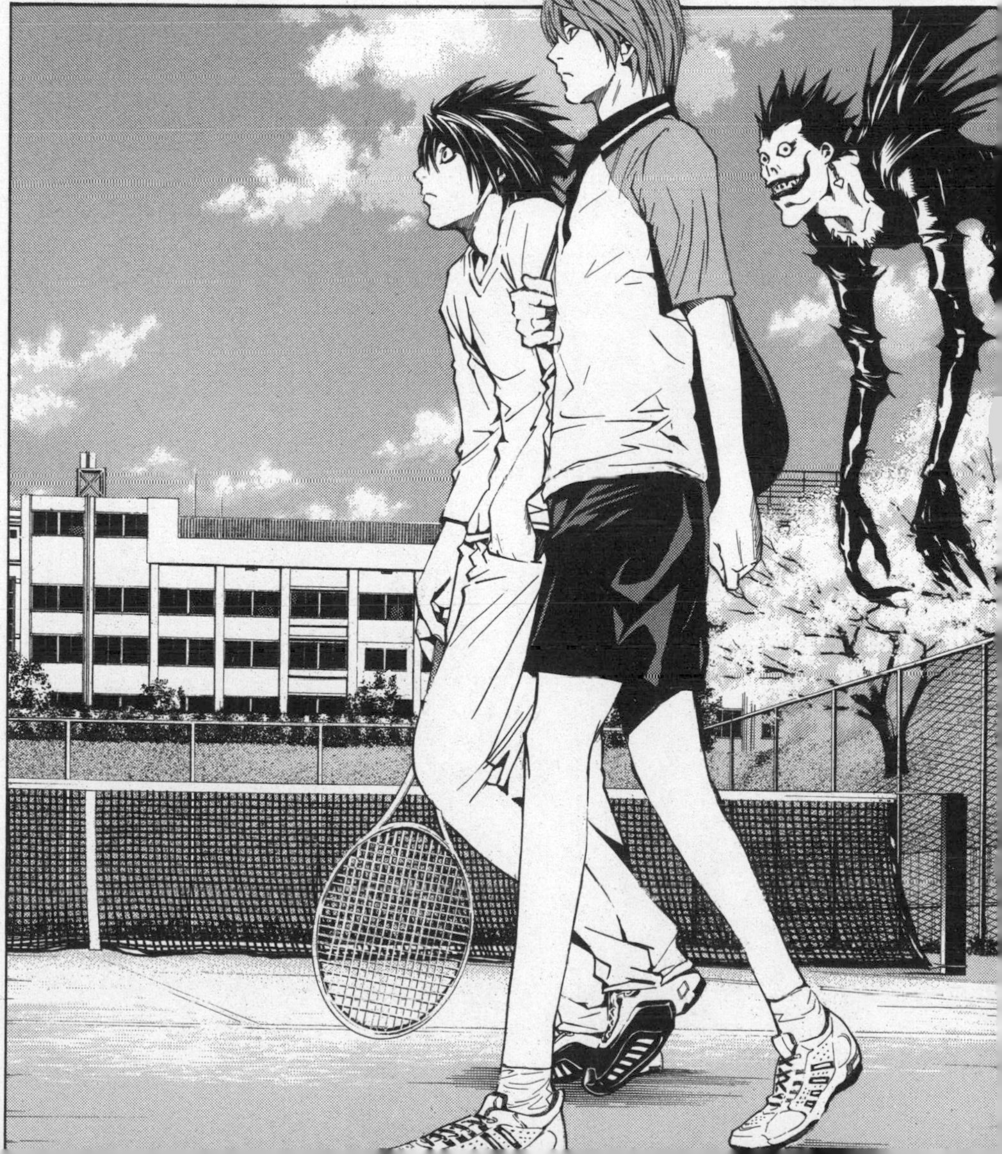

READ THIS WAY

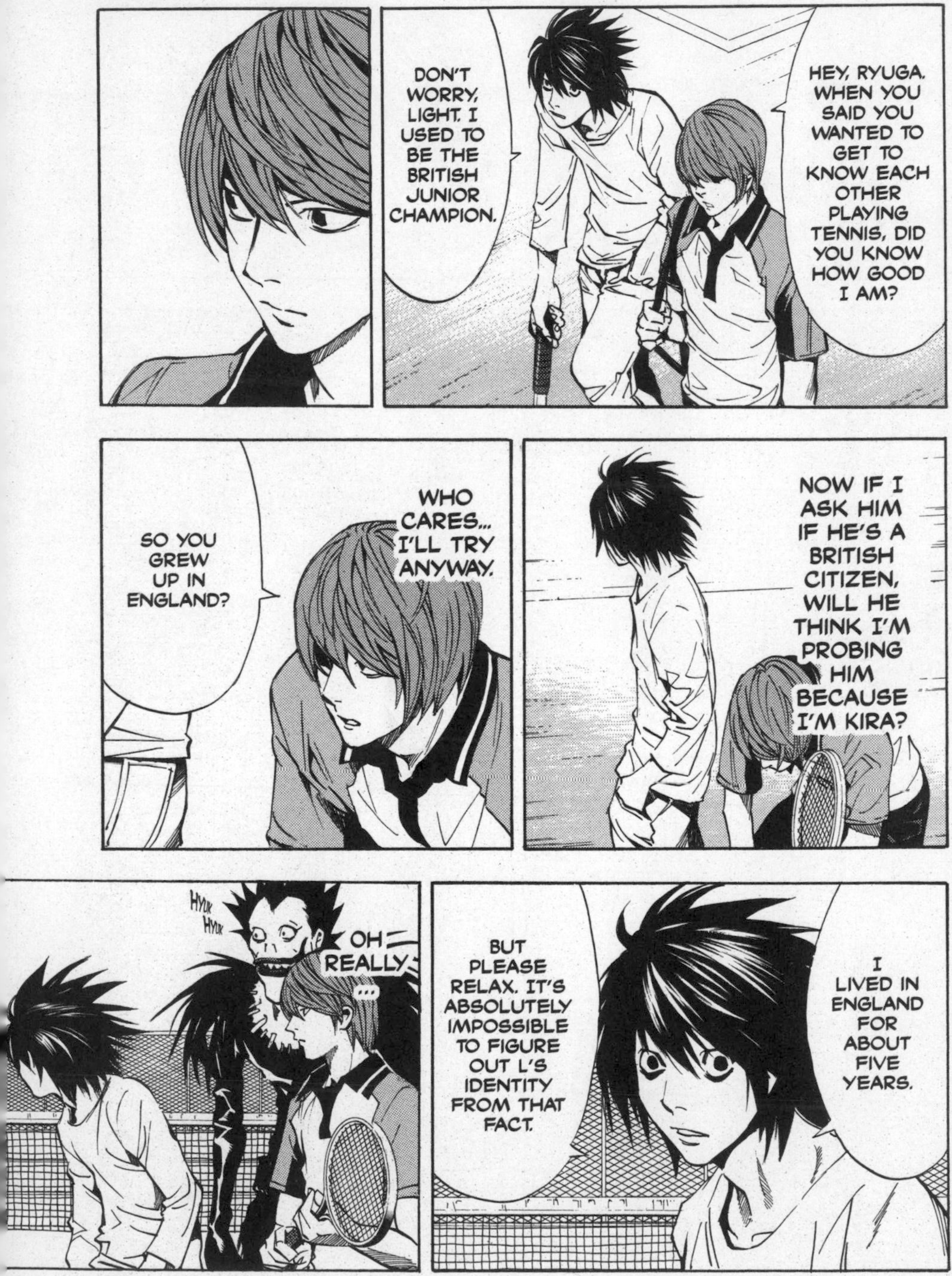
HEY, RYUGA. WHEN YOU SAID YOU WANTED TO GET TO KNOW EACH OTHER PLAYING TENNIS, DID YOU KNOW HOW GOOD I AM?
DON'T WORRY, LIGHT. I USED TO BE THE BRITISH JUNIOR CHAMPION.
NOW IF I ASK HIM IF HE'S A BRITISH CITIZEN, WILL HE THINK I'M PROBING HIM BECAUSE I'M KIRA?
WHO CARES... I'LL TRY ANYWAY.
SO YOU GREW UP IN ENGLAND?
I LIVED IN ENGLAND FOR ABOUT FIVE YEARS.
BUT PLEASE RELAX. IT'S ABSOLUTELY IMPOSSIBLE TO FIGURE OUT L'S IDENTITY FROM THAT FACT.
OH REALLY
...
HYUK HYUK

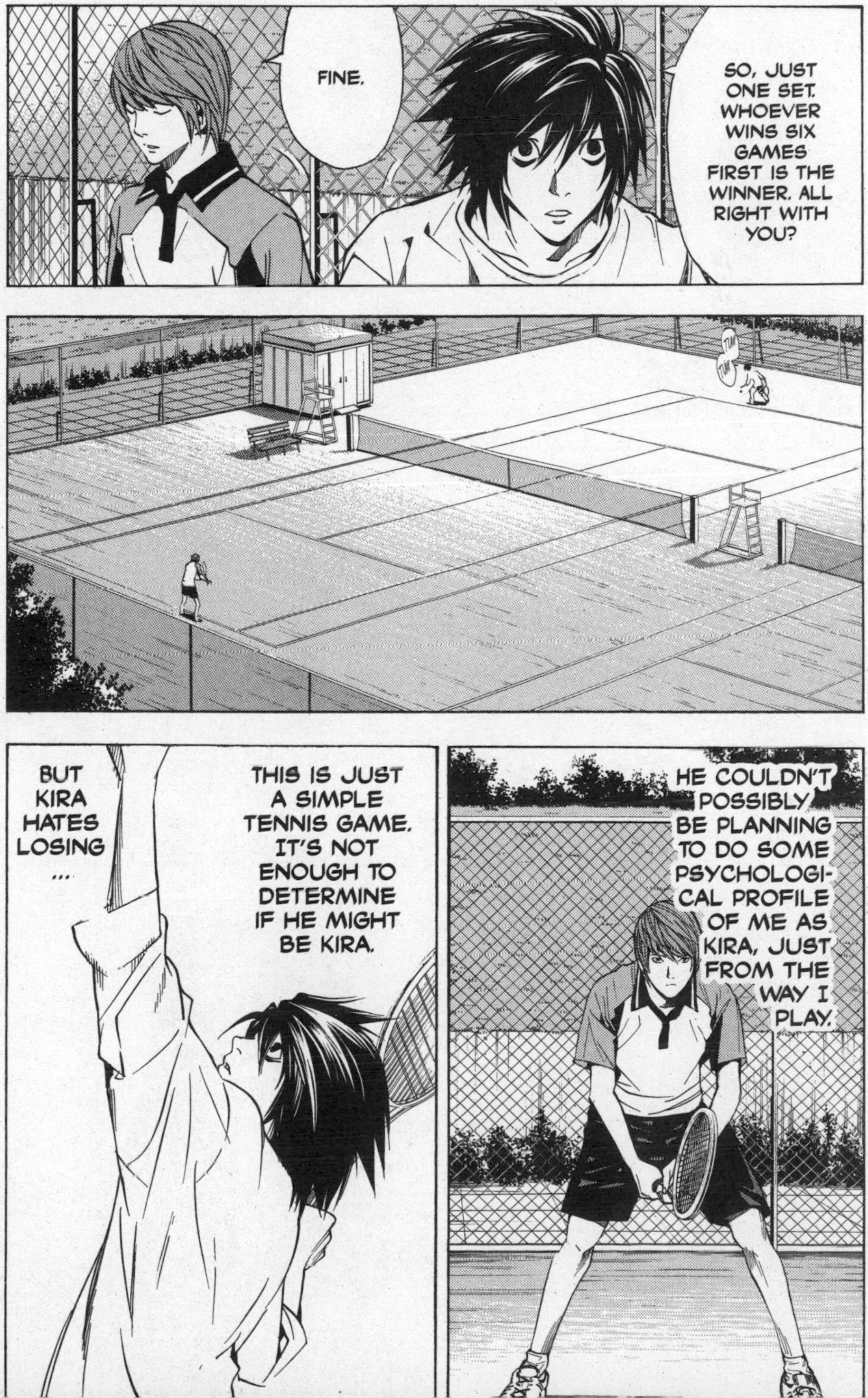
SO, JUST ONE SET. WHOEVER WINS SIX GAMES FIRST IS THE WINNER. ALL RIGHT WITH YOU?
FINE.
HE COULDN'T POSSIBLY BE PLANNING TO DO SOME PSYCHOLOGICAL PROFILE OF ME AS KIRA, JUST FROM THE WAY I PLAY.
THIS IS JUST A SIMPLE TENNIS GAME. IT'S NOT ENOUGH TO DETERMINE IF HE MIGHT BE KIRA.
BUT KIRA HATES LOSING ...

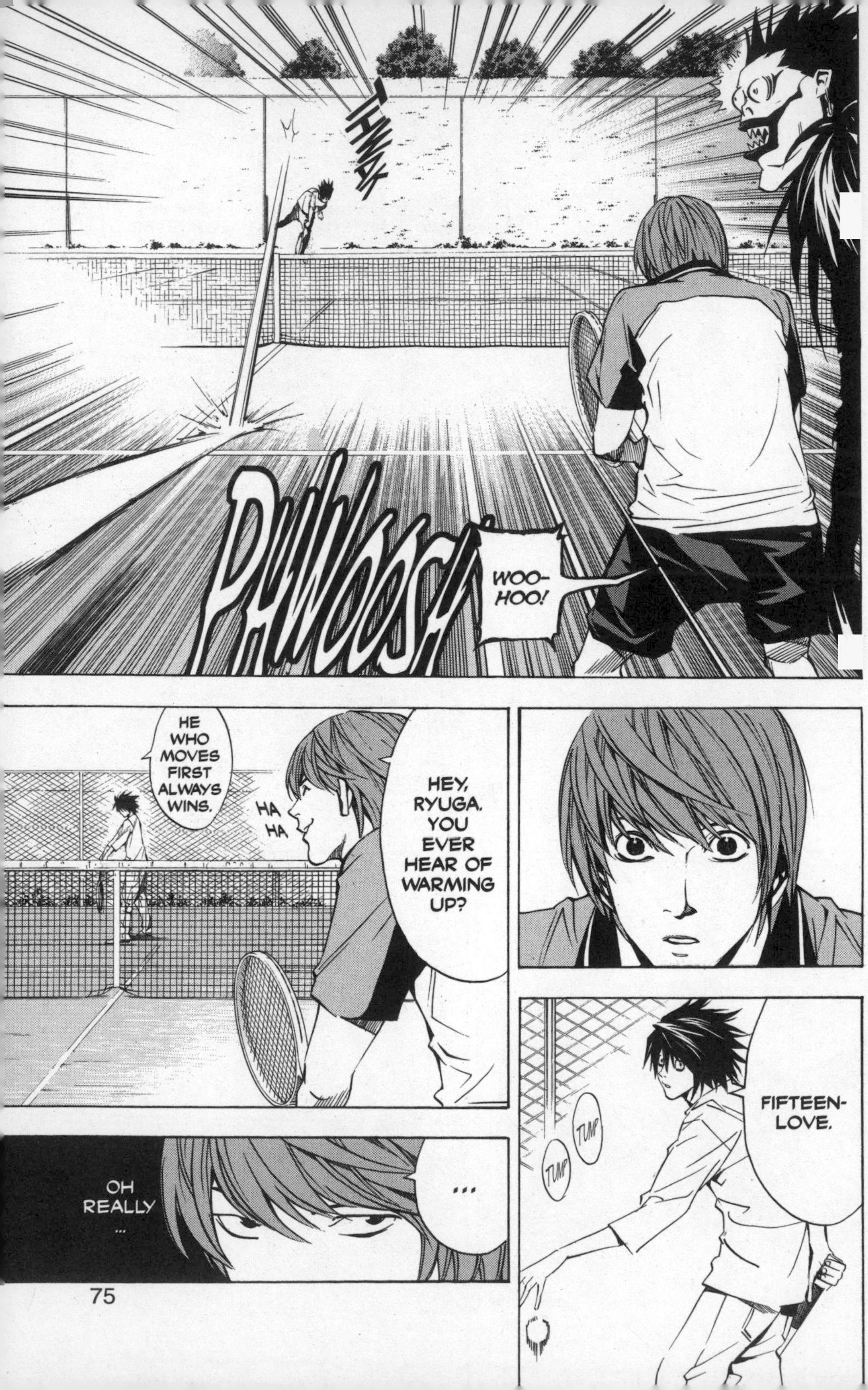
THWACK
PWOOSH
WOO-HOO!
HEY, RYUGA. YOU EVER HEAR OF WARMING UP?
HA HA
HE WHO MOVES FIRST ALWAYS WINS.
FIFTEEN-LOVE.
TUMP
TUMP
TUMP
...
OH REALLY ...

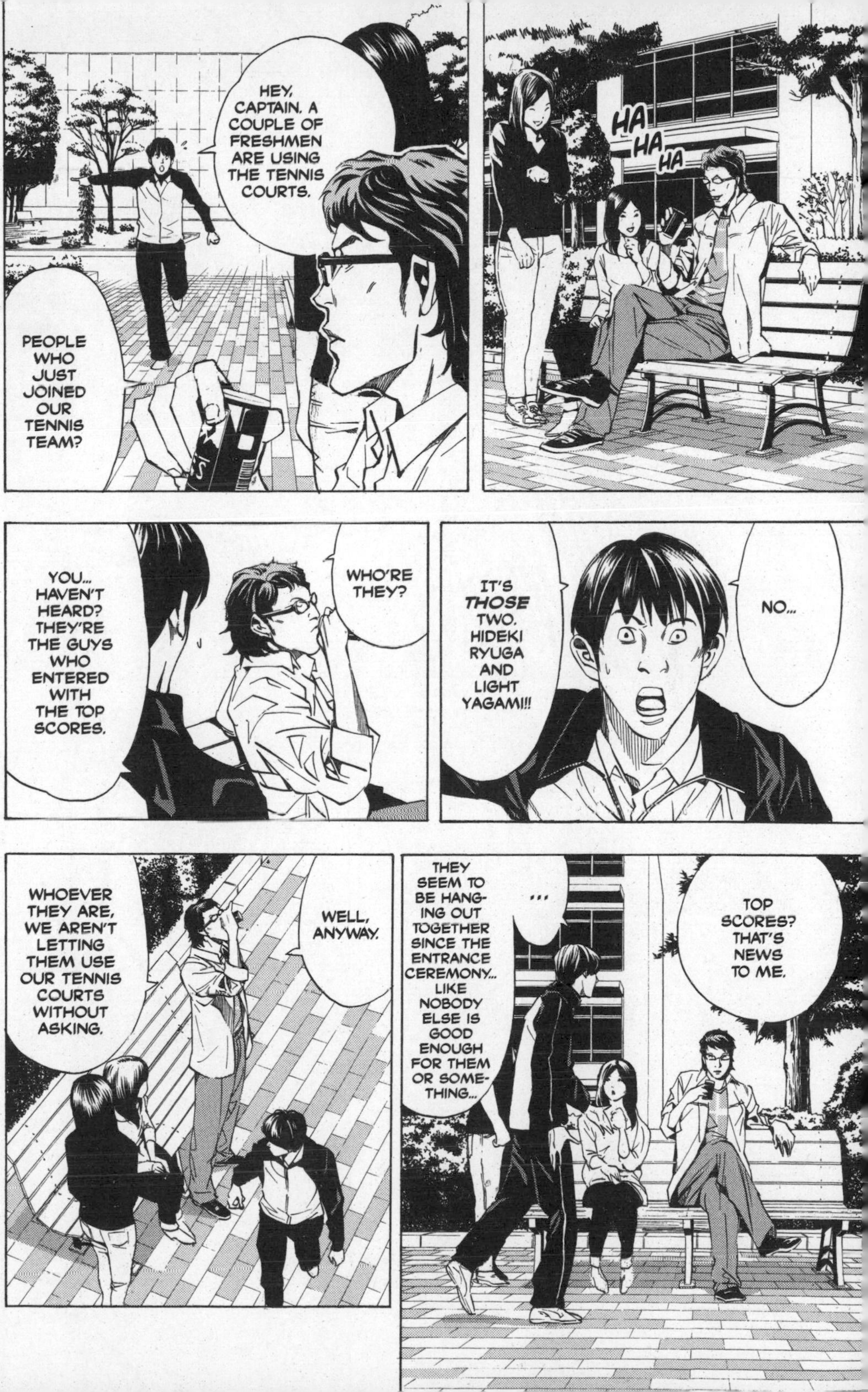
HA HA HA
HEY, CAPTAIN. A COUPLE OF FRESHMEN ARE USING THE TENNIS COURTS.
PEOPLE WHO JUST JOINED OUR TENNIS TEAM?
NO...
IT'S *THOSE* TWO. HIDEKI RYUGA AND LIGHT YAGAMI!!
WHO'RE THEY?
YOU... HAVEN'T HEARD? THEY'RE THE GUYS WHO ENTERED WITH THE TOP SCORES.
TOP SCORES? THAT'S NEWS TO ME.
...
THEY SEEM TO BE HANG-ING OUT TOGETHER SINCE THE ENTRANCE CEREMONY... LIKE NOBODY ELSE IS GOOD ENOUGH FOR THEM OR SOME-THING...
WELL, ANYWAY.
WHOEVER THEY ARE, WE AREN'T LETTING THEM USE OUR TENNIS COURTS WITHOUT ASKING.

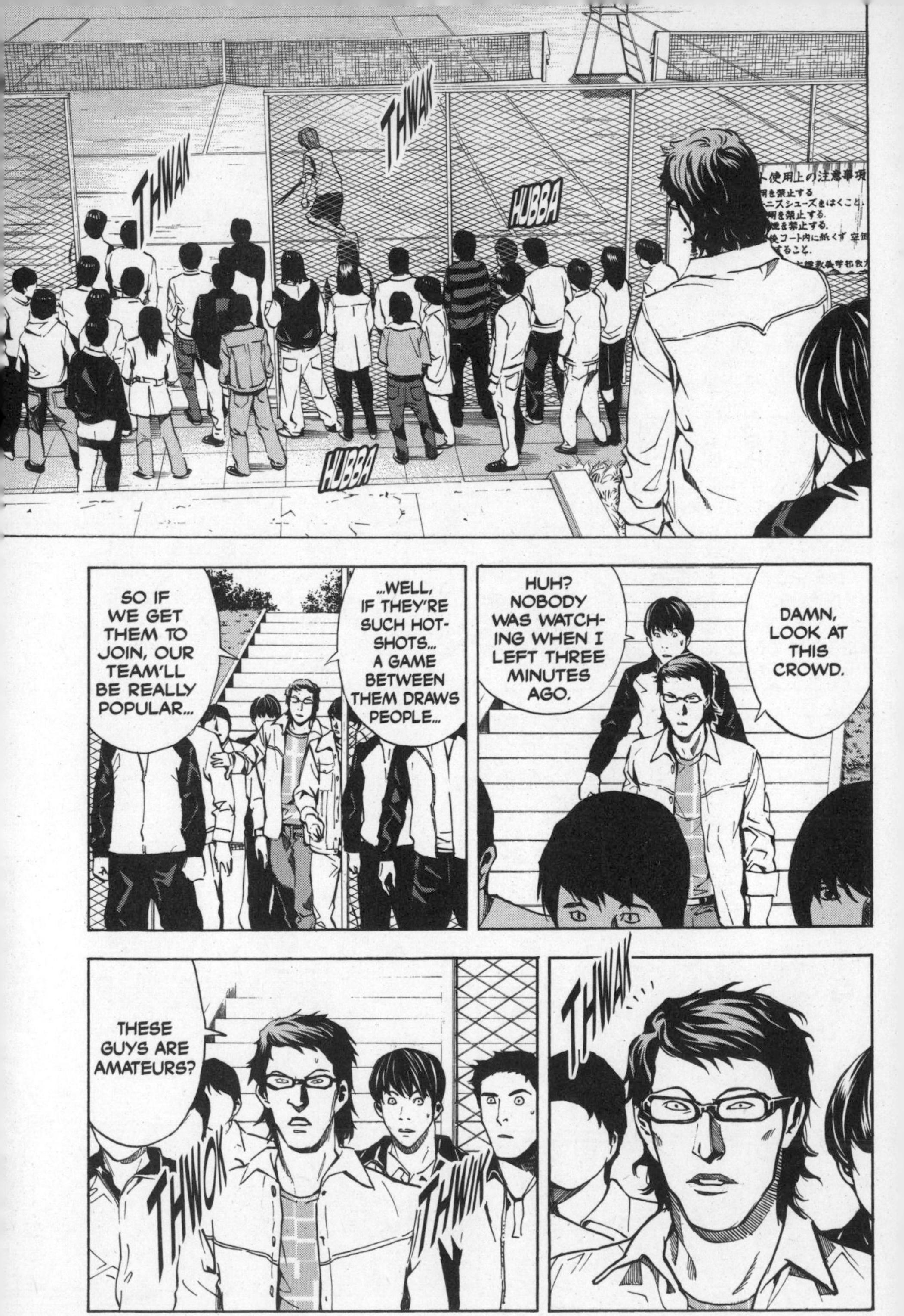
HUBBA
THWAK
THWAK
HUBBA
DAMN, LOOK AT THIS CROWD.
HUH? NOBODY WAS WATCHING WHEN I LEFT THREE MINUTES AGO.
...WELL, IF THEY'RE SUCH HOT-SHOTS... A GAME BETWEEN THEM DRAWS PEOPLE...
SO IF WE GET THEM TO JOIN, OUR TEAM'LL BE REALLY POPULAR...
THWAK
THESE GUYS ARE AMATEURS?
THWOK

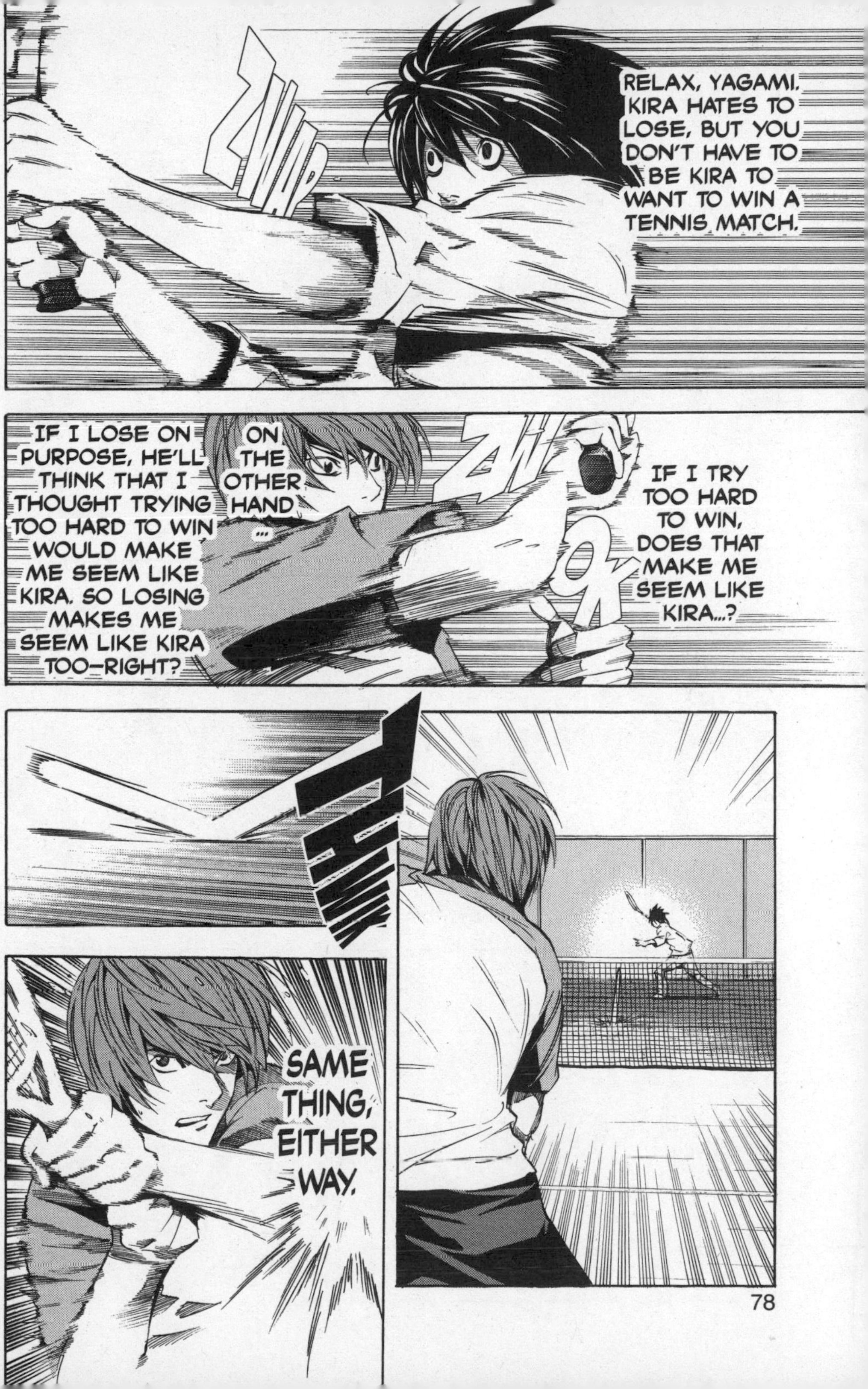
RELAX, YAGAMI. KIRA HATES TO LOSE, BUT YOU DON'T HAVE TO BE KIRA TO WANT TO WIN A TENNIS MATCH.
IF I TRY TOO HARD TO WIN, DOES THAT MAKE ME SEEM LIKE KIRA...?
ON THE OTHER HAND ...
IF I LOSE ON PURPOSE, HE'LL THINK THAT I THOUGHT TRYING TOO HARD TO WIN WOULD MAKE ME SEEM LIKE KIRA. SO LOSING MAKES ME SEEM LIKE KIRA TOO—RIGHT?
SAME THING, EITHER WAY.

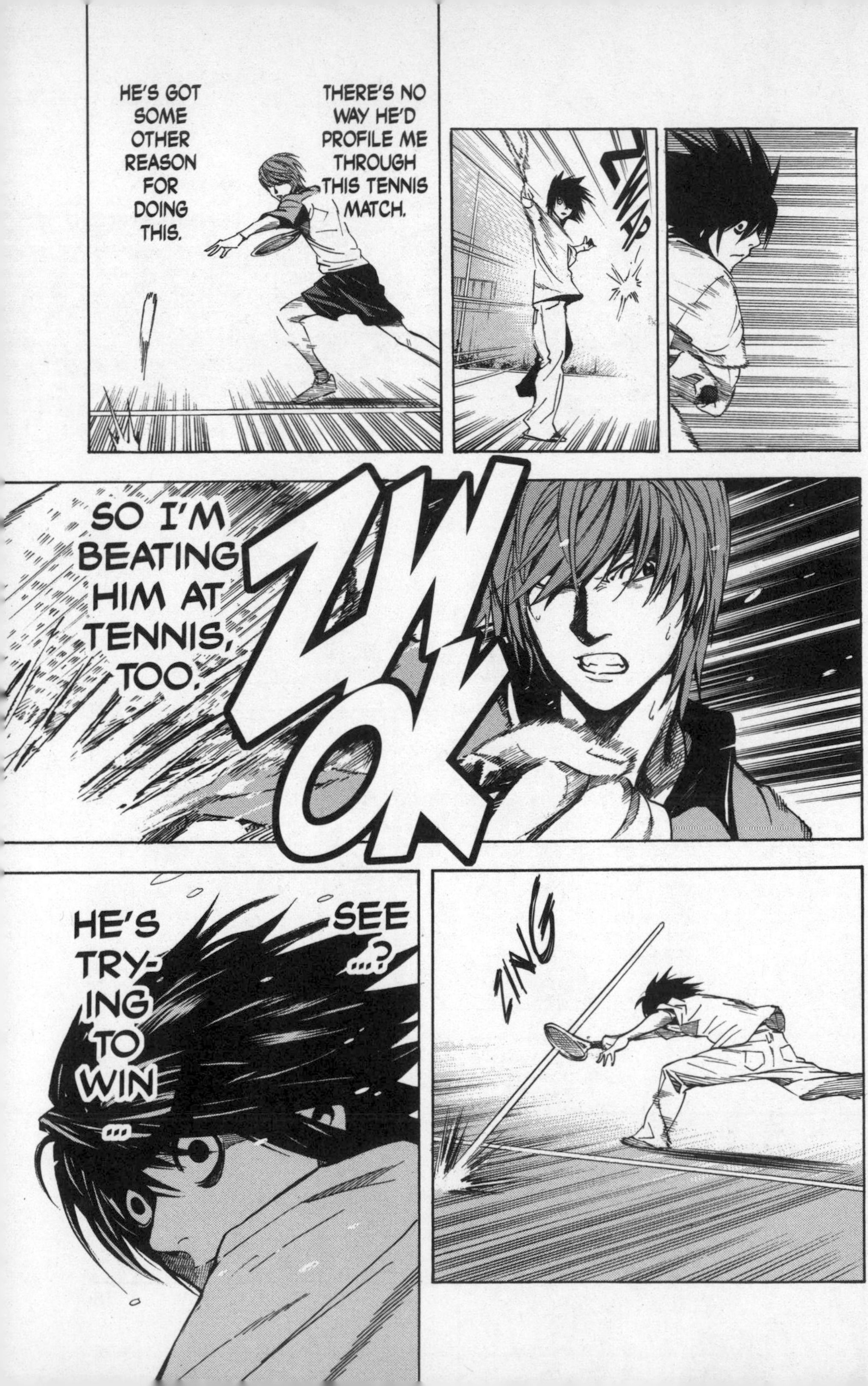
ZWAP
THERE'S NO WAY HE'D PROFILE ME THROUGH THIS TENNIS MATCH.
HE'S GOT SOME OTHER REASON FOR DOING THIS.
ZWOK
SO I'M BEATING HIM AT TENNIS, TOO.
ZING
SEE ...?
HE'S TRY-ING TO WIN ...

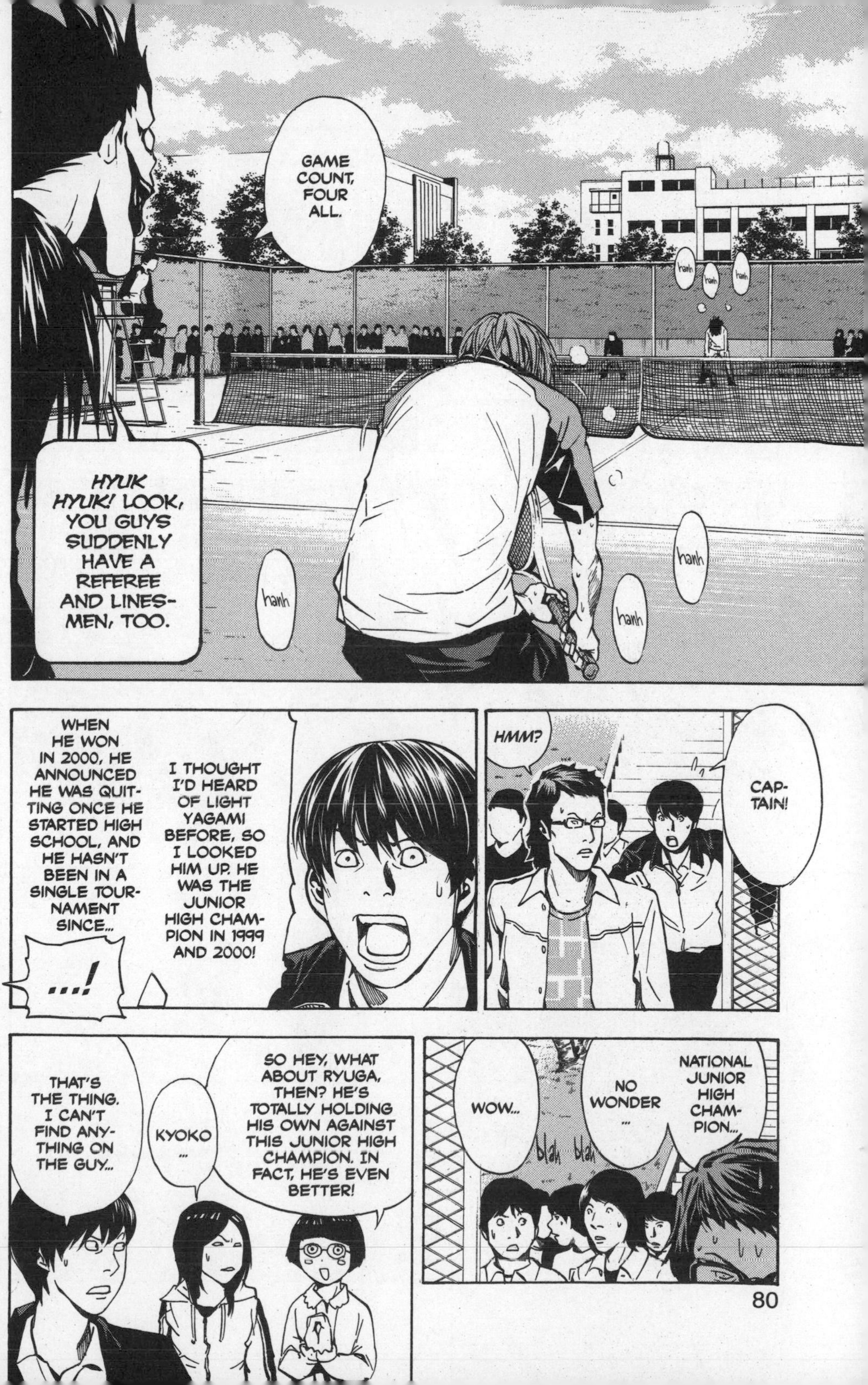
GAME COUNT, FOUR ALL.
hanh
hanh
hanh
HYUK HYUK! LOOK, YOU GUYS SUDDENLY HAVE A REFEREE AND LINES-MEN, TOO.
hanh
hanh
hanh
CAP-TAIN!
HMM?
I THOUGHT I'D HEARD OF LIGHT YAGAMI BEFORE, SO I LOOKED HIM UP. HE WAS THE JUNIOR HIGH CHAM-PION IN 1999 AND 2000!
WHEN HE WON IN 2000, HE ANNOUNCED HE WAS QUIT-TING ONCE HE STARTED HIGH SCHOOL, AND HE HASN'T BEEN IN A SINGLE TOUR-NAMENT SINCE...
...!
NATIONAL JUNIOR HIGH CHAM-PION...
NO WONDER ...
WOW...
blah blah
SO HEY, WHAT ABOUT RYUGA, THEN? HE'S TOTALLY HOLDING HIS OWN AGAINST THIS JUNIOR HIGH CHAMPION. IN FACT, HE'S EVEN BETTER!
KYOKO ...
THAT'S THE THING. I CAN'T FIND ANY-THING ON THE GUY...

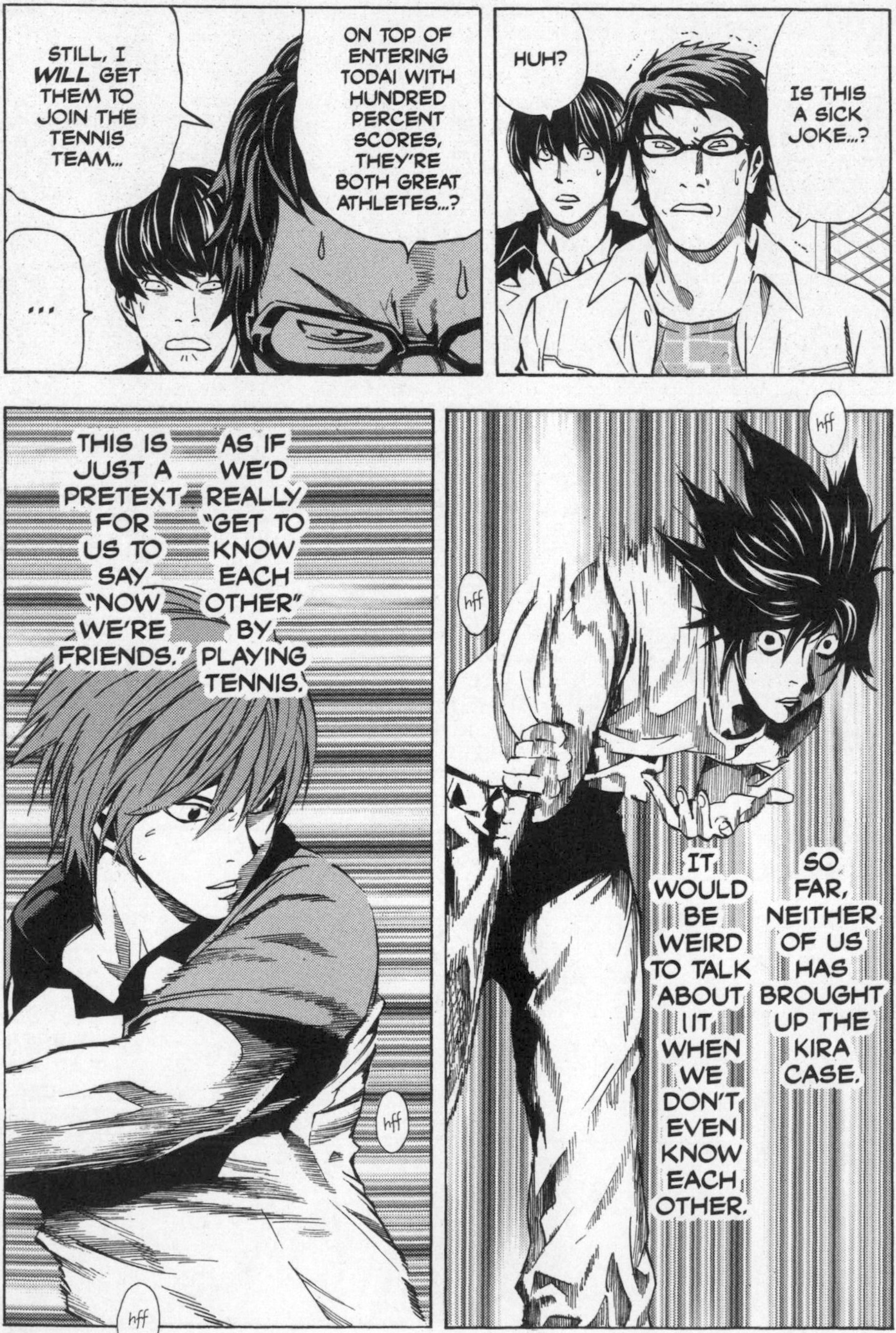
IS THIS A SICK JOKE...?
HUH?
ON TOP OF ENTERING TODAI WITH HUNDRED PERCENT SCORES, THEY'RE BOTH GREAT ATHLETES...?
STILL, I WILL GET THEM TO JOIN THE TENNIS TEAM...
...
hff
SO FAR, NEITHER OF US HAS BROUGHT UP THE KIRA CASE.
IT WOULD BE WEIRD TO TALK ABOUT IT WHEN WE DON'T EVEN KNOW EACH OTHER.
hff
AS IF WE'D REALLY "GET TO KNOW EACH OTHER" BY PLAYING TENNIS.
THIS IS JUST A PRETEXT FOR US TO SAY "NOW WE'RE FRIENDS."
hff
hff

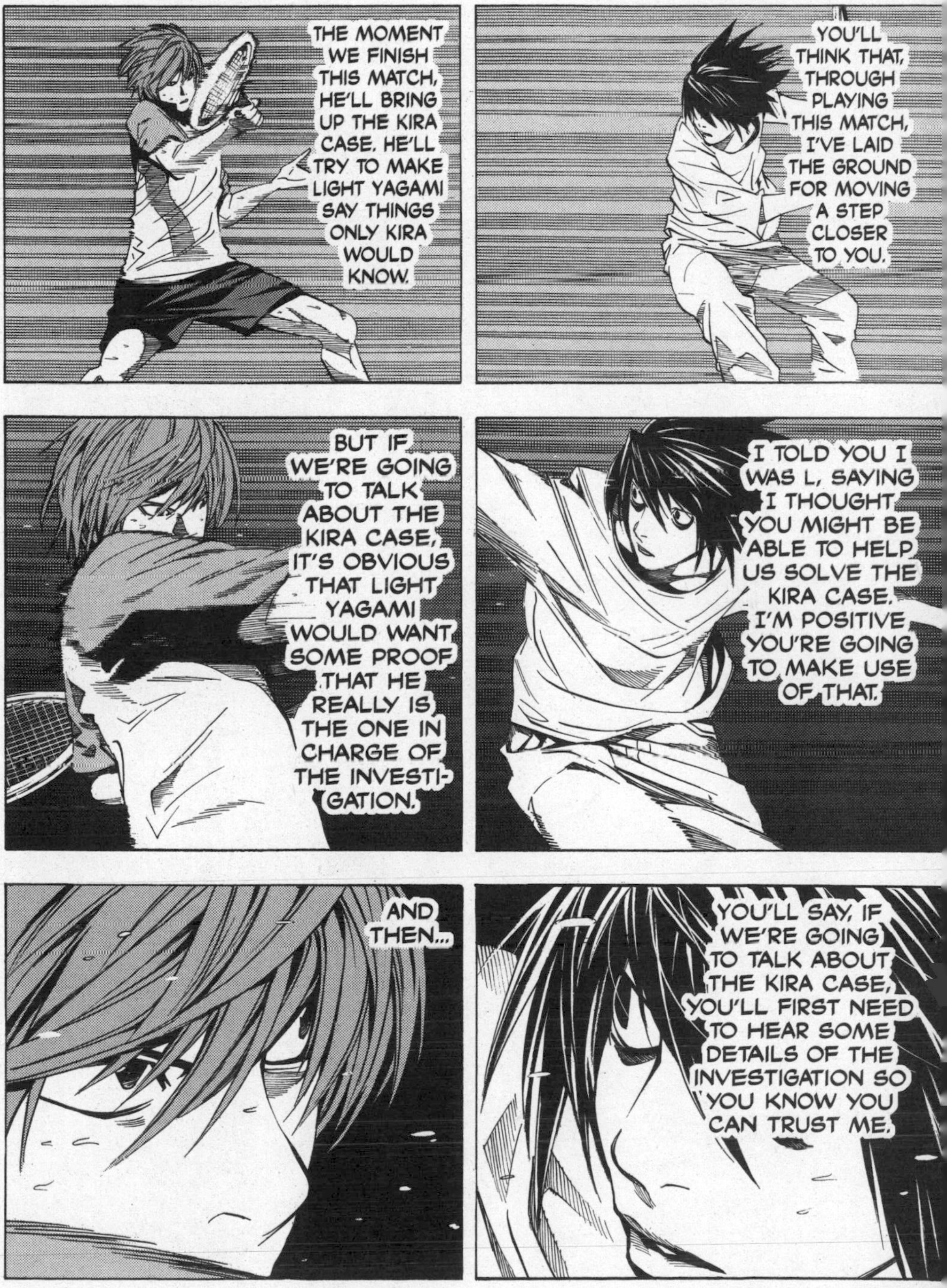
YOU'LL THINK THAT, THROUGH PLAYING THIS MATCH, I'VE LAID THE GROUND FOR MOVING A STEP CLOSER TO YOU.
THE MOMENT WE FINISH THIS MATCH, HE'LL BRING UP THE KIRA CASE. HE'LL TRY TO MAKE LIGHT YAGAMI SAY THINGS ONLY KIRA WOULD KNOW.
I TOLD YOU I WAS L, SAYING I THOUGHT YOU MIGHT BE ABLE TO HELP US SOLVE THE KIRA CASE. I'M POSITIVE YOU'RE GOING TO MAKE USE OF THAT.
BUT IF WE'RE GOING TO TALK ABOUT THE KIRA CASE, IT'S OBVIOUS THAT LIGHT YAGAMI WOULD WANT SOME PROOF THAT HE REALLY IS THE ONE IN CHARGE OF THE INVESTIGATION.
YOU'LL SAY, IF WE'RE GOING TO TALK ABOUT THE KIRA CASE, YOU'LL FIRST NEED TO HEAR SOME DETAILS OF THE INVESTIGATION SO YOU KNOW YOU CAN TRUST ME.
AND THEN...

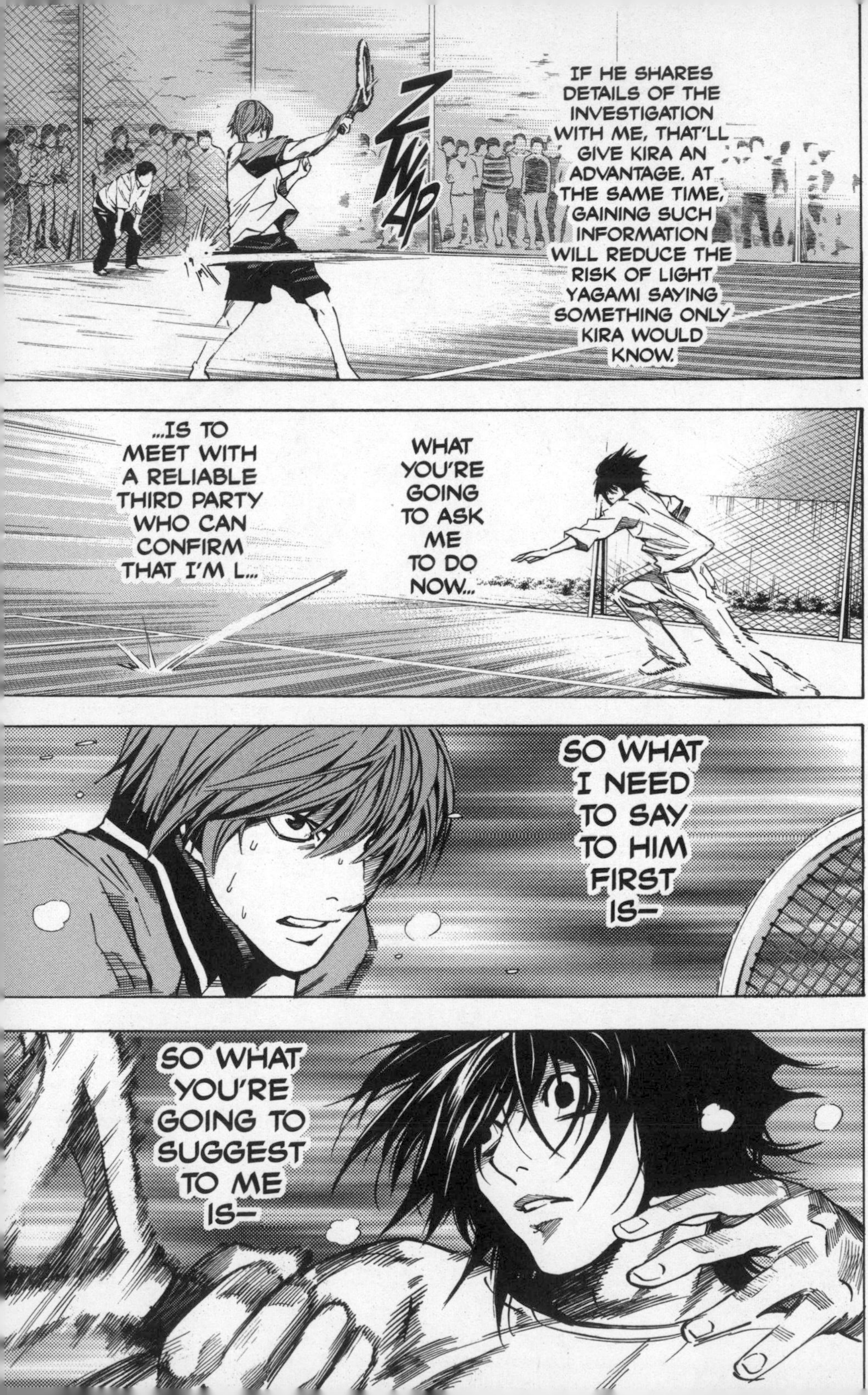

IF HE SHARES DETAILS OF THE INVESTIGATION WITH ME, THAT'LL GIVE KIRA AN ADVANTAGE. AT THE SAME TIME, GAINING SUCH INFORMATION WILL REDUCE THE RISK OF LIGHT YAGAMI SAYING SOMETHING ONLY KIRA WOULD KNOW.
ZWAP
WHAT YOU'RE GOING TO ASK ME TO DO NOW...
...IS TO MEET WITH A RELIABLE THIRD PARTY WHO CAN CONFIRM THAT I'M L...
SO WHAT I NEED TO SAY TO HIM FIRST IS—
SO WHAT YOU'RE GOING TO SUGGEST TO ME IS—

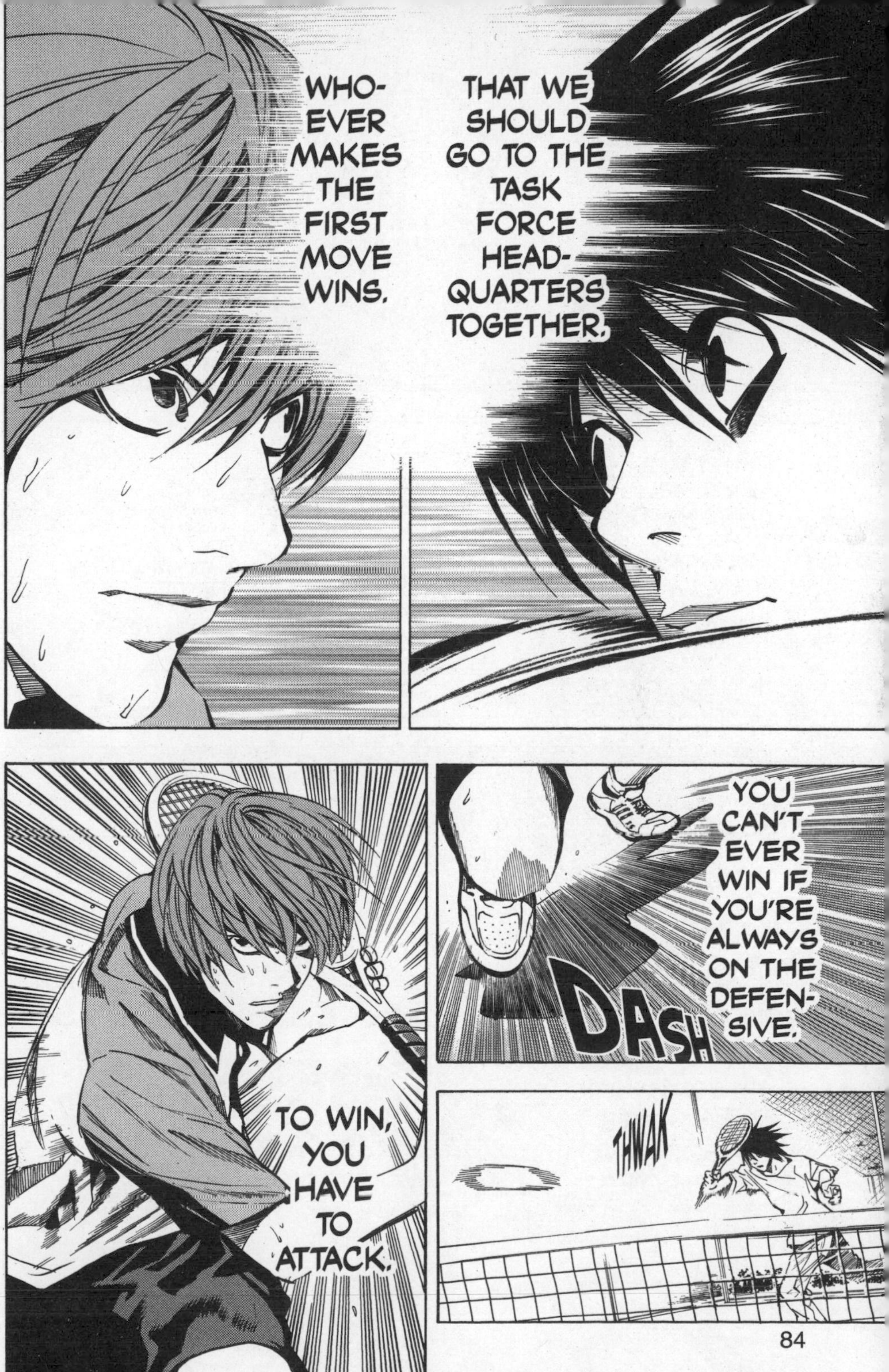
THAT WE SHOULD GO TO THE TASK FORCE HEAD-QUARTERS TOGETHER.
WHO-EVER MAKES THE FIRST MOVE WINS.
YOU CAN'T EVER WIN IF YOU'RE ALWAYS ON THE DEFEN-SIVE.
DASH
THWAK
TO WIN, YOU HAVE TO ATTACK.

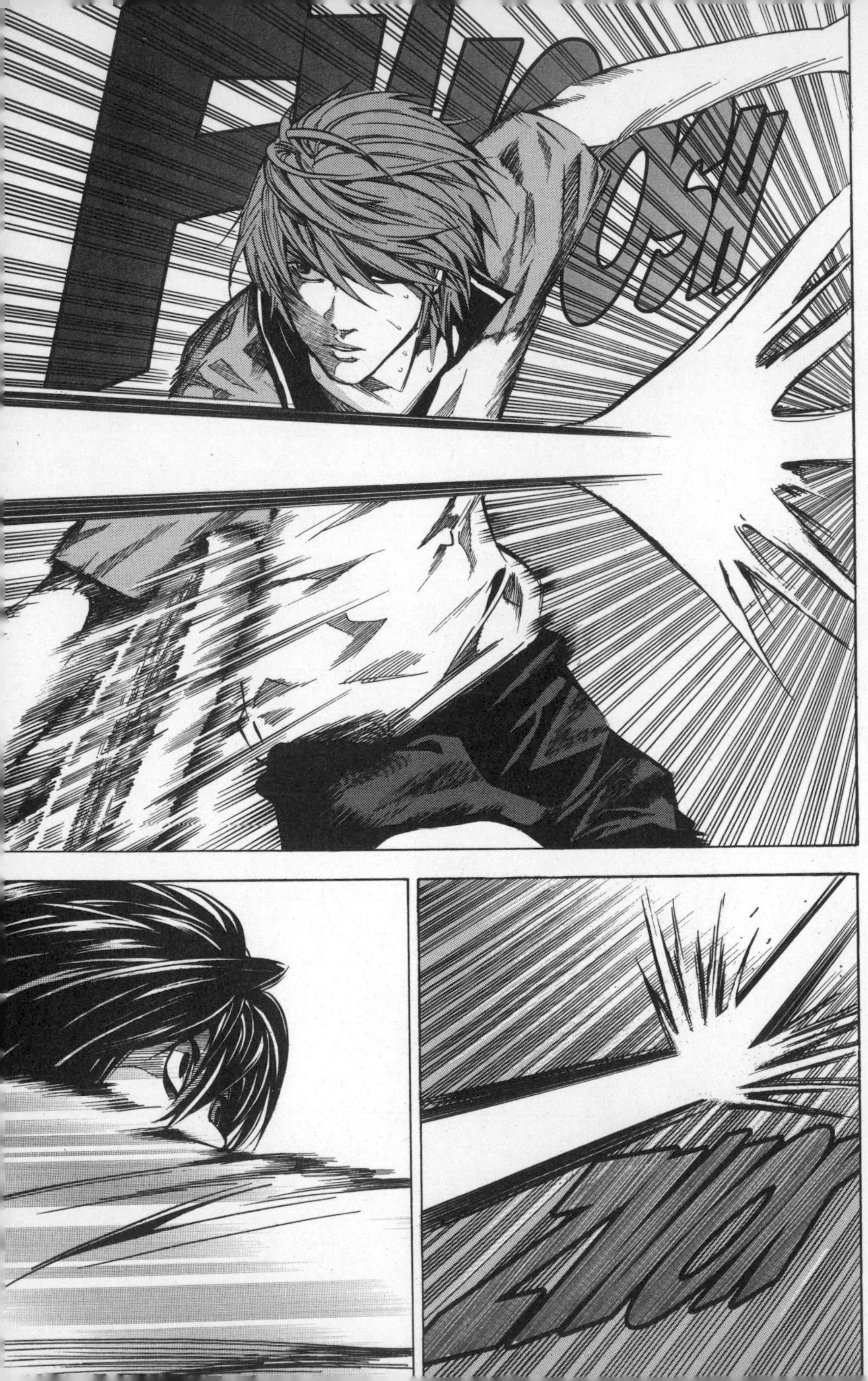
FWOOSH

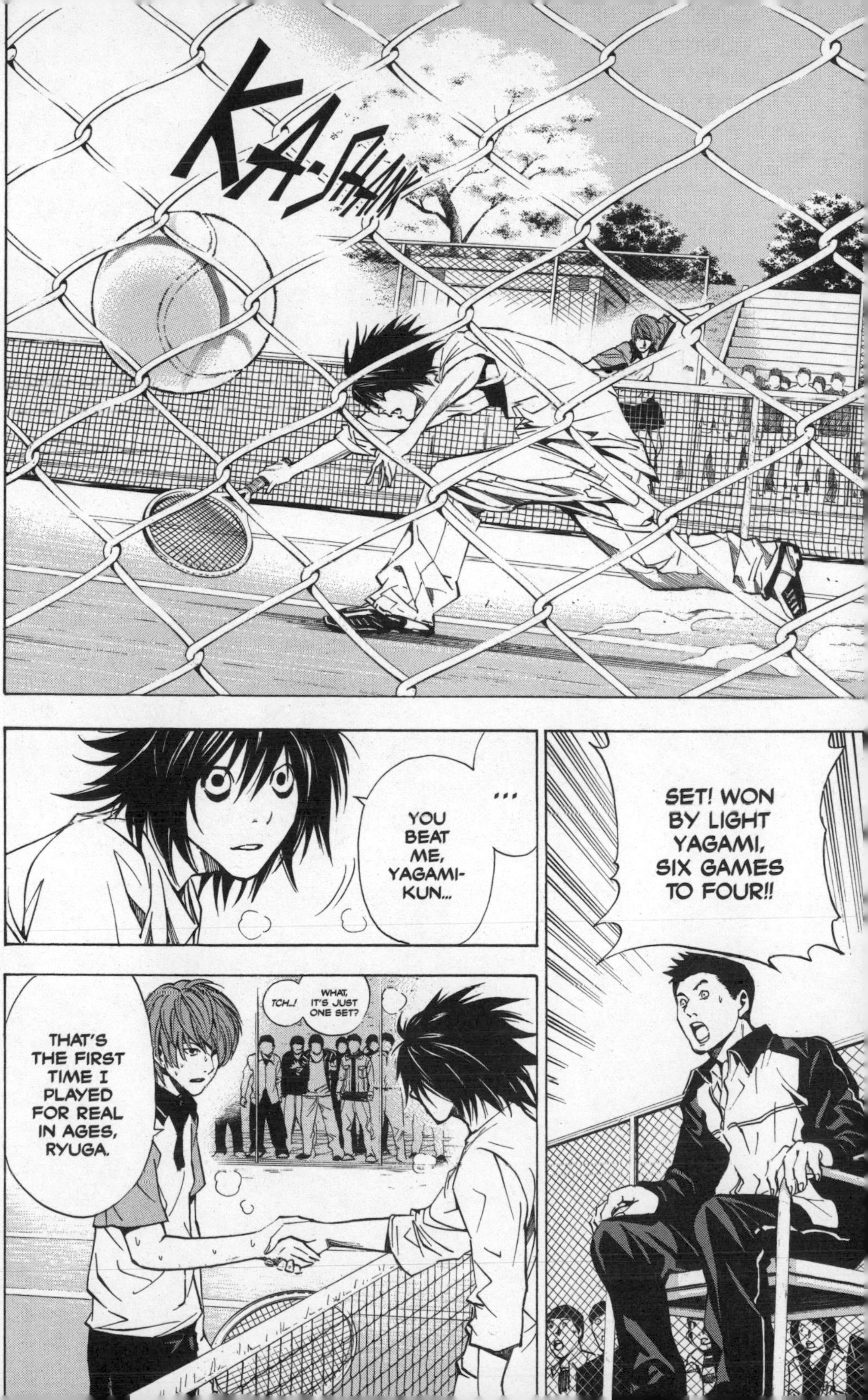
KA-SHANK
SET! WON BY LIGHT YAGAMI, SIX GAMES TO FOUR!!
...
YOU BEAT ME, YAGAMI-KUN...
WHAT, IT'S JUST ONE SET?
TCH..!
THAT'S THE FIRST TIME I PLAYED FOR REAL IN AGES, RYUGA.

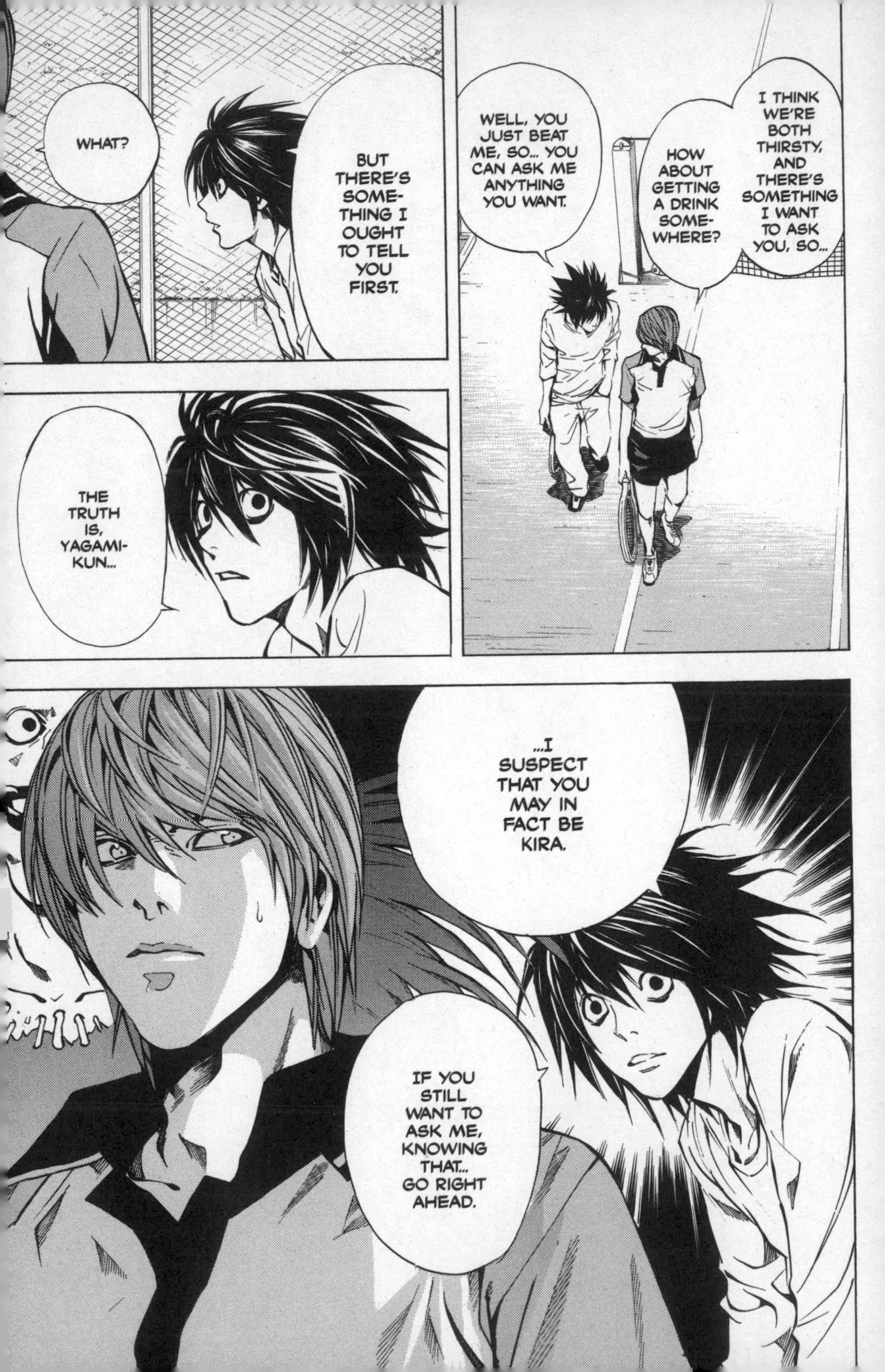
I THINK WE'RE BOTH THIRSTY, AND THERE'S SOMETHING I WANT TO ASK YOU, SO...
HOW ABOUT GETTING A DRINK SOME-WHERE?
WELL, YOU JUST BEAT ME, SO... YOU CAN ASK ME ANYTHING YOU WANT.
BUT THERE'S SOME-THING I OUGHT TO TELL YOU FIRST.
WHAT?
THE TRUTH IS, YAGAMI-KUN...
...I SUSPECT THAT YOU MAY IN FACT BE KIRA.
IF YOU STILL WANT TO ASK ME, KNOWING THAT... GO RIGHT AHEAD.

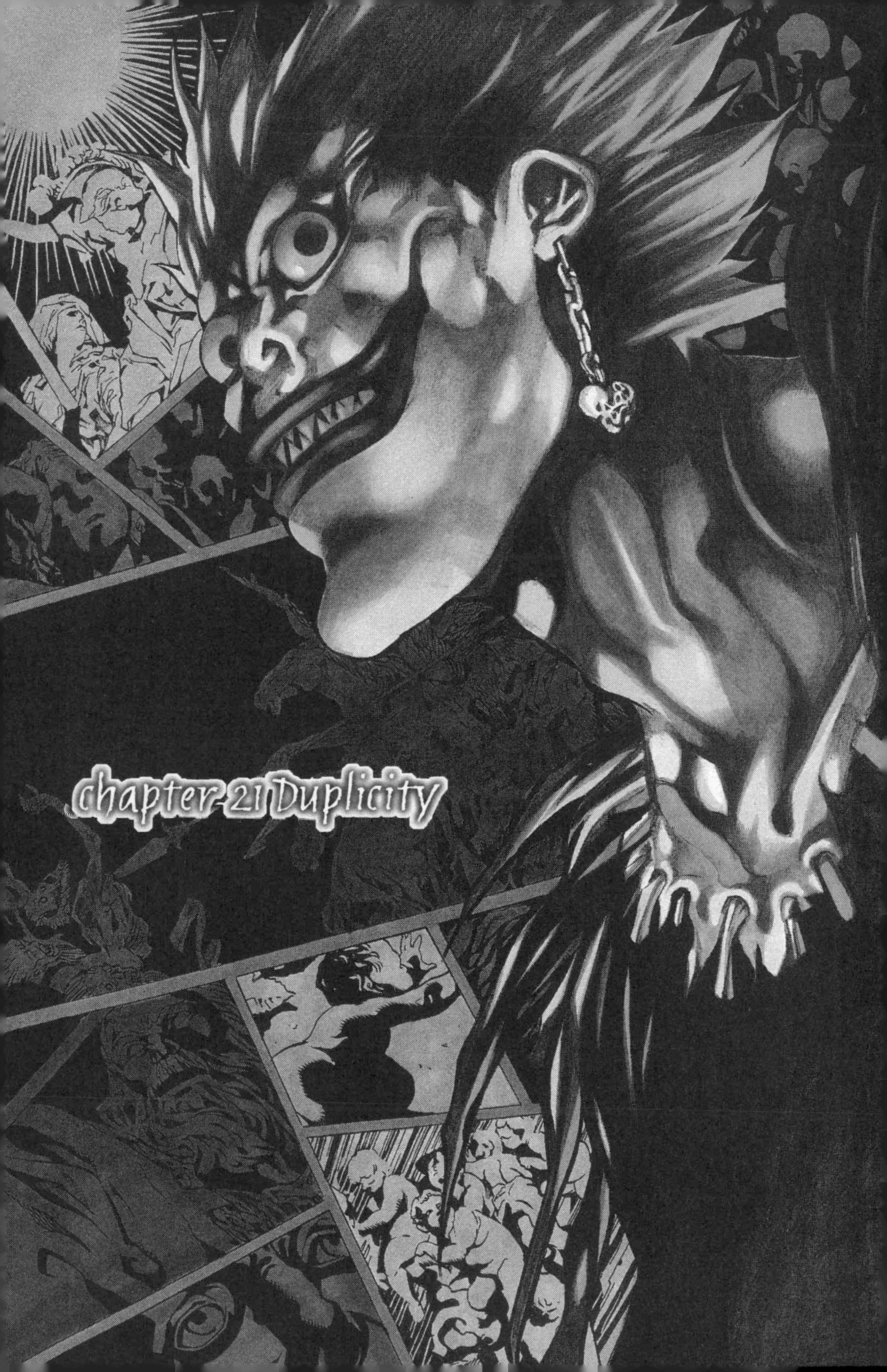
chapter 21 Duplicity

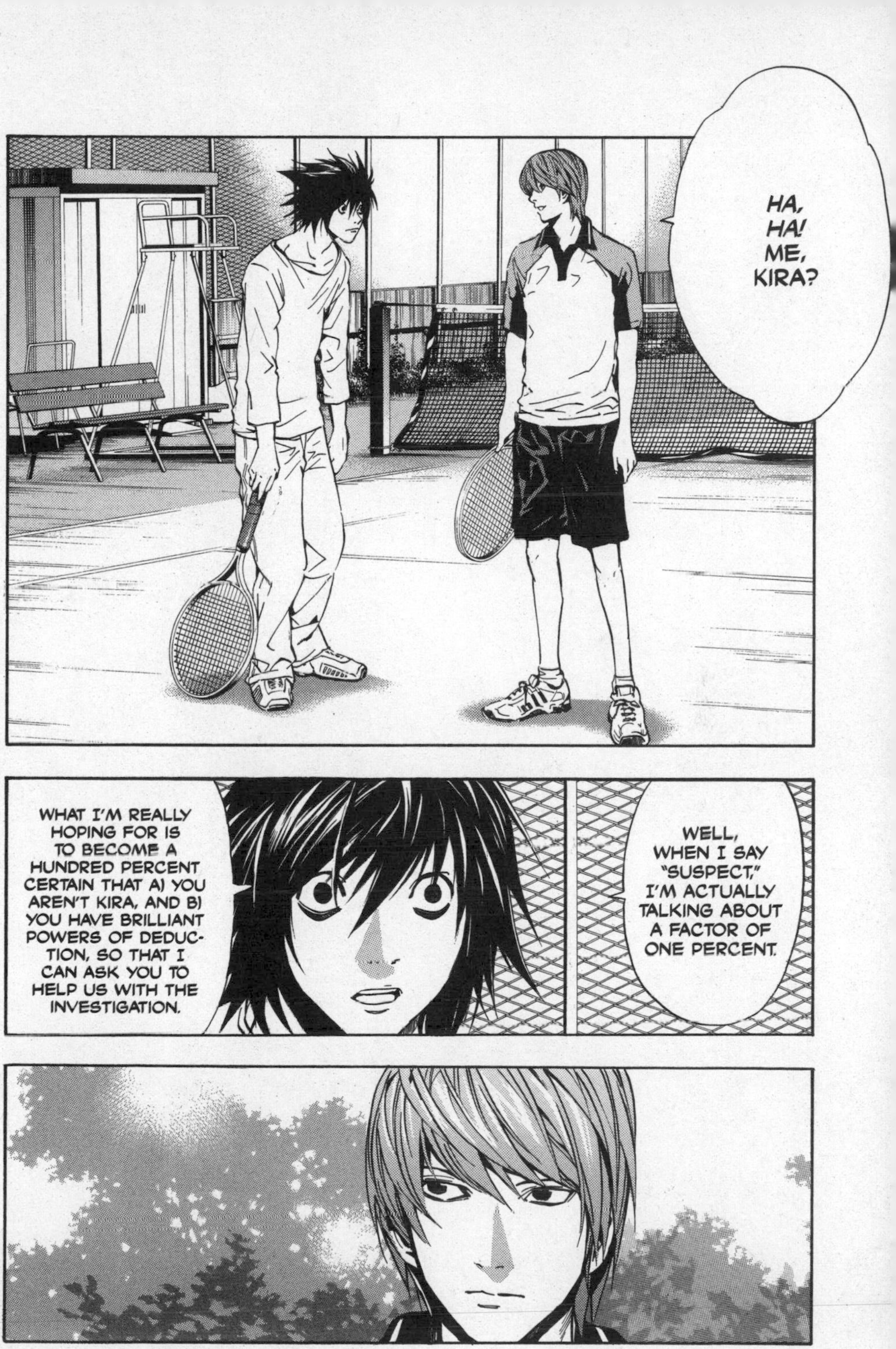
HA, HA! ME, KIRA?
WELL, WHEN I SAY "SUSPECT," I'M ACTUALLY TALKING ABOUT A FACTOR OF ONE PERCENT.
WHAT I'M REALLY HOPING FOR IS TO BECOME A HUNDRED PERCENT CERTAIN THAT A) YOU AREN'T KIRA, AND B) YOU HAVE BRILLIANT POWERS OF DEDUCTION, SO THAT I CAN ASK YOU TO HELP US WITH THE INVESTIGATION.

READ THIS WAY

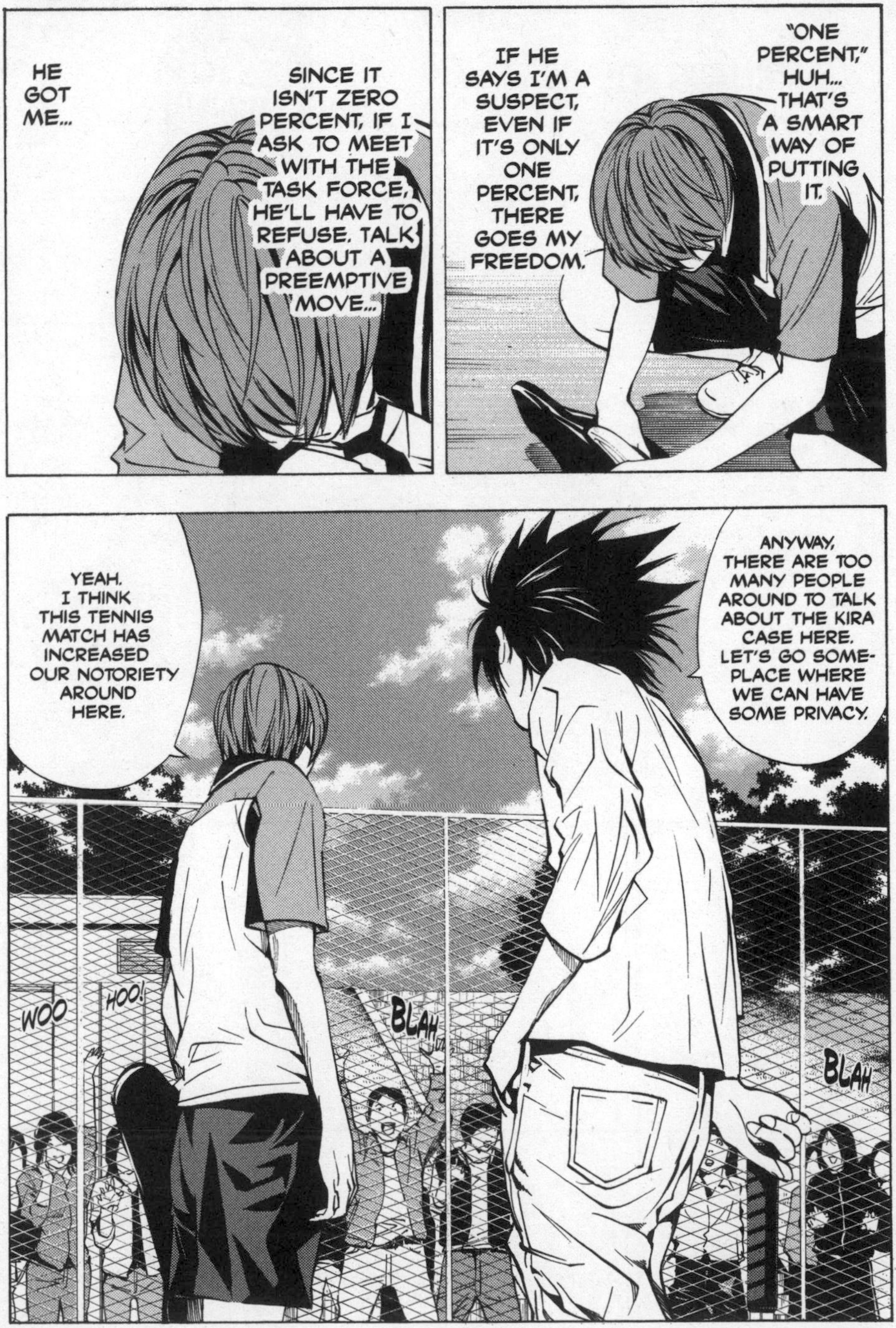
"ONE PERCENT," HUH... THAT'S A SMART WAY OF PUTTING IT.
IF HE SAYS I'M A SUSPECT, EVEN IF IT'S ONLY ONE PERCENT, THERE GOES MY FREEDOM.
SINCE IT ISN'T ZERO PERCENT, IF I ASK TO MEET WITH THE TASK FORCE, HE'LL HAVE TO REFUSE. TALK ABOUT A PREEMPTIVE MOVE...
HE GOT ME...
ANYWAY, THERE ARE TOO MANY PEOPLE AROUND TO TALK ABOUT THE KIRA CASE HERE. LET'S GO SOME-PLACE WHERE WE CAN HAVE SOME PRIVACY.
YEAH. I THINK THIS TENNIS MATCH HAS INCREASED OUR NOTORIETY AROUND HERE.
BLAH
BLAH
WOO HOO!

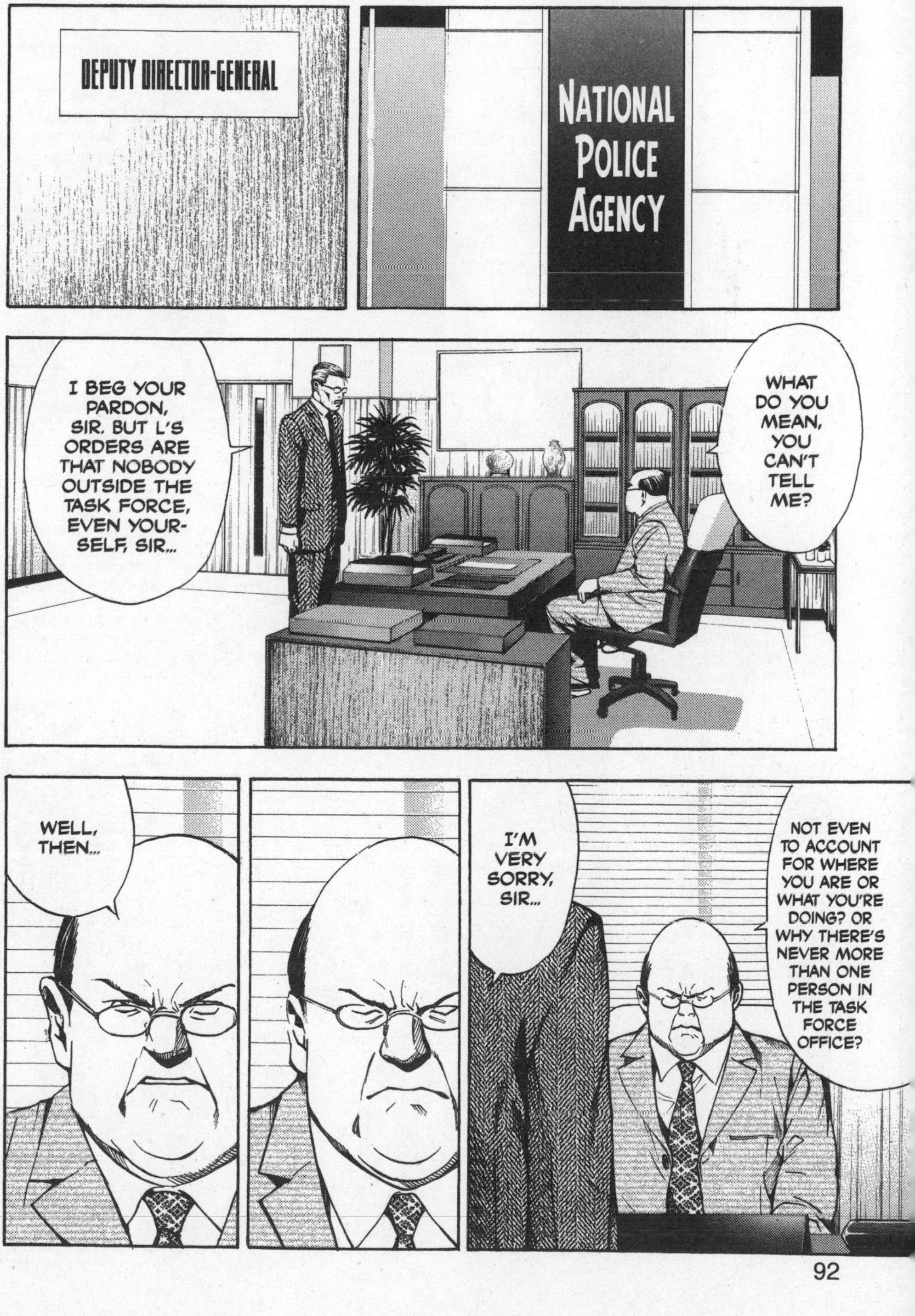
NATIONAL POLICE AGENCY
DEPUTY DIRECTOR-GENERAL
WHAT DO YOU MEAN, YOU CAN'T TELL ME?
I BEG YOUR PARDON, SIR. BUT L'S ORDERS ARE THAT NOBODY OUTSIDE THE TASK FORCE, EVEN YOURSELF, SIR...
NOT EVEN TO ACCOUNT FOR WHERE YOU ARE OR WHAT YOU'RE DOING? OR WHY THERE'S NEVER MORE THAN ONE PERSON IN THE TASK FORCE OFFICE?
I'M VERY SORRY, SIR...
WELL, THEN...

READ THIS WAY

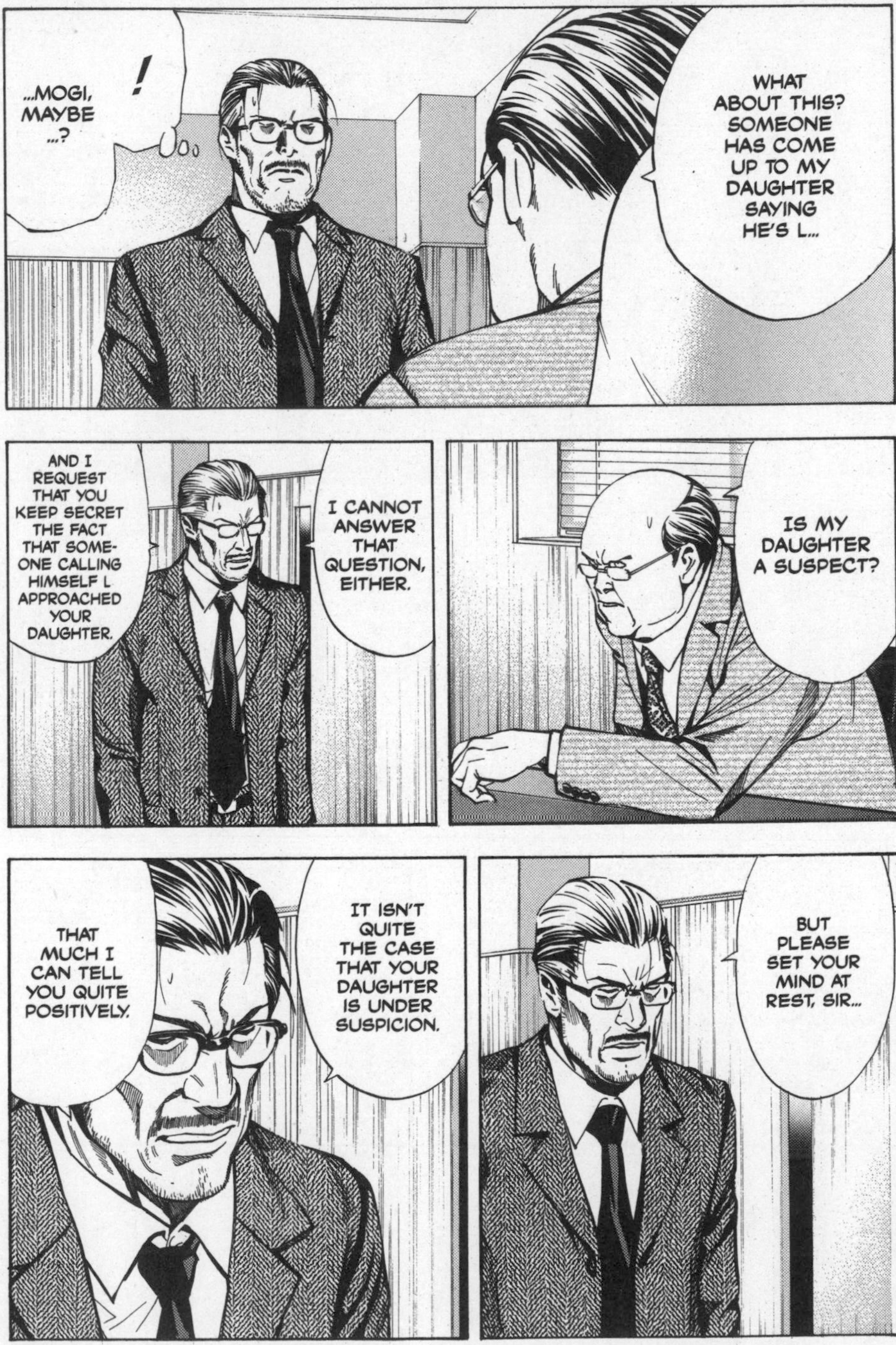
WHAT ABOUT THIS? SOMEONE HAS COME UP TO MY DAUGHTER SAYING HE'S L...
!
...MOGI, MAYBE ...?
IS MY DAUGHTER A SUSPECT?
I CANNOT ANSWER THAT QUESTION, EITHER.
AND I REQUEST THAT YOU KEEP SECRET THE FACT THAT SOME-ONE CALLING HIMSELF L APPROACHED YOUR DAUGHTER.
BUT PLEASE SET YOUR MIND AT REST, SIR...
IT ISN'T QUITE THE CASE THAT YOUR DAUGHTER IS UNDER SUSPICION.
THAT MUCH I CAN TELL YOU QUITE POSITIVELY.

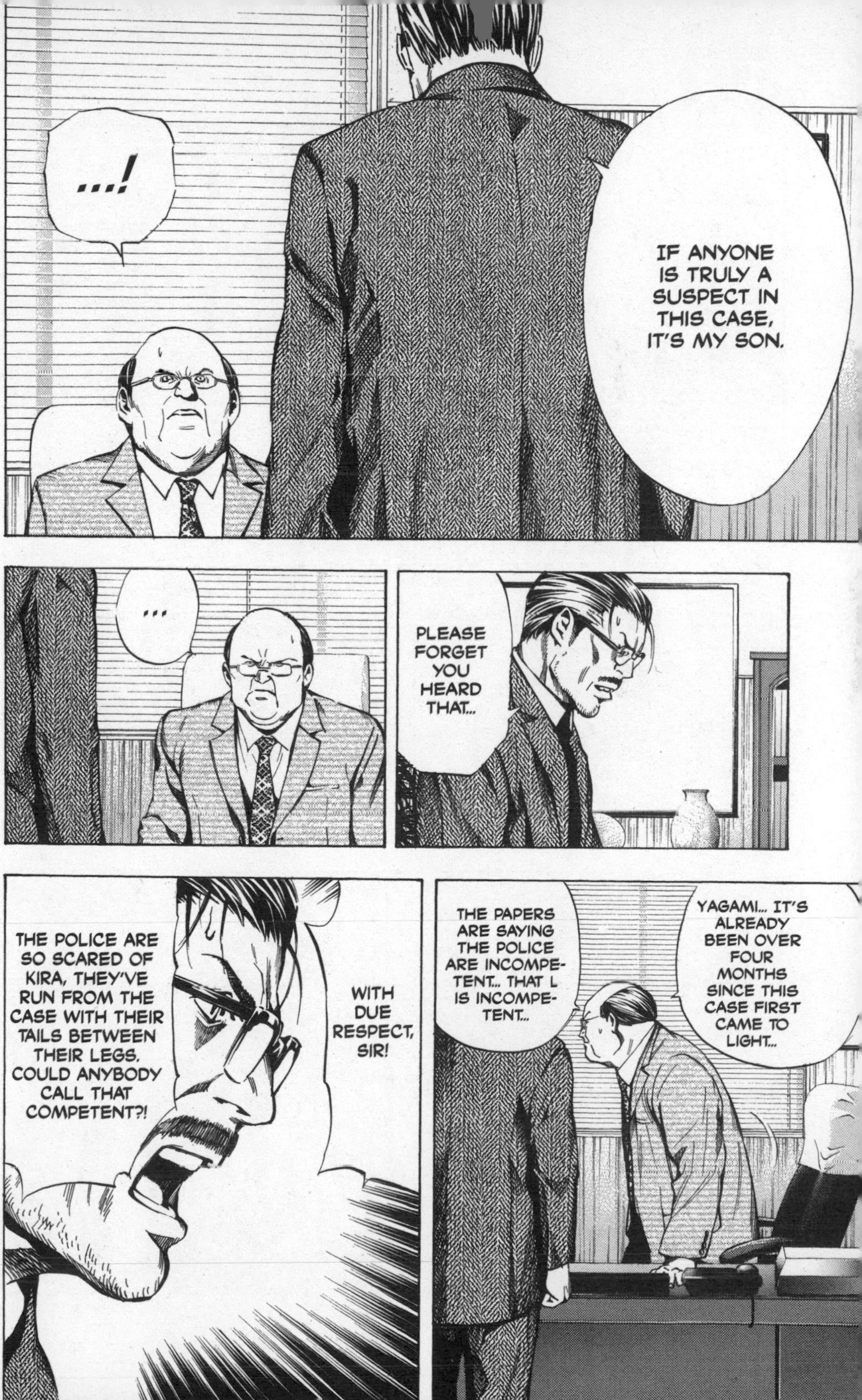
IF ANYONE IS TRULY A SUSPECT IN THIS CASE, IT'S MY SON.
...!
PLEASE FORGET YOU HEARD THAT...
...
YAGAMI... IT'S ALREADY BEEN OVER FOUR MONTHS SINCE THIS CASE FIRST CAME TO LIGHT...
THE PAPERS ARE SAYING THE POLICE ARE INCOMPETENT... THAT L IS INCOMPETENT...
WITH DUE RESPECT, SIR!
THE POLICE ARE SO SCARED OF KIRA, THEY'VE RUN FROM THE CASE WITH THEIR TAILS BETWEEN THEIR LEGS. COULD ANYBODY CALL THAT COMPETENT?!

READ THIS WAY

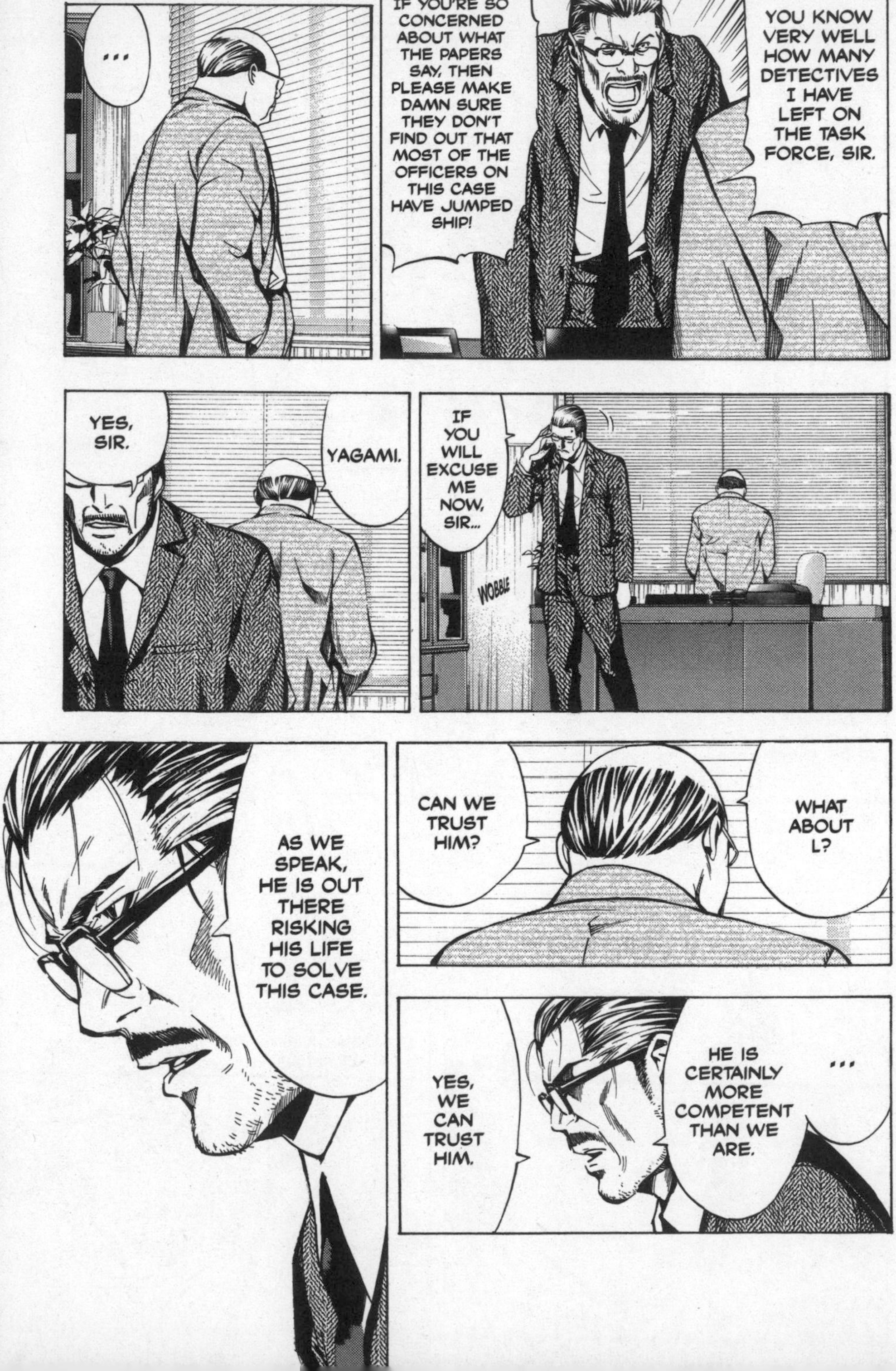

YOU KNOW VERY WELL HOW MANY DETECTIVES I HAVE LEFT ON THE TASK FORCE, SIR.
IF YOU'RE SO CONCERNED ABOUT WHAT THE PAPERS SAY, THEN PLEASE MAKE DAMN SURE THEY DON'T FIND OUT THAT MOST OF THE OFFICERS ON THIS CASE HAVE JUMPED SHIP!
...
IF YOU WILL EXCUSE ME NOW, SIR...
WOBBLE
YAGAMI.
YES, SIR.
WHAT ABOUT L?
CAN WE TRUST HIM?
...
HE IS CERTAINLY MORE COMPETENT THAN WE ARE.
YES, WE CAN TRUST HIM.
AS WE SPEAK, HE IS OUT THERE RISKING HIS LIFE TO SOLVE THIS CASE.

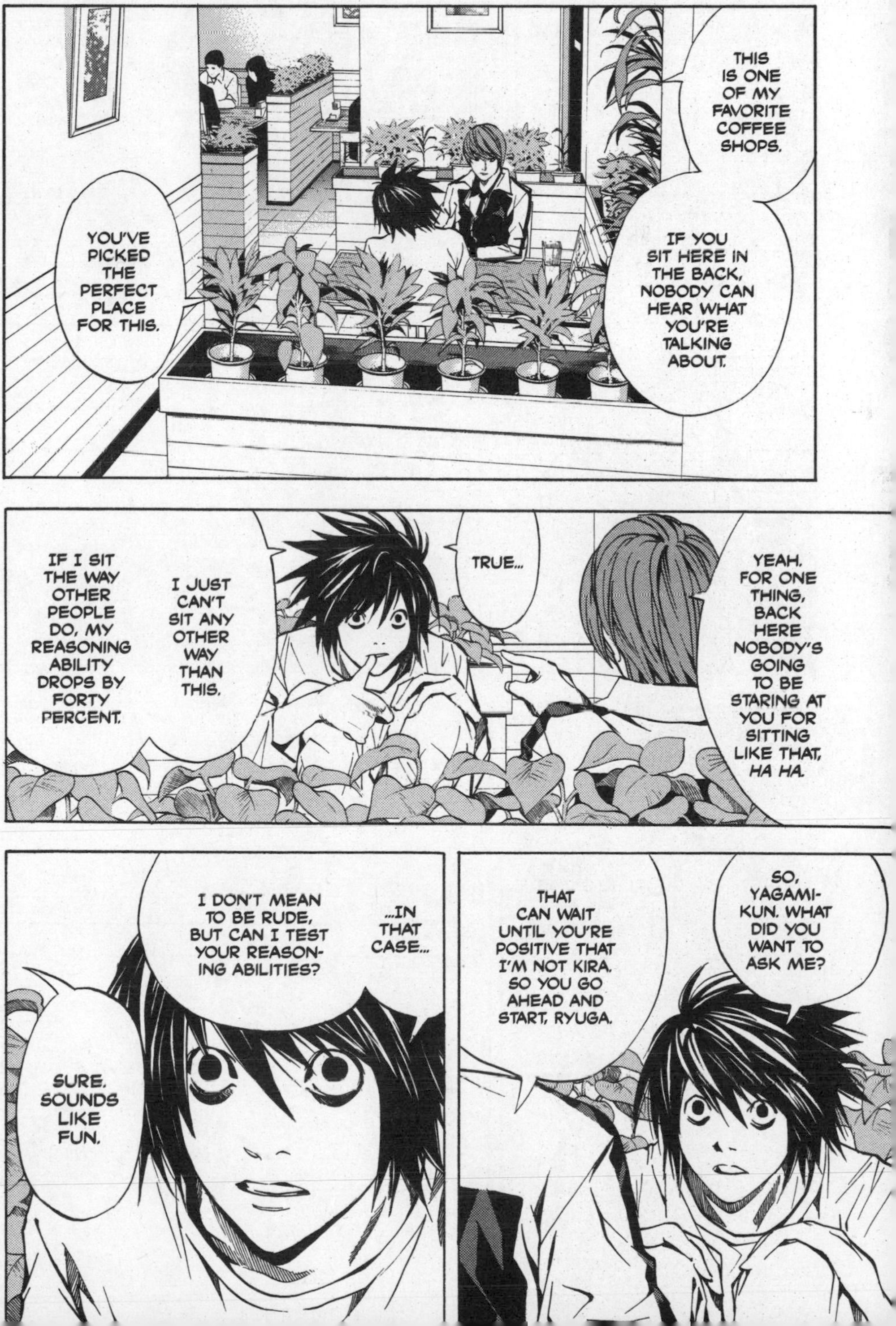
THIS IS ONE OF MY FAVORITE COFFEE SHOPS.
IF YOU SIT HERE IN THE BACK, NOBODY CAN HEAR WHAT YOU'RE TALKING ABOUT.
YOU'VE PICKED THE PERFECT PLACE FOR THIS.
YEAH. FOR ONE THING, BACK HERE NOBODY'S GOING TO BE STARING AT YOU FOR SITTING LIKE THAT, *HA HA*.
TRUE...
I JUST CAN'T SIT ANY OTHER WAY THAN THIS.
IF I SIT THE WAY OTHER PEOPLE DO, MY REASONING ABILITY DROPS BY FORTY PERCENT.
SO, YAGAMI-KUN. WHAT DID YOU WANT TO ASK ME?
THAT CAN WAIT UNTIL YOU'RE POSITIVE THAT I'M NOT KIRA. SO YOU GO AHEAD AND START, RYUGA.
...IN THAT CASE...
I DON'T MEAN TO BE RUDE, BUT CAN I TEST YOUR REASONING ABILITIES?
SURE. SOUNDS LIKE FUN.

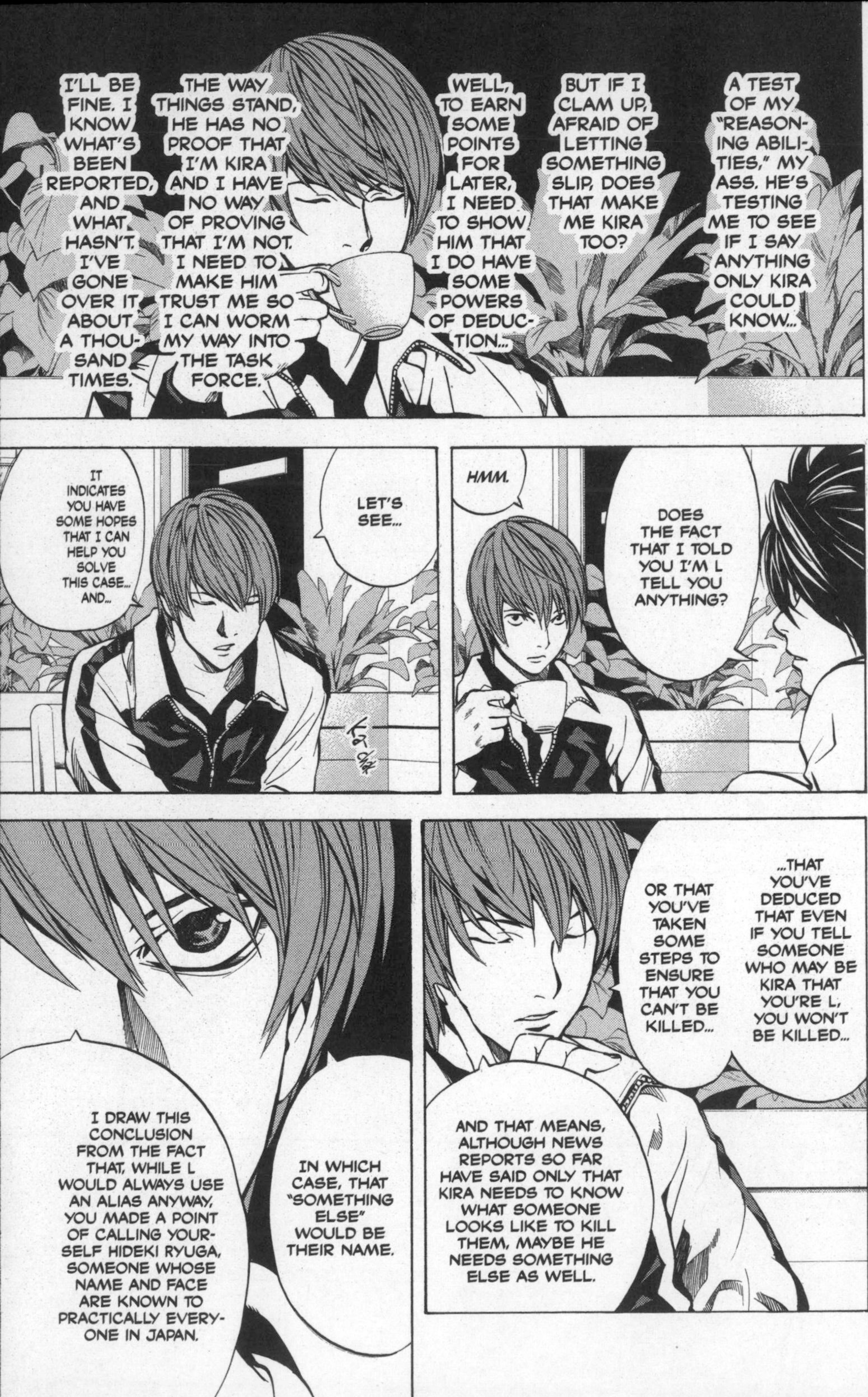
A TEST OF MY "REASONING ABILITIES," MY ASS. HE'S TESTING ME TO SEE IF I SAY ANYTHING ONLY KIRA COULD KNOW...
BUT IF I CLAM UP, AFRAID OF LETTING SOMETHING SLIP, DOES THAT MAKE ME KIRA TOO?
WELL, TO EARN SOME POINTS FOR LATER, I NEED TO SHOW HIM THAT I DO HAVE SOME POWERS OF DEDUCTION...
THE WAY THINGS STAND, HE HAS NO PROOF THAT I'M KIRA AND I HAVE NO WAY OF PROVING THAT I'M NOT. I NEED TO MAKE HIM TRUST ME SO I CAN WORM MY WAY INTO THE TASK FORCE.
I'LL BE FINE. I KNOW WHAT'S BEEN REPORTED, AND WHAT HASN'T. I'VE GONE OVER IT ABOUT A THOUSAND TIMES.
DOES THE FACT THAT I TOLD YOU I'M L TELL YOU ANYTHING?
HMM.
LET'S SEE...
IT INDICATES YOU HAVE SOME HOPES THAT I CAN HELP YOU SOLVE THIS CASE... AND...
...THAT YOU'VE DEDUCED THAT EVEN IF YOU TELL SOMEONE WHO MAY BE KIRA THAT YOU'RE L, YOU WON'T BE KILLED...
OR THAT YOU'VE TAKEN SOME STEPS TO ENSURE THAT YOU CAN'T BE KILLED...
AND THAT MEANS, ALTHOUGH NEWS REPORTS SO FAR HAVE SAID ONLY THAT KIRA NEEDS TO KNOW WHAT SOMEONE LOOKS LIKE TO KILL THEM, MAYBE HE NEEDS SOMETHING ELSE AS WELL.
IN WHICH CASE, THAT "SOMETHING ELSE" WOULD BE THEIR NAME.
I DRAW THIS CONCLUSION FROM THE FACT THAT, WHILE L WOULD ALWAYS USE AN ALIAS ANYWAY, YOU MADE A POINT OF CALLING YOURSELF HIDEKI RYUGA, SOMEONE WHOSE NAME AND FACE ARE KNOWN TO PRACTICALLY EVERYONE IN JAPAN.

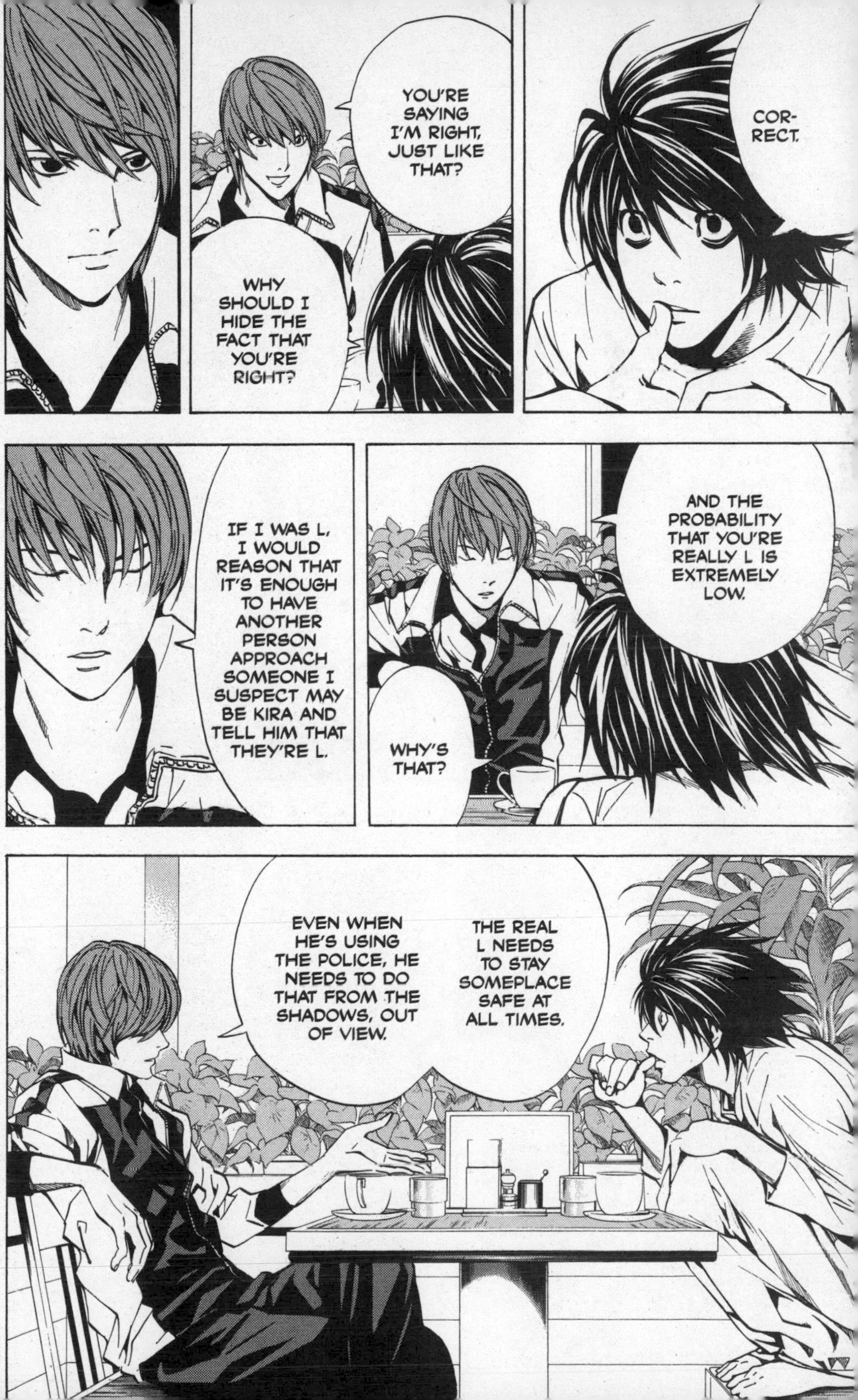
CORRECT.
YOU'RE SAYING I'M RIGHT, JUST LIKE THAT?
WHY SHOULD I HIDE THE FACT THAT YOU'RE RIGHT?
AND THE PROBABILITY THAT YOU'RE REALLY L IS EXTREMELY LOW.
WHY'S THAT?
IF I WAS L, I WOULD REASON THAT IT'S ENOUGH TO HAVE ANOTHER PERSON APPROACH SOMEONE I SUSPECT MAY BE KIRA AND TELL HIM THAT THEY'RE L.
THE REAL L NEEDS TO STAY SOMEPLACE SAFE AT ALL TIMES.
EVEN WHEN HE'S USING THE POLICE, HE NEEDS TO DO THAT FROM THE SHADOWS, OUT OF VIEW.

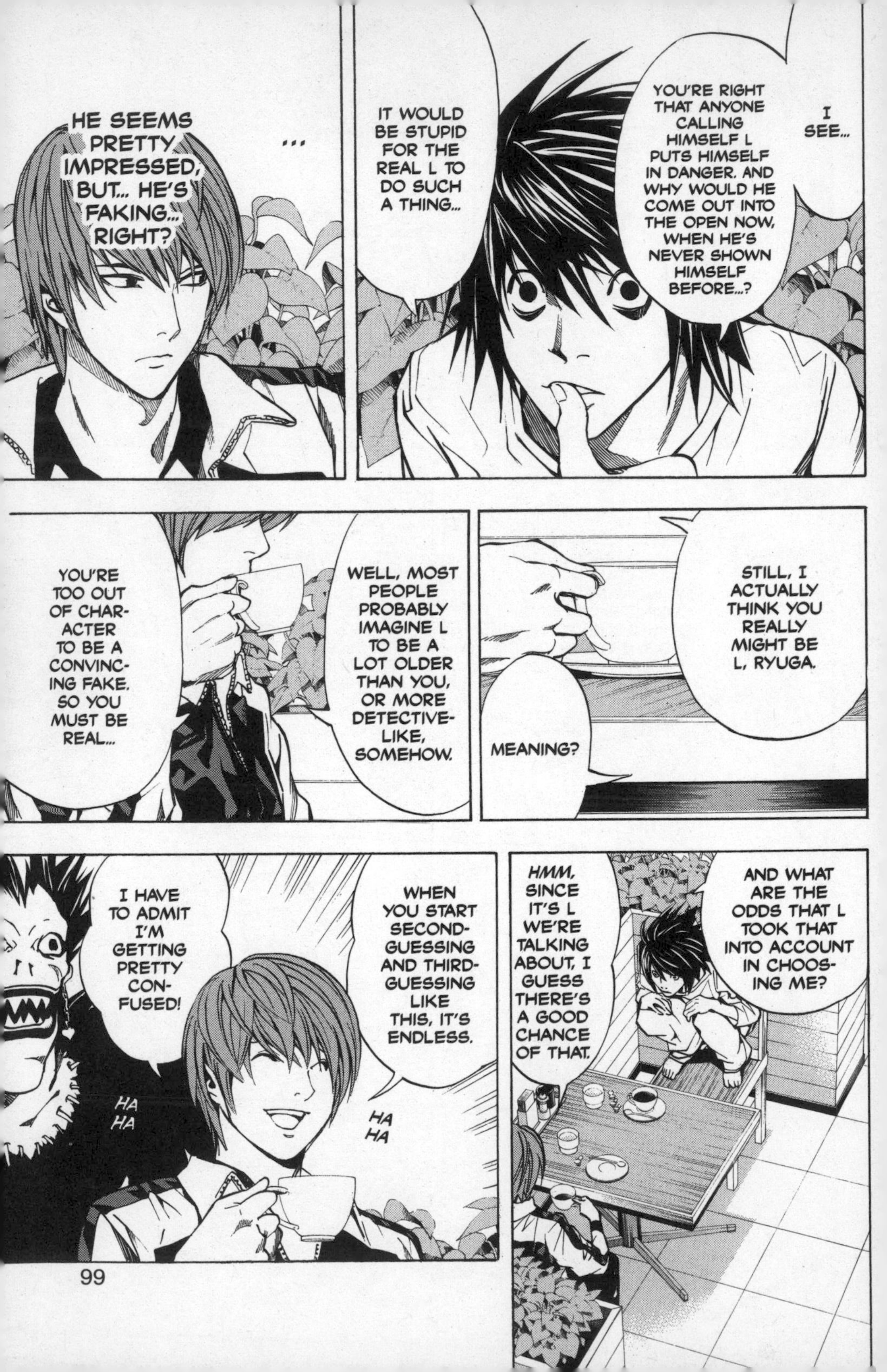
I SEE...
YOU'RE RIGHT THAT ANYONE CALLING HIMSELF L PUTS HIMSELF IN DANGER. AND WHY WOULD HE COME OUT INTO THE OPEN NOW, WHEN HE'S NEVER SHOWN HIMSELF BEFORE...?
IT WOULD BE STUPID FOR THE REAL L TO DO SUCH A THING...
...
HE SEEMS PRETTY IMPRESSED, BUT... HE'S FAKING... RIGHT?
STILL, I ACTUALLY THINK YOU REALLY MIGHT BE L, RYUGA.
MEANING?
WELL, MOST PEOPLE PROBABLY IMAGINE L TO BE A LOT OLDER THAN YOU, OR MORE DETECTIVE-LIKE, SOMEHOW.
YOU'RE TOO OUT OF CHAR-ACTER TO BE A CONVINC-ING FAKE. SO YOU MUST BE REAL...
AND WHAT ARE THE ODDS THAT L TOOK THAT INTO ACCOUNT IN CHOOS-ING ME?
HMM, SINCE IT'S L WE'RE TALKING ABOUT, I GUESS THERE'S A GOOD CHANCE OF THAT.
WHEN YOU START SECOND-GUESSING AND THIRD-GUESSING LIKE THIS, IT'S ENDLESS.
I HAVE TO ADMIT I'M GETTING PRETTY CON-FUSED!
HA HA
HA HA

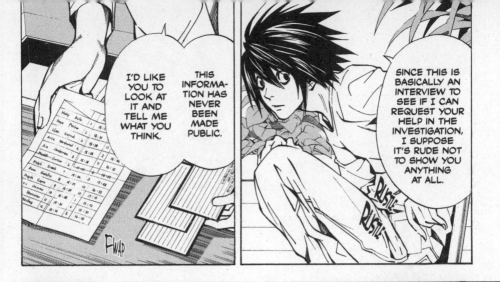

I'D LIKE YOU TO LOOK AT IT AND TELL ME WHAT YOU THINK.

THIS INFORMATION HAS NEVER BEEN MADE PUBLIC.

SINCE THIS IS BASICALLY AN INTERVIEW TO SEE IF I CAN REQUEST YOUR HELP IN THE INVESTIGATION, I SUPPOSE IT'S RUDE NOT TO SHOW YOU ANYTHING AT ALL.

FWAP

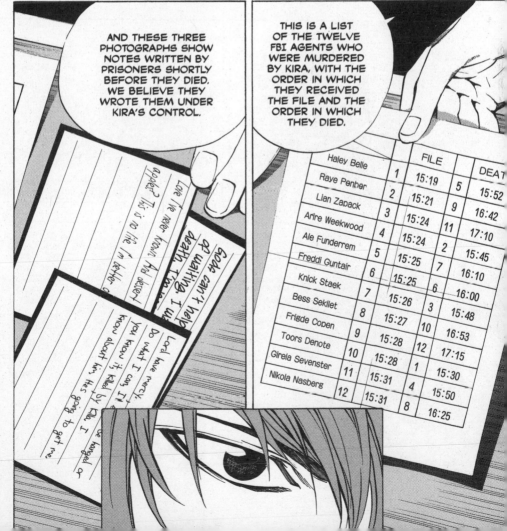

AND THESE THREE PHOTOGRAPHS SHOW NOTES WRITTEN BY PRISONERS SHORTLY BEFORE THEY DIED. WE BELIEVE THEY WROTE THEM UNDER KIRA'S CONTROL.

THIS IS A LIST OF THE TWELVE FBI AGENTS WHO WERE MURDERED BY KIRA, WITH THE ORDER IN WHICH THEY RECEIVED THE FILE AND THE ORDER IN WHICH THEY DIED.

		FILE		DEATH
Haley Belle	1	15:19	5	15:52
Raye Penber	2	15:21	9	16:42
Lian Zapack	3	15:24	11	17:10
Arire Weekwood	4	15:24	2	15:45
Ale Funderrem	5	15:25	7	16:10
Freddi Guntair	6	15:25	6	16:00
Knick Staek	7	15:26	3	15:48
Bess Sekllet	8	15:27	10	16:53
Frisde Coden	9	15:28	12	17:15
Toors Denote	10	15:28	1	15:30
Girela Sevenster	11	15:31	4	15:50
Nikola Nasberg	12	15:31	8	16:25

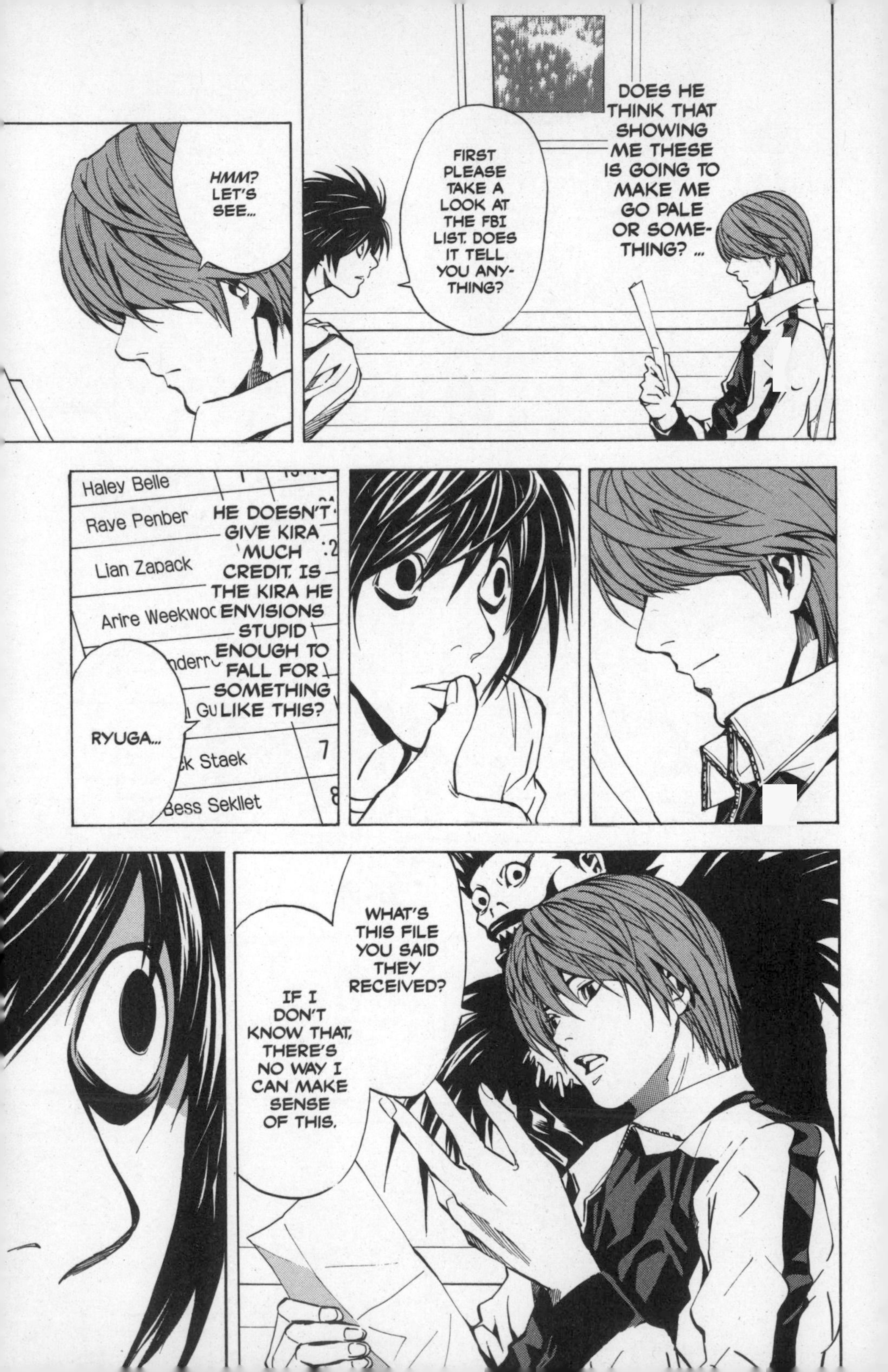

DOES HE THINK THAT SHOWING ME THESE IS GOING TO MAKE ME GO PALE OR SOMETHING? ...
FIRST PLEASE TAKE A LOOK AT THE FBI LIST. DOES IT TELL YOU ANYTHING?
HMM? LET'S SEE...
Haley Belle
Raye Penber
Lian Zapack
HE DOESN'T GIVE KIRA MUCH CREDIT. IS THE KIRA HE ENVISIONS STUPID ENOUGH TO FALL FOR SOMETHING LIKE THIS?
RYUGA...
Bess Seklet
WHAT'S THIS FILE YOU SAID THEY RECEIVED?
IF I DON'T KNOW THAT, THERE'S NO WAY I CAN MAKE SENSE OF THIS.

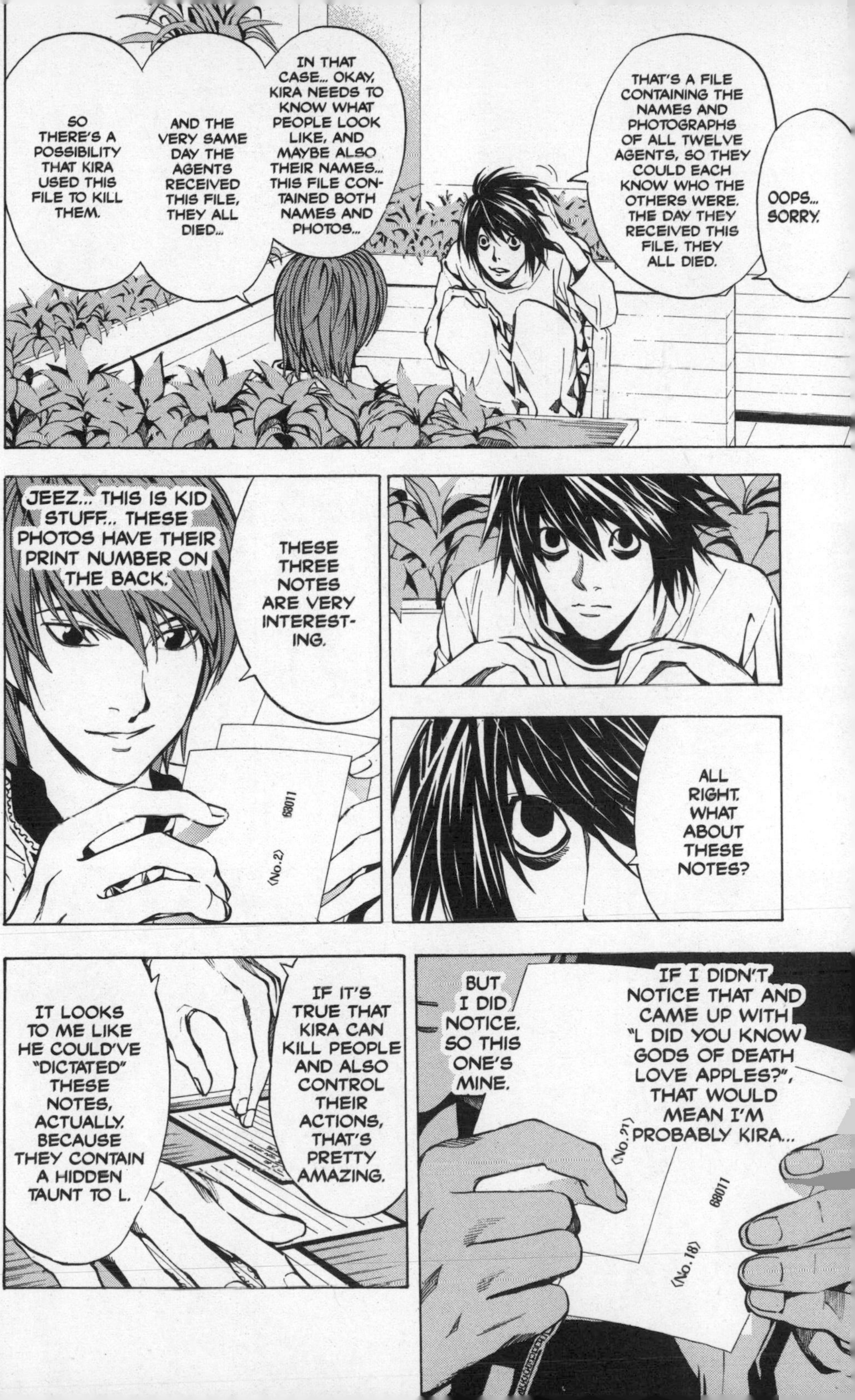
OOPS... SORRY.
THAT'S A FILE CONTAINING THE NAMES AND PHOTOGRAPHS OF ALL TWELVE AGENTS, SO THEY COULD EACH KNOW WHO THE OTHERS WERE. THE DAY THEY RECEIVED THIS FILE, THEY ALL DIED.
IN THAT CASE... OKAY, KIRA NEEDS TO KNOW WHAT PEOPLE LOOK LIKE, AND MAYBE ALSO THEIR NAMES... THIS FILE CONTAINED BOTH NAMES AND PHOTOS...
AND THE VERY SAME DAY THE AGENTS RECEIVED THIS FILE, THEY ALL DIED...
SO THERE'S A POSSIBILITY THAT KIRA USED THIS FILE TO KILL THEM.
ALL RIGHT. WHAT ABOUT THESE NOTES?
THESE THREE NOTES ARE VERY INTEREST-ING.
JEEZ... THIS IS KID STUFF... THESE PHOTOS HAVE THEIR PRINT NUMBER ON THE BACK.
68011
〈No.2〉
IF I DIDN'T NOTICE THAT AND CAME UP WITH "L DID YOU KNOW GODS OF DEATH LOVE APPLES?", THAT WOULD MEAN I'M PROBABLY KIRA...
BUT I DID NOTICE. SO THIS ONE'S MINE.
〈No.21〉
68011
〈No.18〉
IF IT'S TRUE THAT KIRA CAN KILL PEOPLE AND ALSO CONTROL THEIR ACTIONS, THAT'S PRETTY AMAZING.
IT LOOKS TO ME LIKE HE COULD'VE "DICTATED" THESE NOTES, ACTUALLY. BECAUSE THEY CONTAIN A HIDDEN TAUNT TO L.

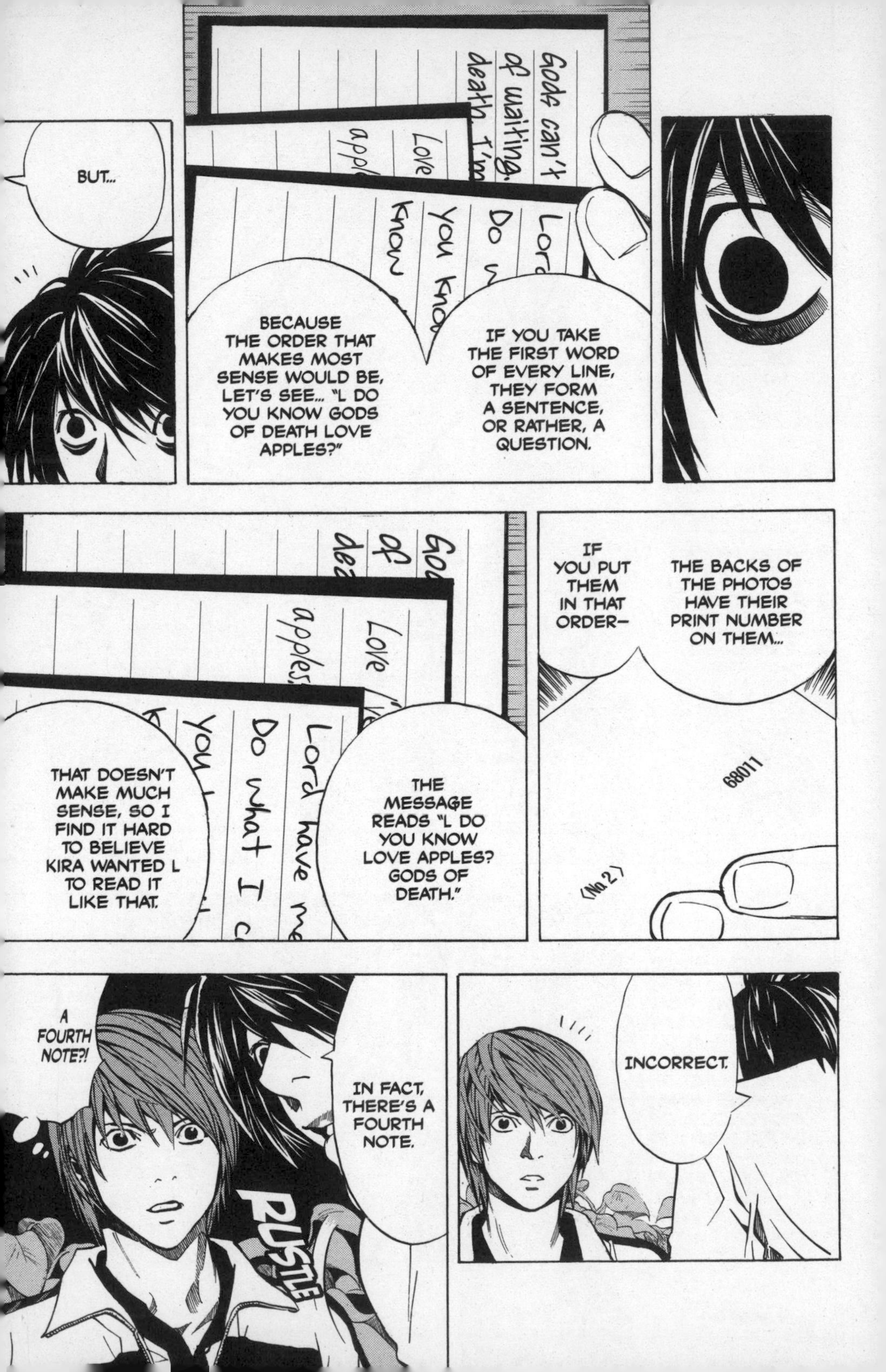
IF YOU TAKE THE FIRST WORD OF EVERY LINE, THEY FORM A SENTENCE, OR RATHER, A QUESTION.
BECAUSE THE ORDER THAT MAKES MOST SENSE WOULD BE, LET'S SEE... "L DO YOU KNOW GODS OF DEATH LOVE APPLES?"
BUT...
THE BACKS OF THE PHOTOS HAVE THEIR PRINT NUMBER ON THEM...
IF YOU PUT THEM IN THAT ORDER—
68011
〈No.2〉
THE MESSAGE READS "L DO YOU KNOW LOVE APPLES? GODS OF DEATH."
THAT DOESN'T MAKE MUCH SENSE, SO I FIND IT HARD TO BELIEVE KIRA WANTED L TO READ IT LIKE THAT.
INCORRECT.
IN FACT, THERE'S A FOURTH NOTE.
RUSTLE
A FOURTH NOTE?!

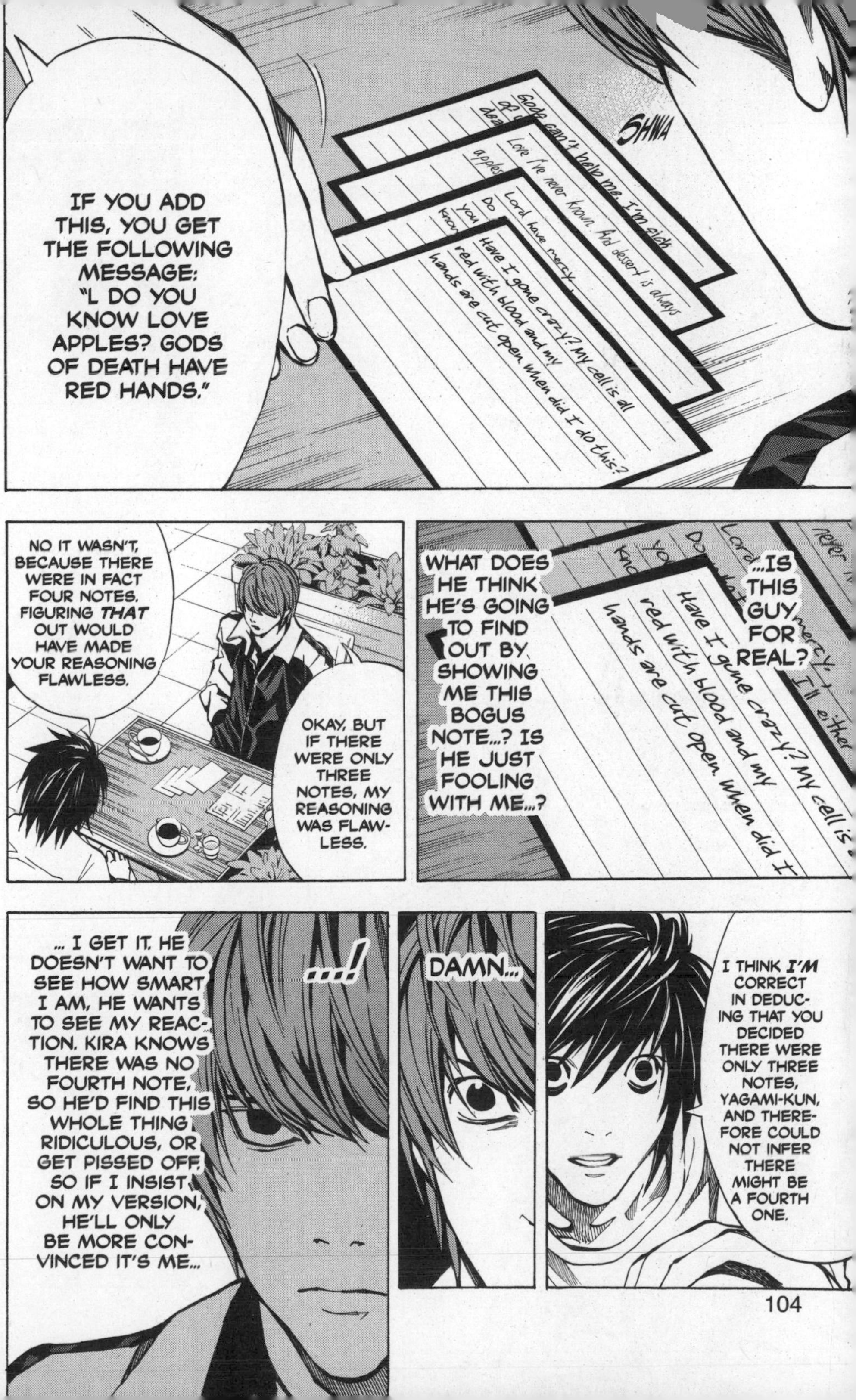
SHWA
Gods can't help me. I'm sick
Love I've never known. And dessert is always
apples
Lord have mercy.
Do
you
know
Have I gone crazy!? My cell is all
red with blood and my
hands are cut open. When did I do this?
IF YOU ADD THIS, YOU GET THE FOLLOWING MESSAGE: "L DO YOU KNOW LOVE APPLES? GODS OF DEATH HAVE RED HANDS."
...IS THIS GUY FOR REAL?
WHAT DOES HE THINK HE'S GOING TO FIND OUT BY SHOWING ME THIS BOGUS NOTE...? IS HE JUST FOOLING WITH ME...?
Have I gone crazy!? My cell is
red with blood and my
hands are cut open. When did I
OKAY, BUT IF THERE WERE ONLY THREE NOTES, MY REASONING WAS FLAWLESS.
NO IT WASN'T, BECAUSE THERE WERE IN FACT FOUR NOTES. FIGURING *THAT* OUT WOULD HAVE MADE YOUR REASONING FLAWLESS.
I THINK *I'M* CORRECT IN DEDUCING THAT YOU DECIDED THERE WERE ONLY THREE NOTES, YAGAMI-KUN, AND THEREFORE COULD NOT INFER THERE MIGHT BE A FOURTH ONE.
DAMN...
...!
... I GET IT. HE DOESN'T WANT TO SEE HOW SMART I AM, HE WANTS TO SEE MY REACTION. KIRA KNOWS THERE WAS NO FOURTH NOTE, SO HE'D FIND THIS WHOLE THING RIDICULOUS, OR GET PISSED OFF. SO IF I INSIST ON MY VERSION, HE'LL ONLY BE MORE CONVINCED IT'S ME...

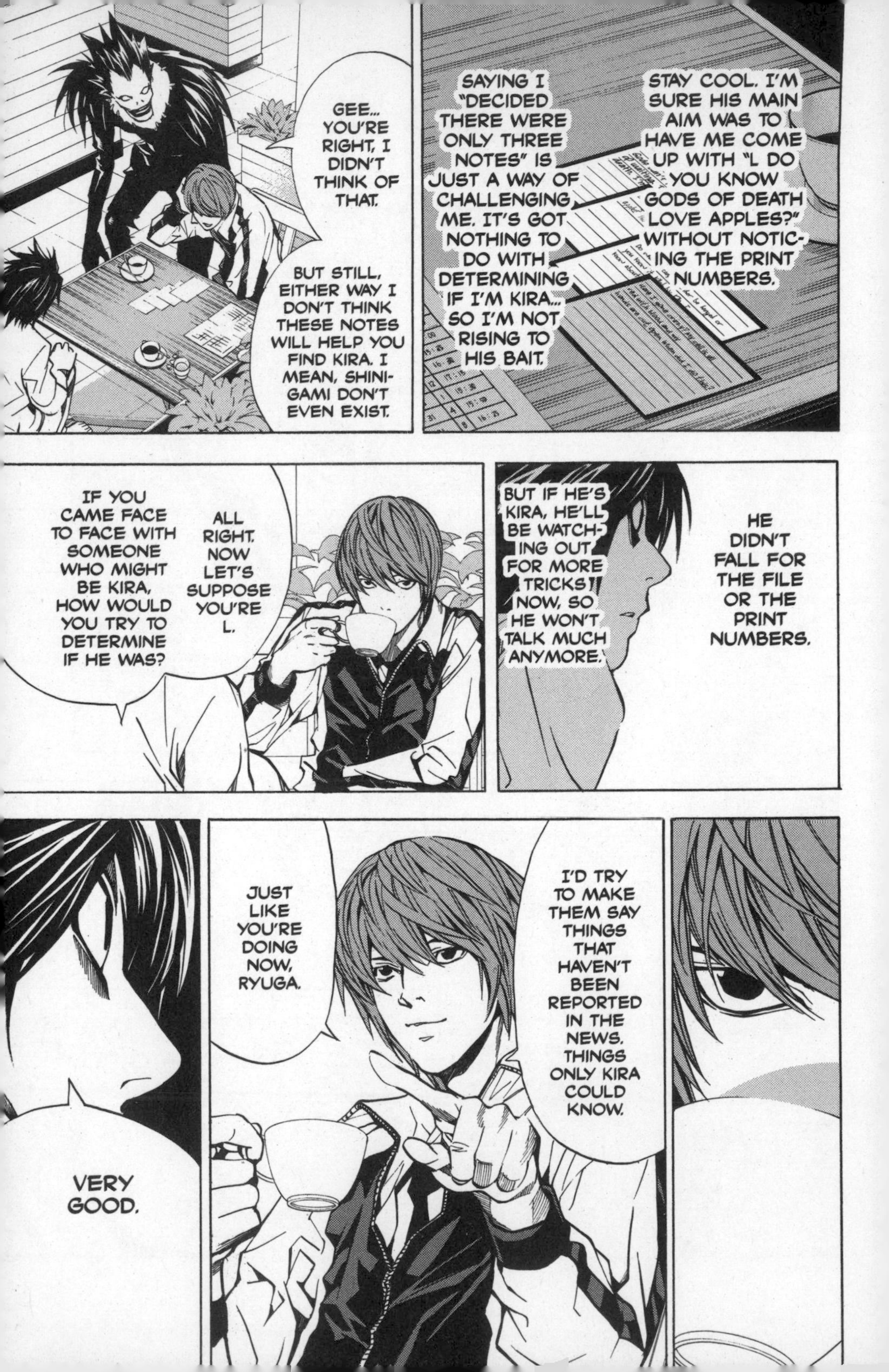
STAY COOL. I'M SURE HIS MAIN AIM WAS TO HAVE ME COME UP WITH "L DO YOU KNOW GODS OF DEATH LOVE APPLES?" WITHOUT NOTICING THE PRINT NUMBERS.
SAYING I "DECIDED THERE WERE ONLY THREE NOTES" IS JUST A WAY OF CHALLENGING ME. IT'S GOT NOTHING TO DO WITH DETERMINING IF I'M KIRA... SO I'M NOT RISING TO HIS BAIT.
GEE... YOU'RE RIGHT, I DIDN'T THINK OF THAT.
BUT STILL, EITHER WAY I DON'T THINK THESE NOTES WILL HELP YOU FIND KIRA. I MEAN, SHINIGAMI DON'T EVEN EXIST.
HE DIDN'T FALL FOR THE FILE OR THE PRINT NUMBERS.
BUT IF HE'S KIRA, HE'LL BE WATCHING OUT FOR MORE TRICKS NOW, SO HE WON'T TALK MUCH ANYMORE.
ALL RIGHT. NOW LET'S SUPPOSE YOU'RE L.
IF YOU CAME FACE TO FACE WITH SOMEONE WHO MIGHT BE KIRA, HOW WOULD YOU TRY TO DETERMINE IF HE WAS?
I'D TRY TO MAKE THEM SAY THINGS THAT HAVEN'T BEEN REPORTED IN THE NEWS. THINGS ONLY KIRA COULD KNOW.
JUST LIKE YOU'RE DOING NOW, RYUGA.
VERY GOOD.

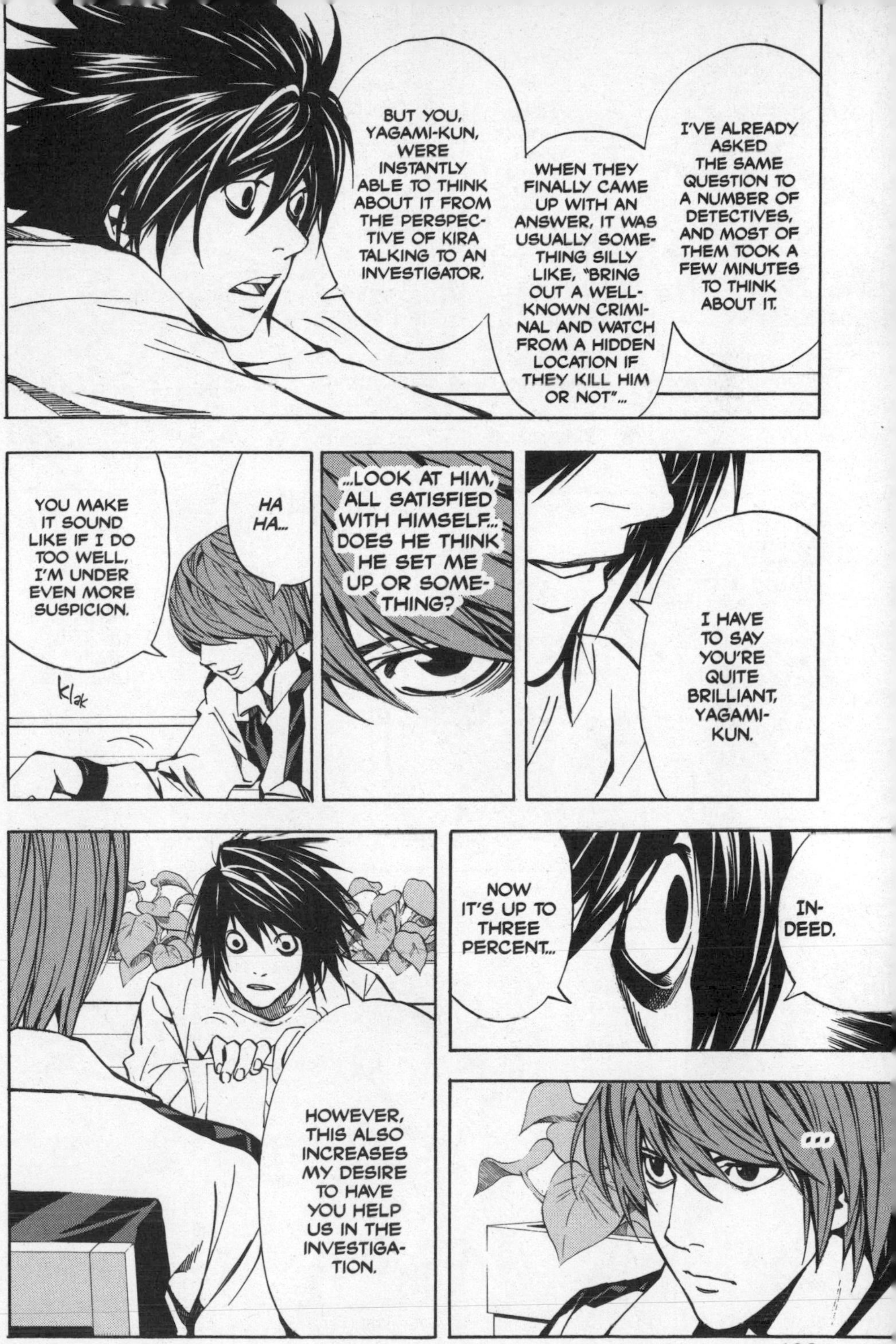
I'VE ALREADY ASKED THE SAME QUESTION TO A NUMBER OF DETECTIVES, AND MOST OF THEM TOOK A FEW MINUTES TO THINK ABOUT IT.
WHEN THEY FINALLY CAME UP WITH AN ANSWER, IT WAS USUALLY SOME-THING SILLY LIKE, "BRING OUT A WELL-KNOWN CRIMI-NAL AND WATCH FROM A HIDDEN LOCATION IF THEY KILL HIM OR NOT"...
BUT YOU, YAGAMI-KUN, WERE INSTANTLY ABLE TO THINK ABOUT IT FROM THE PERSPEC-TIVE OF KIRA TALKING TO AN INVESTIGATOR.
I HAVE TO SAY YOU'RE QUITE BRILLIANT, YAGAMI-KUN.
...LOOK AT HIM, ALL SATISFIED WITH HIMSELF... DOES HE THINK HE SET ME UP OR SOME-THING?
HA HA...
YOU MAKE IT SOUND LIKE IF I DO TOO WELL, I'M UNDER EVEN MORE SUSPICION.
klak
IN-DEED.
NOW IT'S UP TO THREE PERCENT...
...
HOWEVER, THIS ALSO INCREASES MY DESIRE TO HAVE YOU HELP US IN THE INVESTIGA-TION.

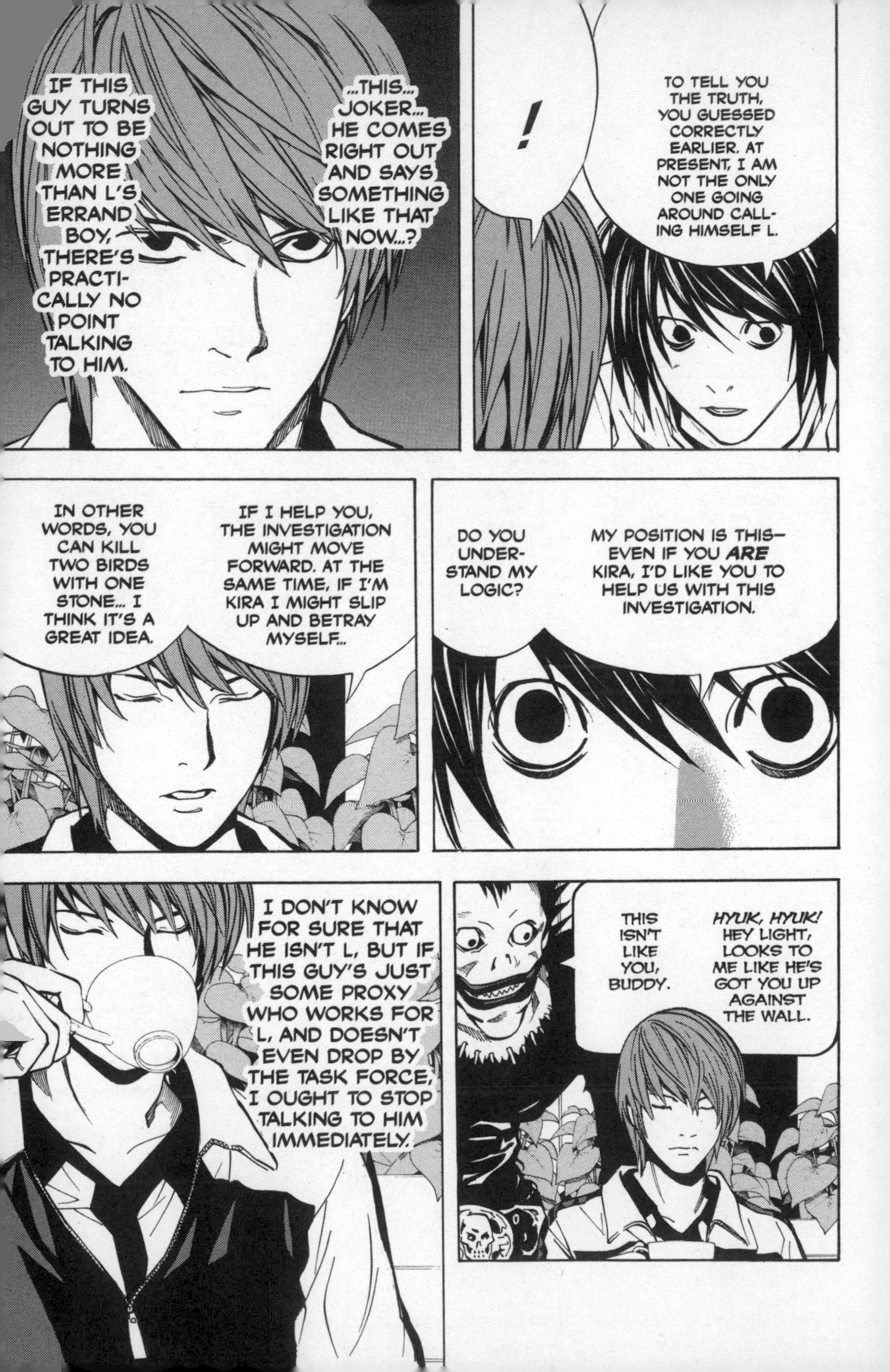
TO TELL YOU THE TRUTH, YOU GUESSED CORRECTLY EARLIER. AT PRESENT, I AM NOT THE ONLY ONE GOING AROUND CALLING HIMSELF L.
!
...THIS... JOKER... HE COMES RIGHT OUT AND SAYS SOMETHING LIKE THAT NOW...?
IF THIS GUY TURNS OUT TO BE NOTHING MORE THAN L'S ERRAND BOY, THERE'S PRACTICALLY NO POINT TALKING TO HIM.
MY POSITION IS THIS—EVEN IF YOU *ARE* KIRA, I'D LIKE YOU TO HELP US WITH THIS INVESTIGATION.
DO YOU UNDERSTAND MY LOGIC?
IF I HELP YOU, THE INVESTIGATION MIGHT MOVE FORWARD. AT THE SAME TIME, IF I'M KIRA I MIGHT SLIP UP AND BETRAY MYSELF...
IN OTHER WORDS, YOU CAN KILL TWO BIRDS WITH ONE STONE... I THINK IT'S A GREAT IDEA.
HYUK, HYUK! HEY LIGHT, LOOKS TO ME LIKE HE'S GOT YOU UP AGAINST THE WALL.
THIS ISN'T LIKE YOU, BUDDY.
I DON'T KNOW FOR SURE THAT HE ISN'T L, BUT IF THIS GUY'S JUST SOME PROXY WHO WORKS FOR L, AND DOESN'T EVEN DROP BY THE TASK FORCE, I OUGHT TO STOP TALKING TO HIM IMMEDIATELY.

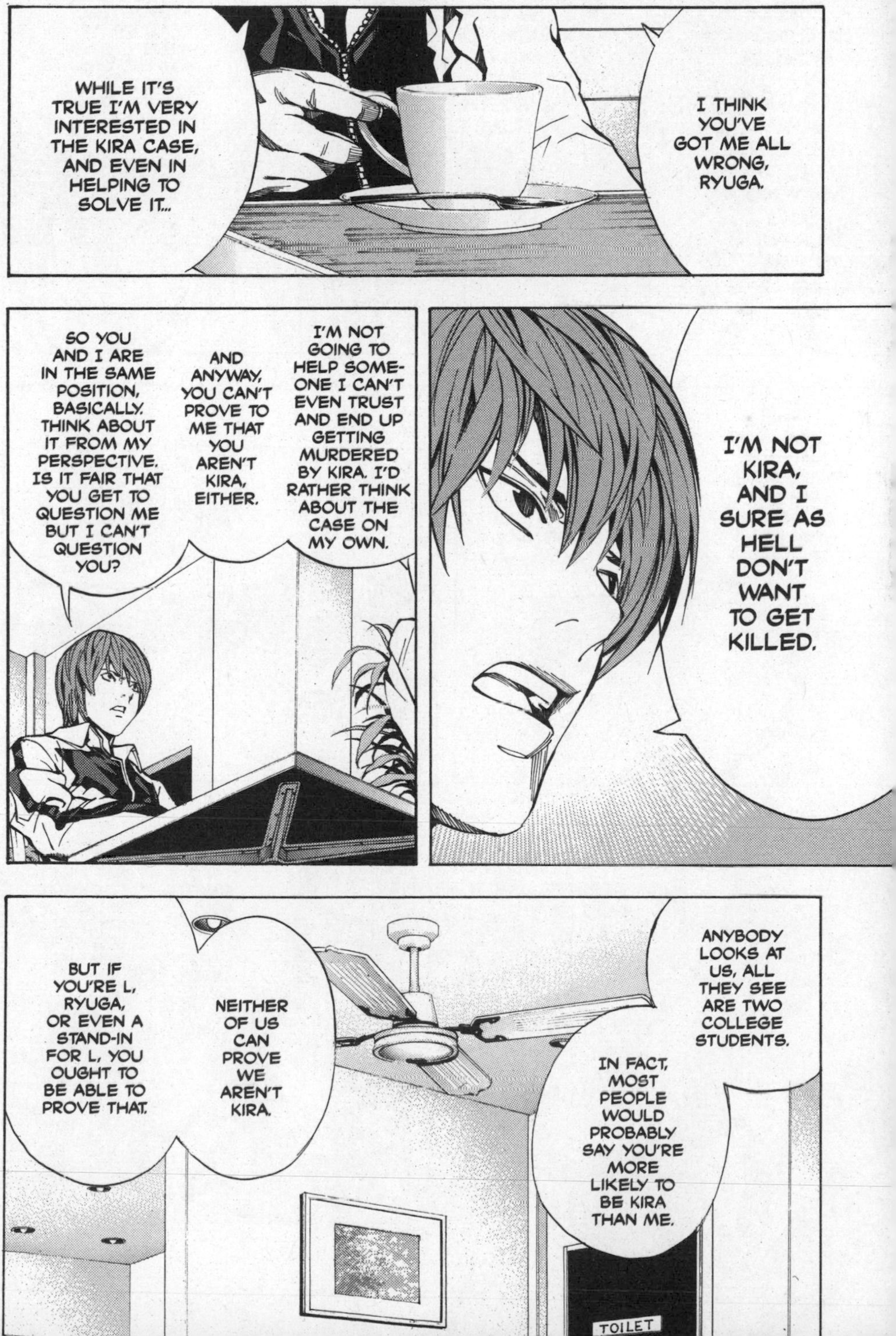
I THINK YOU'VE GOT ME ALL WRONG, RYUGA.
WHILE IT'S TRUE I'M VERY INTERESTED IN THE KIRA CASE, AND EVEN IN HELPING TO SOLVE IT...
I'M NOT KIRA, AND I SURE AS HELL DON'T WANT TO GET KILLED.
I'M NOT GOING TO HELP SOME-ONE I CAN'T EVEN TRUST AND END UP GETTING MURDERED BY KIRA. I'D RATHER THINK ABOUT THE CASE ON MY OWN.
AND ANYWAY, YOU CAN'T PROVE TO ME THAT YOU AREN'T KIRA, EITHER.
SO YOU AND I ARE IN THE SAME POSITION, BASICALLY. THINK ABOUT IT FROM MY PERSPECTIVE. IS IT FAIR THAT YOU GET TO QUESTION ME BUT I CAN'T QUESTION YOU?
ANYBODY LOOKS AT US, ALL THEY SEE ARE TWO COLLEGE STUDENTS.
IN FACT, MOST PEOPLE WOULD PROBABLY SAY YOU'RE MORE LIKELY TO BE KIRA THAN ME.
NEITHER OF US CAN PROVE WE AREN'T KIRA.
BUT IF YOU'RE L, RYUGA, OR EVEN A STAND-IN FOR L, YOU OUGHT TO BE ABLE TO PROVE THAT.
TOILET

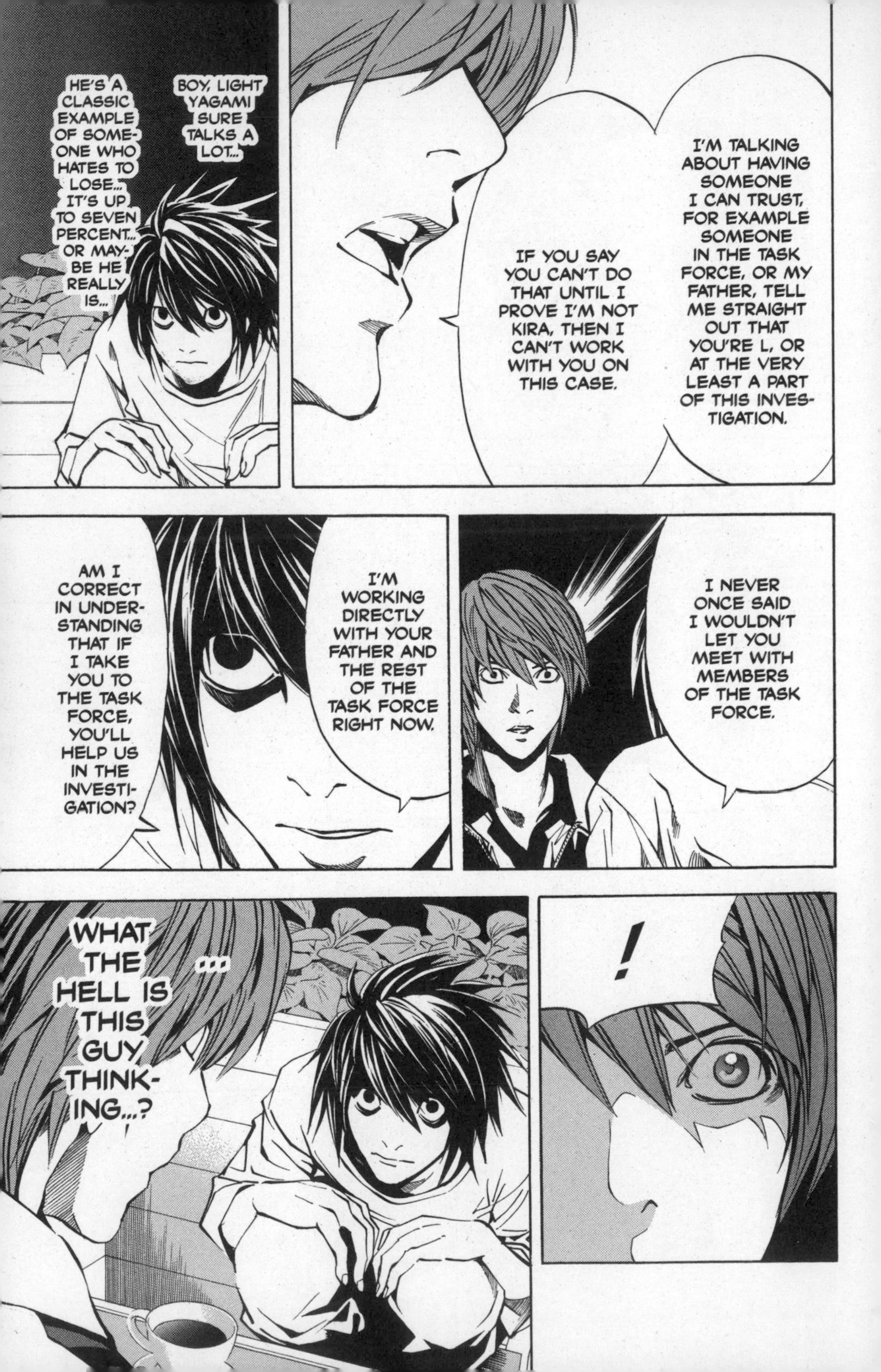
I'M TALKING ABOUT HAVING SOMEONE I CAN TRUST, FOR EXAMPLE SOMEONE IN THE TASK FORCE, OR MY FATHER, TELL ME STRAIGHT OUT THAT YOU'RE L, OR AT THE VERY LEAST A PART OF THIS INVESTIGATION.
IF YOU SAY YOU CAN'T DO THAT UNTIL I PROVE I'M NOT KIRA, THEN I CAN'T WORK WITH YOU ON THIS CASE.
BOY, LIGHT YAGAMI SURE TALKS A LOT...
HE'S A CLASSIC EXAMPLE OF SOMEONE WHO HATES TO LOSE... IT'S UP TO SEVEN PERCENT... OR MAYBE HE REALLY IS...
I NEVER ONCE SAID I WOULDN'T LET YOU MEET WITH MEMBERS OF THE TASK FORCE.
I'M WORKING DIRECTLY WITH YOUR FATHER AND THE REST OF THE TASK FORCE RIGHT NOW.
AM I CORRECT IN UNDERSTANDING THAT IF I TAKE YOU TO THE TASK FORCE, YOU'LL HELP US IN THE INVESTIGATION?
!
...
WHAT THE HELL IS THIS GUY THINKING...?

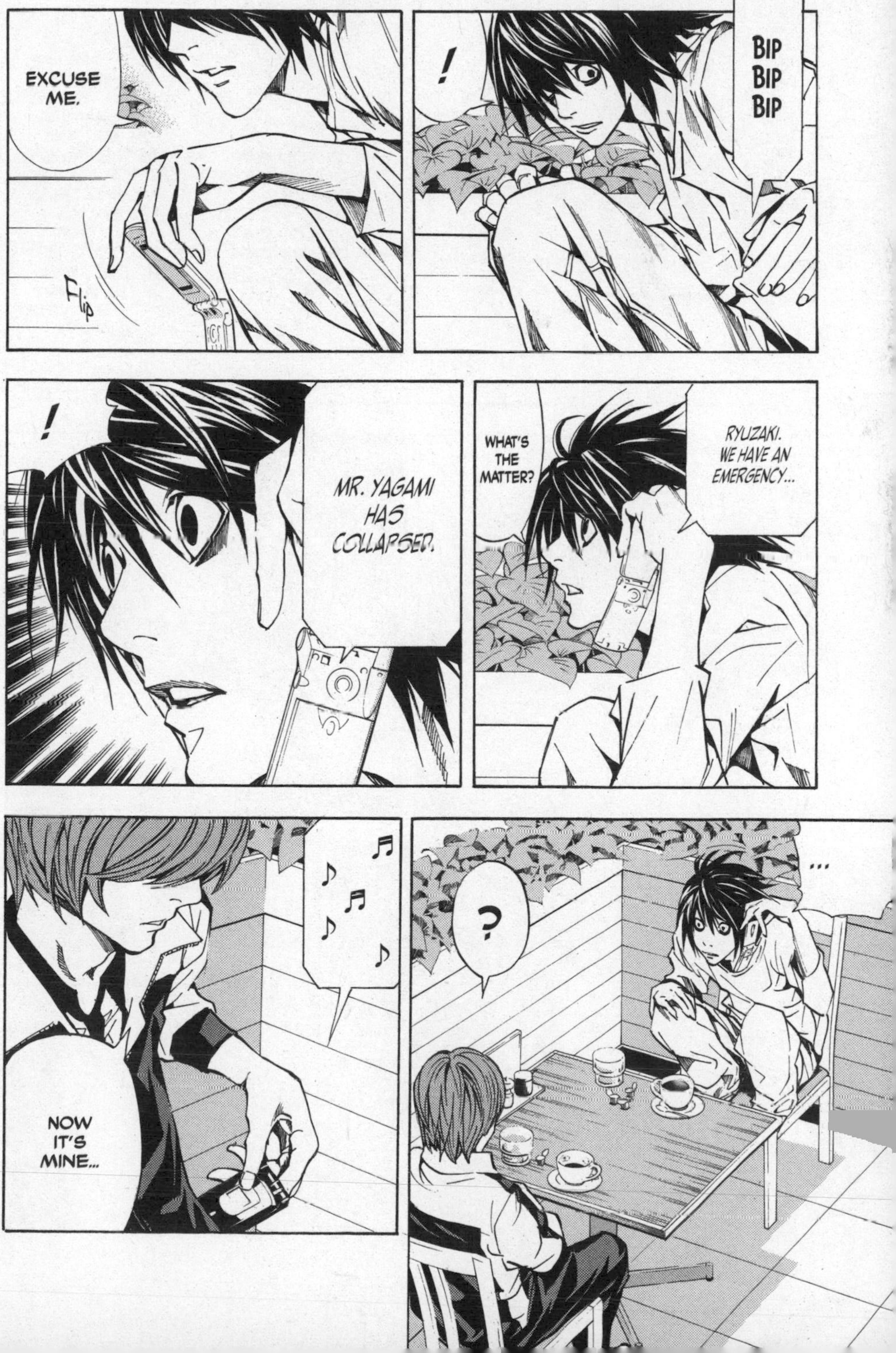
BIP BIP BIP
!
EXCUSE ME.
Flip
RYUZAKI. WE HAVE AN EMERGENCY...
WHAT'S THE MATTER?
!
MR. YAGAMI HAS COLLAPSED.
...
?
NOW IT'S MINE...

READ THIS WAY

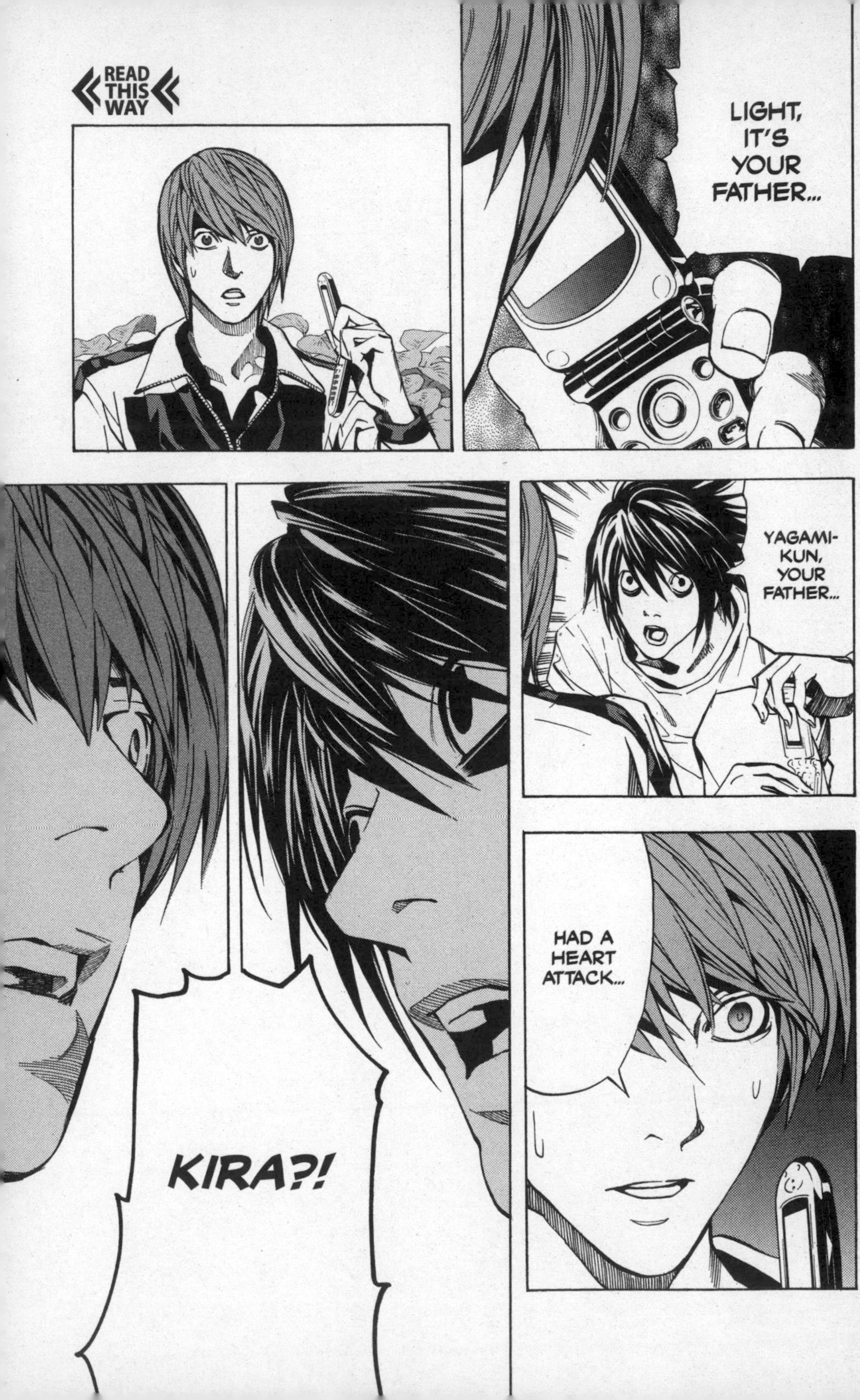
LIGHT, IT'S YOUR FATHER...
YAGAMI-KUN, YOUR FATHER...
HAD A HEART ATTACK...
KIRA?!

DEATH NOTE
How to use it
XIII

○ You may lend the DEATH NOTE to another person while maintaining its ownership.
Subletting it to yet another person is possible, too.

所有権は自分のまま、人にデスノートを貸す事は可能である。
又貸しも構わない。

○ The borrower of the DEATH NOTE will not be followed by a god of death.
The god of death always remains with the owner of the DEATH NOTE.
Also, the borrower cannot trade the eyesight of the god of death.

デスノートを借りた者の方に死神は憑いてこない。
死神は、あくまでも所有者に憑く。
また、借りた者には死神の目の取引はできない。

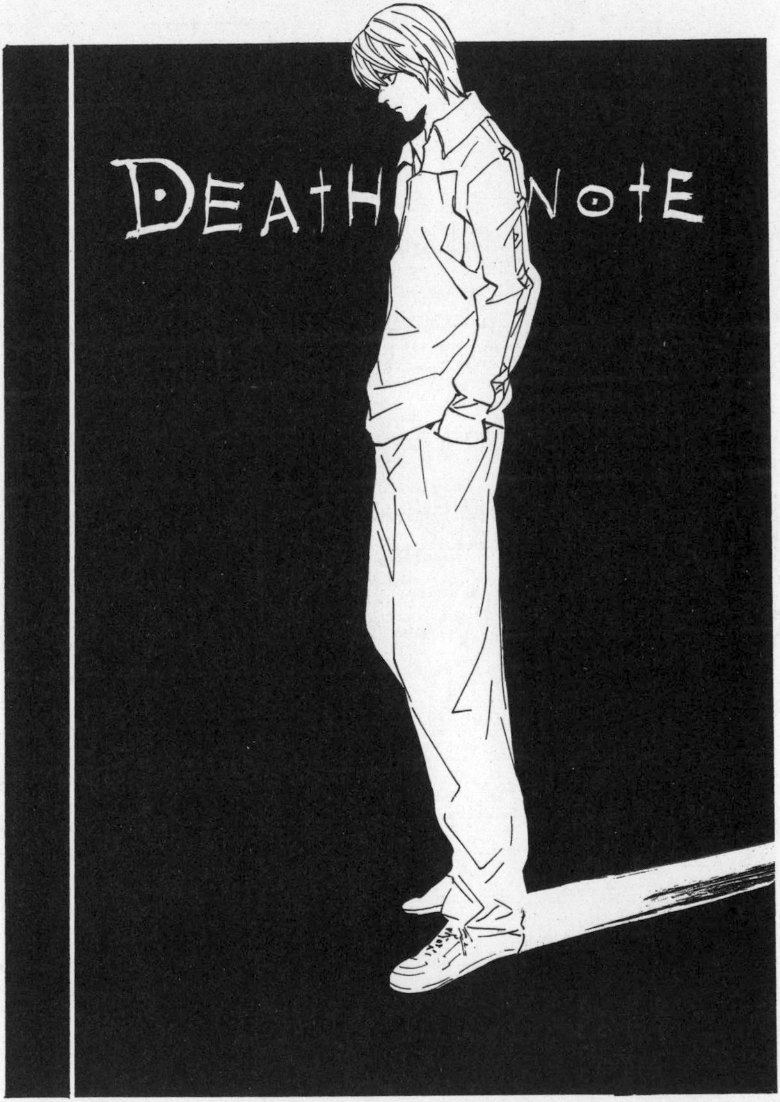
DEATH NOTE

chapter 22 Misfortune

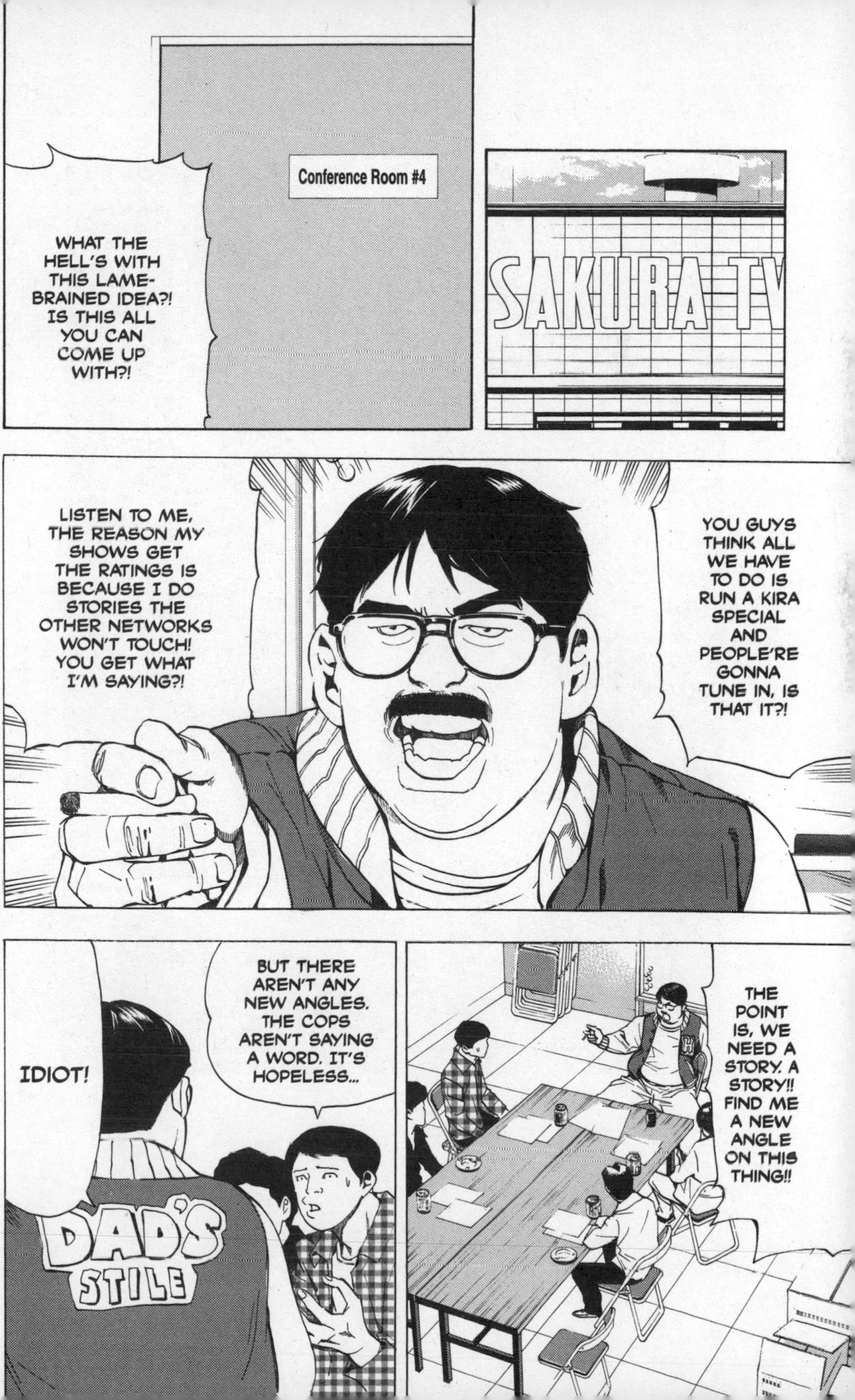
SAKURA TV
Conference Room #4
WHAT THE HELL'S WITH THIS LAME-BRAINED IDEA?! IS THIS ALL YOU CAN COME UP WITH?!
YOU GUYS THINK ALL WE HAVE TO DO IS RUN A KIRA SPECIAL AND PEOPLE'RE GONNA TUNE IN, IS THAT IT?!
LISTEN TO ME, THE REASON MY SHOWS GET THE RATINGS IS BECAUSE I DO STORIES THE OTHER NETWORKS WON'T TOUCH! YOU GET WHAT I'M SAYING?!
THE POINT IS, WE NEED A STORY. A STORY!! FIND ME A NEW ANGLE ON THIS THING!!
BUT THERE AREN'T ANY NEW ANGLES. THE COPS AREN'T SAYING A WORD. IT'S HOPELESS...
IDIOT!
DAD'S STILE

READ THIS WAY

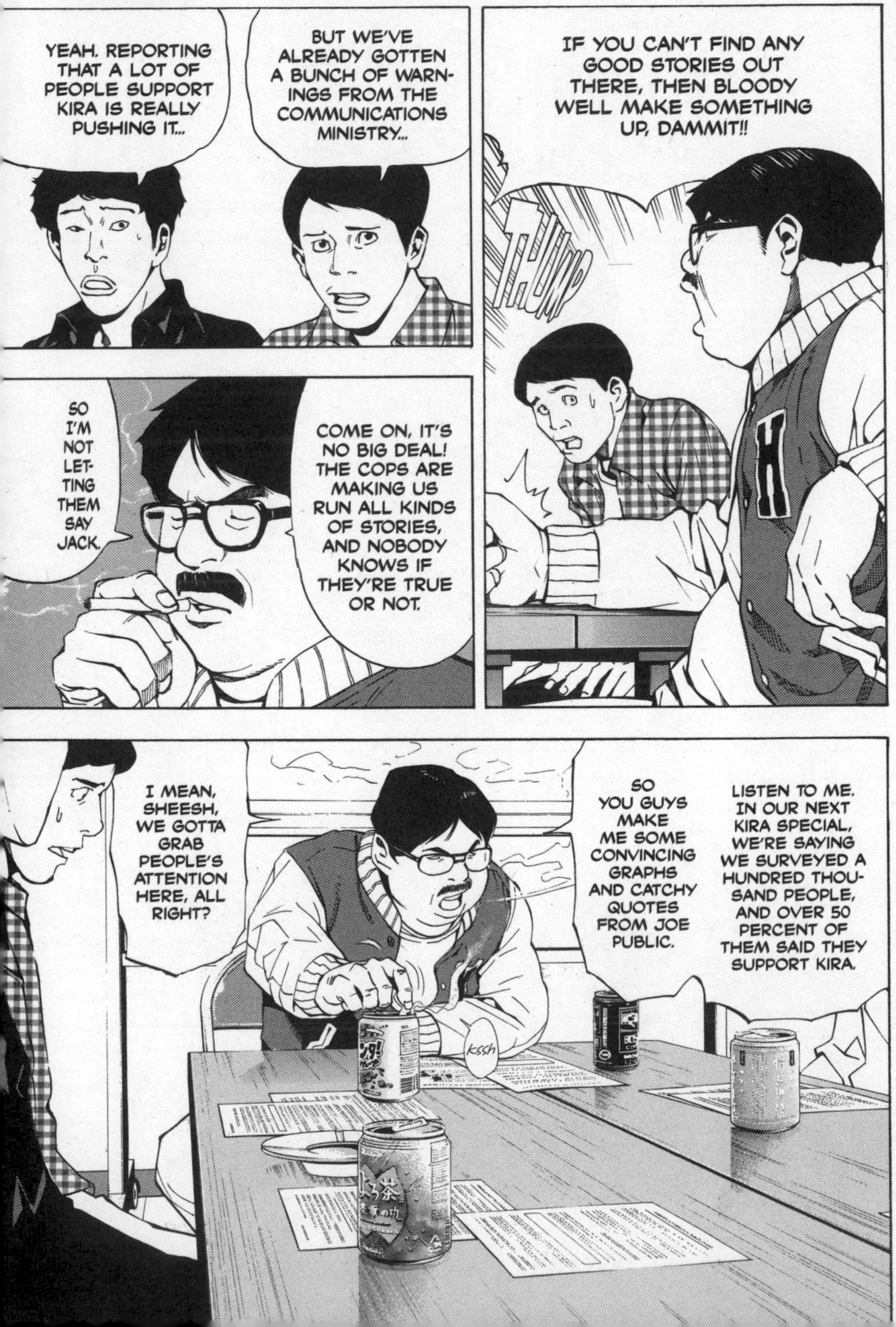
IF YOU CAN'T FIND ANY GOOD STORIES OUT THERE, THEN BLOODY WELL MAKE SOMETHING UP, DAMMIT!!
THUMP
BUT WE'VE ALREADY GOTTEN A BUNCH OF WARN-INGS FROM THE COMMUNICATIONS MINISTRY...
YEAH. REPORTING THAT A LOT OF PEOPLE SUPPORT KIRA IS REALLY PUSHING IT...
COME ON, IT'S NO BIG DEAL! THE COPS ARE MAKING US RUN ALL KINDS OF STORIES, AND NOBODY KNOWS IF THEY'RE TRUE OR NOT.
SO I'M NOT LET-TING THEM SAY JACK.
LISTEN TO ME. IN OUR NEXT KIRA SPECIAL, WE'RE SAYING WE SURVEYED A HUNDRED THOU-SAND PEOPLE, AND OVER 50 PERCENT OF THEM SAID THEY SUPPORT KIRA.
SO YOU GUYS MAKE ME SOME CONVINCING GRAPHS AND CATCHY QUOTES FROM JOE PUBLIC.
I MEAN, SHEESH, WE GOTTA GRAB PEOPLE'S ATTENTION HERE, ALL RIGHT?
kssh

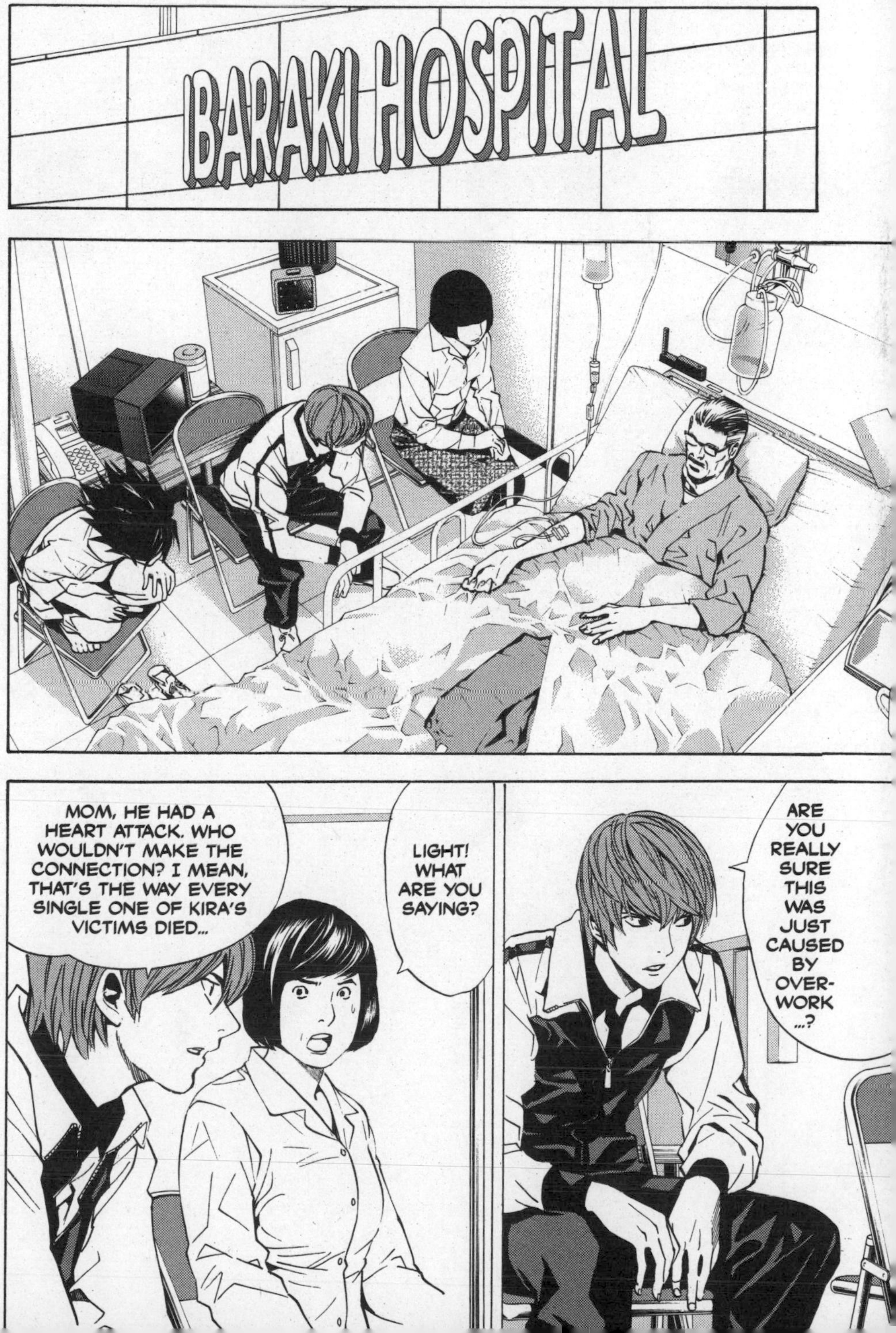
BARAKI HOSPITAL
ARE YOU REALLY SURE THIS WAS JUST CAUSED BY OVER-WORK ...?
LIGHT! WHAT ARE YOU SAYING?
MOM, HE HAD A HEART ATTACK. WHO WOULDN'T MAKE THE CONNECTION? I MEAN, THAT'S THE WAY EVERY SINGLE ONE OF KIRA'S VICTIMS DIED...

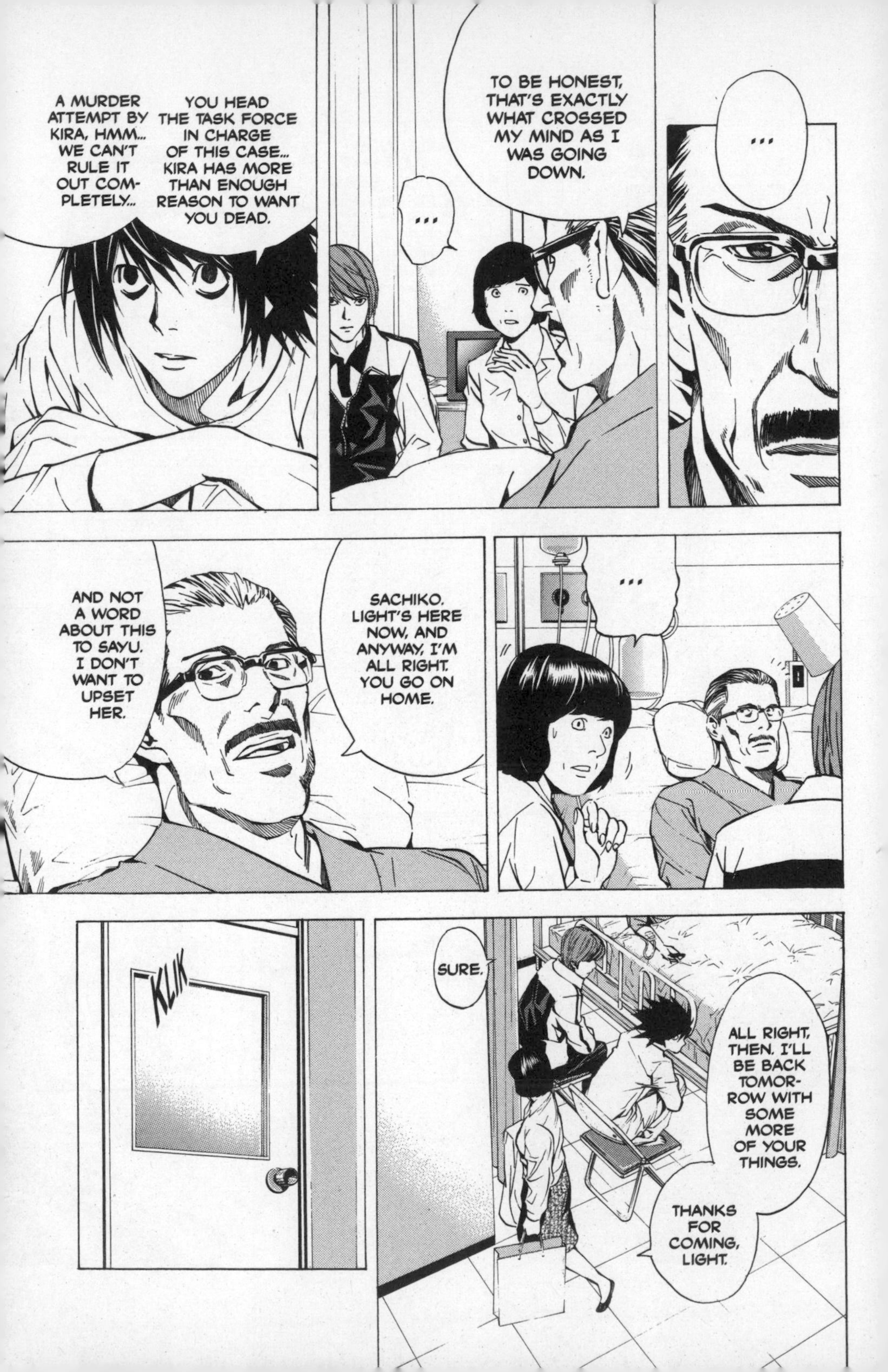
...
TO BE HONEST, THAT'S EXACTLY WHAT CROSSED MY MIND AS I WAS GOING DOWN.
...
YOU HEAD THE TASK FORCE IN CHARGE OF THIS CASE... KIRA HAS MORE THAN ENOUGH REASON TO WANT YOU DEAD.
A MURDER ATTEMPT BY KIRA, HMM... WE CAN'T RULE IT OUT COM-PLETELY...
...
SACHIKO, LIGHT'S HERE NOW, AND ANYWAY, I'M ALL RIGHT. YOU GO ON HOME.
AND NOT A WORD ABOUT THIS TO SAYU. I DON'T WANT TO UPSET HER.
ALL RIGHT, THEN. I'LL BE BACK TOMOR-ROW WITH SOME MORE OF YOUR THINGS.
THANKS FOR COMING, LIGHT.
SURE.
KLIK

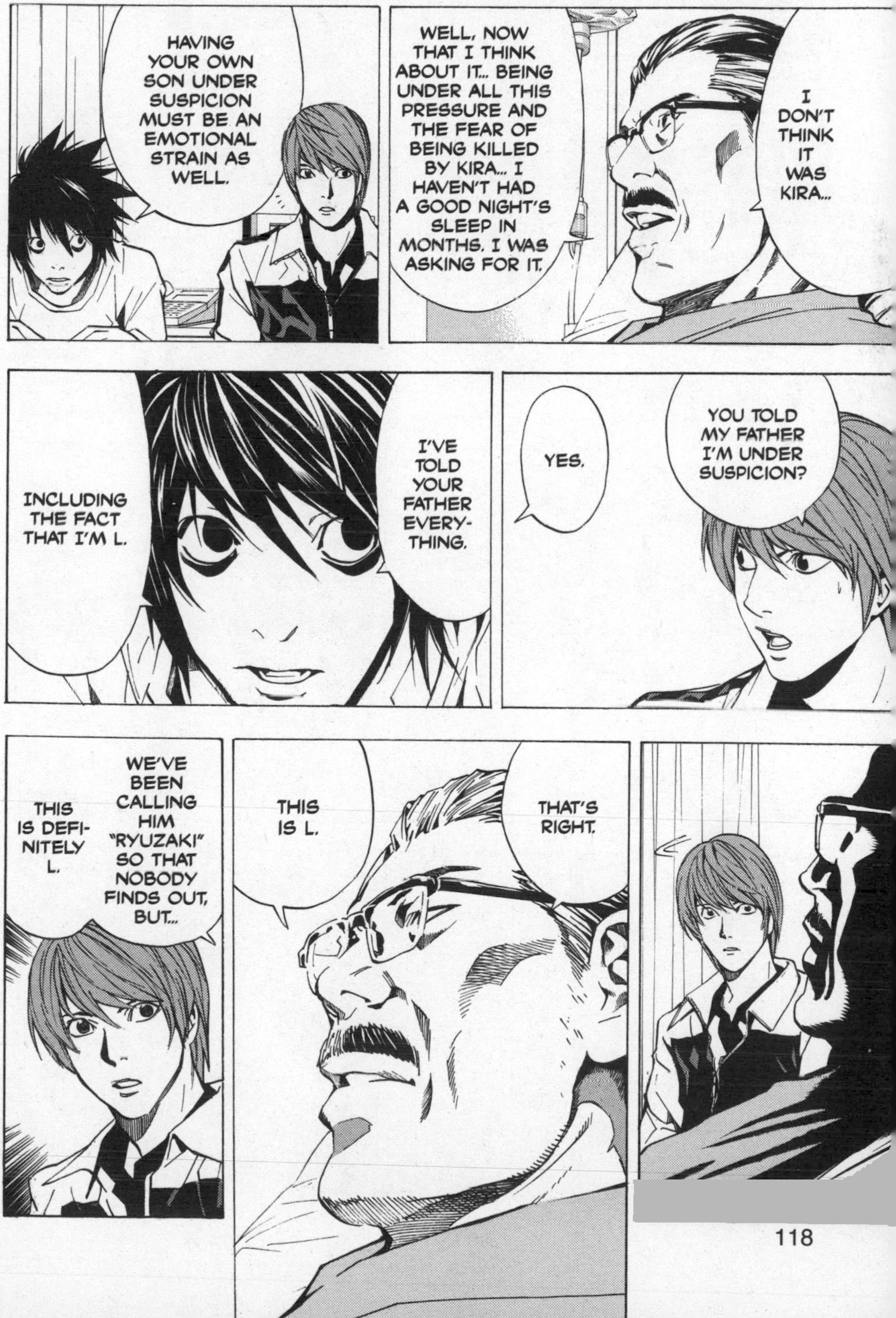
I DON'T THINK IT WAS KIRA...
WELL, NOW THAT I THINK ABOUT IT... BEING UNDER ALL THIS PRESSURE AND THE FEAR OF BEING KILLED BY KIRA... I HAVEN'T HAD A GOOD NIGHT'S SLEEP IN MONTHS. I WAS ASKING FOR IT.
HAVING YOUR OWN SON UNDER SUSPICION MUST BE AN EMOTIONAL STRAIN AS WELL.
YOU TOLD MY FATHER I'M UNDER SUSPICION?
YES.
I'VE TOLD YOUR FATHER EVERY-THING.
INCLUDING THE FACT THAT I'M L.
THAT'S RIGHT.
THIS IS L.
WE'VE BEEN CALLING HIM "RYUZAKI" SO THAT NOBODY FINDS OUT, BUT...
THIS IS DEFI-NITELY L.

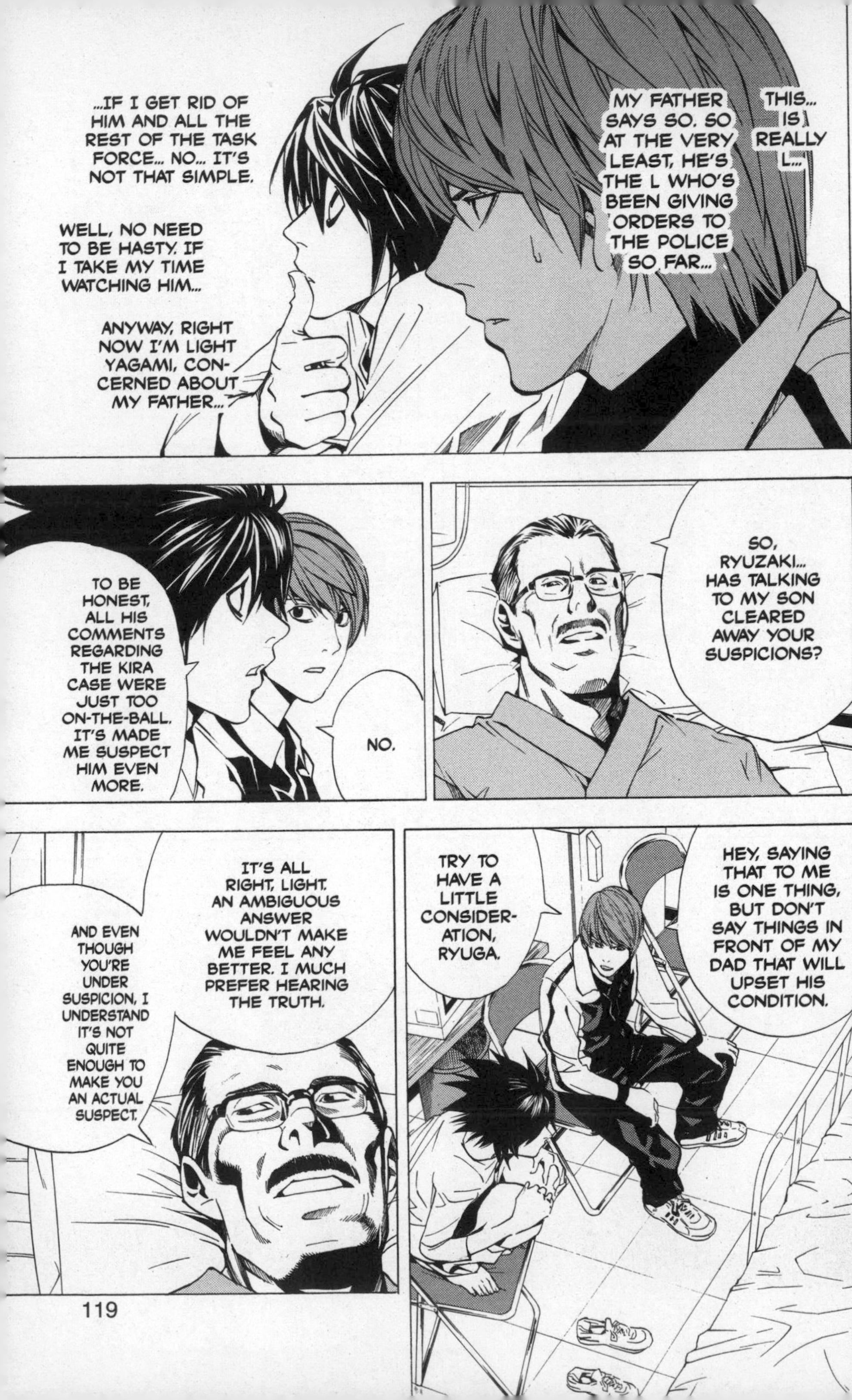

THIS... IS REALLY L...
MY FATHER SAYS SO. SO AT THE VERY LEAST, HE'S THE L WHO'S BEEN GIVING ORDERS TO THE POLICE SO FAR...
...IF I GET RID OF HIM AND ALL THE REST OF THE TASK FORCE... NO... IT'S NOT THAT SIMPLE.
WELL, NO NEED TO BE HASTY. IF I TAKE MY TIME WATCHING HIM...
ANYWAY, RIGHT NOW I'M LIGHT YAGAMI, CONCERNED ABOUT MY FATHER...
SO, RYUZAKI... HAS TALKING TO MY SON CLEARED AWAY YOUR SUSPICIONS?
NO.
TO BE HONEST, ALL HIS COMMENTS REGARDING THE KIRA CASE WERE JUST TOO ON-THE-BALL. IT'S MADE ME SUSPECT HIM EVEN MORE.
HEY, SAYING THAT TO ME IS ONE THING, BUT DON'T SAY THINGS IN FRONT OF MY DAD THAT WILL UPSET HIS CONDITION.
TRY TO HAVE A LITTLE CONSIDERATION, RYUGA.
IT'S ALL RIGHT, LIGHT. AN AMBIGUOUS ANSWER WOULDN'T MAKE ME FEEL ANY BETTER. I MUCH PREFER HEARING THE TRUTH.
AND EVEN THOUGH YOU'RE UNDER SUSPICION, I UNDERSTAND IT'S NOT QUITE ENOUGH TO MAKE YOU AN ACTUAL SUSPECT.

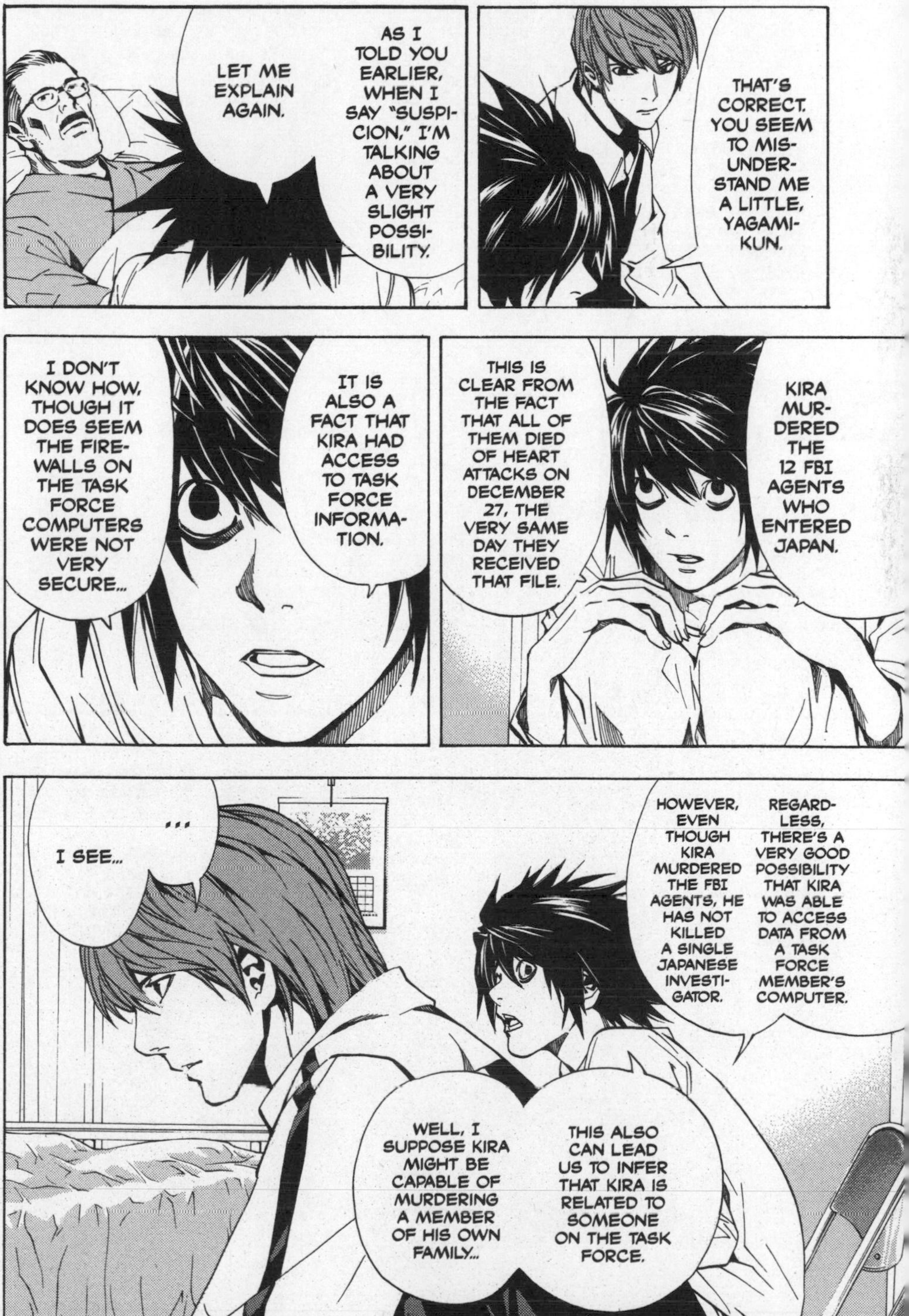
THAT'S CORRECT. YOU SEEM TO MISUNDERSTAND ME A LITTLE, YAGAMI-KUN.
AS I TOLD YOU EARLIER, WHEN I SAY "SUSPICION," I'M TALKING ABOUT A VERY SLIGHT POSSIBILITY.
LET ME EXPLAIN AGAIN.
KIRA MURDERED THE 12 FBI AGENTS WHO ENTERED JAPAN.
THIS IS CLEAR FROM THE FACT THAT ALL OF THEM DIED OF HEART ATTACKS ON DECEMBER 27, THE VERY SAME DAY THEY RECEIVED THAT FILE.
IT IS ALSO A FACT THAT KIRA HAD ACCESS TO TASK FORCE INFORMATION.
I DON'T KNOW HOW, THOUGH IT DOES SEEM THE FIREWALLS ON THE TASK FORCE COMPUTERS WERE NOT VERY SECURE...
REGARDLESS, THERE'S A VERY GOOD POSSIBILITY THAT KIRA WAS ABLE TO ACCESS DATA FROM A TASK FORCE MEMBER'S COMPUTER.
HOWEVER, EVEN THOUGH KIRA MURDERED THE FBI AGENTS, HE HAS NOT KILLED A SINGLE JAPANESE INVESTIGATOR.
...
I SEE...
THIS ALSO CAN LEAD US TO INFER THAT KIRA IS RELATED TO SOMEONE ON THE TASK FORCE.
WELL, I SUPPOSE KIRA MIGHT BE CAPABLE OF MURDERING A MEMBER OF HIS OWN FAMILY...

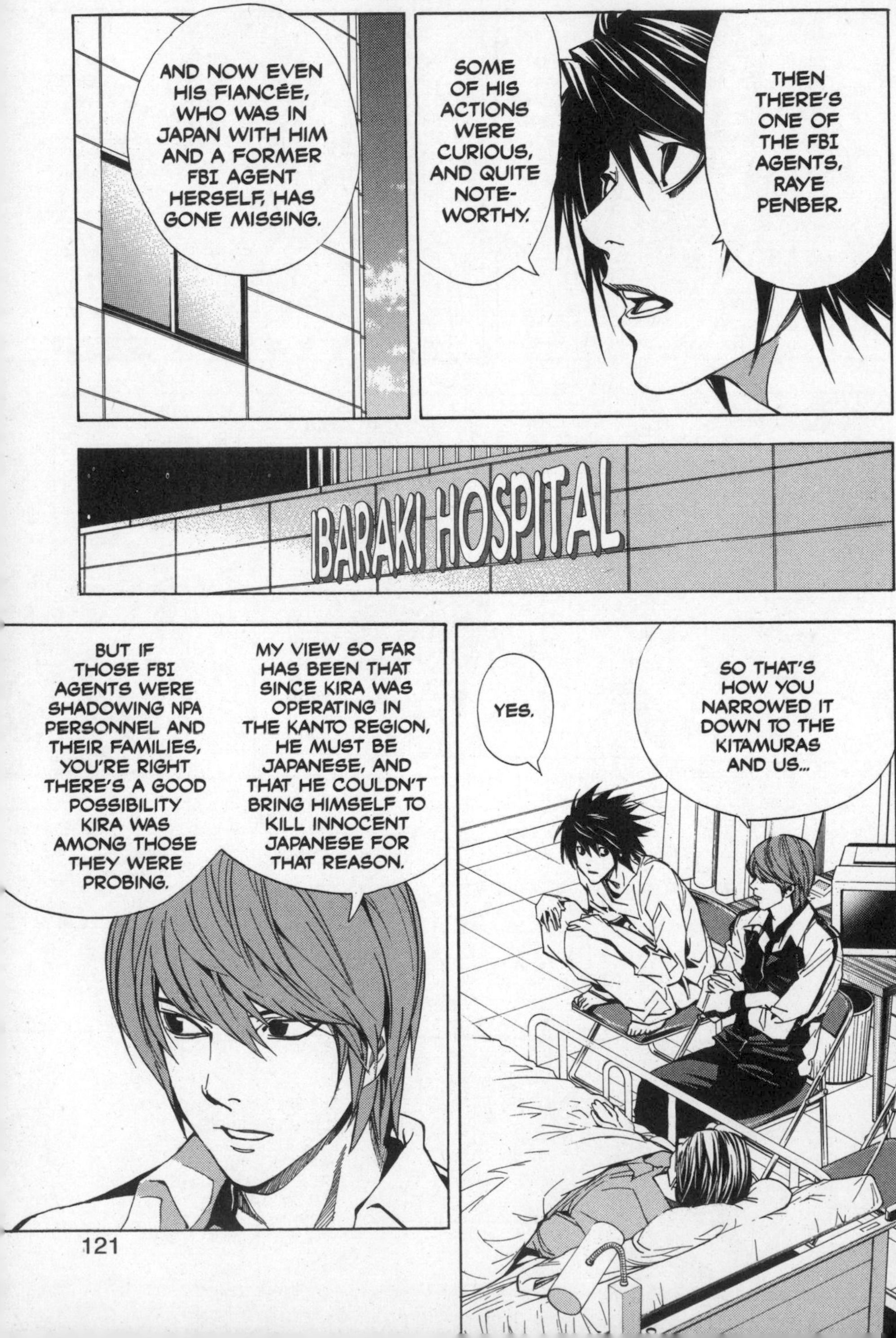
THEN THERE'S ONE OF THE FBI AGENTS, RAYE PENBER.
SOME OF HIS ACTIONS WERE CURIOUS, AND QUITE NOTE-WORTHY.
AND NOW EVEN HIS FIANCÉE, WHO WAS IN JAPAN WITH HIM AND A FORMER FBI AGENT HERSELF, HAS GONE MISSING.
IBARAKI HOSPITAL
SO THAT'S HOW YOU NARROWED IT DOWN TO THE KITAMURAS AND US...
YES.
MY VIEW SO FAR HAS BEEN THAT SINCE KIRA WAS OPERATING IN THE KANTO REGION, HE MUST BE JAPANESE, AND THAT HE COULDN'T BRING HIMSELF TO KILL INNOCENT JAPANESE FOR THAT REASON.
BUT IF THOSE FBI AGENTS WERE SHADOWING NPA PERSONNEL AND THEIR FAMILIES, YOU'RE RIGHT THERE'S A GOOD POSSIBILITY KIRA WAS AMONG THOSE THEY WERE PROBING.

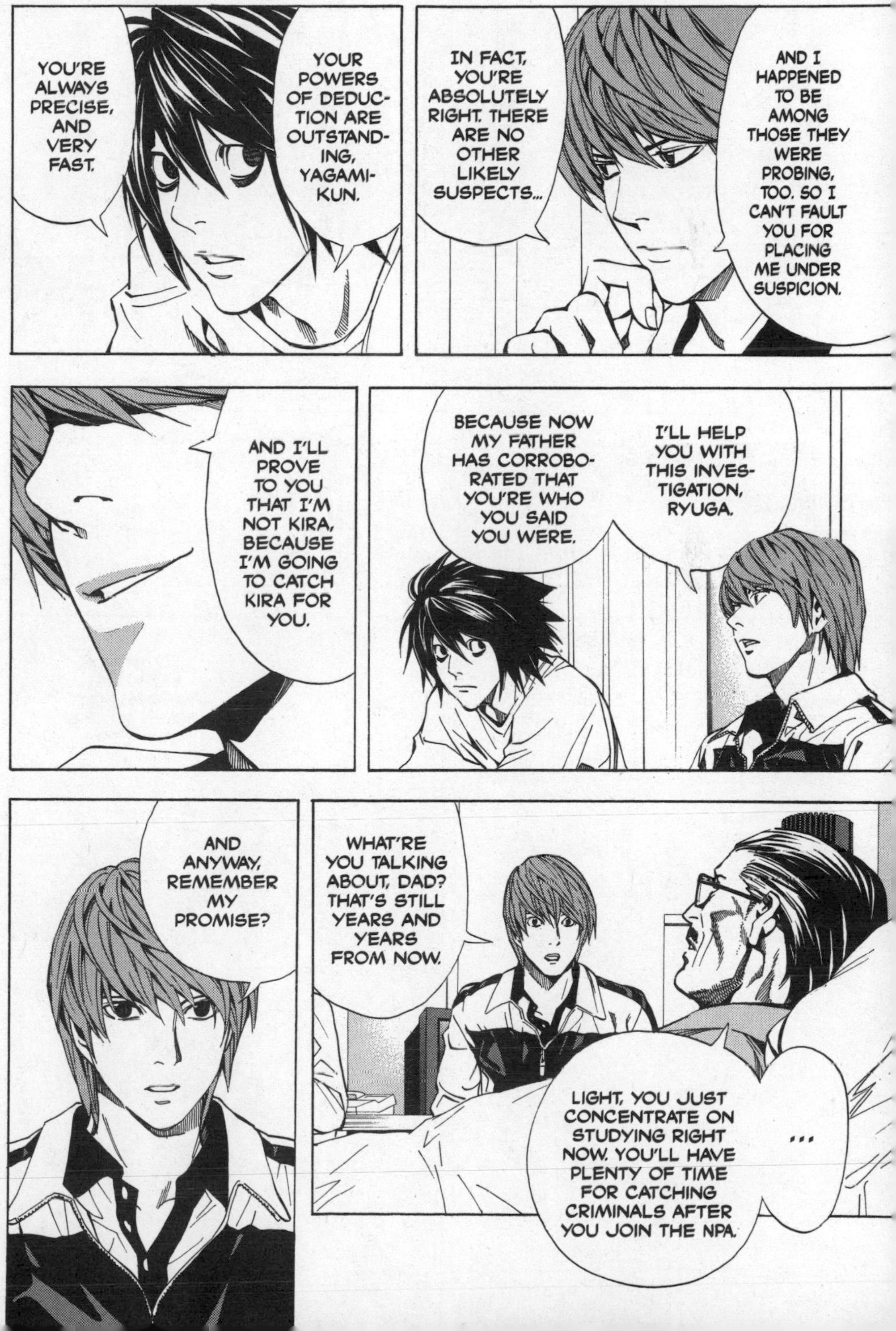
IN FACT, YOU'RE ABSOLUTELY RIGHT. THERE ARE NO OTHER LIKELY SUSPECTS...
AND I HAPPENED TO BE AMONG THOSE THEY WERE PROBING, TOO. SO I CAN'T FAULT YOU FOR PLACING ME UNDER SUSPICION.
YOUR POWERS OF DEDUCTION ARE OUTSTANDING, YAGAMI-KUN.
YOU'RE ALWAYS PRECISE, AND VERY FAST.
I'LL HELP YOU WITH THIS INVESTIGATION, RYUGA.
BECAUSE NOW MY FATHER HAS CORROBORATED THAT YOU'RE WHO YOU SAID YOU WERE.
AND I'LL PROVE TO YOU THAT I'M NOT KIRA, BECAUSE I'M GOING TO CATCH KIRA FOR YOU.
LIGHT, YOU JUST CONCENTRATE ON STUDYING RIGHT NOW. YOU'LL HAVE PLENTY OF TIME FOR CATCHING CRIMINALS AFTER YOU JOIN THE NPA.
WHAT'RE YOU TALKING ABOUT, DAD? THAT'S STILL YEARS AND YEARS FROM NOW.
...
AND ANYWAY, REMEMBER MY PROMISE?

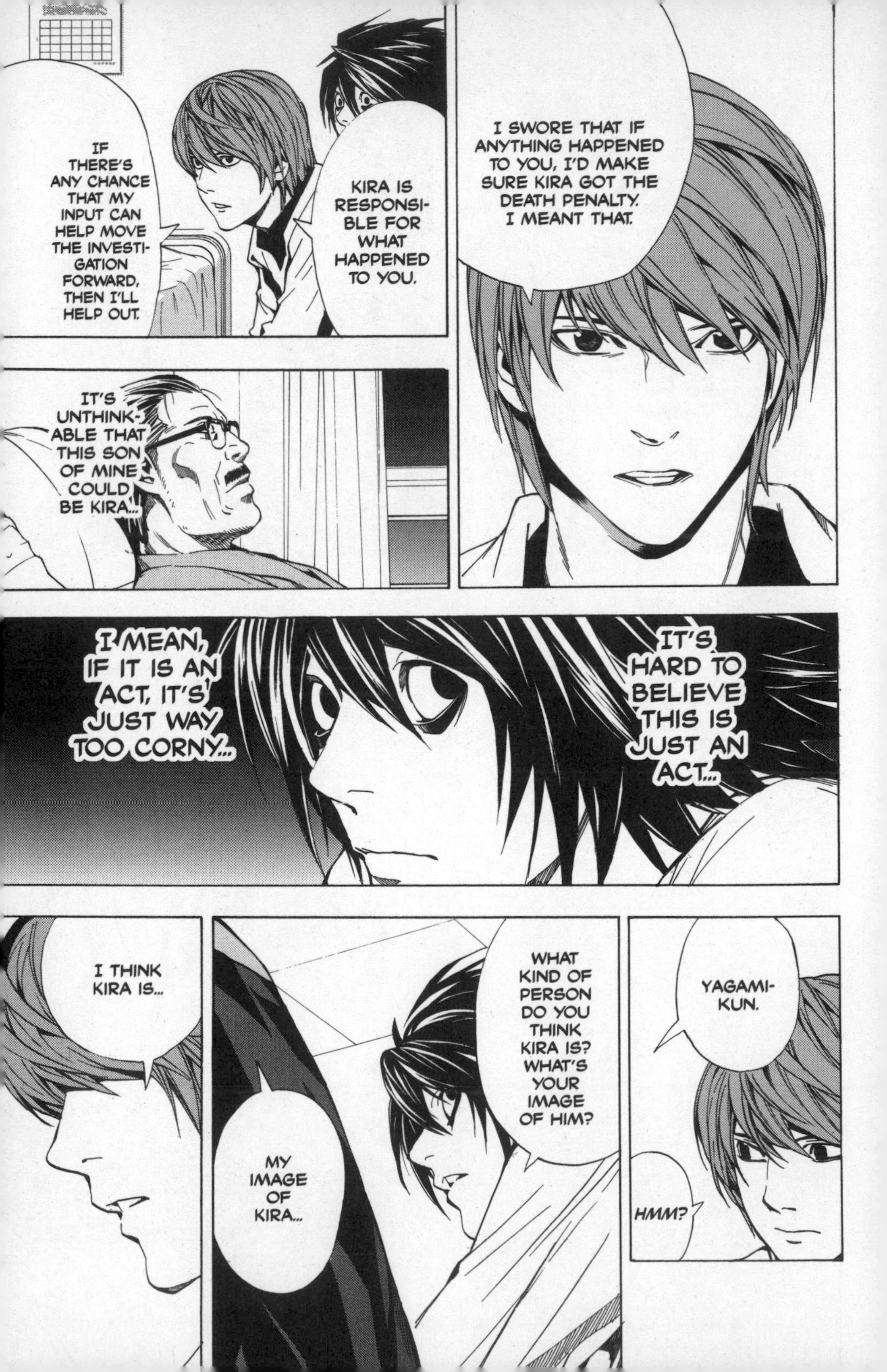
I SWORE THAT IF ANYTHING HAPPENED TO YOU, I'D MAKE SURE KIRA GOT THE DEATH PENALTY. I MEANT THAT.
KIRA IS RESPONSIBLE FOR WHAT HAPPENED TO YOU.
IF THERE'S ANY CHANCE THAT MY INPUT CAN HELP MOVE THE INVESTIGATION FORWARD, THEN I'LL HELP OUT.
IT'S UNTHINKABLE THAT THIS SON OF MINE COULD BE KIRA...
IT'S HARD TO BELIEVE THIS IS JUST AN ACT...
I MEAN, IF IT IS AN ACT, IT'S JUST WAY TOO CORNY...
YAGAMI-KUN.
HMM?
WHAT KIND OF PERSON DO YOU THINK KIRA IS? WHAT'S YOUR IMAGE OF HIM?
MY IMAGE OF KIRA...
I THINK KIRA IS...

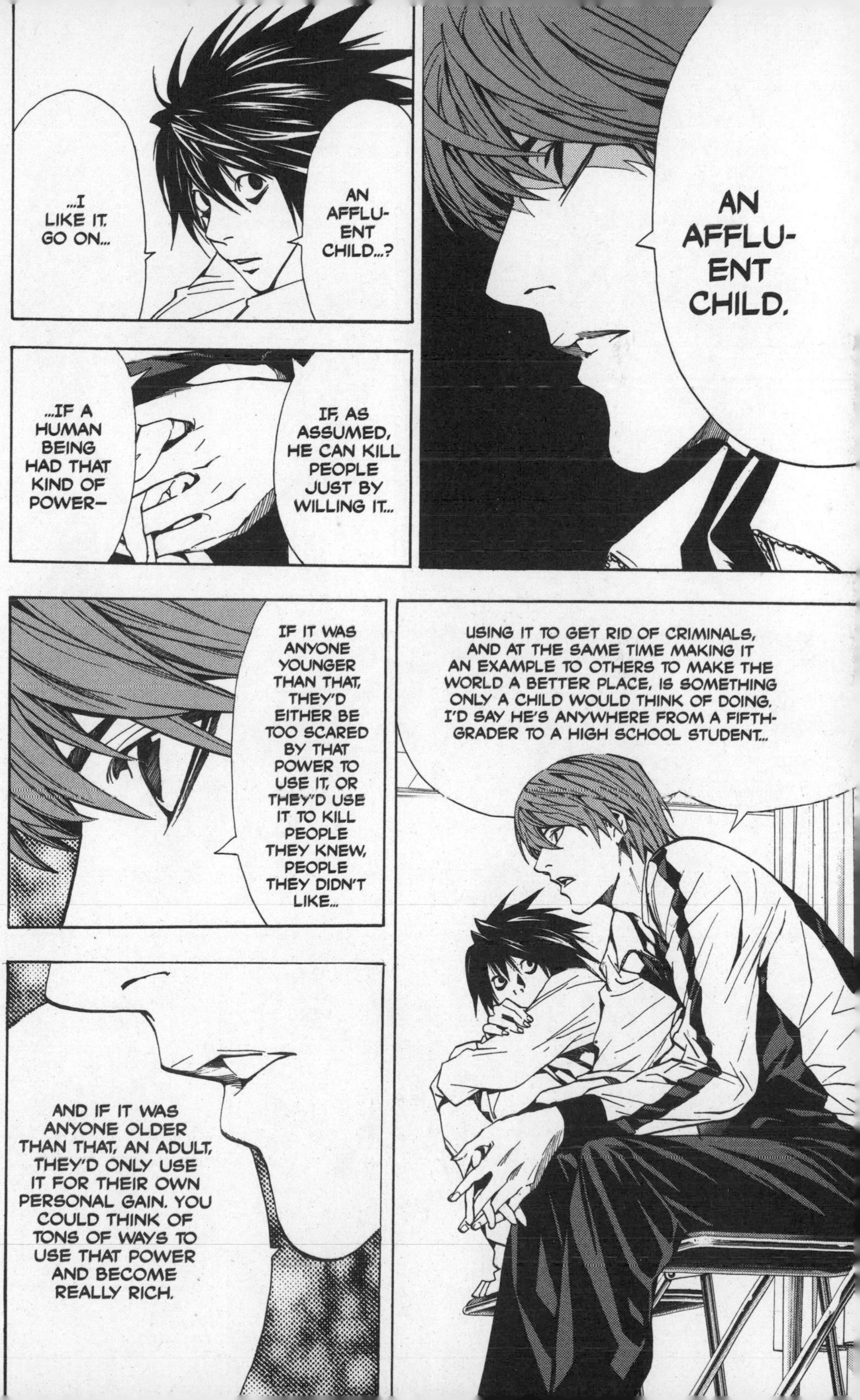
AN AFFLU-ENT CHILD.
AN AFFLU-ENT CHILD...?
...I LIKE IT. GO ON...
IF, AS ASSUMED, HE CAN KILL PEOPLE JUST BY WILLING IT...
...IF A HUMAN BEING HAD THAT KIND OF POWER—
USING IT TO GET RID OF CRIMINALS, AND AT THE SAME TIME MAKING IT AN EXAMPLE TO OTHERS TO MAKE THE WORLD A BETTER PLACE, IS SOMETHING ONLY A CHILD WOULD THINK OF DOING. I'D SAY HE'S ANYWHERE FROM A FIFTH-GRADER TO A HIGH SCHOOL STUDENT...
IF IT WAS ANYONE YOUNGER THAN THAT, THEY'D EITHER BE TOO SCARED BY THAT POWER TO USE IT, OR THEY'D USE IT TO KILL PEOPLE THEY KNEW, PEOPLE THEY DIDN'T LIKE...
AND IF IT WAS ANYONE OLDER THAN THAT, AN ADULT, THEY'D ONLY USE IT FOR THEIR OWN PERSONAL GAIN. YOU COULD THINK OF TONS OF WAYS TO USE THAT POWER AND BECOME REALLY RICH.

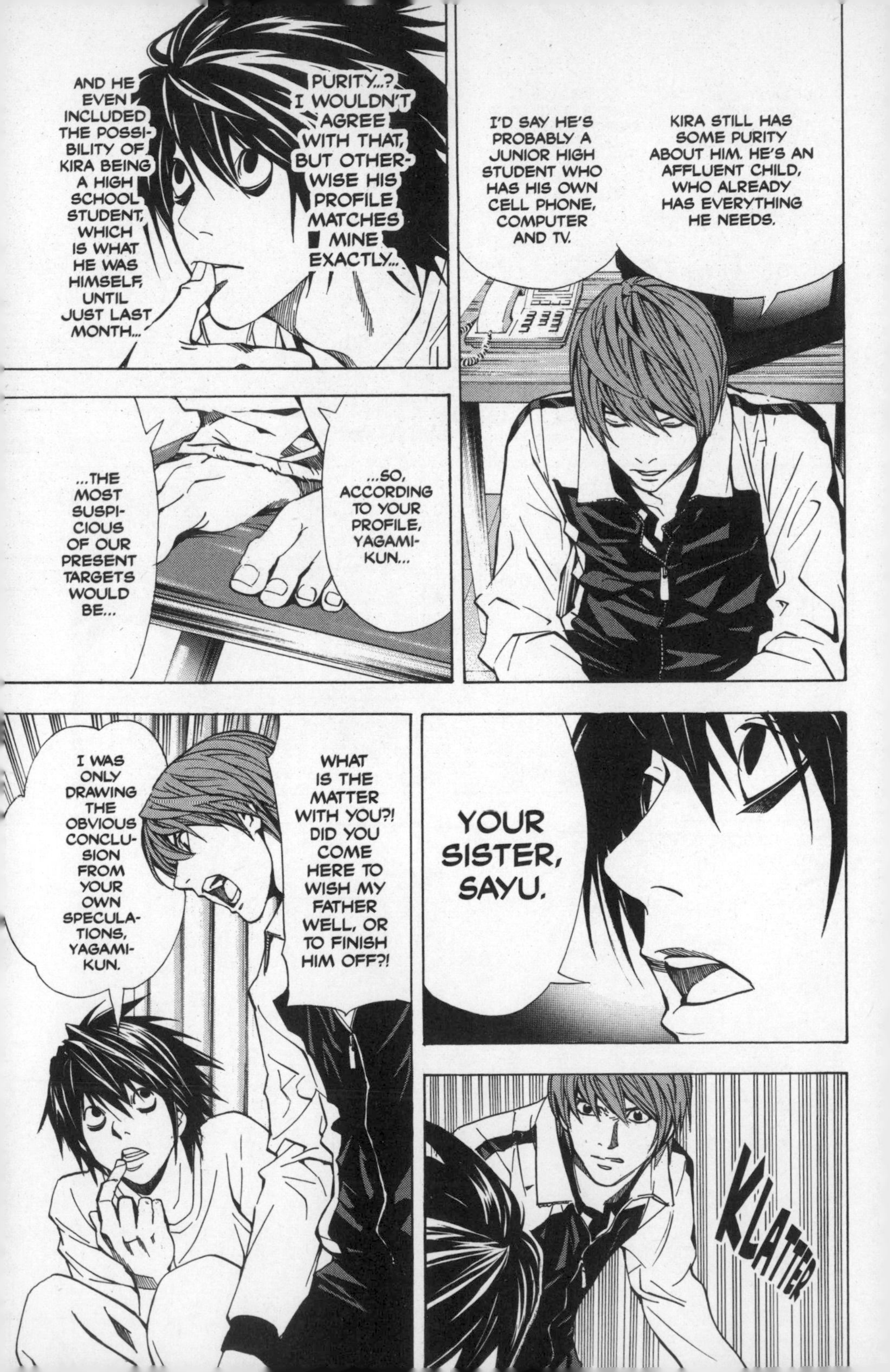
KIRA STILL HAS SOME PURITY ABOUT HIM. HE'S AN AFFLUENT CHILD, WHO ALREADY HAS EVERYTHING HE NEEDS.
I'D SAY HE'S PROBABLY A JUNIOR HIGH STUDENT WHO HAS HIS OWN CELL PHONE, COMPUTER AND TV.
PURITY...? I WOULDN'T AGREE WITH THAT, BUT OTHERWISE HIS PROFILE MATCHES MINE EXACTLY...
AND HE EVEN INCLUDED THE POSSIBILITY OF KIRA BEING A HIGH SCHOOL STUDENT, WHICH IS WHAT HE WAS HIMSELF, UNTIL JUST LAST MONTH...
...SO, ACCORDING TO YOUR PROFILE, YAGAMI-KUN...
...THE MOST SUSPICIOUS OF OUR PRESENT TARGETS WOULD BE...
YOUR SISTER, SAYU.
KLATTER
WHAT IS THE MATTER WITH YOU?! DID YOU COME HERE TO WISH MY FATHER WELL, OR TO FINISH HIM OFF?!
I WAS ONLY DRAWING THE OBVIOUS CONCLUSION FROM YOUR OWN SPECULATIONS, YAGAMI-KUN.

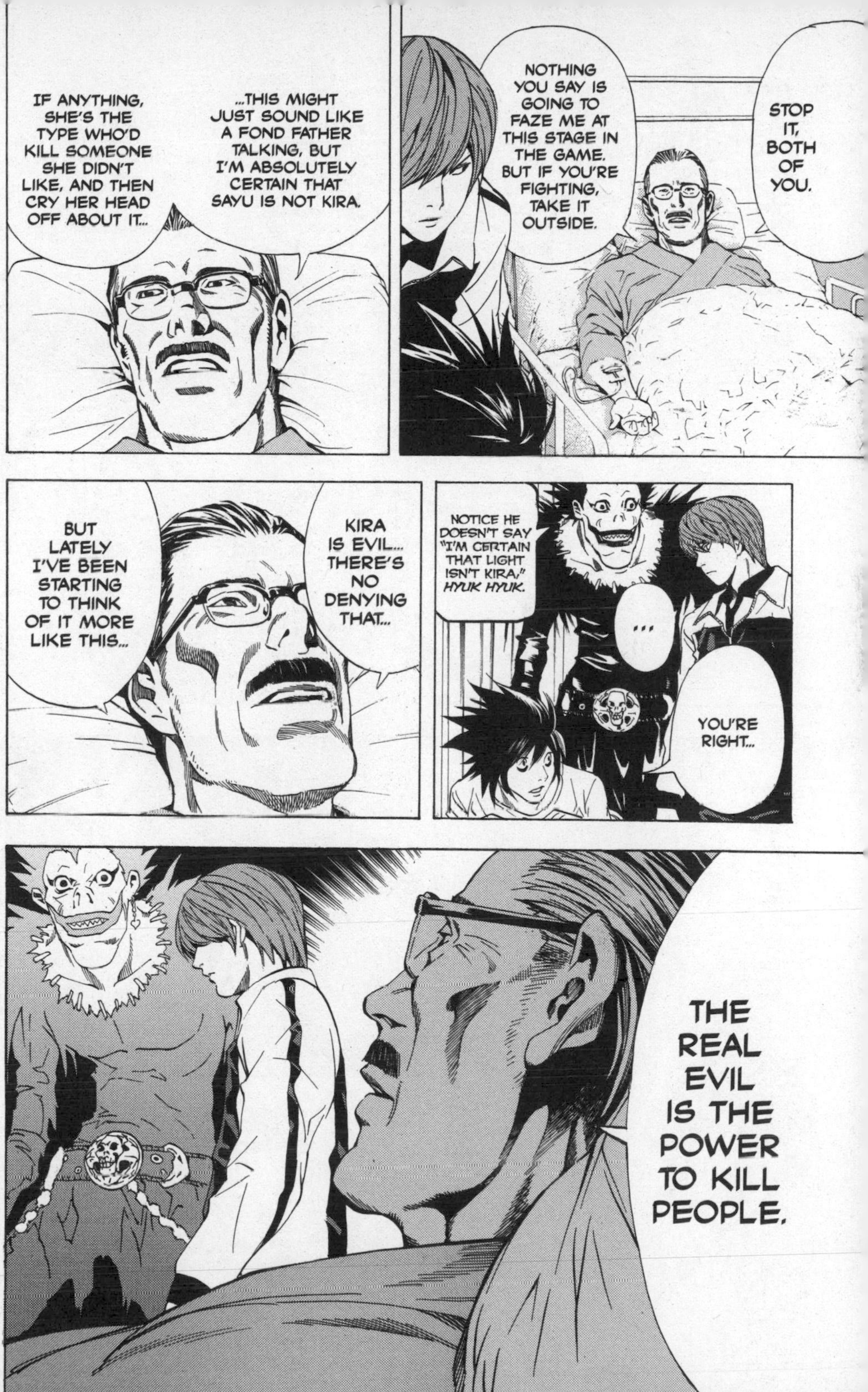
STOP IT, BOTH OF YOU.
NOTHING YOU SAY IS GOING TO FAZE ME AT THIS STAGE IN THE GAME. BUT IF YOU'RE FIGHTING, TAKE IT OUTSIDE.
...THIS MIGHT JUST SOUND LIKE A FOND FATHER TALKING, BUT I'M ABSOLUTELY CERTAIN THAT SAYU IS NOT KIRA.
IF ANYTHING, SHE'S THE TYPE WHO'D KILL SOMEONE SHE DIDN'T LIKE, AND THEN CRY HER HEAD OFF ABOUT IT...
NOTICE HE DOESN'T SAY "I'M CERTAIN THAT LIGHT ISN'T KIRA," HYUK HYUK.
...
YOU'RE RIGHT...
KIRA IS EVIL... THERE'S NO DENYING THAT...
BUT LATELY I'VE BEEN STARTING TO THINK OF IT MORE LIKE THIS...
THE REAL EVIL IS THE POWER TO KILL PEOPLE.

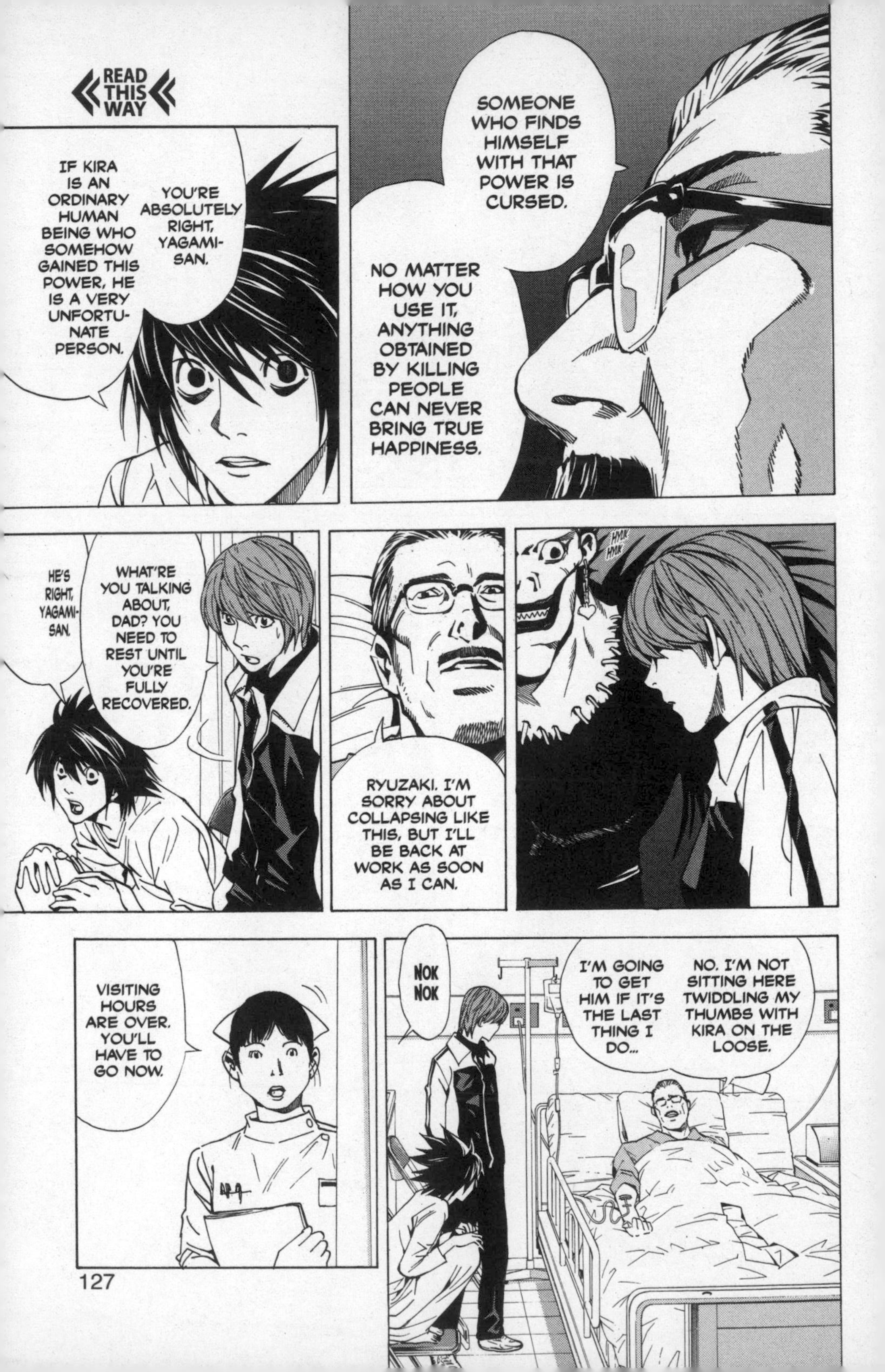
READ THIS WAY
SOMEONE WHO FINDS HIMSELF WITH THAT POWER IS CURSED.
NO MATTER HOW YOU USE IT, ANYTHING OBTAINED BY KILLING PEOPLE CAN NEVER BRING TRUE HAPPINESS.
IF KIRA IS AN ORDINARY HUMAN BEING WHO SOMEHOW GAINED THIS POWER, HE IS A VERY UNFORTUNATE PERSON.
YOU'RE ABSOLUTELY RIGHT, YAGAMI-SAN.
HYUK HYUK
RYUZAKI. I'M SORRY ABOUT COLLAPSING LIKE THIS, BUT I'LL BE BACK AT WORK AS SOON AS I CAN.
WHAT'RE YOU TALKING ABOUT, DAD? YOU NEED TO REST UNTIL YOU'RE FULLY RECOVERED.
HE'S RIGHT, YAGAMI-SAN.
NO. I'M NOT SITTING HERE TWIDDLING MY THUMBS WITH KIRA ON THE LOOSE.
I'M GOING TO GET HIM IF IT'S THE LAST THING I DO...
NOK NOK
VISITING HOURS ARE OVER. YOU'LL HAVE TO GO NOW.

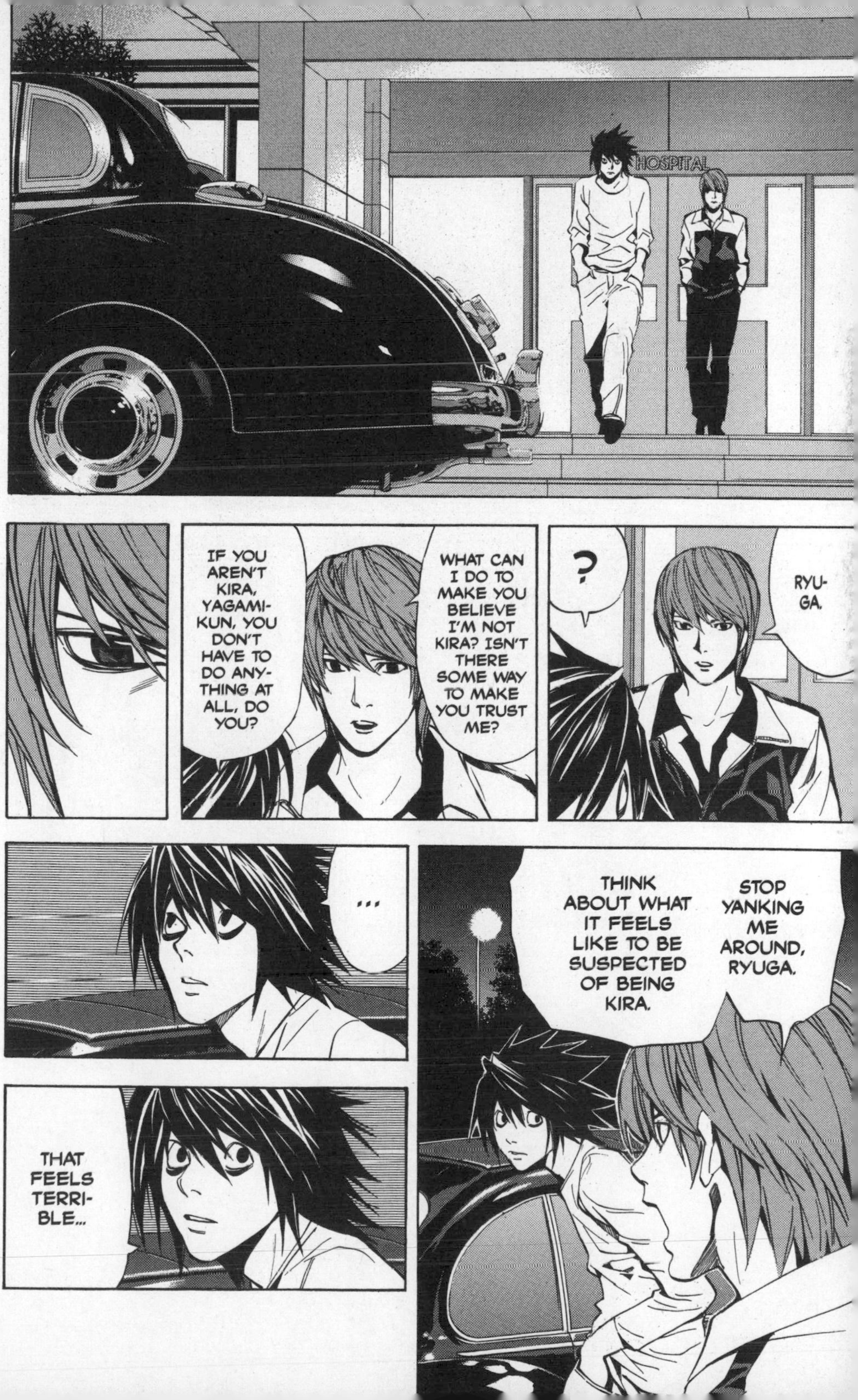
HOSPITAL
RYU-GA.
?
WHAT CAN I DO TO MAKE YOU BELIEVE I'M NOT KIRA? ISN'T THERE SOME WAY TO MAKE YOU TRUST ME?
IF YOU AREN'T KIRA, YAGAMI-KUN, YOU DON'T HAVE TO DO ANY-THING AT ALL, DO YOU?
STOP YANKING ME AROUND, RYUGA.
THINK ABOUT WHAT IT FEELS LIKE TO BE SUSPECTED OF BEING KIRA.
...
THAT FEELS TERRI-BLE...

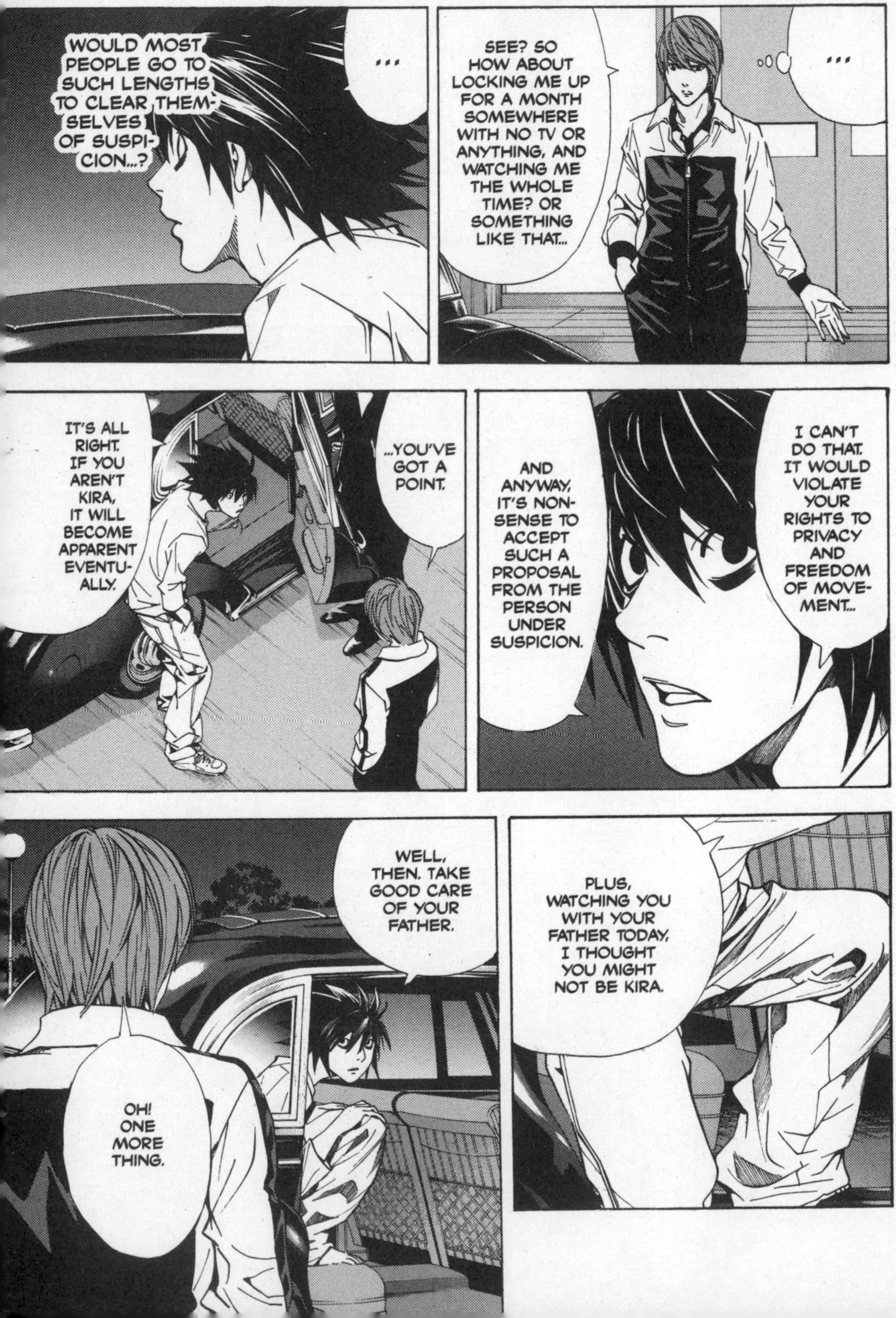
...
SEE? SO HOW ABOUT LOCKING ME UP FOR A MONTH SOMEWHERE WITH NO TV OR ANYTHING, AND WATCHING ME THE WHOLE TIME? OR SOMETHING LIKE THAT...
...
WOULD MOST PEOPLE GO TO SUCH LENGTHS TO CLEAR THEM-SELVES OF SUSPI-CION...?
I CAN'T DO THAT. IT WOULD VIOLATE YOUR RIGHTS TO PRIVACY AND FREEDOM OF MOVE-MENT...
AND ANYWAY, IT'S NON-SENSE TO ACCEPT SUCH A PROPOSAL FROM THE PERSON UNDER SUSPICION.
...YOU'VE GOT A POINT.
IT'S ALL RIGHT. IF YOU AREN'T KIRA, IT WILL BECOME APPARENT EVENTU-ALLY.
PLUS, WATCHING YOU WITH YOUR FATHER TODAY, I THOUGHT YOU MIGHT NOT BE KIRA.
WELL, THEN. TAKE GOOD CARE OF YOUR FATHER.
OH! ONE MORE THING.

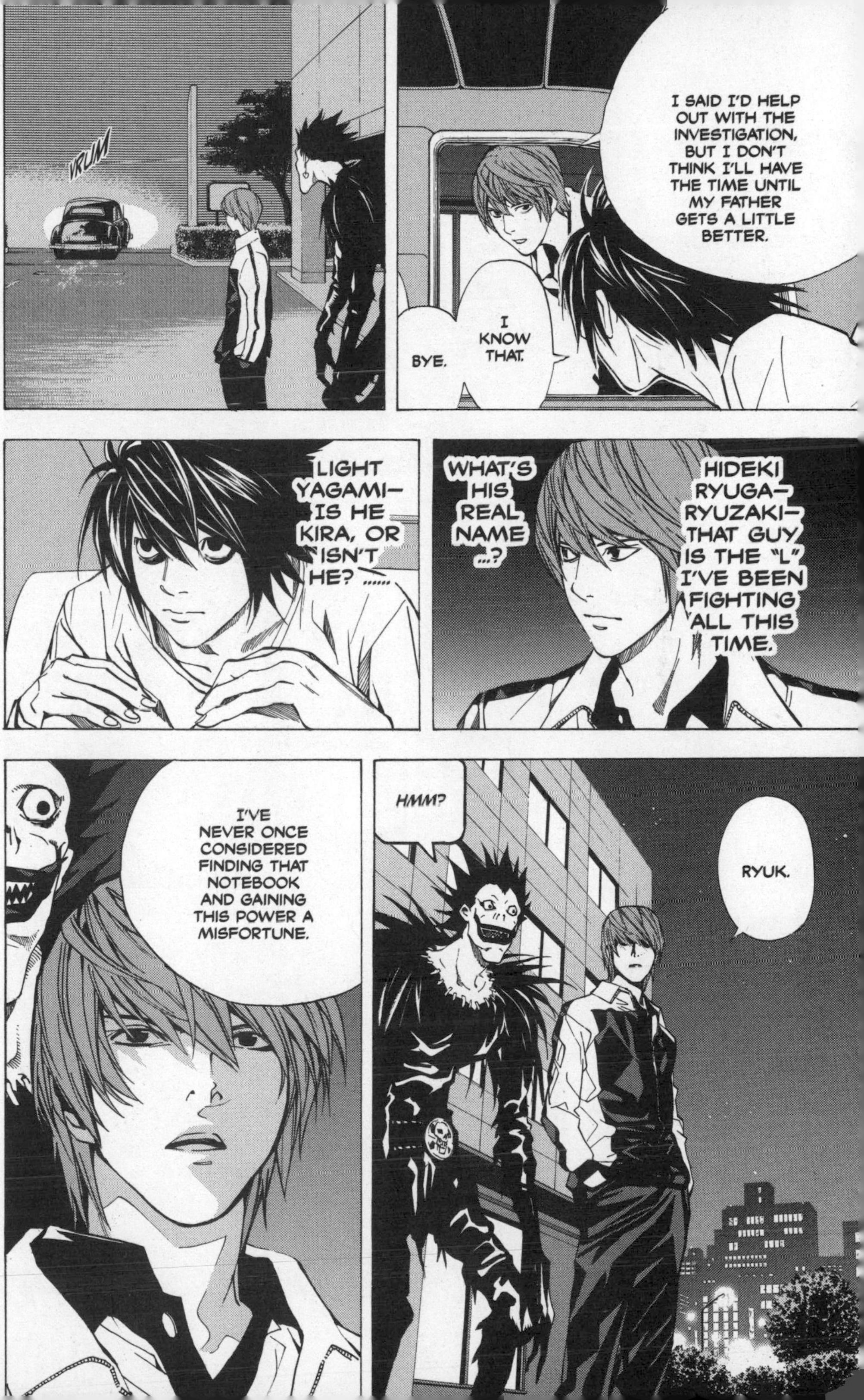
I SAID I'D HELP OUT WITH THE INVESTIGATION, BUT I DON'T THINK I'LL HAVE THE TIME UNTIL MY FATHER GETS A LITTLE BETTER.
I KNOW THAT.
BYE.
VRUM
HIDEKI RYUGA— RYUZAKI— THAT GUY IS THE "L" I'VE BEEN FIGHTING ALL THIS TIME.
WHAT'S HIS REAL NAME ...?
LIGHT YAGAMI— IS HE KIRA, OR ISN'T HE? ......
RYUK.
HMM?
I'VE NEVER ONCE CONSIDERED FINDING THAT NOTEBOOK AND GAINING THIS POWER A MISFORTUNE.

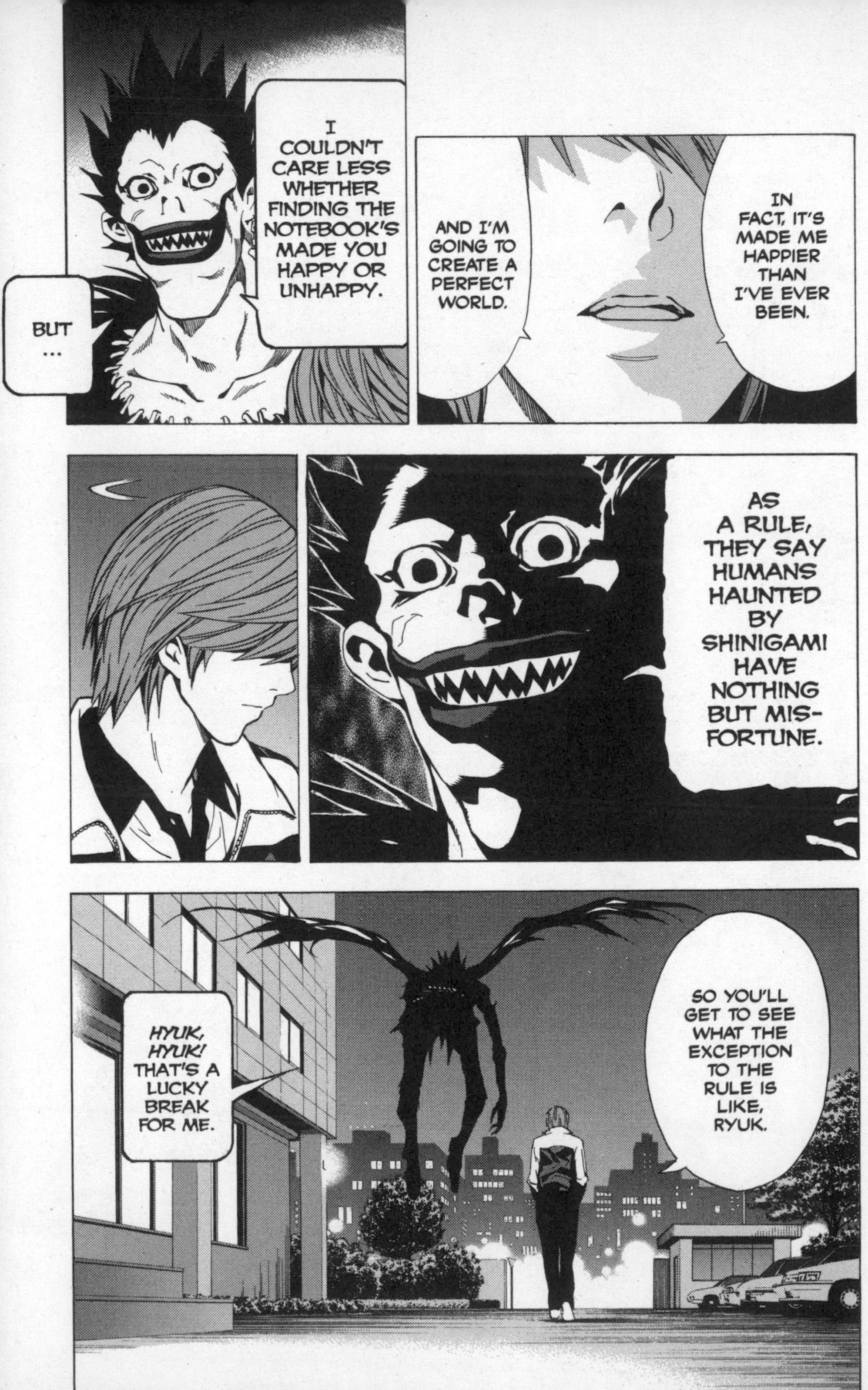
IN FACT, IT'S MADE ME HAPPIER THAN I'VE EVER BEEN.
AND I'M GOING TO CREATE A PERFECT WORLD.
I COULDN'T CARE LESS WHETHER FINDING THE NOTEBOOK'S MADE YOU HAPPY OR UNHAPPY.
BUT ...
AS A RULE, THEY SAY HUMANS HAUNTED BY SHINIGAMI HAVE NOTHING BUT MIS-FORTUNE.
SO YOU'LL GET TO SEE WHAT THE EXCEPTION TO THE RULE IS LIKE, RYUK.
HYUK, HYUK! THAT'S A LUCKY BREAK FOR ME.

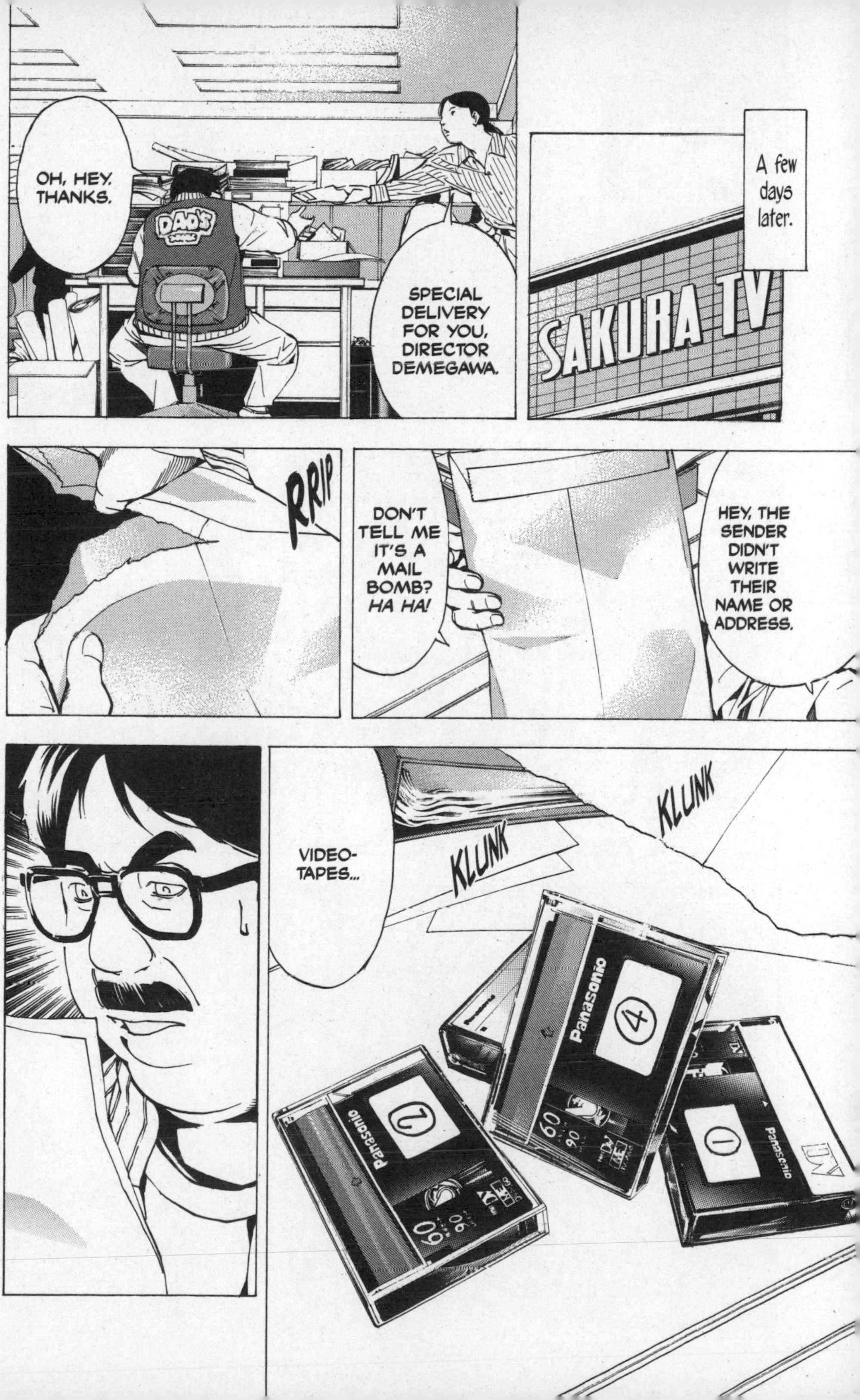
A few days later.
SAKURA TV
SPECIAL DELIVERY FOR YOU, DIRECTOR DEMEGAWA.
OH, HEY. THANKS.
DAD'S
HEY, THE SENDER DIDN'T WRITE THEIR NAME OR ADDRESS.
DON'T TELL ME IT'S A MAIL BOMB? *HA HA!*
RRIP
KLUNK
KLUNK
VIDEO-TAPES...
Panasonic
4
Panasonic
2
Panasonic
1

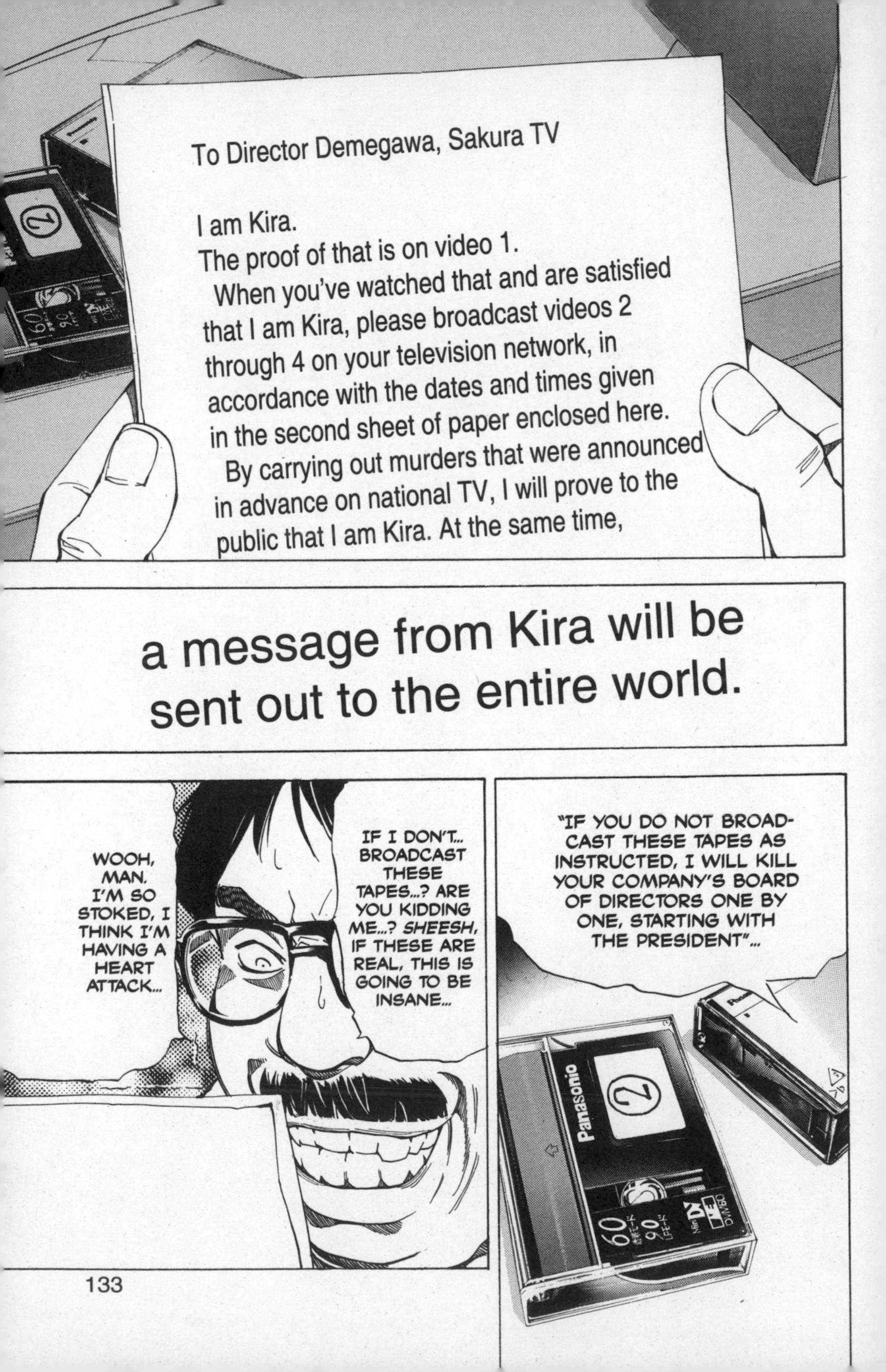
To Director Demegawa, Sakura TV
I am Kira.
The proof of that is on video 1.
When you've watched that and are satisfied that I am Kira, please broadcast videos 2 through 4 on your television network, in accordance with the dates and times given in the second sheet of paper enclosed here.
By carrying out murders that were announced in advance on national TV, I will prove to the public that I am Kira. At the same time,
a message from Kira will be sent out to the entire world.
"IF YOU DO NOT BROADCAST THESE TAPES AS INSTRUCTED, I WILL KILL YOUR COMPANY'S BOARD OF DIRECTORS ONE BY ONE, STARTING WITH THE PRESIDENT"...
Panasonic
IF I DON'T... BROADCAST THESE TAPES...? ARE YOU KIDDING ME...? *SHEESH,* IF THESE ARE REAL, THIS IS GOING TO BE INSANE...
WOOH, MAN. I'M SO STOKED, I THINK I'M HAVING A HEART ATTACK...

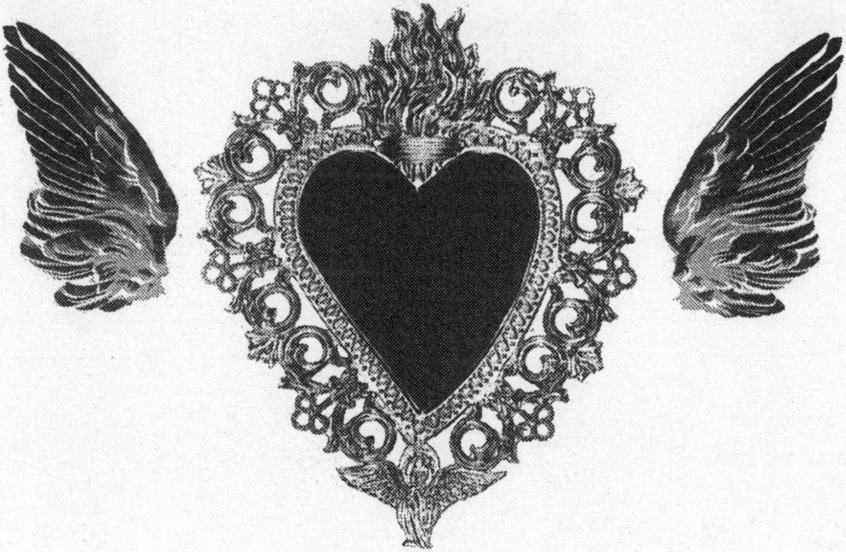

chapter 23 Hard Run

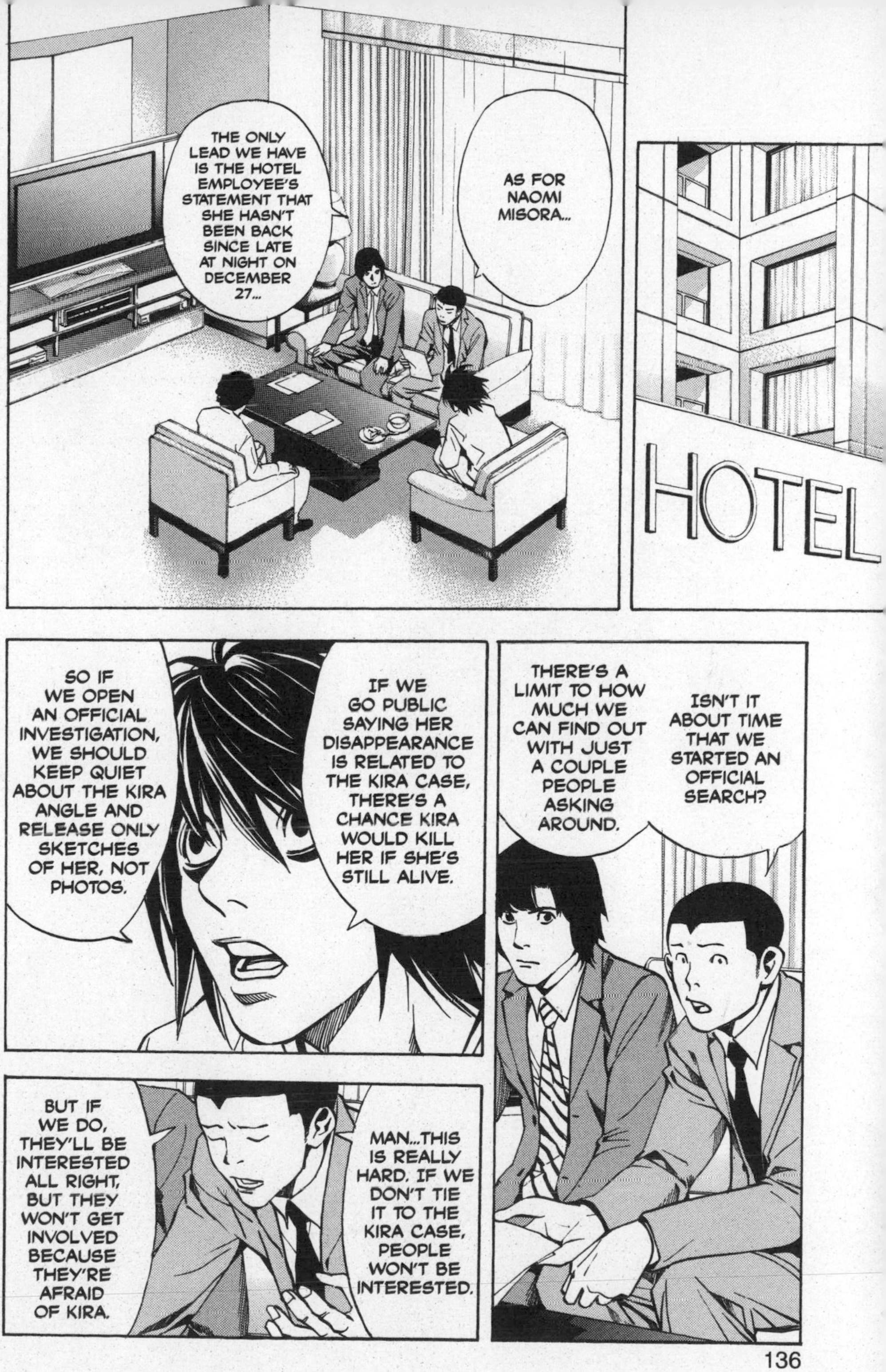
HOTEL
AS FOR NAOMI MISORA...
THE ONLY LEAD WE HAVE IS THE HOTEL EMPLOYEE'S STATEMENT THAT SHE HASN'T BEEN BACK SINCE LATE AT NIGHT ON DECEMBER 27...
ISN'T IT ABOUT TIME THAT WE STARTED AN OFFICIAL SEARCH?
THERE'S A LIMIT TO HOW MUCH WE CAN FIND OUT WITH JUST A COUPLE PEOPLE ASKING AROUND.
IF WE GO PUBLIC SAYING HER DISAPPEARANCE IS RELATED TO THE KIRA CASE, THERE'S A CHANCE KIRA WOULD KILL HER IF SHE'S STILL ALIVE.
SO IF WE OPEN AN OFFICIAL INVESTIGATION, WE SHOULD KEEP QUIET ABOUT THE KIRA ANGLE AND RELEASE ONLY SKETCHES OF HER, NOT PHOTOS.
MAN...THIS IS REALLY HARD. IF WE DON'T TIE IT TO THE KIRA CASE, PEOPLE WON'T BE INTERESTED.
BUT IF WE DO, THEY'LL BE INTERESTED ALL RIGHT, BUT THEY WON'T GET INVOLVED BECAUSE THEY'RE AFRAID OF KIRA.

READ THIS WAY

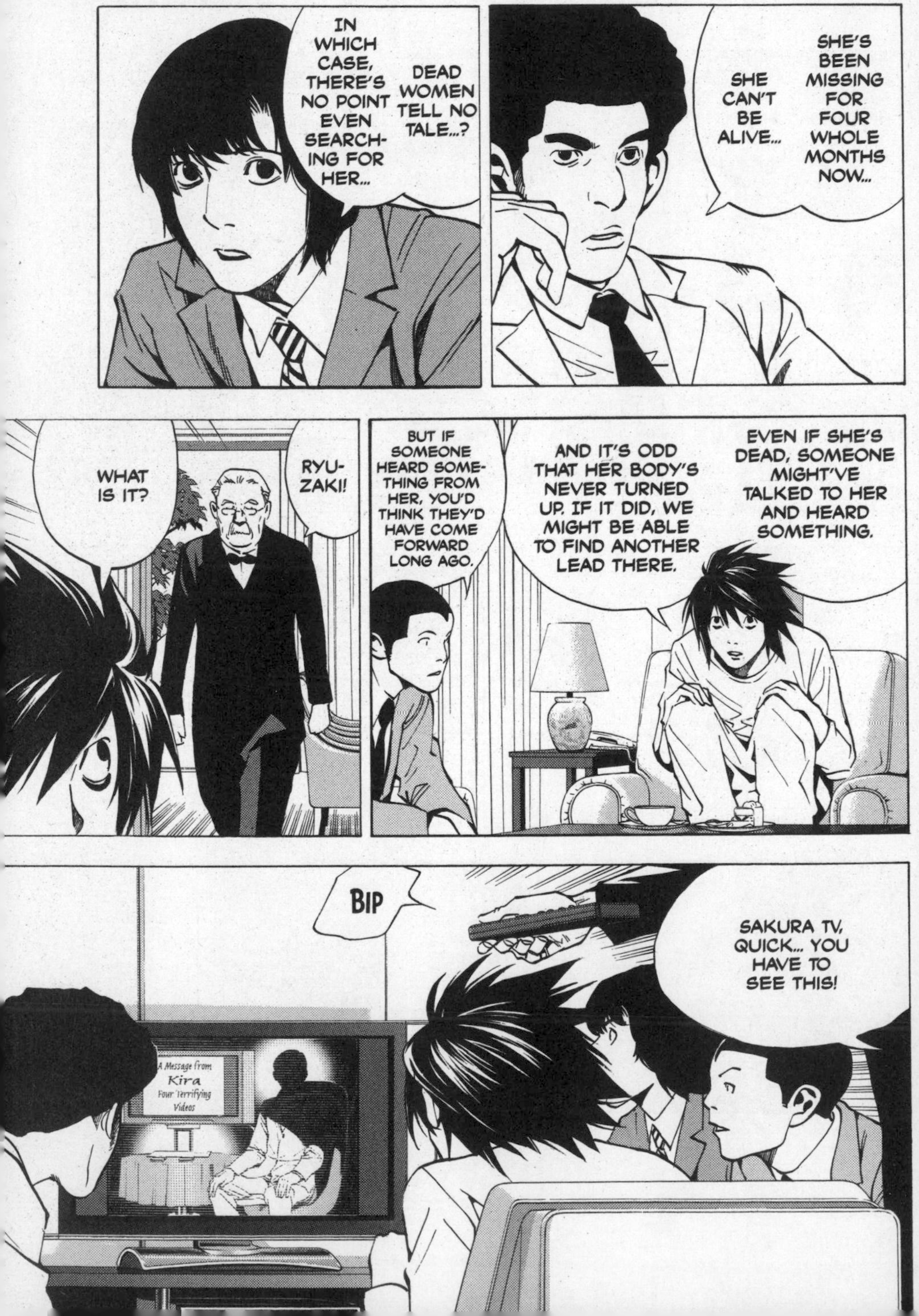

SHE'S BEEN MISSING FOR FOUR WHOLE MONTHS NOW...
SHE CAN'T BE ALIVE...
DEAD WOMEN TELL NO TALE...?
IN WHICH CASE, THERE'S NO POINT EVEN SEARCHING FOR HER...
EVEN IF SHE'S DEAD, SOMEONE MIGHT'VE TALKED TO HER AND HEARD SOMETHING.
AND IT'S ODD THAT HER BODY'S NEVER TURNED UP. IF IT DID, WE MIGHT BE ABLE TO FIND ANOTHER LEAD THERE.
BUT IF SOMEONE HEARD SOMETHING FROM HER, YOU'D THINK THEY'D HAVE COME FORWARD LONG AGO.
RYUZAKI!
WHAT IS IT?
SAKURA TV, QUICK... YOU HAVE TO SEE THIS!
BIP
A Message from Kira Four Terrifying Videos

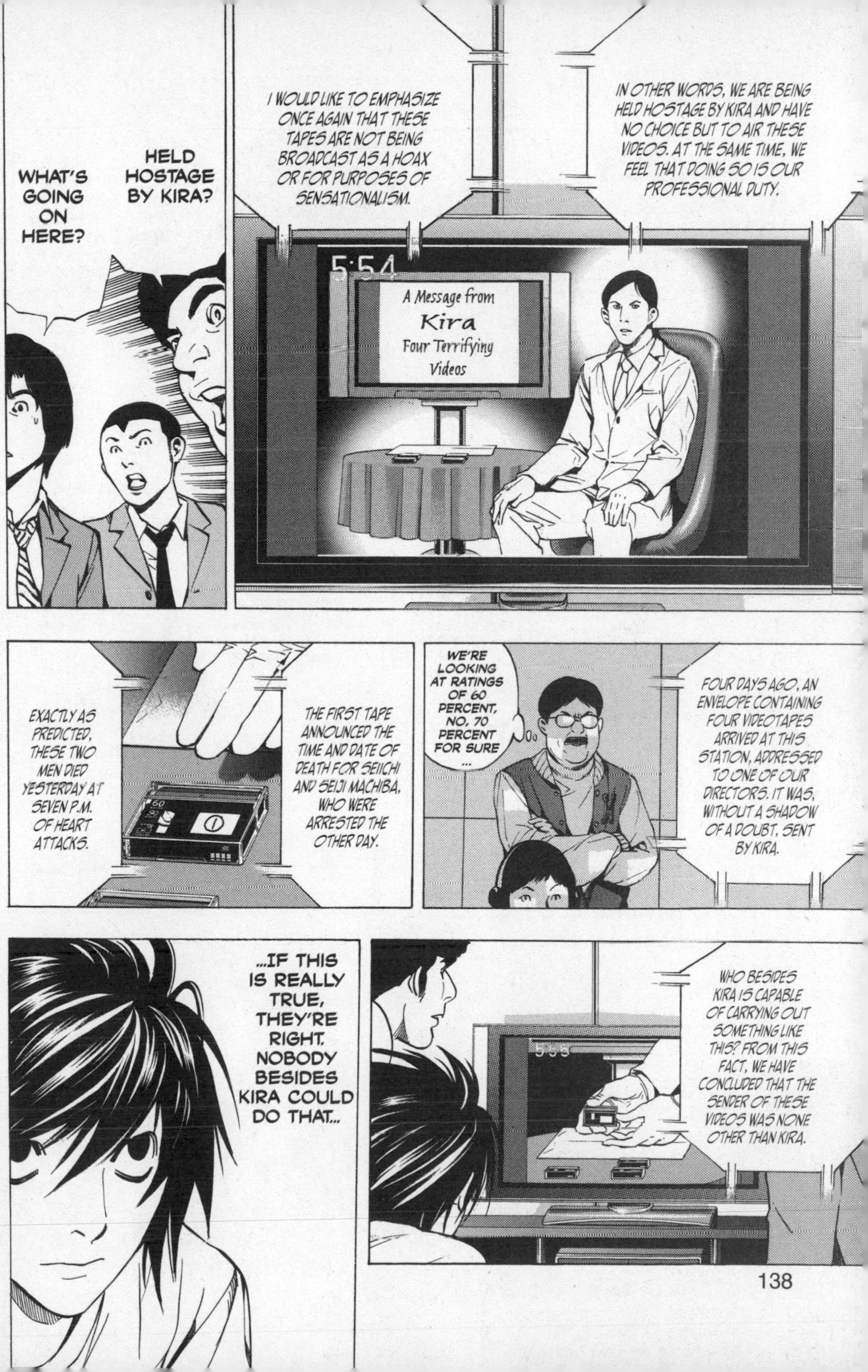
IN OTHER WORDS, WE ARE BEING HELD HOSTAGE BY KIRA AND HAVE NO CHOICE BUT TO AIR THESE VIDEOS. AT THE SAME TIME, WE FEEL THAT DOING SO IS OUR PROFESSIONAL DUTY.
I WOULD LIKE TO EMPHASIZE ONCE AGAIN THAT THESE TAPES ARE NOT BEING BROADCAST AS A HOAX OR FOR PURPOSES OF SENSATIONALISM.
5:54
A Message from Kira Four Terrifying Videos
HELD HOSTAGE BY KIRA?
WHAT'S GOING ON HERE?
FOUR DAYS AGO, AN ENVELOPE CONTAINING FOUR VIDEOTAPES ARRIVED AT THIS STATION, ADDRESSED TO ONE OF OUR DIRECTORS. IT WAS, WITHOUT A SHADOW OF A DOUBT, SENT BY KIRA.
WE'RE LOOKING AT RATINGS OF 60 PERCENT, NO, 70 PERCENT FOR SURE ...
THE FIRST TAPE ANNOUNCED THE TIME AND DATE OF DEATH FOR SEIICHI AND SEIJI MACHIBA, WHO WERE ARRESTED THE OTHER DAY.
EXACTLY AS PREDICTED, THESE TWO MEN DIED YESTERDAY AT SEVEN P.M. OF HEART ATTACKS.
WHO BESIDES KIRA IS CAPABLE OF CARRYING OUT SOMETHING LIKE THIS? FROM THIS FACT, WE HAVE CONCLUDED THAT THE SENDER OF THESE VIDEOS WAS NONE OTHER THAN KIRA.
...IF THIS IS REALLY TRUE, THEY'RE RIGHT. NOBODY BESIDES KIRA COULD DO THAT...

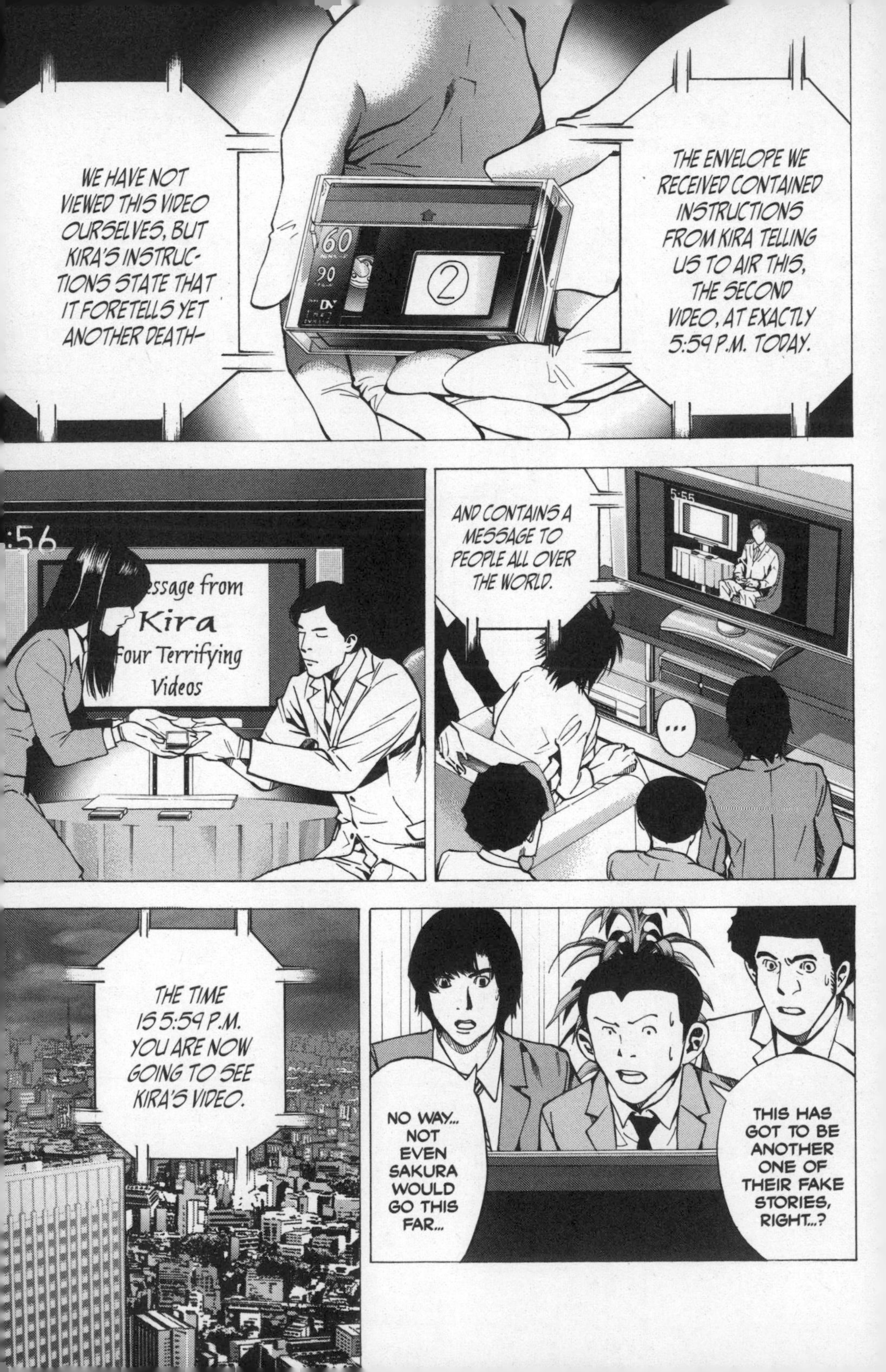
THE ENVELOPE WE RECEIVED CONTAINED INSTRUCTIONS FROM KIRA TELLING US TO AIR THIS, THE SECOND VIDEO, AT EXACTLY 5:59 P.M. TODAY.
WE HAVE NOT VIEWED THIS VIDEO OURSELVES, BUT KIRA'S INSTRUCTIONS STATE THAT IT FORETELLS YET ANOTHER DEATH-
5:55
AND CONTAINS A MESSAGE TO PEOPLE ALL OVER THE WORLD.
...
:56
essage from
Kira
Four Terrifying
Videos
THIS HAS GOT TO BE ANOTHER ONE OF THEIR FAKE STORIES, RIGHT...?
NO WAY... NOT EVEN SAKURA WOULD GO THIS FAR...
THE TIME IS 5:59 P.M. YOU ARE NOW GOING TO SEE KIRA'S VIDEO.

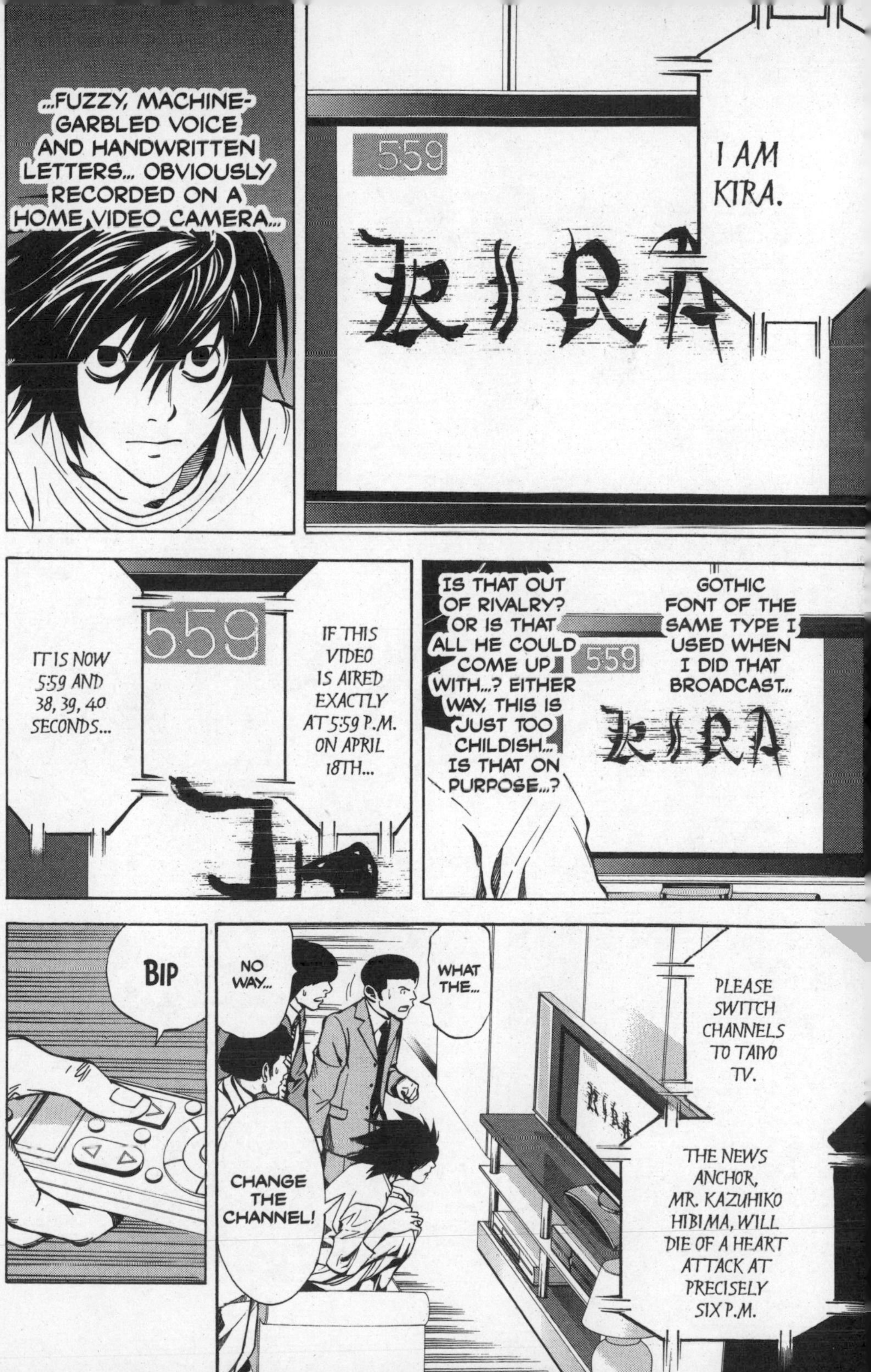
I AM KIRA.
559
KIRA
...FUZZY, MACHINE-GARBLED VOICE AND HANDWRITTEN LETTERS... OBVIOUSLY RECORDED ON A HOME VIDEO CAMERA...
GOTHIC FONT OF THE SAME TYPE I USED WHEN I DID THAT BROADCAST...
IS THAT OUT OF RIVALRY? OR IS THAT ALL HE COULD COME UP WITH...? EITHER WAY, THIS IS JUST TOO CHILDISH... IS THAT ON PURPOSE...?
559
KIRA
IF THIS VIDEO IS AIRED EXACTLY AT 5:59 P.M. ON APRIL 18TH...
559
IT IS NOW 5:59 AND 38, 39, 40 SECONDS...
PLEASE SWITCH CHANNELS TO TAIYO TV.
THE NEWS ANCHOR, MR. KAZUHIKO HIBIMA, WILL DIE OF A HEART ATTACK AT PRECISELY SIX P.M.
WHAT THE...
NO WAY...
CHANGE THE CHANNEL!
KIRA
BIP

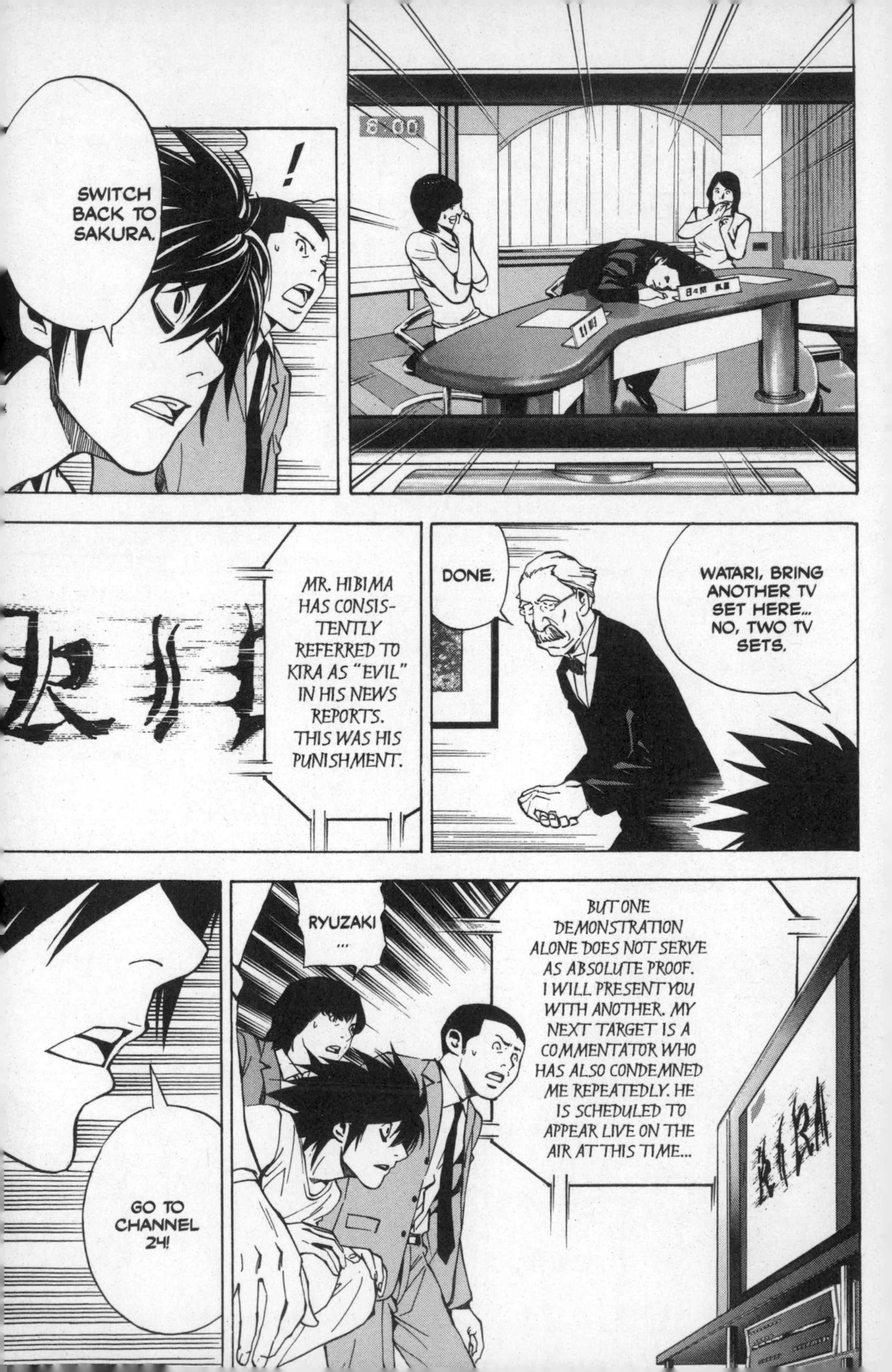
6:00
!
SWITCH BACK TO SAKURA.
WATARI, BRING ANOTHER TV SET HERE... NO, TWO TV SETS.
DONE.
MR. HIBIMA HAS CONSISTENTLY REFERRED TO KIRA AS "EVIL" IN HIS NEWS REPORTS. THIS WAS HIS PUNISHMENT.
KIRA
BUT ONE DEMONSTRATION ALONE DOES NOT SERVE AS ABSOLUTE PROOF. I WILL PRESENT YOU WITH ANOTHER. MY NEXT TARGET IS A COMMENTATOR WHO HAS ALSO CONDEMNED ME REPEATEDLY. HE IS SCHEDULED TO APPEAR LIVE ON THE AIR AT THIS TIME...
RYUZAKI ...
GO TO CHANNEL 24!

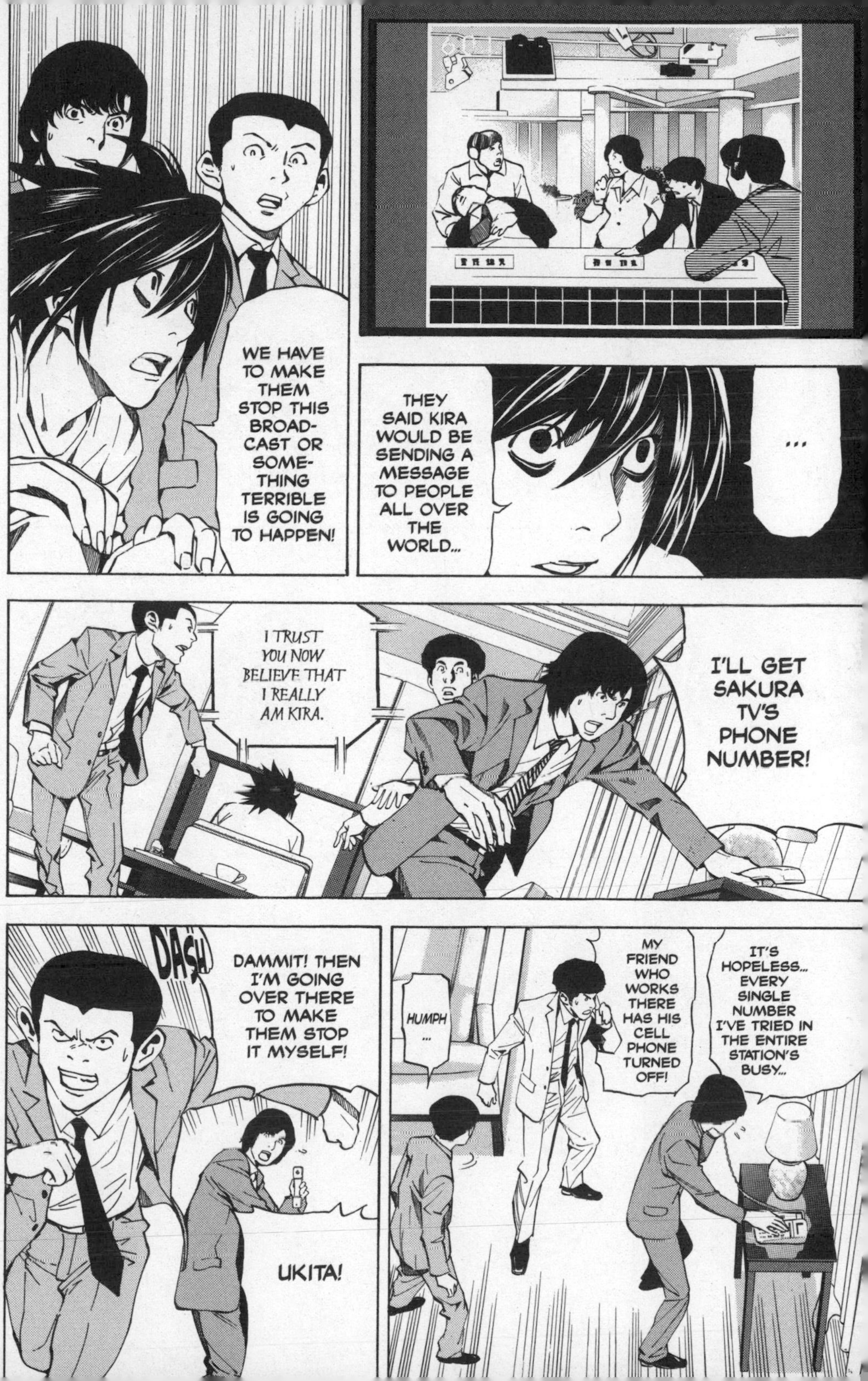
...
THEY SAID KIRA WOULD BE SENDING A MESSAGE TO PEOPLE ALL OVER THE WORLD...
WE HAVE TO MAKE THEM STOP THIS BROADCAST OR SOMETHING TERRIBLE IS GOING TO HAPPEN!
I'LL GET SAKURA TV'S PHONE NUMBER!
I TRUST YOU NOW BELIEVE THAT I REALLY AM KIRA.
IT'S HOPELESS... EVERY SINGLE NUMBER I'VE TRIED IN THE ENTIRE STATION'S BUSY...
MY FRIEND WHO WORKS THERE HAS HIS CELL PHONE TURNED OFF!
HUMPH ...
DASH
DAMMIT! THEN I'M GOING OVER THERE TO MAKE THEM STOP IT MYSELF!
UKITA!

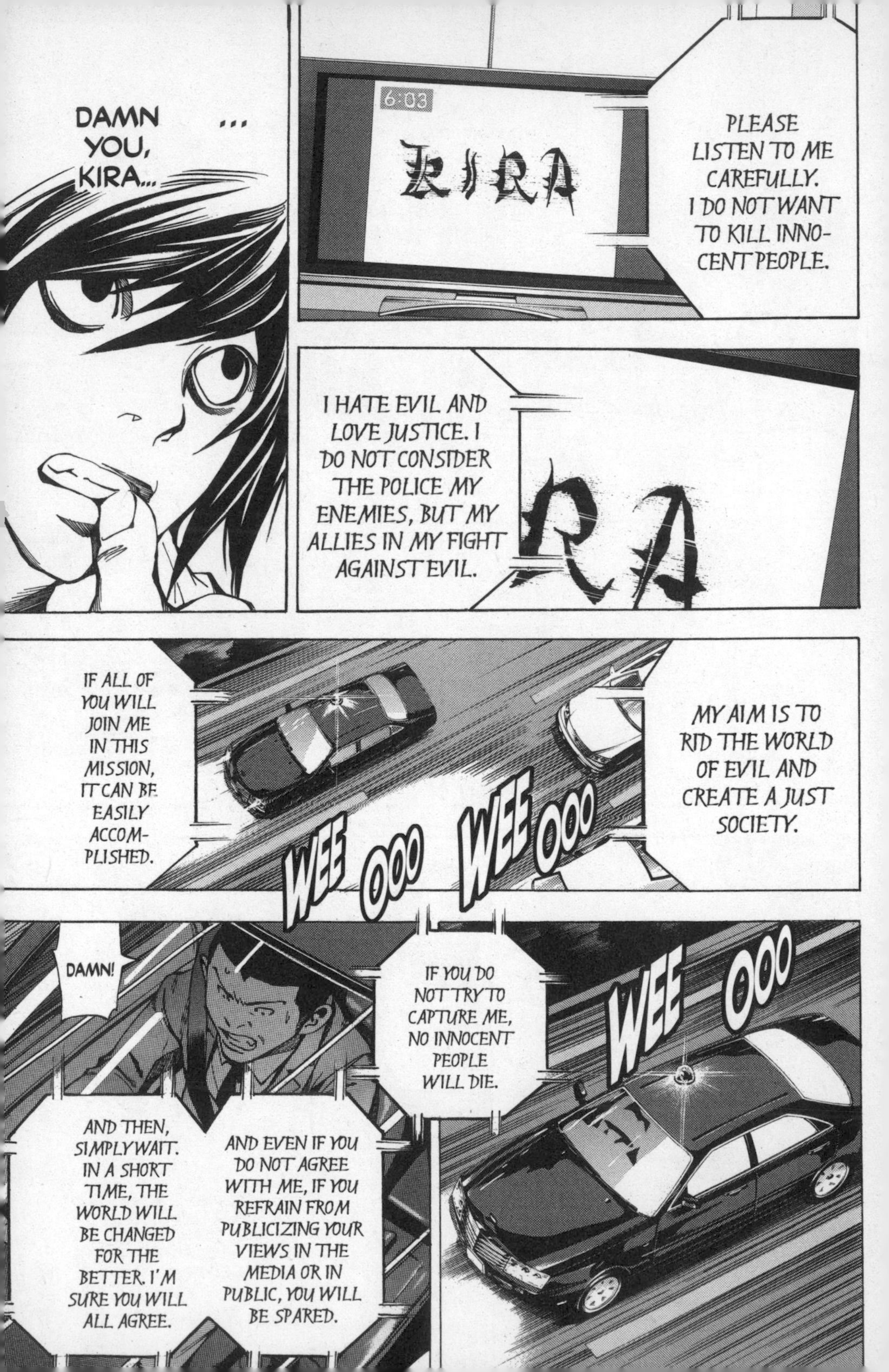
6:03
KIRA
PLEASE LISTEN TO ME CAREFULLY. I DO NOT WANT TO KILL INNOCENT PEOPLE.
I HATE EVIL AND LOVE JUSTICE. I DO NOT CONSIDER THE POLICE MY ENEMIES, BUT MY ALLIES IN MY FIGHT AGAINST EVIL.
RA
...
DAMN YOU, KIRA...
MY AIM IS TO RID THE WORLD OF EVIL AND CREATE A JUST SOCIETY.
WEE OOO WEE OOO
IF ALL OF YOU WILL JOIN ME IN THIS MISSION, IT CAN BE EASILY ACCOMPLISHED.
WEE OOO
IF YOU DO NOT TRY TO CAPTURE ME, NO INNOCENT PEOPLE WILL DIE.
DAMN!
AND EVEN IF YOU DO NOT AGREE WITH ME, IF YOU REFRAIN FROM PUBLICIZING YOUR VIEWS IN THE MEDIA OR IN PUBLIC, YOU WILL BE SPARED.
AND THEN, SIMPLY WAIT. IN A SHORT TIME, THE WORLD WILL BE CHANGED FOR THE BETTER. I'M SURE YOU WILL ALL AGREE.

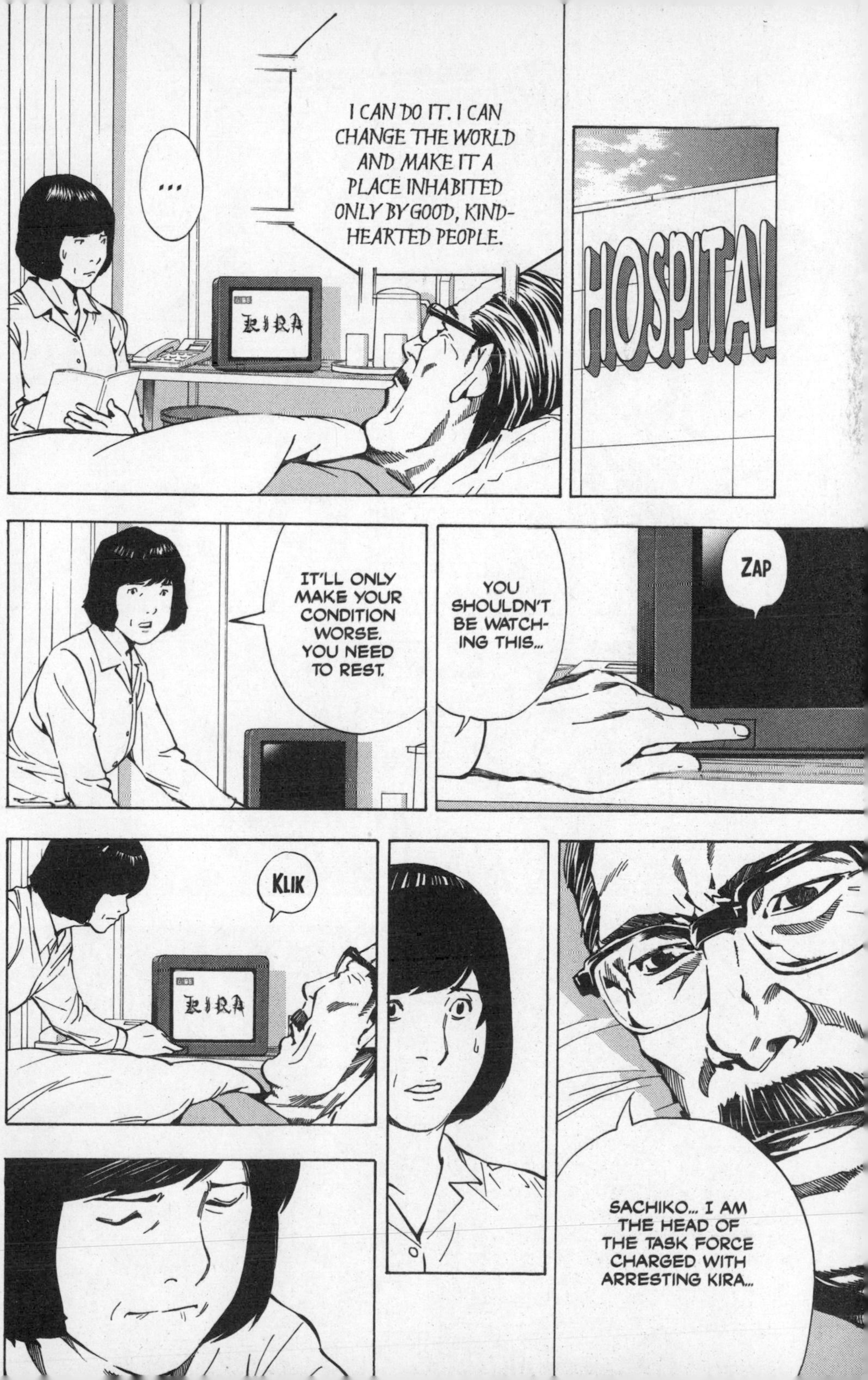
HOSPITAL
I CAN DO IT. I CAN CHANGE THE WORLD AND MAKE IT A PLACE INHABITED ONLY BY GOOD, KIND-HEARTED PEOPLE.
KIRA
...
ZAP
YOU SHOULDN'T BE WATCHING THIS...
IT'LL ONLY MAKE YOUR CONDITION WORSE. YOU NEED TO REST.
SACHIKO... I AM THE HEAD OF THE TASK FORCE CHARGED WITH ARRESTING KIRA...
KLIK
KIRA

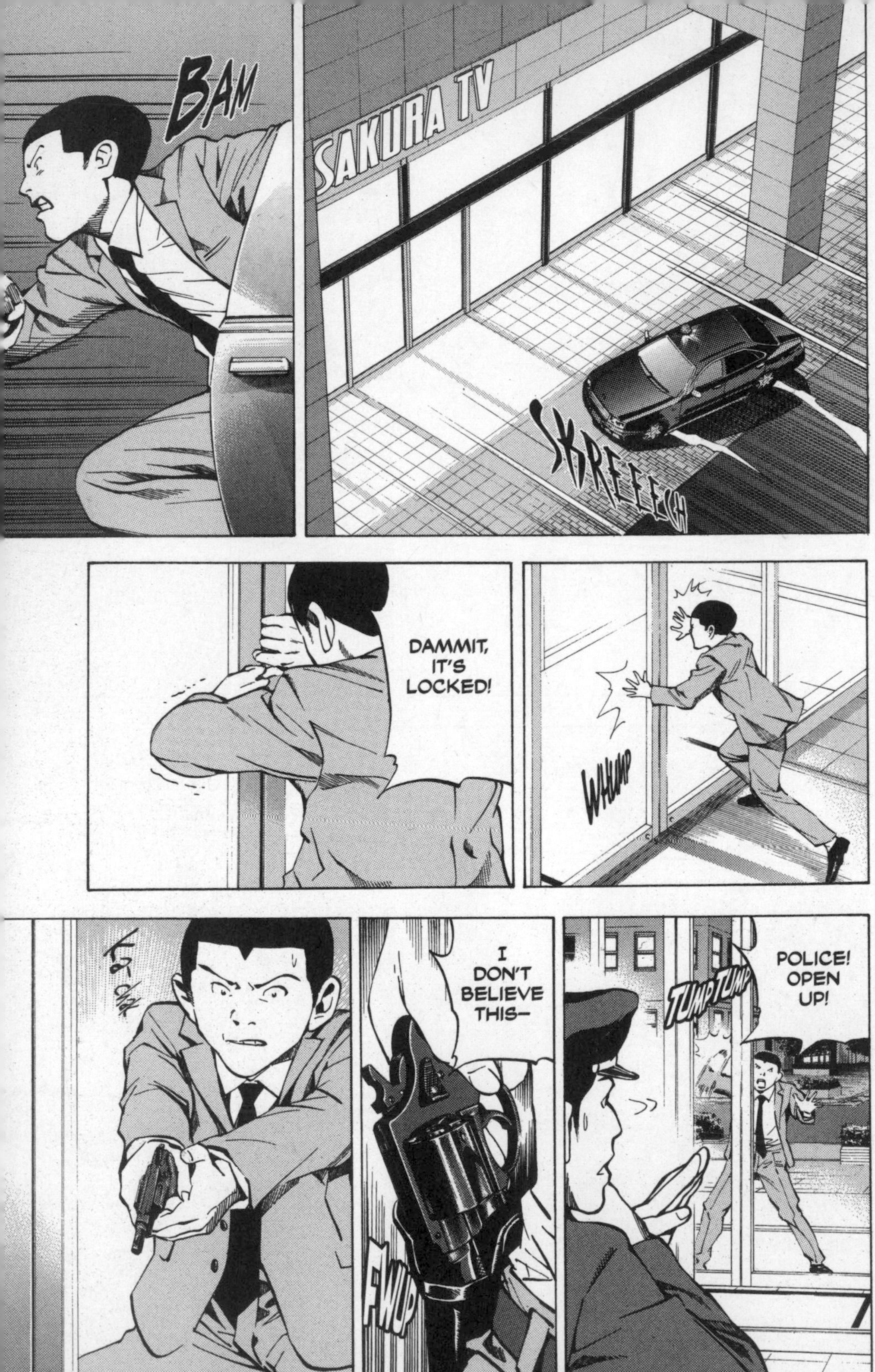
SAKURA TV
SKREEECH
BAM
WHUMP
DAMMIT, IT'S LOCKED!
TUMP TUMP
POLICE! OPEN UP!
I DON'T BELIEVE THIS—
FWUP

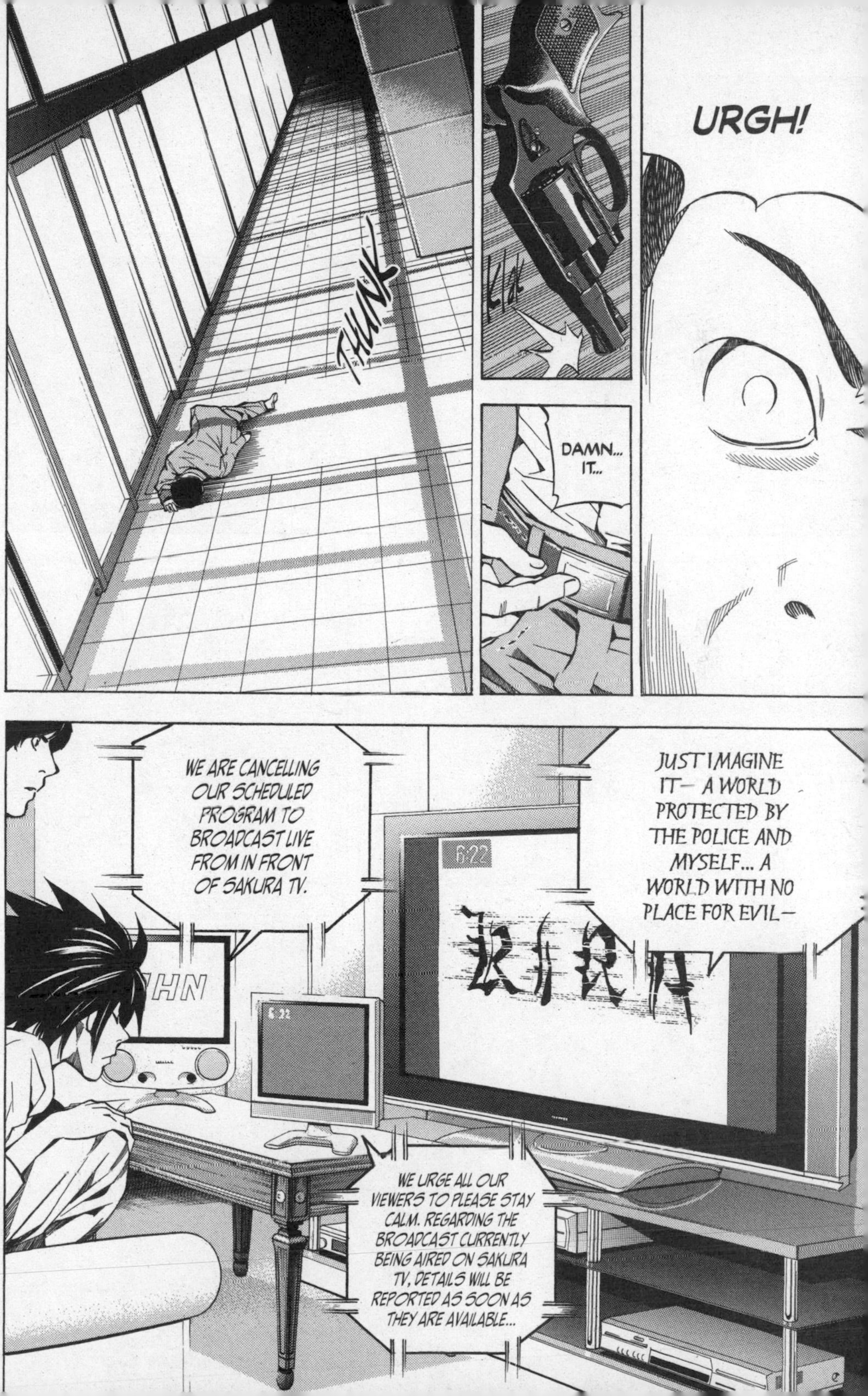
URGH!
DAMN... IT...
THUNK
JUST IMAGINE IT— A WORLD PROTECTED BY THE POLICE AND MYSELF... A WORLD WITH NO PLACE FOR EVIL—
6:22
WE ARE CANCELLING OUR SCHEDULED PROGRAM TO BROADCAST LIVE FROM IN FRONT OF SAKURA TV.
WE URGE ALL OUR VIEWERS TO PLEASE STAY CALM. REGARDING THE BROADCAST CURRENTLY BEING AIRED ON SAKURA TV, DETAILS WILL BE REPORTED AS SOON AS THEY ARE AVAILABLE...

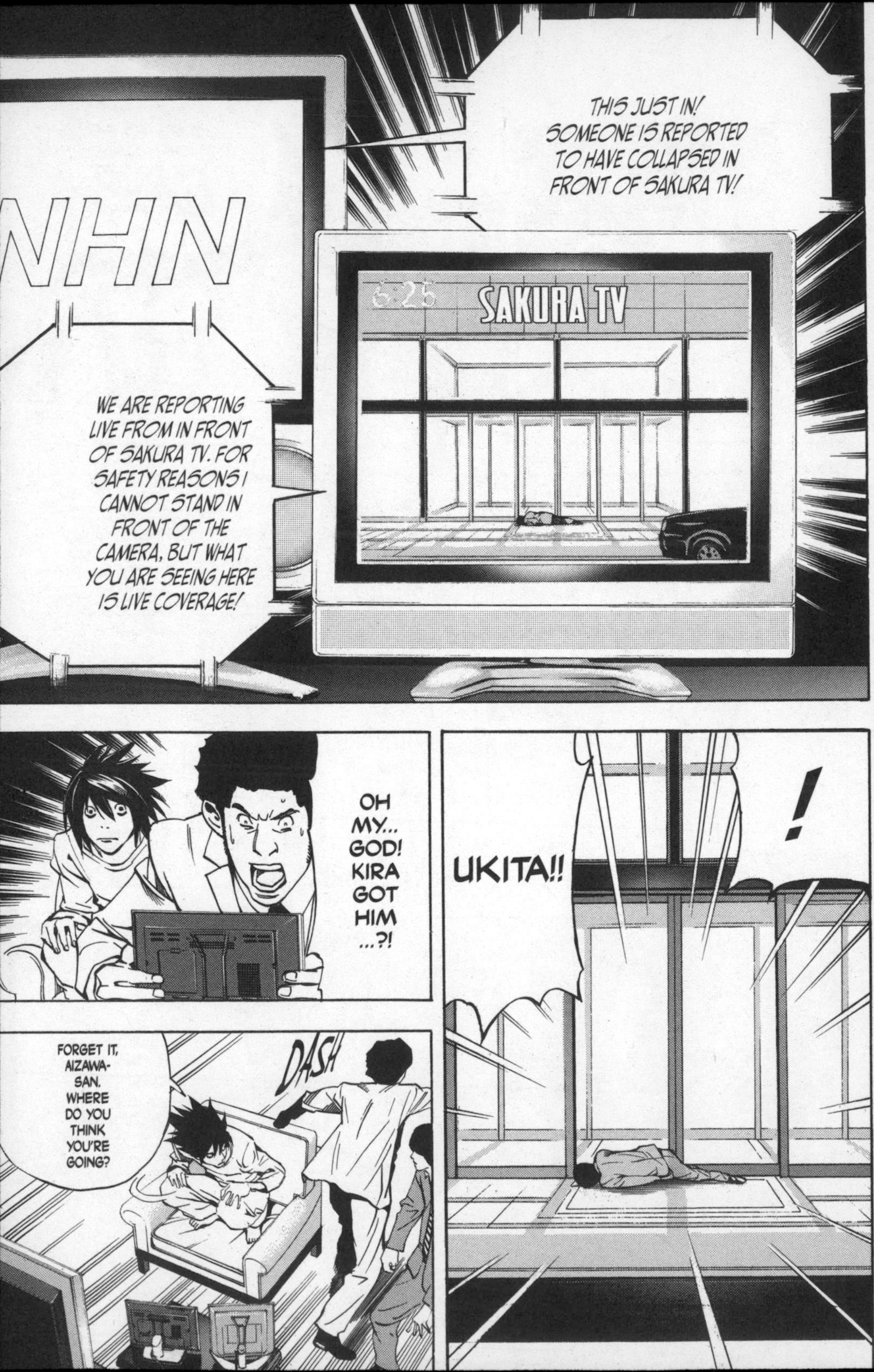
THIS JUST IN! SOMEONE IS REPORTED TO HAVE COLLAPSED IN FRONT OF SAKURA TV!
NHN
6:25
SAKURA TV
WE ARE REPORTING LIVE FROM IN FRONT OF SAKURA TV. FOR SAFETY REASONS I CANNOT STAND IN FRONT OF THE CAMERA, BUT WHAT YOU ARE SEEING HERE IS LIVE COVERAGE!
!
UKITA!!
OH MY... GOD! KIRA GOT HIM ...?!
DASH
FORGET IT, AIZAWA-SAN. WHERE DO YOU THINK YOU'RE GOING?

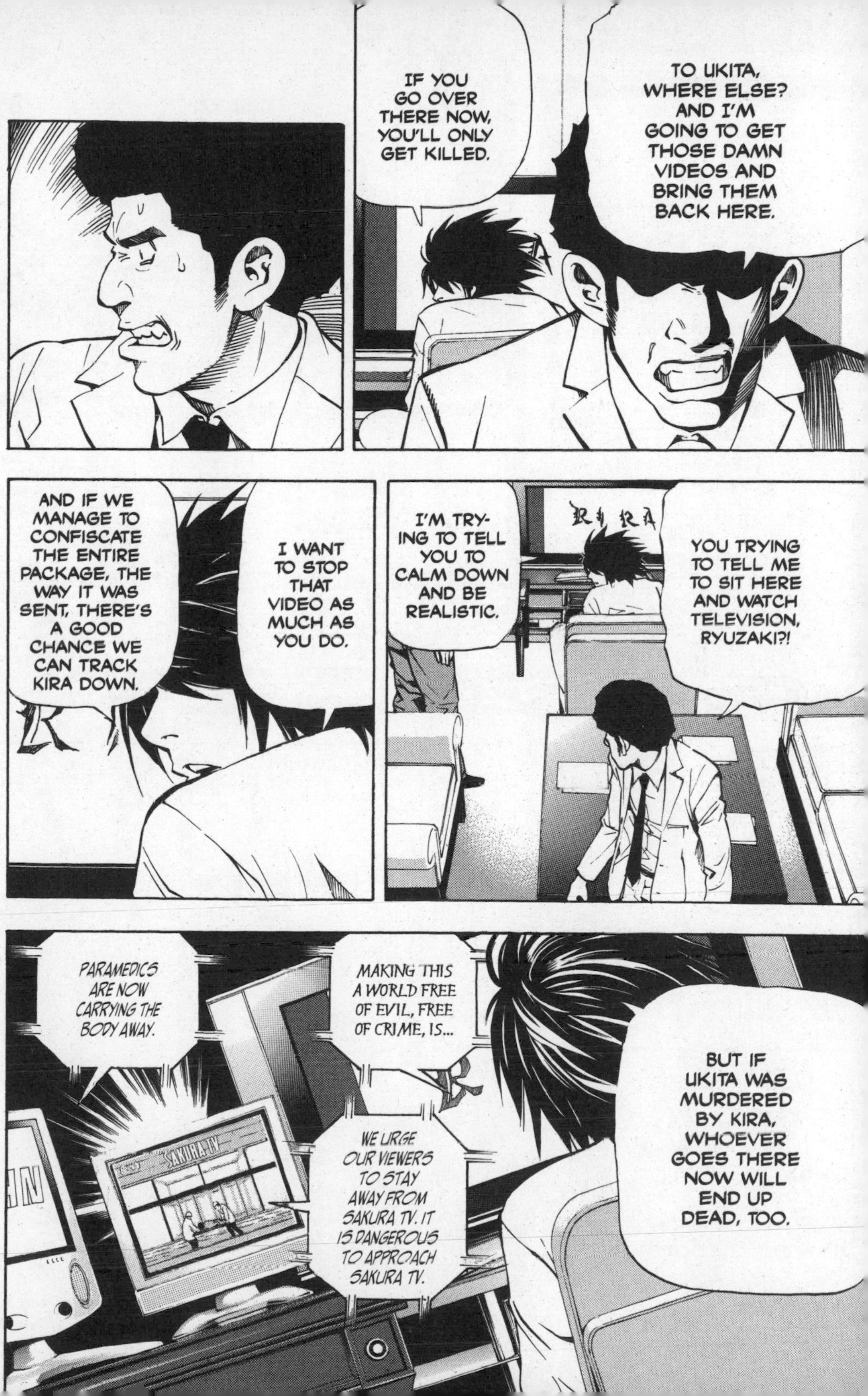
TO UKITA, WHERE ELSE? AND I'M GOING TO GET THOSE DAMN VIDEOS AND BRING THEM BACK HERE.
IF YOU GO OVER THERE NOW, YOU'LL ONLY GET KILLED.
KIRA
YOU TRYING TO TELL ME TO SIT HERE AND WATCH TELEVISION, RYUZAKI?!
I'M TRYING TO TELL YOU TO CALM DOWN AND BE REALISTIC.
I WANT TO STOP THAT VIDEO AS MUCH AS YOU DO.
AND IF WE MANAGE TO CONFISCATE THE ENTIRE PACKAGE, THE WAY IT WAS SENT, THERE'S A GOOD CHANCE WE CAN TRACK KIRA DOWN.
BUT IF UKITA WAS MURDERED BY KIRA, WHOEVER GOES THERE NOW WILL END UP DEAD, TOO.
MAKING THIS A WORLD FREE OF EVIL, FREE OF CRIME, IS...
PARAMEDICS ARE NOW CARRYING THE BODY AWAY.
SAKURA TV
WE URGE OUR VIEWERS TO STAY AWAY FROM SAKURA TV. IT IS DANGEROUS TO APPROACH SAKURA TV.

READ THIS WAY

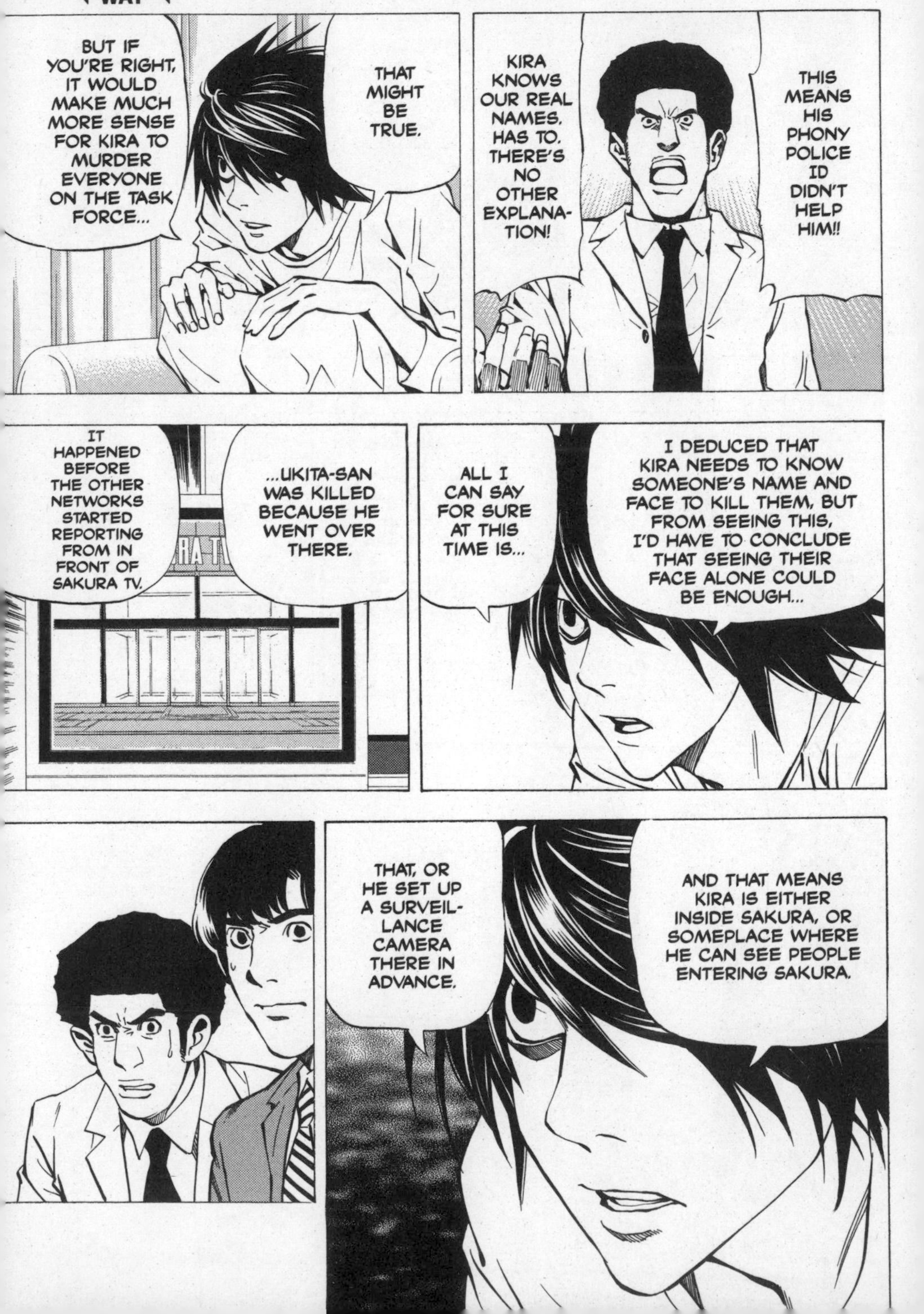
THIS MEANS HIS PHONY POLICE ID DIDN'T HELP HIM!!
KIRA KNOWS OUR REAL NAMES. HAS TO. THERE'S NO OTHER EXPLANATION!
THAT MIGHT BE TRUE.
BUT IF YOU'RE RIGHT, IT WOULD MAKE MUCH MORE SENSE FOR KIRA TO MURDER EVERYONE ON THE TASK FORCE...
I DEDUCED THAT KIRA NEEDS TO KNOW SOMEONE'S NAME AND FACE TO KILL THEM, BUT FROM SEEING THIS, I'D HAVE TO CONCLUDE THAT SEEING THEIR FACE ALONE COULD BE ENOUGH...
ALL I CAN SAY FOR SURE AT THIS TIME IS...
...UKITA-SAN WAS KILLED BECAUSE HE WENT OVER THERE.
IT HAPPENED BEFORE THE OTHER NETWORKS STARTED REPORTING FROM IN FRONT OF SAKURA TV.
AND THAT MEANS KIRA IS EITHER INSIDE SAKURA, OR SOMEPLACE WHERE HE CAN SEE PEOPLE ENTERING SAKURA.
THAT, OR HE SET UP A SURVEIL-LANCE CAMERA THERE IN ADVANCE.

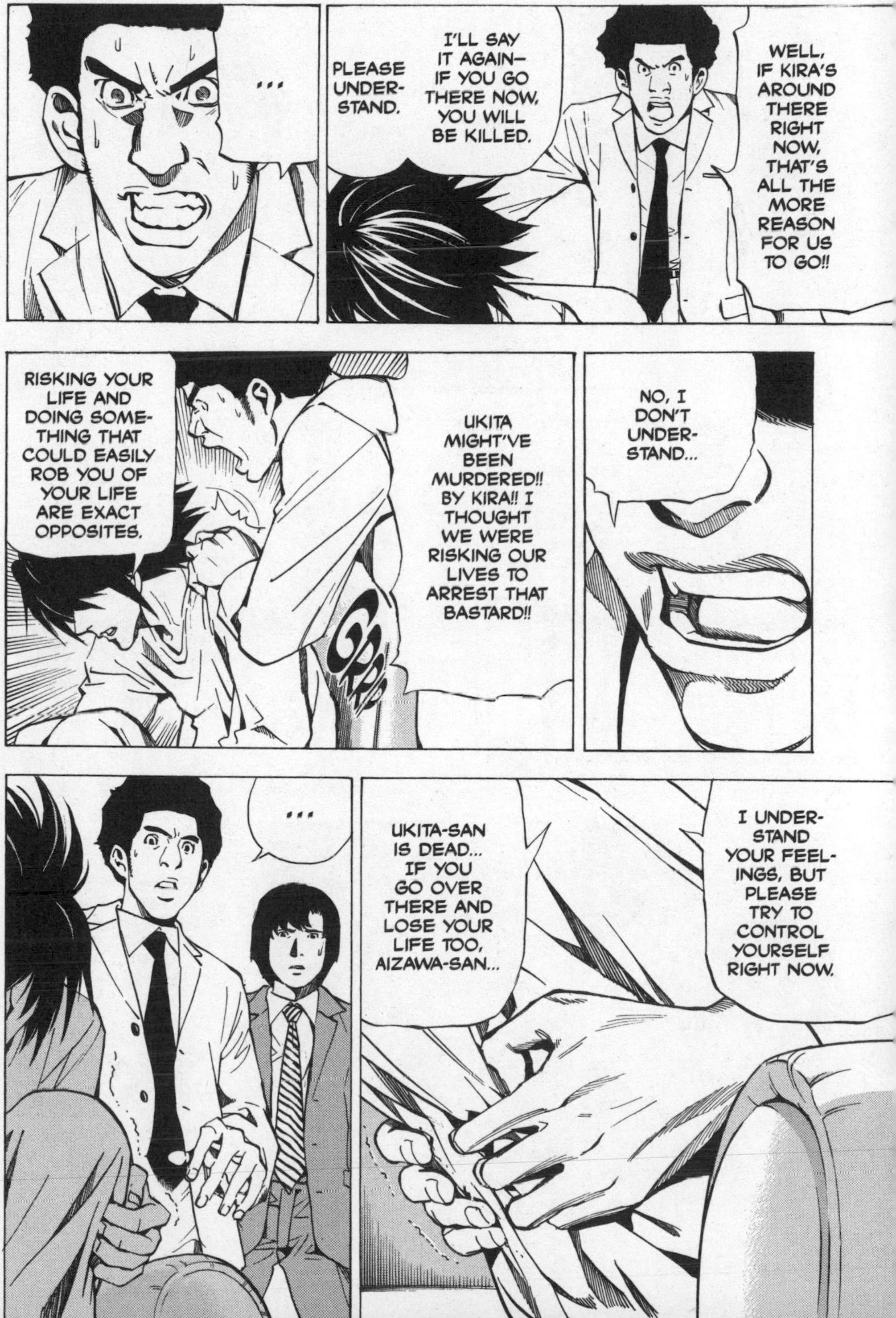
WELL, IF KIRA'S AROUND THERE RIGHT NOW, THAT'S ALL THE MORE REASON FOR US TO GO!!
I'LL SAY IT AGAIN— IF YOU GO THERE NOW, YOU WILL BE KILLED.
PLEASE UNDER-STAND.
...
NO, I DON'T UNDER-STAND...
UKITA MIGHT'VE BEEN MURDERED!! BY KIRA!! I THOUGHT WE WERE RISKING OUR LIVES TO ARREST THAT BASTARD!!
GRR
RISKING YOUR LIFE AND DOING SOME-THING THAT COULD EASILY ROB YOU OF YOUR LIFE ARE EXACT OPPOSITES.
I UNDER-STAND YOUR FEEL-INGS, BUT PLEASE TRY TO CONTROL YOURSELF RIGHT NOW.
UKITA-SAN IS DEAD... IF YOU GO OVER THERE AND LOSE YOUR LIFE TOO, AIZAWA-SAN...
...

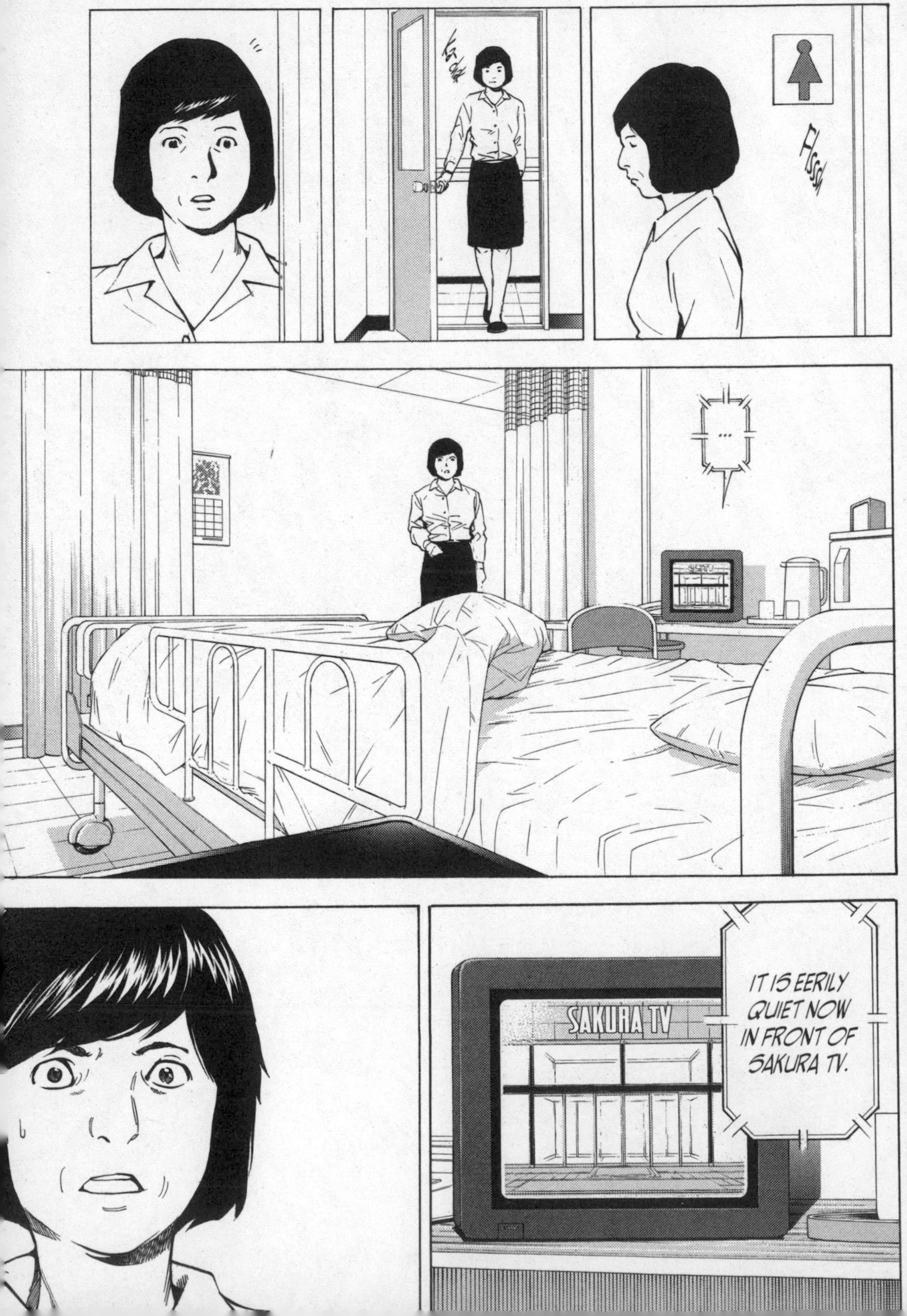
Flsssh
Ka-chak
...
SAKURA TV
IT IS EERILY QUIET NOW IN FRONT OF SAKURA TV.

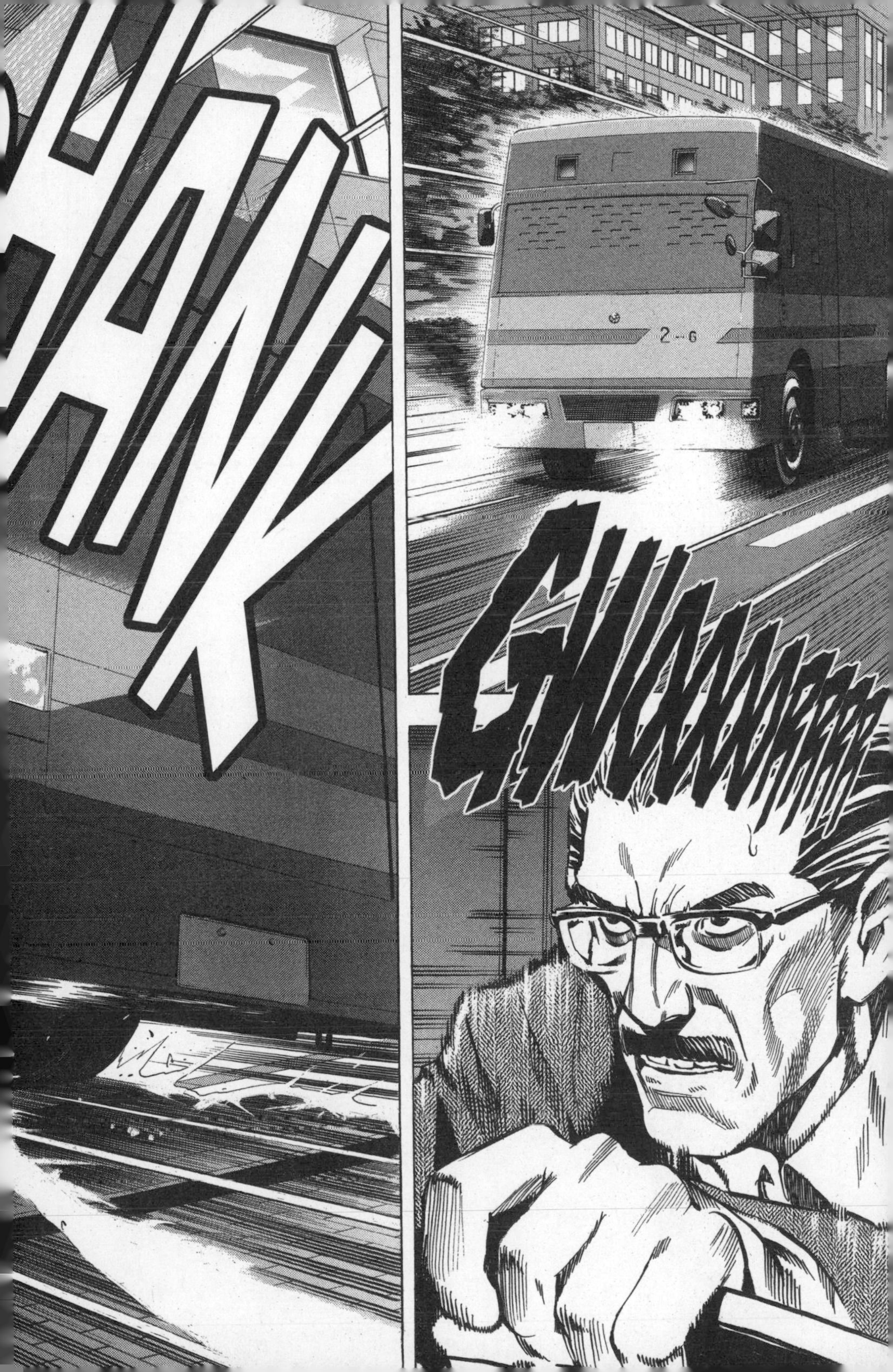
2-G
SHANK

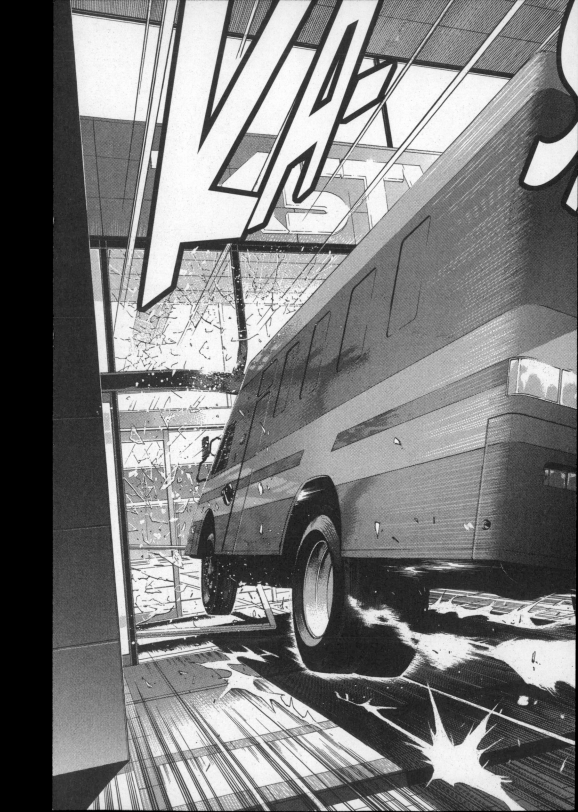

DEATH NOTE
How to use it
— — — XIV — — —

○ When the owner of the DEATH NOTE dies while the Note is being lent, its ownership will be transferred to the person who is holding it at that time.

デスノートを貸している時に所有者が死んだ場合、所有権は、その時、手にしている者に移る。

○ If the DEATH NOTE is stolen and the owner is killed by the thief, its ownership will automatically be transferred to the thief.

デスノートを盗まれ、その盗んだ者に所有者が殺された場合、所有権は自動的にその者に移る。

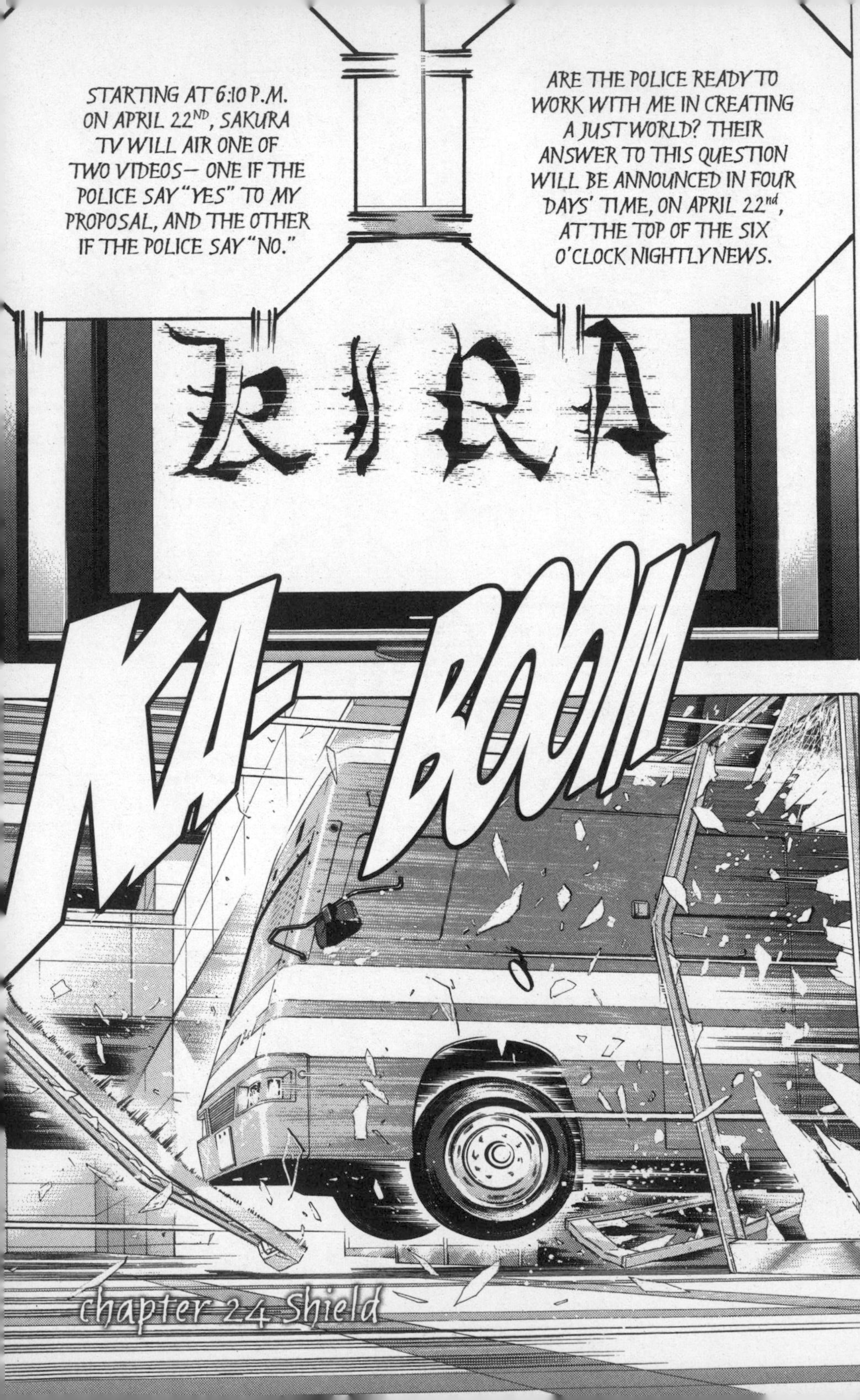
ARE THE POLICE READY TO WORK WITH ME IN CREATING A JUST WORLD? THEIR ANSWER TO THIS QUESTION WILL BE ANNOUNCED IN FOUR DAYS' TIME, ON APRIL 22nd, AT THE TOP OF THE SIX O'CLOCK NIGHTLY NEWS.
STARTING AT 6:10 P.M. ON APRIL 22ND, SAKURA TV WILL AIR ONE OF TWO VIDEOS— ONE IF THE POLICE SAY "YES" TO MY PROPOSAL, AND THE OTHER IF THE POLICE SAY "NO."
KIRA
KA-BOOM
chapter 24 Shield

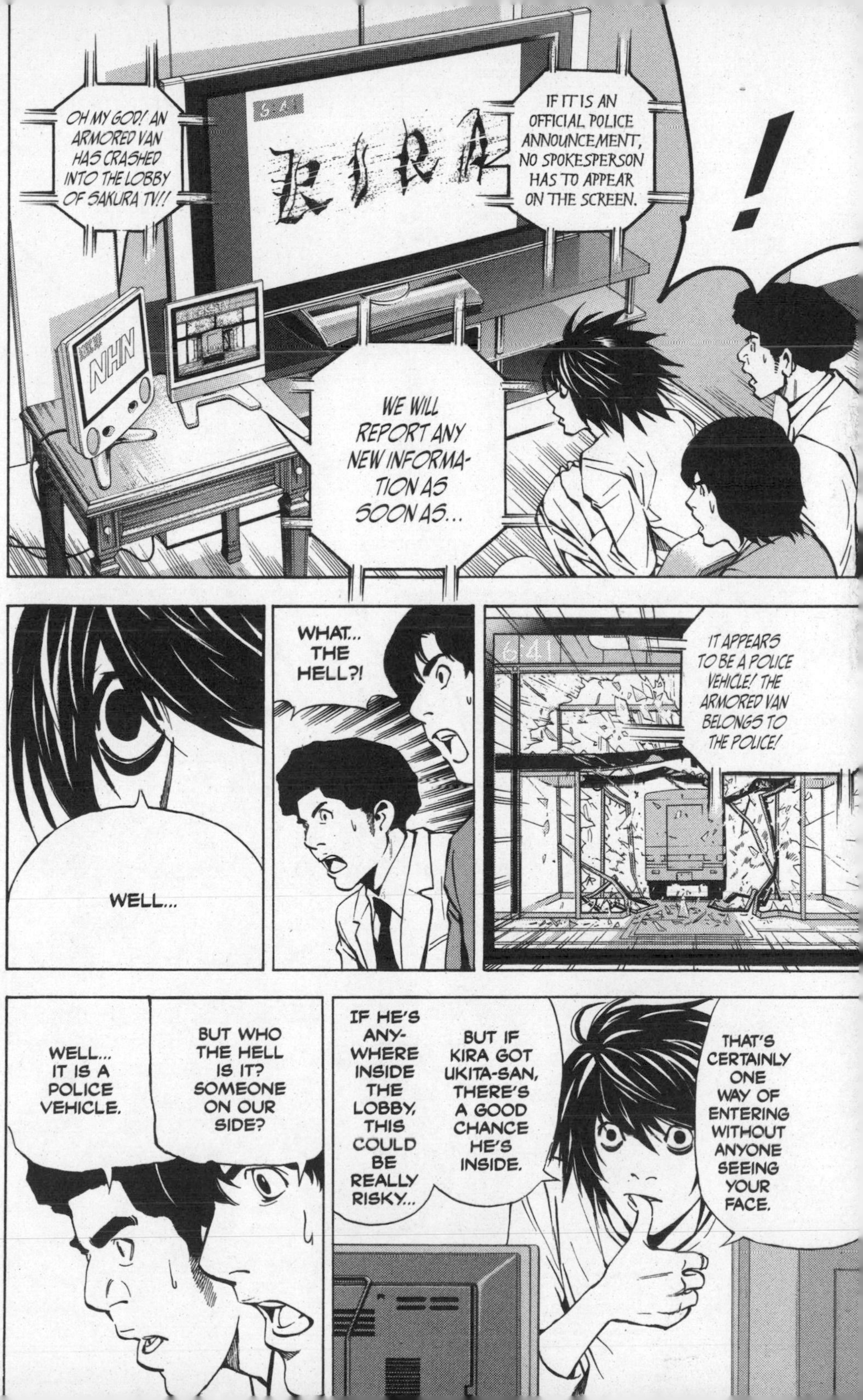
!
IF IT IS AN OFFICIAL POLICE ANNOUNCEMENT, NO SPOKESPERSON HAS TO APPEAR ON THE SCREEN.
OH MY GOD! AN ARMORED VAN HAS CRASHED INTO THE LOBBY OF SAKURA TV!!
WE WILL REPORT ANY NEW INFORMATION AS SOON AS...
IT APPEARS TO BE A POLICE VEHICLE! THE ARMORED VAN BELONGS TO THE POLICE!
WHAT... THE HELL?!
WELL...
THAT'S CERTAINLY ONE WAY OF ENTERING WITHOUT ANYONE SEEING YOUR FACE.
BUT IF KIRA GOT UKITA-SAN, THERE'S A GOOD CHANCE HE'S INSIDE.
IF HE'S ANYWHERE INSIDE THE LOBBY, THIS COULD BE REALLY RISKY...
BUT WHO THE HELL IS IT? SOMEONE ON OUR SIDE?
WELL... IT IS A POLICE VEHICLE.

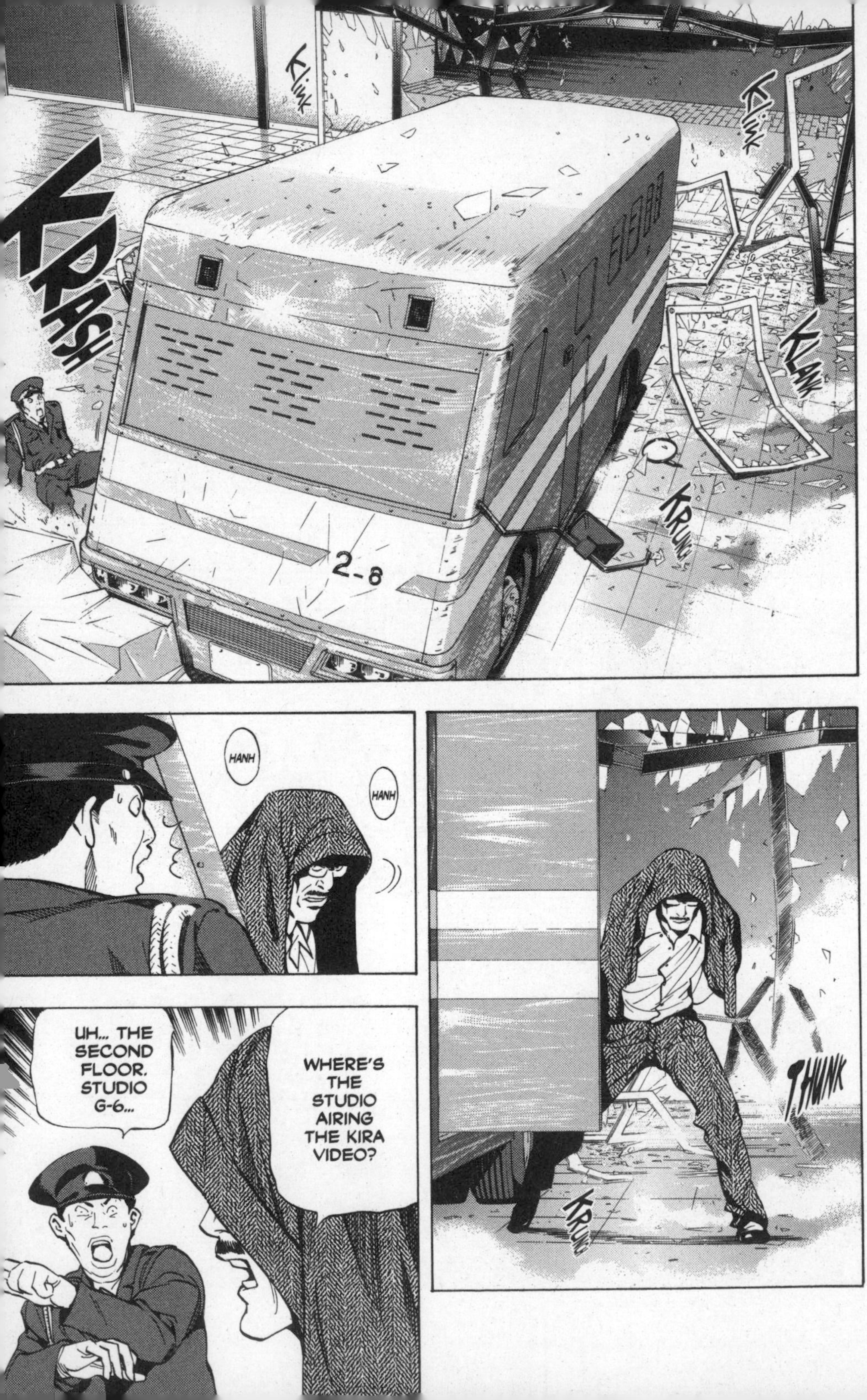
KLINK
KLANK
KRUNCH
KLINK
KRASH
THUNK
KRUNK
HANH
HANH
WHERE'S THE STUDIO AIRING THE KIRA VIDEO?
UH... THE SECOND FLOOR. STUDIO G-6...

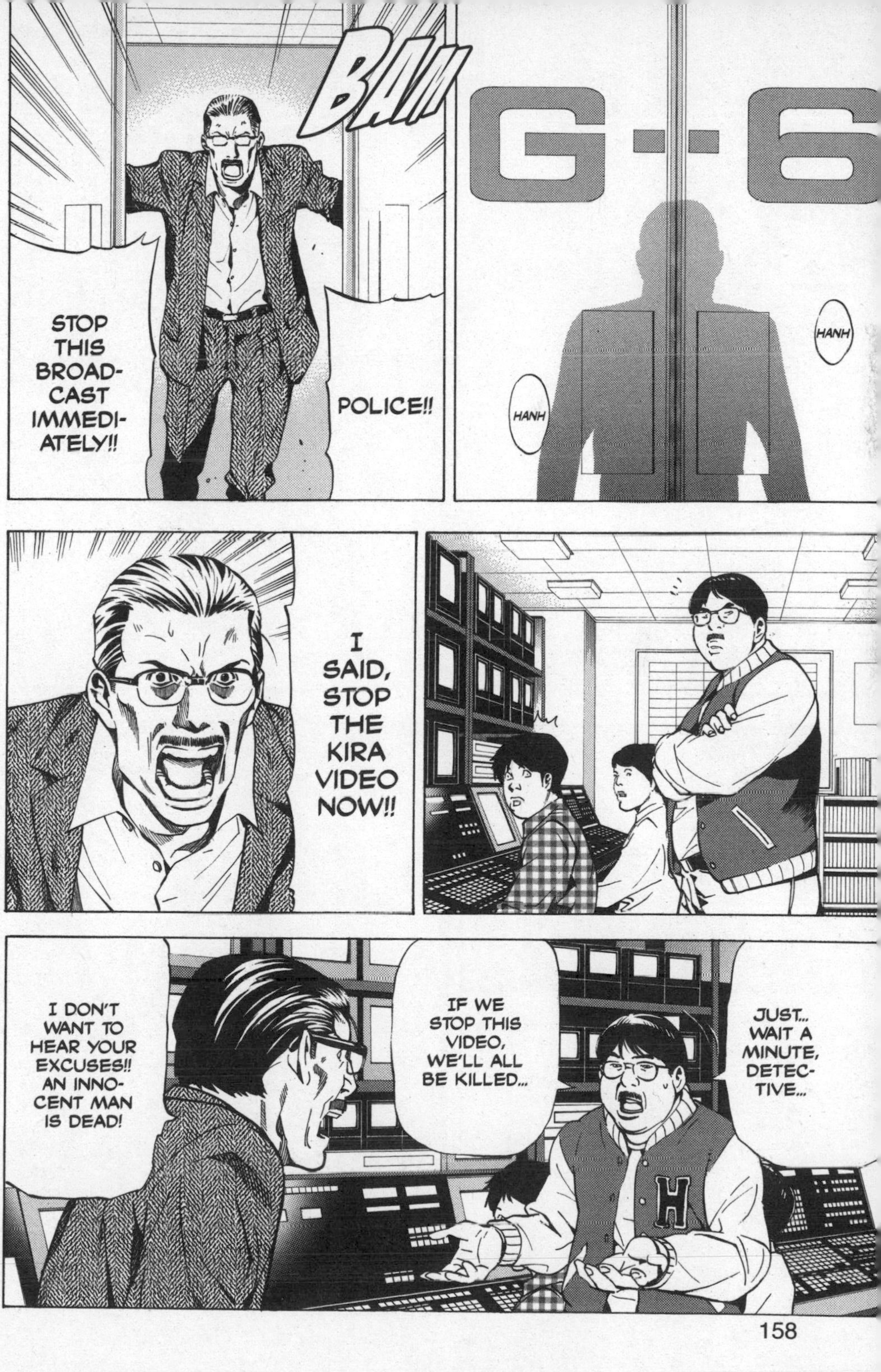
G-6
HANH
HANH
BAM
POLICE!!
STOP THIS BROADCAST IMMEDIATELY!!
I SAID, STOP THE KIRA VIDEO NOW!!
JUST... WAIT A MINUTE, DETECTIVE...
IF WE STOP THIS VIDEO, WE'LL ALL BE KILLED...
I DON'T WANT TO HEAR YOUR EXCUSES!! AN INNOCENT MAN IS DEAD!

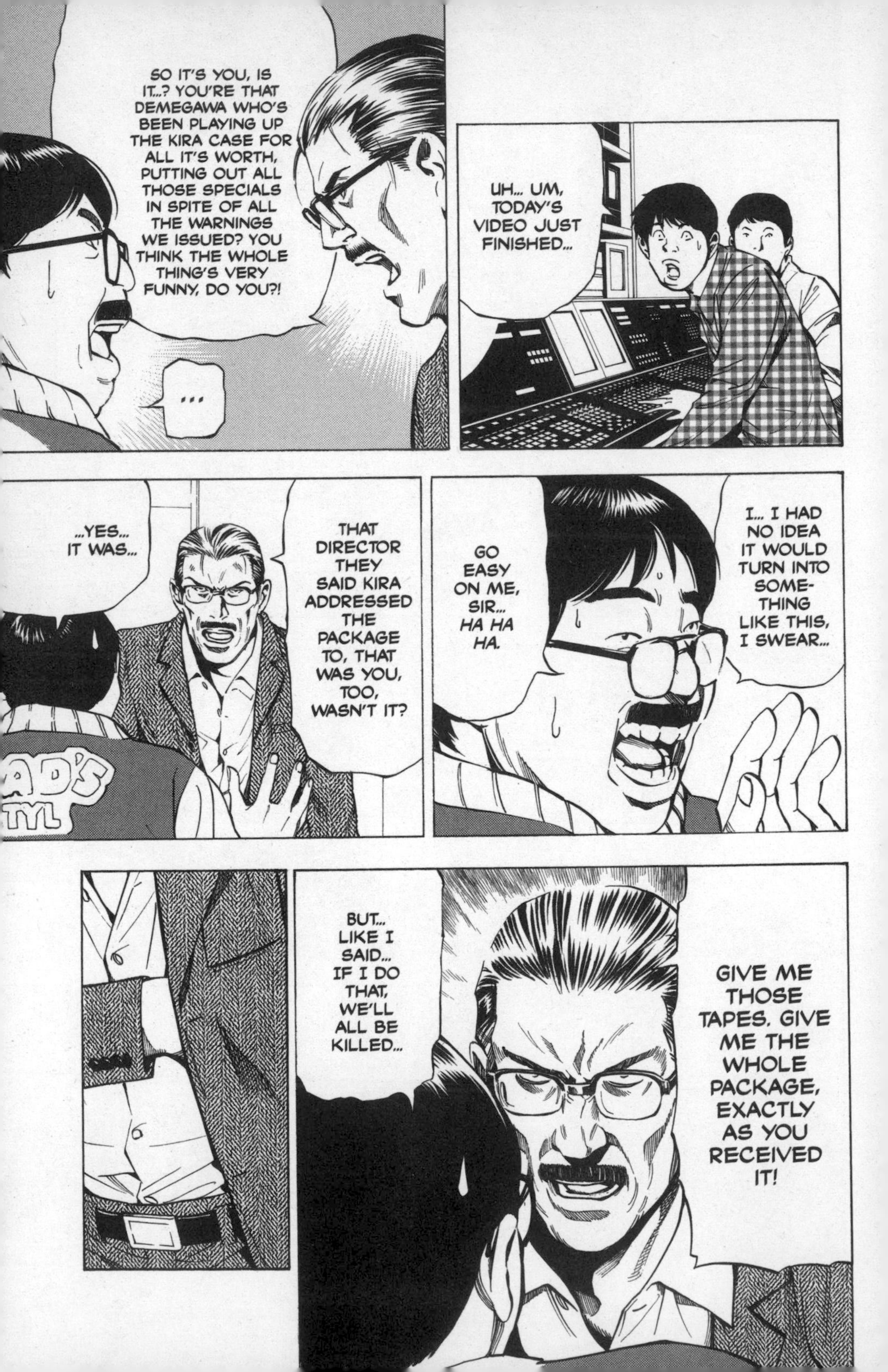
UH... UM, TODAY'S VIDEO JUST FINISHED...
SO IT'S YOU, IS IT...? YOU'RE THAT DEMEGAWA WHO'S BEEN PLAYING UP THE KIRA CASE FOR ALL IT'S WORTH, PUTTING OUT ALL THOSE SPECIALS IN SPITE OF ALL THE WARNINGS WE ISSUED? YOU THINK THE WHOLE THING'S VERY FUNNY, DO YOU?!
...
I... I HAD NO IDEA IT WOULD TURN INTO SOME-THING LIKE THIS, I SWEAR...
GO EASY ON ME, SIR... *HA HA HA.*
THAT DIRECTOR THEY SAID KIRA ADDRESSED THE PACKAGE TO, THAT WAS YOU, TOO, WASN'T IT?
...YES... IT WAS...
GIVE ME THOSE TAPES. GIVE ME THE WHOLE PACKAGE, EXACTLY AS YOU RECEIVED IT!
BUT... LIKE I SAID... IF I DO THAT, WE'LL ALL BE KILLED...

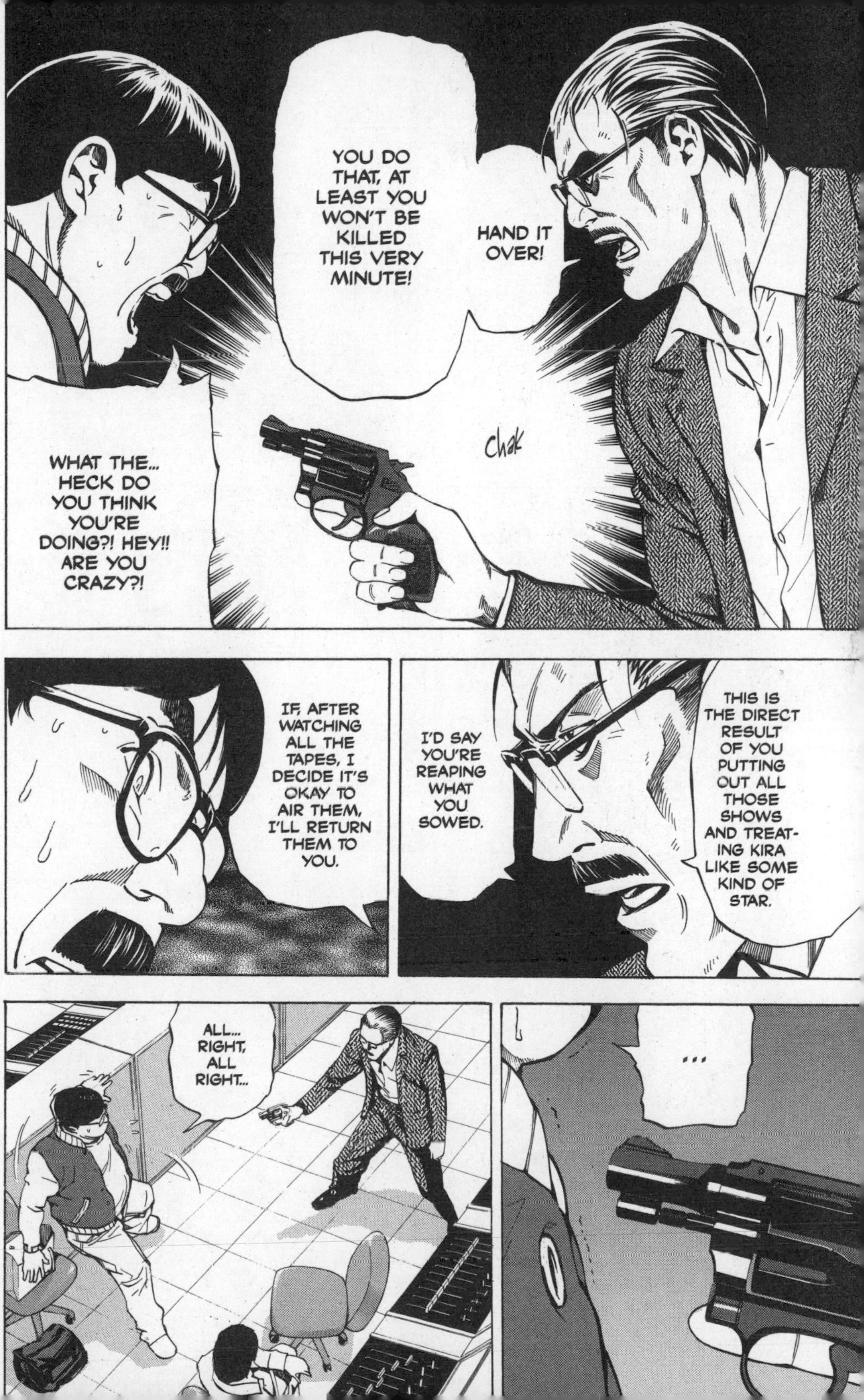
HAND IT OVER!
YOU DO THAT, AT LEAST YOU WON'T BE KILLED THIS VERY MINUTE!
Chak
WHAT THE... HECK DO YOU THINK YOU'RE DOING?! HEY!! ARE YOU CRAZY?!
THIS IS THE DIRECT RESULT OF YOU PUTTING OUT ALL THOSE SHOWS AND TREATING KIRA LIKE SOME KIND OF STAR.
I'D SAY YOU'RE REAPING WHAT YOU SOWED.
IF, AFTER WATCHING ALL THE TAPES, I DECIDE IT'S OKAY TO AIR THEM, I'LL RETURN THEM TO YOU.
...
ALL... RIGHT, ALL RIGHT...

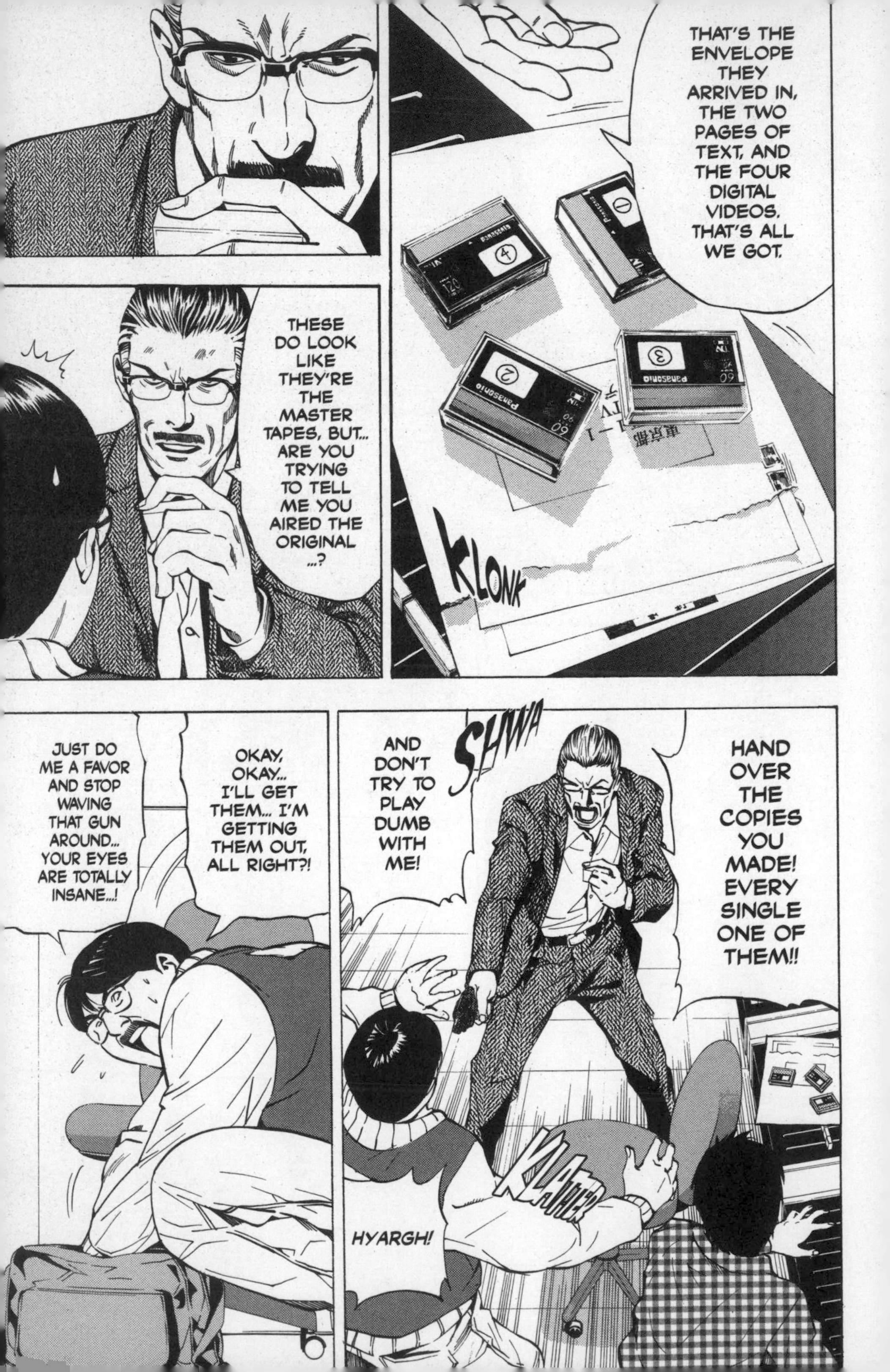
THAT'S THE ENVELOPE THEY ARRIVED IN, THE TWO PAGES OF TEXT, AND THE FOUR DIGITAL VIDEOS. THAT'S ALL WE GOT.
KLONK
THESE DO LOOK LIKE THEY'RE THE MASTER TAPES, BUT... ARE YOU TRYING TO TELL ME YOU AIRED THE ORIGINAL ...?
HAND OVER THE COPIES YOU MADE! EVERY SINGLE ONE OF THEM!!
SHWA
AND DON'T TRY TO PLAY DUMB WITH ME!
HYARGH!
OKAY, OKAY... I'LL GET THEM... I'M GETTING THEM OUT, ALL RIGHT?!
JUST DO ME A FAVOR AND STOP WAVING THAT GUN AROUND... YOUR EYES ARE TOTALLY INSANE...!

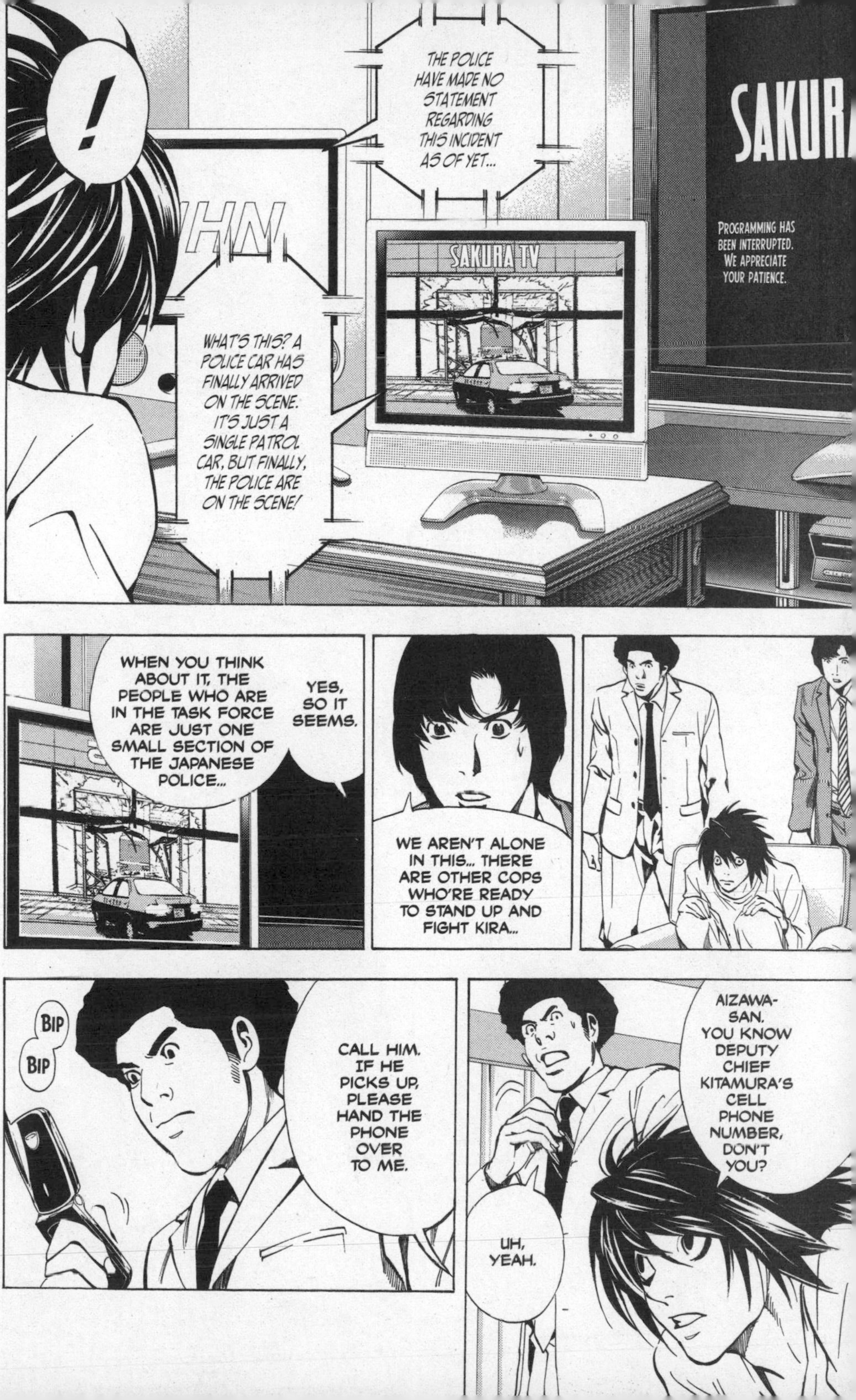
SAKURA
PROGRAMMING HAS BEEN INTERRUPTED. WE APPRECIATE YOUR PATIENCE.
THE POLICE HAVE MADE NO STATEMENT REGARDING THIS INCIDENT AS OF YET...
!
SAKURA TV
WHAT'S THIS? A POLICE CAR HAS FINALLY ARRIVED ON THE SCENE. IT'S JUST A SINGLE PATROL CAR, BUT FINALLY, THE POLICE ARE ON THE SCENE!
WE AREN'T ALONE IN THIS... THERE ARE OTHER COPS WHO'RE READY TO STAND UP AND FIGHT KIRA...
WHEN YOU THINK ABOUT IT, THE PEOPLE WHO ARE IN THE TASK FORCE ARE JUST ONE SMALL SECTION OF THE JAPANESE POLICE...
YES, SO IT SEEMS.
AIZAWA-SAN, YOU KNOW DEPUTY CHIEF KITAMURA'S CELL PHONE NUMBER, DON'T YOU?
UH, YEAH.
CALL HIM. IF HE PICKS UP, PLEASE HAND THE PHONE OVER TO ME.
BIP
BIP

READ THIS WAY

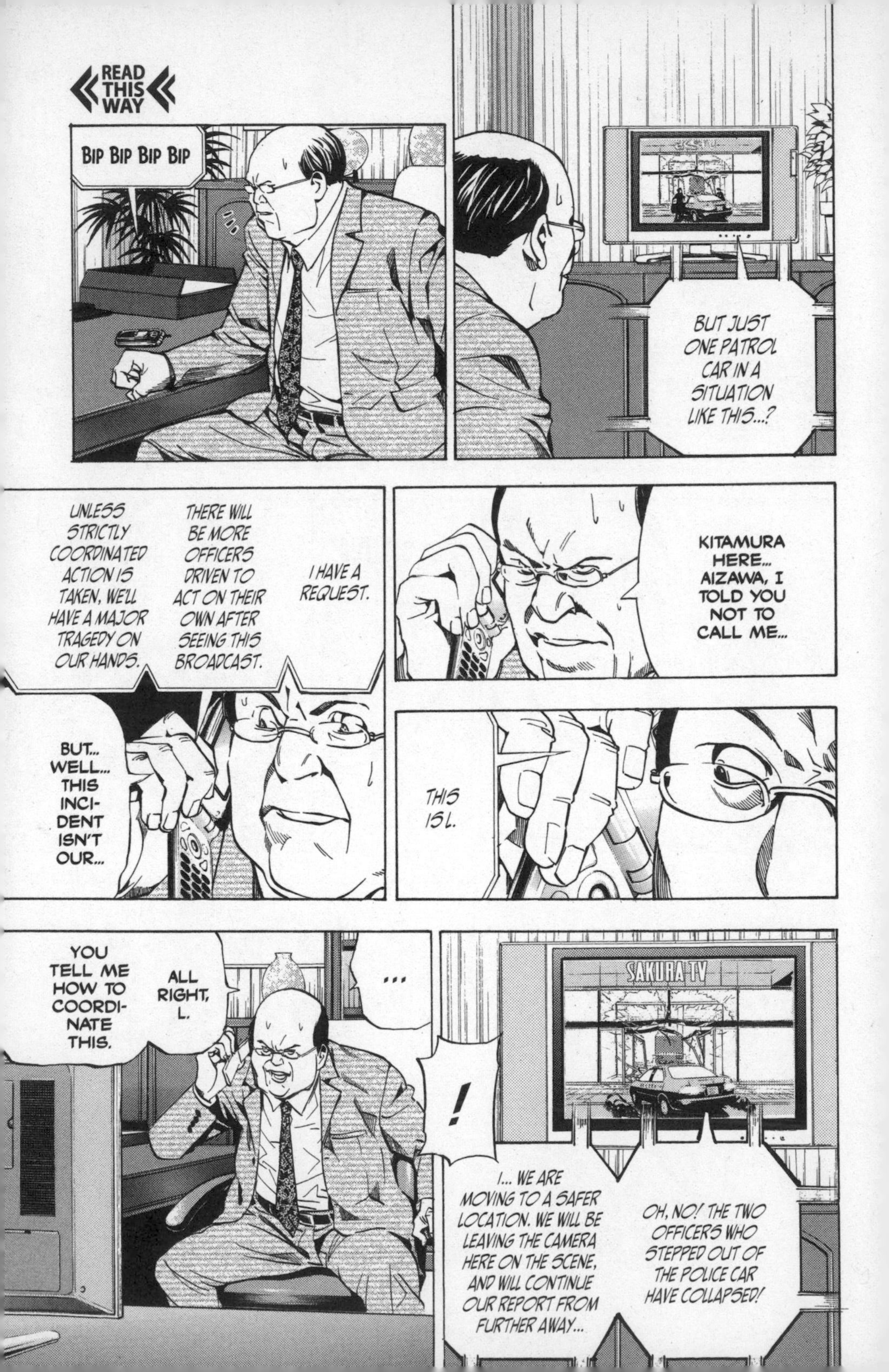
BUT JUST ONE PATROL CAR IN A SITUATION LIKE THIS...?
Bip Bip Bip Bip
KITAMURA HERE... AIZAWA, I TOLD YOU NOT TO CALL ME...
I HAVE A REQUEST.
THERE WILL BE MORE OFFICERS DRIVEN TO ACT ON THEIR OWN AFTER SEEING THIS BROADCAST.
UNLESS STRICTLY COORDINATED ACTION IS TAKEN, WE'LL HAVE A MAJOR TRAGEDY ON OUR HANDS.
THIS IS L.
BUT... WELL... THIS INCI-DENT ISN'T OUR...
SAKURA TV
OH, NO! THE TWO OFFICERS WHO STEPPED OUT OF THE POLICE CAR HAVE COLLAPSED!
I... WE ARE MOVING TO A SAFER LOCATION. WE WILL BE LEAVING THE CAMERA HERE ON THE SCENE, AND WILL CONTINUE OUR REPORT FROM FURTHER AWAY...
!
...
ALL RIGHT, L.
YOU TELL ME HOW TO COORDINATE THIS.

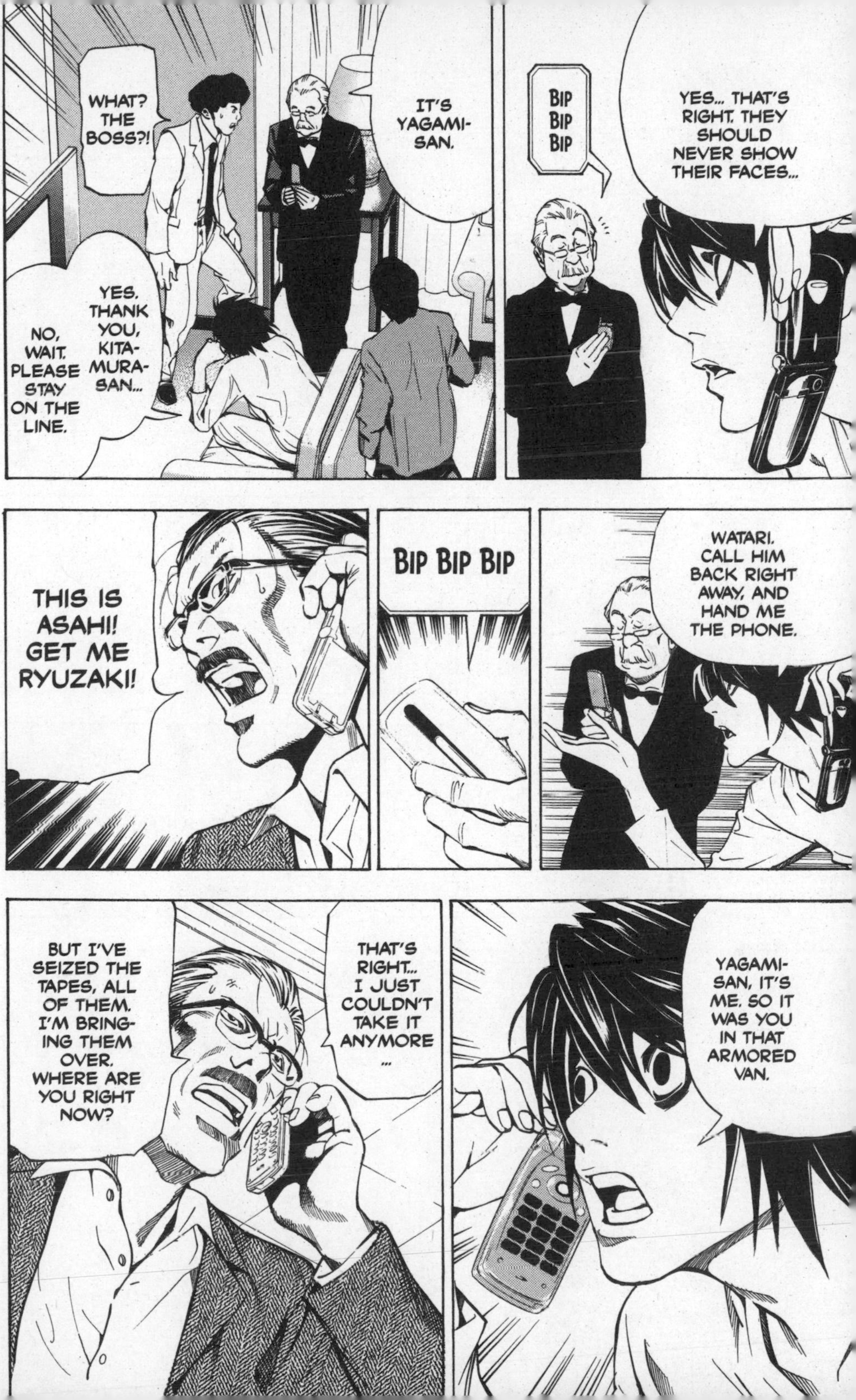

YES... THAT'S RIGHT. THEY SHOULD NEVER SHOW THEIR FACES...
BIP BIP BIP
IT'S YAGAMI-SAN.
WHAT? THE BOSS?!
YES. THANK YOU, KITAMURA-SAN...
NO, WAIT. PLEASE STAY ON THE LINE.
WATARI. CALL HIM BACK RIGHT AWAY, AND HAND ME THE PHONE.
BIP BIP BIP
THIS IS ASAHI! GET ME RYUZAKI!
YAGAMI-SAN, IT'S ME. SO IT WAS YOU IN THAT ARMORED VAN.
THAT'S RIGHT... I JUST COULDN'T TAKE IT ANYMORE ...
BUT I'VE SEIZED THE TAPES, ALL OF THEM. I'M BRINGING THEM OVER. WHERE ARE YOU RIGHT NOW?

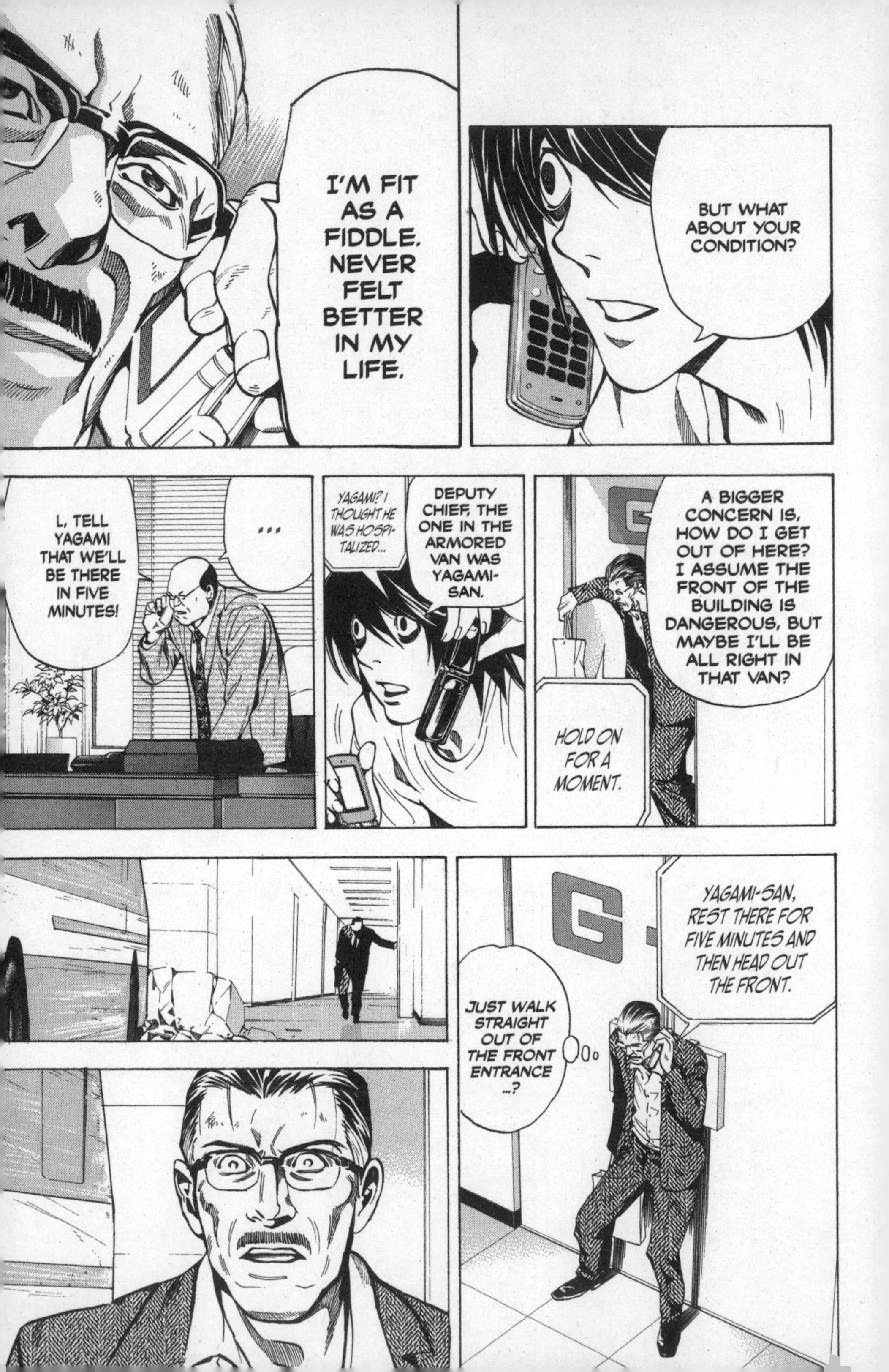
BUT WHAT ABOUT YOUR CONDITION?
I'M FIT AS A FIDDLE. NEVER FELT BETTER IN MY LIFE.
A BIGGER CONCERN IS, HOW DO I GET OUT OF HERE? I ASSUME THE FRONT OF THE BUILDING IS DANGEROUS, BUT MAYBE I'LL BE ALL RIGHT IN THAT VAN?
HOLD ON FOR A MOMENT.
DEPUTY CHIEF, THE ONE IN THE ARMORED VAN WAS YAGAMI-SAN.
YAGAMI? I THOUGHT HE WAS HOSPITALIZED...
...
L, TELL YAGAMI THAT WE'LL BE THERE IN FIVE MINUTES!
YAGAMI-SAN, REST THERE FOR FIVE MINUTES AND THEN HEAD OUT THE FRONT.
JUST WALK STRAIGHT OUT OF THE FRONT ENTRANCE ...?

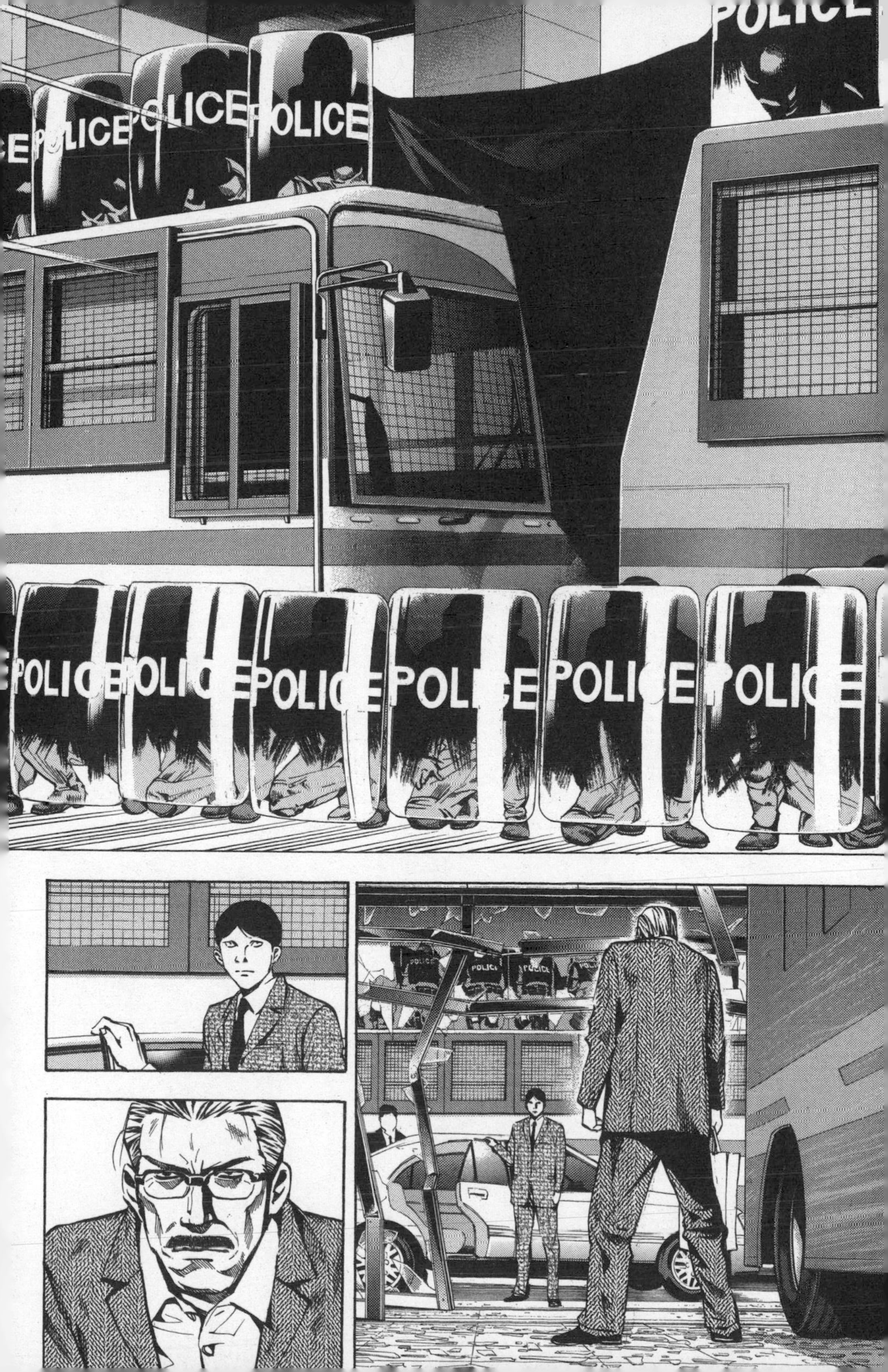
POLICE
POLICE
POLICE
POLICE
POLICE
POLICE
POLICE
POLICE
POLICE
POLICE
POLICE
POLICE

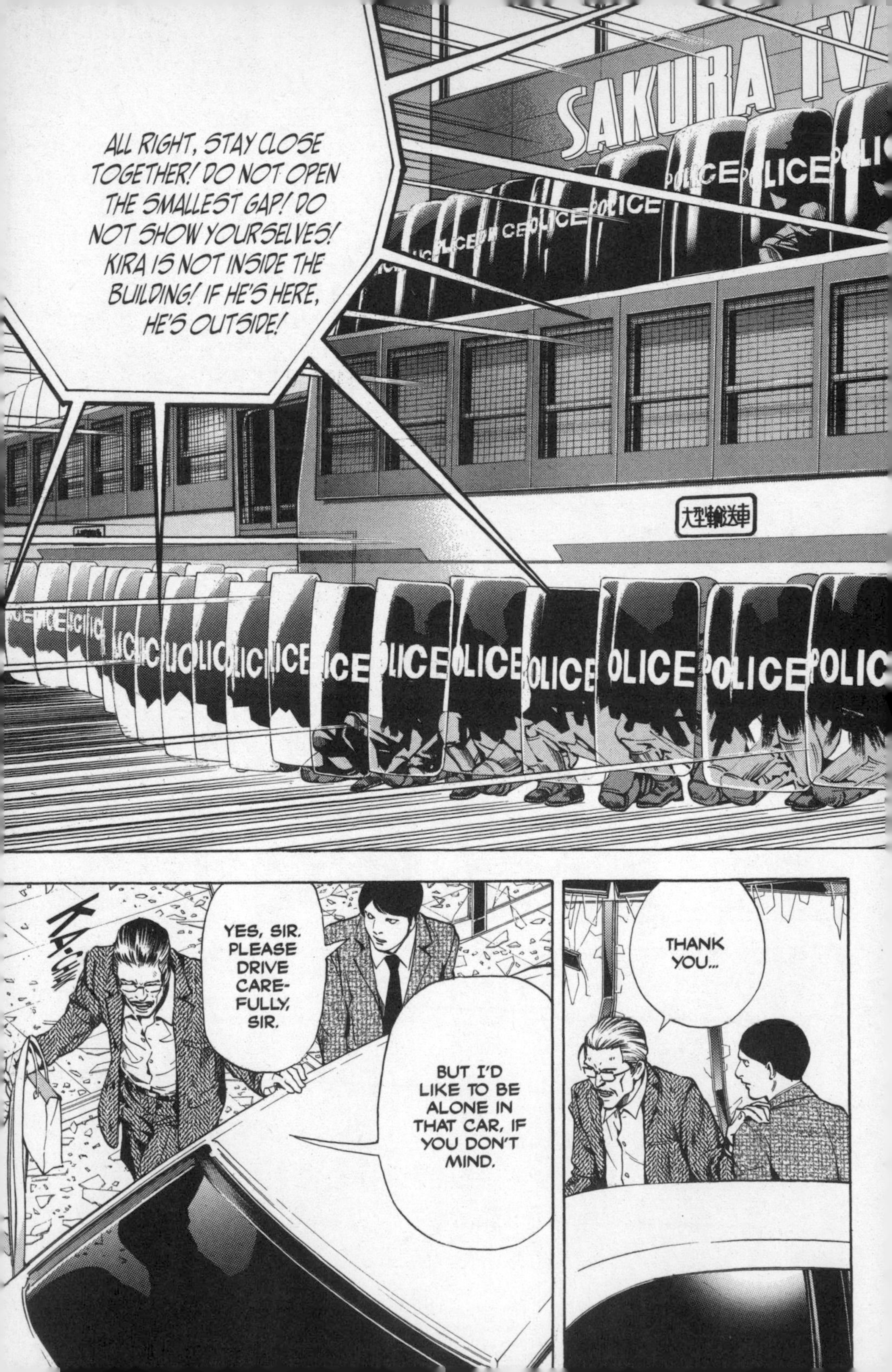
ALL RIGHT, STAY CLOSE TOGETHER! DO NOT OPEN THE SMALLEST GAP! DO NOT SHOW YOURSELVES! KIRA IS NOT INSIDE THE BUILDING! IF HE'S HERE, HE'S OUTSIDE!
SAKURA TV
大型輸送車
THANK YOU...
BUT I'D LIKE TO BE ALONE IN THAT CAR, IF YOU DON'T MIND.
YES, SIR. PLEASE DRIVE CAREFULLY, SIR.

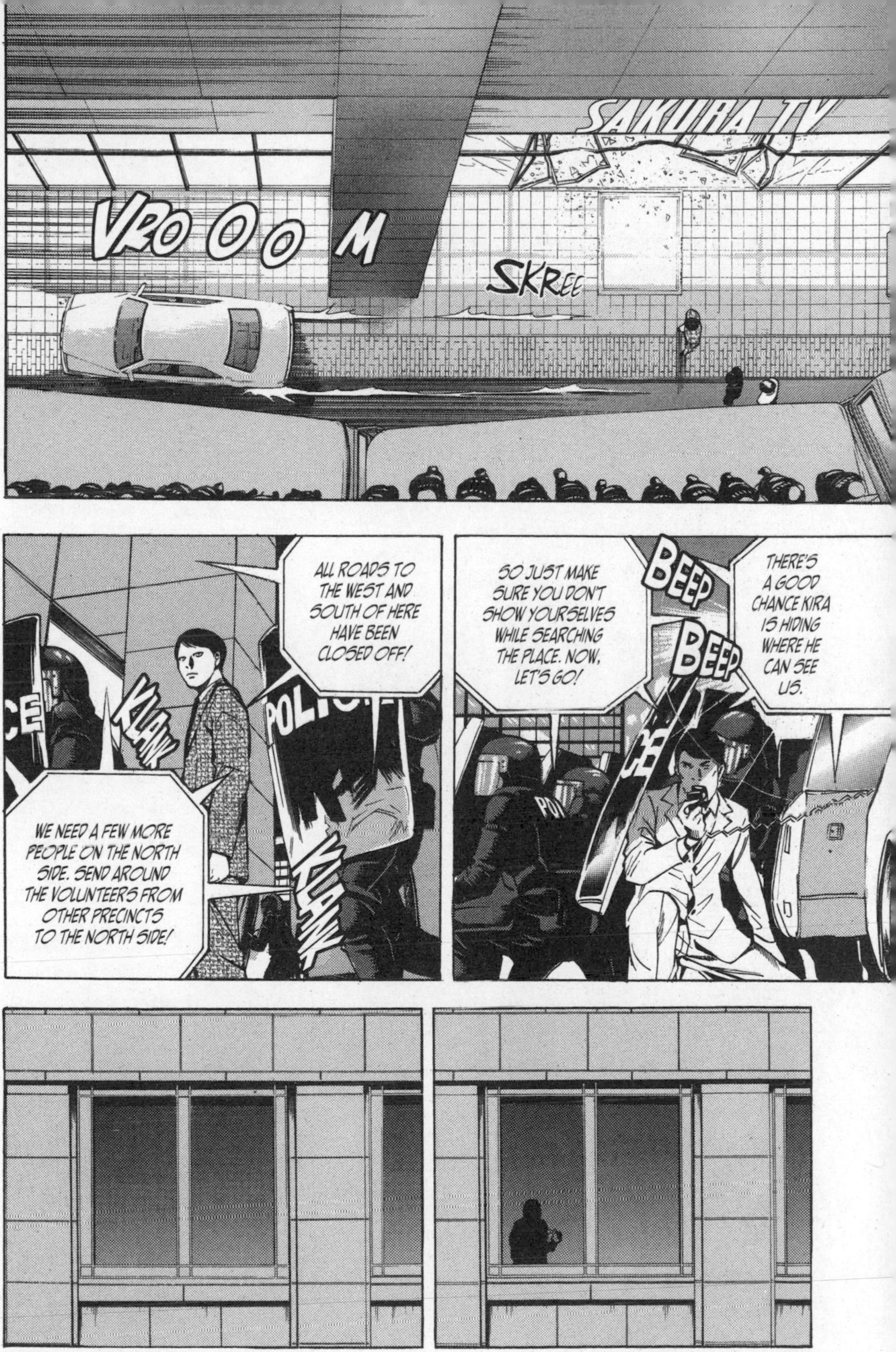
SAKURA TV
VROOOOM
SKREE
BEEP
BEEP
THERE'S A GOOD CHANCE KIRA IS HIDING WHERE HE CAN SEE US.
SO JUST MAKE SURE YOU DON'T SHOW YOURSELVES WHILE SEARCHING THE PLACE. NOW, LET'S GO!
ALL ROADS TO THE WEST AND SOUTH OF HERE HAVE BEEN CLOSED OFF!
KLANK
WE NEED A FEW MORE PEOPLE ON THE NORTH SIDE. SEND AROUND THE VOLUNTEERS FROM OTHER PRECINCTS TO THE NORTH SIDE!
KLANK

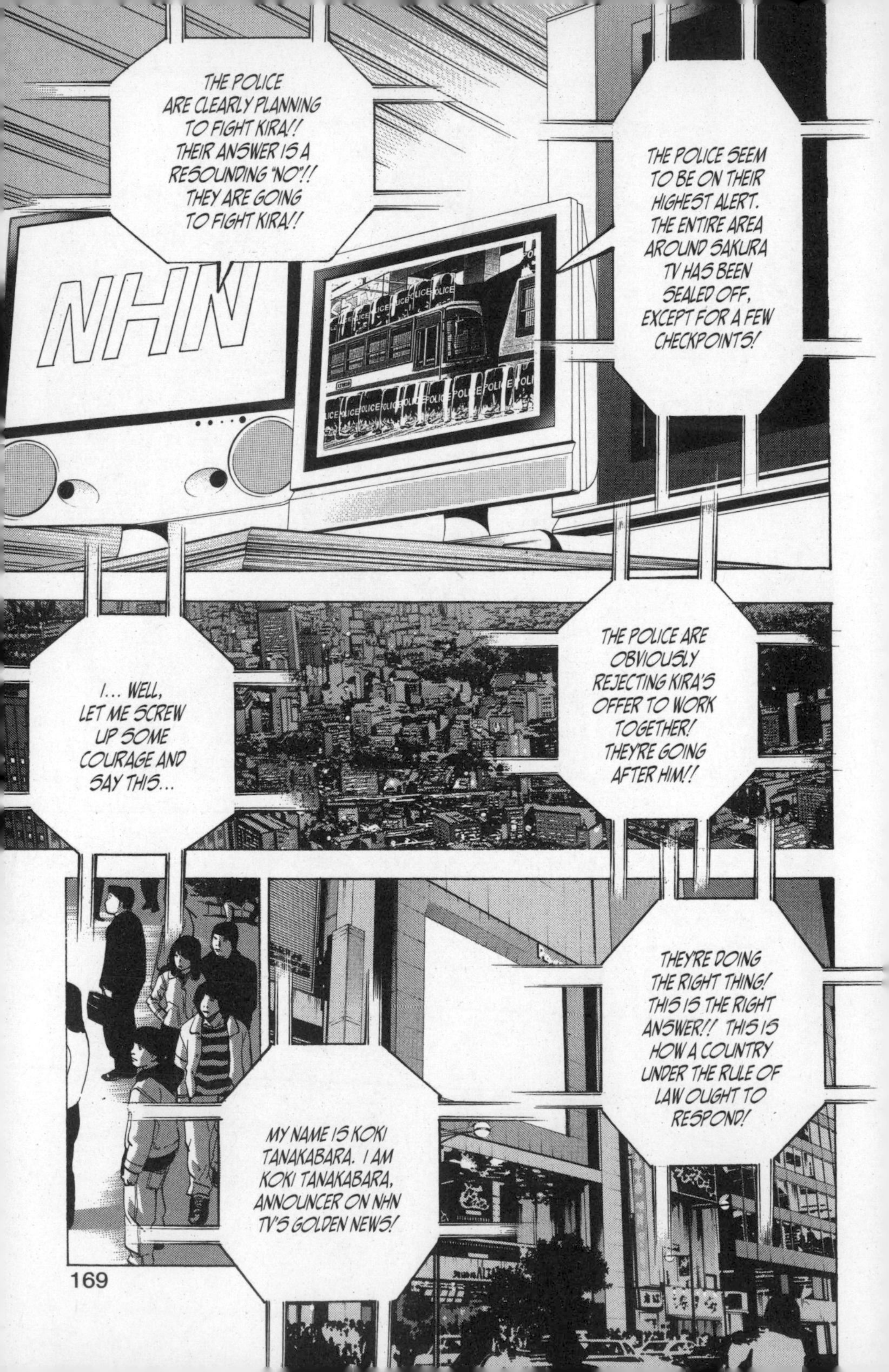
THE POLICE SEEM TO BE ON THEIR HIGHEST ALERT. THE ENTIRE AREA AROUND SAKURA TV HAS BEEN SEALED OFF, EXCEPT FOR A FEW CHECKPOINTS!
THE POLICE ARE CLEARLY PLANNING TO FIGHT KIRA!! THEIR ANSWER IS A RESOUNDING "NO"!! THEY ARE GOING TO FIGHT KIRA!!
NHN
THE POLICE ARE OBVIOUSLY REJECTING KIRA'S OFFER TO WORK TOGETHER! THEY'RE GOING AFTER HIM!!
I... WELL, LET ME SCREW UP SOME COURAGE AND SAY THIS...
THEY'RE DOING THE RIGHT THING! THIS IS THE RIGHT ANSWER!! THIS IS HOW A COUNTRY UNDER THE RULE OF LAW OUGHT TO RESPOND!
MY NAME IS KOKI TANAKABARA. I AM KOKI TANAKABARA, ANNOUNCER ON NHN TV'S GOLDEN NEWS!

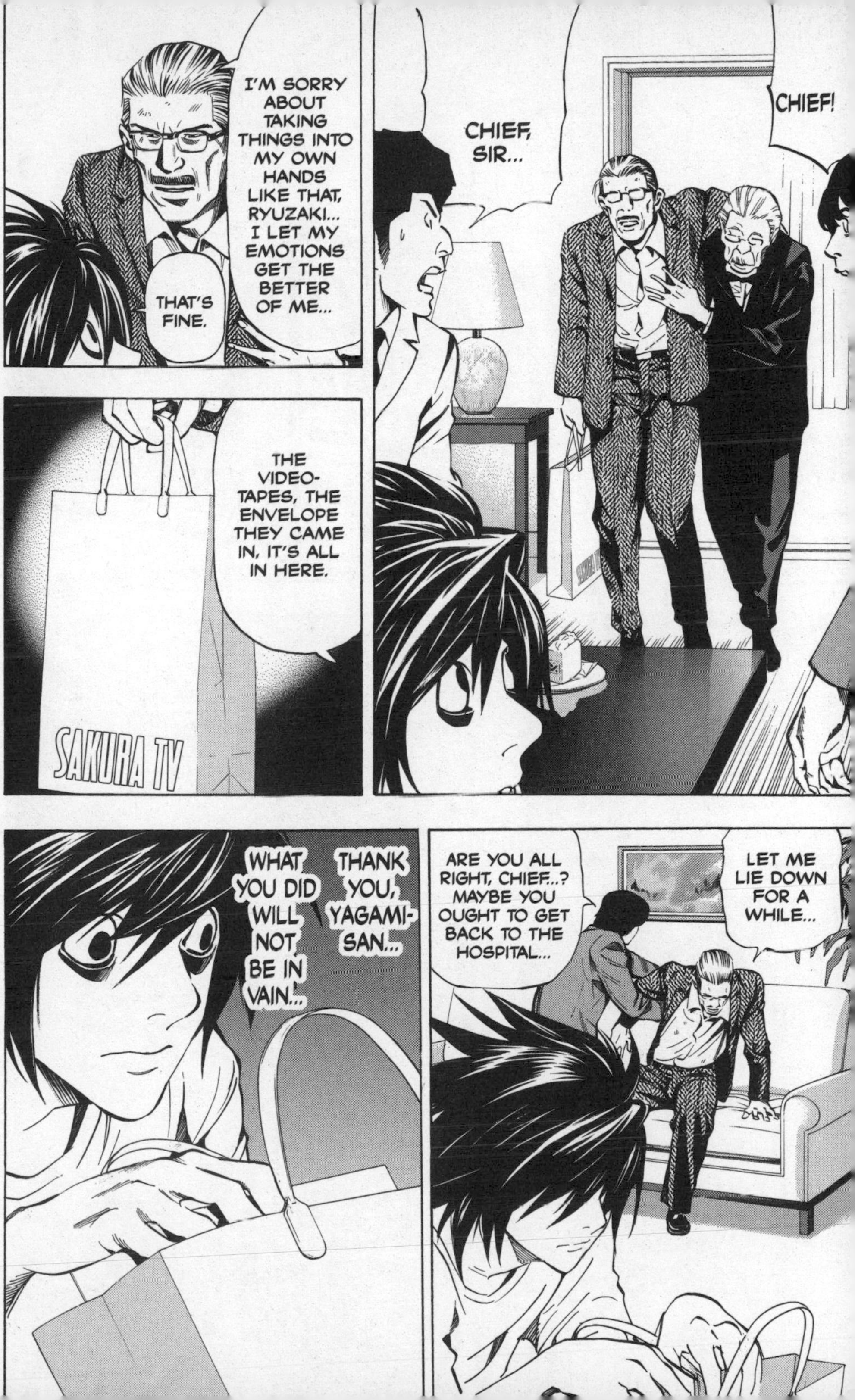
CHIEF!
CHIEF, SIR...
I'M SORRY ABOUT TAKING THINGS INTO MY OWN HANDS LIKE THAT, RYUZAKI... I LET MY EMOTIONS GET THE BETTER OF ME...
THAT'S FINE.
THE VIDEO-TAPES, THE ENVELOPE THEY CAME IN, IT'S ALL IN HERE.
SAKURA TV
LET ME LIE DOWN FOR A WHILE...
ARE YOU ALL RIGHT, CHIEF...? MAYBE YOU OUGHT TO GET BACK TO THE HOSPITAL...
THANK YOU, YAGAMI-SAN...
WHAT YOU DID WILL NOT BE IN VAIN...

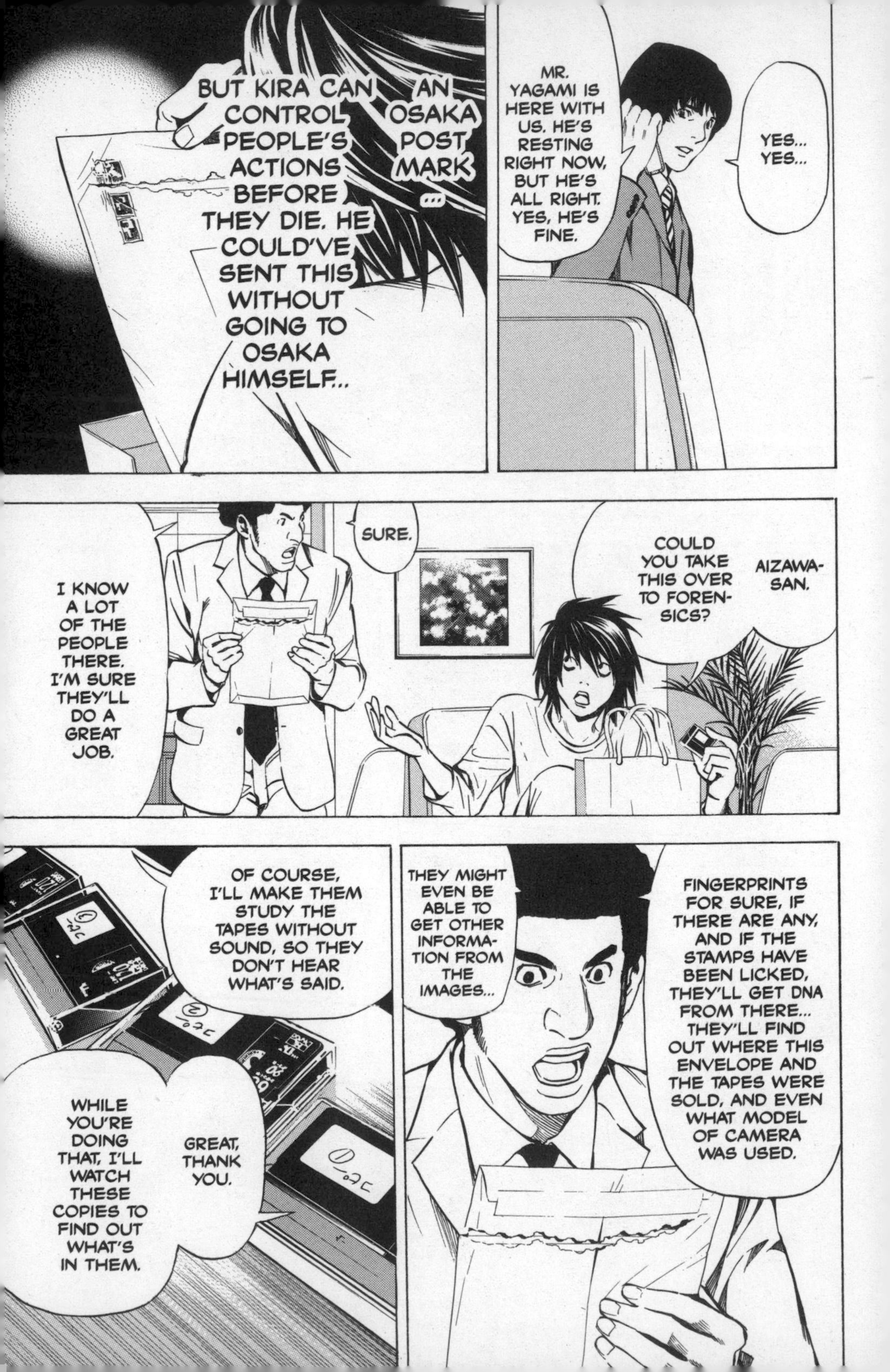
YES... YES...
MR. YAGAMI IS HERE WITH US. HE'S RESTING RIGHT NOW, BUT HE'S ALL RIGHT. YES, HE'S FINE.
AN OSAKA POSTMARK...
BUT KIRA CAN CONTROL PEOPLE'S ACTIONS BEFORE THEY DIE. HE COULD'VE SENT THIS WITHOUT GOING TO OSAKA HIMSELF...
AIZAWA-SAN.
COULD YOU TAKE THIS OVER TO FORENSICS?
SURE.
I KNOW A LOT OF THE PEOPLE THERE. I'M SURE THEY'LL DO A GREAT JOB.
FINGERPRINTS FOR SURE, IF THERE ARE ANY, AND IF THE STAMPS HAVE BEEN LICKED, THEY'LL GET DNA FROM THERE... THEY'LL FIND OUT WHERE THIS ENVELOPE AND THE TAPES WERE SOLD, AND EVEN WHAT MODEL OF CAMERA WAS USED.
THEY MIGHT EVEN BE ABLE TO GET OTHER INFORMATION FROM THE IMAGES...
OF COURSE, I'LL MAKE THEM STUDY THE TAPES WITHOUT SOUND, SO THEY DON'T HEAR WHAT'S SAID.
GREAT, THANK YOU.
WHILE YOU'RE DOING THAT, I'LL WATCH THESE COPIES TO FIND OUT WHAT'S IN THEM.

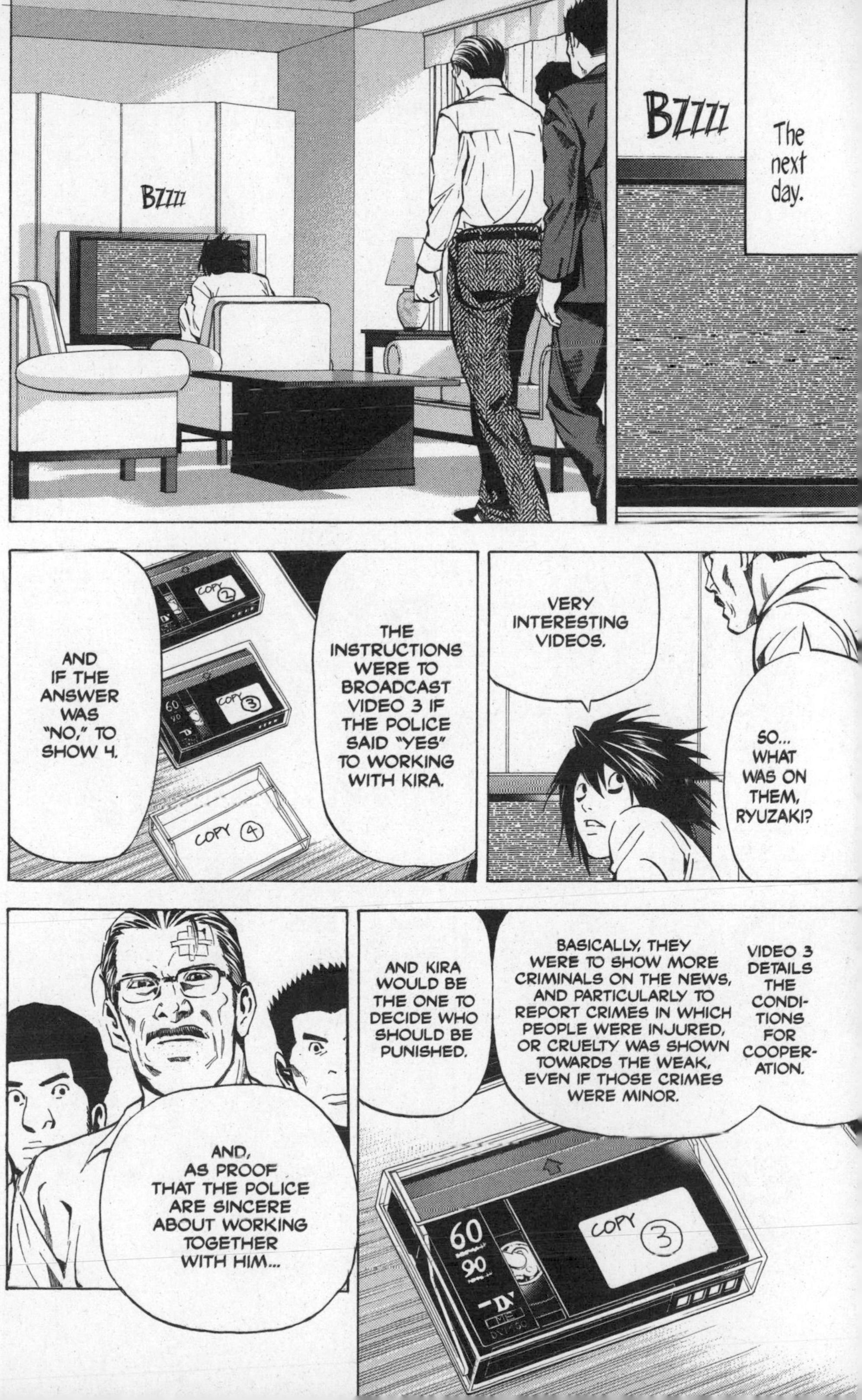
The next day.
BZZZZ
BZZZZ
VERY INTERESTING VIDEOS.
SO... WHAT WAS ON THEM, RYUZAKI?
THE INSTRUCTIONS WERE TO BROADCAST VIDEO 3 IF THE POLICE SAID "YES" TO WORKING WITH KIRA.
AND IF THE ANSWER WAS "NO," TO SHOW 4.
COPY 2
COPY 3
COPY 4
VIDEO 3 DETAILS THE CONDITIONS FOR COOPERATION.
BASICALLY, THEY WERE TO SHOW MORE CRIMINALS ON THE NEWS, AND PARTICULARLY TO REPORT CRIMES IN WHICH PEOPLE WERE INJURED, OR CRUELTY WAS SHOWN TOWARDS THE WEAK, EVEN IF THOSE CRIMES WERE MINOR.
AND KIRA WOULD BE THE ONE TO DECIDE WHO SHOULD BE PUNISHED.
COPY 3
AND, AS PROOF THAT THE POLICE ARE SINCERE ABOUT WORKING TOGETHER WITH HIM...

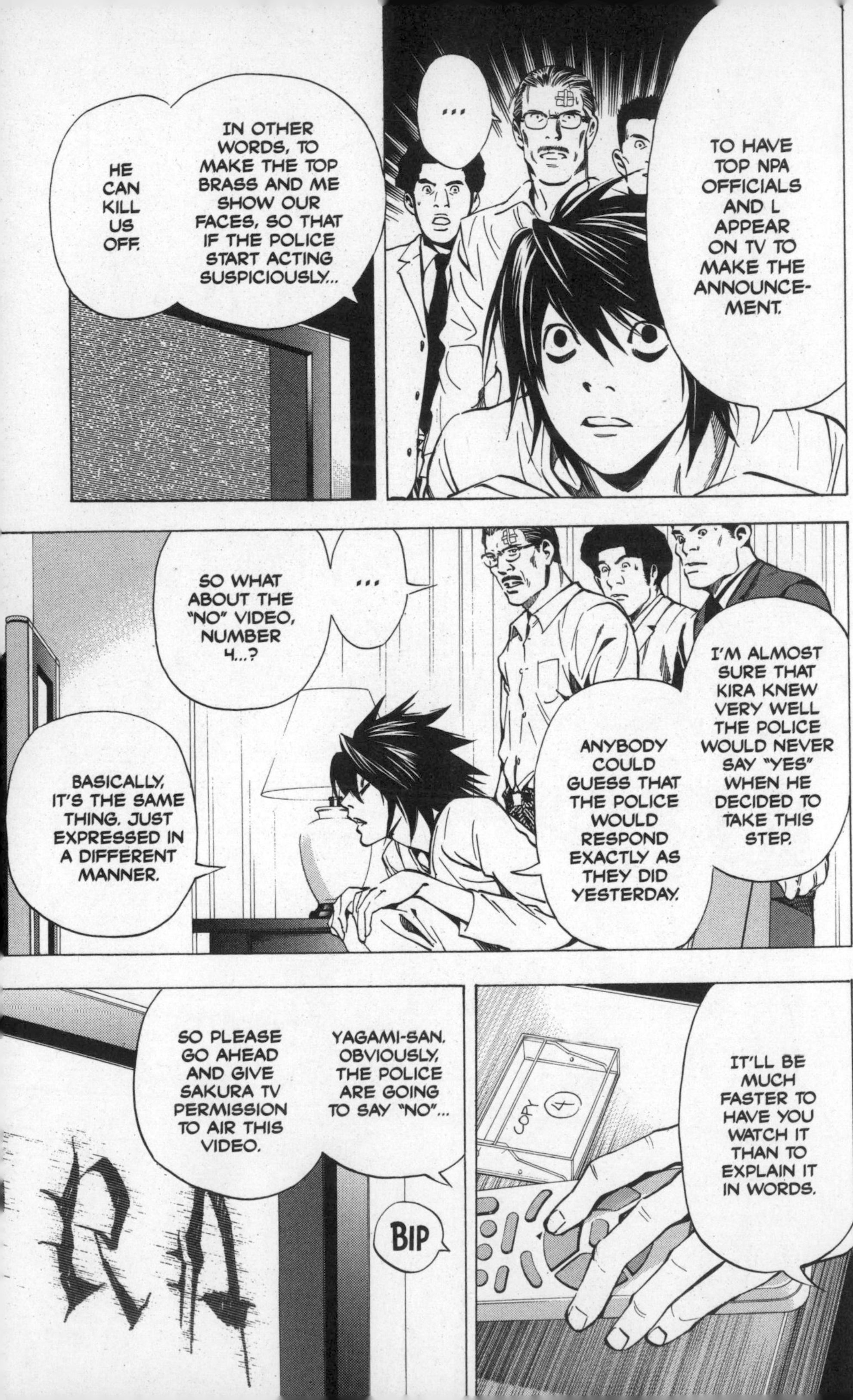
TO HAVE TOP NPA OFFICIALS AND L APPEAR ON TV TO MAKE THE ANNOUNCEMENT.
...
IN OTHER WORDS, TO MAKE THE TOP BRASS AND ME SHOW OUR FACES, SO THAT IF THE POLICE START ACTING SUSPICIOUSLY...
HE CAN KILL US OFF.
...
SO WHAT ABOUT THE "NO" VIDEO, NUMBER 4...?
BASICALLY, IT'S THE SAME THING. JUST EXPRESSED IN A DIFFERENT MANNER.
I'M ALMOST SURE THAT KIRA KNEW VERY WELL THE POLICE WOULD NEVER SAY "YES" WHEN HE DECIDED TO TAKE THIS STEP.
ANYBODY COULD GUESS THAT THE POLICE WOULD RESPOND EXACTLY AS THEY DID YESTERDAY.
IT'LL BE MUCH FASTER TO HAVE YOU WATCH IT THAN TO EXPLAIN IT IN WORDS.
COPY 4
BIP
YAGAMI-SAN. OBVIOUSLY, THE POLICE ARE GOING TO SAY "NO"...
SO PLEASE GO AHEAD AND GIVE SAKURA TV PERMISSION TO AIR THIS VIDEO.

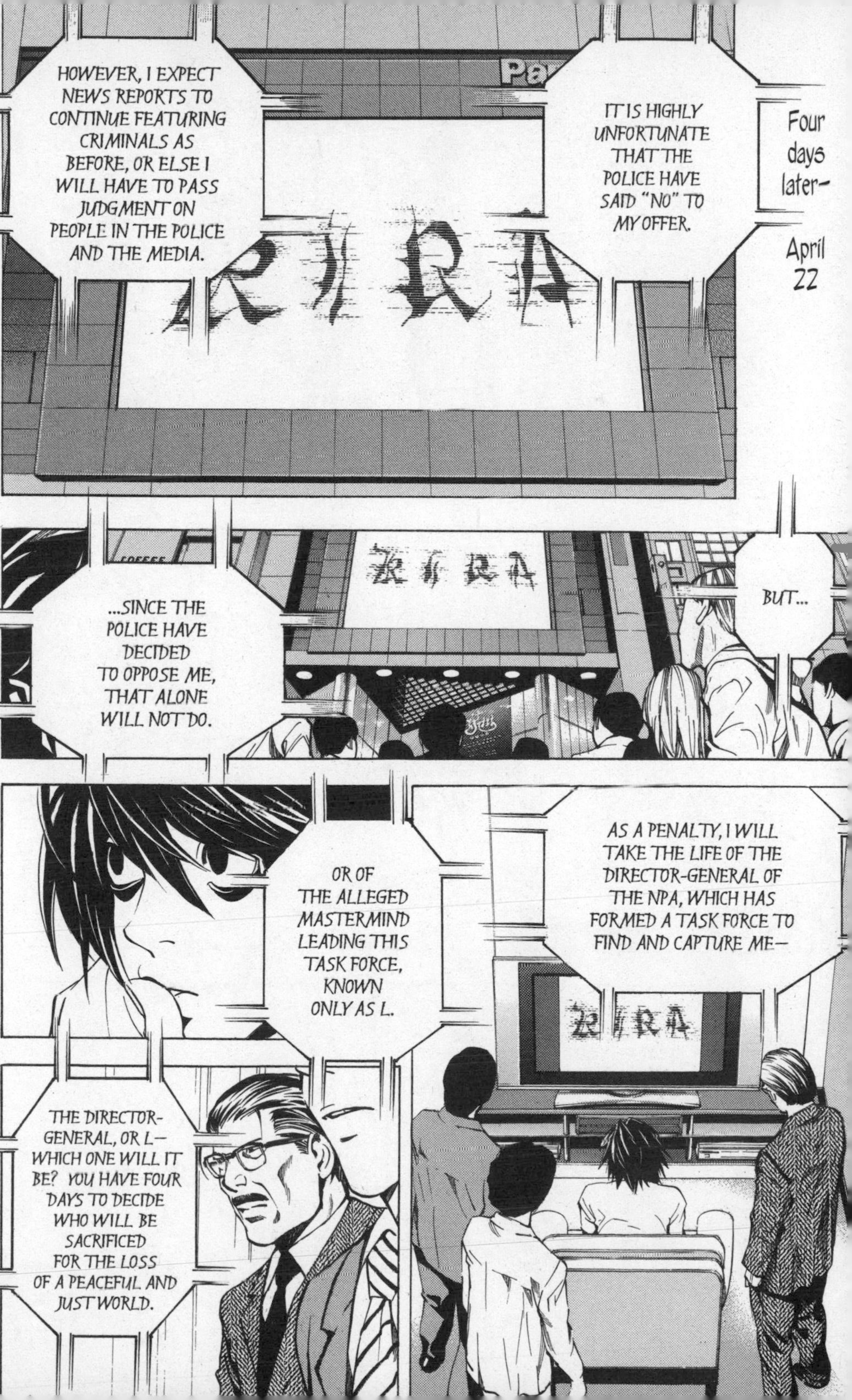
Four days later— April 22
IT IS HIGHLY UNFORTUNATE THAT THE POLICE HAVE SAID "NO" TO MY OFFER.
HOWEVER, I EXPECT NEWS REPORTS TO CONTINUE FEATURING CRIMINALS AS BEFORE, OR ELSE I WILL HAVE TO PASS JUDGMENT ON PEOPLE IN THE POLICE AND THE MEDIA.
KIRA
BUT...
...SINCE THE POLICE HAVE DECIDED TO OPPOSE ME, THAT ALONE WILL NOT DO.
KIRA
AS A PENALTY, I WILL TAKE THE LIFE OF THE DIRECTOR-GENERAL OF THE NPA, WHICH HAS FORMED A TASK FORCE TO FIND AND CAPTURE ME—
OR OF THE ALLEGED MASTERMIND LEADING THIS TASK FORCE, KNOWN ONLY AS L.
KIRA
THE DIRECTOR-GENERAL, OR L— WHICH ONE WILL IT BE? YOU HAVE FOUR DAYS TO DECIDE WHO WILL BE SACRIFICED FOR THE LOSS OF A PEACEFUL AND JUST WORLD.

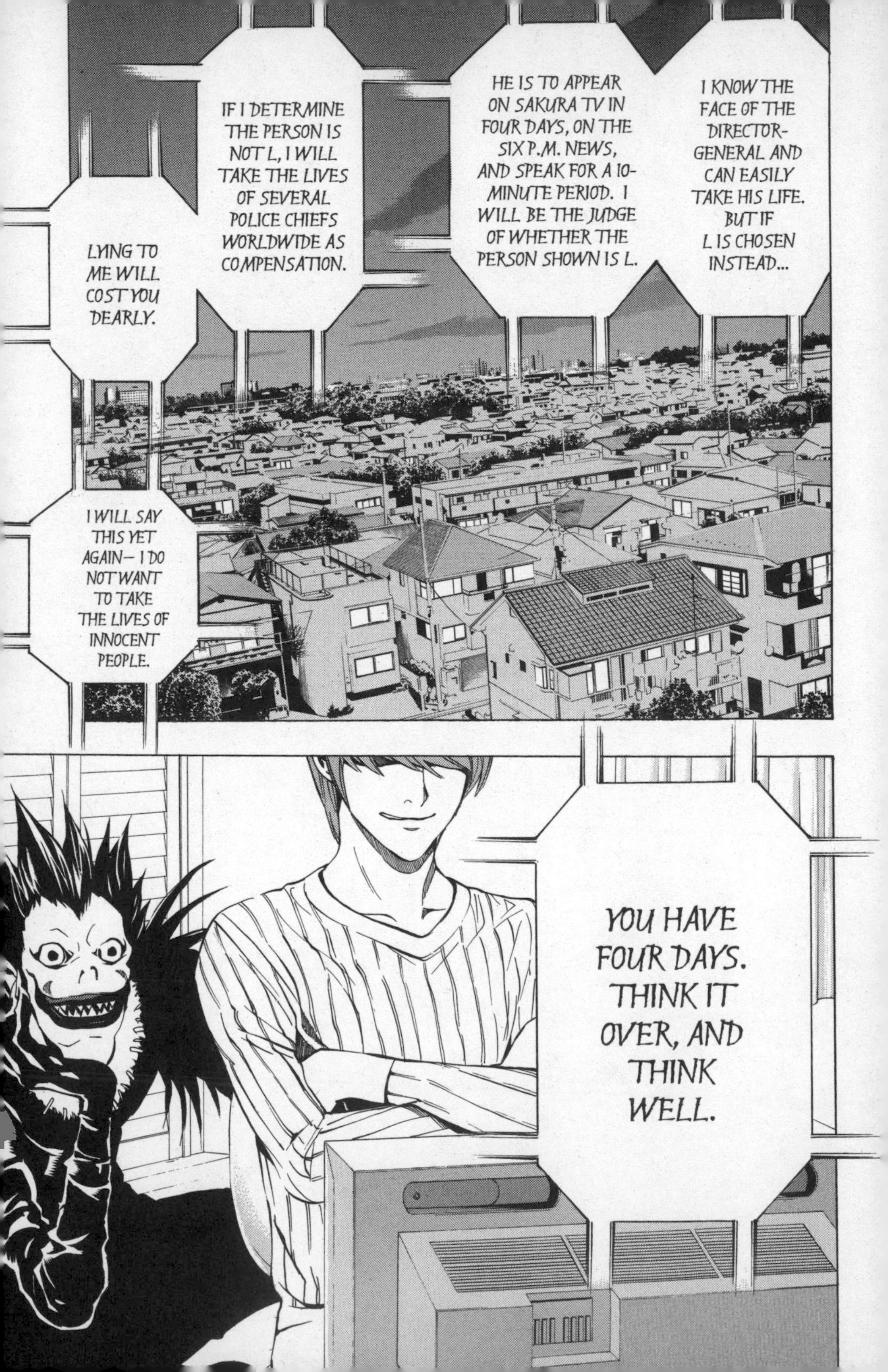
I KNOW THE FACE OF THE DIRECTOR-GENERAL AND CAN EASILY TAKE HIS LIFE. BUT IF L IS CHOSEN INSTEAD...
HE IS TO APPEAR ON SAKURA TV IN FOUR DAYS, ON THE SIX P.M. NEWS, AND SPEAK FOR A 10-MINUTE PERIOD. I WILL BE THE JUDGE OF WHETHER THE PERSON SHOWN IS L.
IF I DETERMINE THE PERSON IS NOT L, I WILL TAKE THE LIVES OF SEVERAL POLICE CHIEFS WORLDWIDE AS COMPENSATION.
LYING TO ME WILL COST YOU DEARLY.
I WILL SAY THIS YET AGAIN— I DO NOT WANT TO TAKE THE LIVES OF INNOCENT PEOPLE.
YOU HAVE FOUR DAYS. THINK IT OVER, AND THINK WELL.

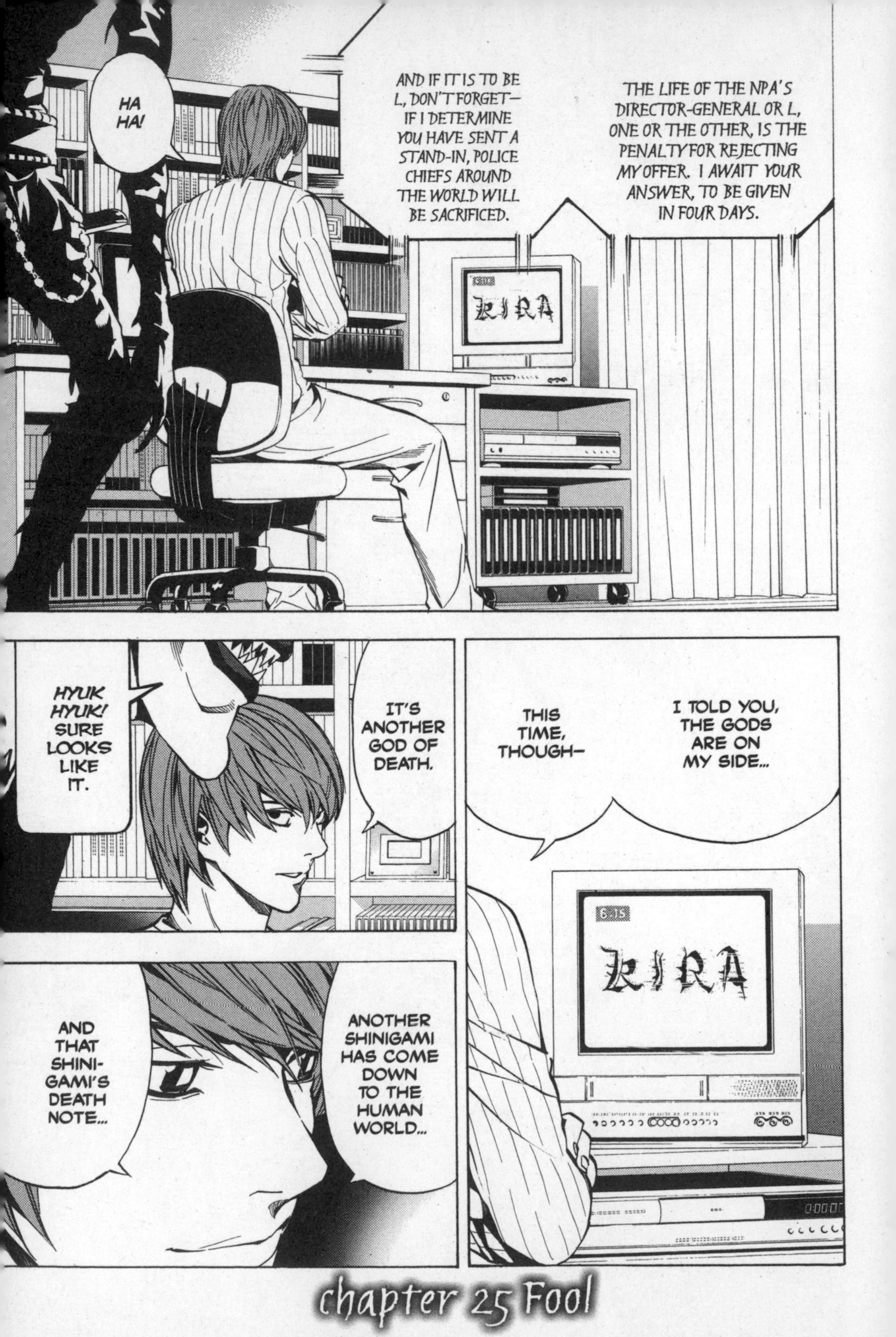

THE LIFE OF THE NPA'S DIRECTOR-GENERAL OR L, ONE OR THE OTHER, IS THE PENALTY FOR REJECTING MY OFFER. I AWAIT YOUR ANSWER, TO BE GIVEN IN FOUR DAYS.
AND IF IT IS TO BE L, DON'T FORGET— IF I DETERMINE YOU HAVE SENT A STAND-IN, POLICE CHIEFS AROUND THE WORLD WILL BE SACRIFICED.
KIRA
HA HA!
I TOLD YOU, THE GODS ARE ON MY SIDE...
THIS TIME, THOUGH—
6.15
KIRA
IT'S ANOTHER GOD OF DEATH.
HYUK HYUK! SURE LOOKS LIKE IT.
ANOTHER SHINIGAMI HAS COME DOWN TO THE HUMAN WORLD...
AND THAT SHINIGAMI'S DEATH NOTE...

chapter 25 Fool

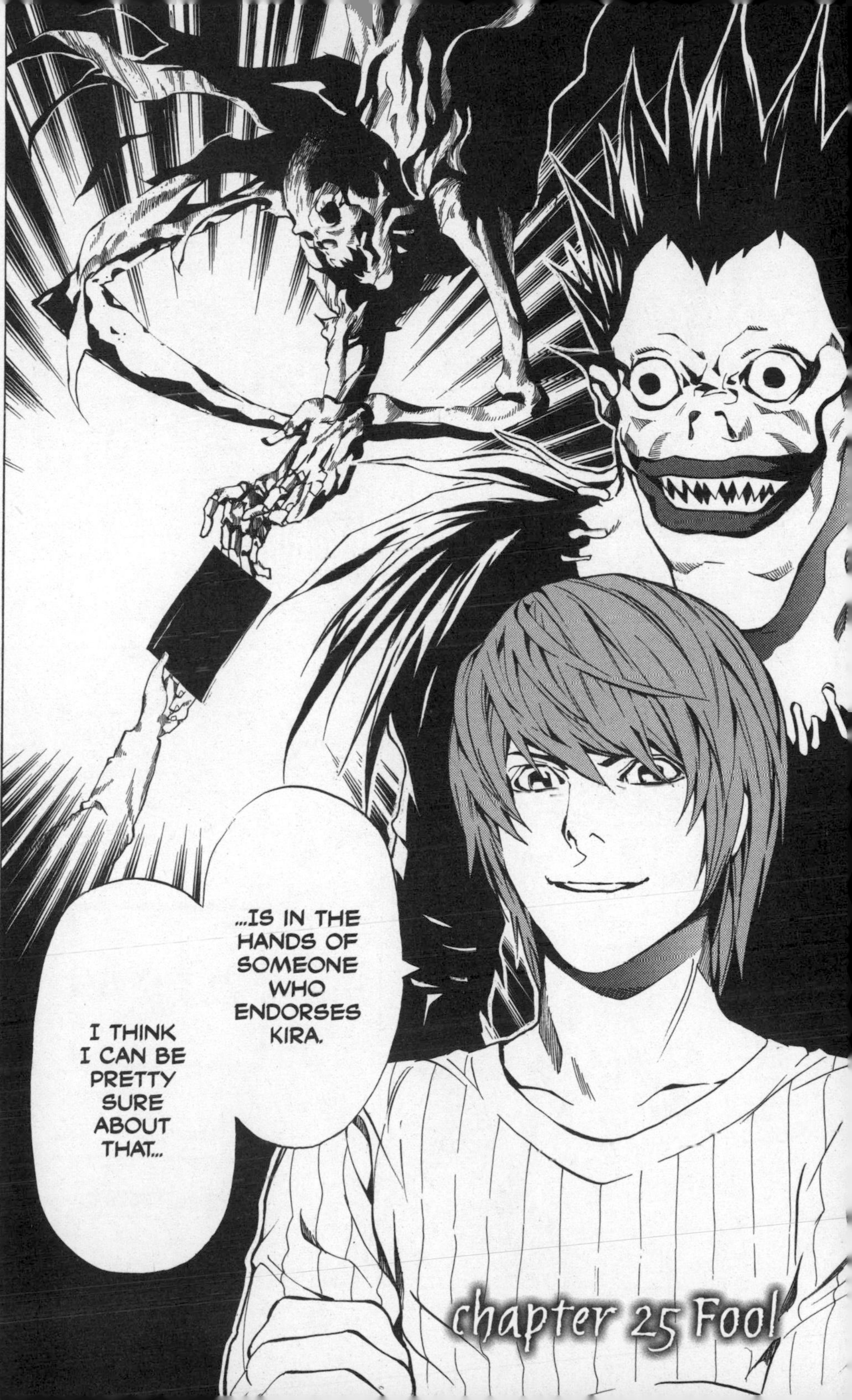
...IS IN THE HANDS OF SOMEONE WHO ENDORSES KIRA.
I THINK I CAN BE PRETTY SURE ABOUT THAT...
chapter 25 Fool

READ THIS WAY

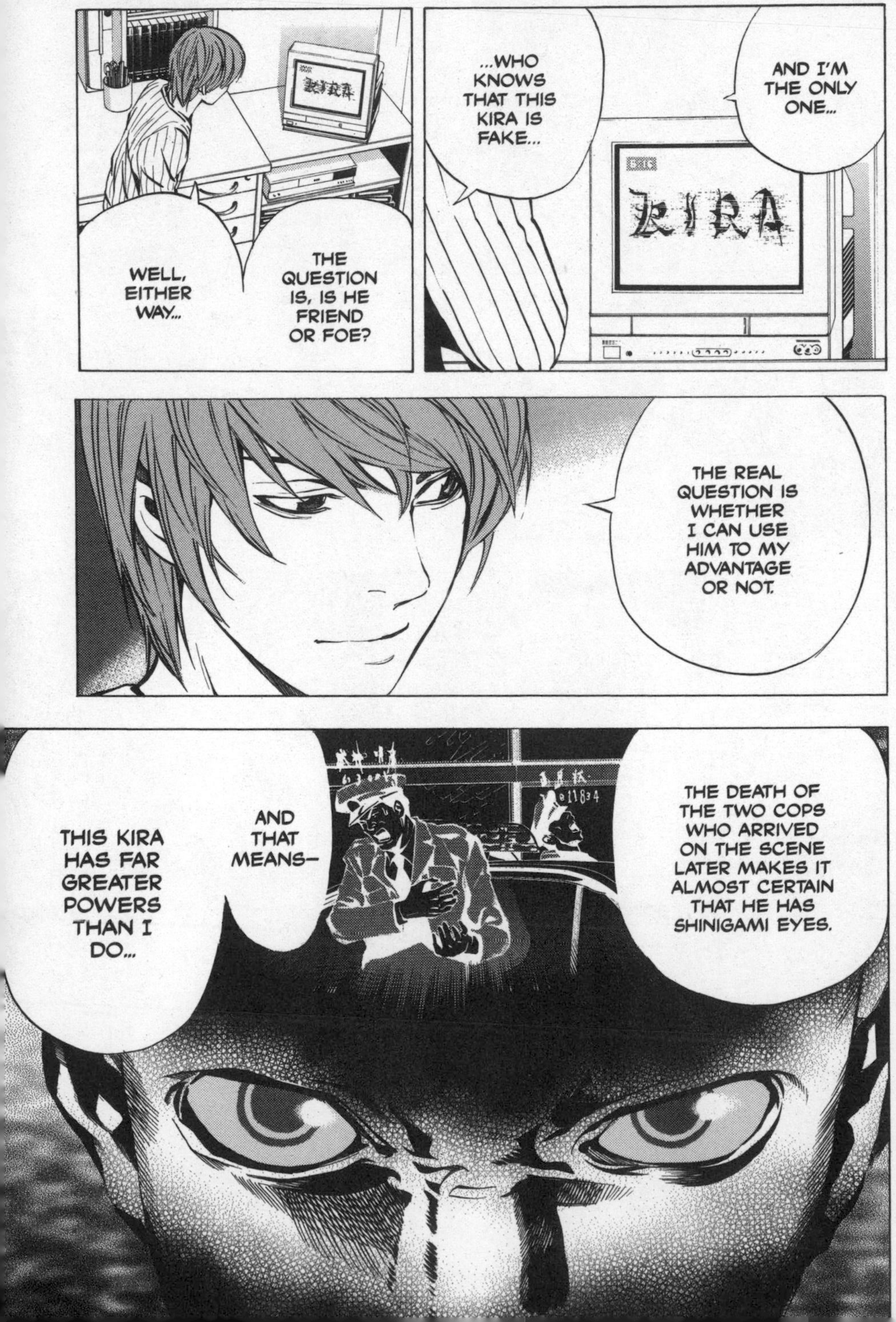
AND I'M THE ONLY ONE...
...WHO KNOWS THAT THIS KIRA IS FAKE...
KIRA
THE QUESTION IS, IS HE FRIEND OR FOE?
WELL, EITHER WAY...
THE REAL QUESTION IS WHETHER I CAN USE HIM TO MY ADVANTAGE OR NOT.
THE DEATH OF THE TWO COPS WHO ARRIVED ON THE SCENE LATER MAKES IT ALMOST CERTAIN THAT HE HAS SHINIGAMI EYES.
AND THAT MEANS—
THIS KIRA HAS FAR GREATER POWERS THAN I DO...

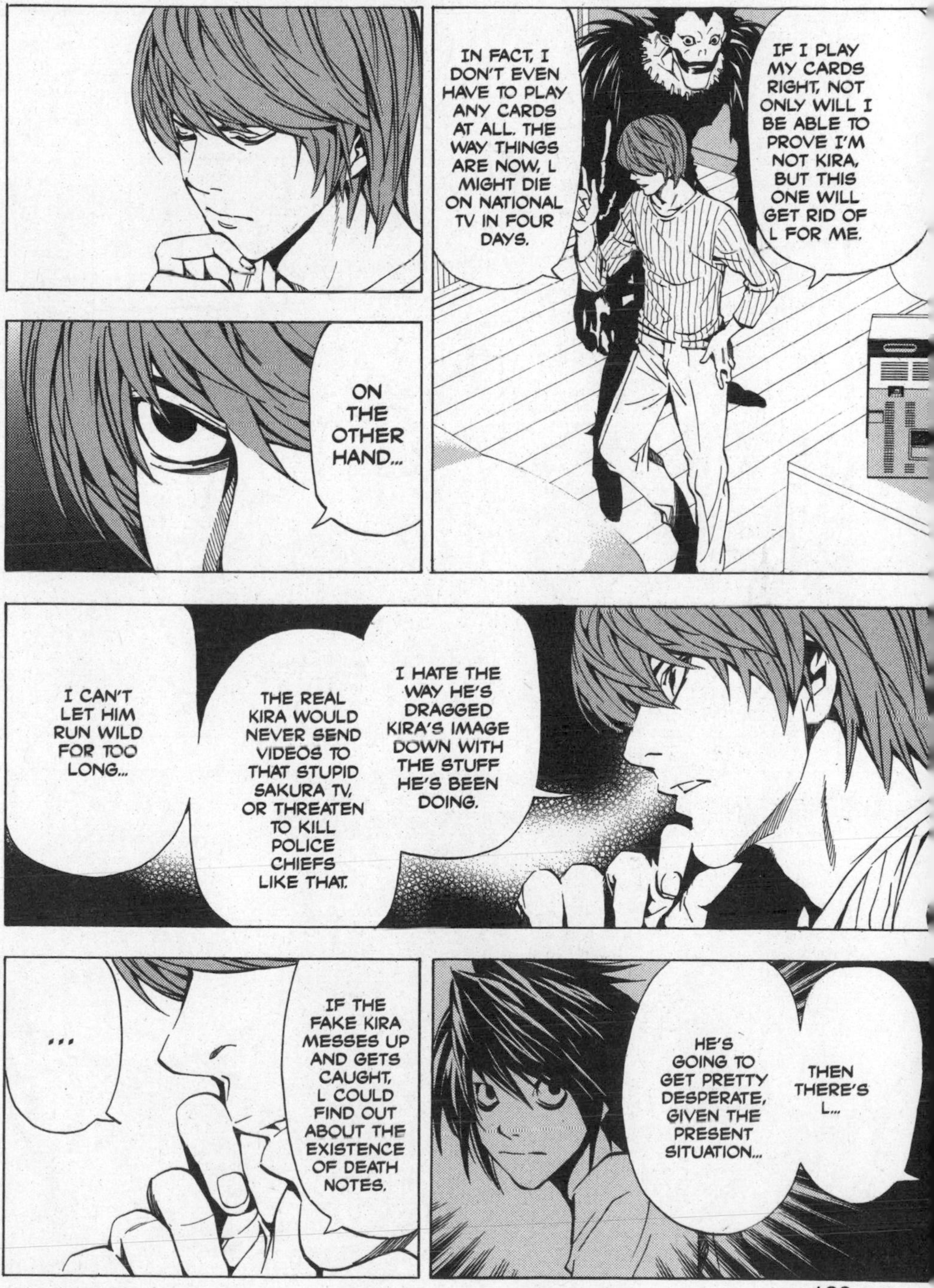
IF I PLAY MY CARDS RIGHT, NOT ONLY WILL I BE ABLE TO PROVE I'M NOT KIRA, BUT THIS ONE WILL GET RID OF L FOR ME.
IN FACT, I DON'T EVEN HAVE TO PLAY ANY CARDS AT ALL. THE WAY THINGS ARE NOW, L MIGHT DIE ON NATIONAL TV IN FOUR DAYS.
ON THE OTHER HAND...
I HATE THE WAY HE'S DRAGGED KIRA'S IMAGE DOWN WITH THE STUFF HE'S BEEN DOING.
THE REAL KIRA WOULD NEVER SEND VIDEOS TO THAT STUPID SAKURA TV, OR THREATEN TO KILL POLICE CHIEFS LIKE THAT.
I CAN'T LET HIM RUN WILD FOR TOO LONG...
THEN THERE'S L...
HE'S GOING TO GET PRETTY DESPERATE, GIVEN THE PRESENT SITUATION...
IF THE FAKE KIRA MESSES UP AND GETS CAUGHT, L COULD FIND OUT ABOUT THE EXISTENCE OF DEATH NOTES.
...

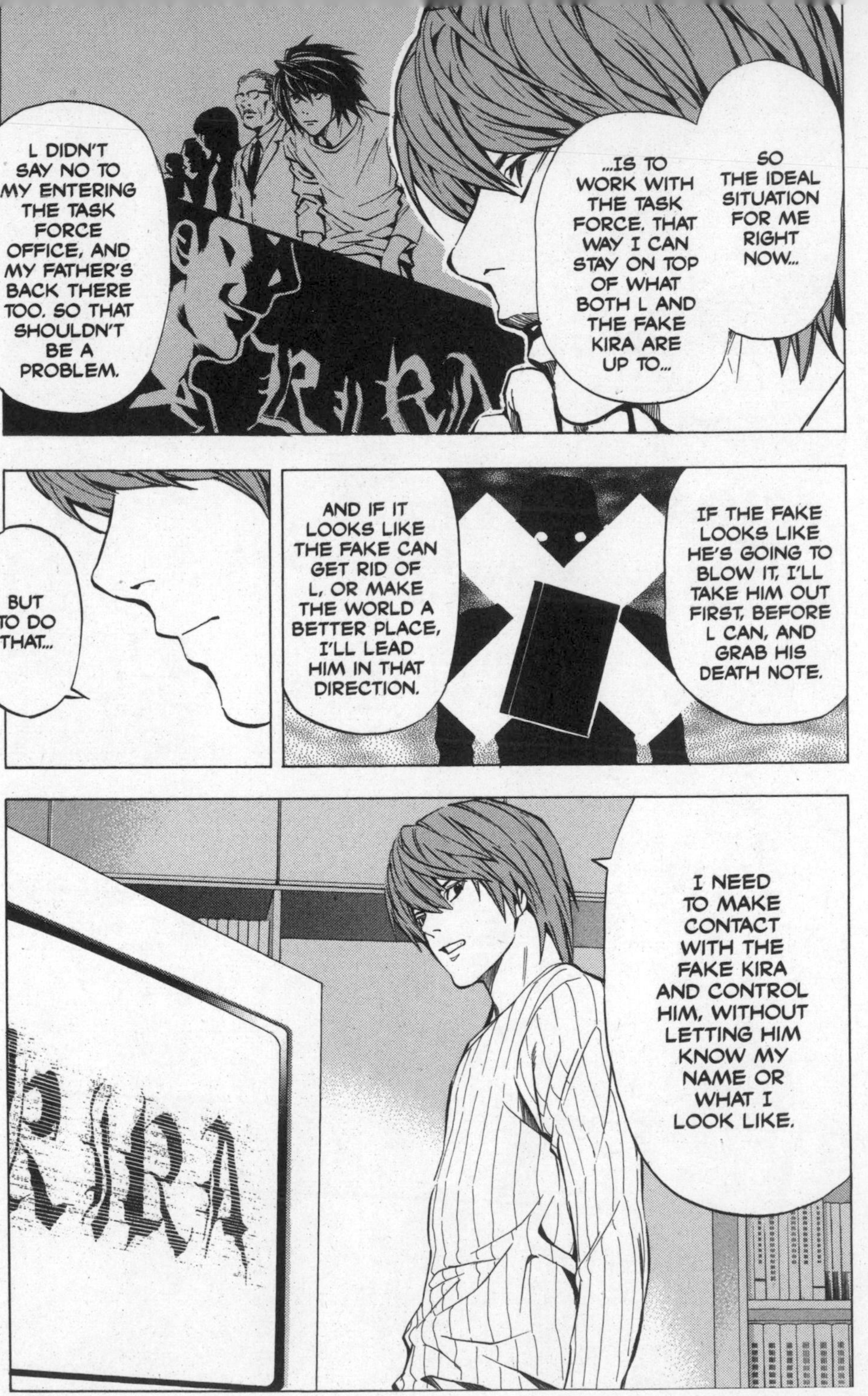
SO THE IDEAL SITUATION FOR ME RIGHT NOW...
...IS TO WORK WITH THE TASK FORCE. THAT WAY I CAN STAY ON TOP OF WHAT BOTH L AND THE FAKE KIRA ARE UP TO...
L DIDN'T SAY NO TO MY ENTERING THE TASK FORCE OFFICE, AND MY FATHER'S BACK THERE TOO. SO THAT SHOULDN'T BE A PROBLEM.
IF THE FAKE LOOKS LIKE HE'S GOING TO BLOW IT, I'LL TAKE HIM OUT FIRST, BEFORE L CAN, AND GRAB HIS DEATH NOTE.
AND IF IT LOOKS LIKE THE FAKE CAN GET RID OF L, OR MAKE THE WORLD A BETTER PLACE, I'LL LEAD HIM IN THAT DIRECTION.
BUT TO DO THAT...
I NEED TO MAKE CONTACT WITH THE FAKE KIRA AND CONTROL HIM, WITHOUT LETTING HIM KNOW MY NAME OR WHAT I LOOK LIKE.

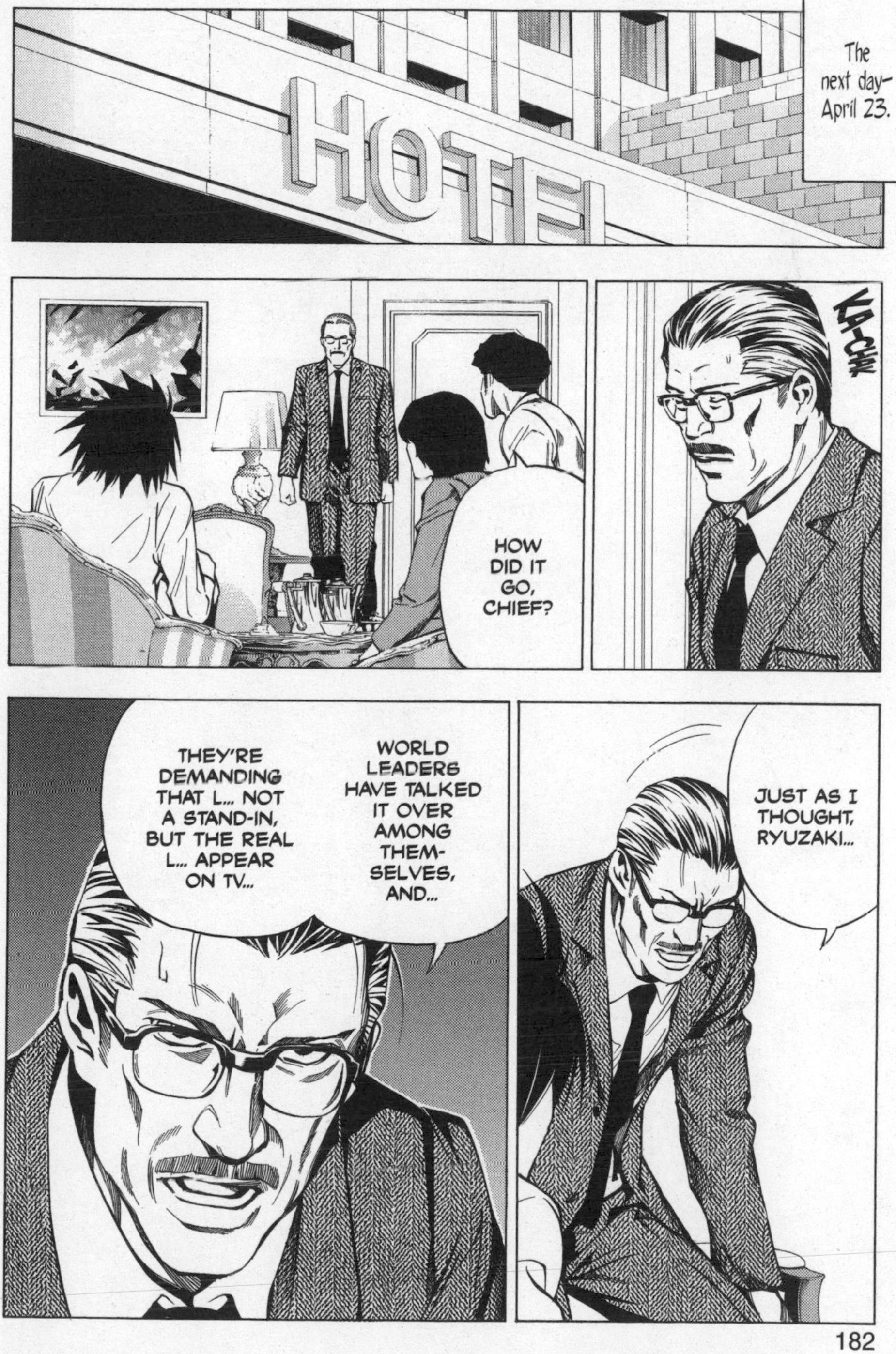
The next day— April 23.
HOTEL
KA-CHAK
HOW DID IT GO, CHIEF?
JUST AS I THOUGHT, RYUZAKI...
WORLD LEADERS HAVE TALKED IT OVER AMONG THEM-SELVES, AND...
THEY'RE DEMANDING THAT L... NOT A STAND-IN, BUT THE REAL L... APPEAR ON TV...

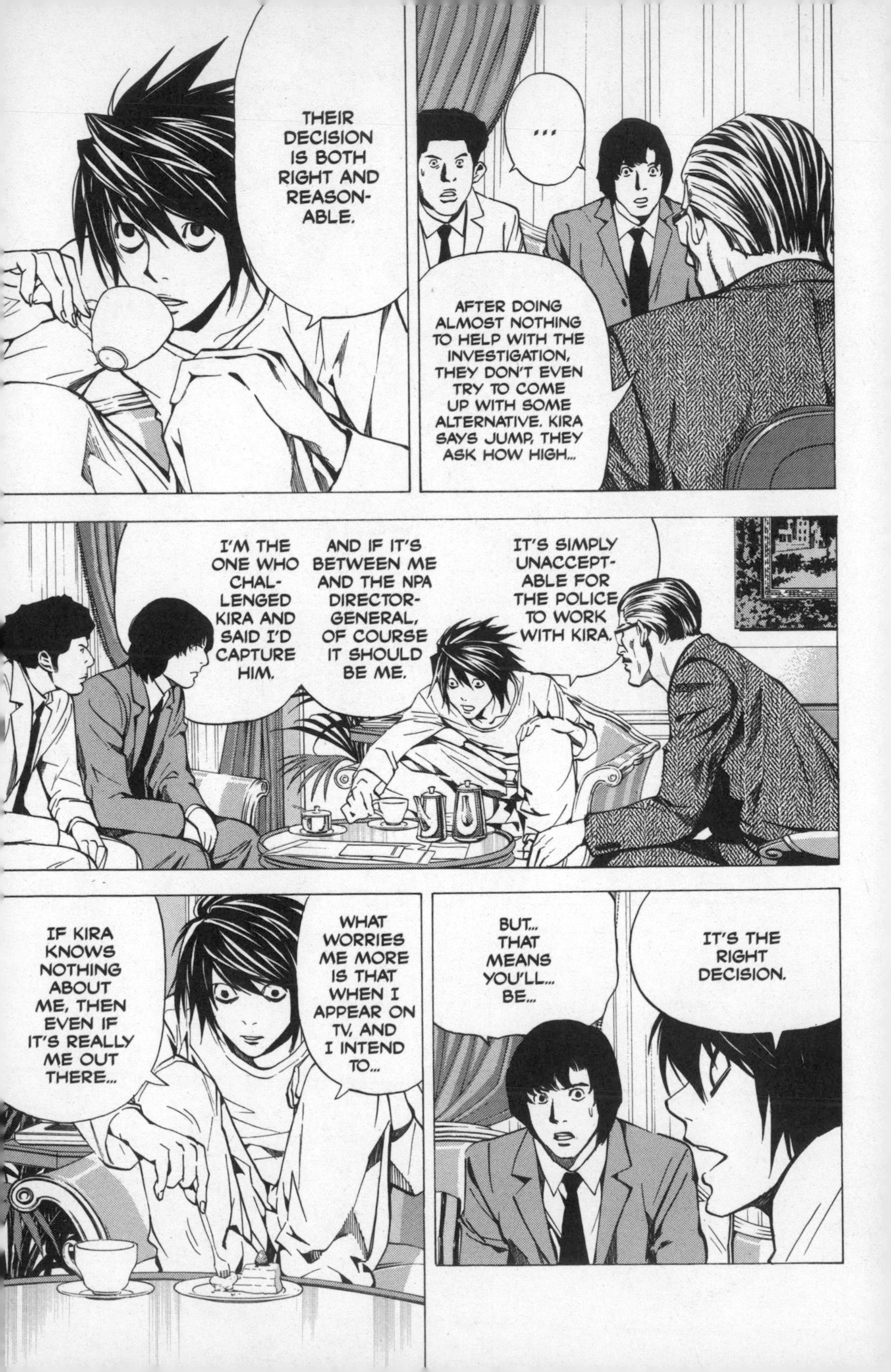
...
AFTER DOING ALMOST NOTHING TO HELP WITH THE INVESTIGATION, THEY DON'T EVEN TRY TO COME UP WITH SOME ALTERNATIVE. KIRA SAYS JUMP, THEY ASK HOW HIGH...
THEIR DECISION IS BOTH RIGHT AND REASON-ABLE.
IT'S SIMPLY UNACCEPT-ABLE FOR THE POLICE TO WORK WITH KIRA.
I'M THE ONE WHO CHAL-LENGED KIRA AND SAID I'D CAPTURE HIM.
AND IF IT'S BETWEEN ME AND THE NPA DIRECTOR-GENERAL, OF COURSE IT SHOULD BE ME.
IT'S THE RIGHT DECISION.
BUT... THAT MEANS YOU'LL... BE...
WHAT WORRIES ME MORE IS THAT WHEN I APPEAR ON TV, AND I INTEND TO...
IF KIRA KNOWS NOTHING ABOUT ME, THEN EVEN IF IT'S REALLY ME OUT THERE...

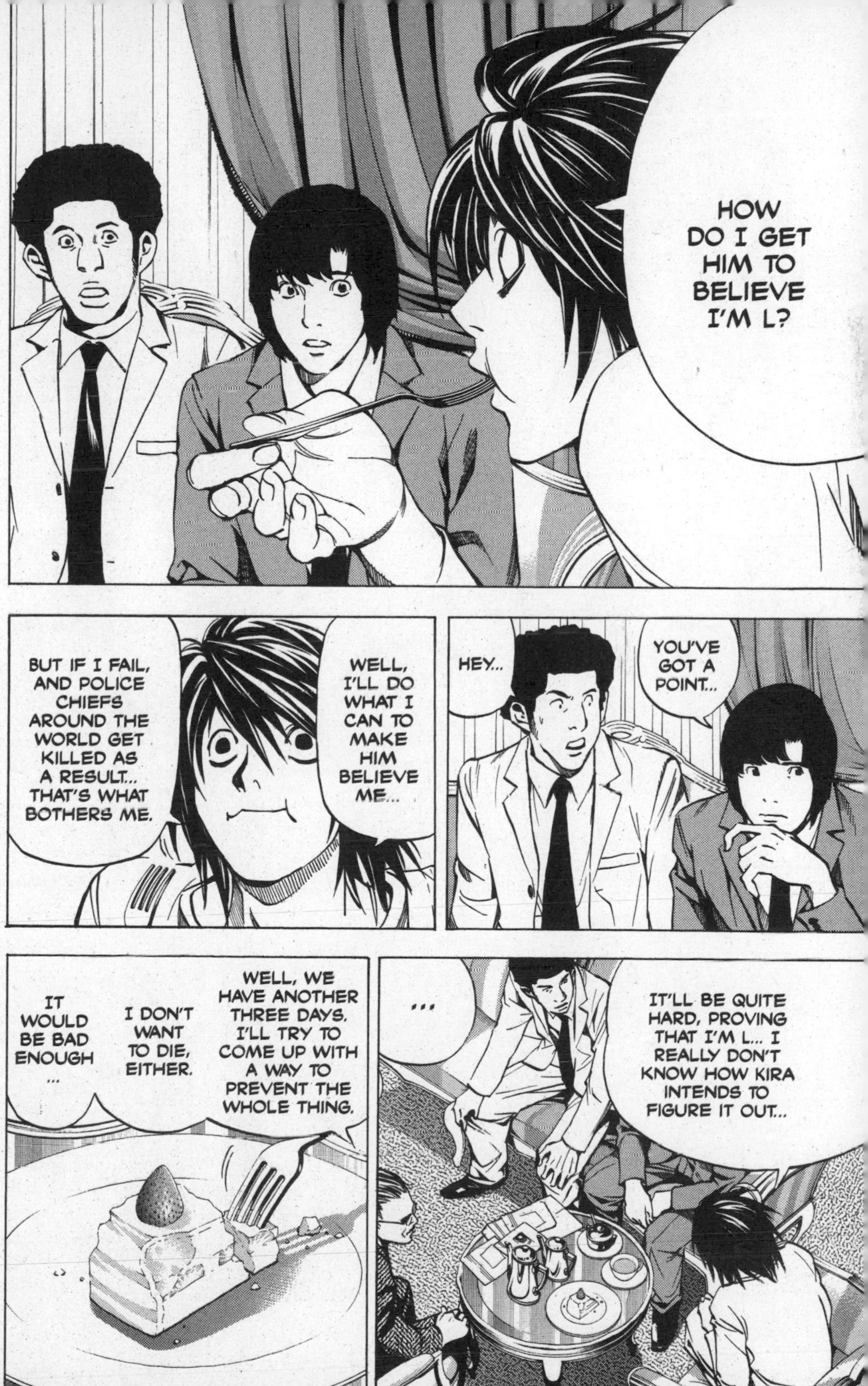
HOW DO I GET HIM TO BELIEVE I'M L?
YOU'VE GOT A POINT...
HEY...
WELL, I'LL DO WHAT I CAN TO MAKE HIM BELIEVE ME...
BUT IF I FAIL, AND POLICE CHIEFS AROUND THE WORLD GET KILLED AS A RESULT... THAT'S WHAT BOTHERS ME.
IT'LL BE QUITE HARD, PROVING THAT I'M L... I REALLY DON'T KNOW HOW KIRA INTENDS TO FIGURE IT OUT...
...
WELL, WE HAVE ANOTHER THREE DAYS. I'LL TRY TO COME UP WITH A WAY TO PREVENT THE WHOLE THING.
I DON'T WANT TO DIE, EITHER.
IT WOULD BE BAD ENOUGH ...

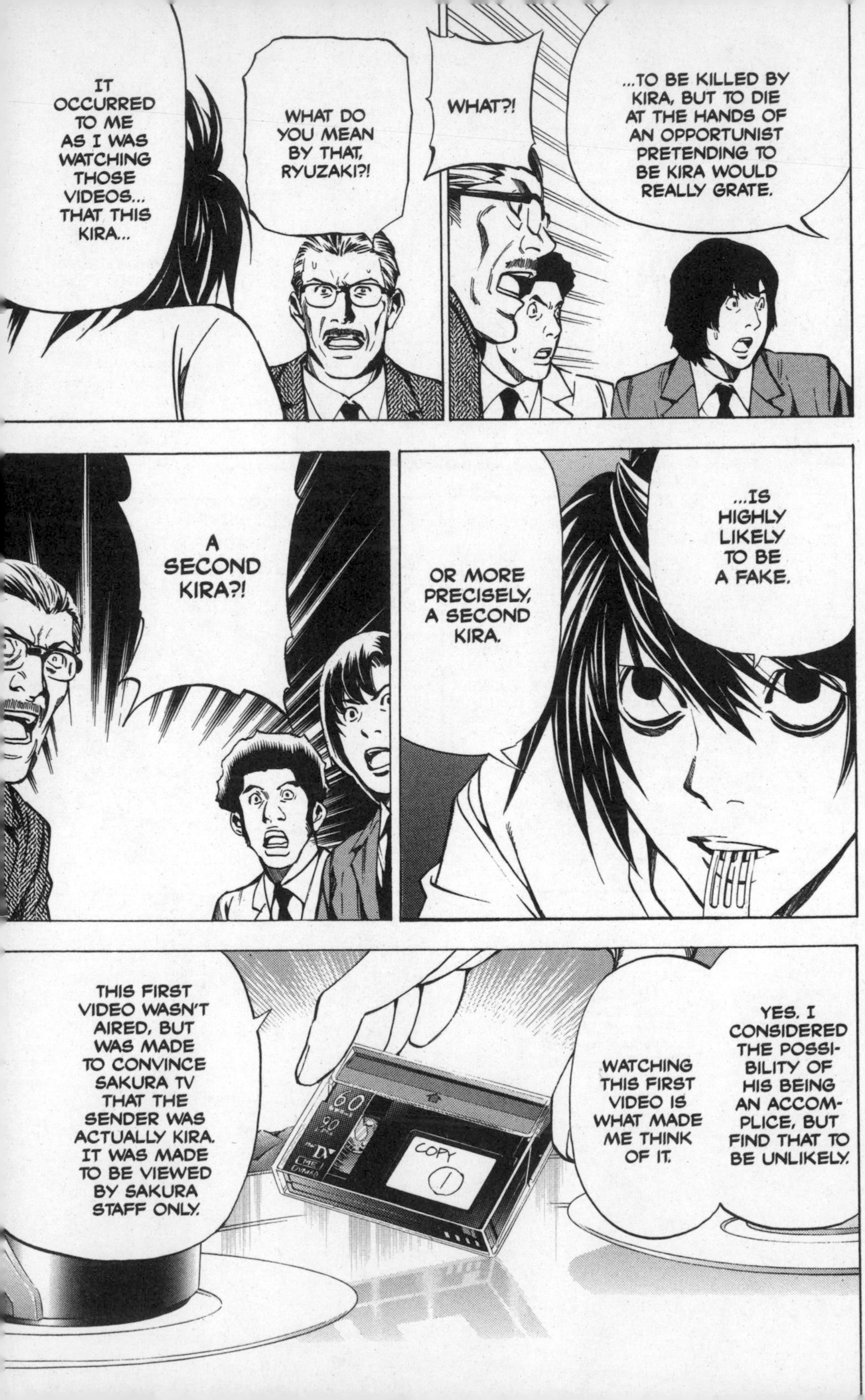
...TO BE KILLED BY KIRA, BUT TO DIE AT THE HANDS OF AN OPPORTUNIST PRETENDING TO BE KIRA WOULD REALLY GRATE.
WHAT?!
WHAT DO YOU MEAN BY THAT, RYUZAKI?!
IT OCCURRED TO ME AS I WAS WATCHING THOSE VIDEOS... THAT THIS KIRA...
...IS HIGHLY LIKELY TO BE A FAKE.
OR MORE PRECISELY, A SECOND KIRA.
A SECOND KIRA?!
YES. I CONSIDERED THE POSSI-BILITY OF HIS BEING AN ACCOM-PLICE, BUT FIND THAT TO BE UNLIKELY.
WATCHING THIS FIRST VIDEO IS WHAT MADE ME THINK OF IT.
COPY 1
THIS FIRST VIDEO WASN'T AIRED, BUT WAS MADE TO CONVINCE SAKURA TV THAT THE SENDER WAS ACTUALLY KIRA. IT WAS MADE TO BE VIEWED BY SAKURA STAFF ONLY.

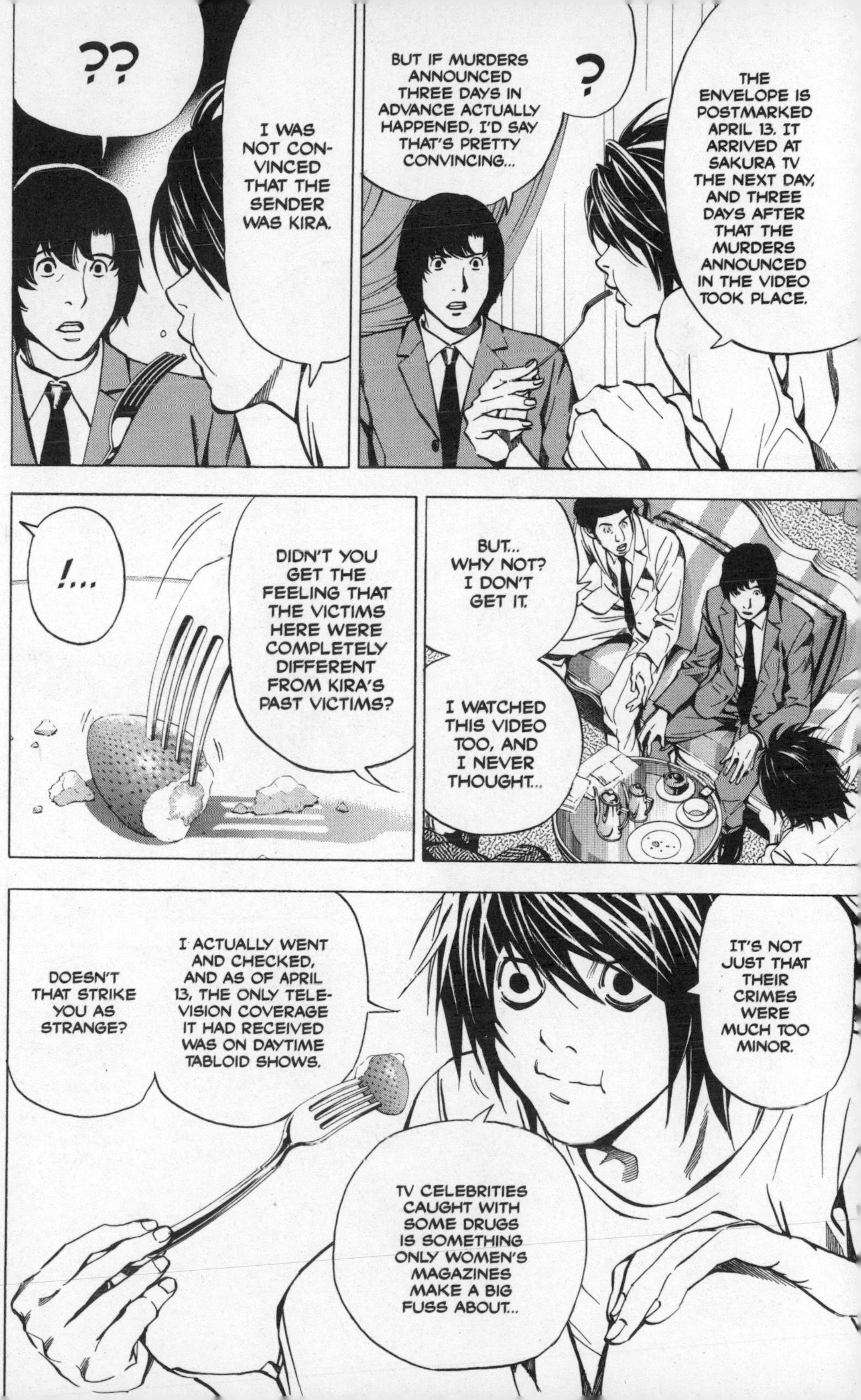
THE ENVELOPE IS POSTMARKED APRIL 13. IT ARRIVED AT SAKURA TV THE NEXT DAY, AND THREE DAYS AFTER THAT THE MURDERS ANNOUNCED IN THE VIDEO TOOK PLACE.
?
BUT IF MURDERS ANNOUNCED THREE DAYS IN ADVANCE ACTUALLY HAPPENED, I'D SAY THAT'S PRETTY CONVINCING...
I WAS NOT CONVINCED THAT THE SENDER WAS KIRA.
??
BUT... WHY NOT? I DON'T GET IT.
I WATCHED THIS VIDEO TOO, AND I NEVER THOUGHT...
DIDN'T YOU GET THE FEELING THAT THE VICTIMS HERE WERE COMPLETELY DIFFERENT FROM KIRA'S PAST VICTIMS?
!...
IT'S NOT JUST THAT THEIR CRIMES WERE MUCH TOO MINOR.
TV CELEBRITIES CAUGHT WITH SOME DRUGS IS SOMETHING ONLY WOMEN'S MAGAZINES MAKE A BIG FUSS ABOUT...
I ACTUALLY WENT AND CHECKED, AND AS OF APRIL 13, THE ONLY TELEVISION COVERAGE IT HAD RECEIVED WAS ON DAYTIME TABLOID SHOWS.
DOESN'T THAT STRIKE YOU AS STRANGE?

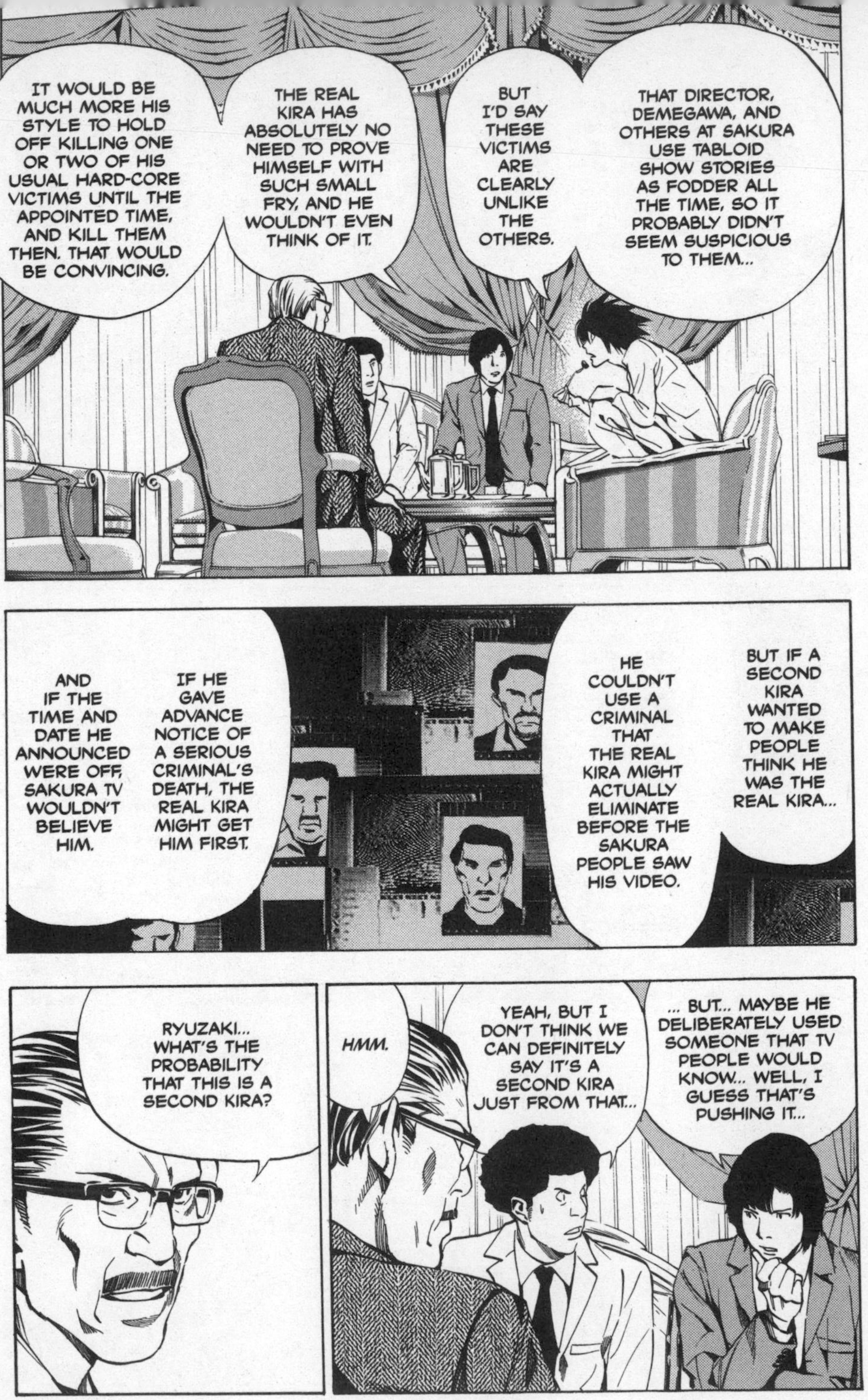
THAT DIRECTOR, DEMEGAWA, AND OTHERS AT SAKURA USE TABLOID SHOW STORIES AS FODDER ALL THE TIME, SO IT PROBABLY DIDN'T SEEM SUSPICIOUS TO THEM...
BUT I'D SAY THESE VICTIMS ARE CLEARLY UNLIKE THE OTHERS.
THE REAL KIRA HAS ABSOLUTELY NO NEED TO PROVE HIMSELF WITH SUCH SMALL FRY, AND HE WOULDN'T EVEN THINK OF IT.
IT WOULD BE MUCH MORE HIS STYLE TO HOLD OFF KILLING ONE OR TWO OF HIS USUAL HARD-CORE VICTIMS UNTIL THE APPOINTED TIME, AND KILL THEM THEN. THAT WOULD BE CONVINCING.
BUT IF A SECOND KIRA WANTED TO MAKE PEOPLE THINK HE WAS THE REAL KIRA...
HE COULDN'T USE A CRIMINAL THAT THE REAL KIRA MIGHT ACTUALLY ELIMINATE BEFORE THE SAKURA PEOPLE SAW HIS VIDEO.
IF HE GAVE ADVANCE NOTICE OF A SERIOUS CRIMINAL'S DEATH, THE REAL KIRA MIGHT GET HIM FIRST.
AND IF THE TIME AND DATE HE ANNOUNCED WERE OFF, SAKURA TV WOULDN'T BELIEVE HIM.
... BUT... MAYBE HE DELIBERATELY USED SOMEONE THAT TV PEOPLE WOULD KNOW... WELL, I GUESS THAT'S PUSHING IT...
YEAH, BUT I DON'T THINK WE CAN DEFINITELY SAY IT'S A SECOND KIRA JUST FROM THAT...
HMM.
RYUZAKI... WHAT'S THE PROBABILITY THAT THIS IS A SECOND KIRA?

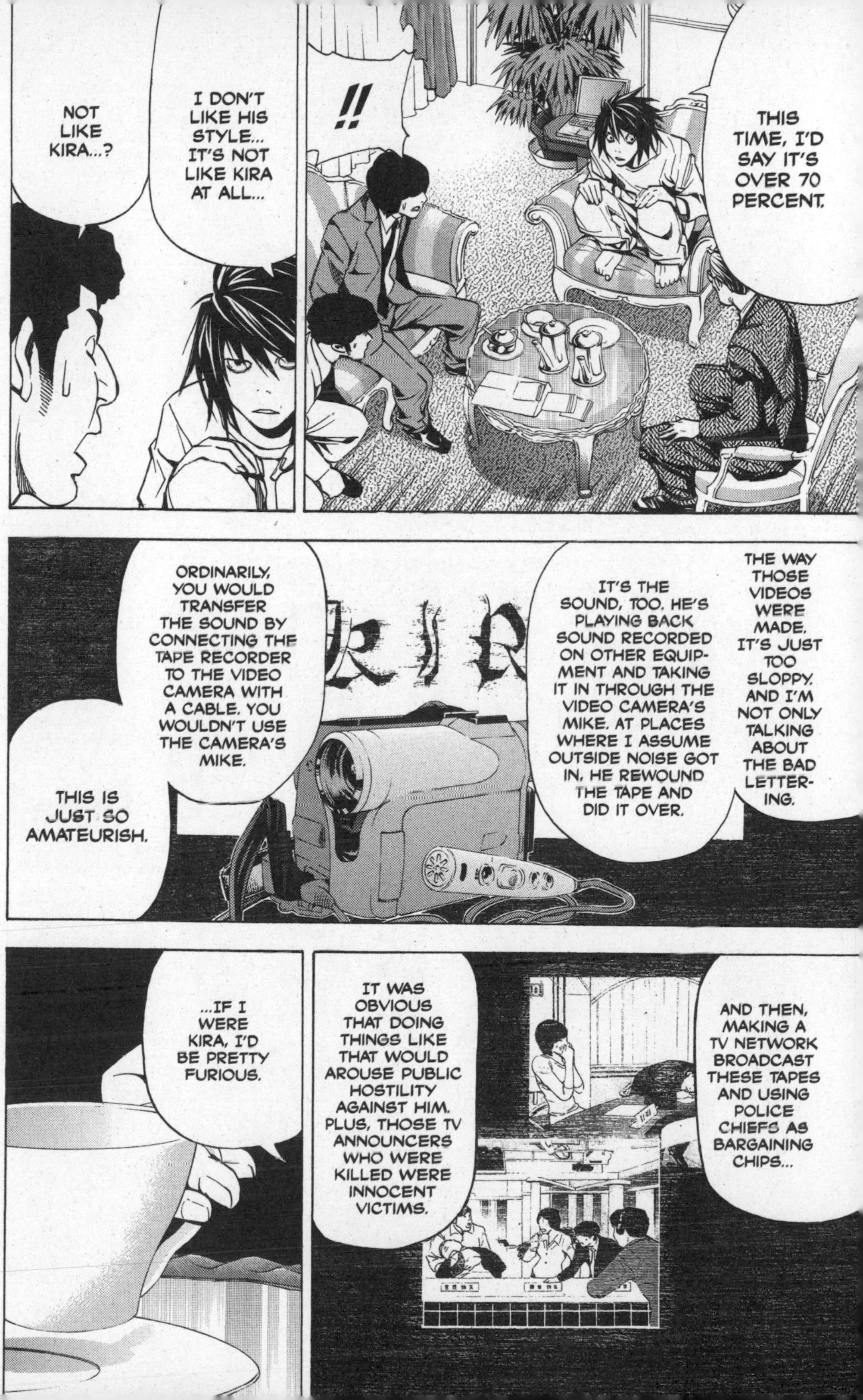
THIS TIME, I'D SAY IT'S OVER 70 PERCENT.
!!
I DON'T LIKE HIS STYLE... IT'S NOT LIKE KIRA AT ALL...
NOT LIKE KIRA...?
THE WAY THOSE VIDEOS WERE MADE. IT'S JUST TOO SLOPPY. AND I'M NOT ONLY TALKING ABOUT THE BAD LETTERING.
IT'S THE SOUND, TOO. HE'S PLAYING BACK SOUND RECORDED ON OTHER EQUIPMENT AND TAKING IT IN THROUGH THE VIDEO CAMERA'S MIKE. AT PLACES WHERE I ASSUME OUTSIDE NOISE GOT IN, HE REWOUND THE TAPE AND DID IT OVER.
ORDINARILY, YOU WOULD TRANSFER THE SOUND BY CONNECTING THE TAPE RECORDER TO THE VIDEO CAMERA WITH A CABLE. YOU WOULDN'T USE THE CAMERA'S MIKE.
THIS IS JUST SO AMATEURISH.
AND THEN, MAKING A TV NETWORK BROADCAST THESE TAPES AND USING POLICE CHIEFS AS BARGAINING CHIPS...
IT WAS OBVIOUS THAT DOING THINGS LIKE THAT WOULD AROUSE PUBLIC HOSTILITY AGAINST HIM. PLUS, THOSE TV ANNOUNCERS WHO WERE KILLED WERE INNOCENT VICTIMS.
...IF I WERE KIRA, I'D BE PRETTY FURIOUS.

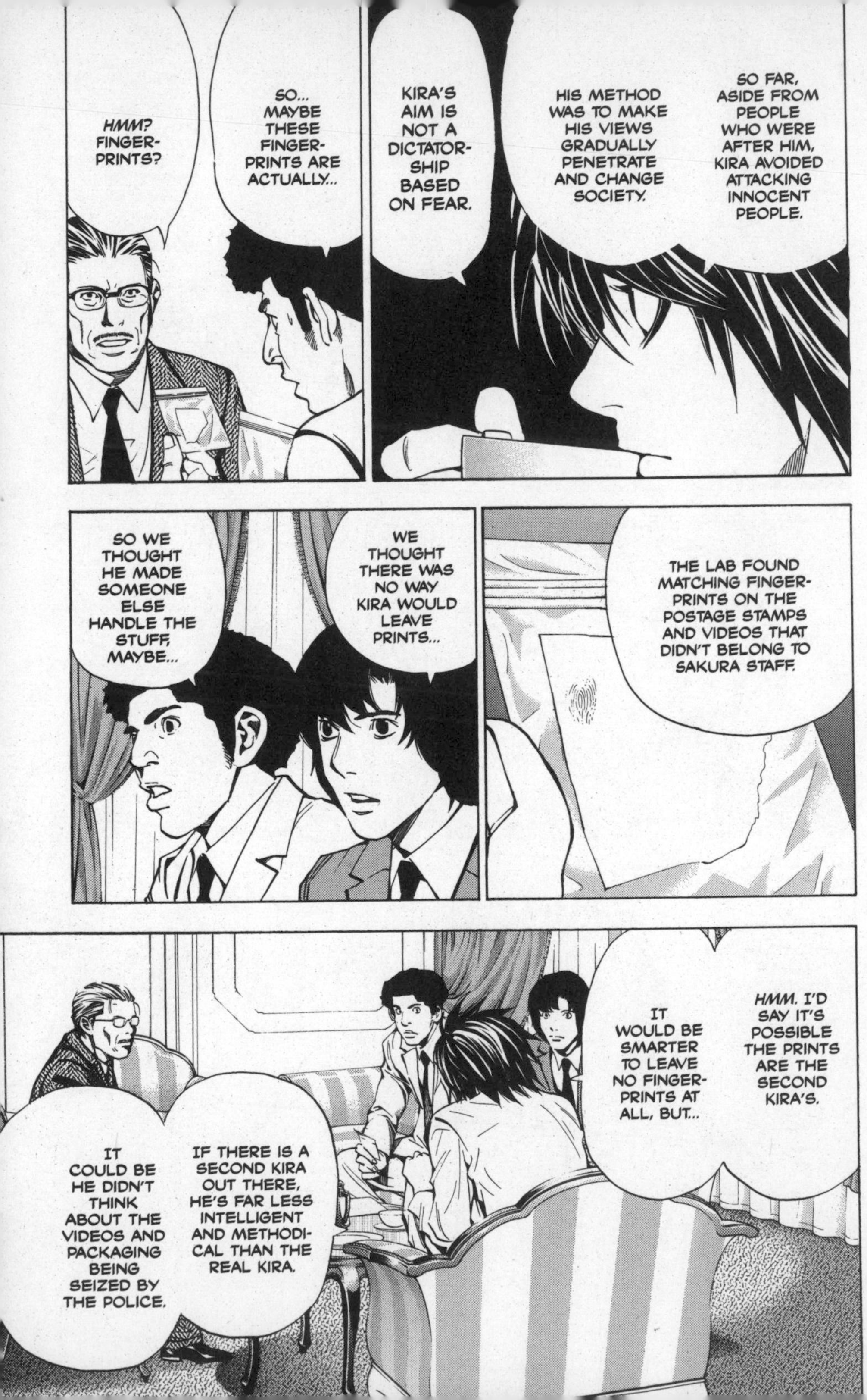
SO FAR, ASIDE FROM PEOPLE WHO WERE AFTER HIM, KIRA AVOIDED ATTACKING INNOCENT PEOPLE.
HIS METHOD WAS TO MAKE HIS VIEWS GRADUALLY PENETRATE AND CHANGE SOCIETY.
KIRA'S AIM IS NOT A DICTATOR-SHIP BASED ON FEAR.
SO... MAYBE THESE FINGER-PRINTS ARE ACTUALLY...
HMM? FINGER-PRINTS?
THE LAB FOUND MATCHING FINGER-PRINTS ON THE POSTAGE STAMPS AND VIDEOS THAT DIDN'T BELONG TO SAKURA STAFF.
WE THOUGHT THERE WAS NO WAY KIRA WOULD LEAVE PRINTS...
SO WE THOUGHT HE MADE SOMEONE ELSE HANDLE THE STUFF, MAYBE...
HMM. I'D SAY IT'S POSSIBLE THE PRINTS ARE THE SECOND KIRA'S.
IT WOULD BE SMARTER TO LEAVE NO FINGER-PRINTS AT ALL, BUT...
IF THERE IS A SECOND KIRA OUT THERE, HE'S FAR LESS INTELLIGENT AND METHODI-CAL THAN THE REAL KIRA.
IT COULD BE HE DIDN'T THINK ABOUT THE VIDEOS AND PACKAGING BEING SEIZED BY THE POLICE.

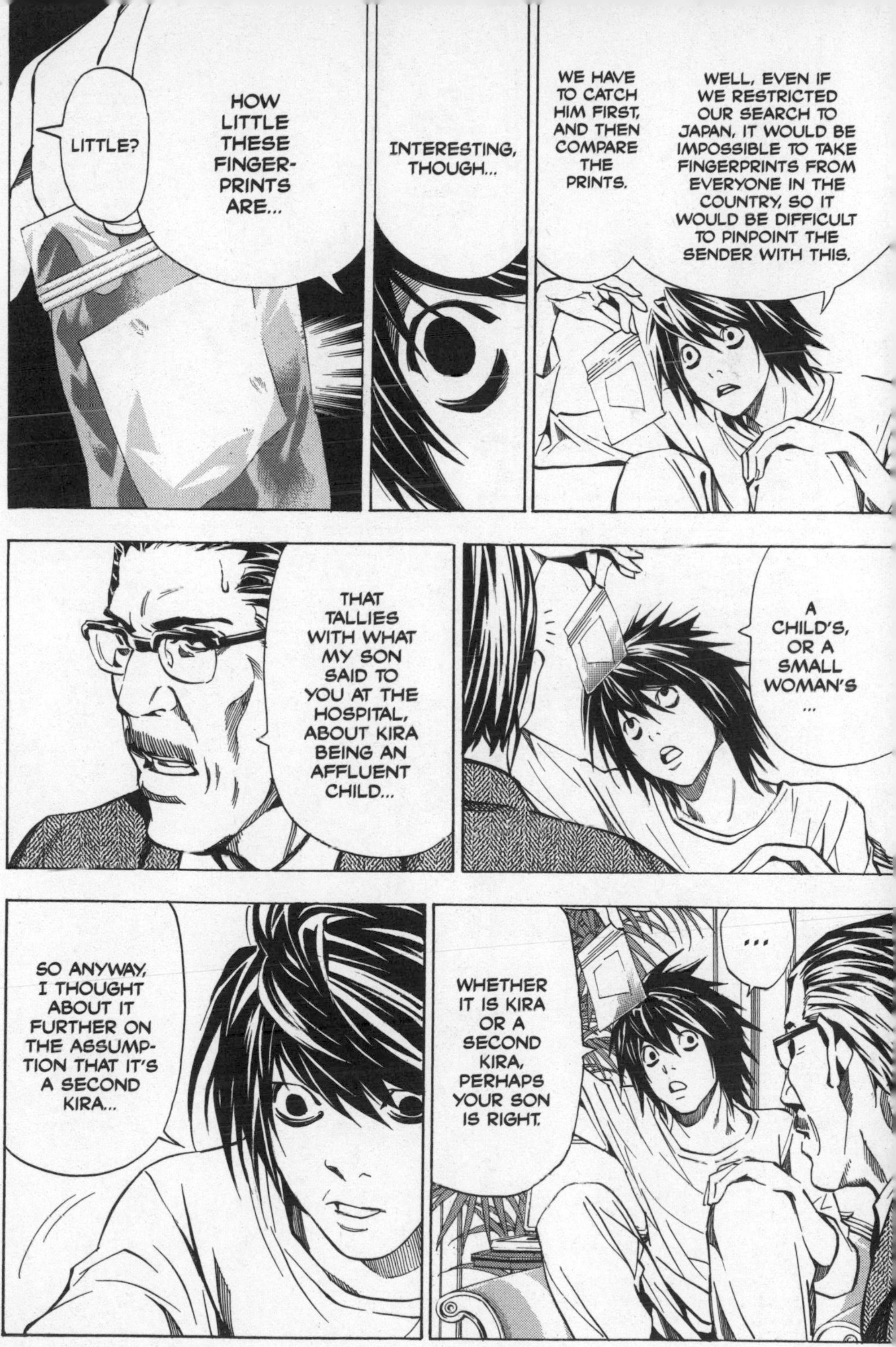
WELL, EVEN IF WE RESTRICTED OUR SEARCH TO JAPAN, IT WOULD BE IMPOSSIBLE TO TAKE FINGERPRINTS FROM EVERYONE IN THE COUNTRY, SO IT WOULD BE DIFFICULT TO PINPOINT THE SENDER WITH THIS.
WE HAVE TO CATCH HIM FIRST, AND THEN COMPARE THE PRINTS.
INTERESTING, THOUGH...
HOW LITTLE THESE FINGER-PRINTS ARE...
LITTLE?
A CHILD'S, OR A SMALL WOMAN'S ...
THAT TALLIES WITH WHAT MY SON SAID TO YOU AT THE HOSPITAL, ABOUT KIRA BEING AN AFFLUENT CHILD...
...
WHETHER IT IS KIRA OR A SECOND KIRA, PERHAPS YOUR SON IS RIGHT.
SO ANYWAY, I THOUGHT ABOUT IT FURTHER ON THE ASSUMP-TION THAT IT'S A SECOND KIRA...

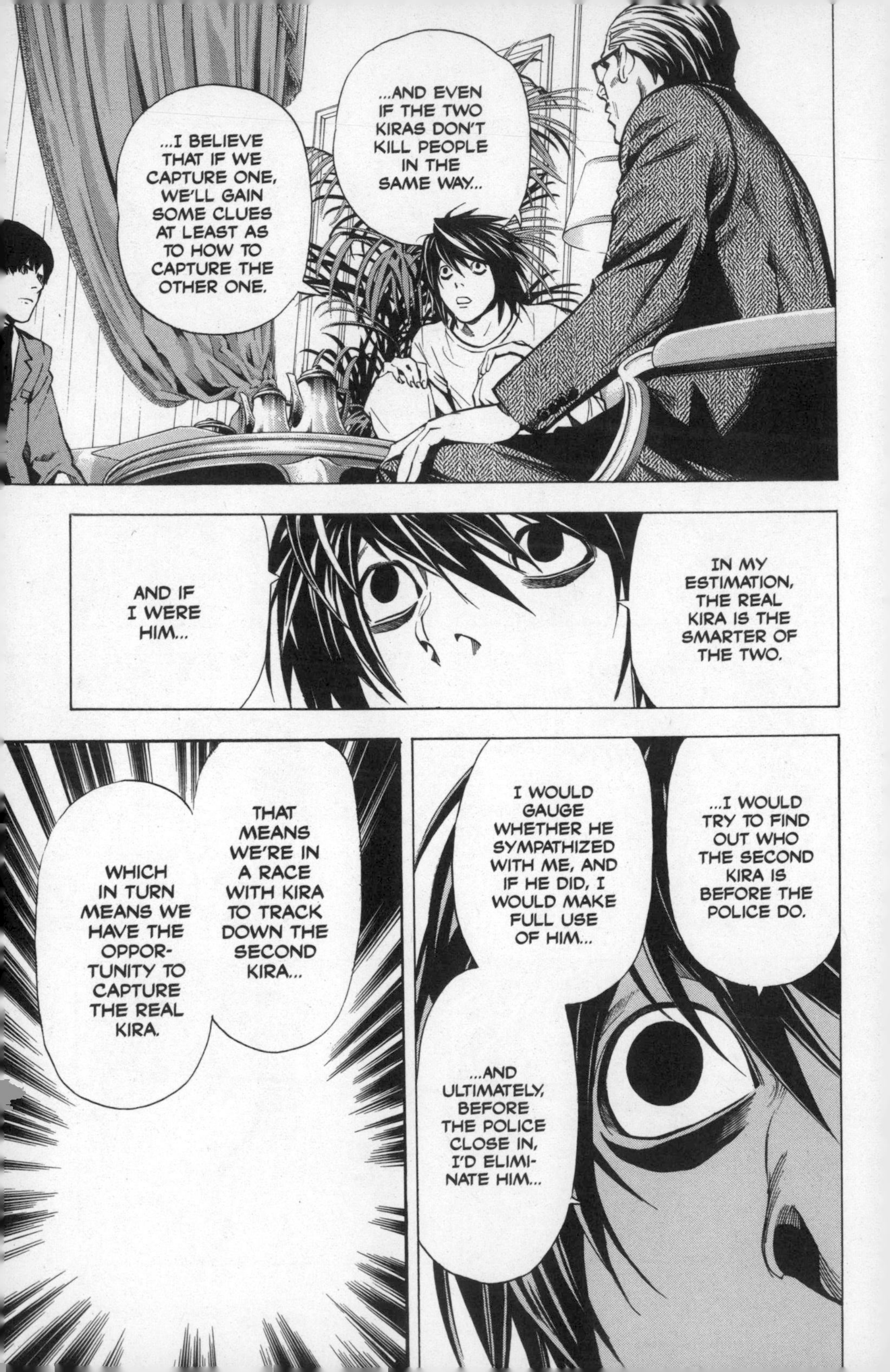
...AND EVEN IF THE TWO KIRAS DON'T KILL PEOPLE IN THE SAME WAY...
...I BELIEVE THAT IF WE CAPTURE ONE, WE'LL GAIN SOME CLUES AT LEAST AS TO HOW TO CAPTURE THE OTHER ONE.
IN MY ESTIMATION, THE REAL KIRA IS THE SMARTER OF THE TWO.
AND IF I WERE HIM...
...I WOULD TRY TO FIND OUT WHO THE SECOND KIRA IS BEFORE THE POLICE DO.
I WOULD GAUGE WHETHER HE SYMPATHIZED WITH ME, AND IF HE DID, I WOULD MAKE FULL USE OF HIM...
...AND ULTIMATELY, BEFORE THE POLICE CLOSE IN, I'D ELIMI-NATE HIM...
THAT MEANS WE'RE IN A RACE WITH KIRA TO TRACK DOWN THE SECOND KIRA...
WHICH IN TURN MEANS WE HAVE THE OPPOR-TUNITY TO CAPTURE THE REAL KIRA.

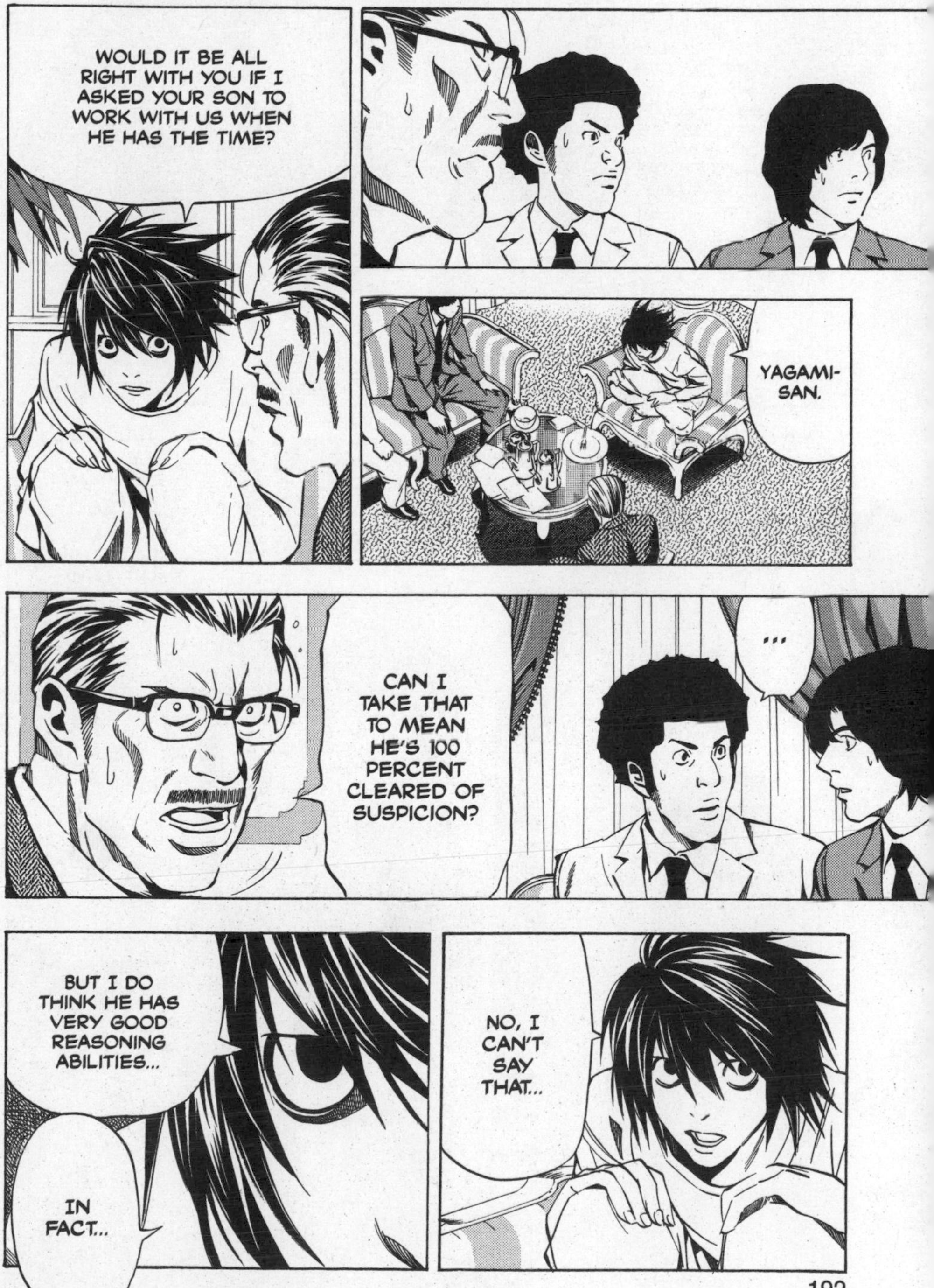
YAGAMI-SAN.
WOULD IT BE ALL RIGHT WITH YOU IF I ASKED YOUR SON TO WORK WITH US WHEN HE HAS THE TIME?
...
CAN I TAKE THAT TO MEAN HE'S 100 PERCENT CLEARED OF SUSPICION?
NO, I CAN'T SAY THAT...
BUT I DO THINK HE HAS VERY GOOD REASONING ABILITIES...
IN FACT...

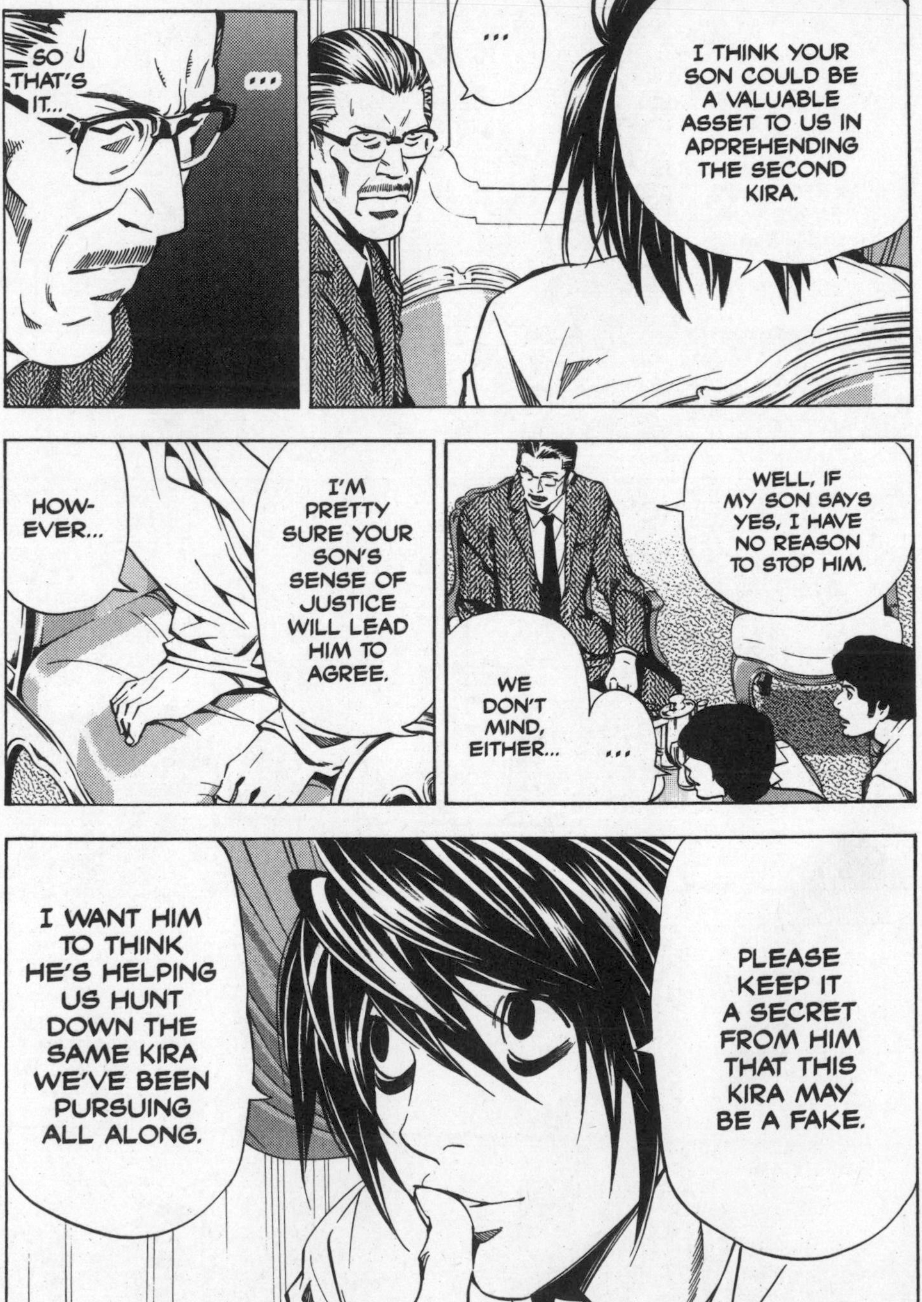
I THINK YOUR SON COULD BE A VALUABLE ASSET TO US IN APPREHENDING THE SECOND KIRA.
...
...
SO THAT'S IT...
WELL, IF MY SON SAYS YES, I HAVE NO REASON TO STOP HIM.
WE DON'T MIND, EITHER...
...
I'M PRETTY SURE YOUR SON'S SENSE OF JUSTICE WILL LEAD HIM TO AGREE.
HOW-EVER...
PLEASE KEEP IT A SECRET FROM HIM THAT THIS KIRA MAY BE A FAKE.
I WANT HIM TO THINK HE'S HELPING US HUNT DOWN THE SAME KIRA WE'VE BEEN PURSUING ALL ALONG.

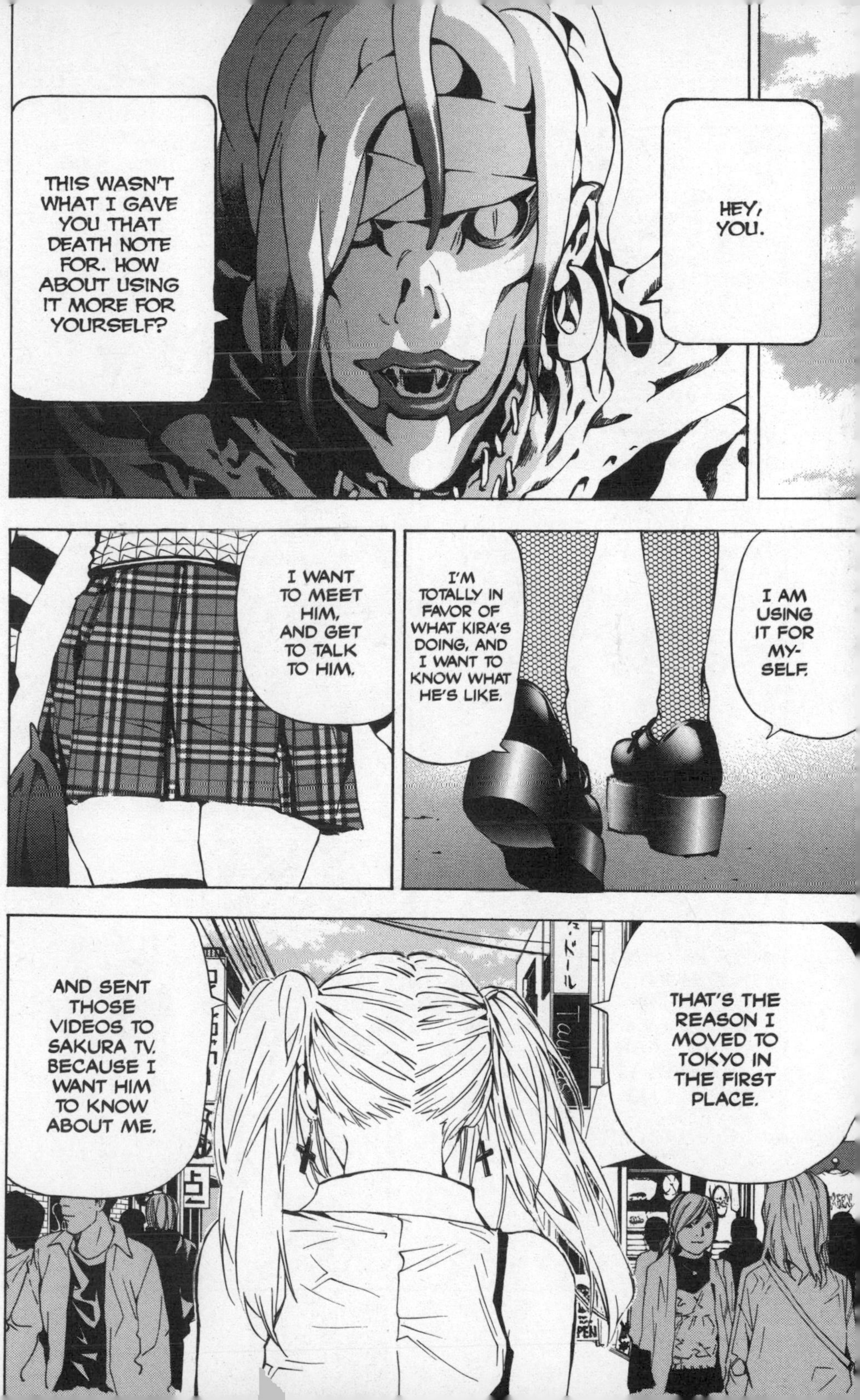
HEY, YOU.
THIS WASN'T WHAT I GAVE YOU THAT DEATH NOTE FOR. HOW ABOUT USING IT MORE FOR YOURSELF?
I AM USING IT FOR MY-SELF.
I'M TOTALLY IN FAVOR OF WHAT KIRA'S DOING, AND I WANT TO KNOW WHAT HE'S LIKE.
I WANT TO MEET HIM, AND GET TO TALK TO HIM.
THAT'S THE REASON I MOVED TO TOKYO IN THE FIRST PLACE.
AND SENT THOSE VIDEOS TO SAKURA TV. BECAUSE I WANT HIM TO KNOW ABOUT ME.

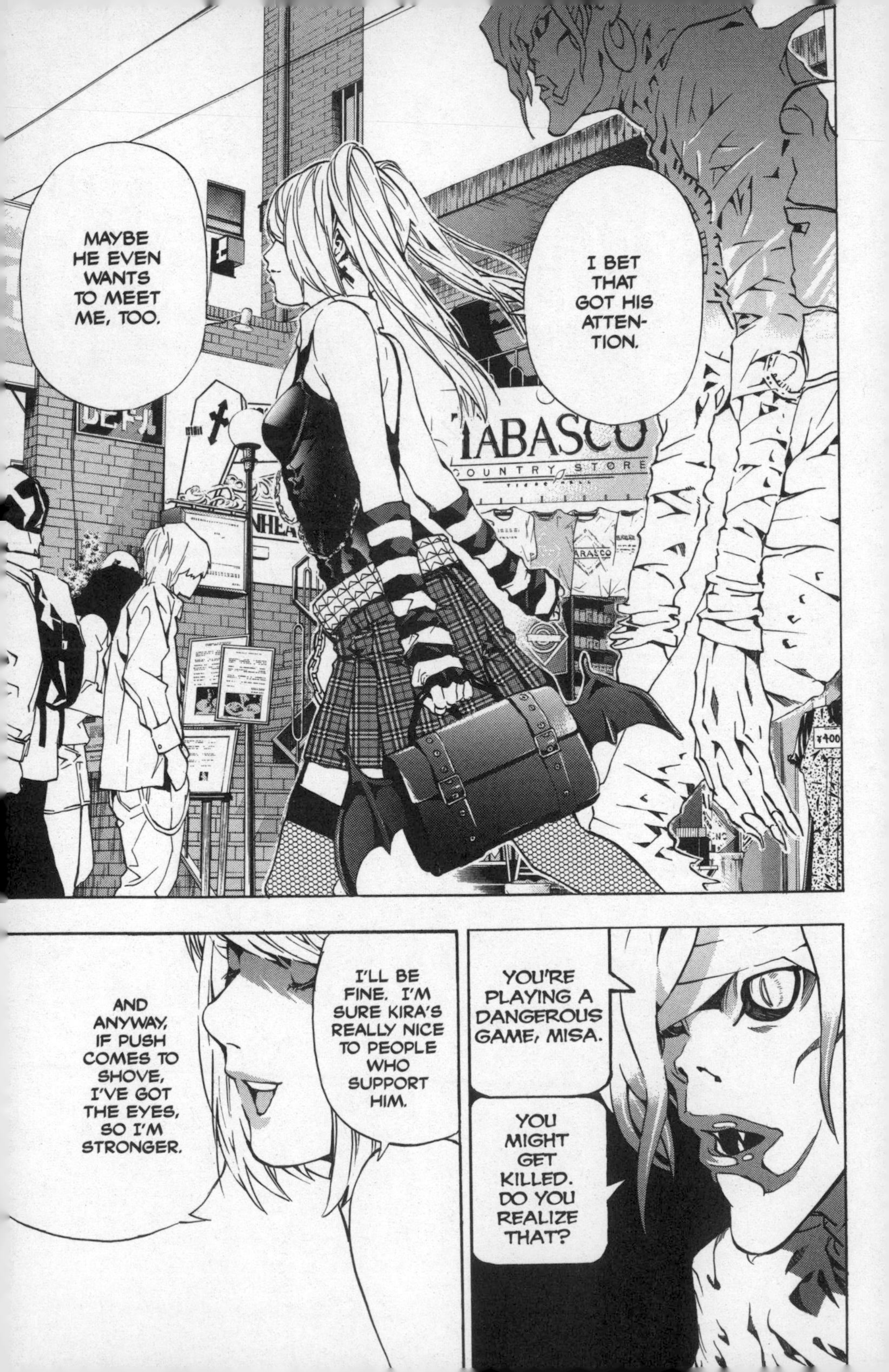
I BET THAT GOT HIS ATTENTION.
MAYBE HE EVEN WANTS TO MEET ME, TOO.
TABASCO
COUNTRY STORE
YOU'RE PLAYING A DANGEROUS GAME, MISA.
YOU MIGHT GET KILLED. DO YOU REALIZE THAT?
I'LL BE FINE. I'M SURE KIRA'S REALLY NICE TO PEOPLE WHO SUPPORT HIM.
AND ANYWAY, IF PUSH COMES TO SHOVE, I'VE GOT THE EYES, SO I'M STRONGER.

DEATH NOTE
How to use it
XV

○ When the same name is written on more than two DEATH NOTES, the Note which was first filled in will take effect. regard less of the time of death,.

二冊以上のデスノートに同じ人間の名前が書かれた場合、記してある死亡時刻には関係なく、一番先に書かれたものが優先される。

○ If writing the same name on more than two DEATH NOTES is completed within a 0.06-second difference, it is regarded as simultaneous; the DEATH NOTE will not take effect and the individual written will not die.

二冊以上のデスノートで名前を書き終える時間の差が0.06秒以内の場合は同時とみなされ、それらのノートに書かれた事は無効になり、名前を書かれた人間は死なない。

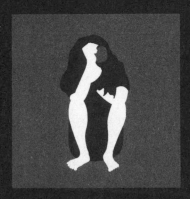

Walking along a street in a small town, I come to a
T-intersection and turn right. At the next T-intersection
I turn left. I keep repeating this pattern, wondering how
far I'll get. Finally I end up on a large road, where I'm not
going to come to any T-intersections for a long time, so I
turn around and head back. But on the return journey, all
the T-intersections I'd turned at have been transformed
into plain old side streets. "This is a mystery. This is a
trick!" I think, as I ask passersby for help going home.
Just one memory from a foolish childhood.

-Tsugumi Ohba

chapter 26 Reversal

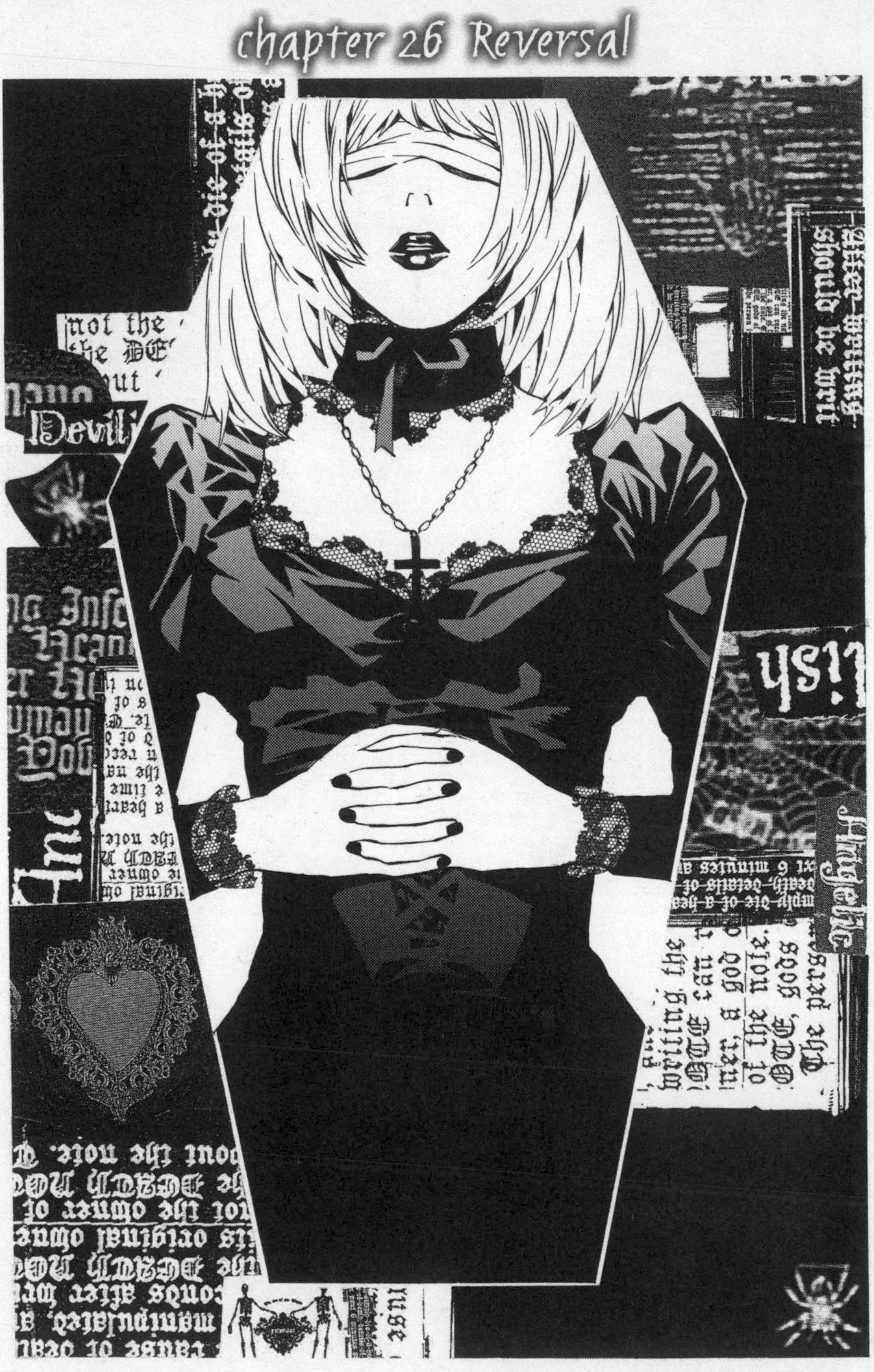
Devil

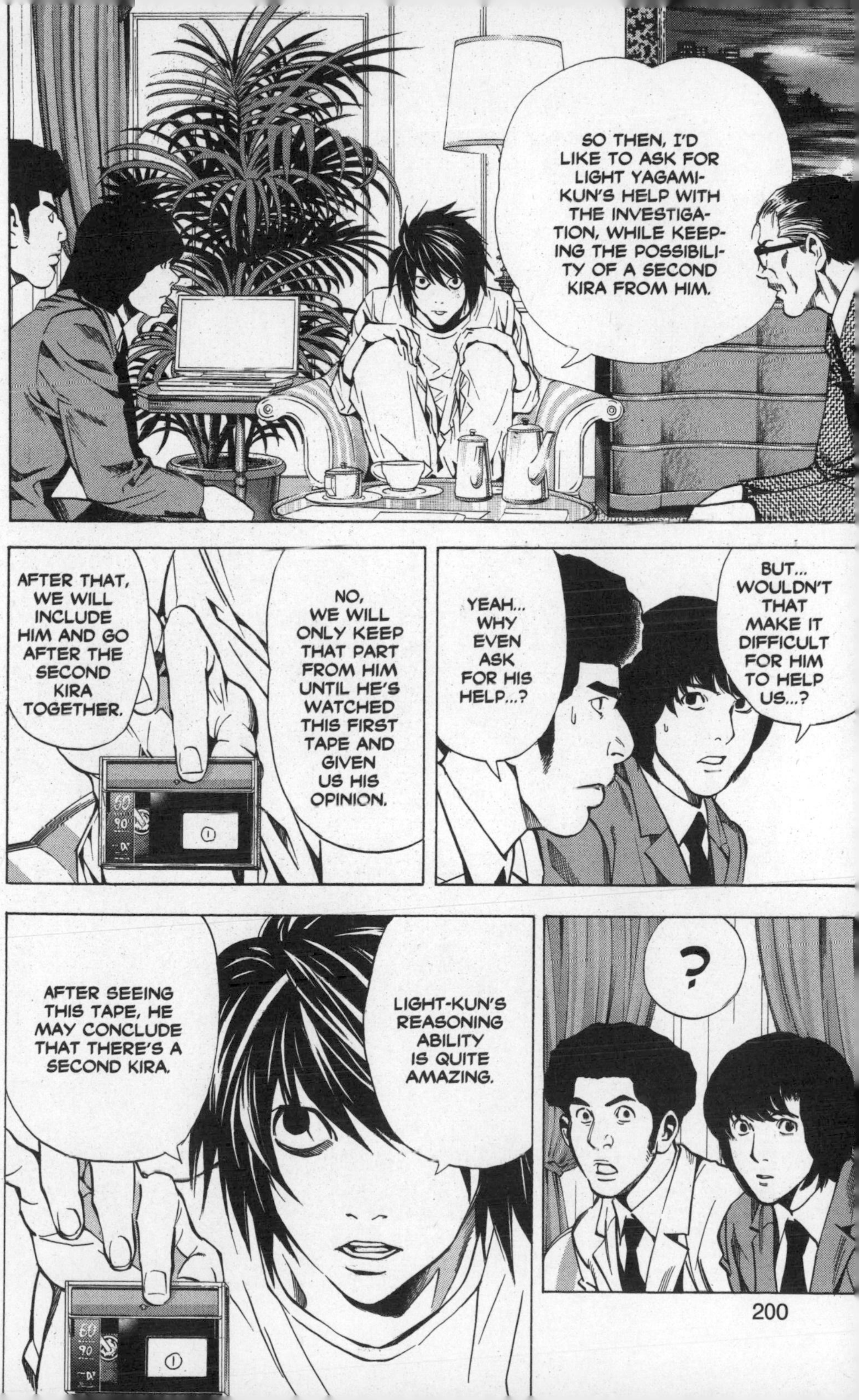
SO THEN, I'D LIKE TO ASK FOR LIGHT YAGAMI-KUN'S HELP WITH THE INVESTIGATION, WHILE KEEPING THE POSSIBILITY OF A SECOND KIRA FROM HIM.
BUT... WOULDN'T THAT MAKE IT DIFFICULT FOR HIM TO HELP US...?
YEAH... WHY EVEN ASK FOR HIS HELP...?
NO, WE WILL ONLY KEEP THAT PART FROM HIM UNTIL HE'S WATCHED THIS FIRST TAPE AND GIVEN US HIS OPINION.
AFTER THAT, WE WILL INCLUDE HIM AND GO AFTER THE SECOND KIRA TOGETHER.
?
LIGHT-KUN'S REASONING ABILITY IS QUITE AMAZING.
AFTER SEEING THIS TAPE, HE MAY CONCLUDE THAT THERE'S A SECOND KIRA.

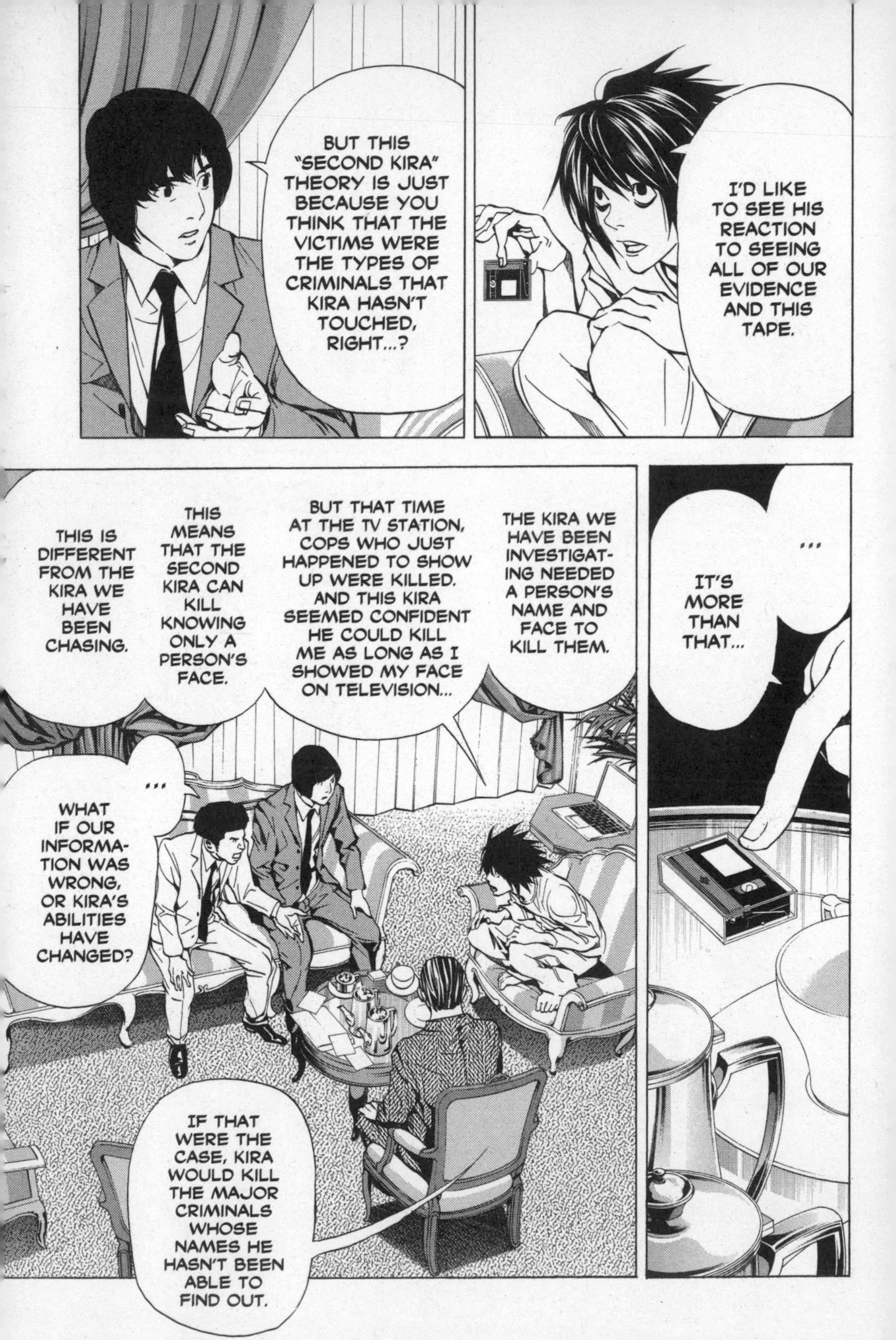
I'D LIKE TO SEE HIS REACTION TO SEEING ALL OF OUR EVIDENCE AND THIS TAPE.
BUT THIS "SECOND KIRA" THEORY IS JUST BECAUSE YOU THINK THAT THE VICTIMS WERE THE TYPES OF CRIMINALS THAT KIRA HASN'T TOUCHED, RIGHT...?
...
IT'S MORE THAN THAT...
THE KIRA WE HAVE BEEN INVESTIGATING NEEDED A PERSON'S NAME AND FACE TO KILL THEM.
BUT THAT TIME AT THE TV STATION, COPS WHO JUST HAPPENED TO SHOW UP WERE KILLED. AND THIS KIRA SEEMED CONFIDENT HE COULD KILL ME AS LONG AS I SHOWED MY FACE ON TELEVISION...
THIS MEANS THAT THE SECOND KIRA CAN KILL KNOWING ONLY A PERSON'S FACE.
THIS IS DIFFERENT FROM THE KIRA WE HAVE BEEN CHASING.
...
WHAT IF OUR INFORMATION WAS WRONG, OR KIRA'S ABILITIES HAVE CHANGED?
IF THAT WERE THE CASE, KIRA WOULD KILL THE MAJOR CRIMINALS WHOSE NAMES HE HASN'T BEEN ABLE TO FIND OUT.

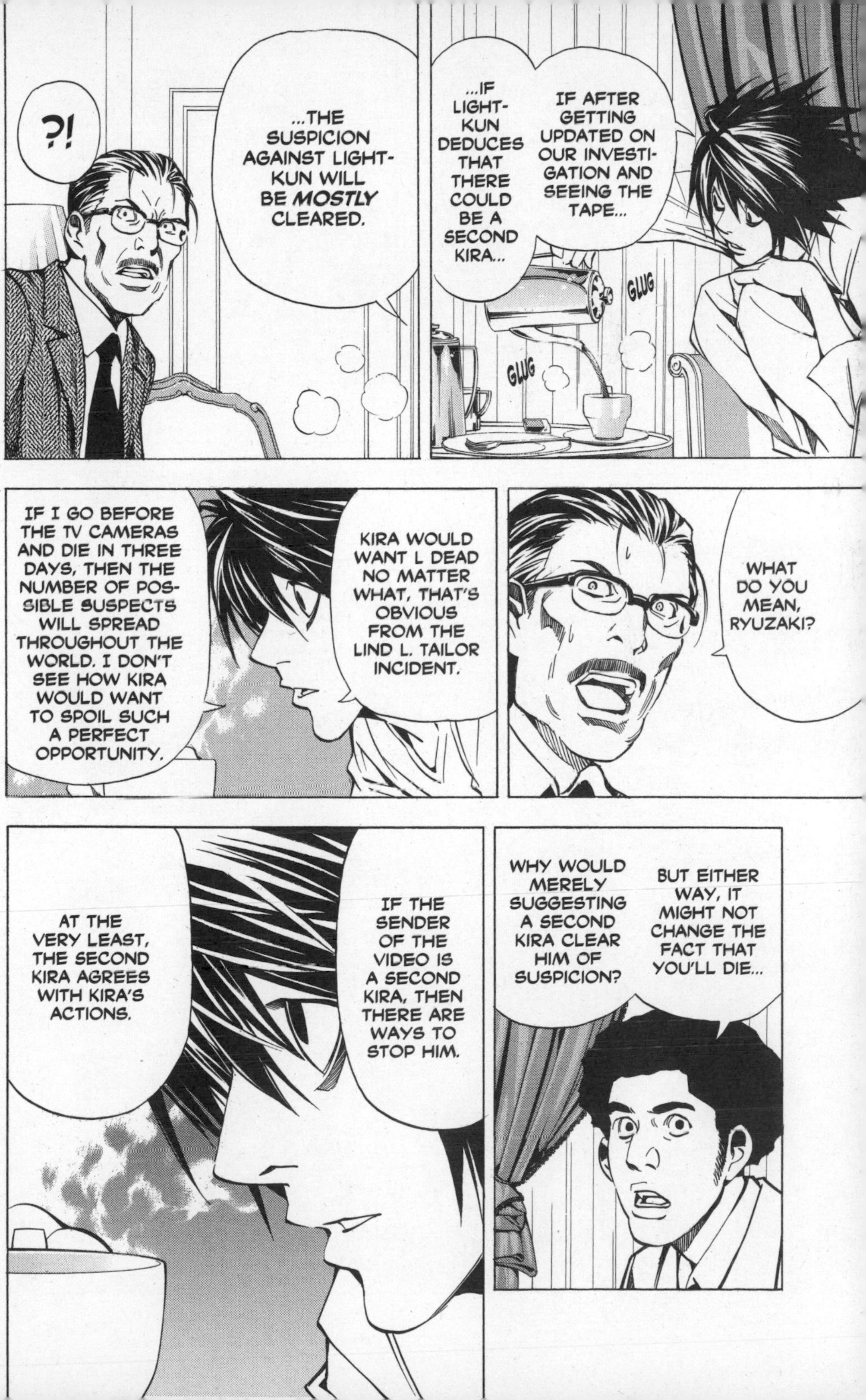
IF AFTER GETTING UPDATED ON OUR INVESTIGATION AND SEEING THE TAPE...
...IF LIGHT-KUN DEDUCES THAT THERE COULD BE A SECOND KIRA...
GLUG
GLUG
...THE SUSPICION AGAINST LIGHT-KUN WILL BE *MOSTLY* CLEARED.
?!
WHAT DO YOU MEAN, RYUZAKI?
KIRA WOULD WANT L DEAD NO MATTER WHAT, THAT'S OBVIOUS FROM THE LIND L. TAILOR INCIDENT.
IF I GO BEFORE THE TV CAMERAS AND DIE IN THREE DAYS, THEN THE NUMBER OF POSSIBLE SUSPECTS WILL SPREAD THROUGHOUT THE WORLD. I DON'T SEE HOW KIRA WOULD WANT TO SPOIL SUCH A PERFECT OPPORTUNITY.
BUT EITHER WAY, IT MIGHT NOT CHANGE THE FACT THAT YOU'LL DIE...
WHY WOULD MERELY SUGGESTING A SECOND KIRA CLEAR HIM OF SUSPICION?
IF THE SENDER OF THE VIDEO IS A SECOND KIRA, THEN THERE ARE WAYS TO STOP HIM.
AT THE VERY LEAST, THE SECOND KIRA AGREES WITH KIRA'S ACTIONS.

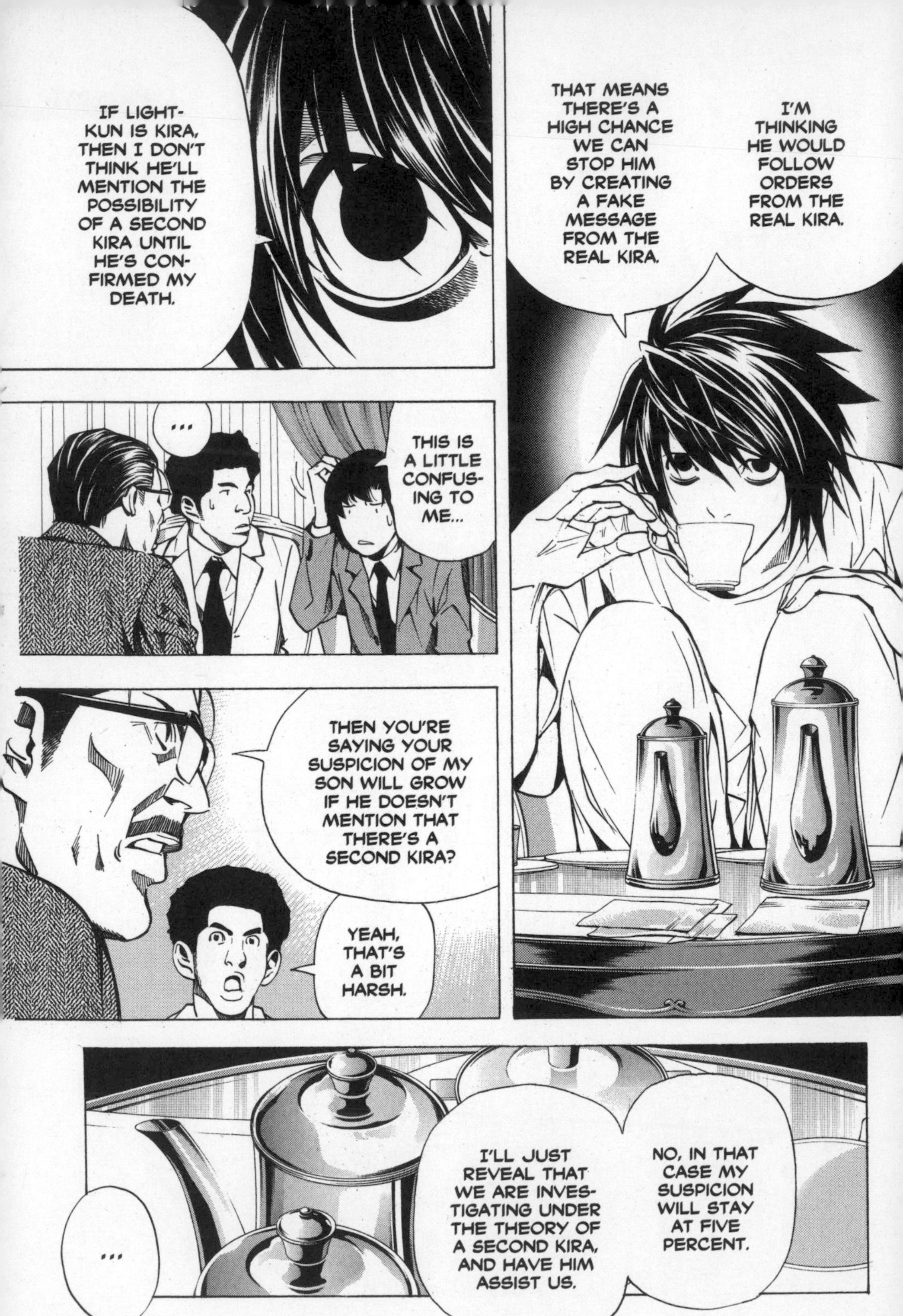
I'M THINKING HE WOULD FOLLOW ORDERS FROM THE REAL KIRA.
THAT MEANS THERE'S A HIGH CHANCE WE CAN STOP HIM BY CREATING A FAKE MESSAGE FROM THE REAL KIRA.
IF LIGHT-KUN IS KIRA, THEN I DON'T THINK HE'LL MENTION THE POSSIBILITY OF A SECOND KIRA UNTIL HE'S CONFIRMED MY DEATH.
THIS IS A LITTLE CONFUSING TO ME...
...
THEN YOU'RE SAYING YOUR SUSPICION OF MY SON WILL GROW IF HE DOESN'T MENTION THAT THERE'S A SECOND KIRA?
YEAH, THAT'S A BIT HARSH.
NO, IN THAT CASE MY SUSPICION WILL STAY AT FIVE PERCENT.
I'LL JUST REVEAL THAT WE ARE INVESTIGATING UNDER THE THEORY OF A SECOND KIRA, AND HAVE HIM ASSIST US.
...

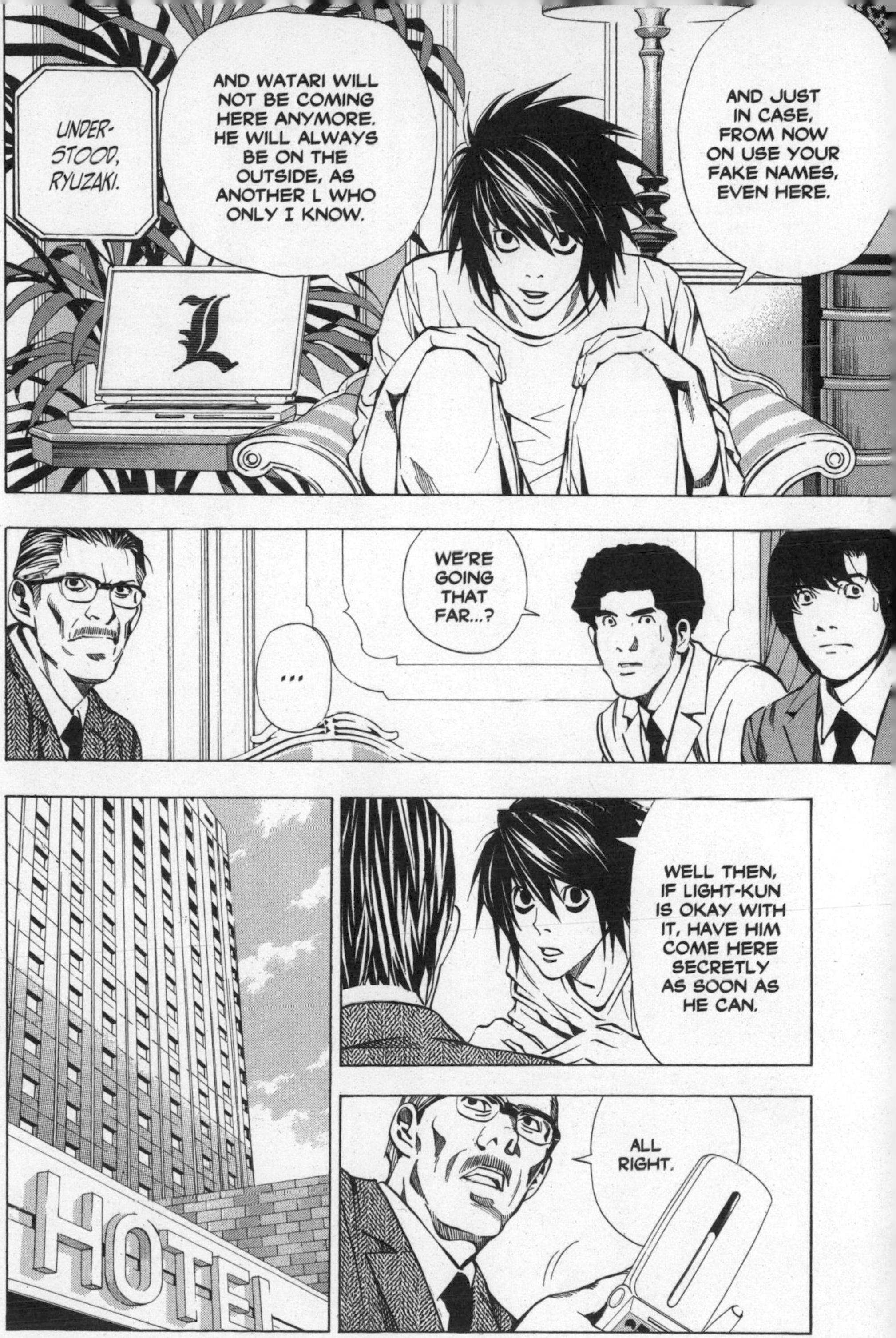
AND JUST IN CASE, FROM NOW ON USE YOUR FAKE NAMES, EVEN HERE.
AND WATARI WILL NOT BE COMING HERE ANYMORE. HE WILL ALWAYS BE ON THE OUTSIDE, AS ANOTHER L WHO ONLY I KNOW.
UNDER-STOOD, RYUZAKI.
L
WE'RE GOING THAT FAR...?
...
WELL THEN, IF LIGHT-KUN IS OKAY WITH IT, HAVE HIM COME HERE SECRETLY AS SOON AS HE CAN.
ALL RIGHT.
HOTEL

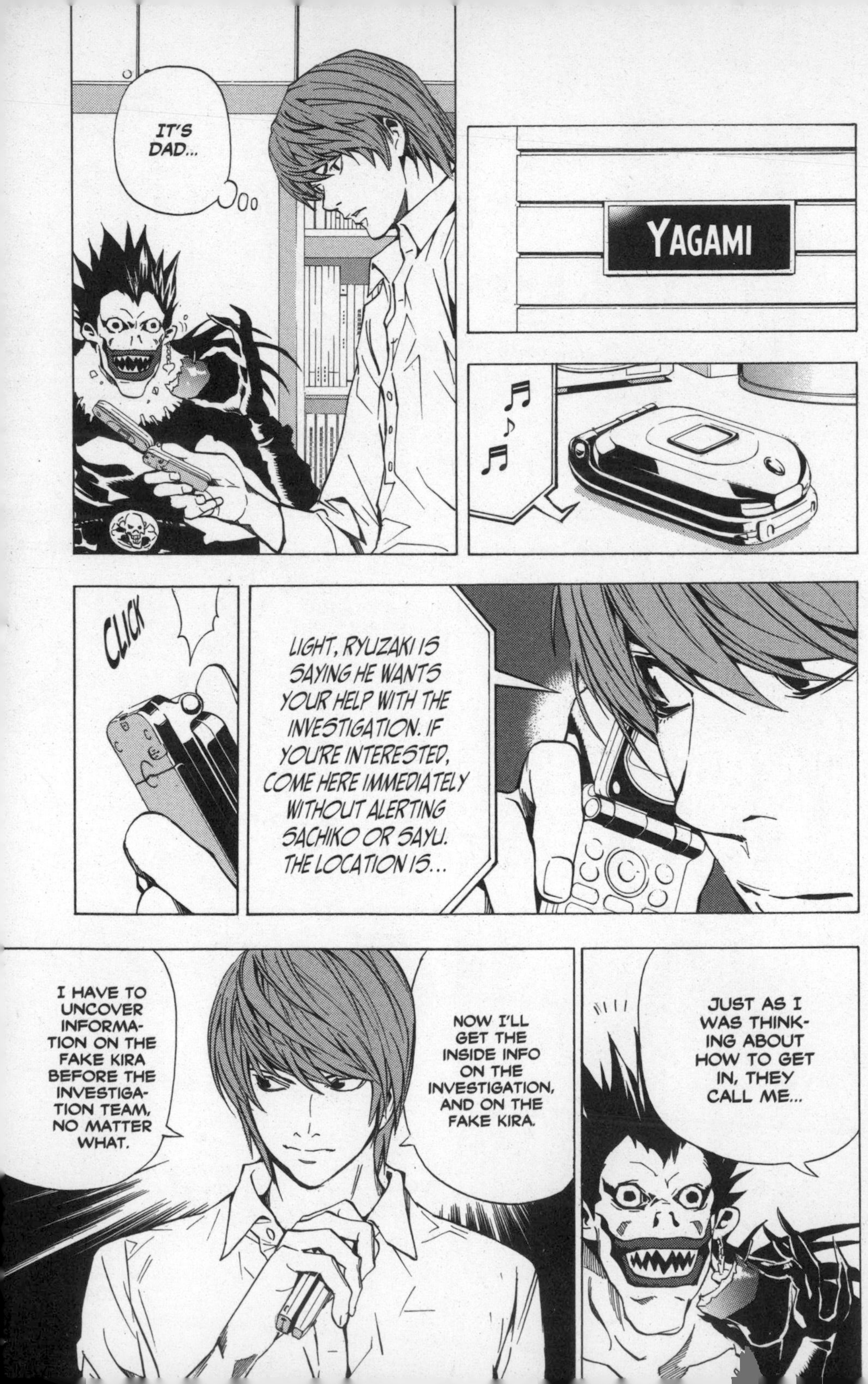
YAGAMI
IT'S DAD...
LIGHT, RYUZAKI IS SAYING HE WANTS YOUR HELP WITH THE INVESTIGATION. IF YOU'RE INTERESTED, COME HERE IMMEDIATELY WITHOUT ALERTING SACHIKO OR SAYU. THE LOCATION IS...
CLICK
JUST AS I WAS THINKING ABOUT HOW TO GET IN, THEY CALL ME...
NOW I'LL GET THE INSIDE INFO ON THE INVESTIGATION, AND ON THE FAKE KIRA.
I HAVE TO UNCOVER INFORMATION ON THE FAKE KIRA BEFORE THE INVESTIGATION TEAM, NO MATTER WHAT.

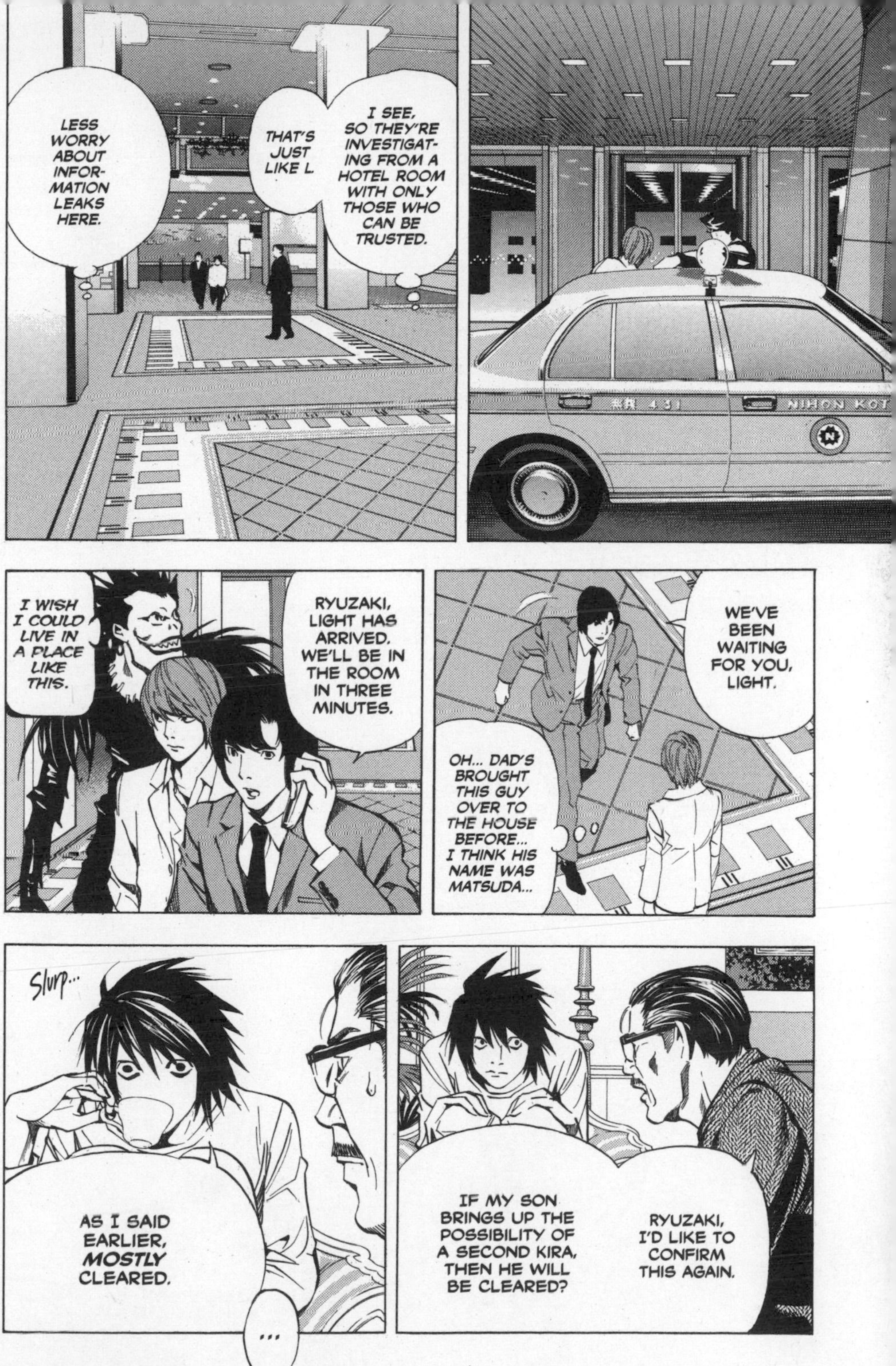
I SEE, SO THEY'RE INVESTIGATING FROM A HOTEL ROOM WITH ONLY THOSE WHO CAN BE TRUSTED.
THAT'S JUST LIKE L.
LESS WORRY ABOUT INFORMATION LEAKS HERE.
WE'VE BEEN WAITING FOR YOU, LIGHT.
OH... DAD'S BROUGHT THIS GUY OVER TO THE HOUSE BEFORE... I THINK HIS NAME WAS MATSUDA...
RYUZAKI, LIGHT HAS ARRIVED. WE'LL BE IN THE ROOM IN THREE MINUTES.
I WISH I COULD LIVE IN A PLACE LIKE THIS.
RYUZAKI, I'D LIKE TO CONFIRM THIS AGAIN.
IF MY SON BRINGS UP THE POSSIBILITY OF A SECOND KIRA, THEN HE WILL BE CLEARED?
Slurp...
AS I SAID EARLIER, **MOSTLY** CLEARED.
...

READ THIS WAY

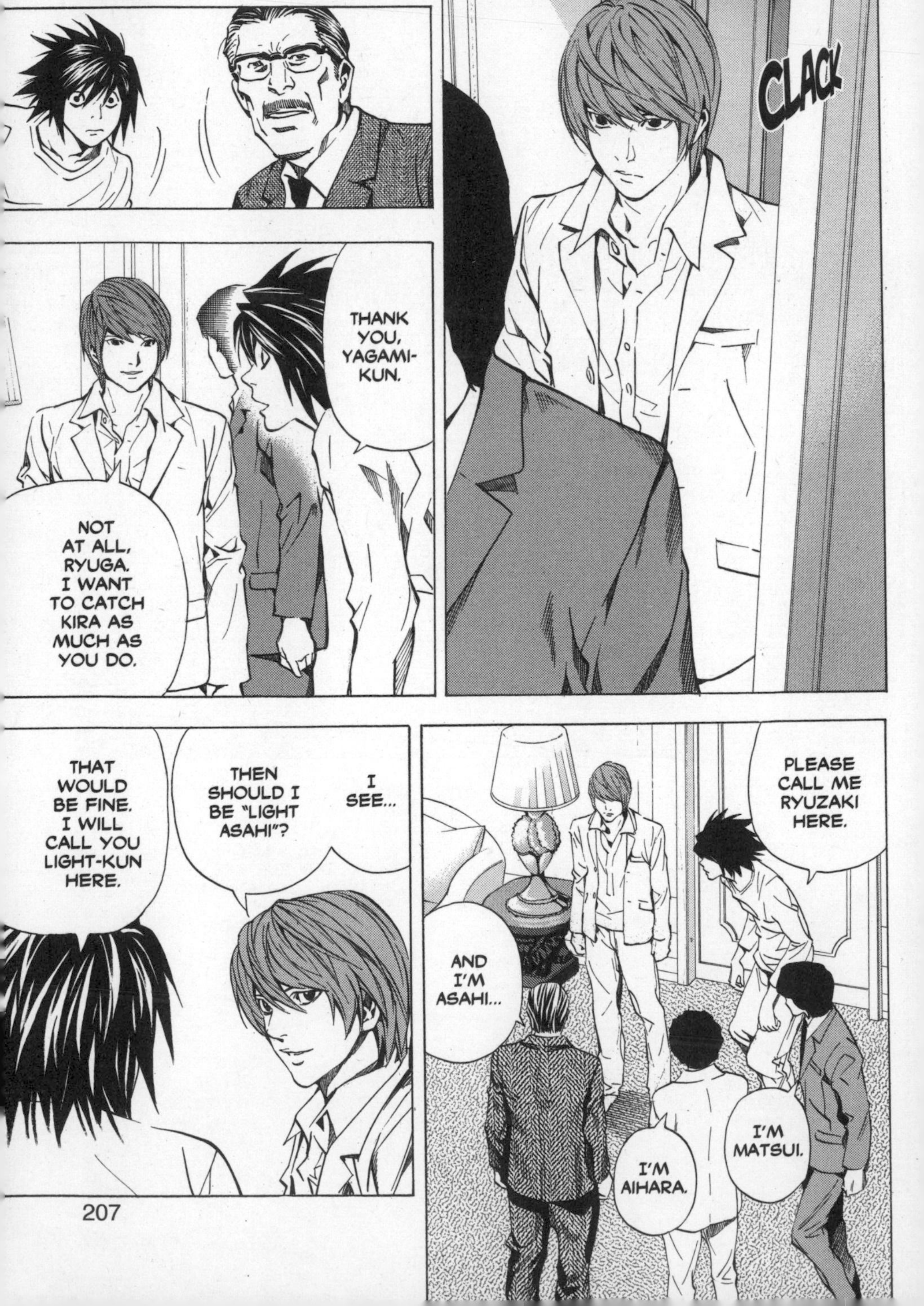
CLACK
THANK YOU, YAGAMI-KUN.
NOT AT ALL, RYUGA. I WANT TO CATCH KIRA AS MUCH AS YOU DO.
PLEASE CALL ME RYUZAKI HERE.
AND I'M ASAHI...
I'M MATSUI.
I'M AIHARA.
I SEE...
THEN SHOULD I BE "LIGHT ASAHI"?
THAT WOULD BE FINE. I WILL CALL YOU LIGHT-KUN HERE.

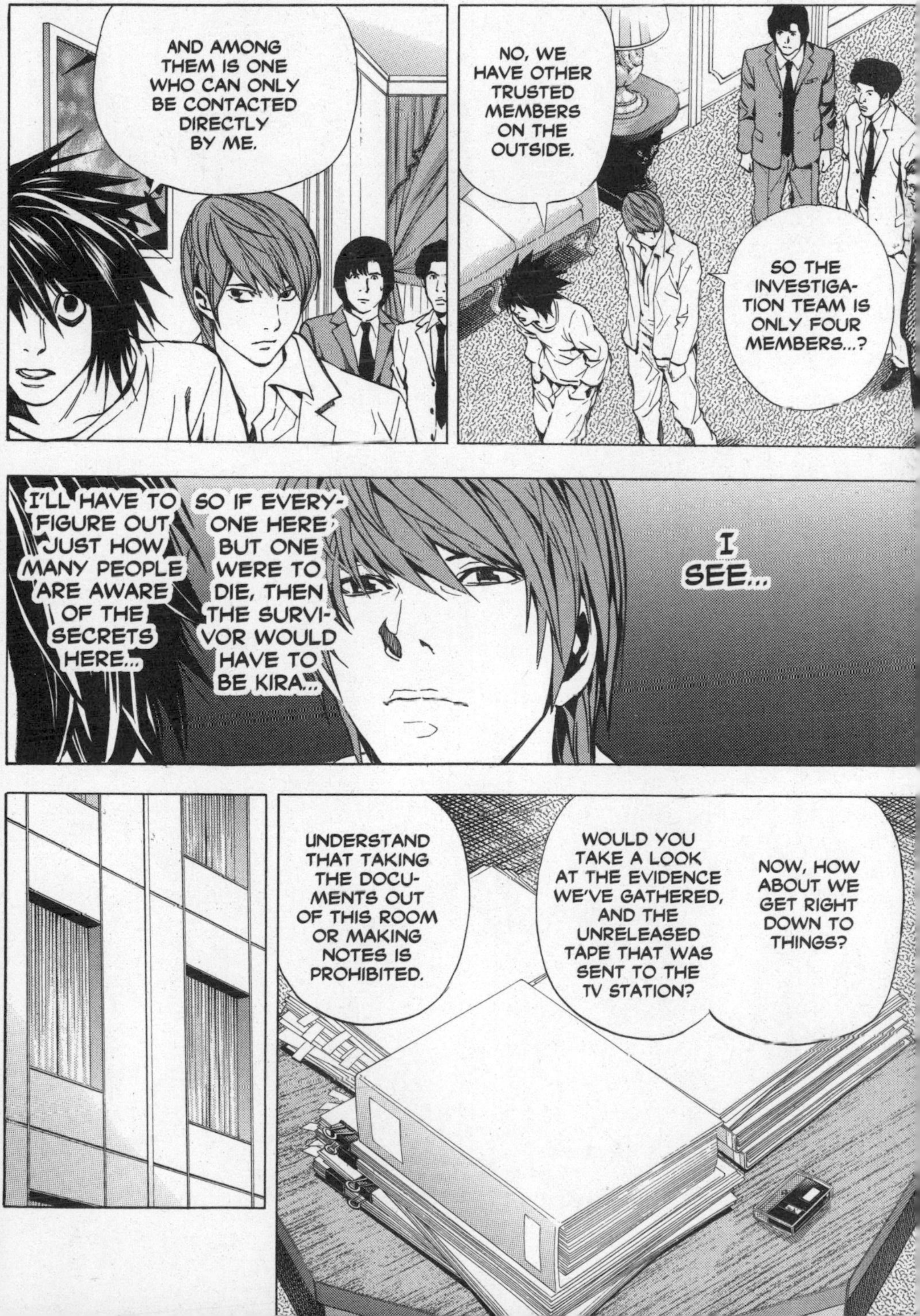
SO THE INVESTIGATION TEAM IS ONLY FOUR MEMBERS...?
NO, WE HAVE OTHER TRUSTED MEMBERS ON THE OUTSIDE.
AND AMONG THEM IS ONE WHO CAN ONLY BE CONTACTED DIRECTLY BY ME.
I SEE...
SO IF EVERYONE HERE BUT ONE WERE TO DIE, THEN THE SURVIVOR WOULD HAVE TO BE KIRA...
I'LL HAVE TO FIGURE OUT JUST HOW MANY PEOPLE ARE AWARE OF THE SECRETS HERE...
NOW, HOW ABOUT WE GET RIGHT DOWN TO THINGS?
WOULD YOU TAKE A LOOK AT THE EVIDENCE WE'VE GATHERED, AND THE UNRELEASED TAPE THAT WAS SENT TO THE TV STATION?
UNDERSTAND THAT TAKING THE DOCUMENTS OUT OF THIS ROOM OR MAKING NOTES IS PROHIBITED.

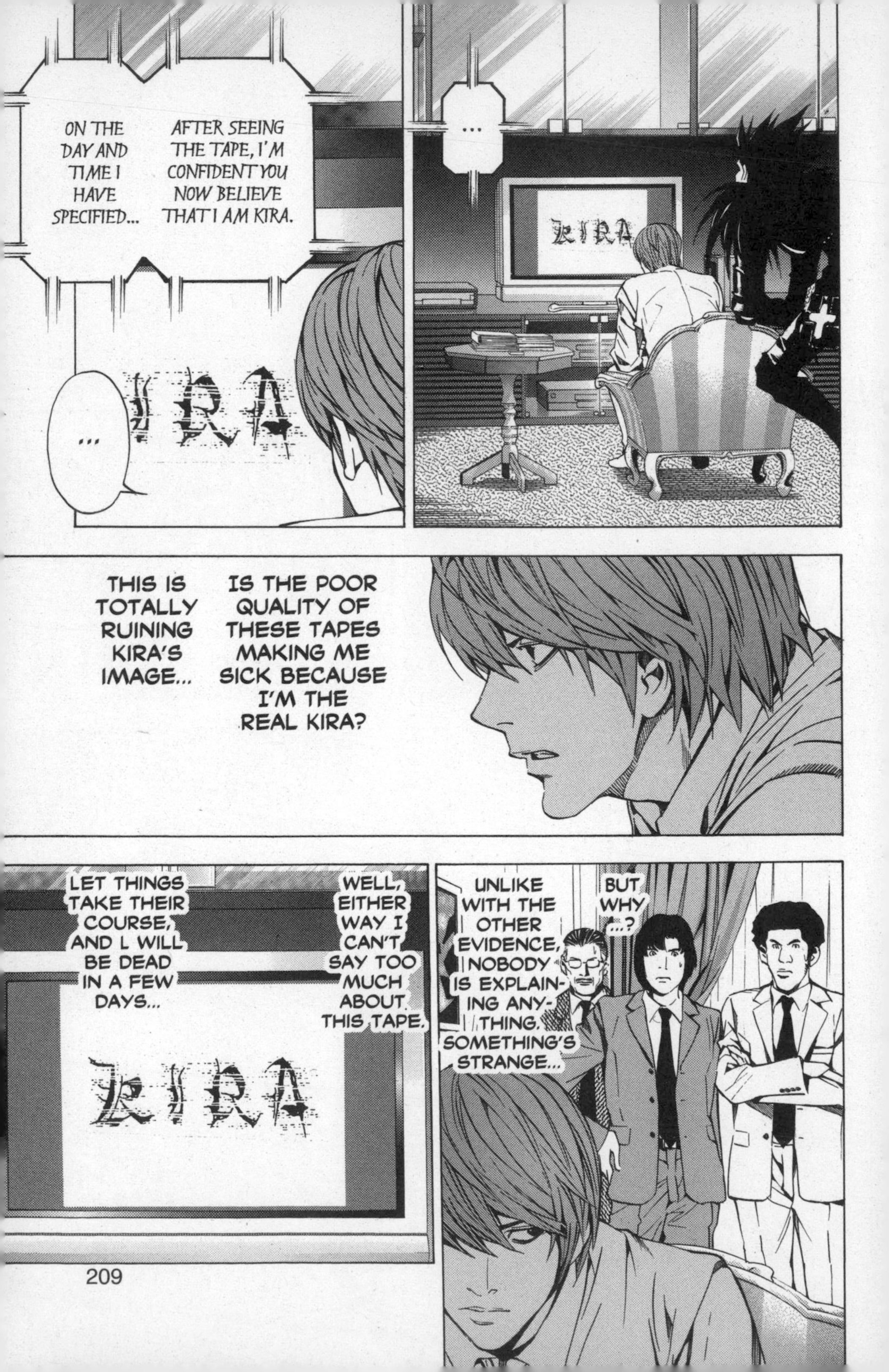
...
AFTER SEEING THE TAPE, I'M CONFIDENT YOU NOW BELIEVE THAT I AM KIRA.
ON THE DAY AND TIME I HAVE SPECIFIED...
KIRA
...
IS THE POOR QUALITY OF THESE TAPES MAKING ME SICK BECAUSE I'M THE REAL KIRA?
THIS IS TOTALLY RUINING KIRA'S IMAGE...
BUT WHY ...?
UNLIKE WITH THE OTHER EVIDENCE, NOBODY IS EXPLAINING ANYTHING. SOMETHING'S STRANGE...
WELL, EITHER WAY I CAN'T SAY TOO MUCH ABOUT THIS TAPE.
LET THINGS TAKE THEIR COURSE, AND L WILL BE DEAD IN A FEW DAYS...
KIRA

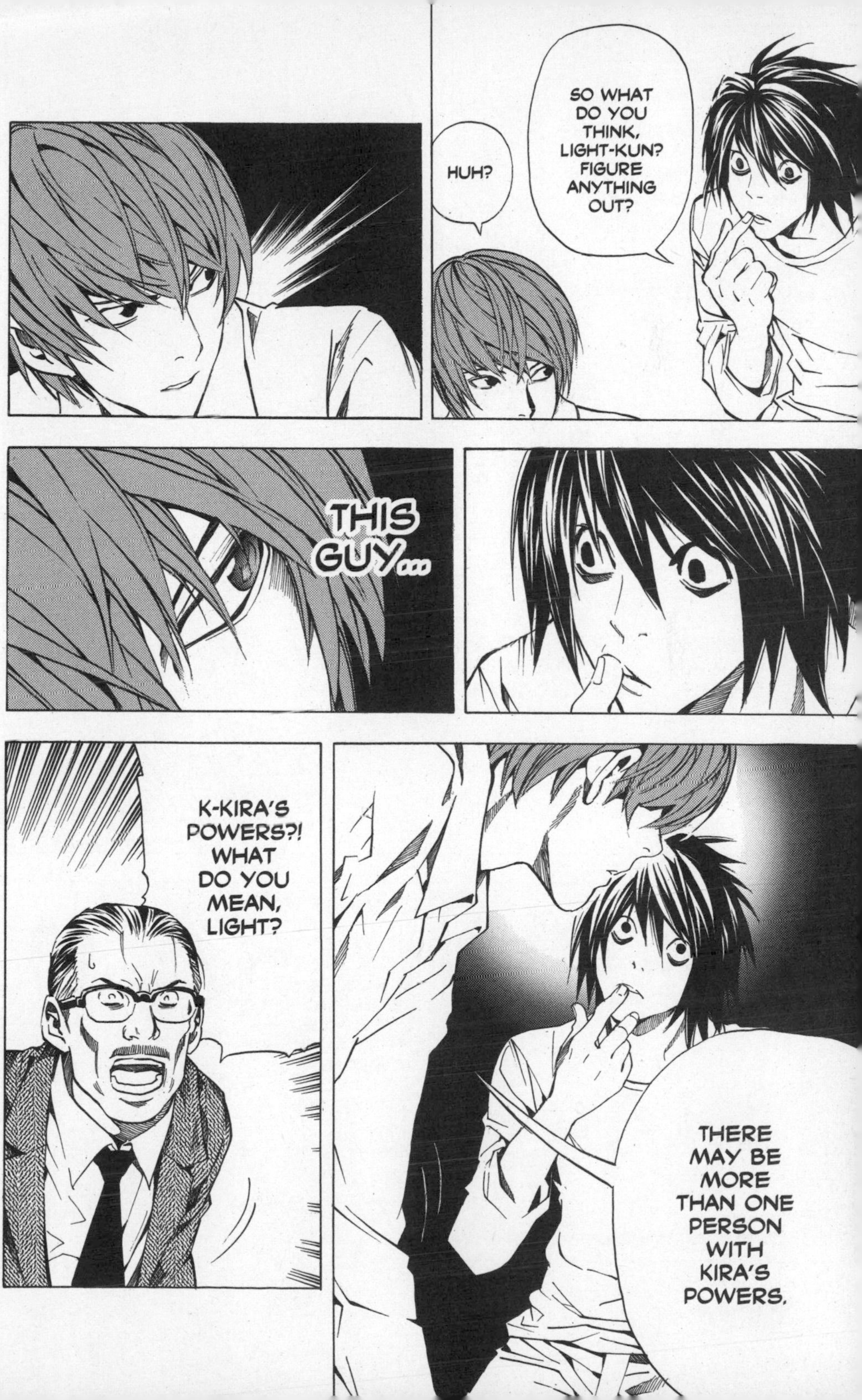
SO WHAT DO YOU THINK, LIGHT-KUN? FIGURE ANYTHING OUT?
HUH?
THIS GUY...
THERE MAY BE MORE THAN ONE PERSON WITH KIRA'S POWERS.
K-KIRA'S POWERS?! WHAT DO YOU MEAN, LIGHT?

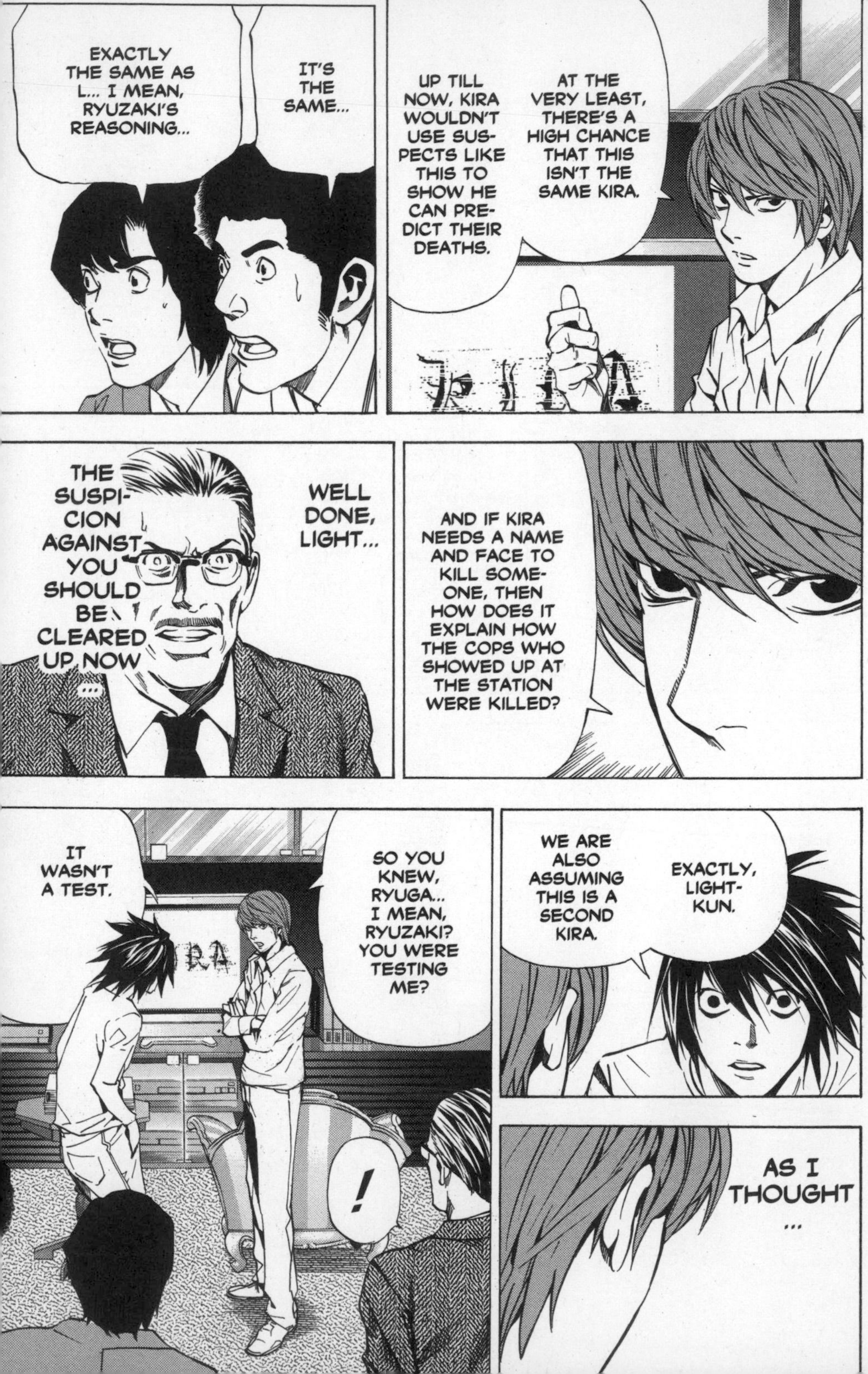
AT THE VERY LEAST, THERE'S A HIGH CHANCE THAT THIS ISN'T THE SAME KIRA.
UP TILL NOW, KIRA WOULDN'T USE SUSPECTS LIKE THIS TO SHOW HE CAN PREDICT THEIR DEATHS.
IT'S THE SAME...
EXACTLY THE SAME AS L... I MEAN, RYUZAKI'S REASONING...
AND IF KIRA NEEDS A NAME AND FACE TO KILL SOMEONE, THEN HOW DOES IT EXPLAIN HOW THE COPS WHO SHOWED UP AT THE STATION WERE KILLED?
WELL DONE, LIGHT...
THE SUSPICION AGAINST YOU SHOULD BE CLEARED UP NOW...
EXACTLY, LIGHT-KUN.
WE ARE ALSO ASSUMING THIS IS A SECOND KIRA.
AS I THOUGHT...
SO YOU KNEW, RYUGA... I MEAN, RYUZAKI? YOU WERE TESTING ME?
IT WASN'T A TEST.
!

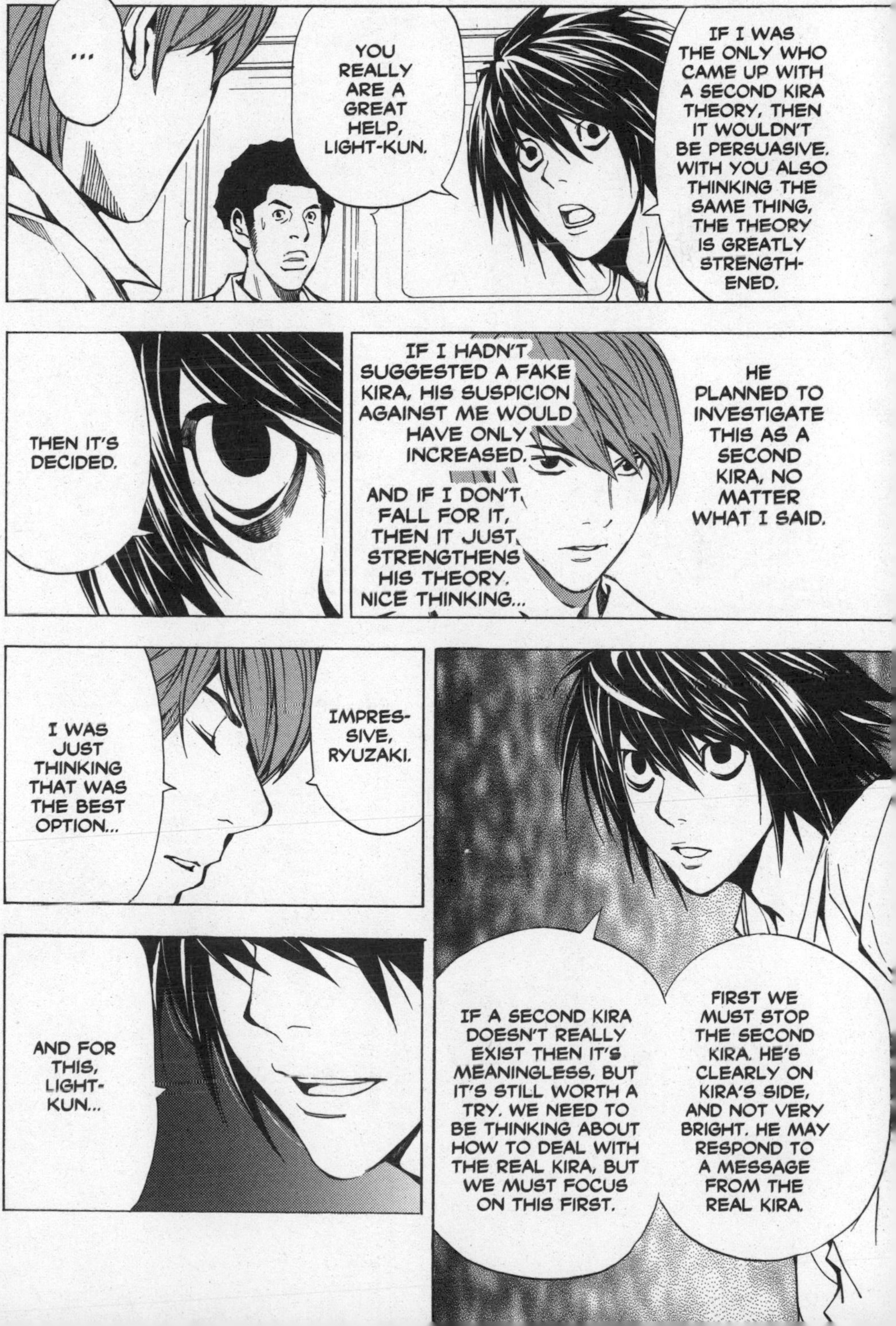
IF I WAS THE ONLY WHO CAME UP WITH A SECOND KIRA THEORY, THEN IT WOULDN'T BE PERSUASIVE. WITH YOU ALSO THINKING THE SAME THING, THE THEORY IS GREATLY STRENGTH-ENED.
YOU REALLY ARE A GREAT HELP, LIGHT-KUN.
...
HE PLANNED TO INVESTIGATE THIS AS A SECOND KIRA, NO MATTER WHAT I SAID.
IF I HADN'T SUGGESTED A FAKE KIRA, HIS SUSPICION AGAINST ME WOULD HAVE ONLY INCREASED.
AND IF I DON'T FALL FOR IT, THEN IT JUST STRENGTHENS HIS THEORY. NICE THINKING...
THEN IT'S DECIDED.
FIRST WE MUST STOP THE SECOND KIRA. HE'S CLEARLY ON KIRA'S SIDE, AND NOT VERY BRIGHT. HE MAY RESPOND TO A MESSAGE FROM THE REAL KIRA.
IF A SECOND KIRA DOESN'T REALLY EXIST THEN IT'S MEANINGLESS, BUT IT'S STILL WORTH A TRY. WE NEED TO BE THINKING ABOUT HOW TO DEAL WITH THE REAL KIRA, BUT WE MUST FOCUS ON THIS FIRST.
IMPRES-SIVE, RYUZAKI.
I WAS JUST THINKING THAT WAS THE BEST OPTION...
AND FOR THIS, LIGHT-KUN...

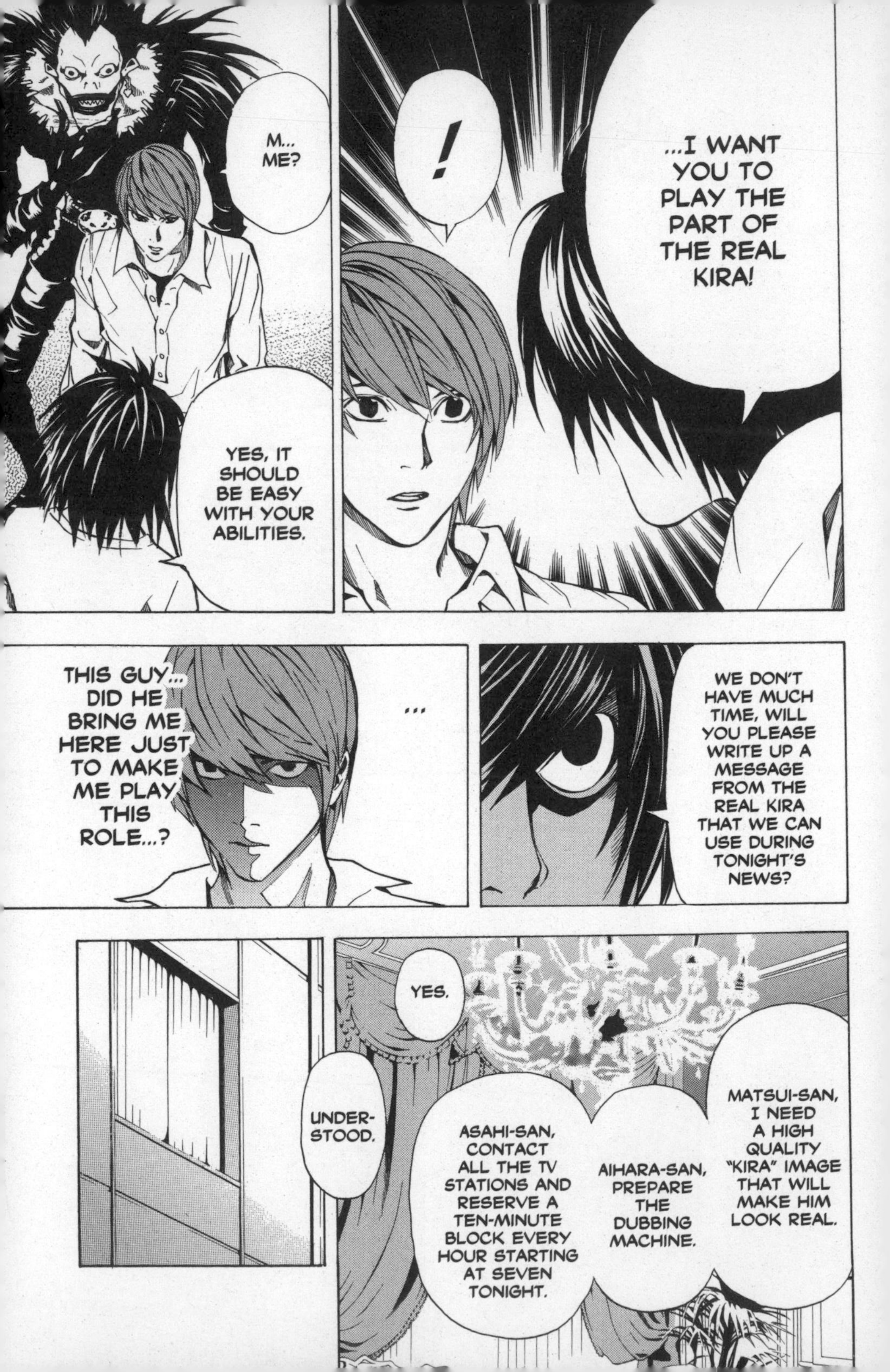
...I WANT YOU TO PLAY THE PART OF THE REAL KIRA!
!
M... ME?
YES, IT SHOULD BE EASY WITH YOUR ABILITIES.
WE DON'T HAVE MUCH TIME, WILL YOU PLEASE WRITE UP A MESSAGE FROM THE REAL KIRA THAT WE CAN USE DURING TONIGHT'S NEWS?
...
THIS GUY... DID HE BRING ME HERE JUST TO MAKE ME PLAY THIS ROLE...?
MATSUI-SAN, I NEED A HIGH QUALITY "KIRA" IMAGE THAT WILL MAKE HIM LOOK REAL.
AIHARA-SAN, PREPARE THE DUBBING MACHINE.
ASAHI-SAN, CONTACT ALL THE TV STATIONS AND RESERVE A TEN-MINUTE BLOCK EVERY HOUR STARTING AT SEVEN TONIGHT.
YES.
UNDER-STOOD.

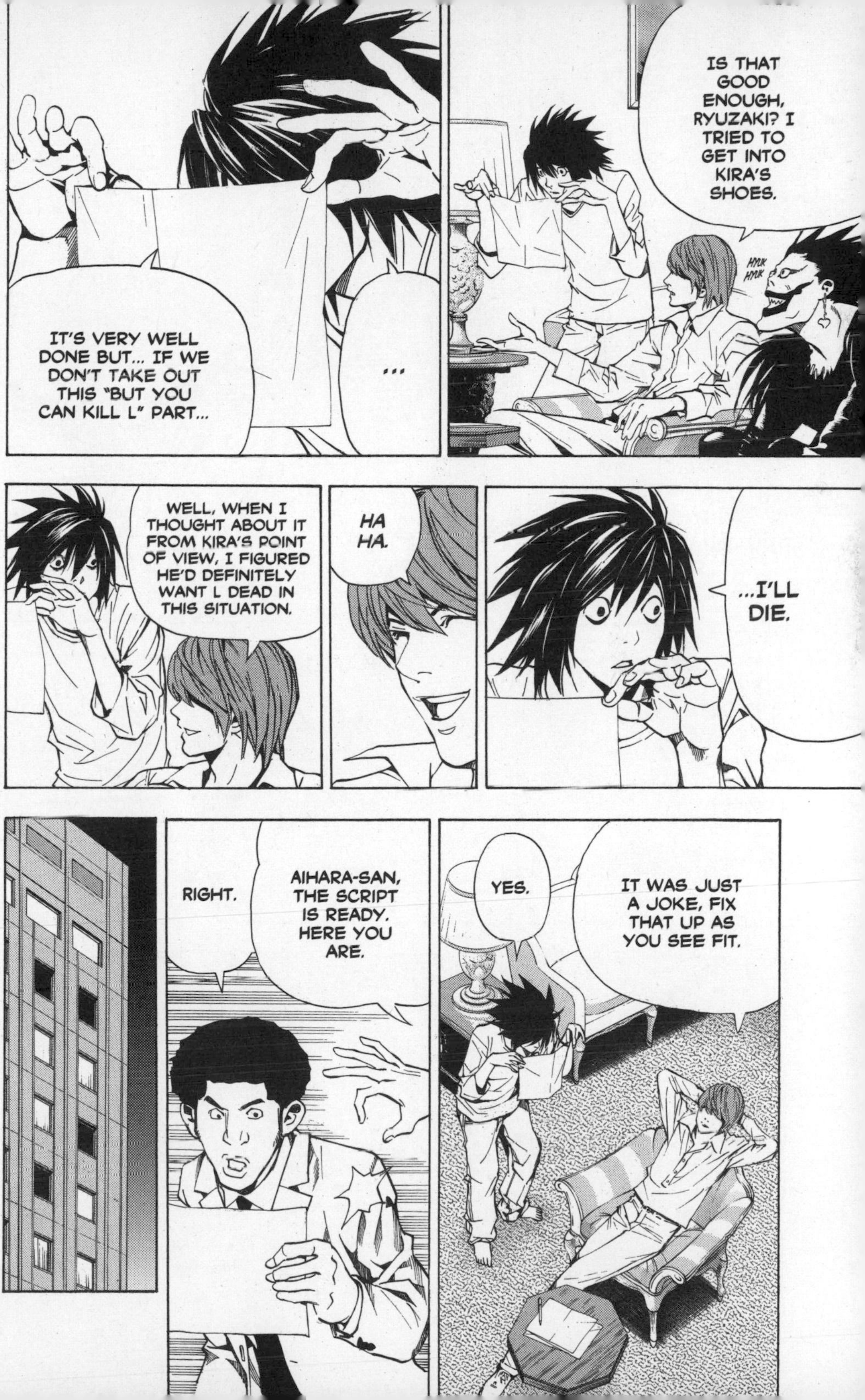
IS THAT GOOD ENOUGH, RYUZAKI? I TRIED TO GET INTO KIRA'S SHOES.
HYUK HYUK
...
IT'S VERY WELL DONE BUT... IF WE DON'T TAKE OUT THIS "BUT YOU CAN KILL L" PART...
...I'LL DIE.
HA HA.
WELL, WHEN I THOUGHT ABOUT IT FROM KIRA'S POINT OF VIEW, I FIGURED HE'D DEFINITELY WANT L DEAD IN THIS SITUATION.
IT WAS JUST A JOKE, FIX THAT UP AS YOU SEE FIT.
YES.
AIHARA-SAN, THE SCRIPT IS READY. HERE YOU ARE.
RIGHT.

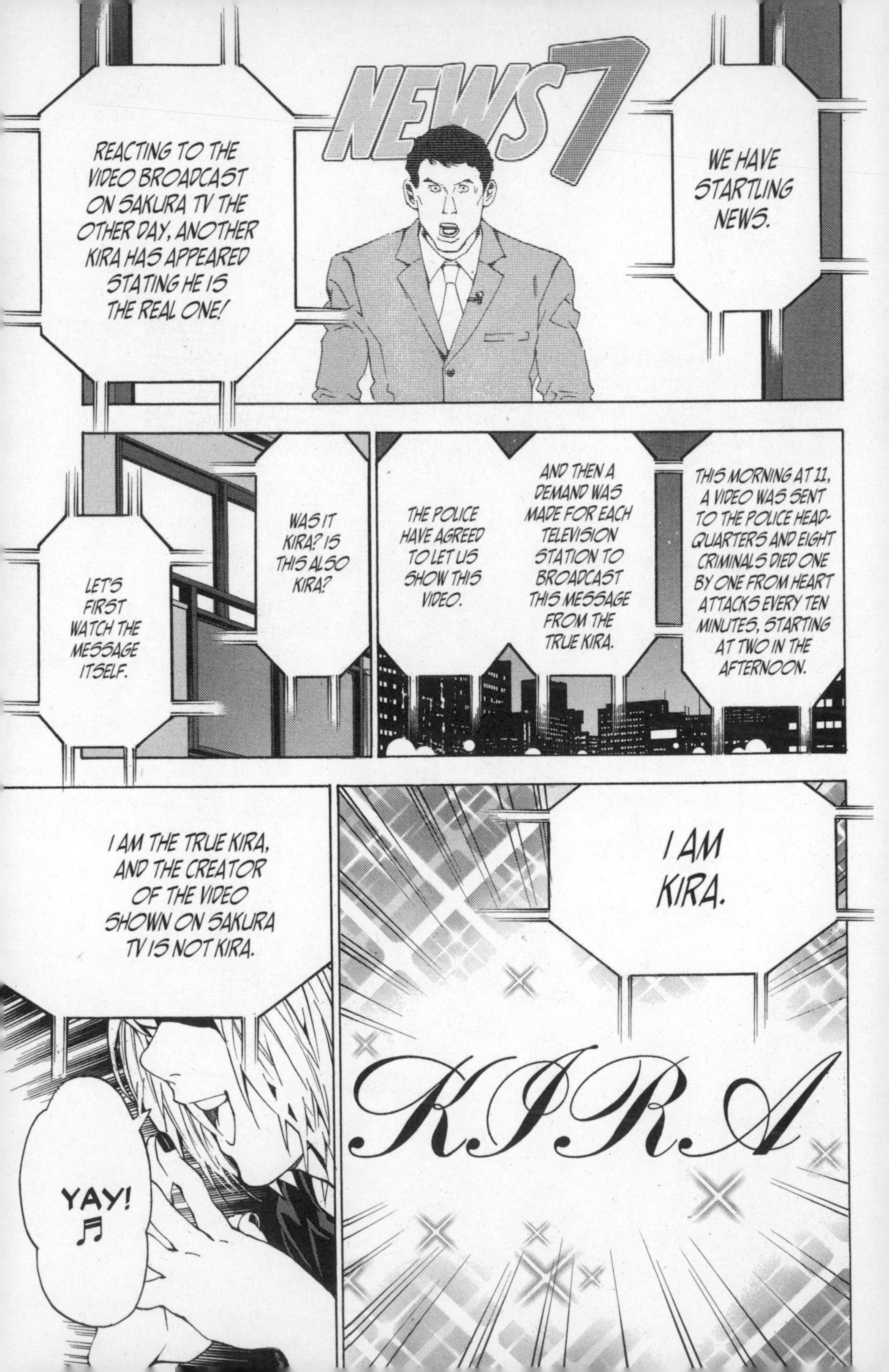
NEWS 7
WE HAVE STARTLING NEWS.
REACTING TO THE VIDEO BROADCAST ON SAKURA TV THE OTHER DAY, ANOTHER KIRA HAS APPEARED STATING HE IS THE REAL ONE!
THIS MORNING AT 11, A VIDEO WAS SENT TO THE POLICE HEAD-QUARTERS AND EIGHT CRIMINALS DIED ONE BY ONE FROM HEART ATTACKS EVERY TEN MINUTES, STARTING AT TWO IN THE AFTERNOON.
AND THEN A DEMAND WAS MADE FOR EACH TELEVISION STATION TO BROADCAST THIS MESSAGE FROM THE TRUE KIRA.
THE POLICE HAVE AGREED TO LET US SHOW THIS VIDEO.
WAS IT KIRA? IS THIS ALSO KIRA?
LET'S FIRST WATCH THE MESSAGE ITSELF.
I AM KIRA.
KIRA
I AM THE TRUE KIRA, AND THE CREATOR OF THE VIDEO SHOWN ON SAKURA TV IS NOT KIRA.
YAY! ♬

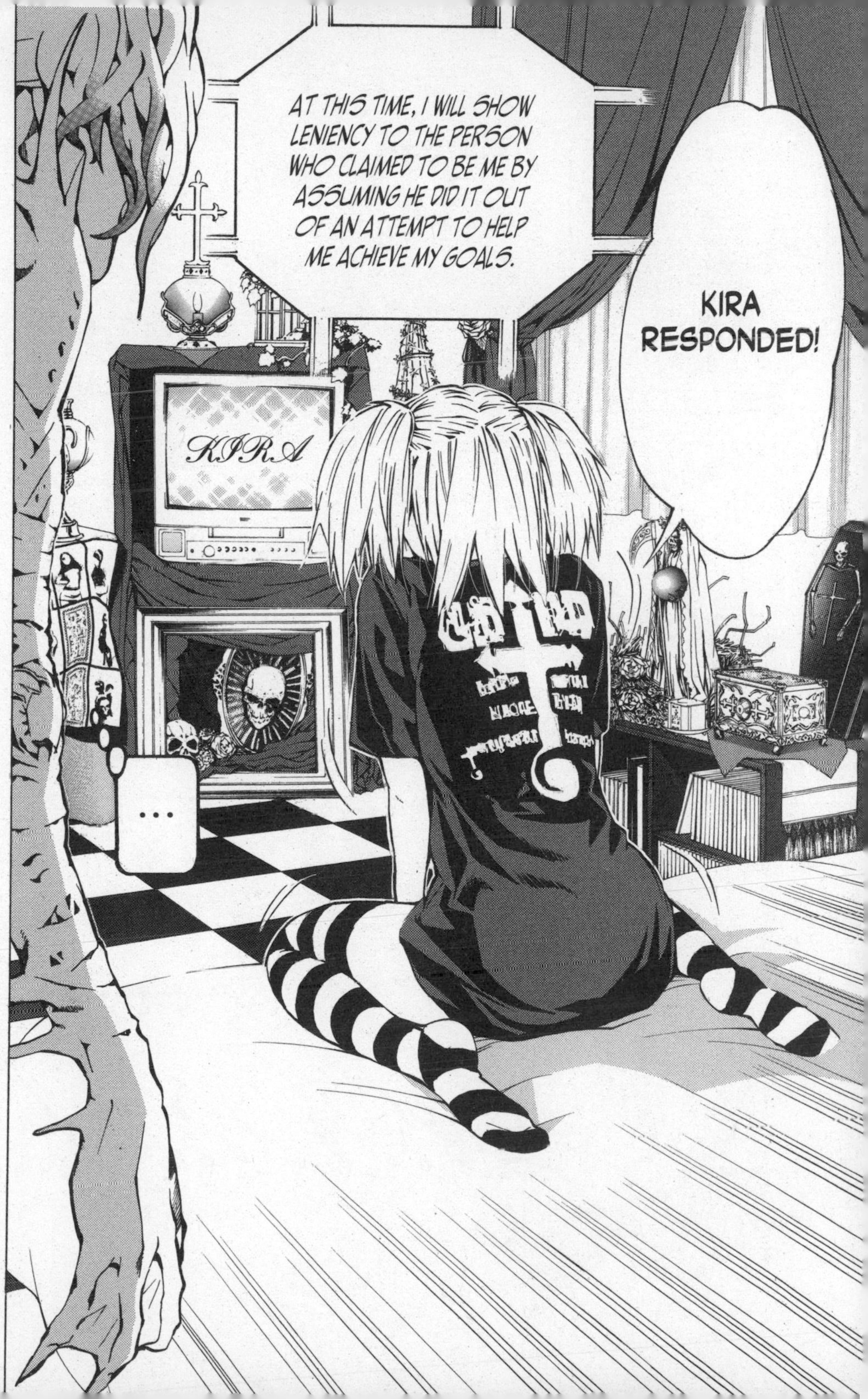
KIRA RESPONDED!
AT THIS TIME, I WILL SHOW LENIENCY TO THE PERSON WHO CLAIMED TO BE ME BY ASSUMING HE DID IT OUT OF AN ATTEMPT TO HELP ME ACHIEVE MY GOALS.
KIRA
...

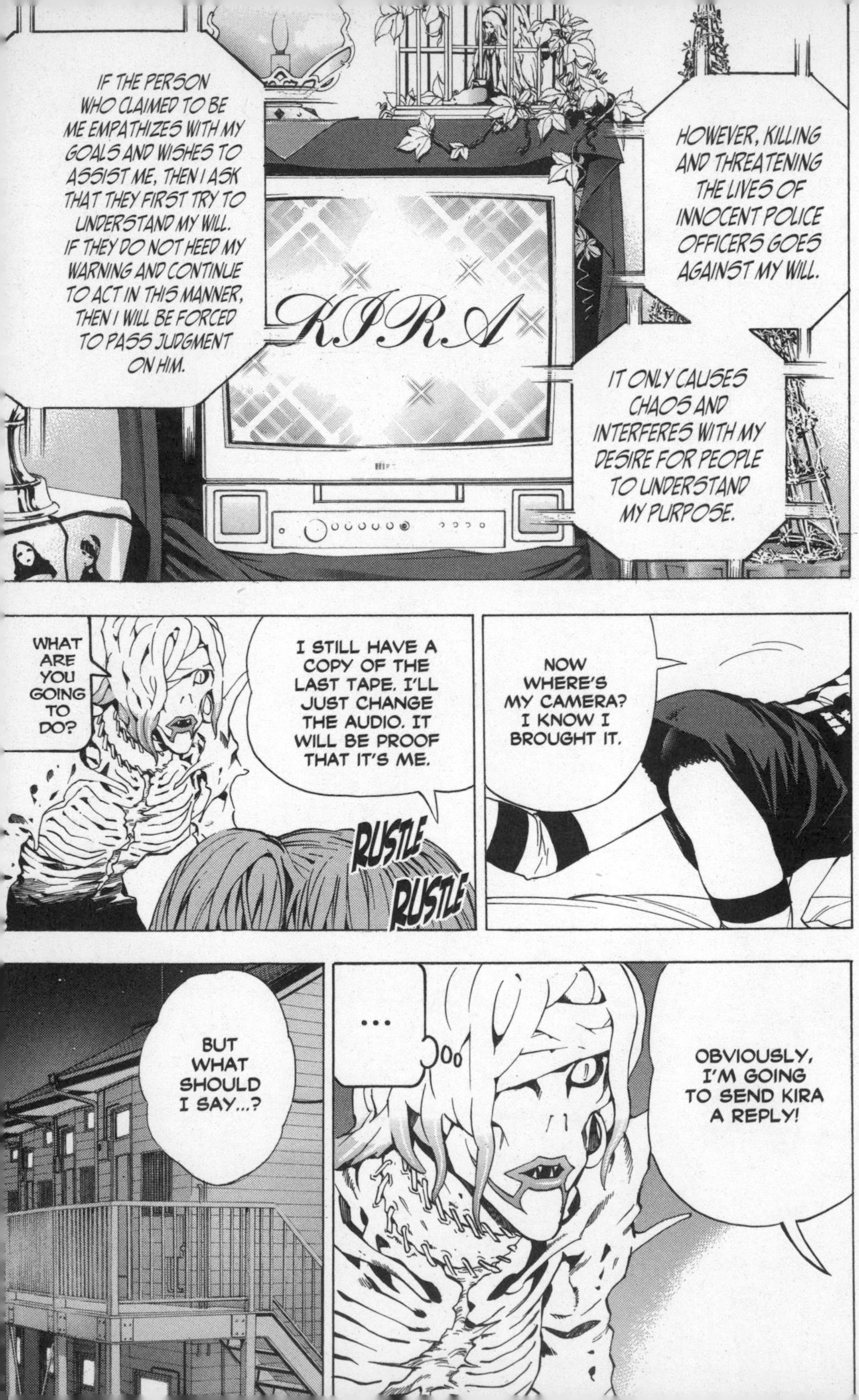
HOWEVER, KILLING AND THREATENING THE LIVES OF INNOCENT POLICE OFFICERS GOES AGAINST MY WILL.
IT ONLY CAUSES CHAOS AND INTERFERES WITH MY DESIRE FOR PEOPLE TO UNDERSTAND MY PURPOSE.
IF THE PERSON WHO CLAIMED TO BE ME EMPATHIZES WITH MY GOALS AND WISHES TO ASSIST ME, THEN I ASK THAT THEY FIRST TRY TO UNDERSTAND MY WILL. IF THEY DO NOT HEED MY WARNING AND CONTINUE TO ACT IN THIS MANNER, THEN I WILL BE FORCED TO PASS JUDGMENT ON HIM.
KIRA
NOW WHERE'S MY CAMERA? I KNOW I BROUGHT IT.
WHAT ARE YOU GOING TO DO?
I STILL HAVE A COPY OF THE LAST TAPE. I'LL JUST CHANGE THE AUDIO. IT WILL BE PROOF THAT IT'S ME.
RUSTLE
RUSTLE
OBVIOUSLY, I'M GOING TO SEND KIRA A REPLY!
...
BUT WHAT SHOULD I SAY...?

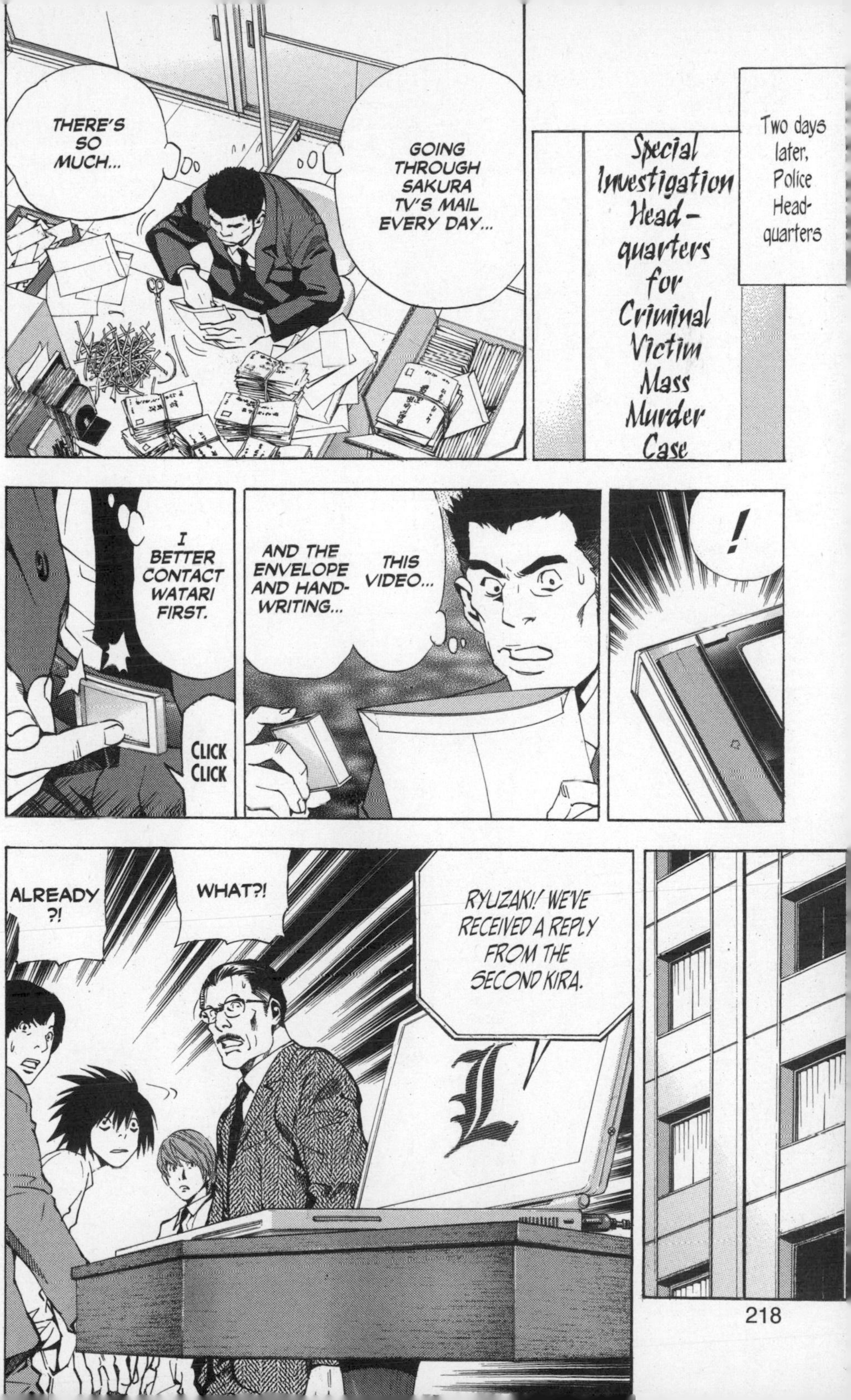
Two days later, Police Headquarters
Special Investigation Headquarters for Criminal Victim Mass Murder Case
GOING THROUGH SAKURA TV'S MAIL EVERY DAY...
THERE'S SO MUCH...
!
THIS VIDEO...
AND THE ENVELOPE AND HANDWRITING...
I BETTER CONTACT WATARI FIRST.
CLICK CLICK
RYUZAKI! WE'VE RECEIVED A REPLY FROM THE SECOND KIRA.
WHAT?!
ALREADY?!

READ THIS WAY

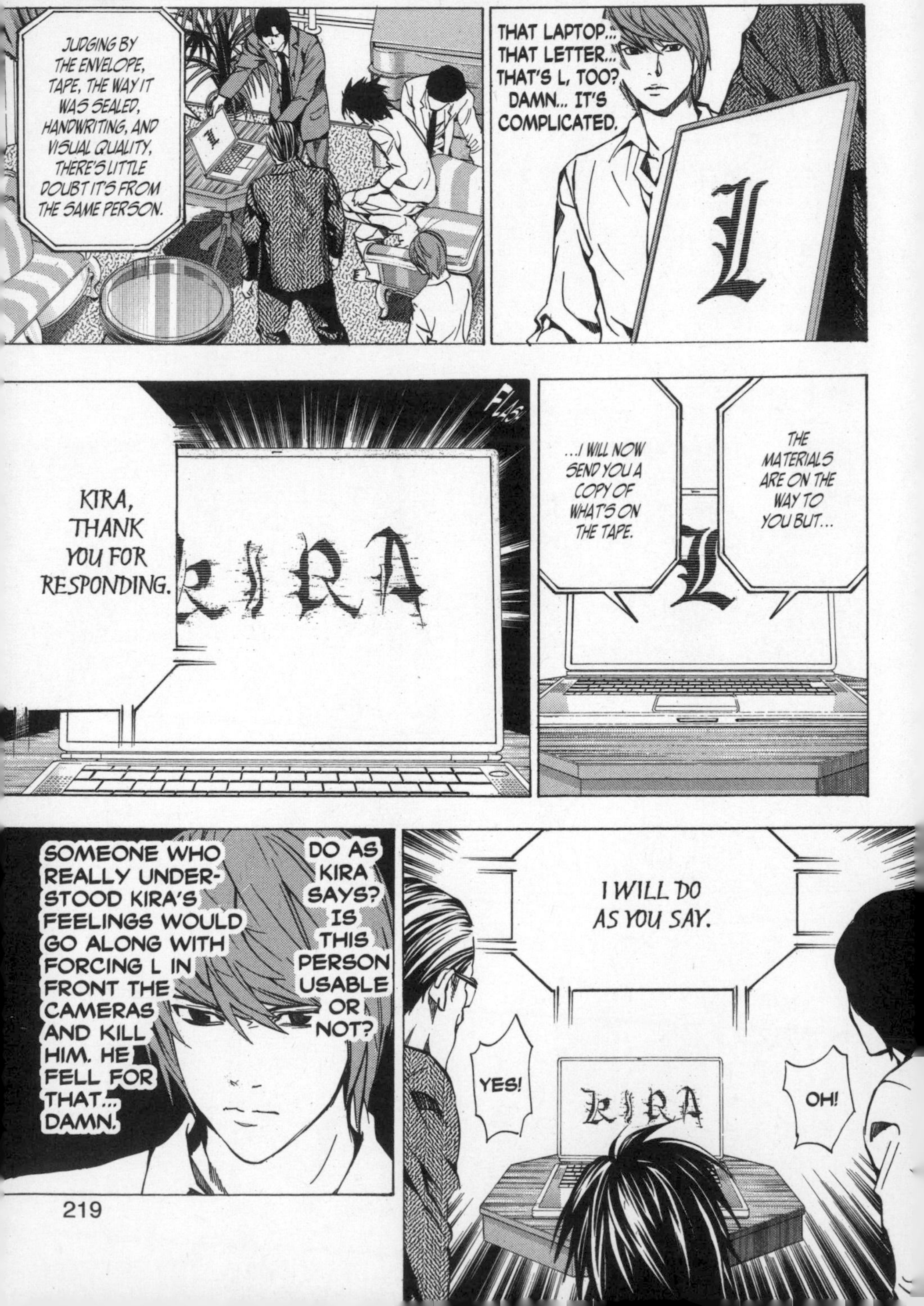

THAT LAPTOP... THAT LETTER... THAT'S L, TOO? DAMN... IT'S COMPLICATED.
JUDGING BY THE ENVELOPE, TAPE, THE WAY IT WAS SEALED, HANDWRITING, AND VISUAL QUALITY, THERE'S LITTLE DOUBT IT'S FROM THE SAME PERSON.
THE MATERIALS ARE ON THE WAY TO YOU BUT...
...I WILL NOW SEND YOU A COPY OF WHAT'S ON THE TAPE.
FLASH
KIRA, THANK YOU FOR RESPONDING.
I WILL DO AS YOU SAY.
OH!
YES!
DO AS KIRA SAYS? IS THIS PERSON USABLE OR NOT?
SOMEONE WHO REALLY UNDER-STOOD KIRA'S FEELINGS WOULD GO ALONG WITH FORCING L IN FRONT THE CAMERAS AND KILL HIM. HE FELL FOR THAT... DAMN.

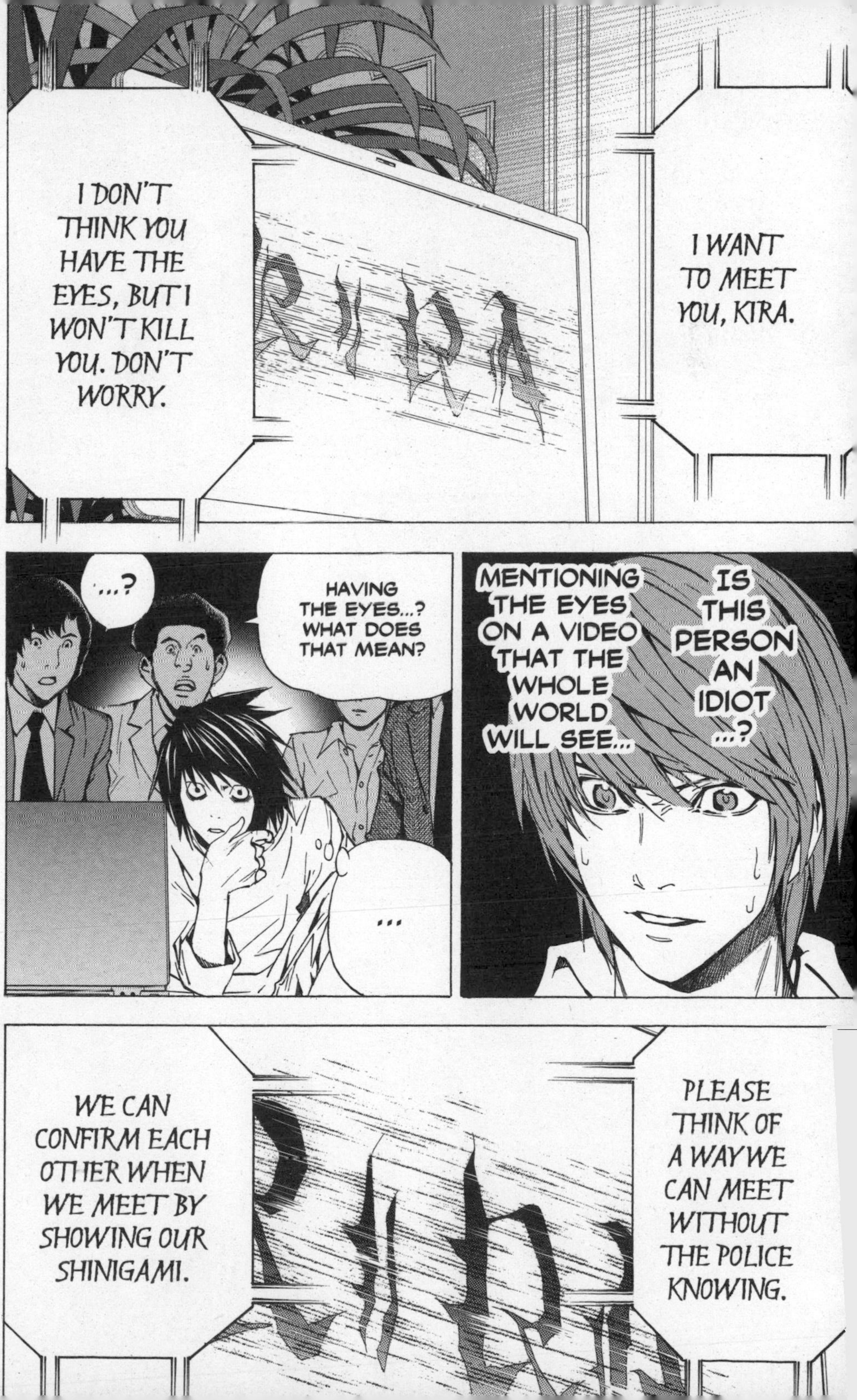
I WANT TO MEET YOU, KIRA.
I DON'T THINK YOU HAVE THE EYES, BUT I WON'T KILL YOU. DON'T WORRY.
IS THIS PERSON AN IDIOT ...?
MENTIONING THE EYES ON A VIDEO THAT THE WHOLE WORLD WILL SEE...
HAVING THE EYES...? WHAT DOES THAT MEAN?
...?
...
PLEASE THINK OF A WAY WE CAN MEET WITHOUT THE POLICE KNOWING.
WE CAN CONFIRM EACH OTHER WHEN WE MEET BY SHOWING OUR SHINIGAMI.

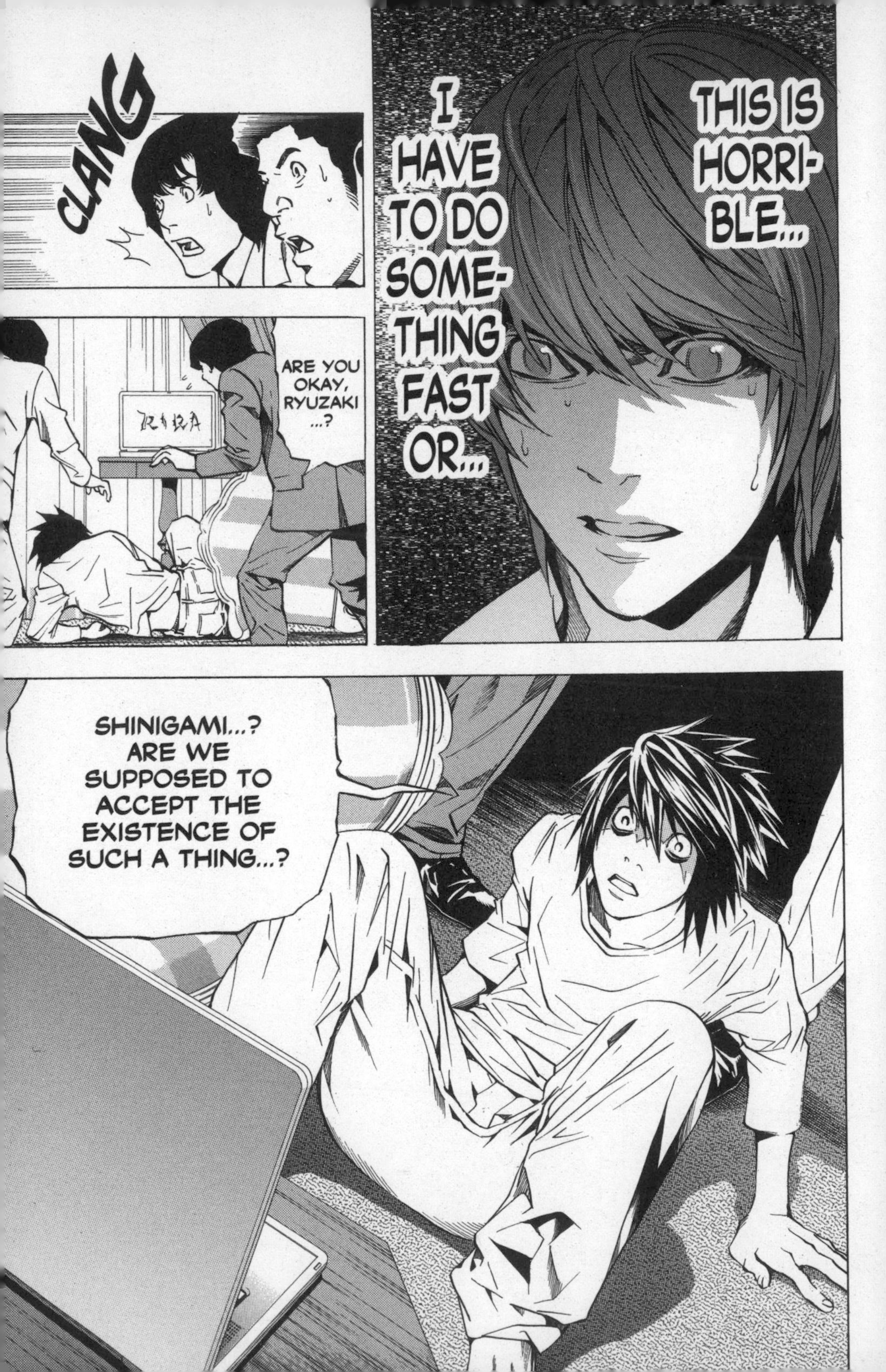
THIS IS HORRI-BLE...
I HAVE TO DO SOME-THING FAST OR...
CLANG
ARE YOU OKAY, RYUZAKI ...?
SHINIGAMI...? ARE WE SUPPOSED TO ACCEPT THE EXISTENCE OF SUCH A THING...?

DEATH NOTE
How to use it
XVI

○ The god of death must at least own one DEATH NOTE.
That DEATH NOTE must never be lent to or written on
by a human.

死神は必ずデスノートを一冊は所有していなければならない。
その一冊は人間に譲渡できないし、人間に書き込ませる事も許されない。

○ Exchanging and writing on the DEATH NOTE

between the gods of death is no problem.

死神同士のデスノートの交換や他の死神のノートへの書き込みは、
なんら問題ない。

chapter 27 Love

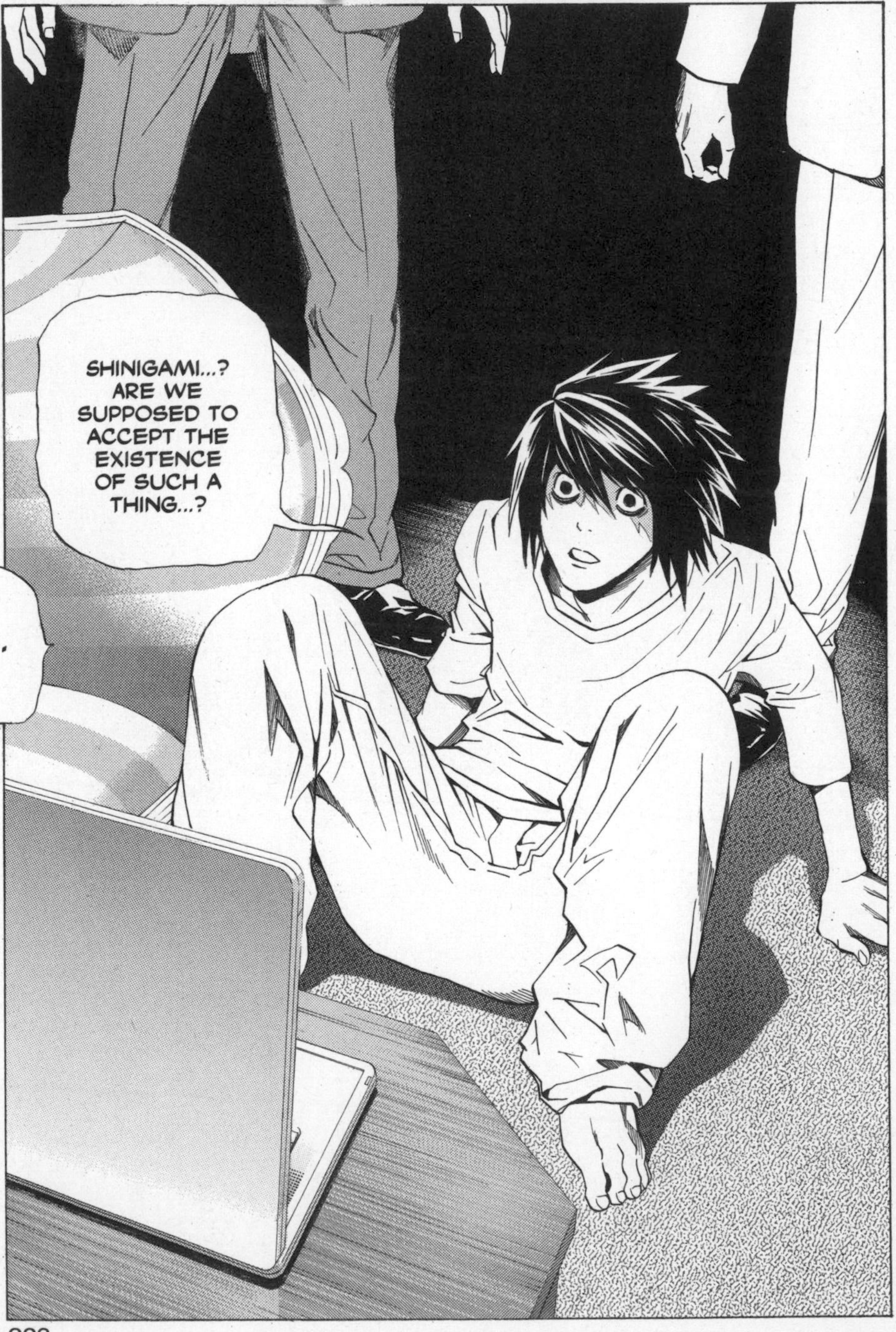
SHINIGAMI...? ARE WE SUPPOSED TO ACCEPT THE EXISTENCE OF SUCH A THING...?
...

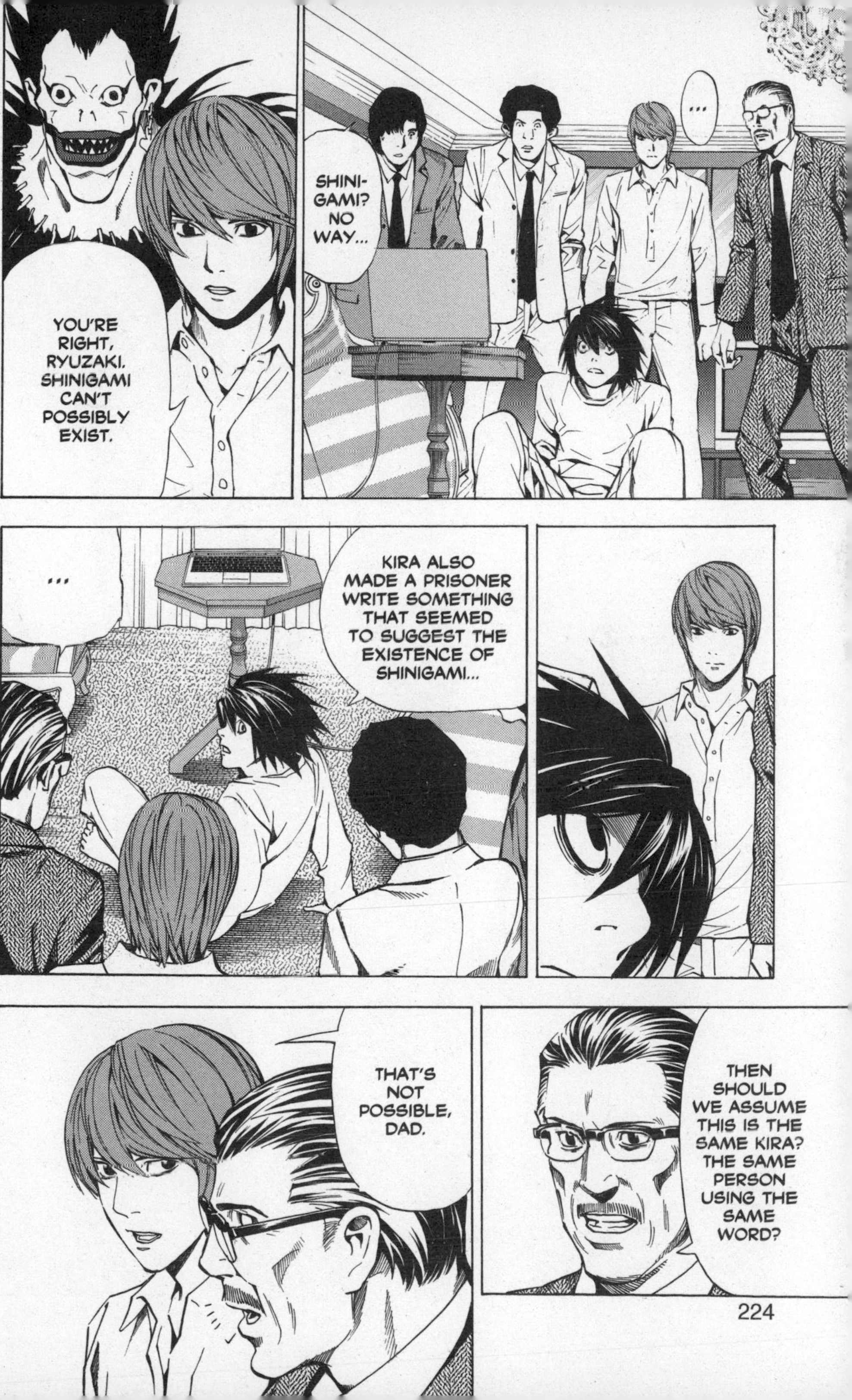
...
SHINI-GAMI? NO WAY...
YOU'RE RIGHT, RYUZAKI. SHINIGAMI CAN'T POSSIBLY EXIST.
KIRA ALSO MADE A PRISONER WRITE SOMETHING THAT SEEMED TO SUGGEST THE EXISTENCE OF SHINIGAMI...
...
THEN SHOULD WE ASSUME THIS IS THE SAME KIRA? THE SAME PERSON USING THE SAME WORD?
THAT'S NOT POSSIBLE, DAD.

READ THIS WAY

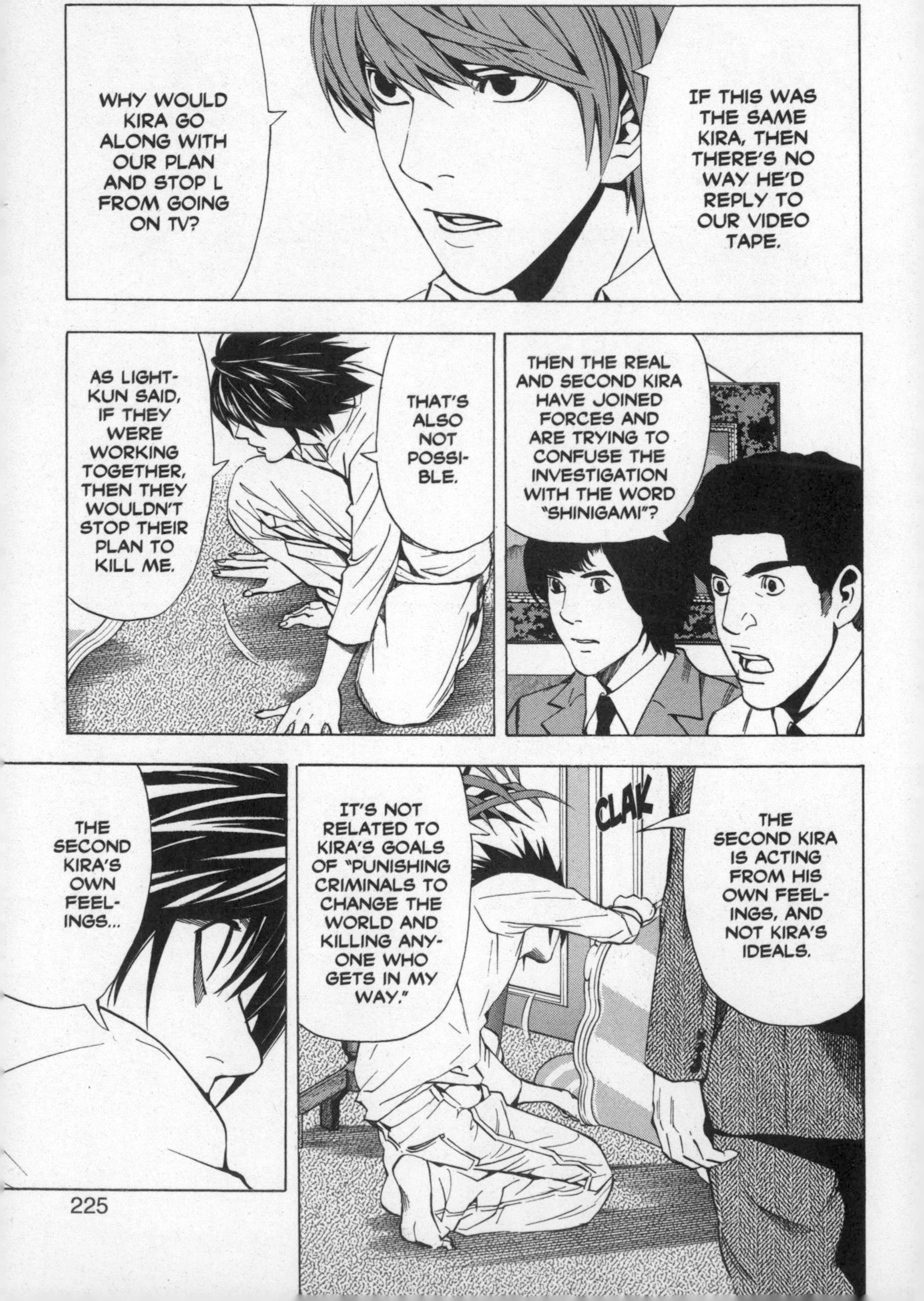
IF THIS WAS THE SAME KIRA, THEN THERE'S NO WAY HE'D REPLY TO OUR VIDEO TAPE.
WHY WOULD KIRA GO ALONG WITH OUR PLAN AND STOP L FROM GOING ON TV?
THEN THE REAL AND SECOND KIRA HAVE JOINED FORCES AND ARE TRYING TO CONFUSE THE INVESTIGATION WITH THE WORD "SHINIGAMI"?
THAT'S ALSO NOT POSSIBLE.
AS LIGHT-KUN SAID, IF THEY WERE WORKING TOGETHER, THEN THEY WOULDN'T STOP THEIR PLAN TO KILL ME.
CLAK
THE SECOND KIRA IS ACTING FROM HIS OWN FEELINGS, AND NOT KIRA'S IDEALS.
IT'S NOT RELATED TO KIRA'S GOALS OF "PUNISHING CRIMINALS TO CHANGE THE WORLD AND KILLING ANYONE WHO GETS IN MY WAY."
THE SECOND KIRA'S OWN FEELINGS...

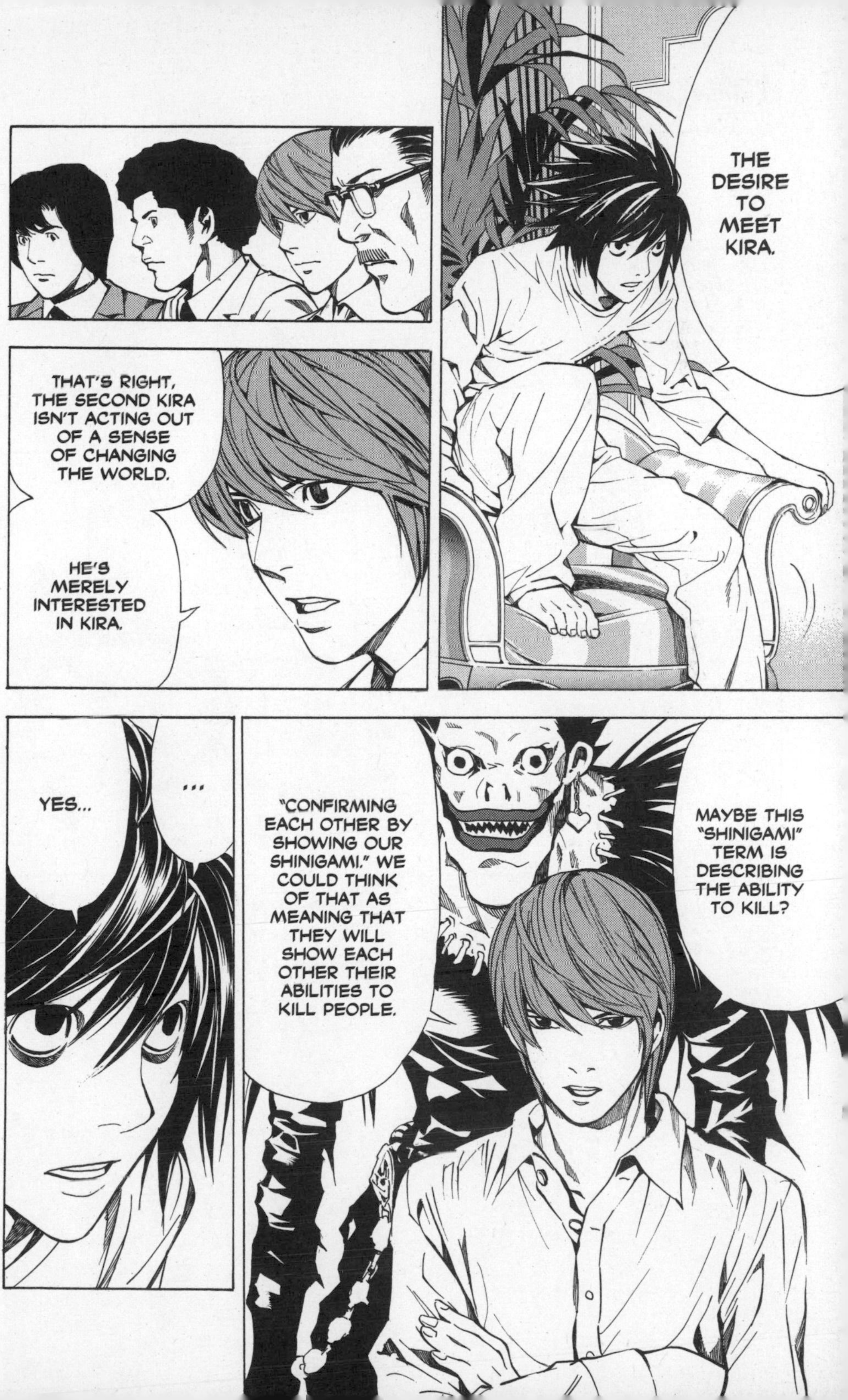
THE DESIRE TO MEET KIRA.
THAT'S RIGHT, THE SECOND KIRA ISN'T ACTING OUT OF A SENSE OF CHANGING THE WORLD.
HE'S MERELY INTERESTED IN KIRA.
MAYBE THIS "SHINIGAMI" TERM IS DESCRIBING THE ABILITY TO KILL?
"CONFIRMING EACH OTHER BY SHOWING OUR SHINIGAMI." WE COULD THINK OF THAT AS MEANING THAT THEY WILL SHOW EACH OTHER THEIR ABILITIES TO KILL PEOPLE.
...
YES...

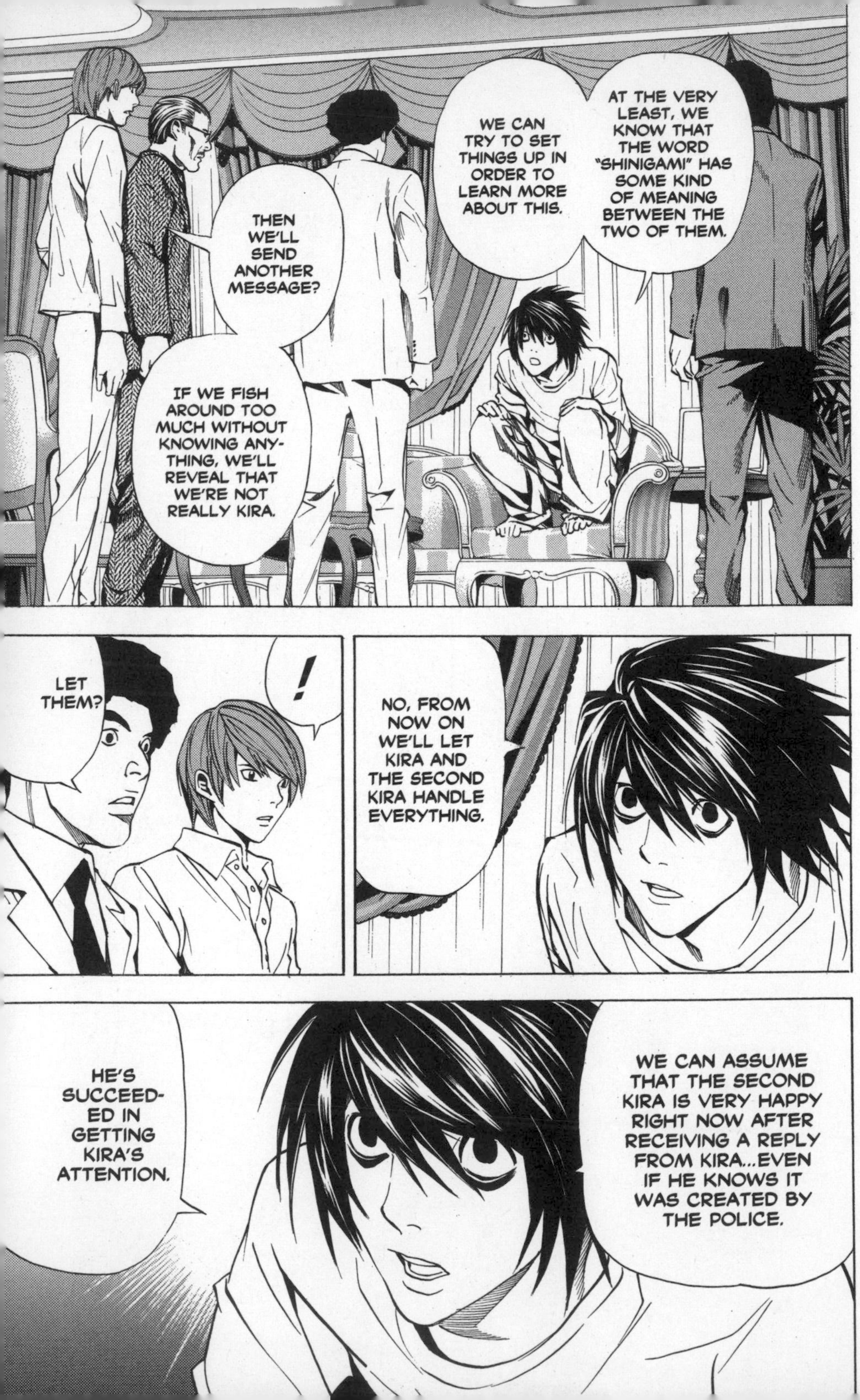
AT THE VERY LEAST, WE KNOW THAT THE WORD "SHINIGAMI" HAS SOME KIND OF MEANING BETWEEN THE TWO OF THEM.
WE CAN TRY TO SET THINGS UP IN ORDER TO LEARN MORE ABOUT THIS.
THEN WE'LL SEND ANOTHER MESSAGE?
IF WE FISH AROUND TOO MUCH WITHOUT KNOWING ANY-THING, WE'LL REVEAL THAT WE'RE NOT REALLY KIRA.
NO, FROM NOW ON WE'LL LET KIRA AND THE SECOND KIRA HANDLE EVERYTHING.
!
LET THEM?
WE CAN ASSUME THAT THE SECOND KIRA IS VERY HAPPY RIGHT NOW AFTER RECEIVING A REPLY FROM KIRA...EVEN IF HE KNOWS IT WAS CREATED BY THE POLICE.
HE'S SUCCEED-ED IN GETTING KIRA'S ATTENTION.

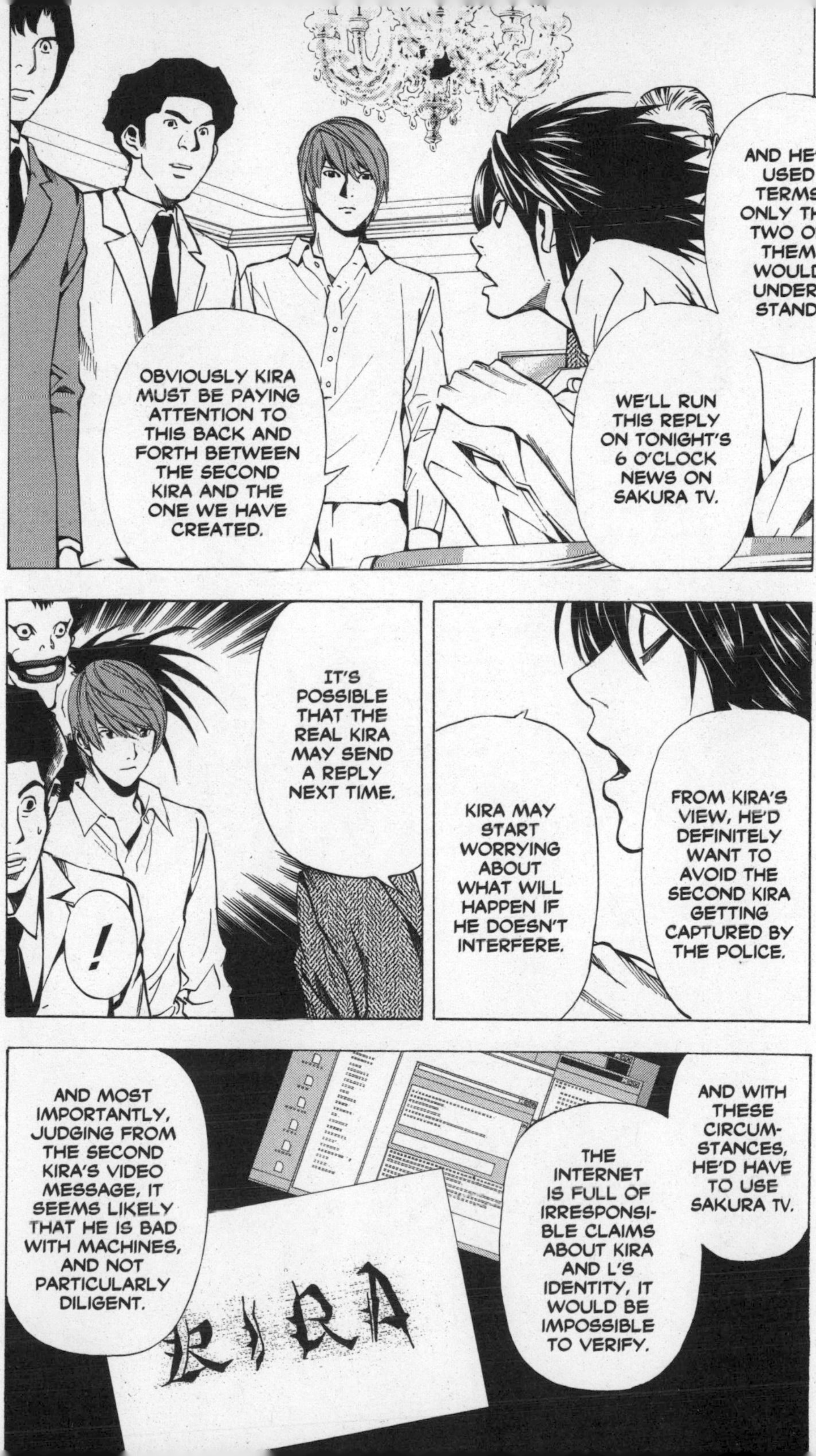
AND HE'S USED TERMS ONLY THE TWO OF THEM WOULD UNDER-STAND.
WE'LL RUN THIS REPLY ON TONIGHT'S 6 O'CLOCK NEWS ON SAKURA TV.
OBVIOUSLY KIRA MUST BE PAYING ATTENTION TO THIS BACK AND FORTH BETWEEN THE SECOND KIRA AND THE ONE WE HAVE CREATED.
FROM KIRA'S VIEW, HE'D DEFINITELY WANT TO AVOID THE SECOND KIRA GETTING CAPTURED BY THE POLICE.
KIRA MAY START WORRYING ABOUT WHAT WILL HAPPEN IF HE DOESN'T INTERFERE.
IT'S POSSIBLE THAT THE REAL KIRA MAY SEND A REPLY NEXT TIME.
!
AND WITH THESE CIRCUM-STANCES, HE'D HAVE TO USE SAKURA TV.
THE INTERNET IS FULL OF IRRESPONSI-BLE CLAIMS ABOUT KIRA AND L'S IDENTITY, IT WOULD BE IMPOSSIBLE TO VERIFY.
AND MOST IMPORTANTLY, JUDGING FROM THE SECOND KIRA'S VIDEO MESSAGE, IT SEEMS LIKELY THAT HE IS BAD WITH MACHINES, AND NOT PARTICULARLY DILIGENT.
KIRA

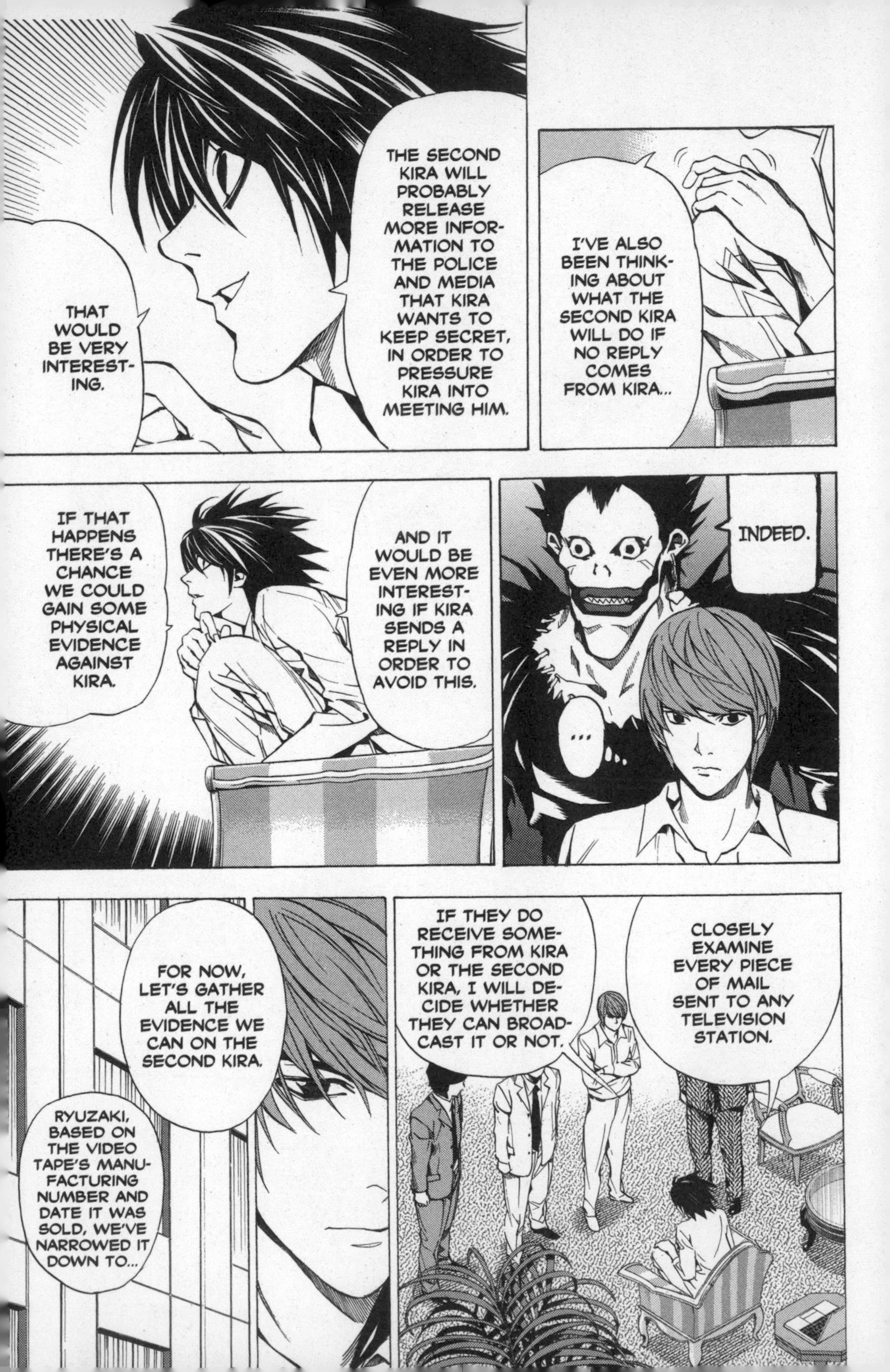
I'VE ALSO BEEN THINKING ABOUT WHAT THE SECOND KIRA WILL DO IF NO REPLY COMES FROM KIRA...
THE SECOND KIRA WILL PROBABLY RELEASE MORE INFORMATION TO THE POLICE AND MEDIA THAT KIRA WANTS TO KEEP SECRET, IN ORDER TO PRESSURE KIRA INTO MEETING HIM.
THAT WOULD BE VERY INTERESTING.
INDEED.
...
AND IT WOULD BE EVEN MORE INTERESTING IF KIRA SENDS A REPLY IN ORDER TO AVOID THIS.
IF THAT HAPPENS THERE'S A CHANCE WE COULD GAIN SOME PHYSICAL EVIDENCE AGAINST KIRA.
CLOSELY EXAMINE EVERY PIECE OF MAIL SENT TO ANY TELEVISION STATION.
IF THEY DO RECEIVE SOMETHING FROM KIRA OR THE SECOND KIRA, I WILL DECIDE WHETHER THEY CAN BROADCAST IT OR NOT.
FOR NOW, LET'S GATHER ALL THE EVIDENCE WE CAN ON THE SECOND KIRA.
RYUZAKI, BASED ON THE VIDEO TAPE'S MANUFACTURING NUMBER AND DATE IT WAS SOLD, WE'VE NARROWED IT DOWN TO...

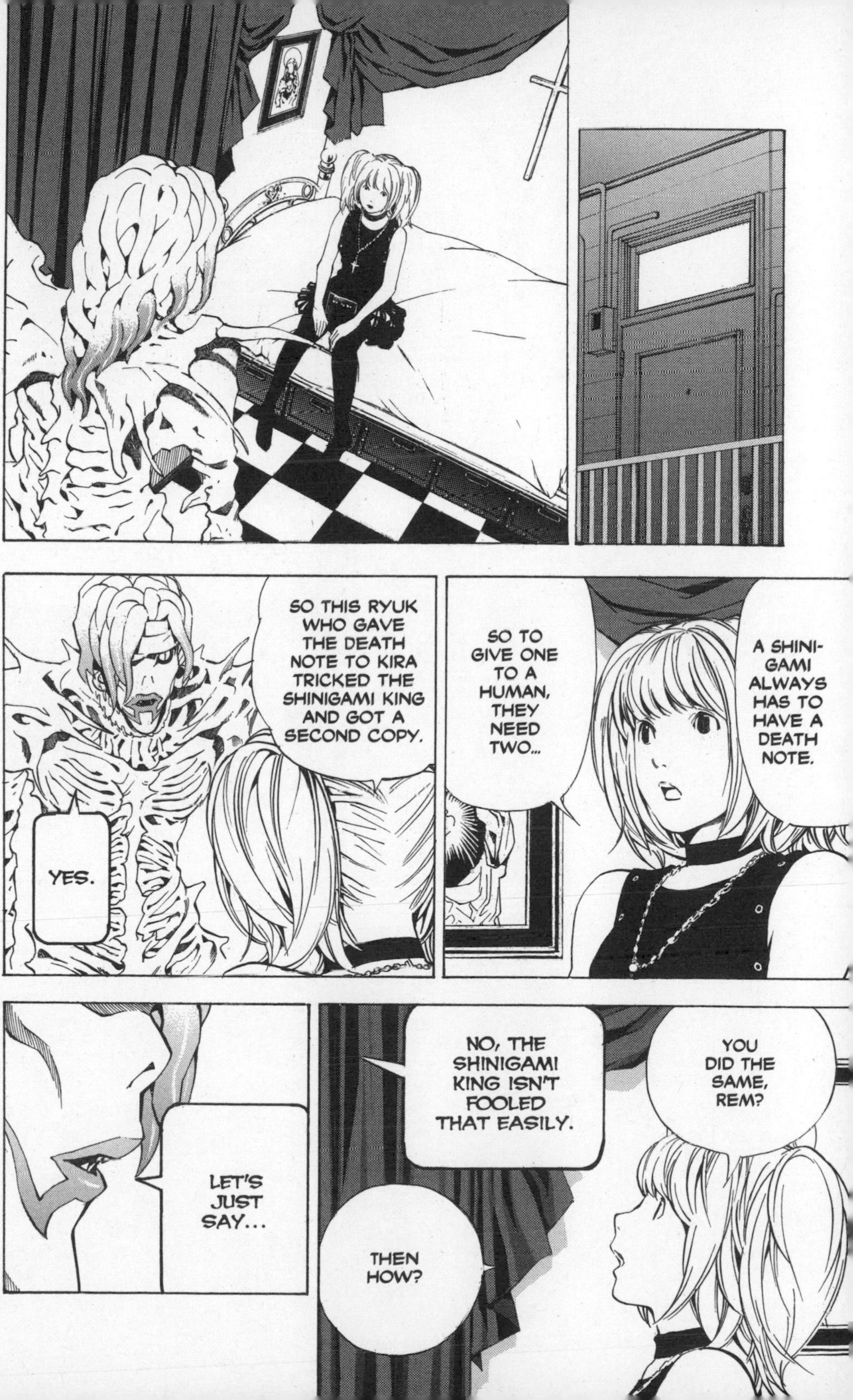
A SHINIGAMI ALWAYS HAS TO HAVE A DEATH NOTE.
SO TO GIVE ONE TO A HUMAN, THEY NEED TWO...
SO THIS RYUK WHO GAVE THE DEATH NOTE TO KIRA TRICKED THE SHINIGAMI KING AND GOT A SECOND COPY.
YES.
YOU DID THE SAME, REM?
NO, THE SHINIGAMI KING ISN'T FOOLED THAT EASILY.
THEN HOW?
LET'S JUST SAY...

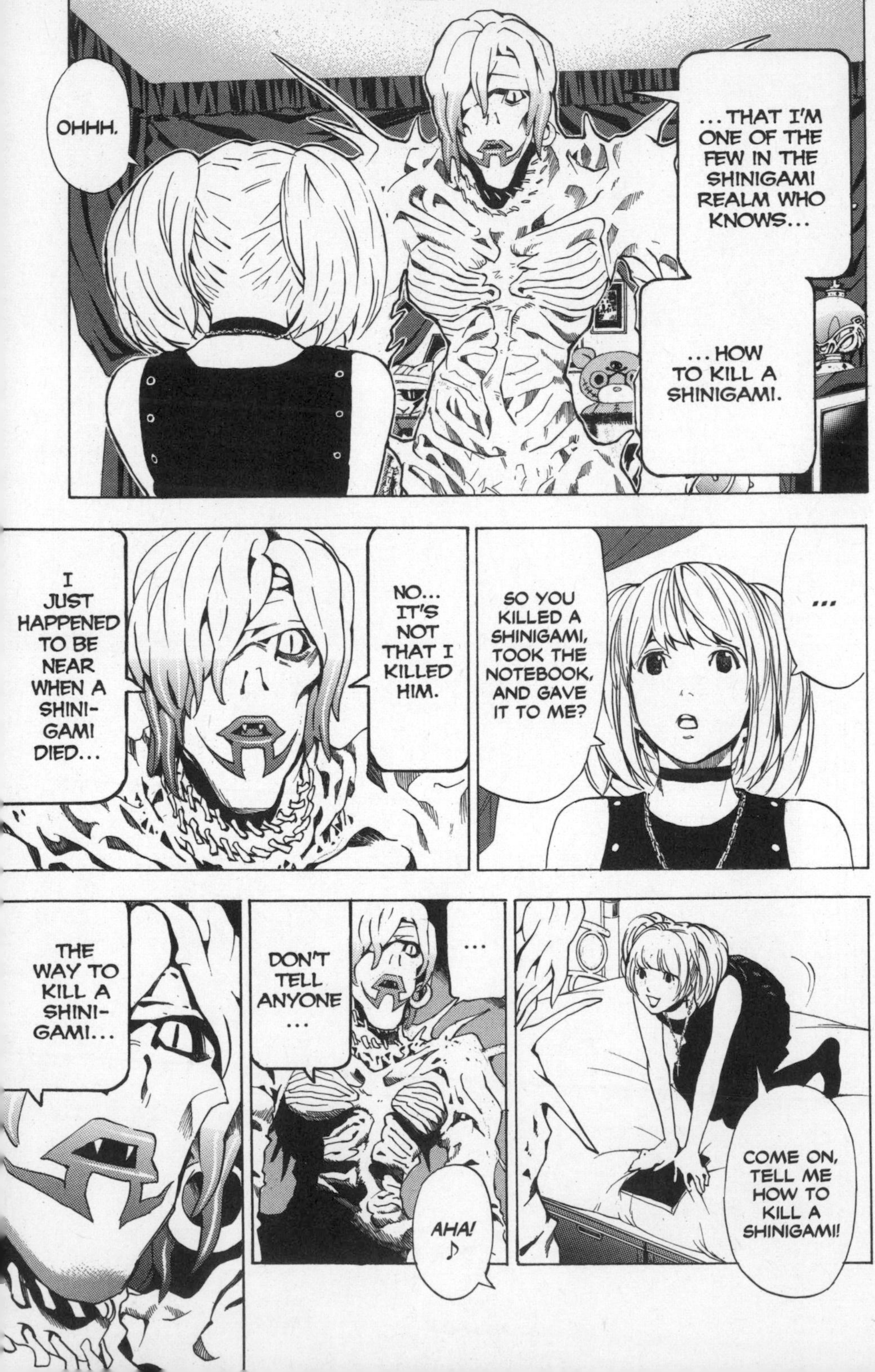
...THAT I'M ONE OF THE FEW IN THE SHINIGAMI REALM WHO KNOWS...
...HOW TO KILL A SHINIGAMI.
OHHH.
...
SO YOU KILLED A SHINIGAMI, TOOK THE NOTEBOOK, AND GAVE IT TO ME?
NO... IT'S NOT THAT I KILLED HIM.
I JUST HAPPENED TO BE NEAR WHEN A SHINI-GAMI DIED...
COME ON, TELL ME HOW TO KILL A SHINIGAMI!
...
DON'T TELL ANYONE ...
AHA! ♪
THE WAY TO KILL A SHINI-GAMI...

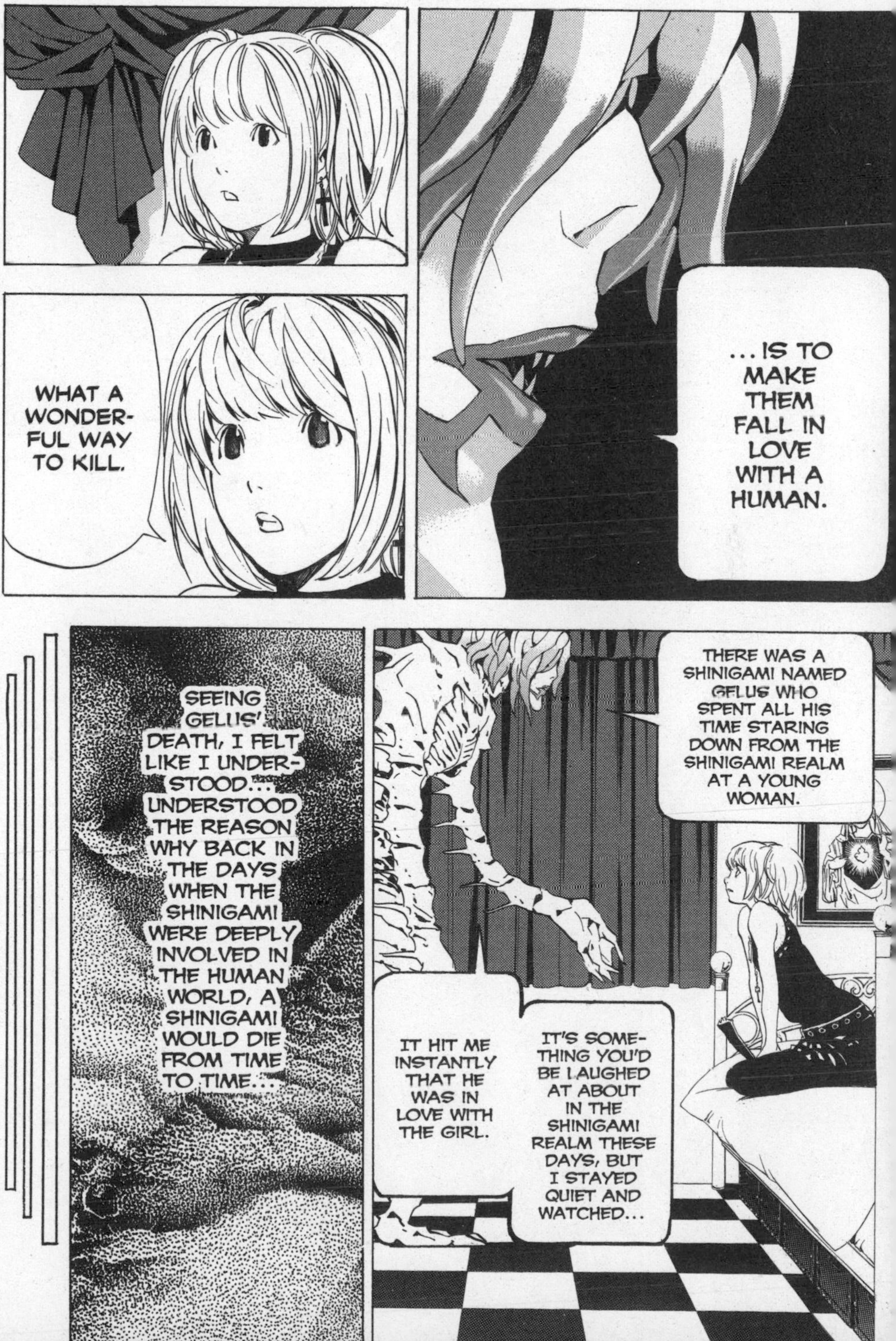
...IS TO MAKE THEM FALL IN LOVE WITH A HUMAN.
WHAT A WONDERFUL WAY TO KILL.
THERE WAS A SHINIGAMI NAMED GELUS WHO SPENT ALL HIS TIME STARING DOWN FROM THE SHINIGAMI REALM AT A YOUNG WOMAN.
IT'S SOMETHING YOU'D BE LAUGHED AT ABOUT IN THE SHINIGAMI REALM THESE DAYS, BUT I STAYED QUIET AND WATCHED...
IT HIT ME INSTANTLY THAT HE WAS IN LOVE WITH THE GIRL.
SEEING GELUS' DEATH, I FELT LIKE I UNDERSTOOD... UNDERSTOOD THE REASON WHY BACK IN THE DAYS WHEN THE SHINIGAMI WERE DEEPLY INVOLVED IN THE HUMAN WORLD, A SHINIGAMI WOULD DIE FROM TIME TO TIME...

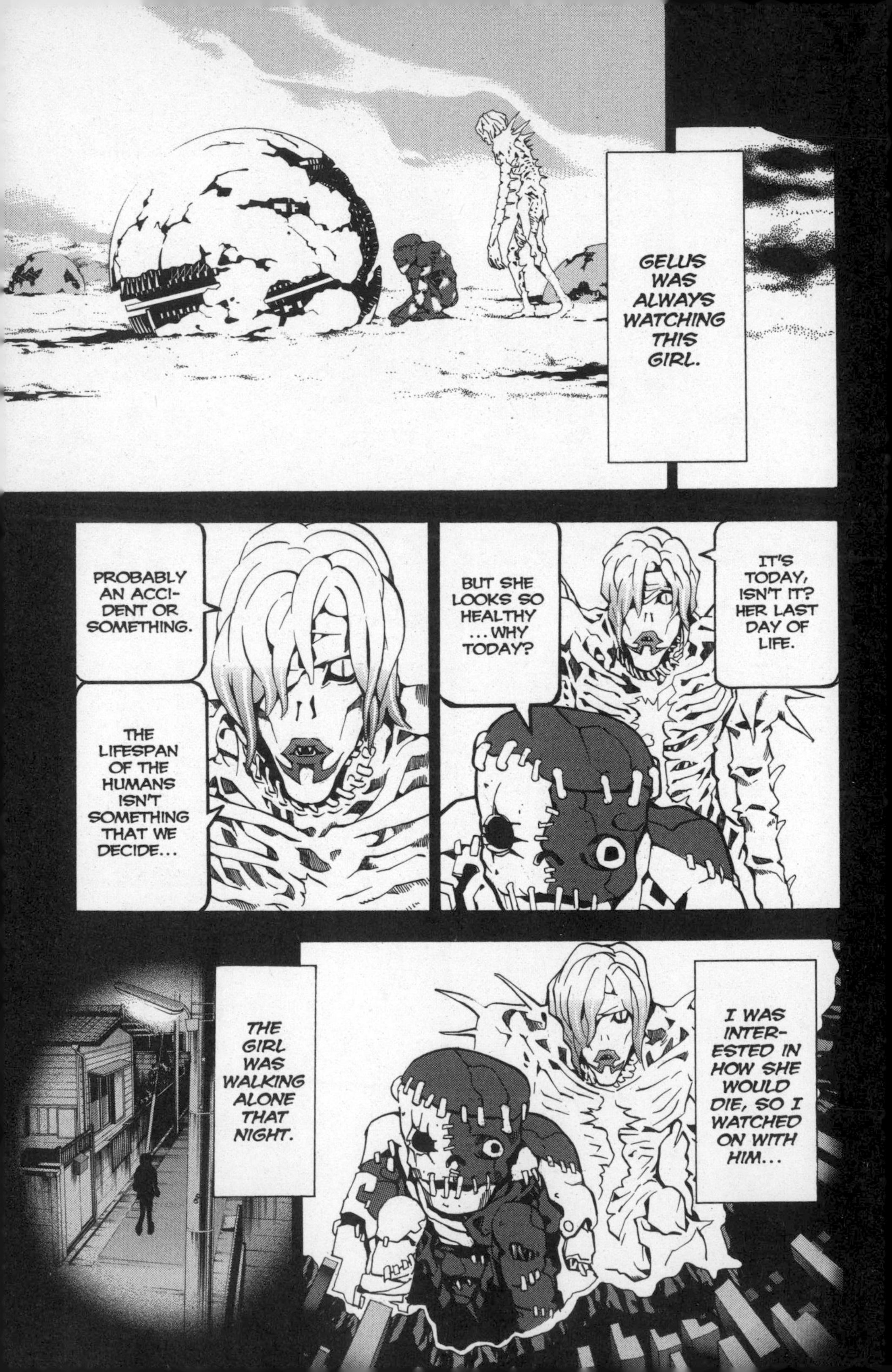
GELUS WAS ALWAYS WATCHING THIS GIRL.
IT'S TODAY, ISN'T IT? HER LAST DAY OF LIFE.
BUT SHE LOOKS SO HEALTHY ...WHY TODAY?
PROBABLY AN ACCIDENT OR SOMETHING.
THE LIFESPAN OF THE HUMANS ISN'T SOMETHING THAT WE DECIDE...
I WAS INTERESTED IN HOW SHE WOULD DIE, SO I WATCHED ON WITH HIM...
THE GIRL WAS WALKING ALONE THAT NIGHT.

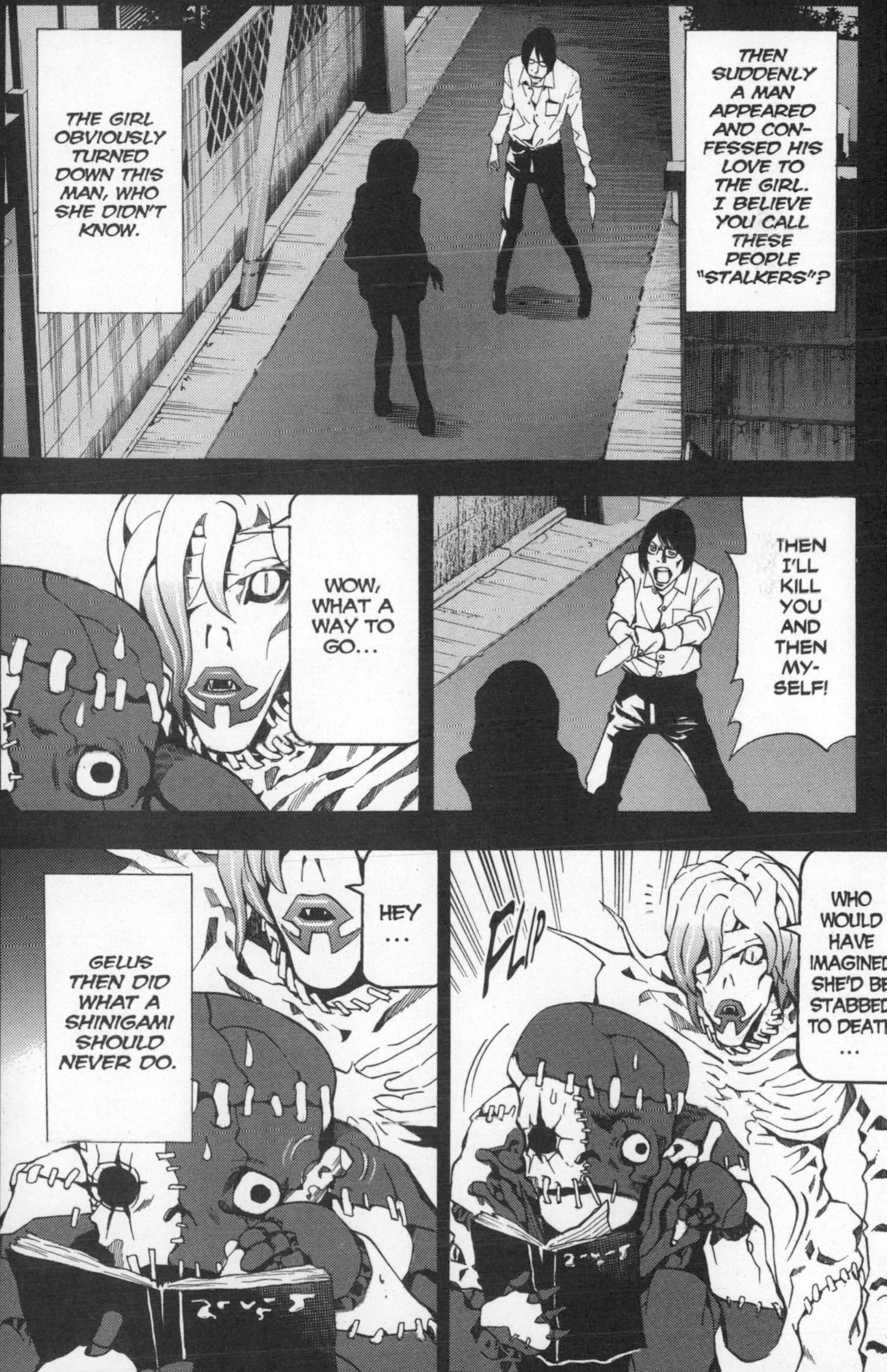
THEN SUDDENLY A MAN APPEARED AND CONFESSED HIS LOVE TO THE GIRL. I BELIEVE YOU CALL THESE PEOPLE "STALKERS"?
THE GIRL OBVIOUSLY TURNED DOWN THIS MAN, WHO SHE DIDN'T KNOW.
THEN I'LL KILL YOU AND THEN MYSELF!
WOW, WHAT A WAY TO GO...
WHO WOULD HAVE IMAGINED SHE'D BE STABBED TO DEATH...
FLIP
HEY...
GELUS THEN DID WHAT A SHINIGAMI SHOULD NEVER DO.

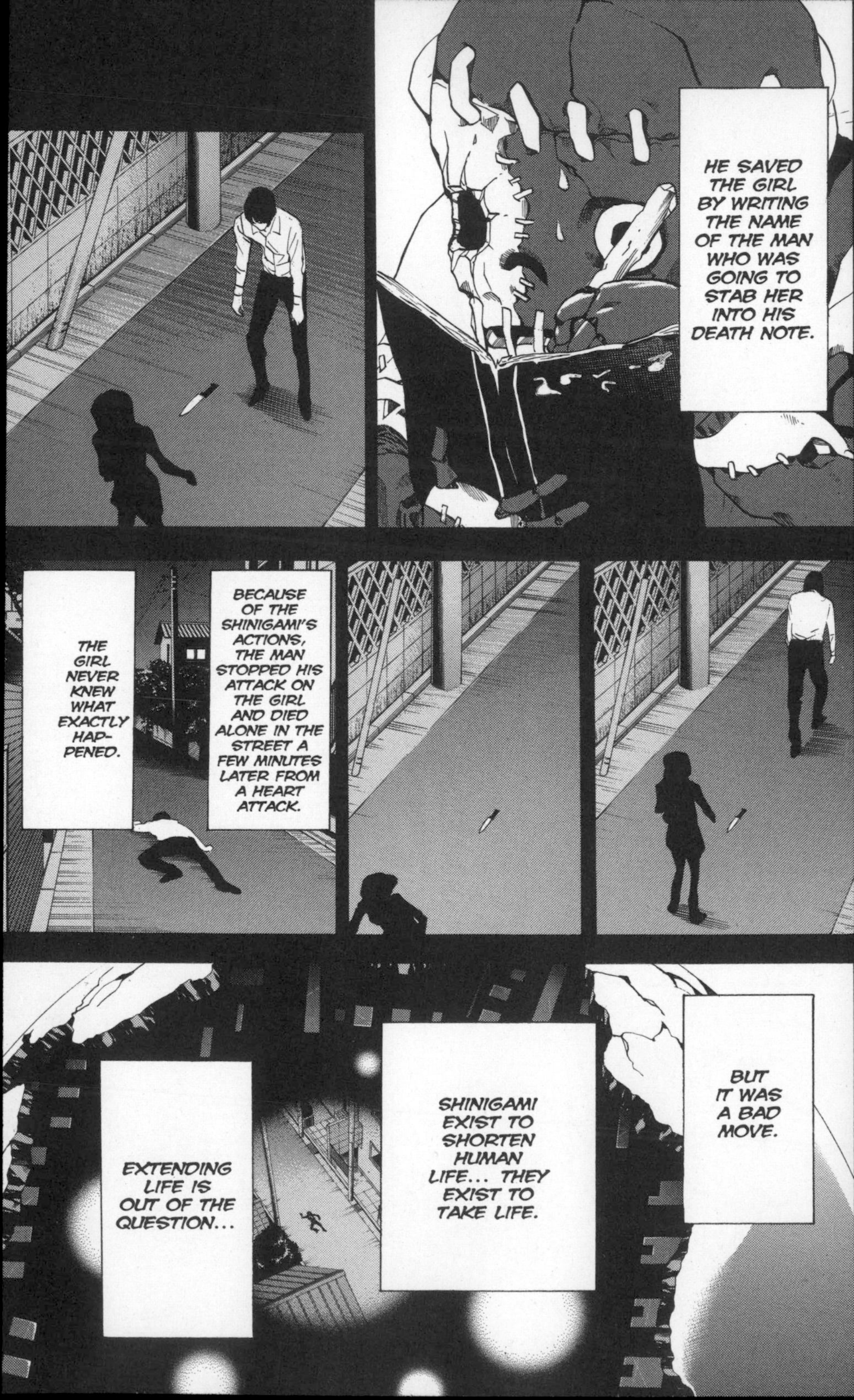
HE SAVED THE GIRL BY WRITING THE NAME OF THE MAN WHO WAS GOING TO STAB HER INTO HIS DEATH NOTE.
BECAUSE OF THE SHINIGAMI'S ACTIONS, THE MAN STOPPED HIS ATTACK ON THE GIRL AND DIED ALONE IN THE STREET A FEW MINUTES LATER FROM A HEART ATTACK.
THE GIRL NEVER KNEW WHAT EXACTLY HAP-PENED.
BUT IT WAS A BAD MOVE.
SHINIGAMI EXIST TO SHORTEN HUMAN LIFE... THEY EXIST TO TAKE LIFE.
EXTENDING LIFE IS OUT OF THE QUESTION...

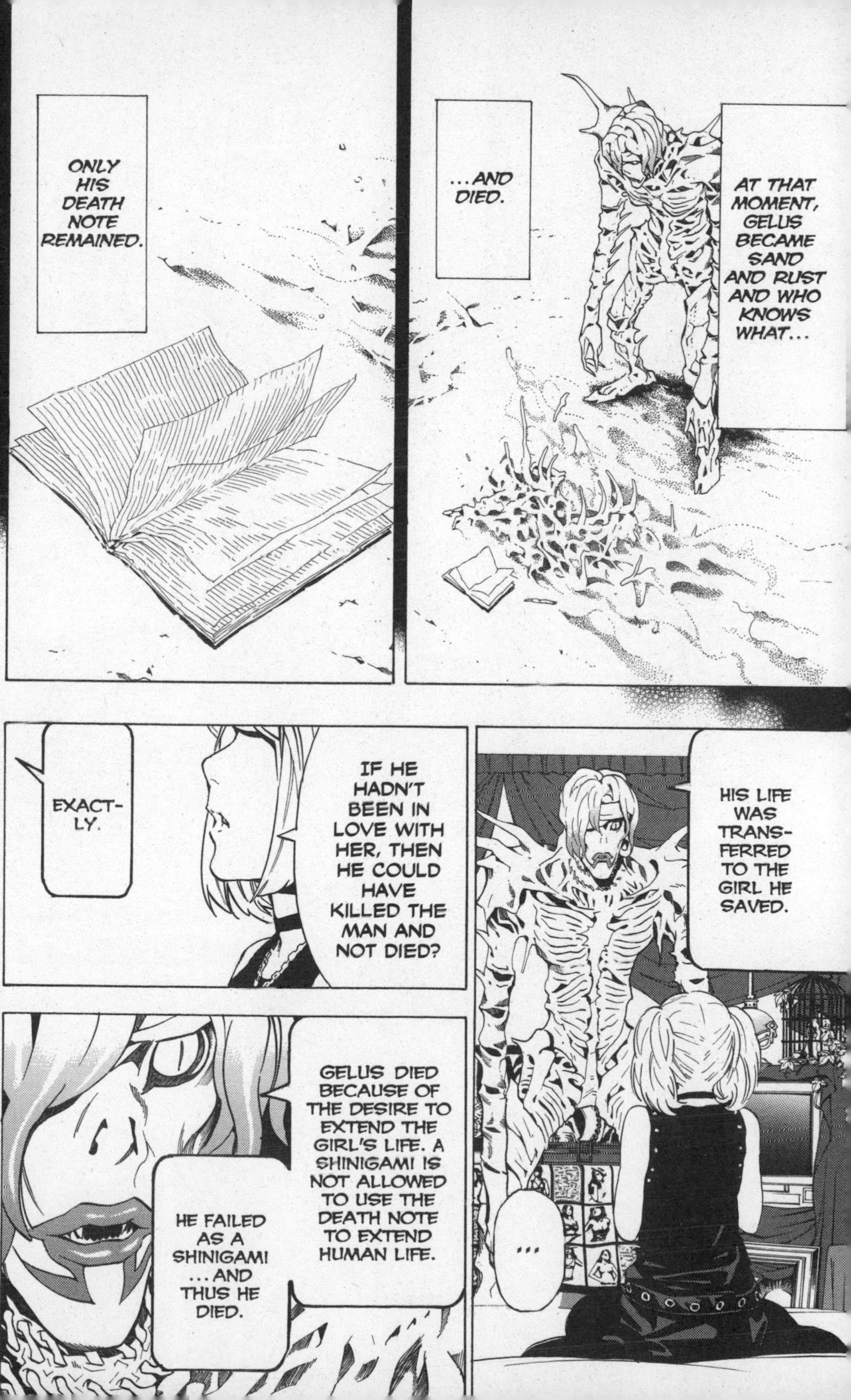
AT THAT MOMENT, GELUS BECAME SAND AND RUST AND WHO KNOWS WHAT...
...AND DIED.
ONLY HIS DEATH NOTE REMAINED.
HIS LIFE WAS TRANS-FERRED TO THE GIRL HE SAVED.
...
IF HE HADN'T BEEN IN LOVE WITH HER, THEN HE COULD HAVE KILLED THE MAN AND NOT DIED?
EXACT-LY.
GELUS DIED BECAUSE OF THE DESIRE TO EXTEND THE GIRL'S LIFE. A SHINIGAMI IS NOT ALLOWED TO USE THE DEATH NOTE TO EXTEND HUMAN LIFE.
HE FAILED AS A SHINIGAMI ...AND THUS HE DIED.

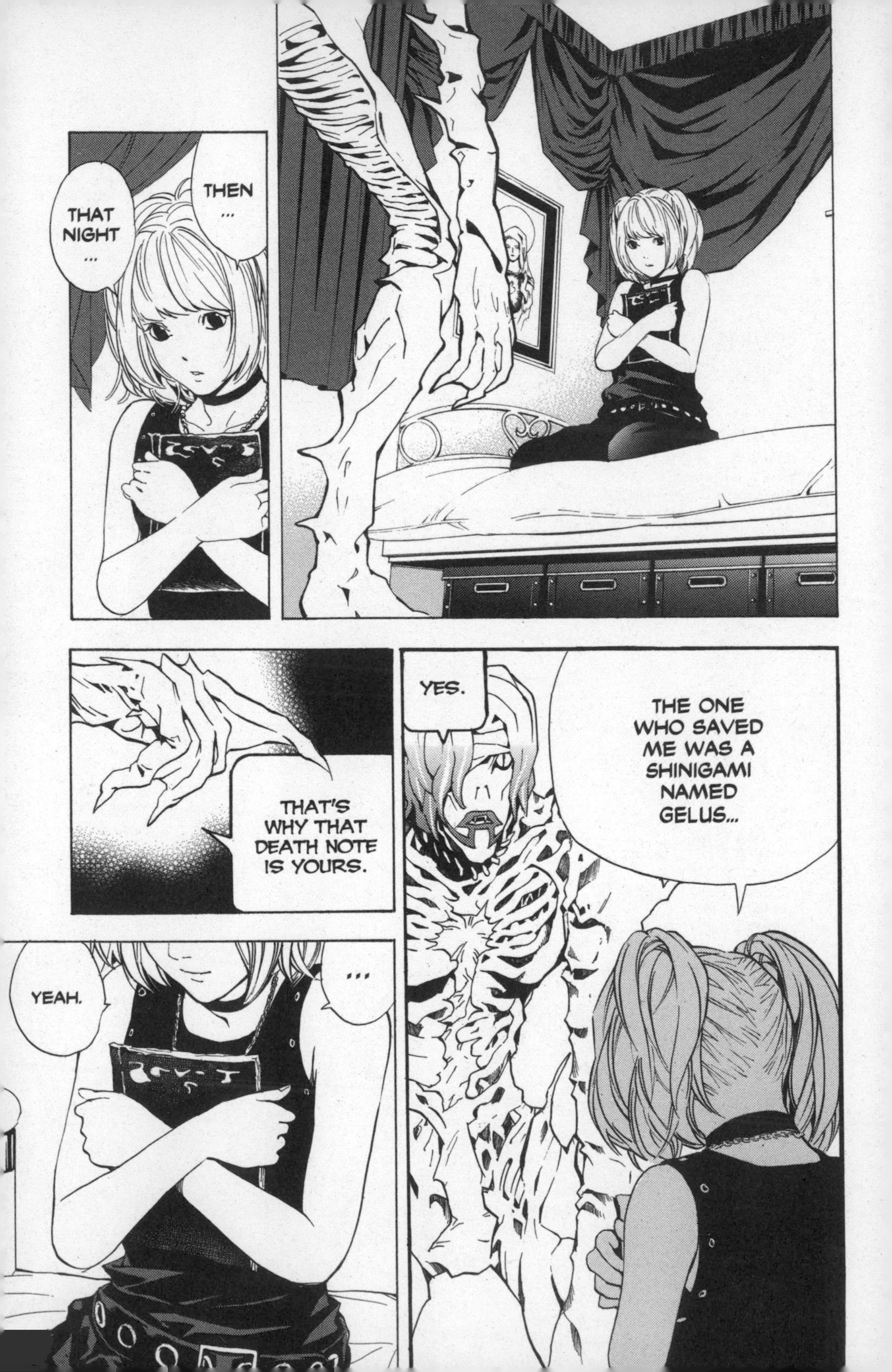
THEN ...
THAT NIGHT ...
THE ONE WHO SAVED ME WAS A SHINIGAMI NAMED GELUS...
YES.
THAT'S WHY THAT DEATH NOTE IS YOURS.
...
YEAH.

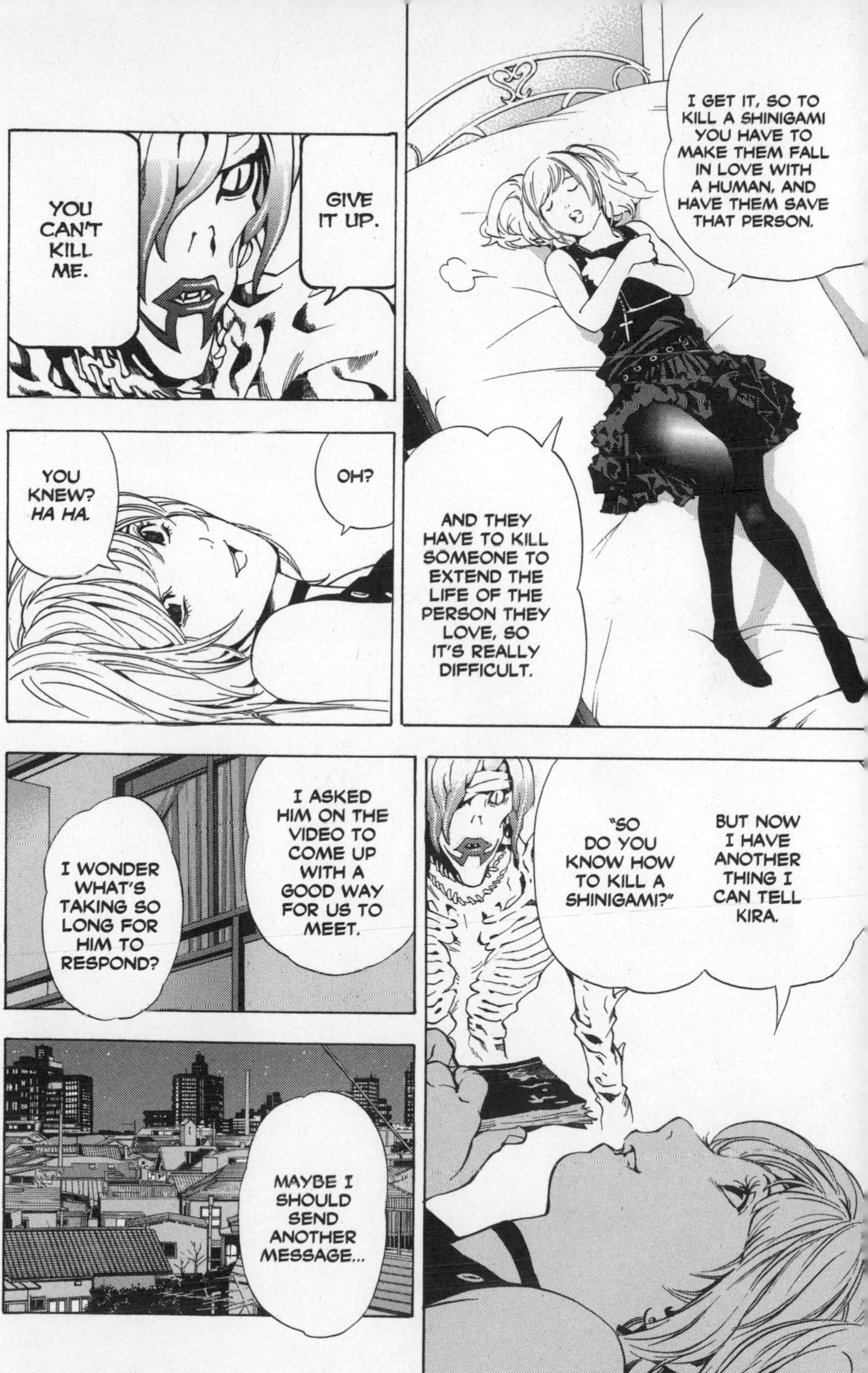
I GET IT, SO TO KILL A SHINIGAMI YOU HAVE TO MAKE THEM FALL IN LOVE WITH A HUMAN, AND HAVE THEM SAVE THAT PERSON.
AND THEY HAVE TO KILL SOMEONE TO EXTEND THE LIFE OF THE PERSON THEY LOVE, SO IT'S REALLY DIFFICULT.
GIVE IT UP.
YOU CAN'T KILL ME.
OH?
YOU KNEW? *HA HA.*
BUT NOW I HAVE ANOTHER THING I CAN TELL KIRA.
"SO DO YOU KNOW HOW TO KILL A SHINIGAMI?"
I ASKED HIM ON THE VIDEO TO COME UP WITH A GOOD WAY FOR US TO MEET.
I WONDER WHAT'S TAKING SO LONG FOR HIM TO RESPOND?
MAYBE I SHOULD SEND ANOTHER MESSAGE...

READ THIS WAY

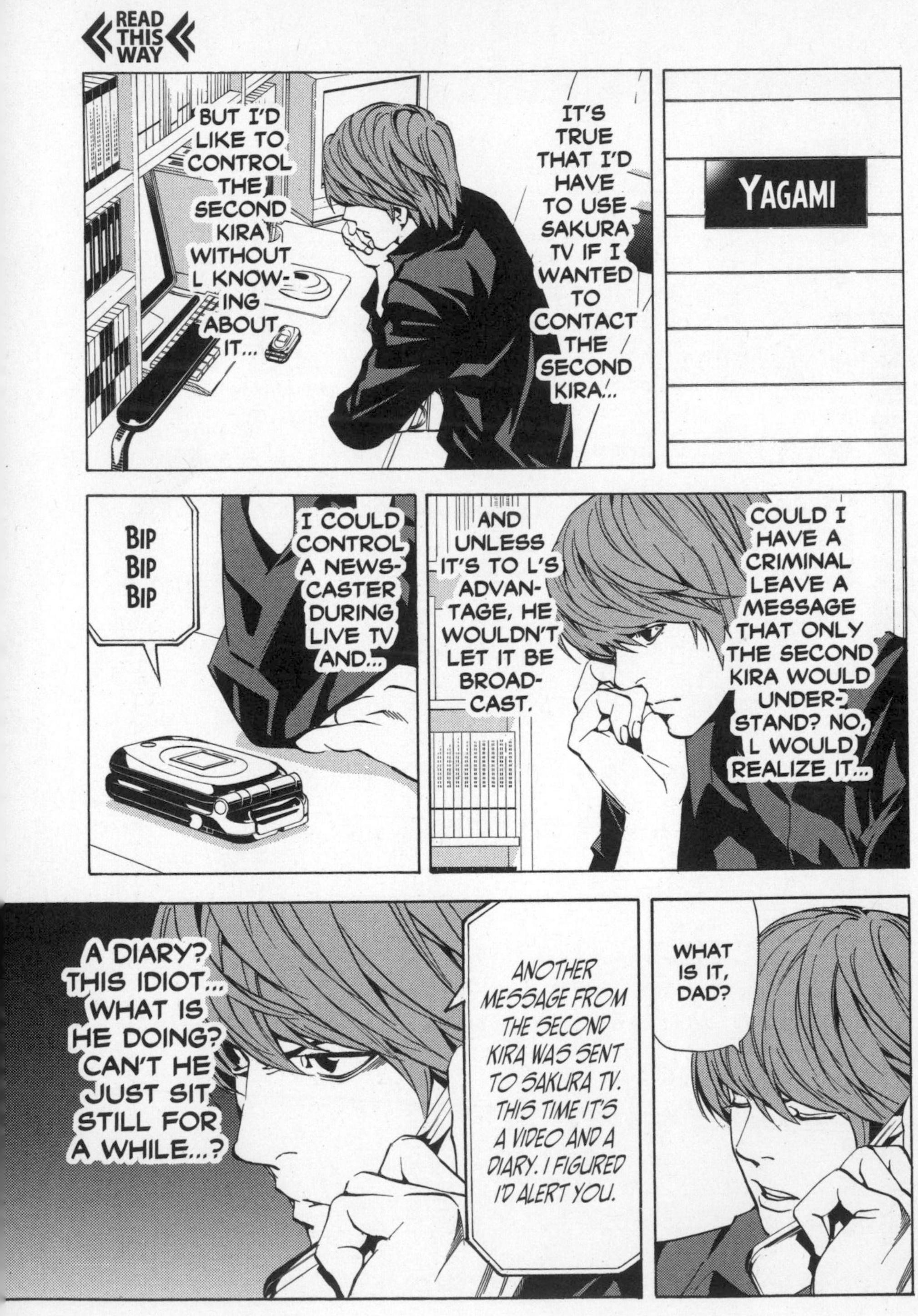
YAGAMI
IT'S TRUE THAT I'D HAVE TO USE SAKURA TV IF I WANTED TO CONTACT THE SECOND KIRA...
BUT I'D LIKE TO CONTROL THE SECOND KIRA WITHOUT L KNOW-ING ABOUT IT...
COULD I HAVE A CRIMINAL LEAVE A MESSAGE THAT ONLY THE SECOND KIRA WOULD UNDER-STAND? NO, L WOULD REALIZE IT...
AND UNLESS IT'S TO L'S ADVAN-TAGE, HE WOULDN'T LET IT BE BROAD-CAST.
I COULD CONTROL A NEWS-CASTER DURING LIVE TV AND...
BIP BIP BIP
WHAT IS IT, DAD?
ANOTHER MESSAGE FROM THE SECOND KIRA WAS SENT TO SAKURA TV. THIS TIME IT'S A VIDEO AND A DIARY. I FIGURED I'D ALERT YOU.
A DIARY? THIS IDIOT... WHAT IS HE DOING? CAN'T HE JUST SIT STILL FOR A WHILE...?

May 2003

1st   I said I wouldn't be participating in club activities during Golden Week but my friend called and invited me anyway.

4th   I went to the Saitama Super Arena with a friend to see the Morning Musume concert.

5th   It was the last day of vacation but I just sat around the house being lazy.

7th   School has started but I just borrowed my friend's notes and skipped class.

10th My friend invited me to go drinking but I declined. Yokohama is too far.

13th The friend I promised to lend a CD to came by so I let her borrow it.

16th I forgot to do my report so I copied it off my friend.

19th I bought Jump for the first time in a while. The short story was really good.

22nd My friend and I showed off our notebooks in Aoyama.

23rd I ran into **HIM** in the cafeteria. He was eating pork curry rice.

24th I met a friend in Shibuya. We bought some clothes to wear this summer.

28th I heard they're coming out with something better than the PS2 called the PSX. WOW!

30th We confirmed our Shinigami at the Giants game at the Tokyo Dome.

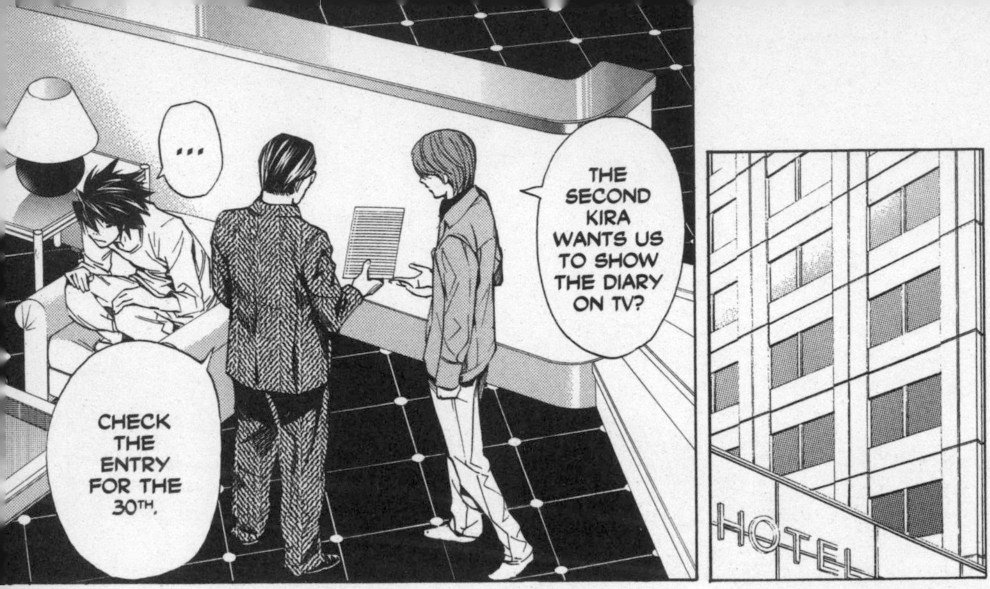
HOTEL
THE SECOND KIRA WANTS US TO SHOW THE DIARY ON TV?
...
CHECK THE ENTRY FOR THE 30TH.

30th We confirmed our Shinigami at the Giants game at the Tokyo Dome.

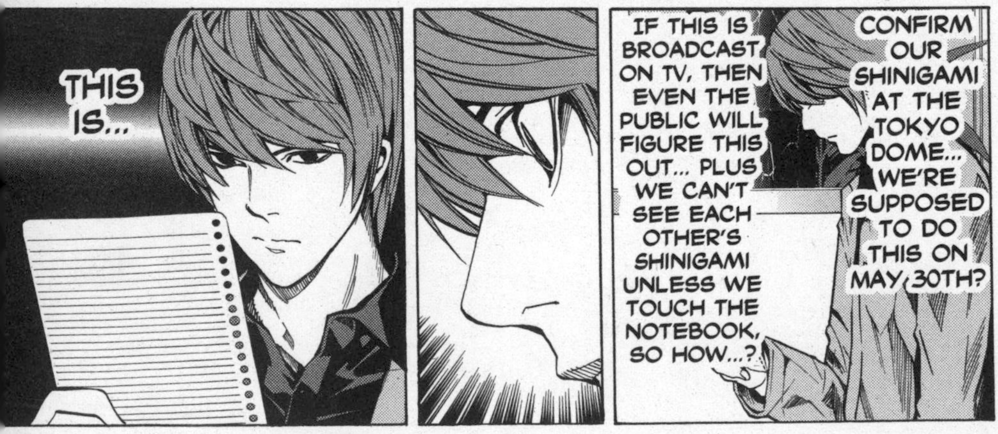
CONFIRM OUR SHINIGAMI AT THE TOKYO DOME... WE'RE SUPPOSED TO DO THIS ON MAY 30TH?
IF THIS IS BROADCAST ON TV, THEN EVEN THE PUBLIC WILL FIGURE THIS OUT... PLUS WE CAN'T SEE EACH OTHER'S SHINIGAMI UNLESS WE TOUCH THE NOTEBOOK, SO HOW...?
THIS IS...

22nd My friend and I showed off our notebooks in Aoyama.

23rd I ran into **HIM** in the cafeteria. He was eating pork cur

DEATH NOTE
How to use it
XVII

○ If the god of death decides to use the DEATH NOTE to kill the assassin of an individual he favors, the individual's life will be extended, but the god of death will die.

死神は特定の人間に好意を持ち、その人間の寿命を延ばす為に
デスノートを使い、人間を殺すと死ぬ。

○ The dead god of death will disappear, but the DEATH NOTE will remain. The ownership of this DEATH NOTE is usually carried over to the next god of death that touches it, but it is common sense that it is returned to the Great god of death.

死んだ死神は消えるが、デスノートは残る。
そのノートの所有権は、通常、次にノートに触れた死神に移るが、
死神大王に返上するのが常識とされている。

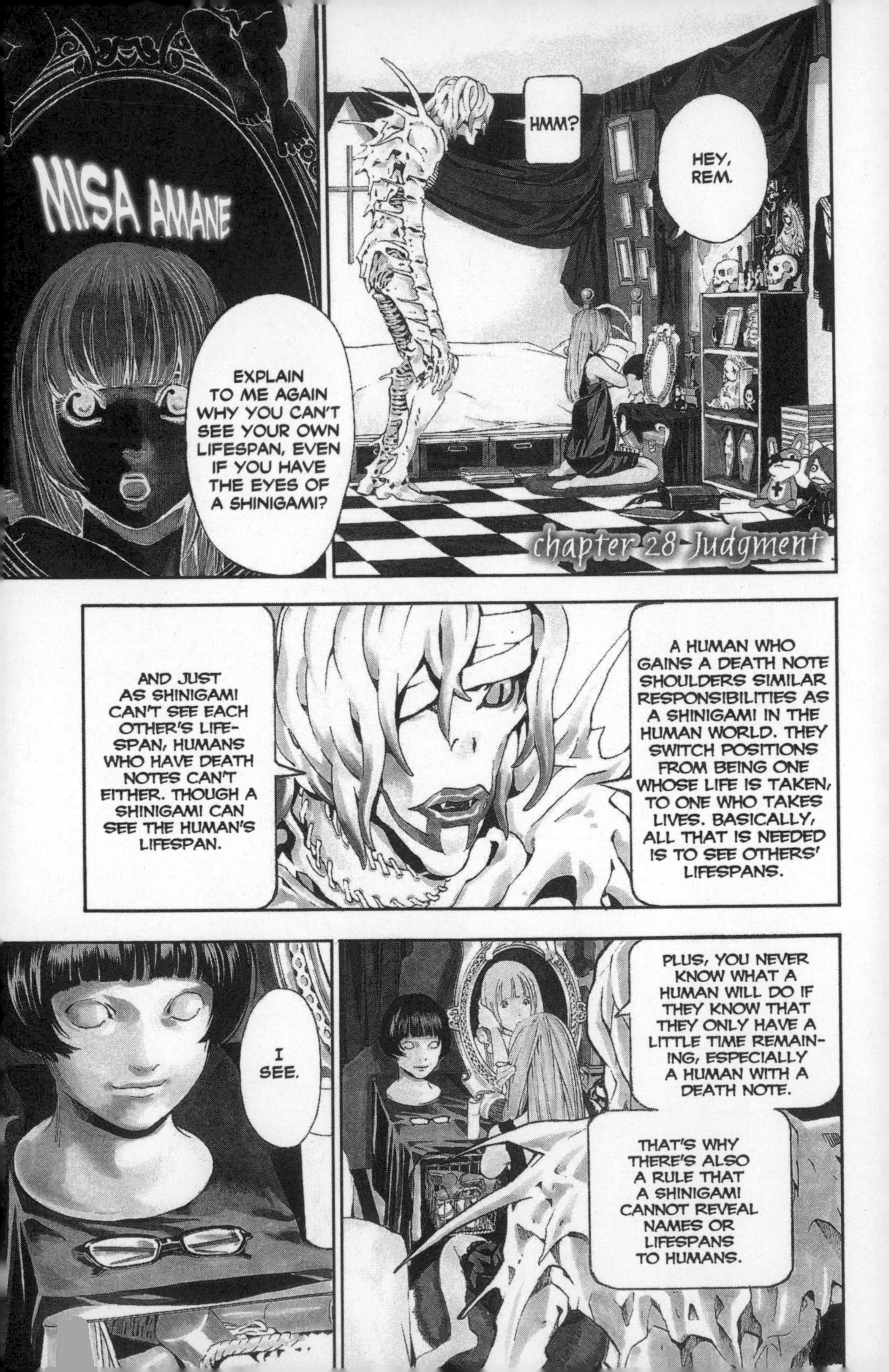
HEY, REM.
HMM?
chapter 28 Judgment
MISA AMANE
EXPLAIN TO ME AGAIN WHY YOU CAN'T SEE YOUR OWN LIFESPAN, EVEN IF YOU HAVE THE EYES OF A SHINIGAMI?
A HUMAN WHO GAINS A DEATH NOTE SHOULDERS SIMILAR RESPONSIBILITIES AS A SHINIGAMI IN THE HUMAN WORLD. THEY SWITCH POSITIONS FROM BEING ONE WHOSE LIFE IS TAKEN, TO ONE WHO TAKES LIVES. BASICALLY, ALL THAT IS NEEDED IS TO SEE OTHERS' LIFESPANS.
AND JUST AS SHINIGAMI CAN'T SEE EACH OTHER'S LIFE-SPAN, HUMANS WHO HAVE DEATH NOTES CAN'T EITHER. THOUGH A SHINIGAMI CAN SEE THE HUMAN'S LIFESPAN.
PLUS, YOU NEVER KNOW WHAT A HUMAN WILL DO IF THEY KNOW THAT THEY ONLY HAVE A LITTLE TIME REMAIN-ING, ESPECIALLY A HUMAN WITH A DEATH NOTE.
THAT'S WHY THERE'S ALSO A RULE THAT A SHINIGAMI CANNOT REVEAL NAMES OR LIFESPANS TO HUMANS.
I SEE.

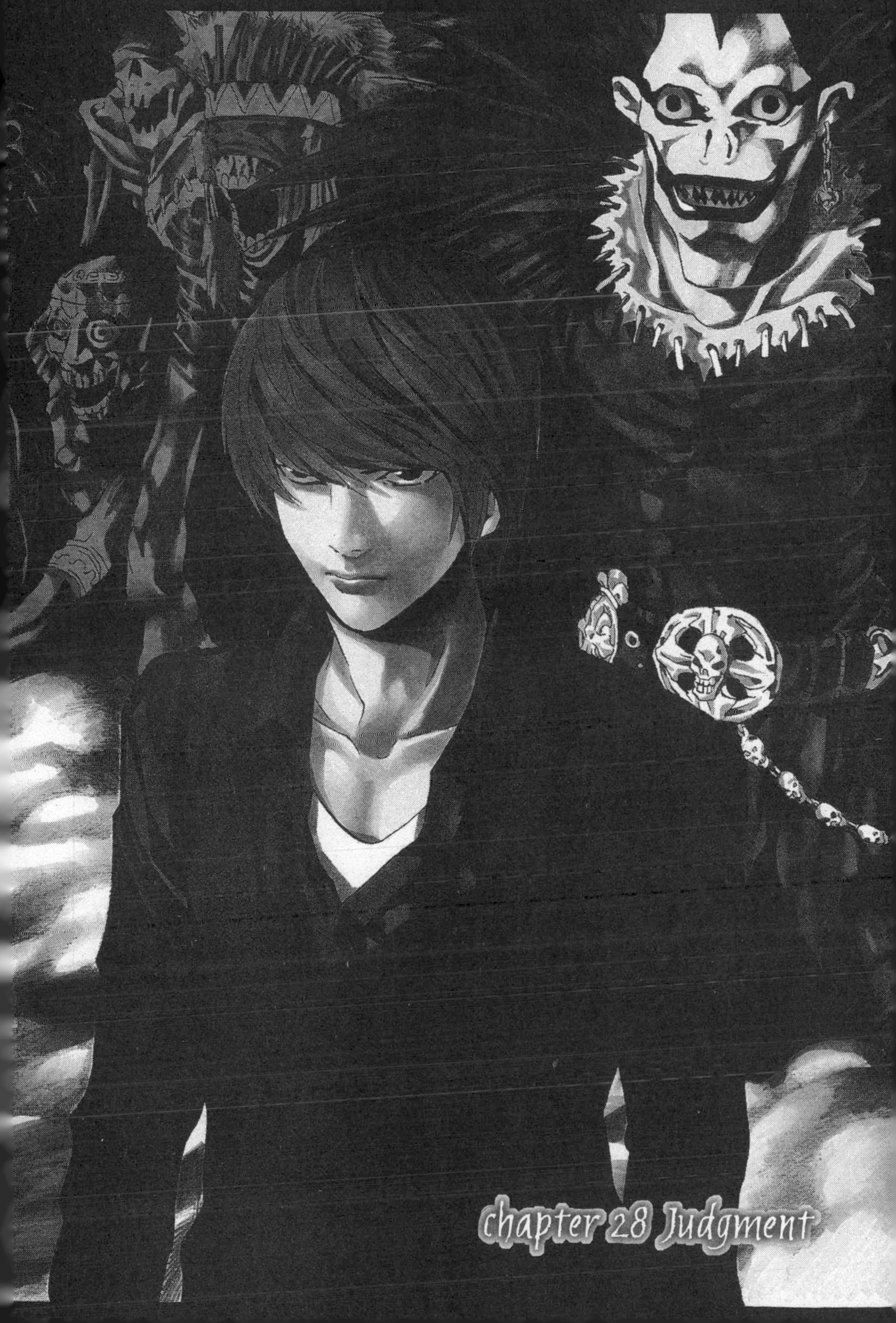
chapter 28 Judgment

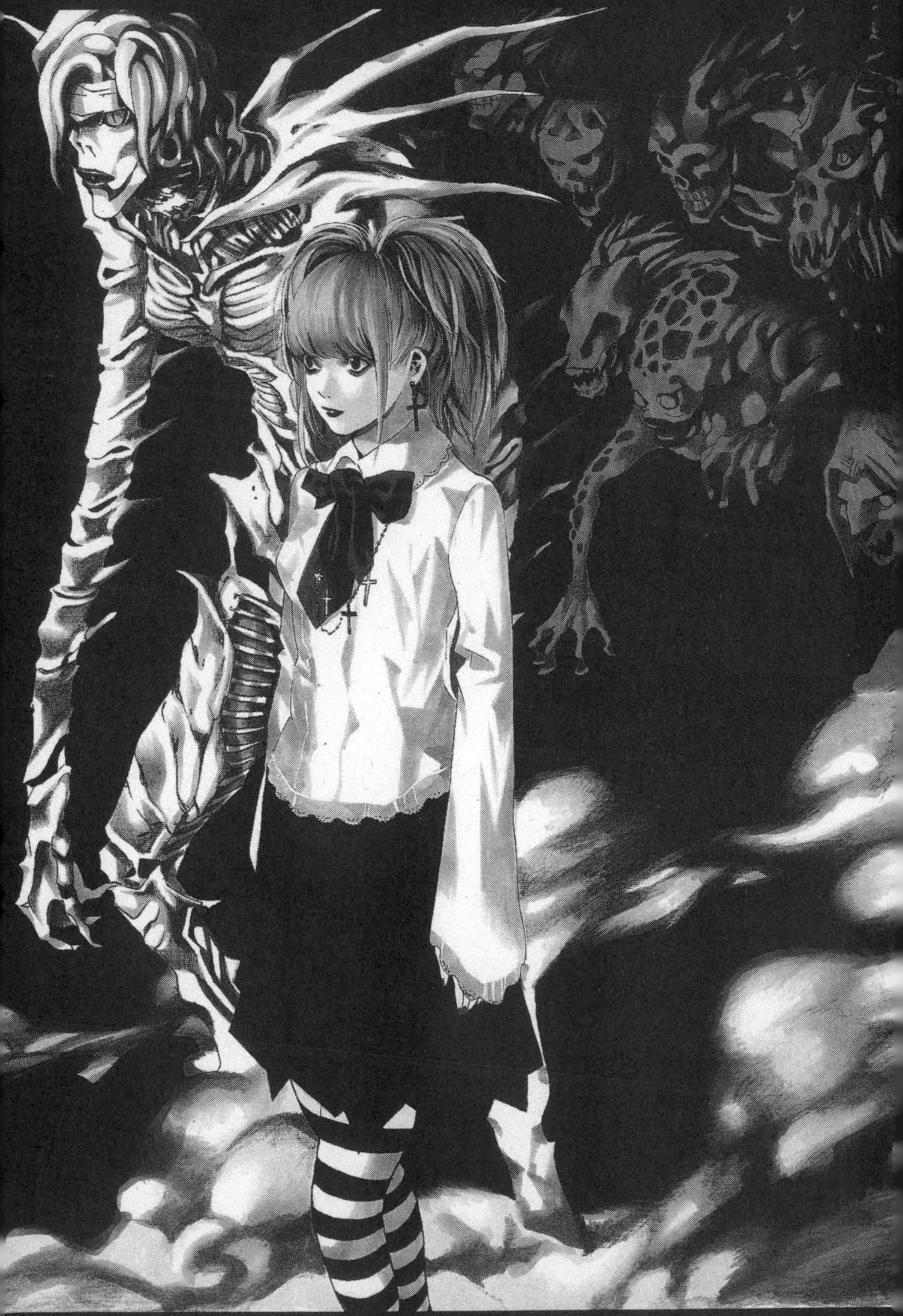

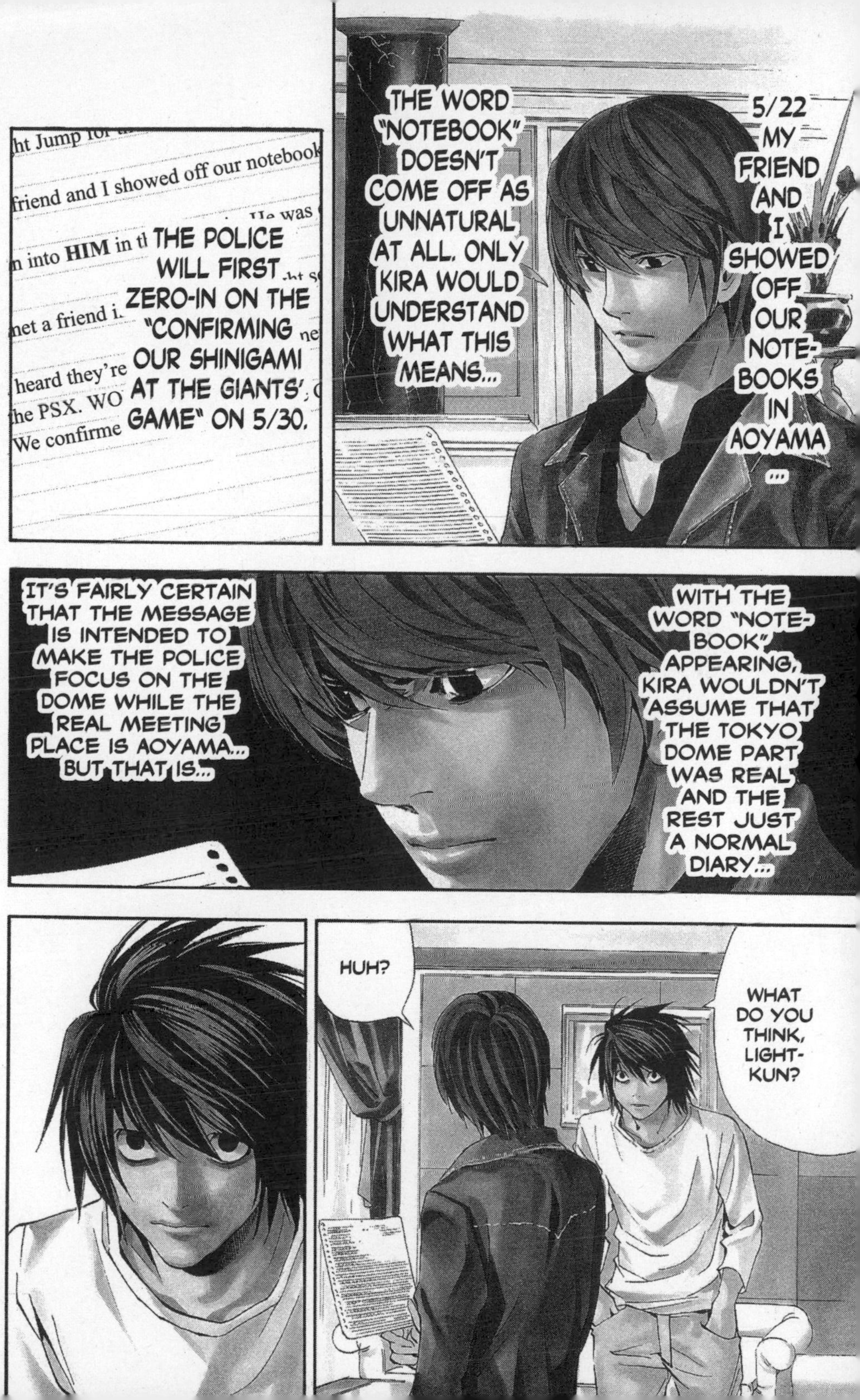
5/22 MY FRIEND AND I SHOWED OFF OUR NOTEBOOKS IN AOYAMA...
THE WORD "NOTEBOOK" DOESN'T COME OFF AS UNNATURAL AT ALL. ONLY KIRA WOULD UNDERSTAND WHAT THIS MEANS...
friend and I showed off our notebook
n into HIM in t
net a friend i
heard they're
the PSX. WO
We confirme
THE POLICE WILL FIRST ZERO-IN ON THE "CONFIRMING OUR SHINIGAMI AT THE GIANTS' GAME" ON 5/30.
WITH THE WORD "NOTEBOOK" APPEARING, KIRA WOULDN'T ASSUME THAT THE TOKYO DOME PART WAS REAL AND THE REST JUST A NORMAL DIARY...
IT'S FAIRLY CERTAIN THAT THE MESSAGE IS INTENDED TO MAKE THE POLICE FOCUS ON THE DOME WHILE THE REAL MEETING PLACE IS AOYAMA... BUT THAT IS...
WHAT DO YOU THINK, LIGHT-KUN?
HUH?

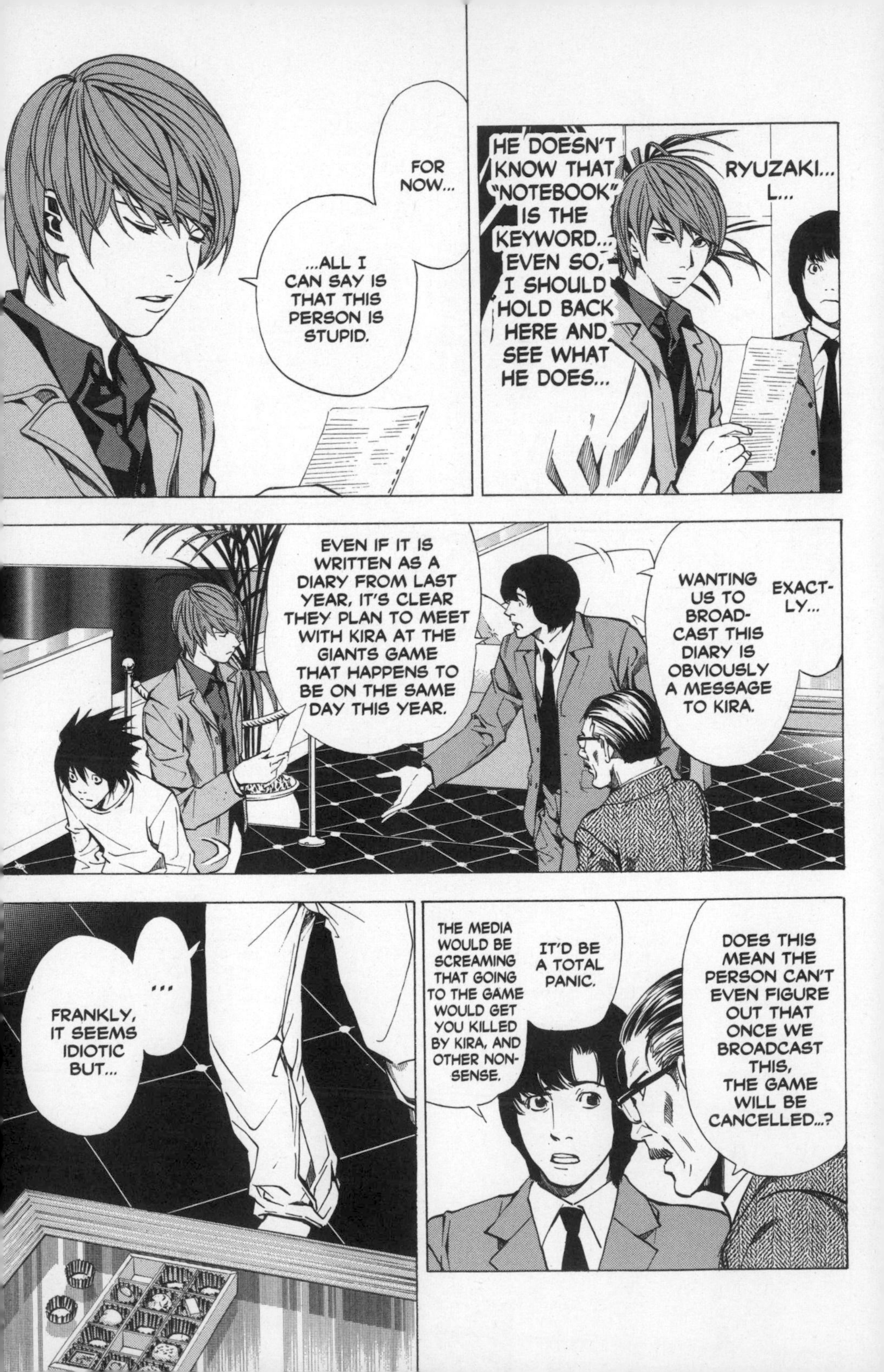
RYUZAKI... L...
HE DOESN'T KNOW THAT "NOTEBOOK" IS THE KEYWORD... EVEN SO, I SHOULD HOLD BACK HERE AND SEE WHAT HE DOES...
FOR NOW...
...ALL I CAN SAY IS THAT THIS PERSON IS STUPID.
EXACT-LY...
WANTING US TO BROAD-CAST THIS DIARY IS OBVIOUSLY A MESSAGE TO KIRA.
EVEN IF IT IS WRITTEN AS A DIARY FROM LAST YEAR, IT'S CLEAR THEY PLAN TO MEET WITH KIRA AT THE GIANTS GAME THAT HAPPENS TO BE ON THE SAME DAY THIS YEAR.
DOES THIS MEAN THE PERSON CAN'T EVEN FIGURE OUT THAT ONCE WE BROADCAST THIS, THE GAME WILL BE CANCELLED...?
IT'D BE A TOTAL PANIC.
THE MEDIA WOULD BE SCREAMING THAT GOING TO THE GAME WOULD GET YOU KILLED BY KIRA, AND OTHER NON-SENSE.
...
FRANKLY, IT SEEMS IDIOTIC BUT...

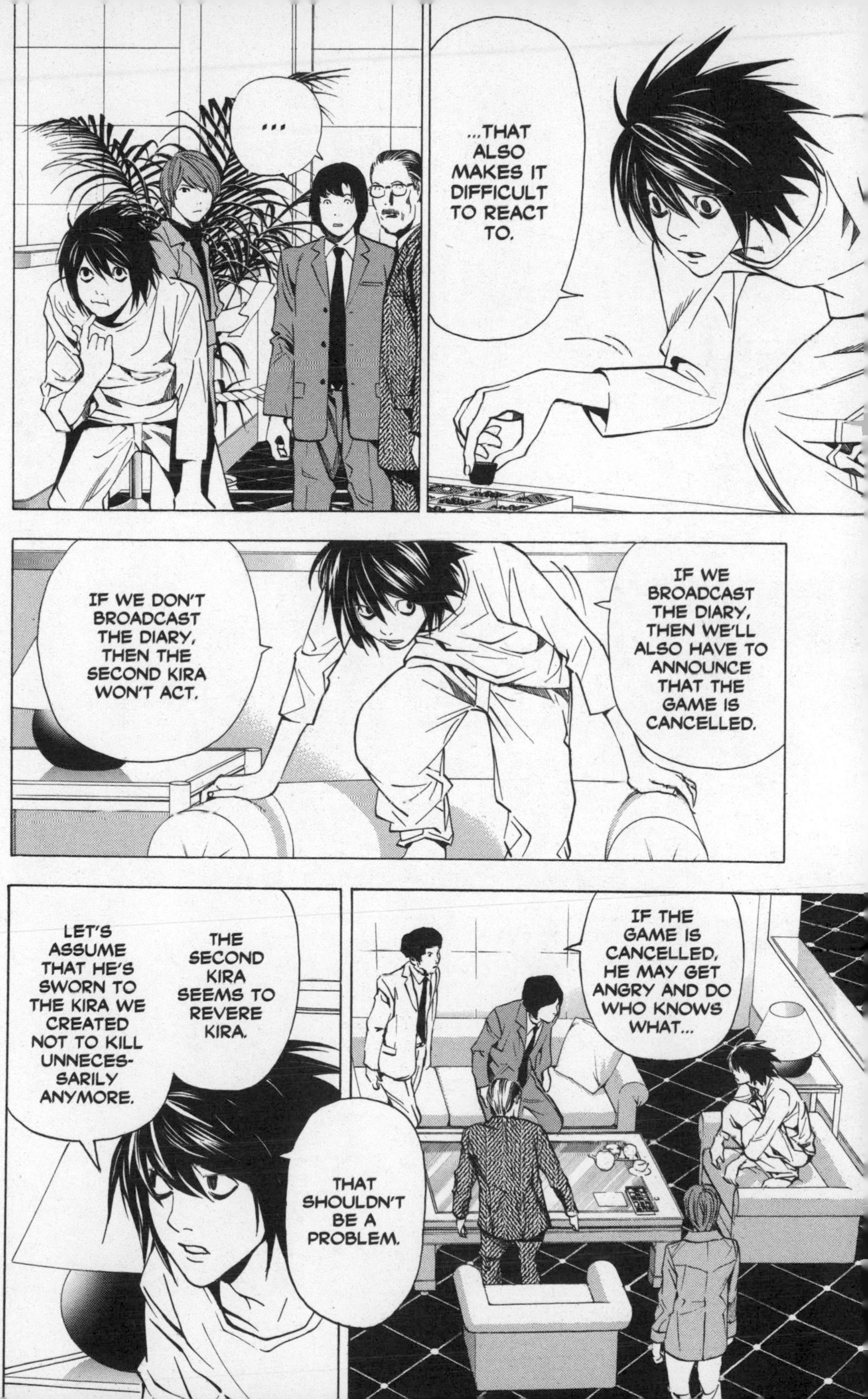
...THAT ALSO MAKES IT DIFFICULT TO REACT TO.
...
IF WE BROADCAST THE DIARY, THEN WE'LL ALSO HAVE TO ANNOUNCE THAT THE GAME IS CANCELLED.
IF WE DON'T BROADCAST THE DIARY, THEN THE SECOND KIRA WON'T ACT.
IF THE GAME IS CANCELLED, HE MAY GET ANGRY AND DO WHO KNOWS WHAT...
THE SECOND KIRA SEEMS TO REVERE KIRA.
LET'S ASSUME THAT HE'S SWORN TO THE KIRA WE CREATED NOT TO KILL UNNECES-SARILY ANYMORE.
THAT SHOULDN'T BE A PROBLEM.

READ THIS WAY

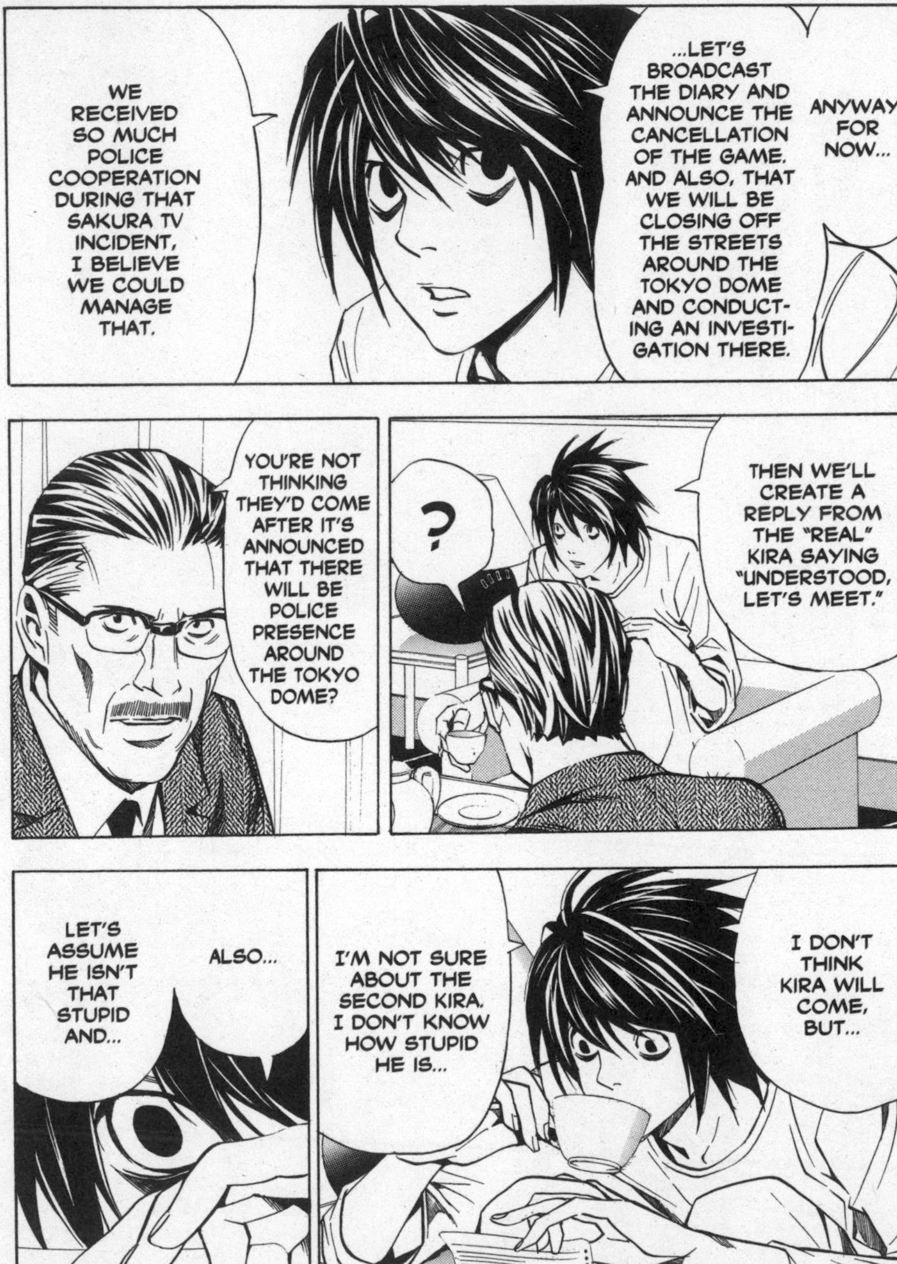

ANYWAY, FOR NOW...
...LET'S BROADCAST THE DIARY AND ANNOUNCE THE CANCELLATION OF THE GAME. AND ALSO, THAT WE WILL BE CLOSING OFF THE STREETS AROUND THE TOKYO DOME AND CONDUCTING AN INVESTIGATION THERE.
WE RECEIVED SO MUCH POLICE COOPERATION DURING THAT SAKURA TV INCIDENT, I BELIEVE WE COULD MANAGE THAT.
THEN WE'LL CREATE A REPLY FROM THE "REAL" KIRA SAYING "UNDERSTOOD, LET'S MEET."
?
YOU'RE NOT THINKING THEY'D COME AFTER IT'S ANNOUNCED THAT THERE WILL BE POLICE PRESENCE AROUND THE TOKYO DOME?
I DON'T THINK KIRA WILL COME, BUT...
I'M NOT SURE ABOUT THE SECOND KIRA. I DON'T KNOW HOW STUPID HE IS...
ALSO...
LET'S ASSUME HE ISN'T THAT STUPID AND...

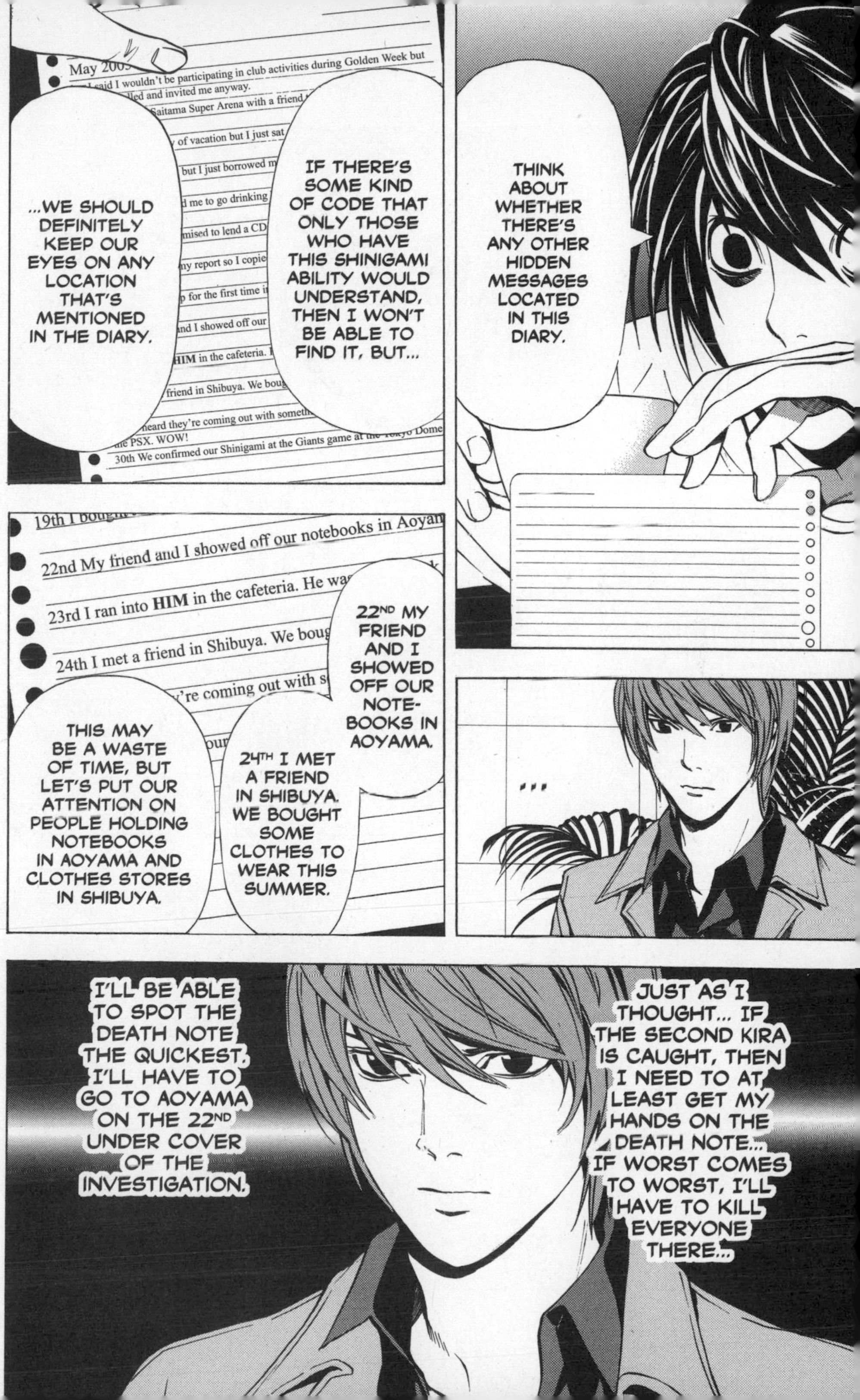
THINK ABOUT WHETHER THERE'S ANY OTHER HIDDEN MESSAGES LOCATED IN THIS DIARY.
IF THERE'S SOME KIND OF CODE THAT ONLY THOSE WHO HAVE THIS SHINIGAMI ABILITY WOULD UNDERSTAND, THEN I WON'T BE ABLE TO FIND IT, BUT...
...WE SHOULD DEFINITELY KEEP OUR EYES ON ANY LOCATION THAT'S MENTIONED IN THE DIARY.
...
22ND MY FRIEND AND I SHOWED OFF OUR NOTE-BOOKS IN AOYAMA.
24TH I MET A FRIEND IN SHIBUYA. WE BOUGHT SOME CLOTHES TO WEAR THIS SUMMER.
THIS MAY BE A WASTE OF TIME, BUT LET'S PUT OUR ATTENTION ON PEOPLE HOLDING NOTEBOOKS IN AOYAMA AND CLOTHES STORES IN SHIBUYA.
JUST AS I THOUGHT... IF THE SECOND KIRA IS CAUGHT, THEN I NEED TO AT LEAST GET MY HANDS ON THE DEATH NOTE... IF WORST COMES TO WORST, I'LL HAVE TO KILL EVERYONE THERE...
I'LL BE ABLE TO SPOT THE DEATH NOTE THE QUICKEST. I'LL HAVE TO GO TO AOYAMA ON THE 22ND UNDER COVER OF THE INVESTIGATION.

READ THIS WAY

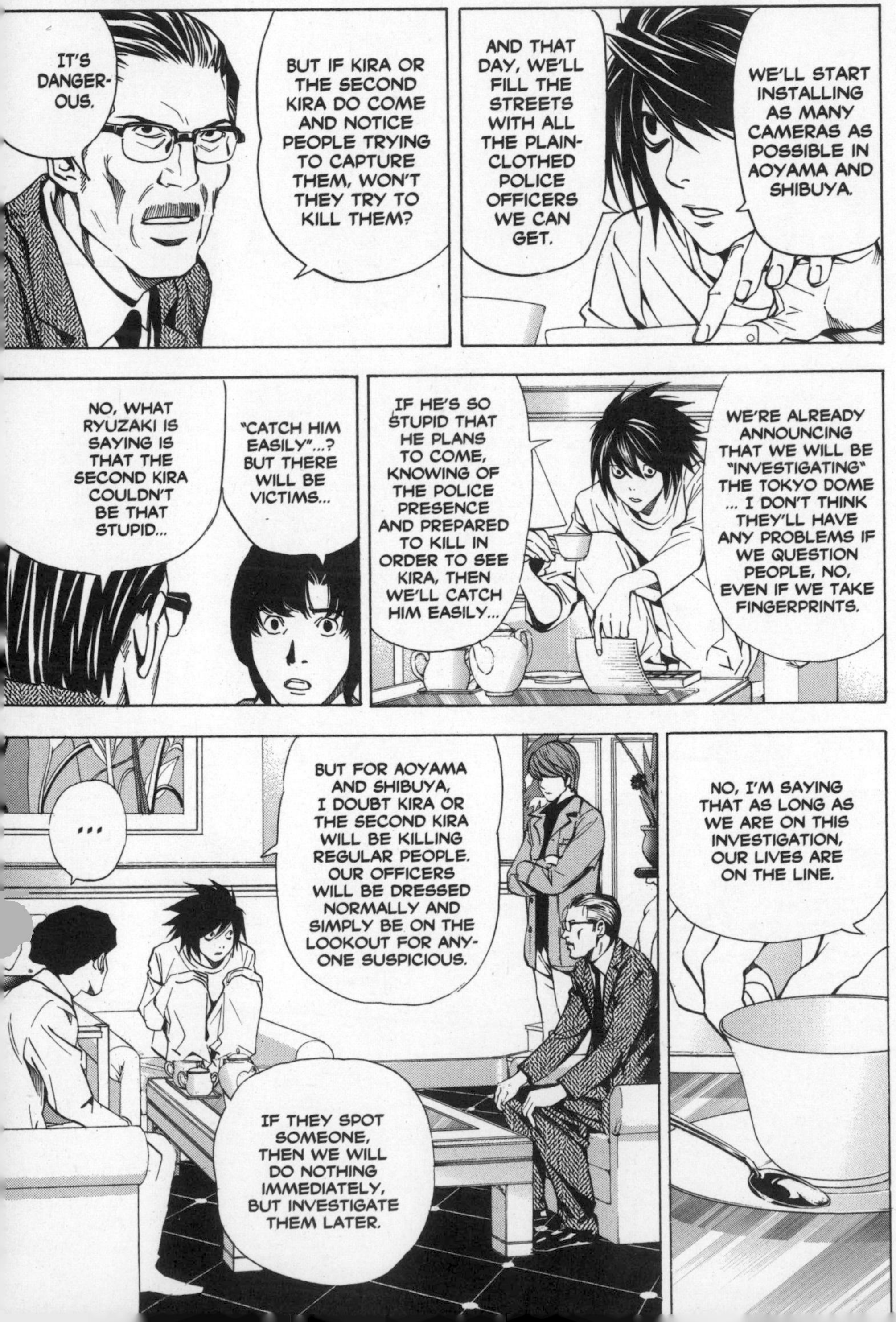

WE'LL START INSTALLING AS MANY CAMERAS AS POSSIBLE IN AOYAMA AND SHIBUYA.
AND THAT DAY, WE'LL FILL THE STREETS WITH ALL THE PLAIN-CLOTHED POLICE OFFICERS WE CAN GET.
BUT IF KIRA OR THE SECOND KIRA DO COME AND NOTICE PEOPLE TRYING TO CAPTURE THEM, WON'T THEY TRY TO KILL THEM?
IT'S DANGER-OUS.
WE'RE ALREADY ANNOUNCING THAT WE WILL BE "INVESTIGATING" THE TOKYO DOME ... I DON'T THINK THEY'LL HAVE ANY PROBLEMS IF WE QUESTION PEOPLE, NO, EVEN IF WE TAKE FINGERPRINTS.
IF HE'S SO STUPID THAT HE PLANS TO COME, KNOWING OF THE POLICE PRESENCE AND PREPARED TO KILL IN ORDER TO SEE KIRA, THEN WE'LL CATCH HIM EASILY...
"CATCH HIM EASILY"...? BUT THERE WILL BE VICTIMS...
NO, WHAT RYUZAKI IS SAYING IS THAT THE SECOND KIRA COULDN'T BE THAT STUPID...
NO, I'M SAYING THAT AS LONG AS WE ARE ON THIS INVESTIGATION, OUR LIVES ARE ON THE LINE.
BUT FOR AOYAMA AND SHIBUYA, I DOUBT KIRA OR THE SECOND KIRA WILL BE KILLING REGULAR PEOPLE. OUR OFFICERS WILL BE DRESSED NORMALLY AND SIMPLY BE ON THE LOOKOUT FOR ANY-ONE SUSPICIOUS.
IF THEY SPOT SOMEONE, THEN WE WILL DO NOTHING IMMEDIATELY, BUT INVESTIGATE THEM LATER.
...

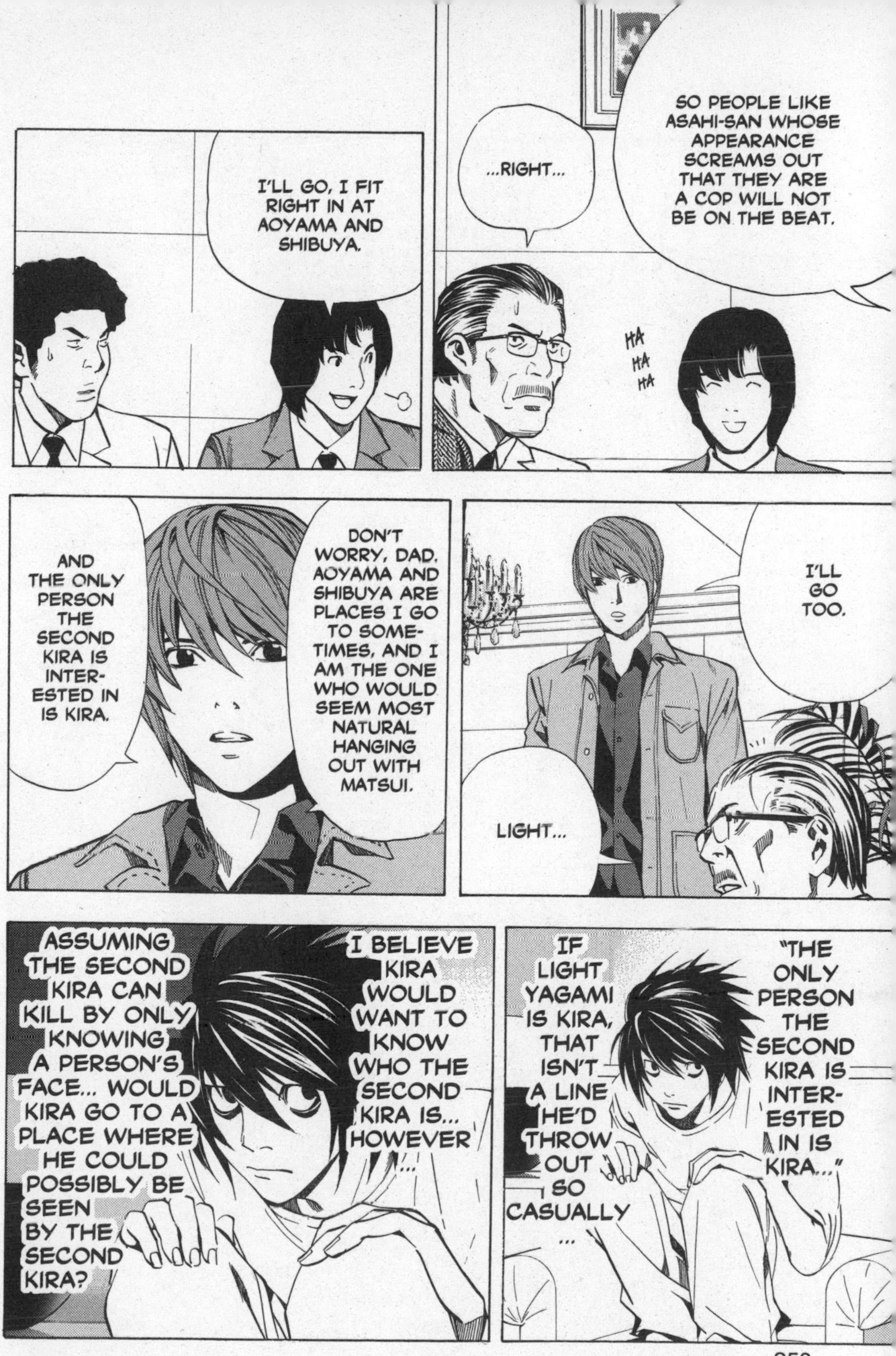
SO PEOPLE LIKE ASAHI-SAN WHOSE APPEARANCE SCREAMS OUT THAT THEY ARE A COP WILL NOT BE ON THE BEAT.
...RIGHT...
HA HA HA
I'LL GO, I FIT RIGHT IN AT AOYAMA AND SHIBUYA.
I'LL GO TOO.
LIGHT...
DON'T WORRY, DAD. AOYAMA AND SHIBUYA ARE PLACES I GO TO SOME-TIMES, AND I AM THE ONE WHO WOULD SEEM MOST NATURAL HANGING OUT WITH MATSUI.
AND THE ONLY PERSON THE SECOND KIRA IS INTER-ESTED IN IS KIRA.
"THE ONLY PERSON THE SECOND KIRA IS INTER-ESTED IN IS KIRA..."
IF LIGHT YAGAMI IS KIRA, THAT ISN'T A LINE HE'D THROW OUT SO CASUALLY...
I BELIEVE KIRA WOULD WANT TO KNOW WHO THE SECOND KIRA IS... HOWEVER...
ASSUMING THE SECOND KIRA CAN KILL BY ONLY KNOWING A PERSON'S FACE... WOULD KIRA GO TO A PLACE WHERE HE COULD POSSIBLY BE SEEN BY THE SECOND KIRA?

READ THIS WAY

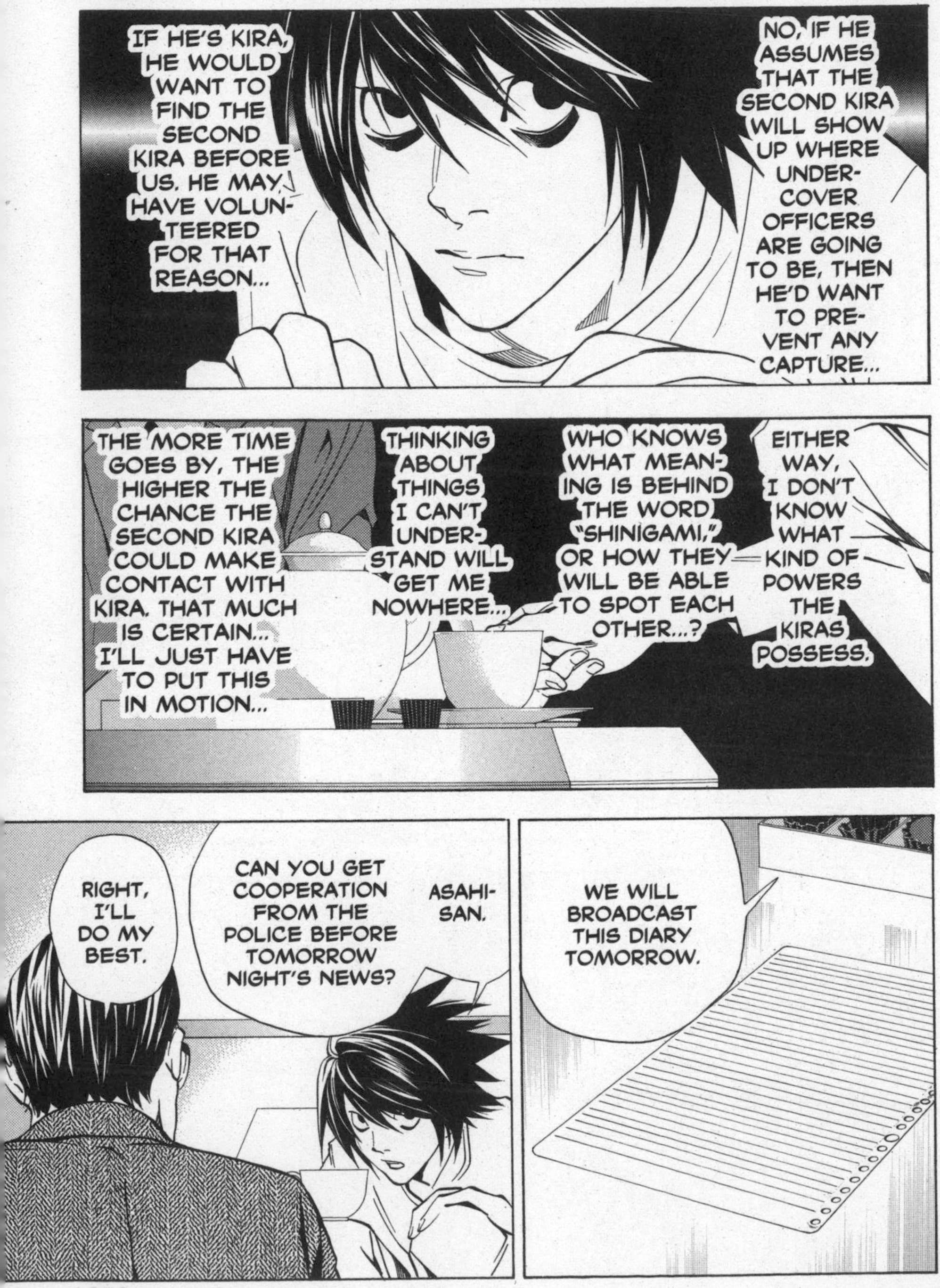
NO, IF HE ASSUMES THAT THE SECOND KIRA WILL SHOW UP WHERE UNDER-COVER OFFICERS ARE GOING TO BE, THEN HE'D WANT TO PRE-VENT ANY CAPTURE...
IF HE'S KIRA, HE WOULD WANT TO FIND THE SECOND KIRA BEFORE US. HE MAY HAVE VOLUN-TEERED FOR THAT REASON...
EITHER WAY, I DON'T KNOW WHAT KIND OF POWERS THE KIRAS POSSESS.
WHO KNOWS WHAT MEAN-ING IS BEHIND THE WORD "SHINIGAMI," OR HOW THEY WILL BE ABLE TO SPOT EACH OTHER...?
THINKING ABOUT THINGS I CAN'T UNDER-STAND WILL GET ME NOWHERE...
THE MORE TIME GOES BY, THE HIGHER THE CHANCE THE SECOND KIRA COULD MAKE CONTACT WITH KIRA. THAT MUCH IS CERTAIN... I'LL JUST HAVE TO PUT THIS IN MOTION...
WE WILL BROADCAST THIS DIARY TOMORROW.
ASAHI-SAN.
CAN YOU GET COOPERATION FROM THE POLICE BEFORE TOMORROW NIGHT'S NEWS?
RIGHT, I'LL DO MY BEST.

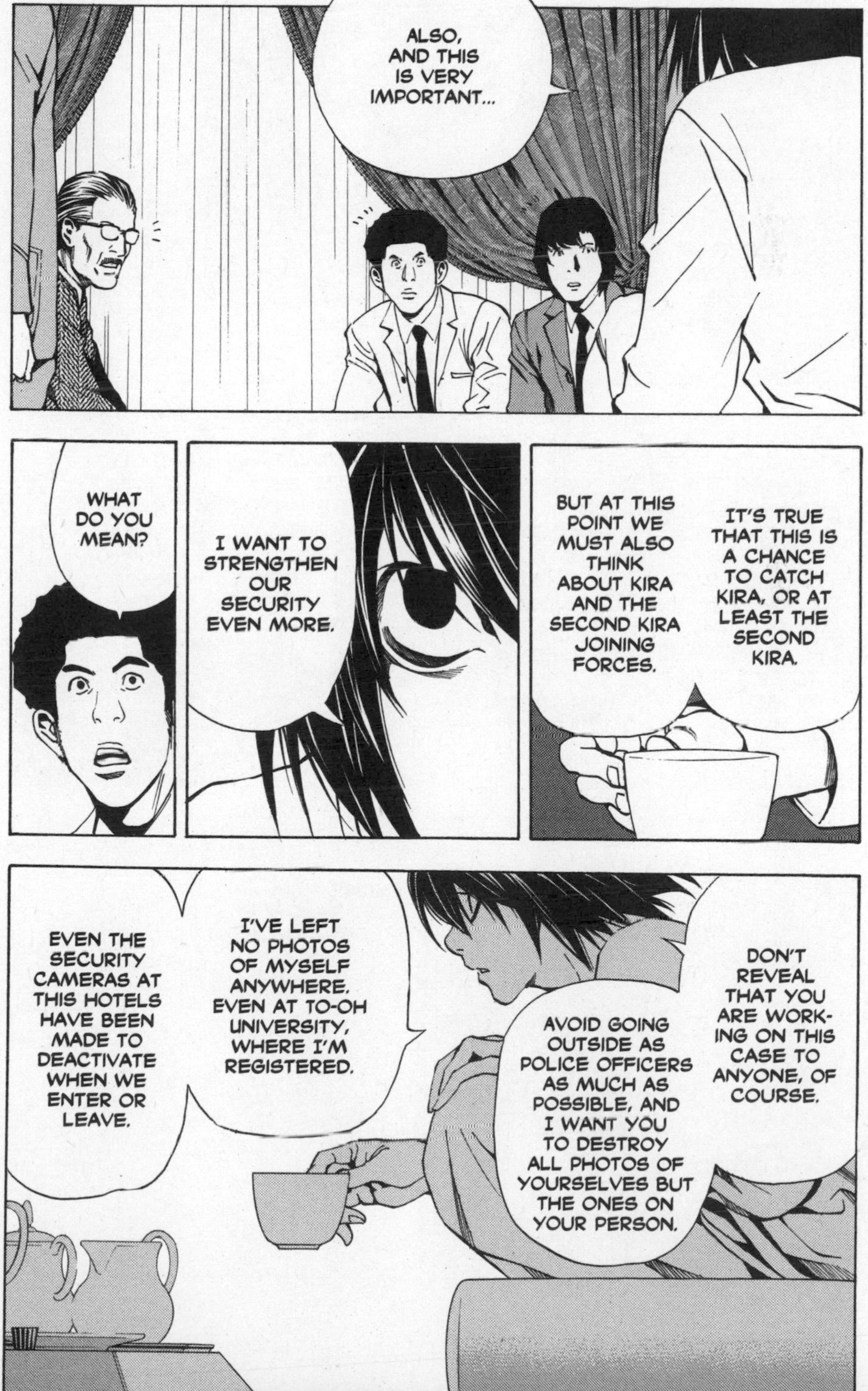
ALSO, AND THIS IS VERY IMPORTANT...
IT'S TRUE THAT THIS IS A CHANCE TO CATCH KIRA, OR AT LEAST THE SECOND KIRA.
BUT AT THIS POINT WE MUST ALSO THINK ABOUT KIRA AND THE SECOND KIRA JOINING FORCES.
I WANT TO STRENGTHEN OUR SECURITY EVEN MORE.
WHAT DO YOU MEAN?
DON'T REVEAL THAT YOU ARE WORKING ON THIS CASE TO ANYONE, OF COURSE.
AVOID GOING OUTSIDE AS POLICE OFFICERS AS MUCH AS POSSIBLE, AND I WANT YOU TO DESTROY ALL PHOTOS OF YOURSELVES BUT THE ONES ON YOUR PERSON.
I'VE LEFT NO PHOTOS OF MYSELF ANYWHERE. EVEN AT TO-OH UNIVERSITY, WHERE I'M REGISTERED.
EVEN THE SECURITY CAMERAS AT THIS HOTELS HAVE BEEN MADE TO DEACTIVATE WHEN WE ENTER OR LEAVE.

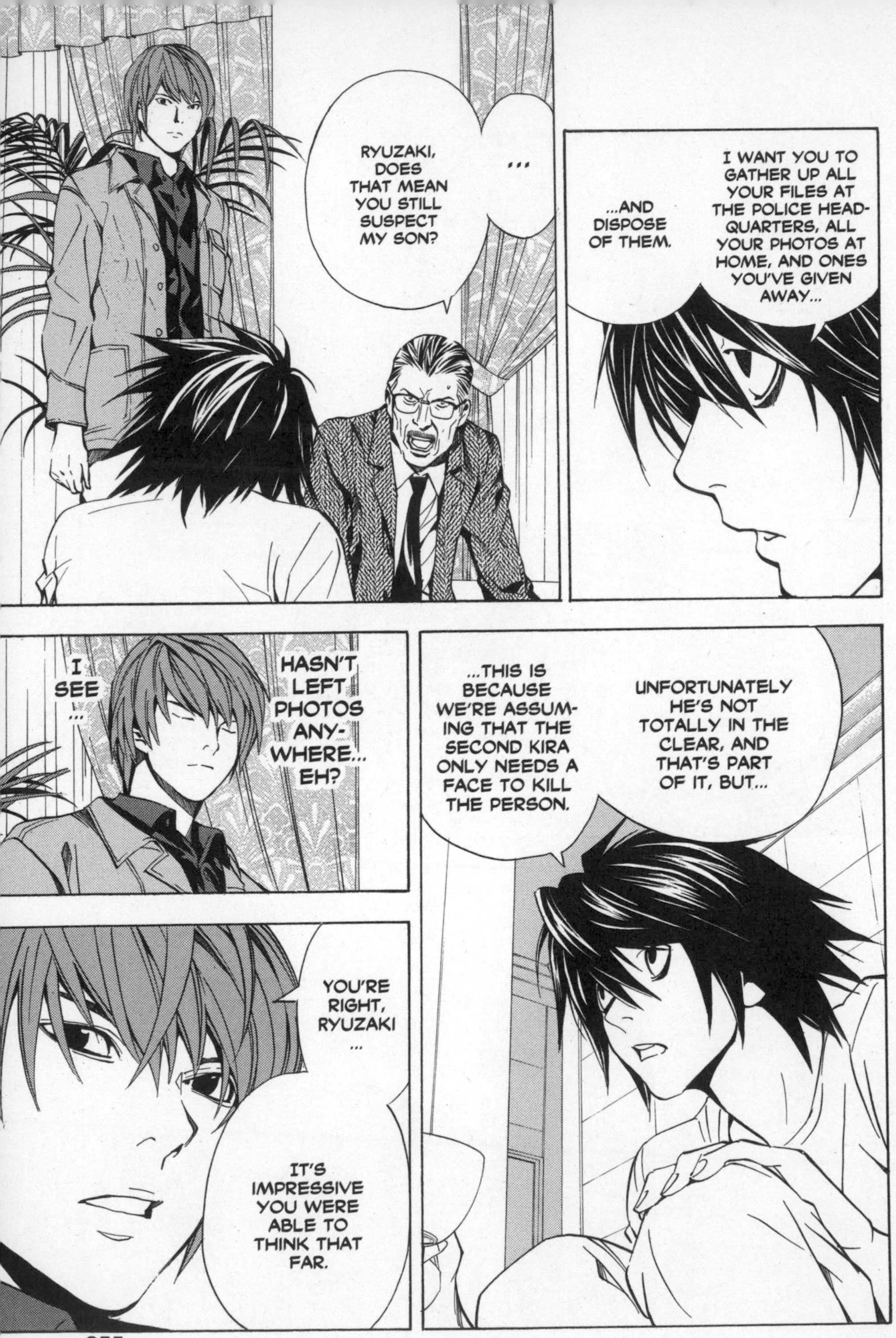
I WANT YOU TO GATHER UP ALL YOUR FILES AT THE POLICE HEAD-QUARTERS, ALL YOUR PHOTOS AT HOME, AND ONES YOU'VE GIVEN AWAY...
...AND DISPOSE OF THEM.
RYUZAKI, DOES THAT MEAN YOU STILL SUSPECT MY SON?
...
UNFORTUNATELY HE'S NOT TOTALLY IN THE CLEAR, AND THAT'S PART OF IT, BUT...
...THIS IS BECAUSE WE'RE ASSUM-ING THAT THE SECOND KIRA ONLY NEEDS A FACE TO KILL THE PERSON.
HASN'T LEFT PHOTOS ANY-WHERE... EH?
I SEE ...
YOU'RE RIGHT, RYUZAKI ...
IT'S IMPRESSIVE YOU WERE ABLE TO THINK THAT FAR.

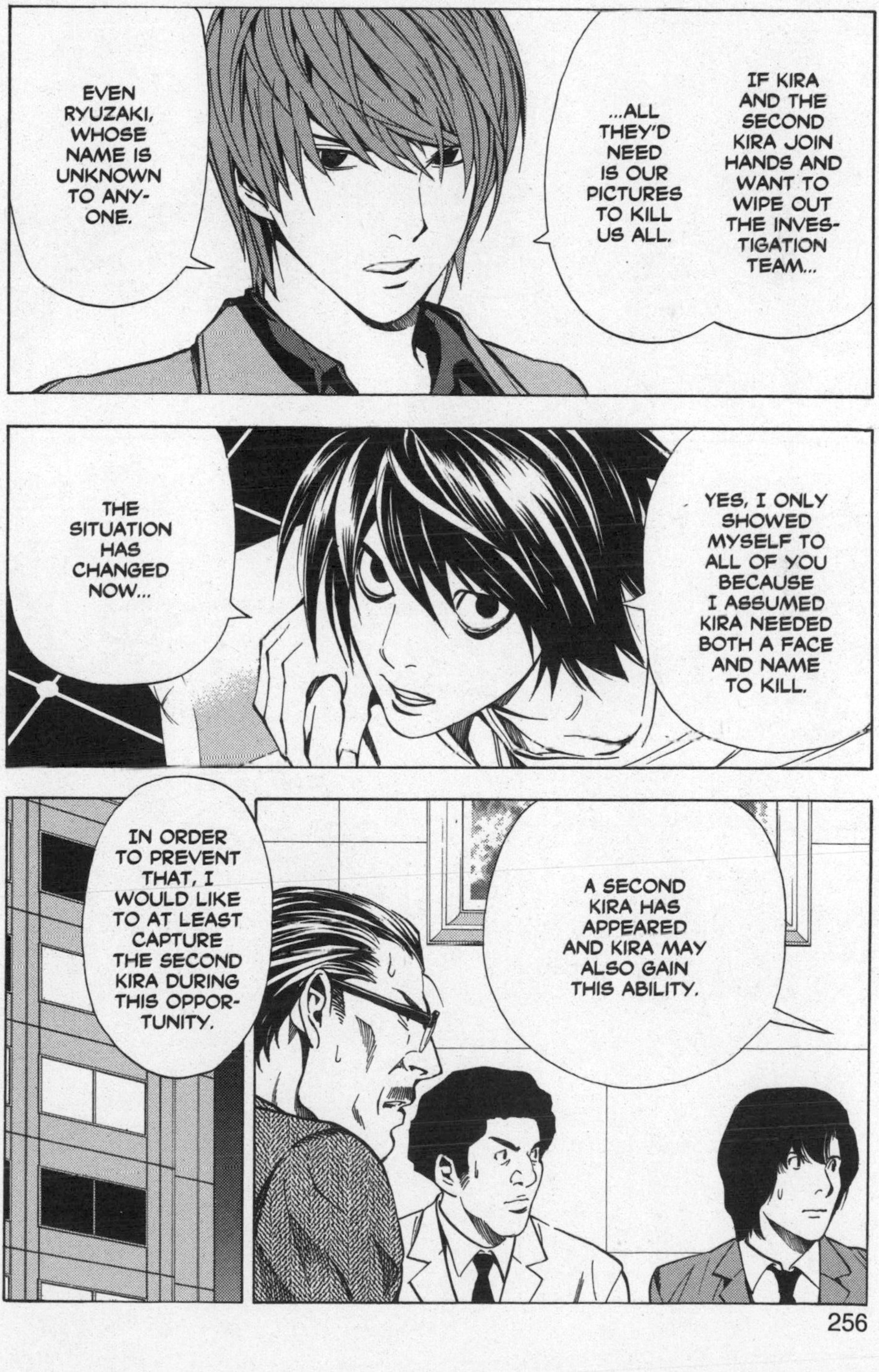
IF KIRA AND THE SECOND KIRA JOIN HANDS AND WANT TO WIPE OUT THE INVESTIGATION TEAM...
...ALL THEY'D NEED IS OUR PICTURES TO KILL US ALL.
EVEN RYUZAKI, WHOSE NAME IS UNKNOWN TO ANYONE.
YES, I ONLY SHOWED MYSELF TO ALL OF YOU BECAUSE I ASSUMED KIRA NEEDED BOTH A FACE AND NAME TO KILL.
THE SITUATION HAS CHANGED NOW...
A SECOND KIRA HAS APPEARED AND KIRA MAY ALSO GAIN THIS ABILITY.
IN ORDER TO PREVENT THAT, I WOULD LIKE TO AT LEAST CAPTURE THE SECOND KIRA DURING THIS OPPORTUNITY.

READ THIS WAY

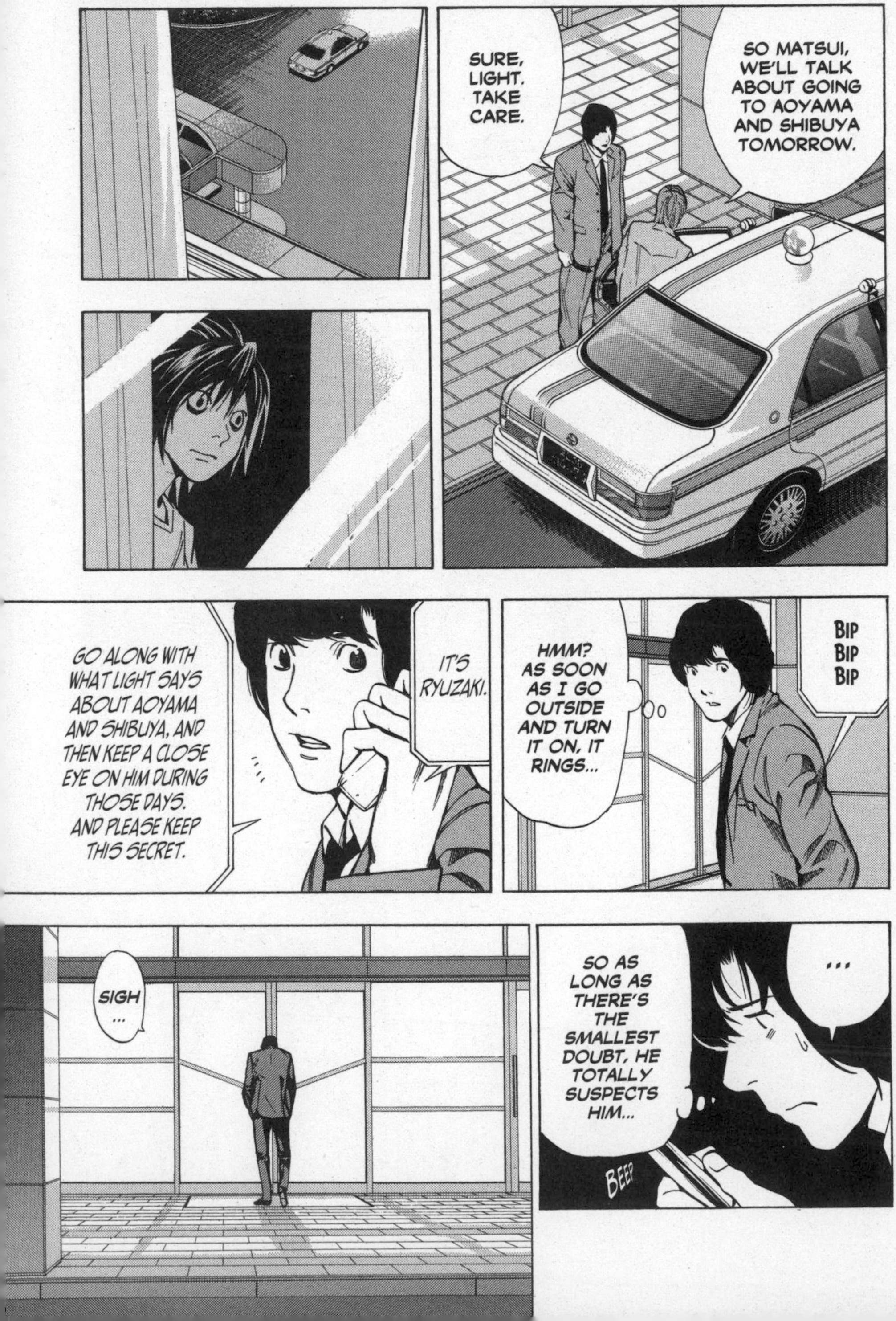
SO MATSUI, WE'LL TALK ABOUT GOING TO AOYAMA AND SHIBUYA TOMORROW.
SURE, LIGHT. TAKE CARE.
BIP BIP BIP
HMM? AS SOON AS I GO OUTSIDE AND TURN IT ON, IT RINGS...
IT'S RYUZAKI.
GO ALONG WITH WHAT LIGHT SAYS ABOUT AOYAMA AND SHIBUYA, AND THEN KEEP A CLOSE EYE ON HIM DURING THOSE DAYS. AND PLEASE KEEP THIS SECRET.
...
SO AS LONG AS THERE'S THE SMALLEST DOUBT, HE TOTALLY SUSPECTS HIM...
BEEP
SIGH ...

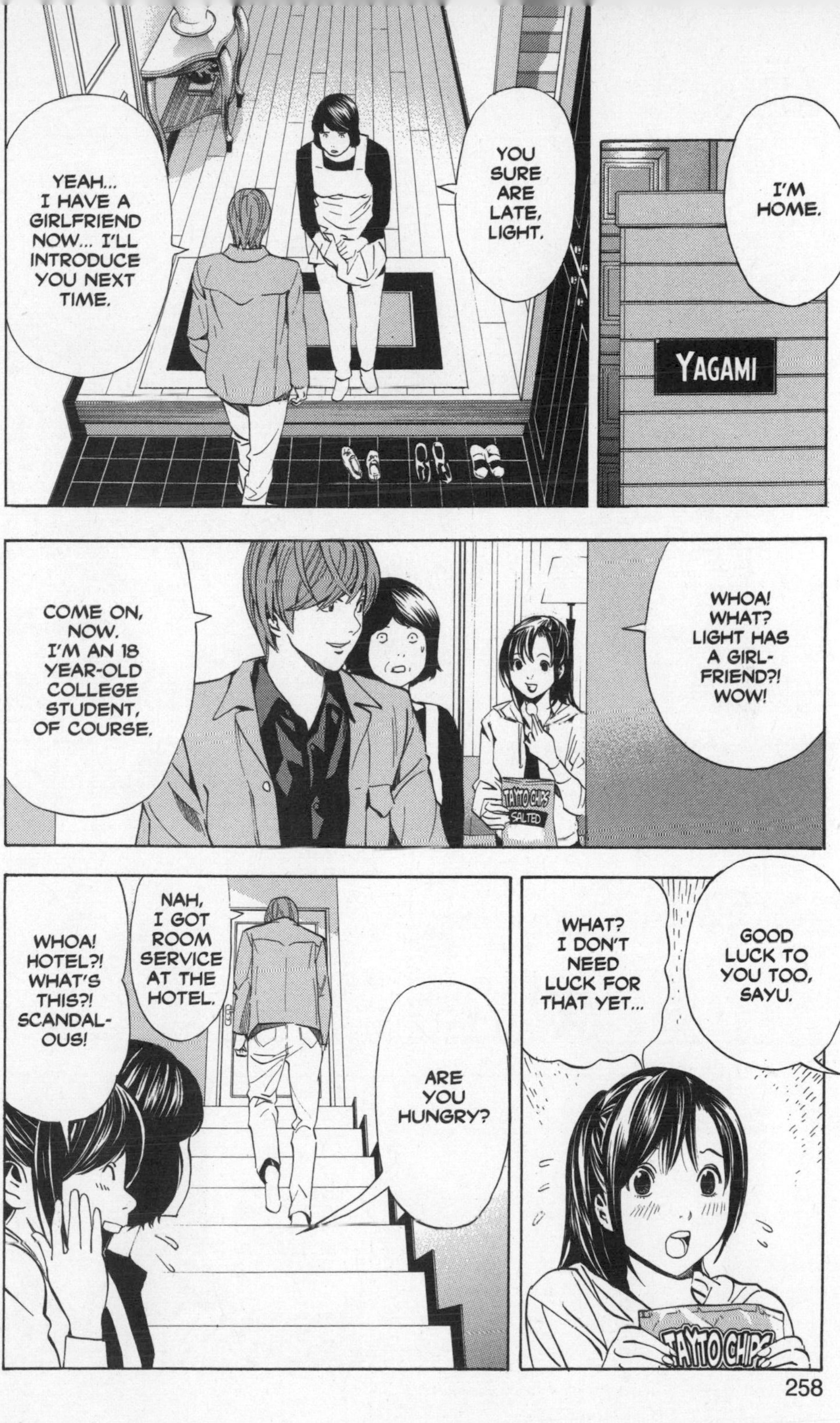
I'M HOME.
YAGAMI
YOU SURE ARE LATE, LIGHT.
YEAH... I HAVE A GIRLFRIEND NOW... I'LL INTRODUCE YOU NEXT TIME.
WHOA! WHAT? LIGHT HAS A GIRL-FRIEND?! WOW!
COME ON, NOW. I'M AN 18 YEAR-OLD COLLEGE STUDENT, OF COURSE.
TAYTO CHIPS
SALTED
GOOD LUCK TO YOU TOO, SAYU.
WHAT? I DON'T NEED LUCK FOR THAT YET...
TAYTO CHIPS
ARE YOU HUNGRY?
NAH, I GOT ROOM SERVICE AT THE HOTEL.
WHOA! HOTEL?! WHAT'S THIS?! SCANDAL-OUS!

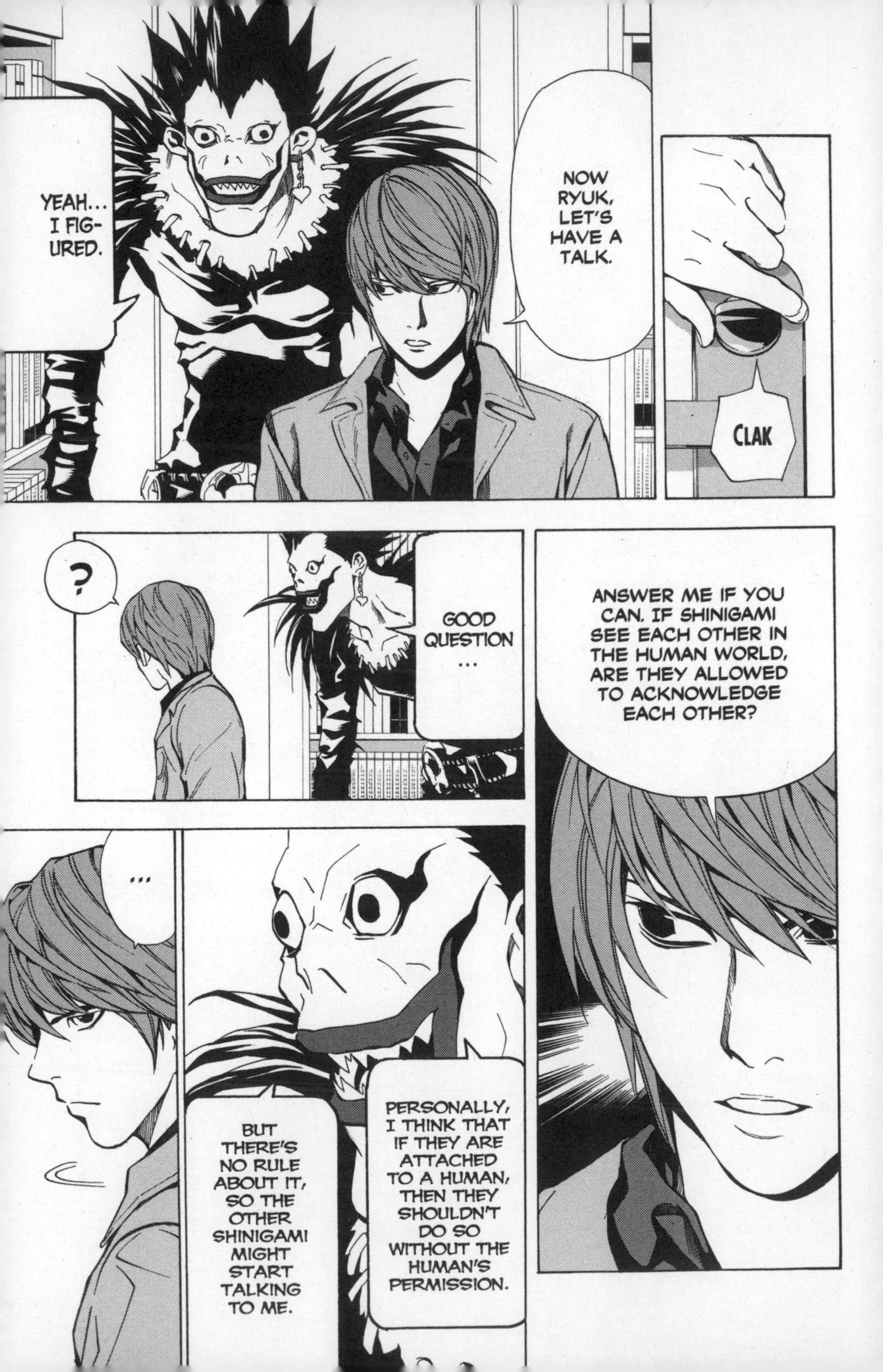
CLAK
NOW RYUK, LET'S HAVE A TALK.
YEAH... I FIGURED.
ANSWER ME IF YOU CAN. IF SHINIGAMI SEE EACH OTHER IN THE HUMAN WORLD, ARE THEY ALLOWED TO ACKNOWLEDGE EACH OTHER?
GOOD QUESTION ...
?
PERSONALLY, I THINK THAT IF THEY ARE ATTACHED TO A HUMAN, THEN THEY SHOULDN'T DO SO WITHOUT THE HUMAN'S PERMISSION.
BUT THERE'S NO RULE ABOUT IT, SO THE OTHER SHINIGAMI MIGHT START TALKING TO ME.
...

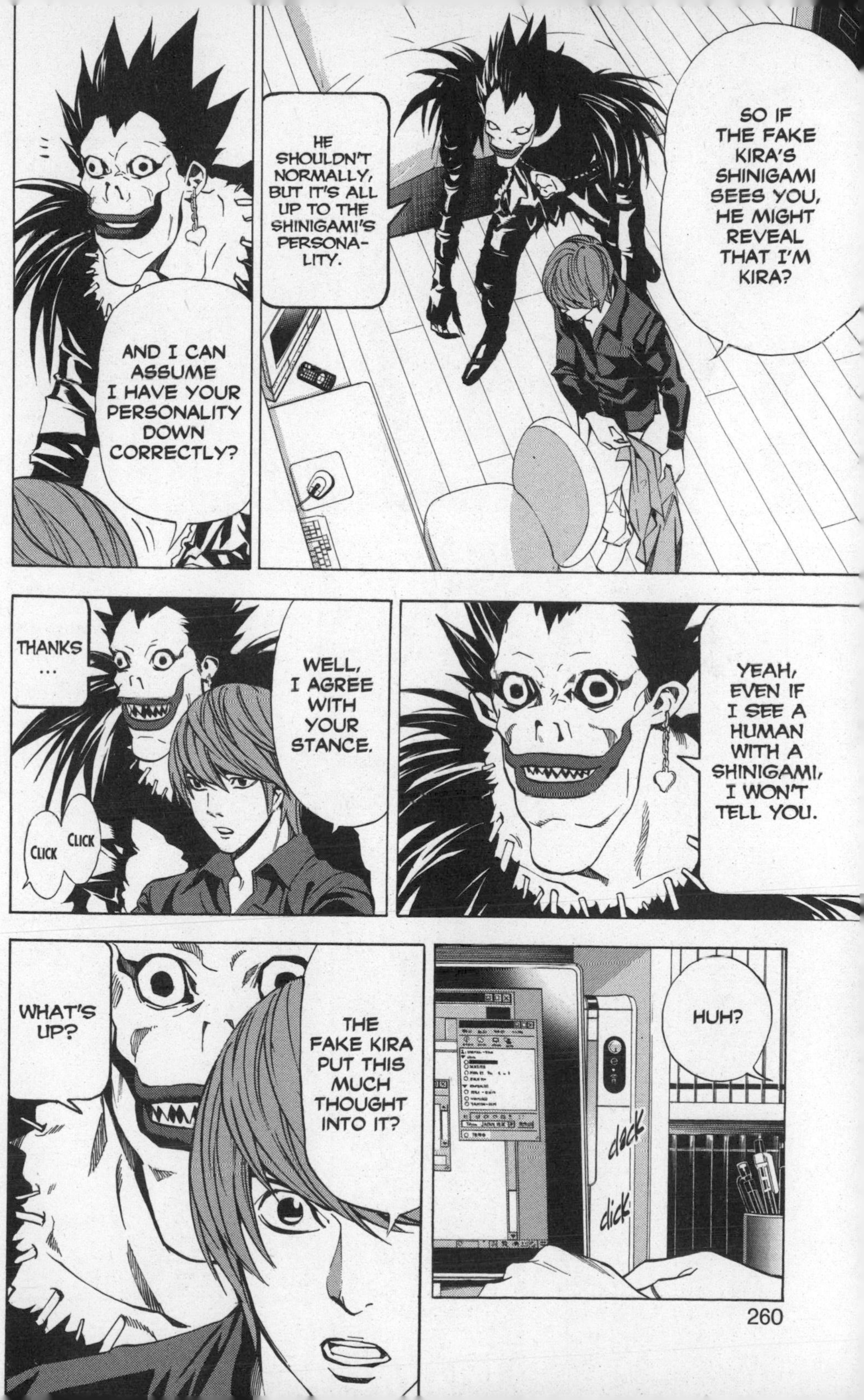
SO IF THE FAKE KIRA'S SHINIGAMI SEES YOU, HE MIGHT REVEAL THAT I'M KIRA?
HE SHOULDN'T NORMALLY, BUT IT'S ALL UP TO THE SHINIGAMI'S PERSONALITY.
AND I CAN ASSUME I HAVE YOUR PERSONALITY DOWN CORRECTLY?
YEAH, EVEN IF I SEE A HUMAN WITH A SHINIGAMI, I WON'T TELL YOU.
WELL, I AGREE WITH YOUR STANCE.
THANKS ...
CLICK
CLICK
HUH?
click
click
THE FAKE KIRA PUT THIS MUCH THOUGHT INTO IT?
WHAT'S UP?

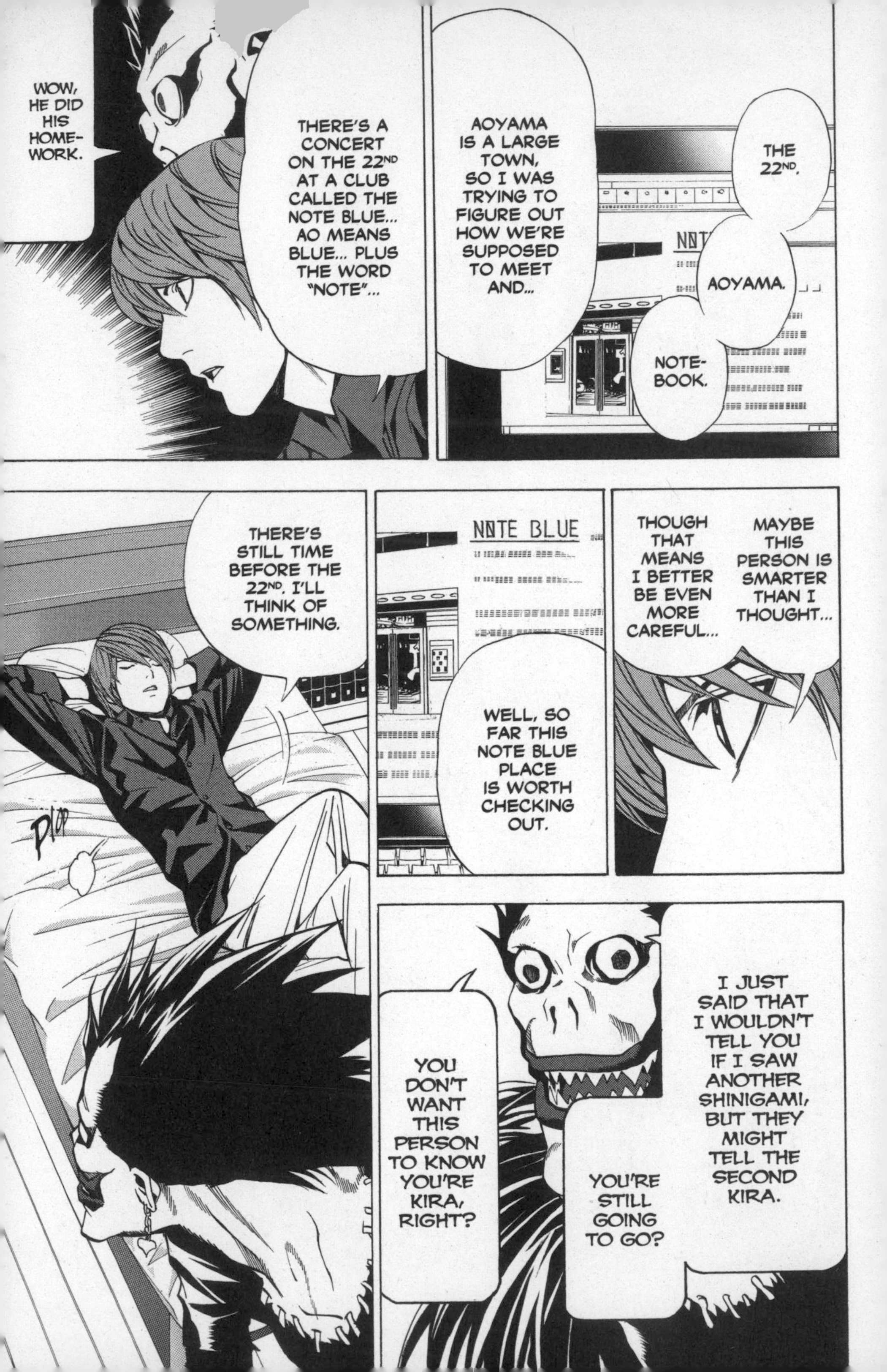
THE 22ND.
AOYAMA.
NOTE-BOOK.
AOYAMA IS A LARGE TOWN, SO I WAS TRYING TO FIGURE OUT HOW WE'RE SUPPOSED TO MEET AND...
THERE'S A CONCERT ON THE 22ND AT A CLUB CALLED THE NOTE BLUE... AO MEANS BLUE... PLUS THE WORD "NOTE"...
WOW, HE DID HIS HOMEWORK.
MAYBE THIS PERSON IS SMARTER THAN I THOUGHT...
THOUGH THAT MEANS I BETTER BE EVEN MORE CAREFUL...
NOTE BLUE
WELL, SO FAR THIS NOTE BLUE PLACE IS WORTH CHECKING OUT.
I JUST SAID THAT I WOULDN'T TELL YOU IF I SAW ANOTHER SHINIGAMI, BUT THEY MIGHT TELL THE SECOND KIRA.
YOU'RE STILL GOING TO GO?
YOU DON'T WANT THIS PERSON TO KNOW YOU'RE KIRA, RIGHT?
THERE'S STILL TIME BEFORE THE 22ND. I'LL THINK OF SOMETHING.
PLOP

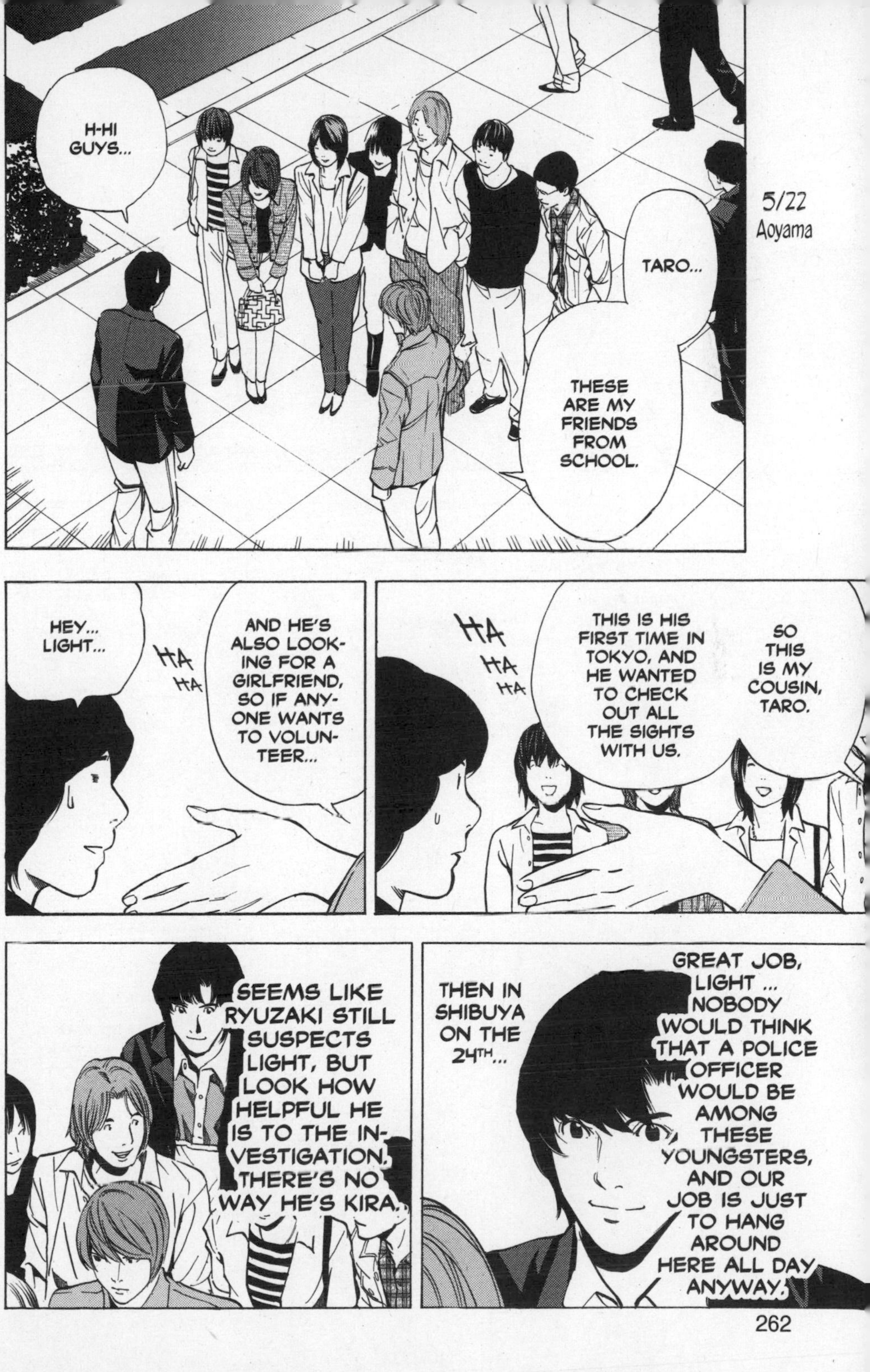
5/22 Aoyama
TARO...
THESE ARE MY FRIENDS FROM SCHOOL.
H-HI GUYS...
SO THIS IS MY COUSIN, TARO.
THIS IS HIS FIRST TIME IN TOKYO, AND HE WANTED TO CHECK OUT ALL THE SIGHTS WITH US.
HA HA HA
AND HE'S ALSO LOOKING FOR A GIRLFRIEND, SO IF ANYONE WANTS TO VOLUNTEER...
HA HA
HEY... LIGHT...
GREAT JOB, LIGHT ... NOBODY WOULD THINK THAT A POLICE OFFICER WOULD BE AMONG THESE YOUNGSTERS, AND OUR JOB IS JUST TO HANG AROUND HERE ALL DAY ANYWAY.
THEN IN SHIBUYA ON THE 24TH...
SEEMS LIKE RYUZAKI STILL SUSPECTS LIGHT, BUT LOOK HOW HELPFUL HE IS TO THE INVESTIGATION, THERE'S NO WAY HE'S KIRA.

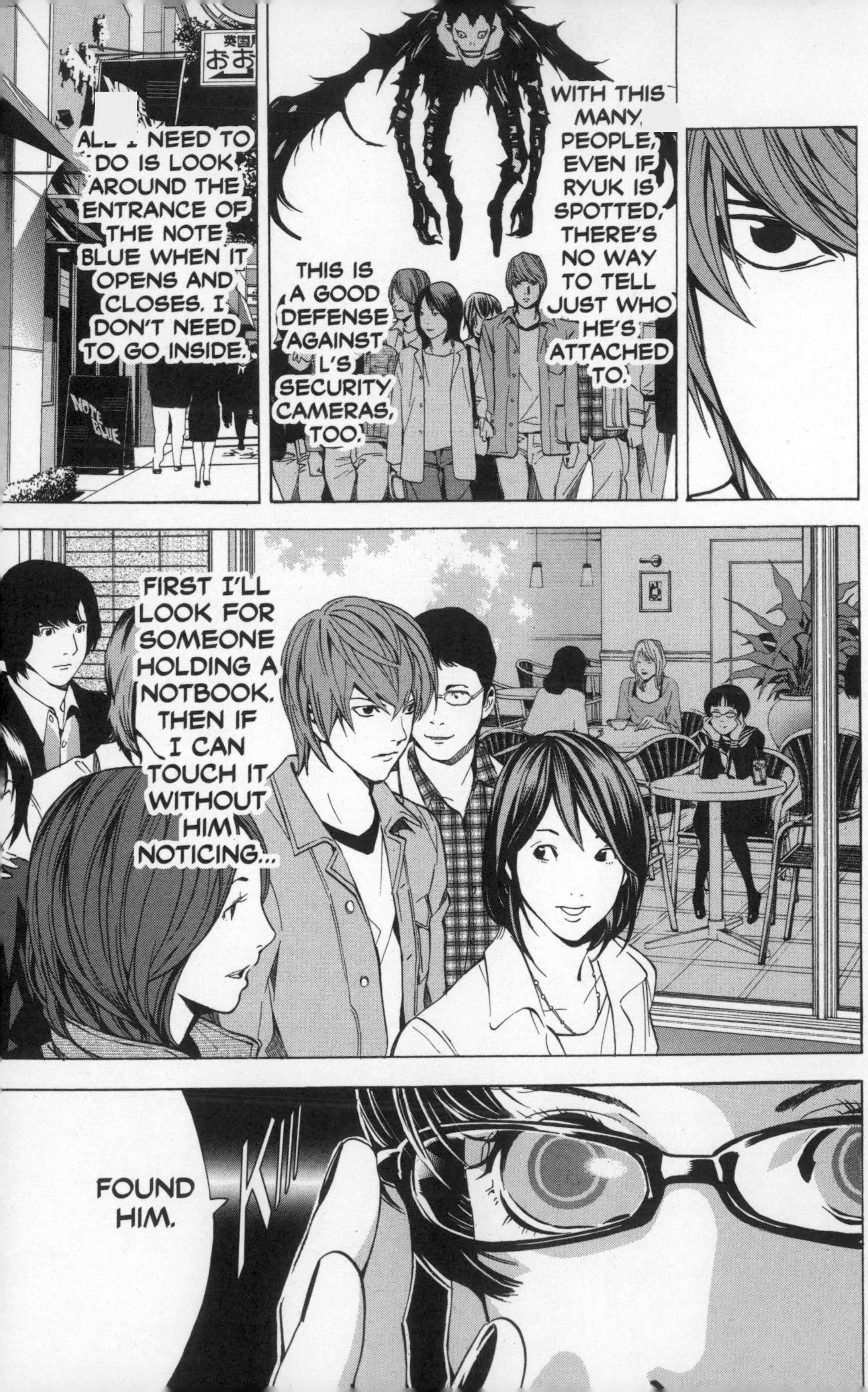
WITH THIS MANY PEOPLE, EVEN IF RYUK IS SPOTTED, THERE'S NO WAY TO TELL JUST WHO HE'S ATTACHED TO.
THIS IS A GOOD DEFENSE AGAINST L'S SECURITY CAMERAS, TOO.
ALL I NEED TO DO IS LOOK AROUND THE ENTRANCE OF THE NOTE BLUE WHEN IT OPENS AND CLOSES. I DON'T NEED TO GO INSIDE.
FIRST I'LL LOOK FOR SOMEONE HOLDING A NOTBOOK. THEN IF I CAN TOUCH IT WITHOUT HIM NOTICING...
FOUND HIM.

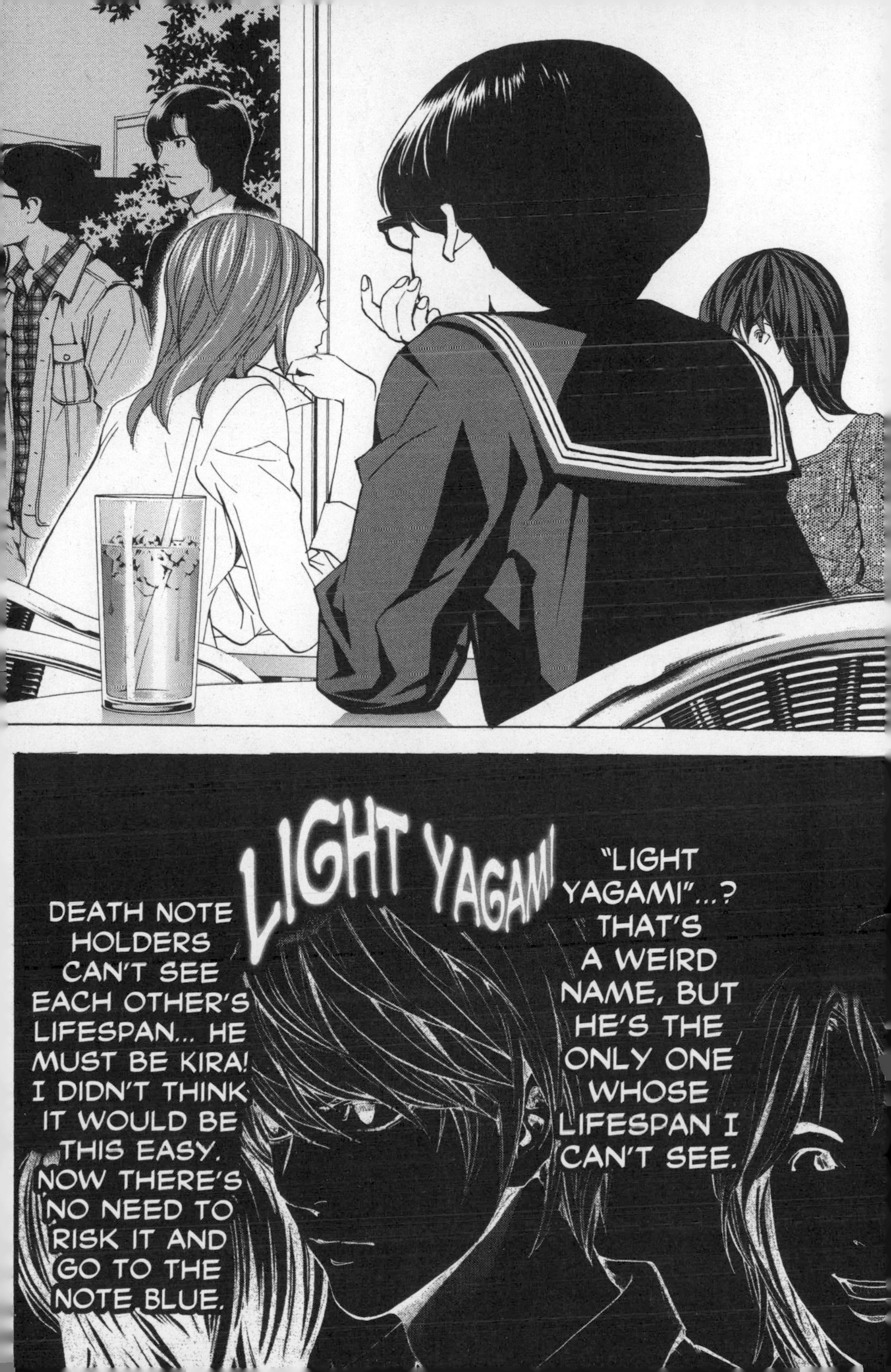
LIGHT YAGAMI
"LIGHT YAGAMI"...? THAT'S A WEIRD NAME, BUT HE'S THE ONLY ONE WHOSE LIFESPAN I CAN'T SEE.
DEATH NOTE HOLDERS CAN'T SEE EACH OTHER'S LIFESPAN... HE MUST BE KIRA! I DIDN'T THINK IT WOULD BE THIS EASY. NOW THERE'S NO NEED TO RISK IT AND GO TO THE NOTE BLUE.

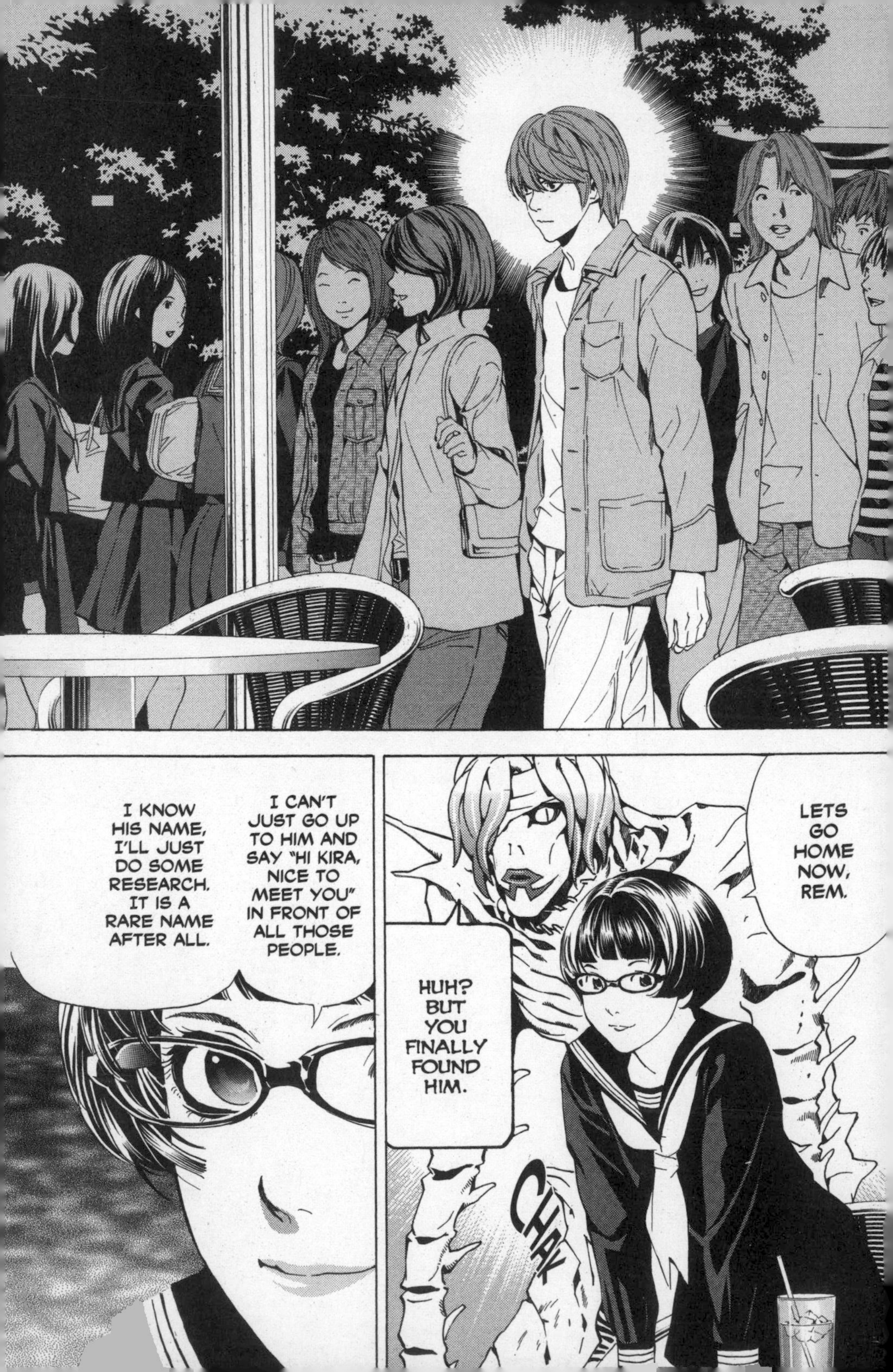
LETS GO HOME NOW, REM.
HUH? BUT YOU FINALLY FOUND HIM.
CHAK
I CAN'T JUST GO UP TO HIM AND SAY "HI KIRA, NICE TO MEET YOU" IN FRONT OF ALL THOSE PEOPLE.
I KNOW HIS NAME, I'LL JUST DO SOME RESEARCH. IT IS A RARE NAME AFTER ALL.

DEATH NOTE
How to use it

XVIII

○ Only by touching each other's DEATH NOTE can human individuals who own the DEATH NOTE in the human world recognize the appearance or voice of each other's god of death.

人間界でデスノートを持った人間同士でも、相手のデスノートに触らなければ、相手に憑いている死神の姿や声は認知できない。

○ An individual with the eye power of a god of death can tell the name and life span of other humans by looking at that person's face.

By possessing the DEATH NOTE, an individual gains the ability to kill and stops being a victim. From this point, a person with the DEATH NOTE cannot see the life span of other DEATH NOTE owners, including him/herself. But, it is not really necessary for the individual to view the life span of him/herself nor other DEATH NOTE owners.

死神の目を持った人間は顔を見た人間の名前と寿命を見る事ができるが、デスノートを持つ事によって、命を取られる側から取る側になる為、殺す人間の寿命だけが見えていればいいという考え方から、自分を含め、他のデスノートを持った人間の寿命の方は見る事ができない。

○ The god of death must not tell humans the names or life spans of individuals he sees. This is to avoid confusion in the human world.

死神は人間に死神の目で見える名前や寿命を教えてはならない。
これは人間界の混乱を避ける配慮である。

chapter 29 Weapon

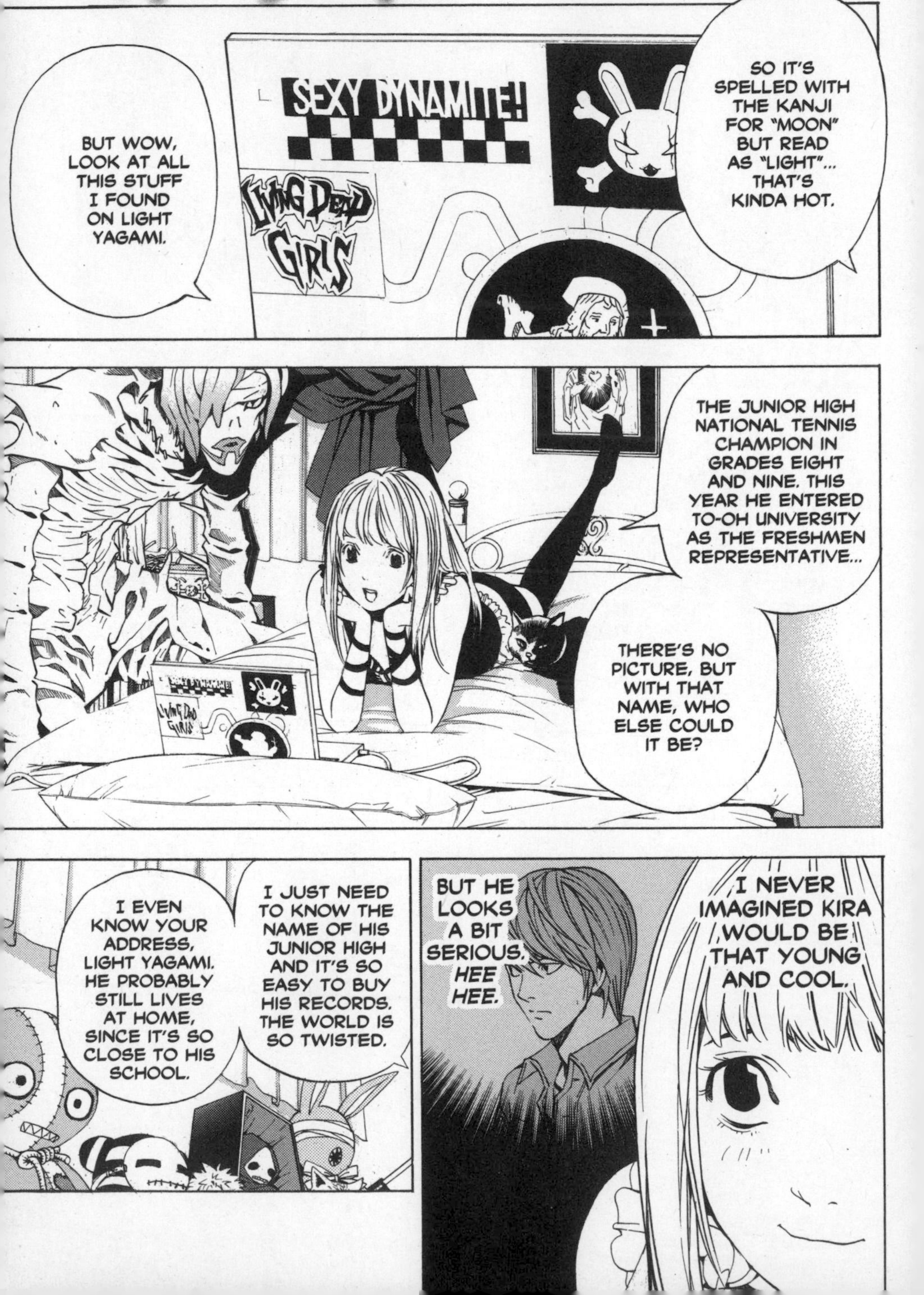

SO IT'S SPELLED WITH THE KANJI FOR "MOON" BUT READ AS "LIGHT"... THAT'S KINDA HOT.
SEXY DYNAMITE!!
LIVING DEAD GIRLS
BUT WOW, LOOK AT ALL THIS STUFF I FOUND ON LIGHT YAGAMI.
THE JUNIOR HIGH NATIONAL TENNIS CHAMPION IN GRADES EIGHT AND NINE. THIS YEAR HE ENTERED TO-OH UNIVERSITY AS THE FRESHMEN REPRESENTATIVE...
THERE'S NO PICTURE, BUT WITH THAT NAME, WHO ELSE COULD IT BE?
I NEVER IMAGINED KIRA WOULD BE THAT YOUNG AND COOL.
BUT HE LOOKS A BIT SERIOUS. HEE HEE.
I JUST NEED TO KNOW THE NAME OF HIS JUNIOR HIGH AND IT'S SO EASY TO BUY HIS RECORDS. THE WORLD IS SO TWISTED.
I EVEN KNOW YOUR ADDRESS, LIGHT YAGAMI. HE PROBABLY STILL LIVES AT HOME, SINCE IT'S SO CLOSE TO HIS SCHOOL.

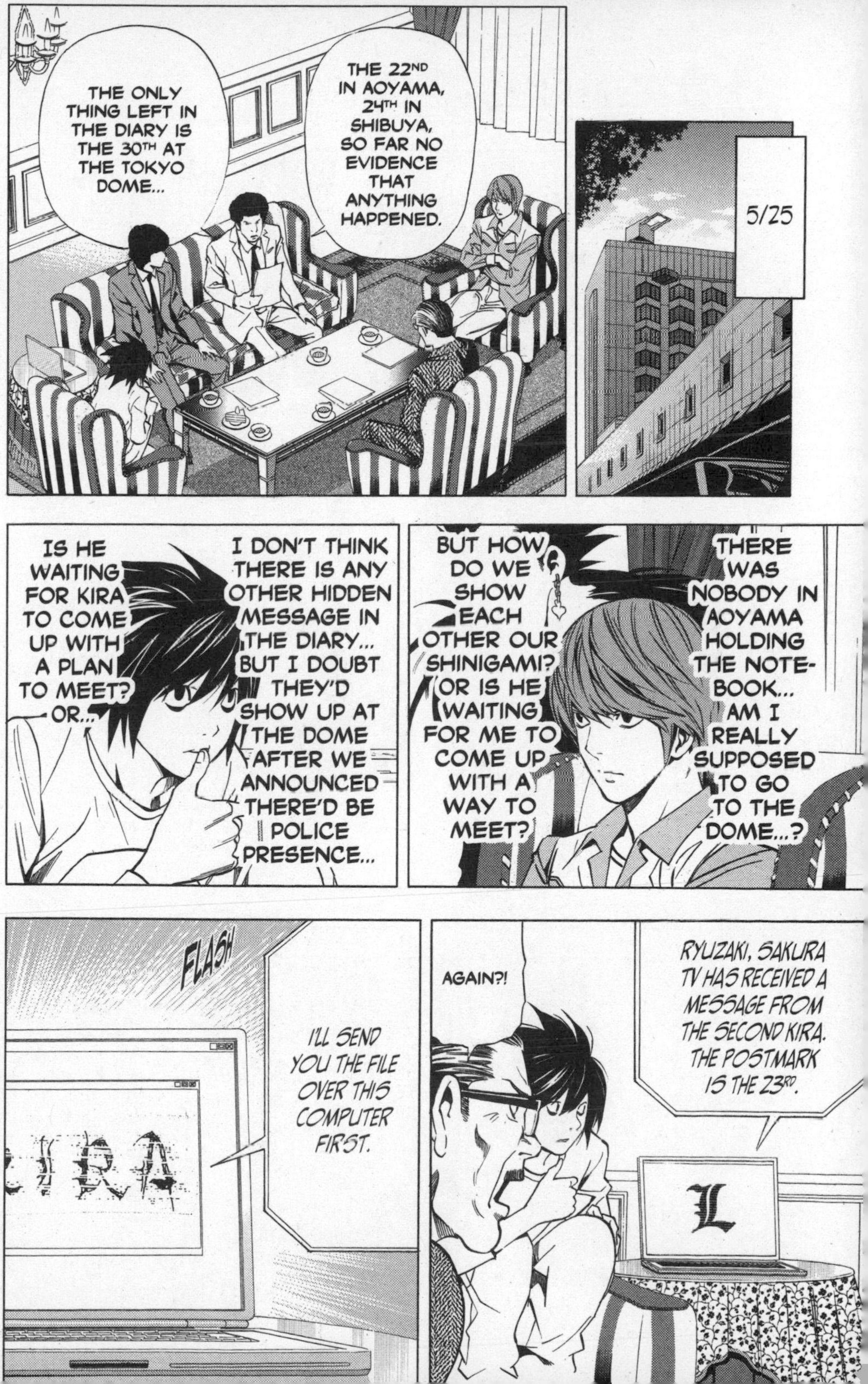
5/25
THE 22ND IN AOYAMA, 24TH IN SHIBUYA, SO FAR NO EVIDENCE THAT ANYTHING HAPPENED.
THE ONLY THING LEFT IN THE DIARY IS THE 30TH AT THE TOKYO DOME...
THERE WAS NOBODY IN AOYAMA HOLDING THE NOTE-BOOK... AM I REALLY SUPPOSED TO GO TO THE DOME...?
BUT HOW DO WE SHOW EACH OTHER OUR SHINIGAMI? OR IS HE WAITING FOR ME TO COME UP WITH A WAY TO MEET?
I DON'T THINK THERE IS ANY OTHER HIDDEN MESSAGE IN THE DIARY... BUT I DOUBT THEY'D SHOW UP AT THE DOME AFTER WE ANNOUNCED THERE'D BE POLICE PRESENCE...
IS HE WAITING FOR KIRA TO COME UP WITH A PLAN TO MEET? OR...
RYUZAKI, SAKURA TV HAS RECEIVED A MESSAGE FROM THE SECOND KIRA. THE POSTMARK IS THE 23RD.
AGAIN?!
FLASH
I'LL SEND YOU THE FILE OVER THIS COMPUTER FIRST.

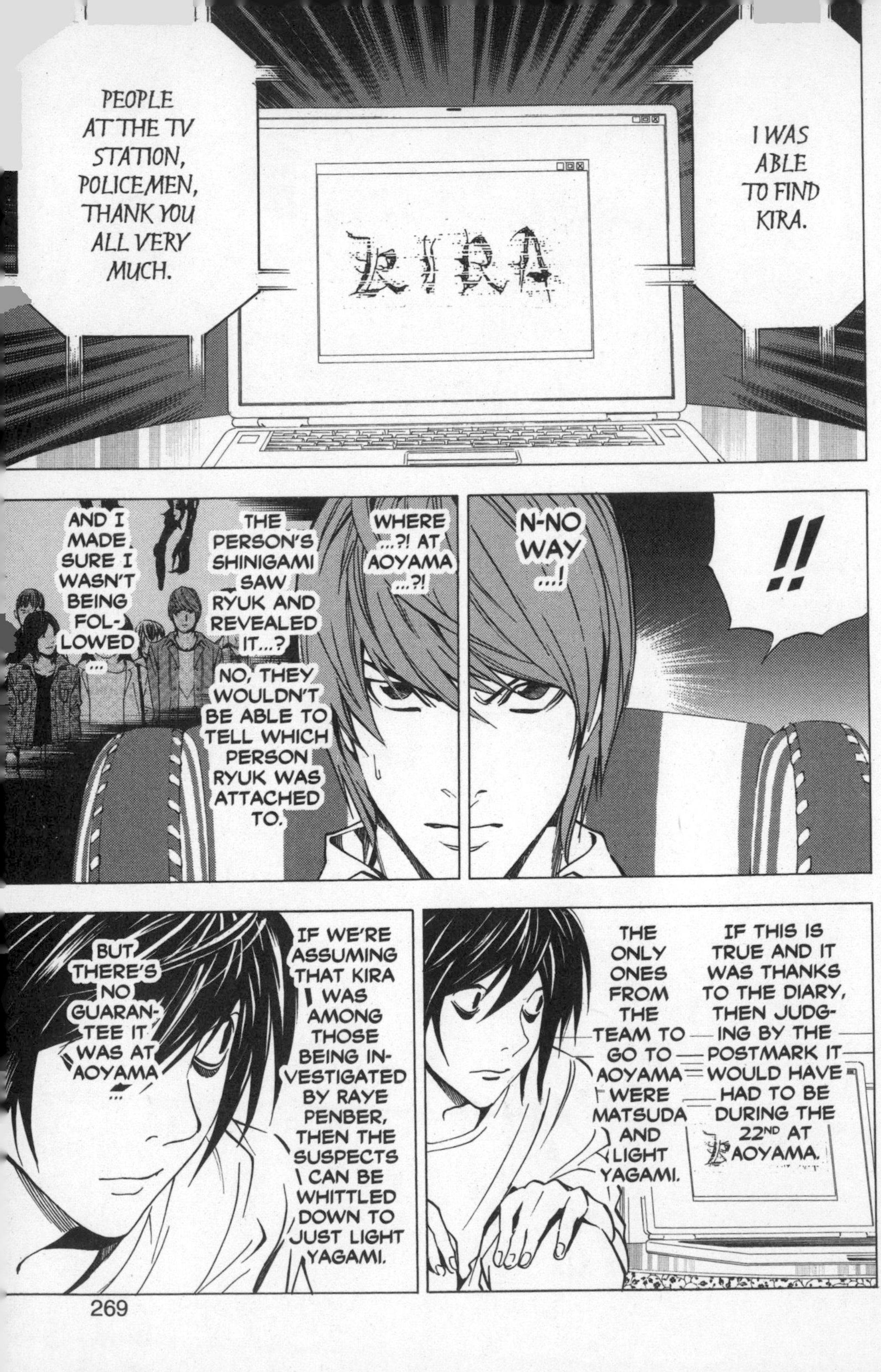
I WAS ABLE TO FIND KIRA.
PEOPLE AT THE TV STATION, POLICEMEN, THANK YOU ALL VERY MUCH.
KIRA
!!
N-NO WAY...!
WHERE...?! AT AOYAMA...?!
THE PERSON'S SHINIGAMI SAW RYUK AND REVEALED IT...?
NO, THEY WOULDN'T BE ABLE TO TELL WHICH PERSON RYUK WAS ATTACHED TO.
AND I MADE SURE I WASN'T BEING FOL-LOWED...
IF THIS IS TRUE AND IT WAS THANKS TO THE DIARY, THEN JUDG-ING BY THE POSTMARK IT WOULD HAVE HAD TO BE DURING THE 22ND AT AOYAMA.
THE ONLY ONES FROM THE TEAM TO GO TO AOYAMA WERE MATSUDA AND LIGHT YAGAMI.
IF WE'RE ASSUMING THAT KIRA WAS AMONG THOSE BEING IN-VESTIGATED BY RAYE PENBER, THEN THE SUSPECTS CAN BE WHITTLED DOWN TO JUST LIGHT YAGAMI.
BUT THERE'S NO GUARAN-TEE IT WAS AT AOYAMA...

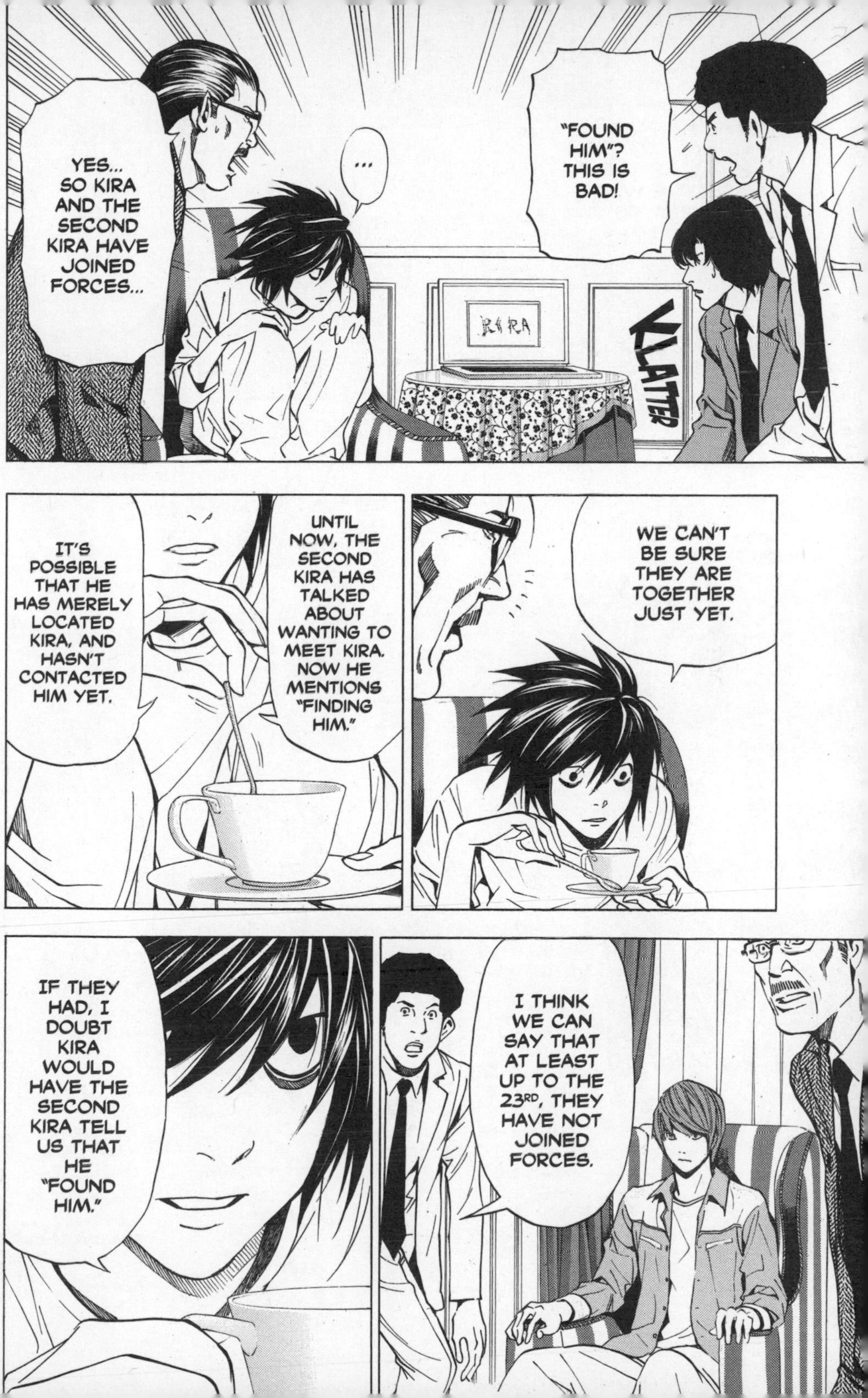
"FOUND HIM"? THIS IS BAD!
KLATTER
...
YES... SO KIRA AND THE SECOND KIRA HAVE JOINED FORCES...
WE CAN'T BE SURE THEY ARE TOGETHER JUST YET.
UNTIL NOW, THE SECOND KIRA HAS TALKED ABOUT WANTING TO MEET KIRA. NOW HE MENTIONS "FINDING HIM."
IT'S POSSIBLE THAT HE HAS MERELY LOCATED KIRA, AND HASN'T CONTACTED HIM YET.
I THINK WE CAN SAY THAT AT LEAST UP TO THE 23RD, THEY HAVE NOT JOINED FORCES.
IF THEY HAD, I DOUBT KIRA WOULD HAVE THE SECOND KIRA TELL US THAT HE "FOUND HIM."

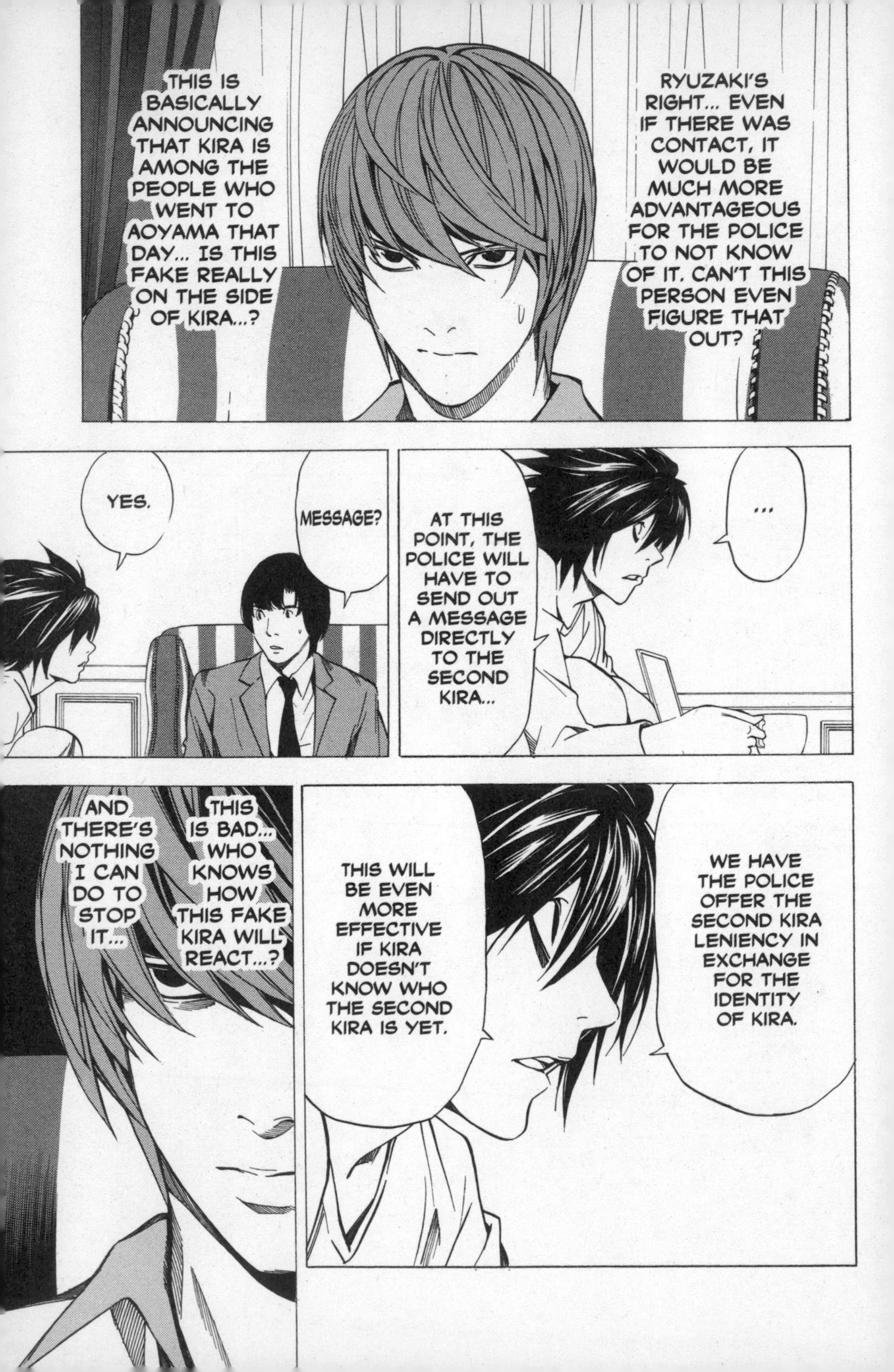
RYUZAKI'S RIGHT... EVEN IF THERE WAS CONTACT, IT WOULD BE MUCH MORE ADVANTAGEOUS FOR THE POLICE TO NOT KNOW OF IT. CAN'T THIS PERSON EVEN FIGURE THAT OUT?
THIS IS BASICALLY ANNOUNCING THAT KIRA IS AMONG THE PEOPLE WHO WENT TO AOYAMA THAT DAY... IS THIS FAKE REALLY ON THE SIDE OF KIRA...?
...
AT THIS POINT, THE POLICE WILL HAVE TO SEND OUT A MESSAGE DIRECTLY TO THE SECOND KIRA...
MESSAGE?
YES.
WE HAVE THE POLICE OFFER THE SECOND KIRA LENIENCY IN EXCHANGE FOR THE IDENTITY OF KIRA.
THIS WILL BE EVEN MORE EFFECTIVE IF KIRA DOESN'T KNOW WHO THE SECOND KIRA IS YET.
THIS IS BAD... WHO KNOWS HOW THIS FAKE KIRA WILL REACT...?
AND THERE'S NOTHING I CAN DO TO STOP IT...

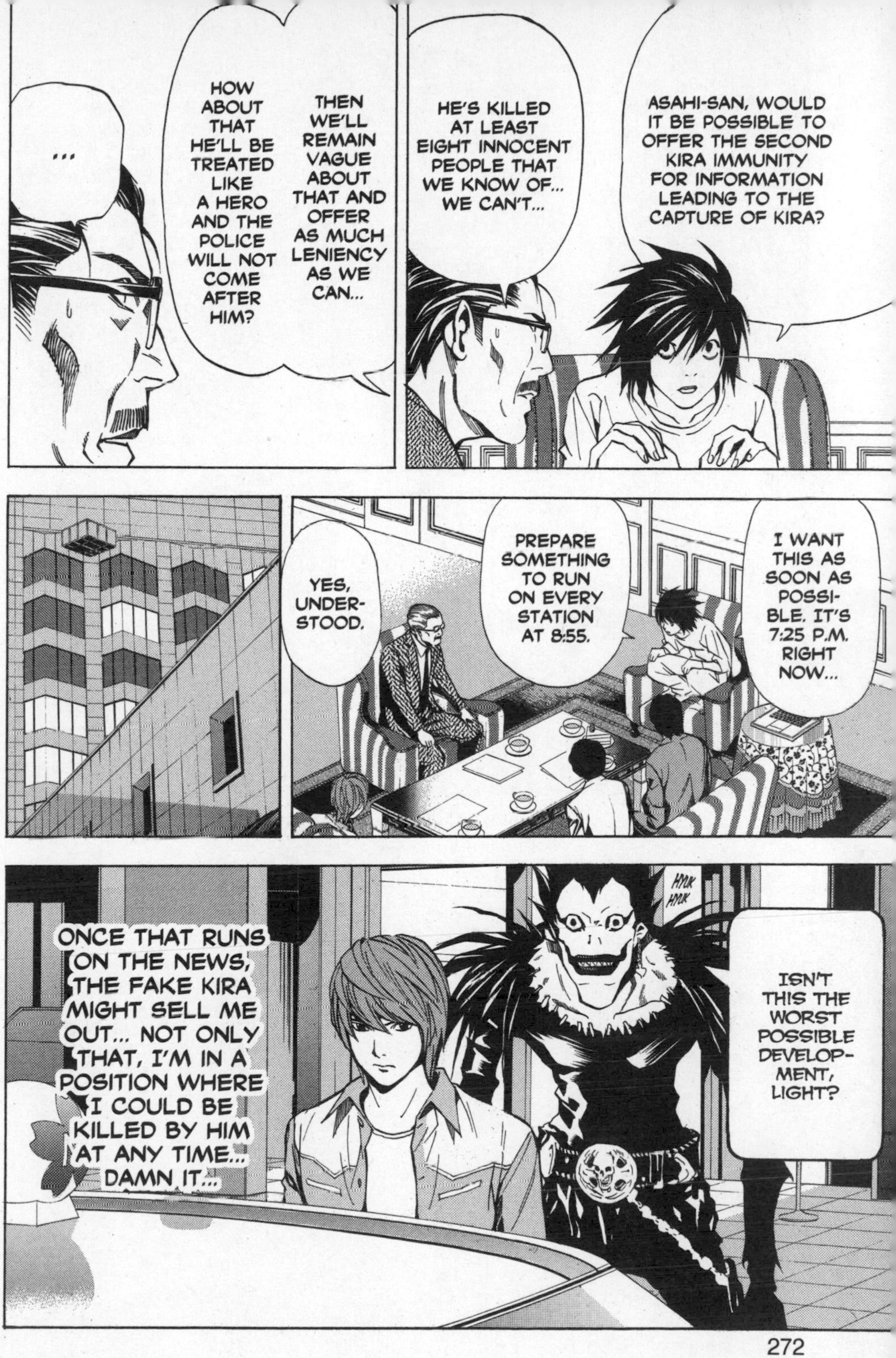
ASAHI-SAN, WOULD IT BE POSSIBLE TO OFFER THE SECOND KIRA IMMUNITY FOR INFORMATION LEADING TO THE CAPTURE OF KIRA?
HE'S KILLED AT LEAST EIGHT INNOCENT PEOPLE THAT WE KNOW OF... WE CAN'T...
THEN WE'LL REMAIN VAGUE ABOUT THAT AND OFFER AS MUCH LENIENCY AS WE CAN...
HOW ABOUT THAT HE'LL BE TREATED LIKE A HERO AND THE POLICE WILL NOT COME AFTER HIM?
...
I WANT THIS AS SOON AS POSSI-BLE. IT'S 7:25 P.M. RIGHT NOW...
PREPARE SOMETHING TO RUN ON EVERY STATION AT 8:55.
YES, UNDER-STOOD.
HYUK HYUK
ISN'T THIS THE WORST POSSIBLE DEVELOP-MENT, LIGHT?
ONCE THAT RUNS ON THE NEWS, THE FAKE KIRA MIGHT SELL ME OUT... NOT ONLY THAT, I'M IN A POSITION WHERE I COULD BE KILLED BY HIM AT ANY TIME... DAMN IT...

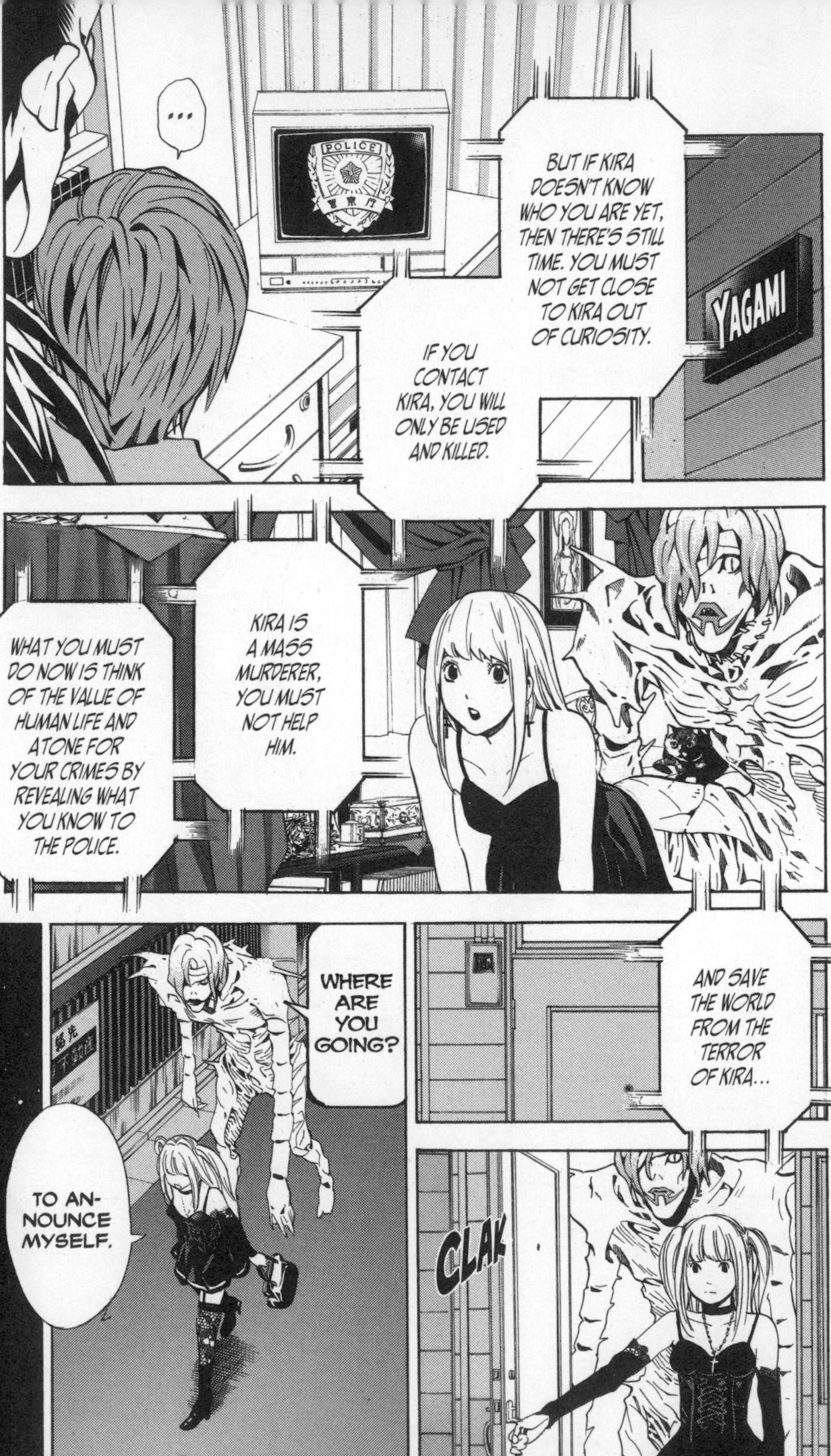
POLICE
YAGAMI
BUT IF KIRA DOESN'T KNOW WHO YOU ARE YET, THEN THERE'S STILL TIME. YOU MUST NOT GET CLOSE TO KIRA OUT OF CURIOSITY.
IF YOU CONTACT KIRA, YOU WILL ONLY BE USED AND KILLED.
...
KIRA IS A MASS MURDERER, YOU MUST NOT HELP HIM.
WHAT YOU MUST DO NOW IS THINK OF THE VALUE OF HUMAN LIFE AND ATONE FOR YOUR CRIMES BY REVEALING WHAT YOU KNOW TO THE POLICE.
AND SAVE THE WORLD FROM THE TERROR OF KIRA...
CLAK
WHERE ARE YOU GOING?
TO AN-NOUNCE MYSELF.
...

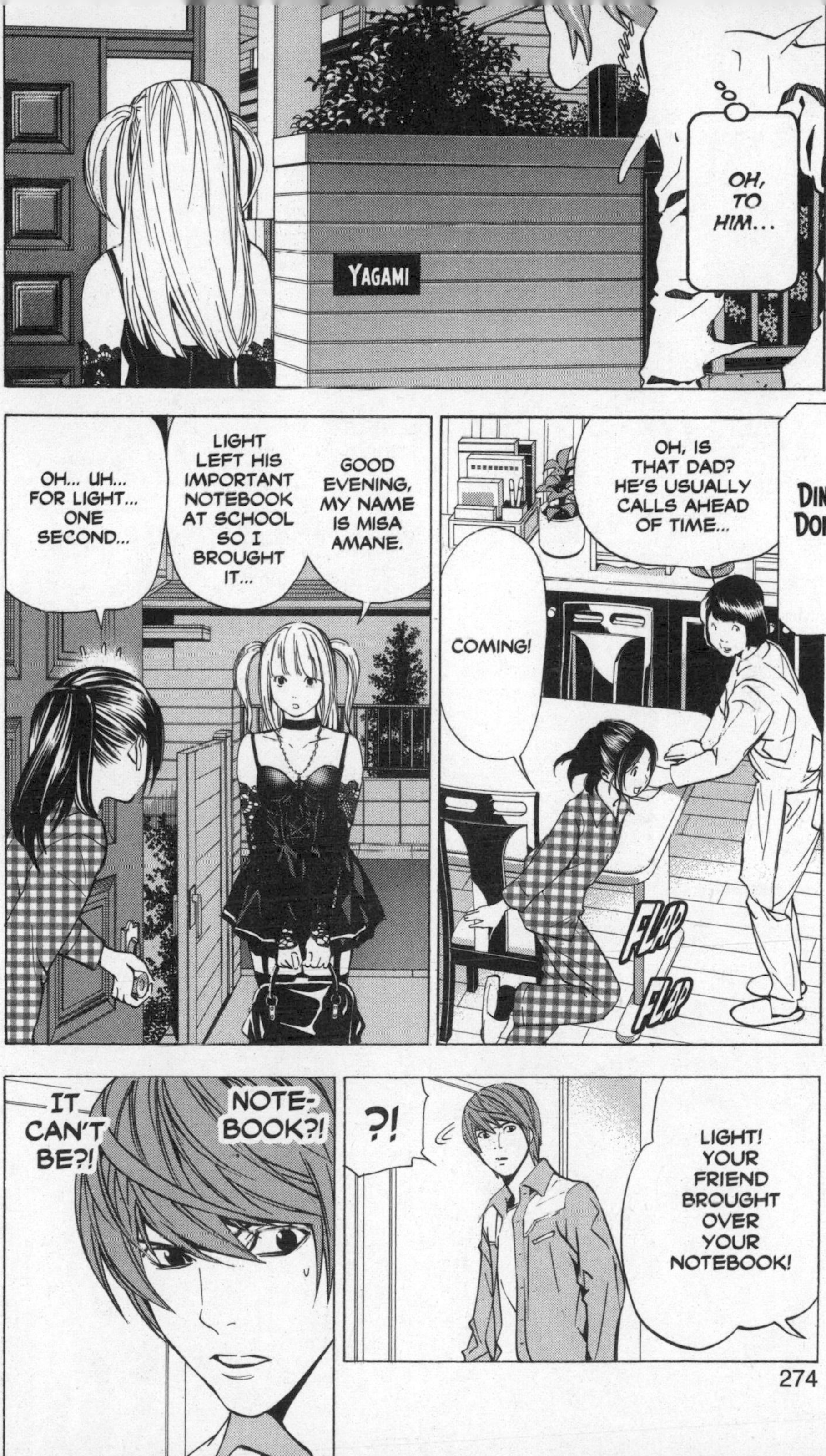

OH, TO HIM...
YAGAMI
DING DONG
OH, IS THAT DAD? HE'S USUALLY CALLS AHEAD OF TIME...
COMING!
FLAP
FLAP
GOOD EVENING, MY NAME IS MISA AMANE.
LIGHT LEFT HIS IMPORTANT NOTEBOOK AT SCHOOL SO I BROUGHT IT...
OH... UH... FOR LIGHT... ONE SECOND...
LIGHT! YOUR FRIEND BROUGHT OVER YOUR NOTEBOOK!
?!
NOTE-BOOK?!
IT CAN'T BE?!

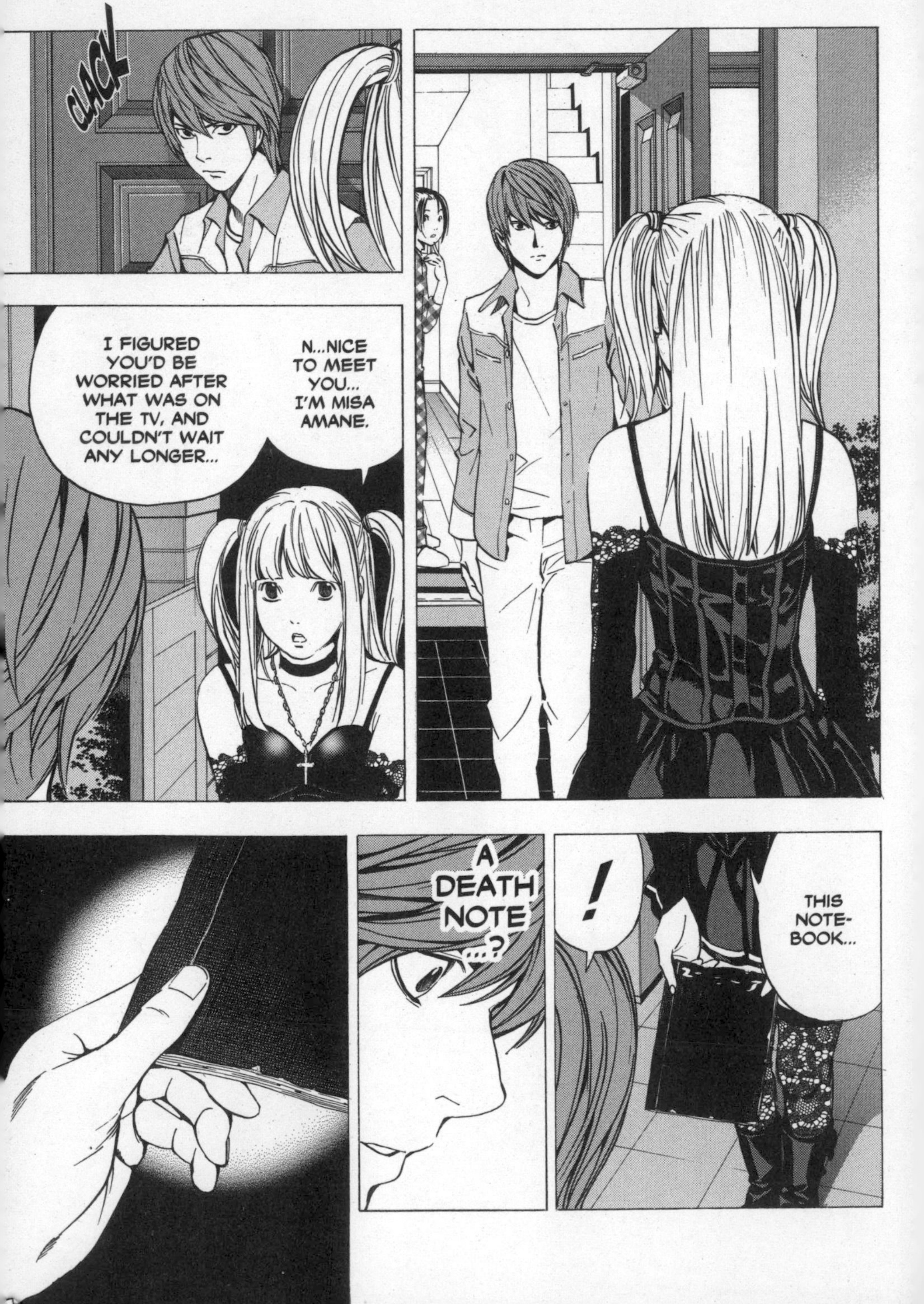
CLACK
N...NICE TO MEET YOU... I'M MISA AMANE.
I FIGURED YOU'D BE WORRIED AFTER WHAT WAS ON THE TV, AND COULDN'T WAIT ANY LONGER...
THIS NOTE-BOOK...
!
A DEATH NOTE ...?

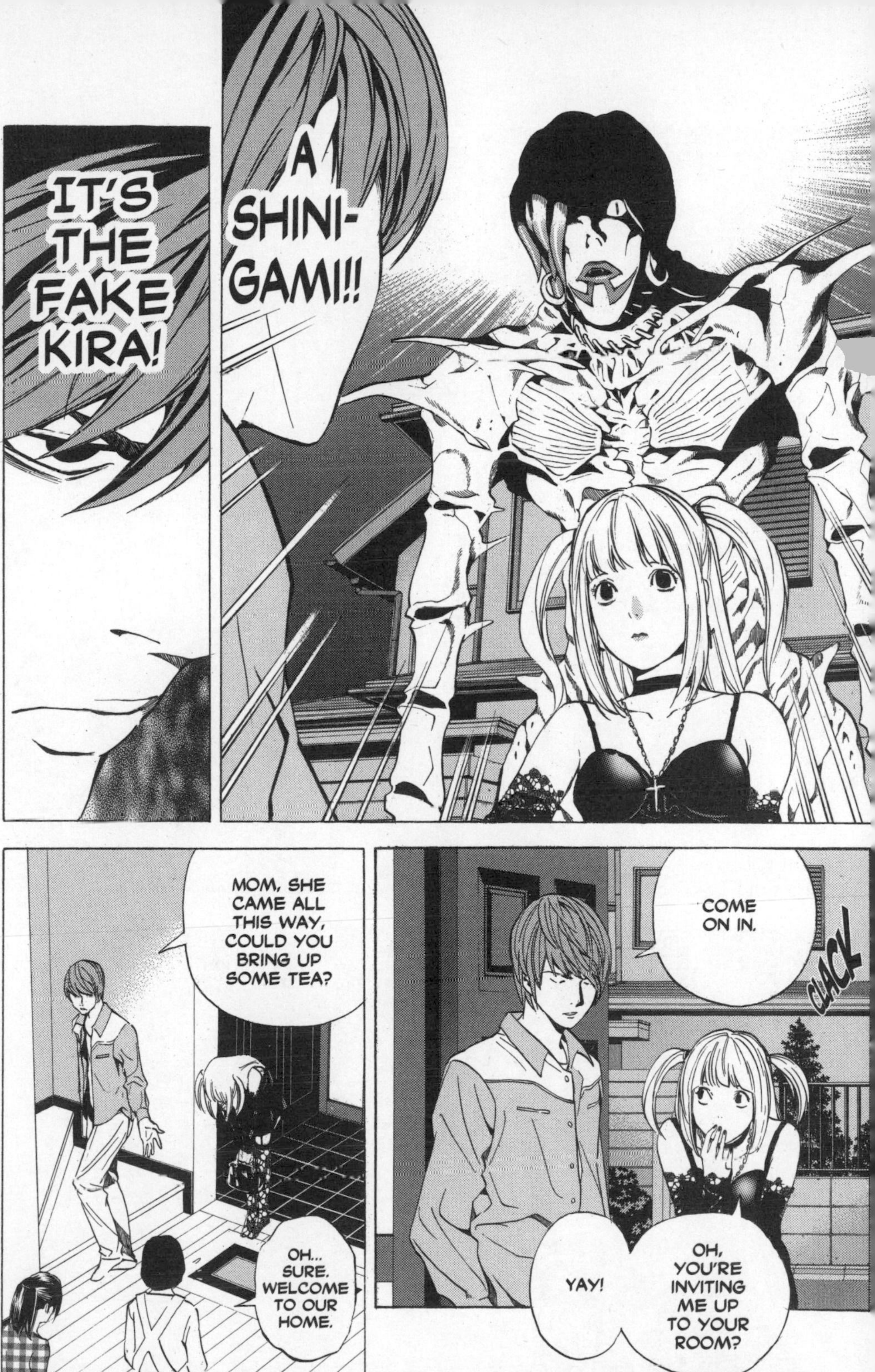
A SHINI-GAMI!!
IT'S THE FAKE KIRA!
COME ON IN.
CLACK
OH, YOU'RE INVITING ME UP TO YOUR ROOM?
YAY!
MOM, SHE CAME ALL THIS WAY, COULD YOU BRING UP SOME TEA?
OH... SURE. WELCOME TO OUR HOME.

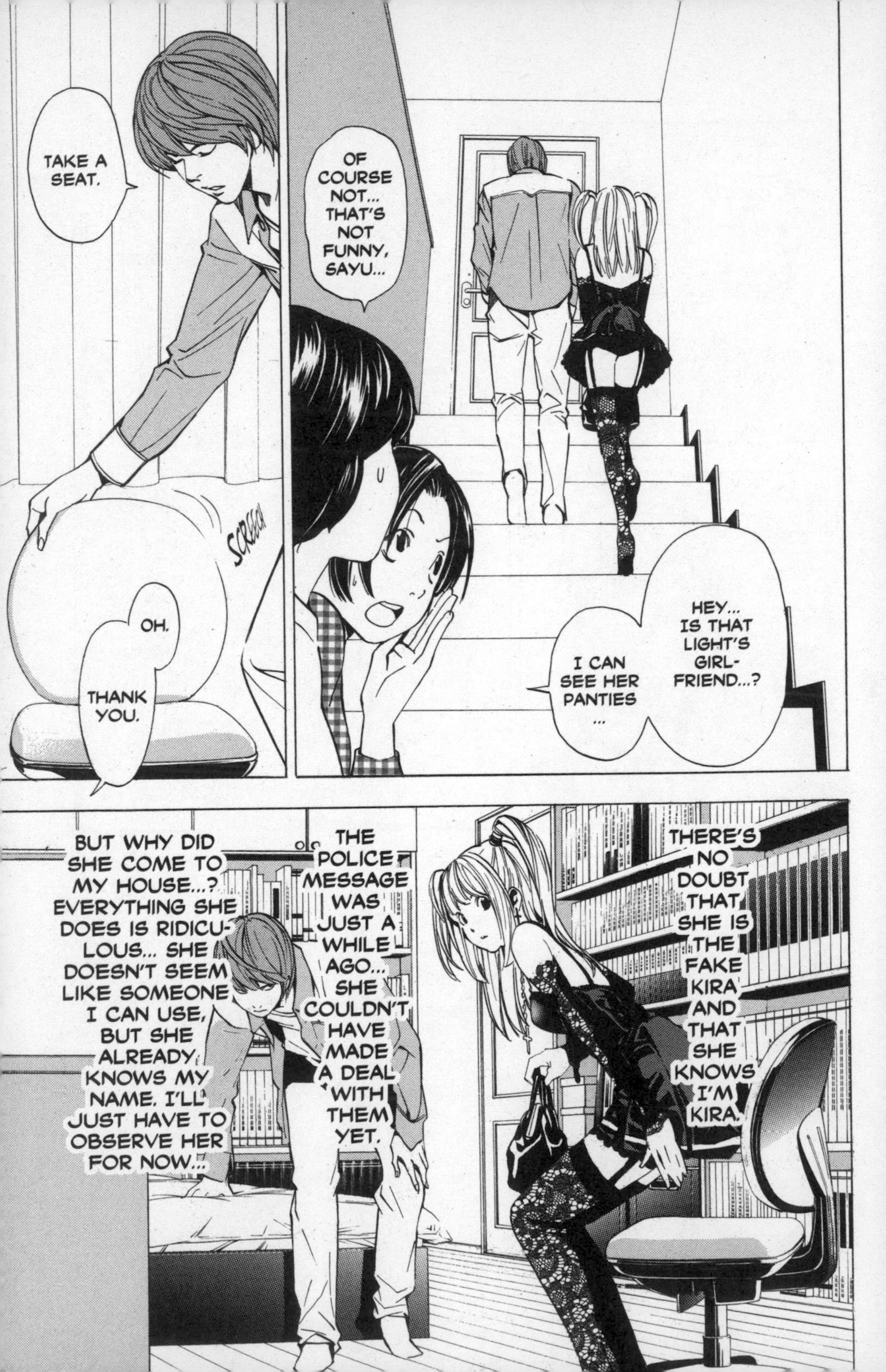
HEY... IS THAT LIGHT'S GIRL-FRIEND...?
I CAN SEE HER PANTIES ...
OF COURSE NOT... THAT'S NOT FUNNY, SAYU...
TAKE A SEAT.
SCREECH
OH.
THANK YOU.
THERE'S NO DOUBT THAT SHE IS THE FAKE KIRA AND THAT SHE KNOWS I'M KIRA.
THE POLICE MESSAGE WAS JUST A WHILE AGO... SHE COULDN'T HAVE MADE A DEAL WITH THEM YET.
BUT WHY DID SHE COME TO MY HOUSE...? EVERYTHING SHE DOES IS RIDICU-LOUS... SHE DOESN'T SEEM LIKE SOMEONE I CAN USE, BUT SHE ALREADY KNOWS MY NAME. I'LL JUST HAVE TO OBSERVE HER FOR NOW...

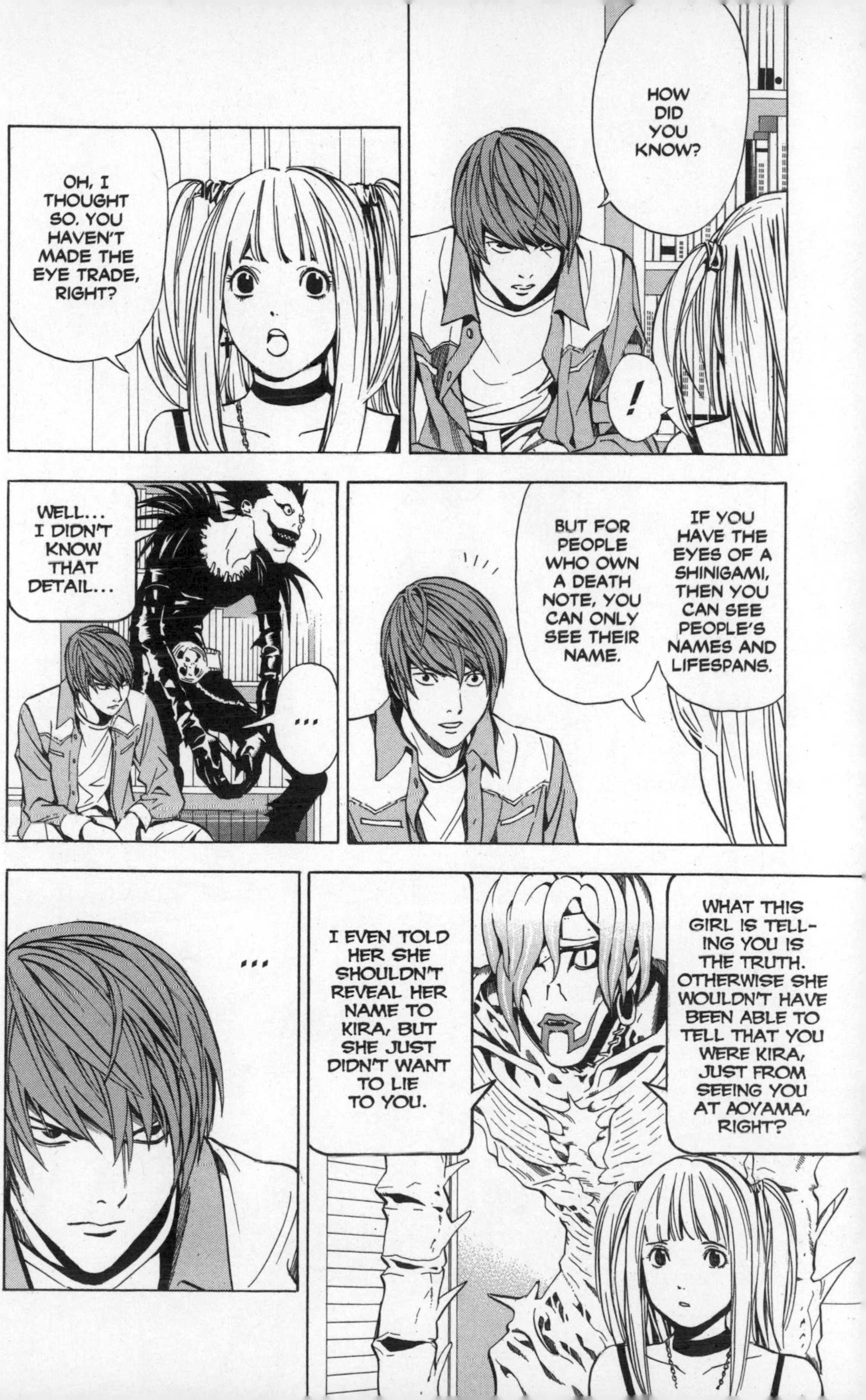
HOW DID YOU KNOW?
!
OH, I THOUGHT SO. YOU HAVEN'T MADE THE EYE TRADE, RIGHT?
IF YOU HAVE THE EYES OF A SHINIGAMI, THEN YOU CAN SEE PEOPLE'S NAMES AND LIFESPANS.
BUT FOR PEOPLE WHO OWN A DEATH NOTE, YOU CAN ONLY SEE THEIR NAME.
WELL... I DIDN'T KNOW THAT DETAIL...
...
WHAT THIS GIRL IS TELL-ING YOU IS THE TRUTH. OTHERWISE SHE WOULDN'T HAVE BEEN ABLE TO TELL THAT YOU WERE KIRA, JUST FROM SEEING YOU AT AOYAMA, RIGHT?
I EVEN TOLD HER SHE SHOULDN'T REVEAL HER NAME TO KIRA, BUT SHE JUST DIDN'T WANT TO LIE TO YOU.
...

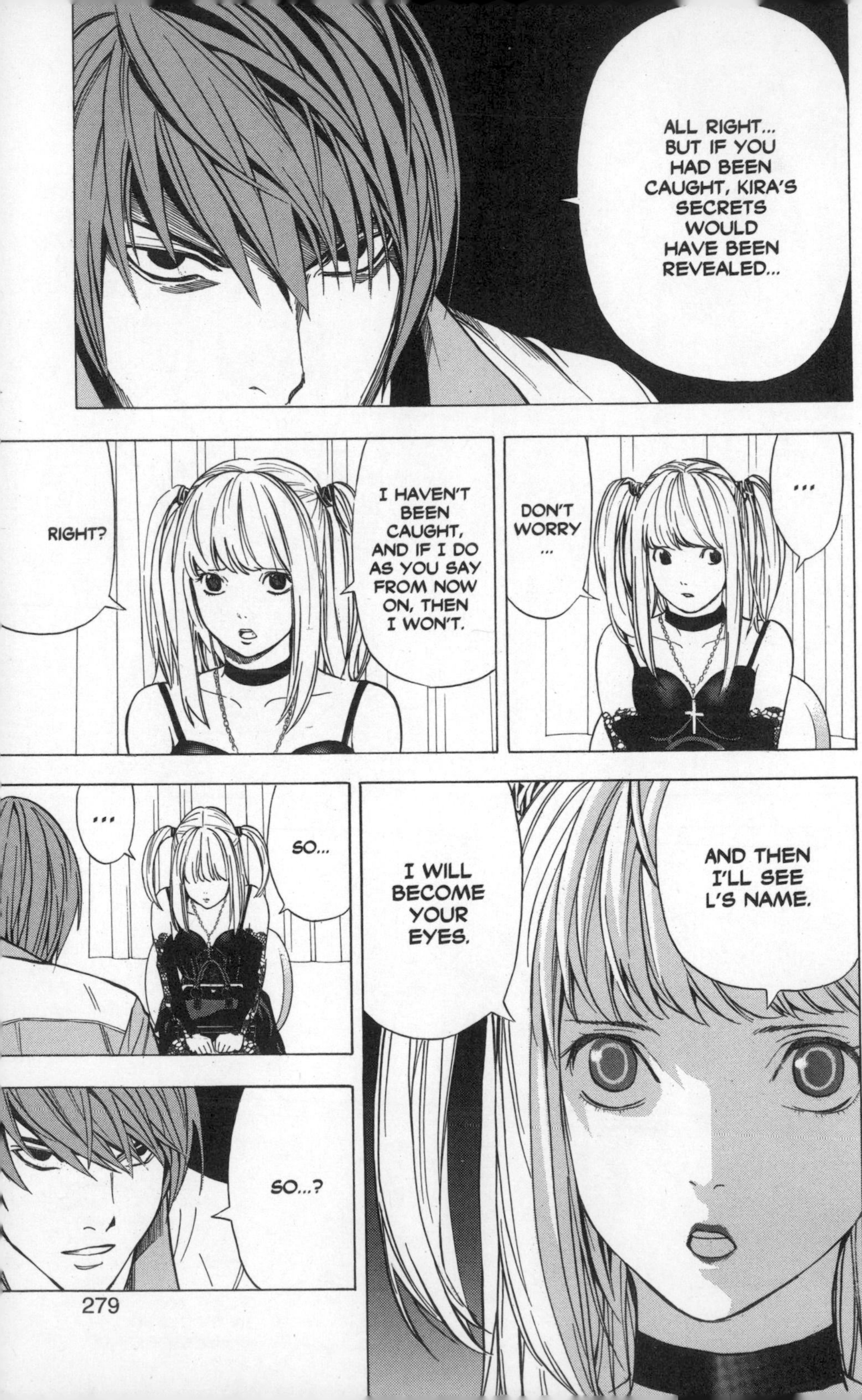
ALL RIGHT... BUT IF YOU HAD BEEN CAUGHT, KIRA'S SECRETS WOULD HAVE BEEN REVEALED...
...
DON'T WORRY ...
I HAVEN'T BEEN CAUGHT, AND IF I DO AS YOU SAY FROM NOW ON, THEN I WON'T.
RIGHT?
AND THEN I'LL SEE L'S NAME.
I WILL BECOME YOUR EYES.
SO...
...
SO...?

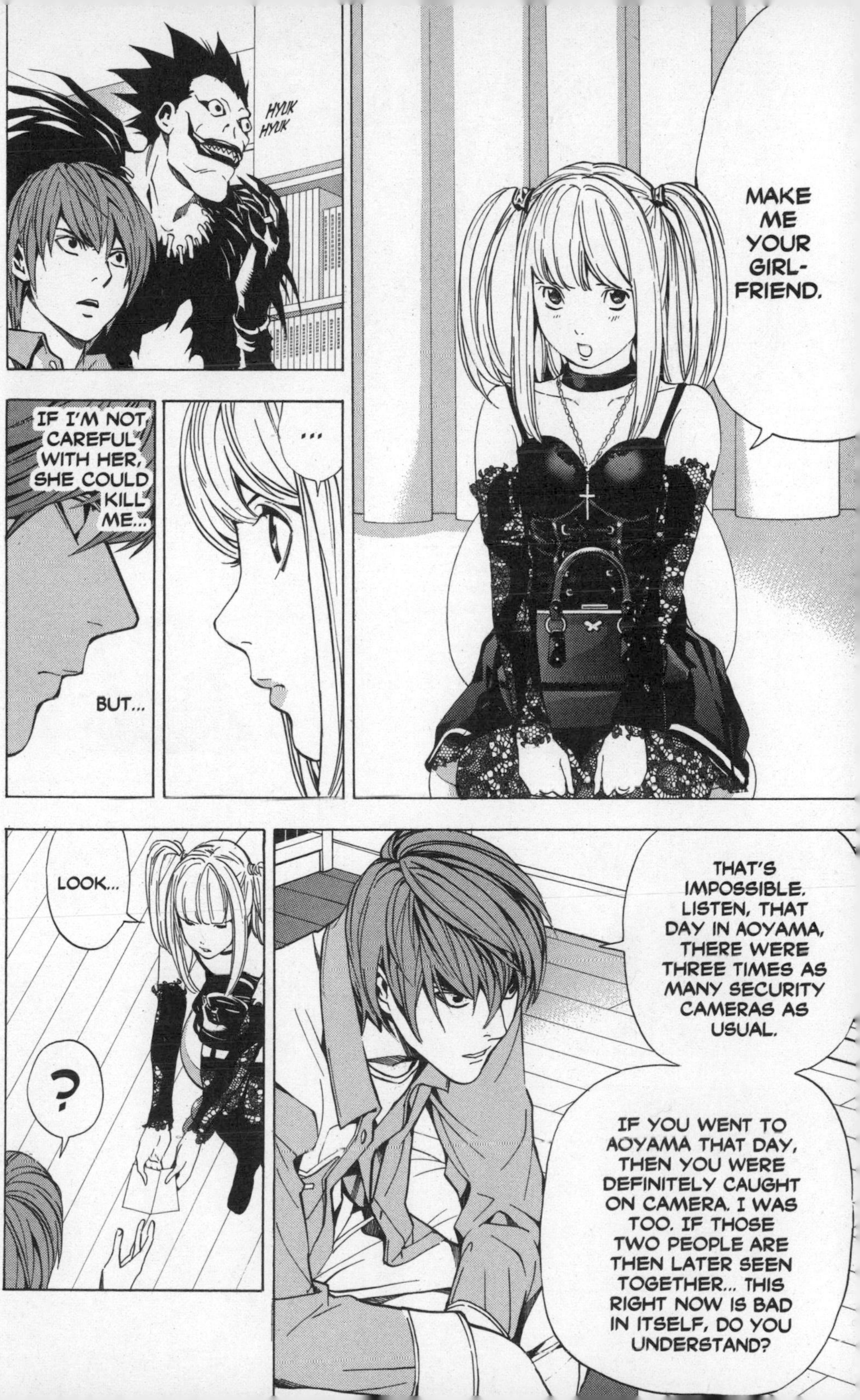
MAKE ME YOUR GIRL-FRIEND.
HYUK HYUK
...
IF I'M NOT CAREFUL WITH HER, SHE COULD KILL ME...
BUT...
THAT'S IMPOSSIBLE. LISTEN, THAT DAY IN AOYAMA, THERE WERE THREE TIMES AS MANY SECURITY CAMERAS AS USUAL.
IF YOU WENT TO AOYAMA THAT DAY, THEN YOU WERE DEFINITELY CAUGHT ON CAMERA. I WAS TOO. IF THOSE TWO PEOPLE ARE THEN LATER SEEN TOGETHER... THIS RIGHT NOW IS BAD IN ITSELF, DO YOU UNDERSTAND?
LOOK...
?

READ THIS WAY

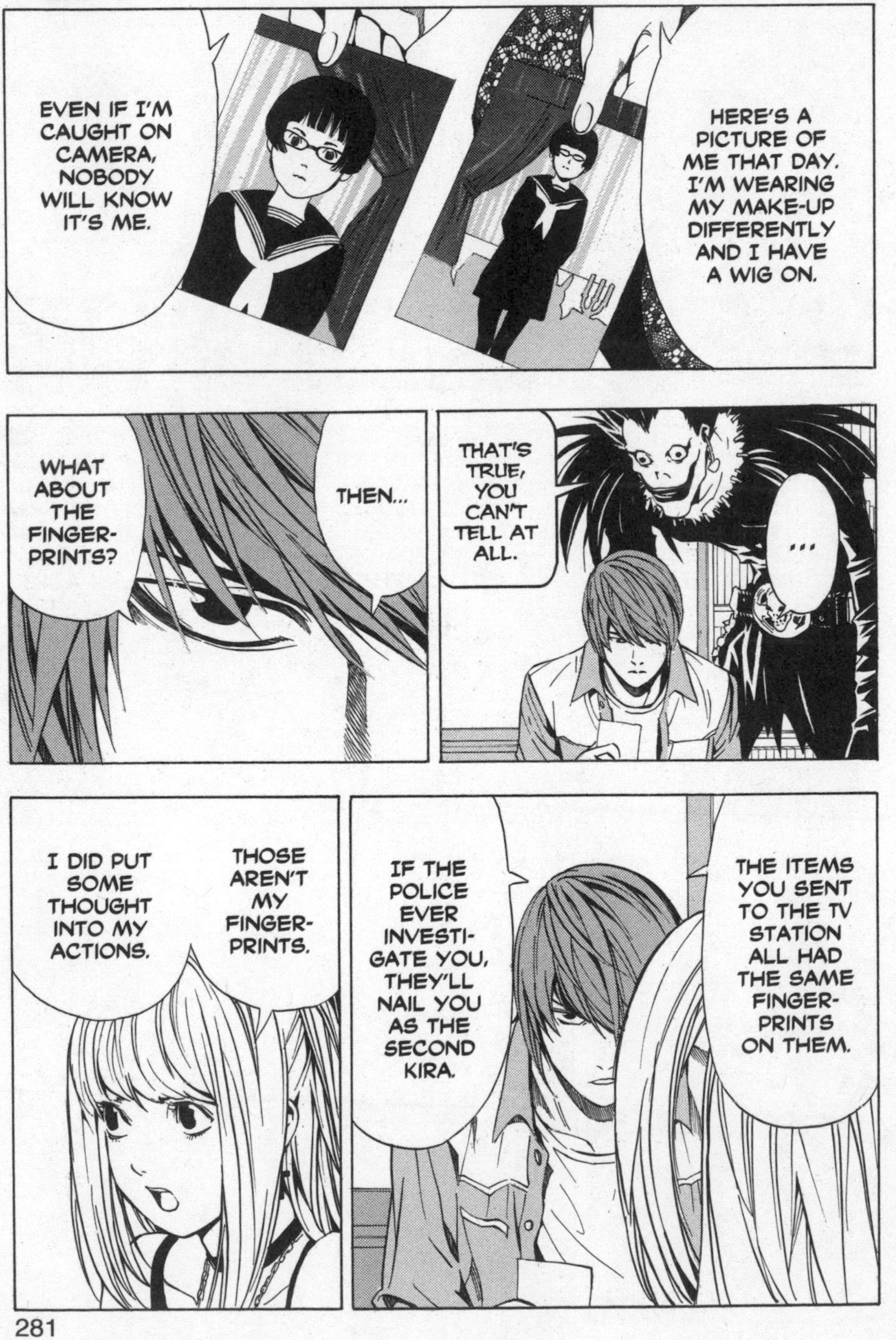
HERE'S A PICTURE OF ME THAT DAY. I'M WEARING MY MAKE-UP DIFFERENTLY AND I HAVE A WIG ON.
EVEN IF I'M CAUGHT ON CAMERA, NOBODY WILL KNOW IT'S ME.
THAT'S TRUE, YOU CAN'T TELL AT ALL.
...
THEN...
WHAT ABOUT THE FINGER-PRINTS?
THE ITEMS YOU SENT TO THE TV STATION ALL HAD THE SAME FINGER-PRINTS ON THEM.
IF THE POLICE EVER INVESTI-GATE YOU, THEY'LL NAIL YOU AS THE SECOND KIRA.
THOSE AREN'T MY FINGER-PRINTS.
I DID PUT SOME THOUGHT INTO MY ACTIONS.

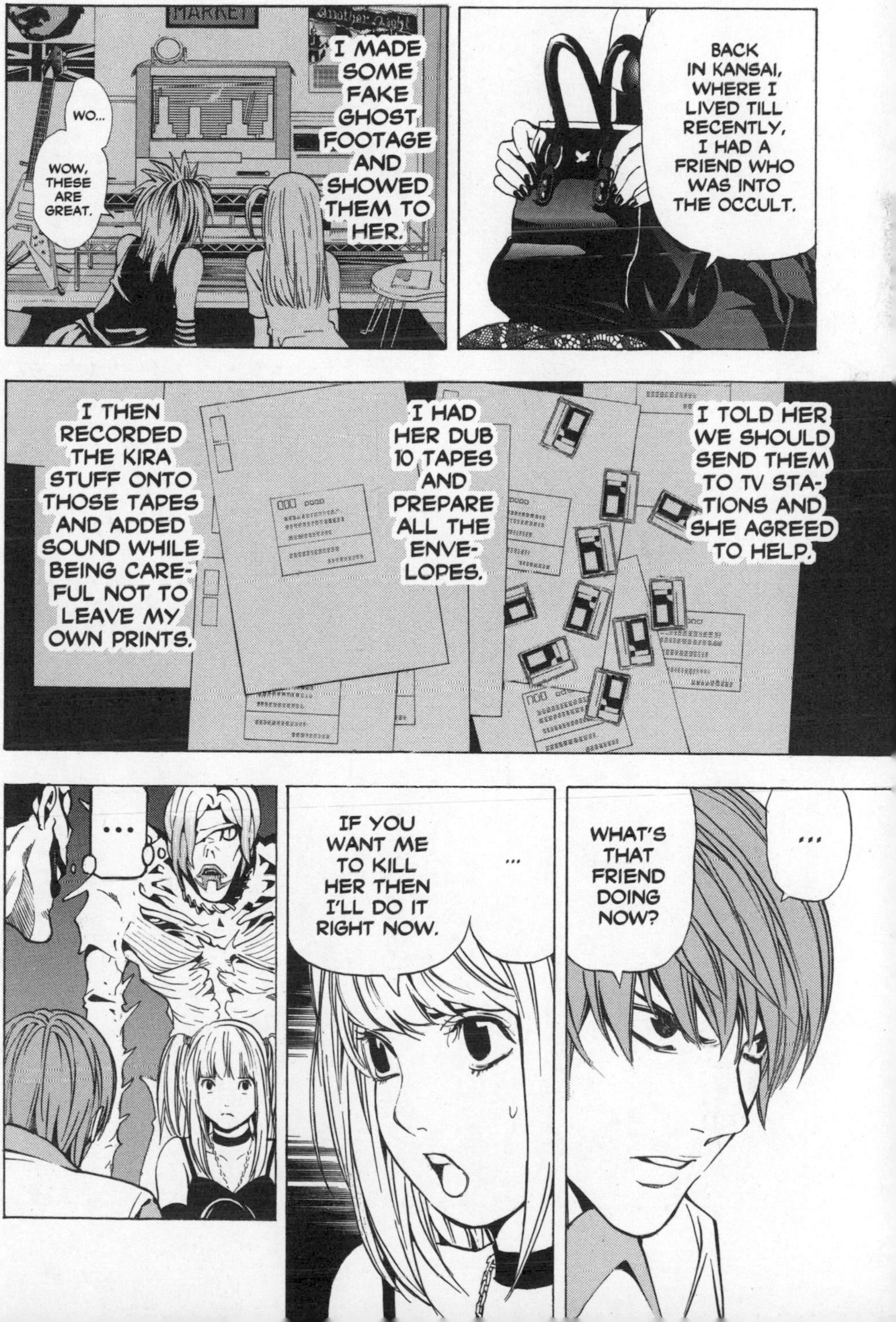
BACK IN KANSAI, WHERE I LIVED TILL RECENTLY, I HAD A FRIEND WHO WAS INTO THE OCCULT.
I MADE SOME FAKE GHOST FOOTAGE AND SHOWED THEM TO HER.
WO...
WOW, THESE ARE GREAT.
I TOLD HER WE SHOULD SEND THEM TO TV STATIONS AND SHE AGREED TO HELP.
I HAD HER DUB 10 TAPES AND PREPARE ALL THE ENVELOPES.
I THEN RECORDED THE KIRA STUFF ONTO THOSE TAPES AND ADDED SOUND WHILE BEING CAREFUL NOT TO LEAVE MY OWN PRINTS.
...
WHAT'S THAT FRIEND DOING NOW?
...
IF YOU WANT ME TO KILL HER THEN I'LL DO IT RIGHT NOW.
...

READ THIS WAY

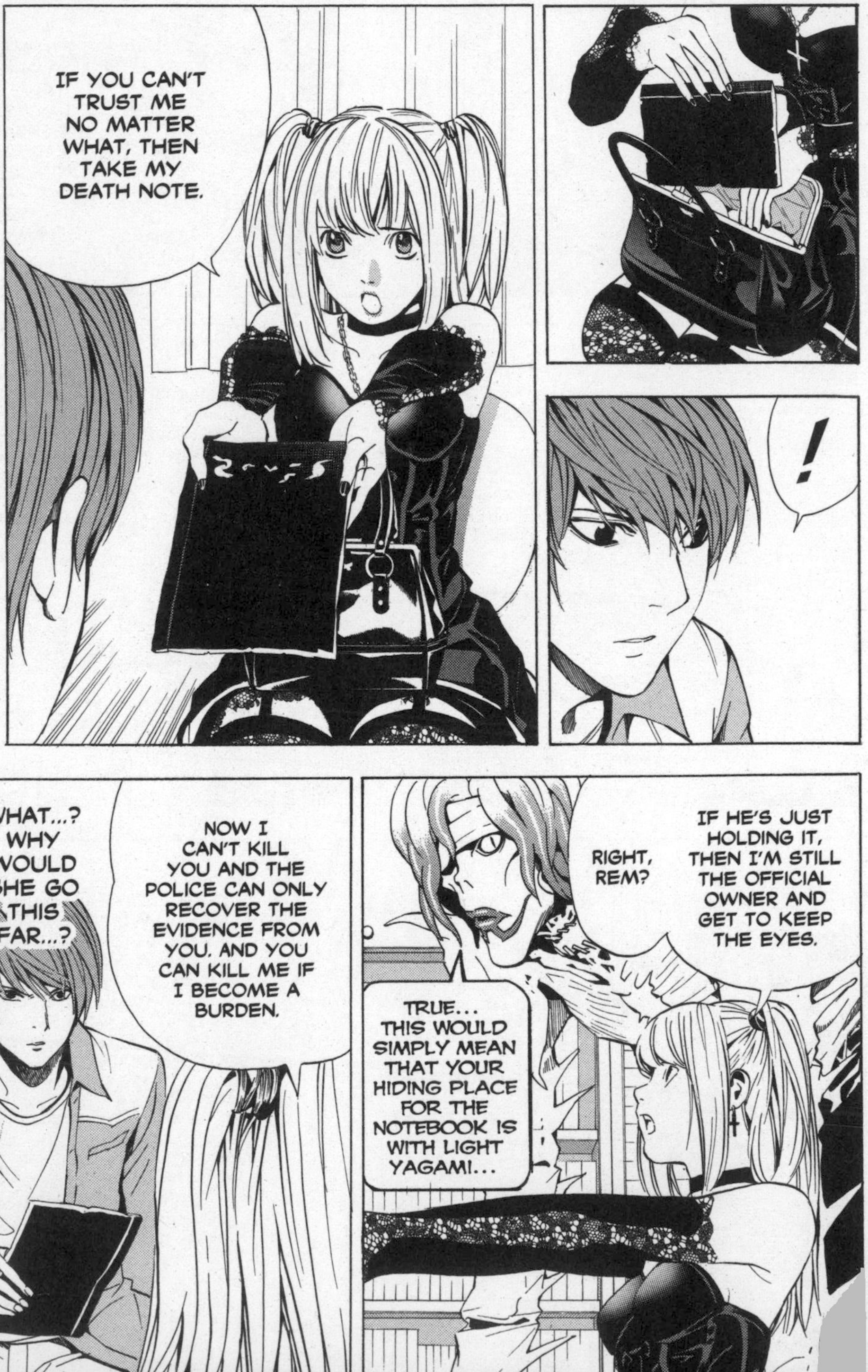
!
IF YOU CAN'T TRUST ME NO MATTER WHAT, THEN TAKE MY DEATH NOTE.
IF HE'S JUST HOLDING IT, THEN I'M STILL THE OFFICIAL OWNER AND GET TO KEEP THE EYES.
RIGHT, REM?
TRUE... THIS WOULD SIMPLY MEAN THAT YOUR HIDING PLACE FOR THE NOTEBOOK IS WITH LIGHT YAGAMI...
NOW I CAN'T KILL YOU AND THE POLICE CAN ONLY RECOVER THE EVIDENCE FROM YOU, AND YOU CAN KILL ME IF I BECOME A BURDEN.
WHAT...? WHY WOULD SHE GO THIS FAR...?

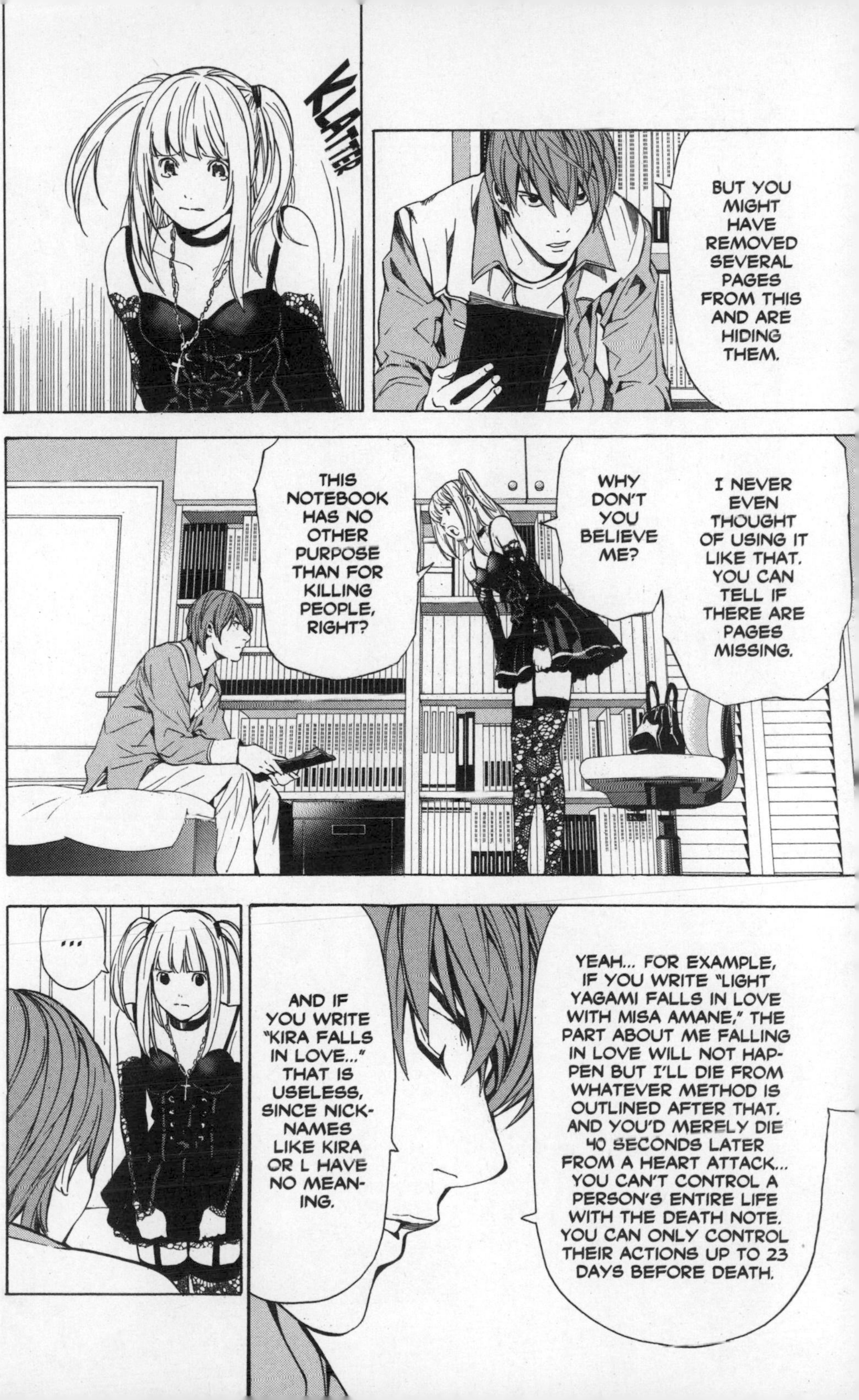
BUT YOU MIGHT HAVE REMOVED SEVERAL PAGES FROM THIS AND ARE HIDING THEM.
KLATTER
I NEVER EVEN THOUGHT OF USING IT LIKE THAT. YOU CAN TELL IF THERE ARE PAGES MISSING.
WHY DON'T YOU BELIEVE ME?
THIS NOTEBOOK HAS NO OTHER PURPOSE THAN FOR KILLING PEOPLE, RIGHT?
YEAH... FOR EXAMPLE, IF YOU WRITE "LIGHT YAGAMI FALLS IN LOVE WITH MISA AMANE," THE PART ABOUT ME FALLING IN LOVE WILL NOT HAPPEN BUT I'LL DIE FROM WHATEVER METHOD IS OUTLINED AFTER THAT. AND YOU'D MERELY DIE 40 SECONDS LATER FROM A HEART ATTACK... YOU CAN'T CONTROL A PERSON'S ENTIRE LIFE WITH THE DEATH NOTE. YOU CAN ONLY CONTROL THEIR ACTIONS UP TO 23 DAYS BEFORE DEATH.
AND IF YOU WRITE "KIRA FALLS IN LOVE..." THAT IS USELESS, SINCE NICKNAMES LIKE KIRA OR L HAVE NO MEANING.
...

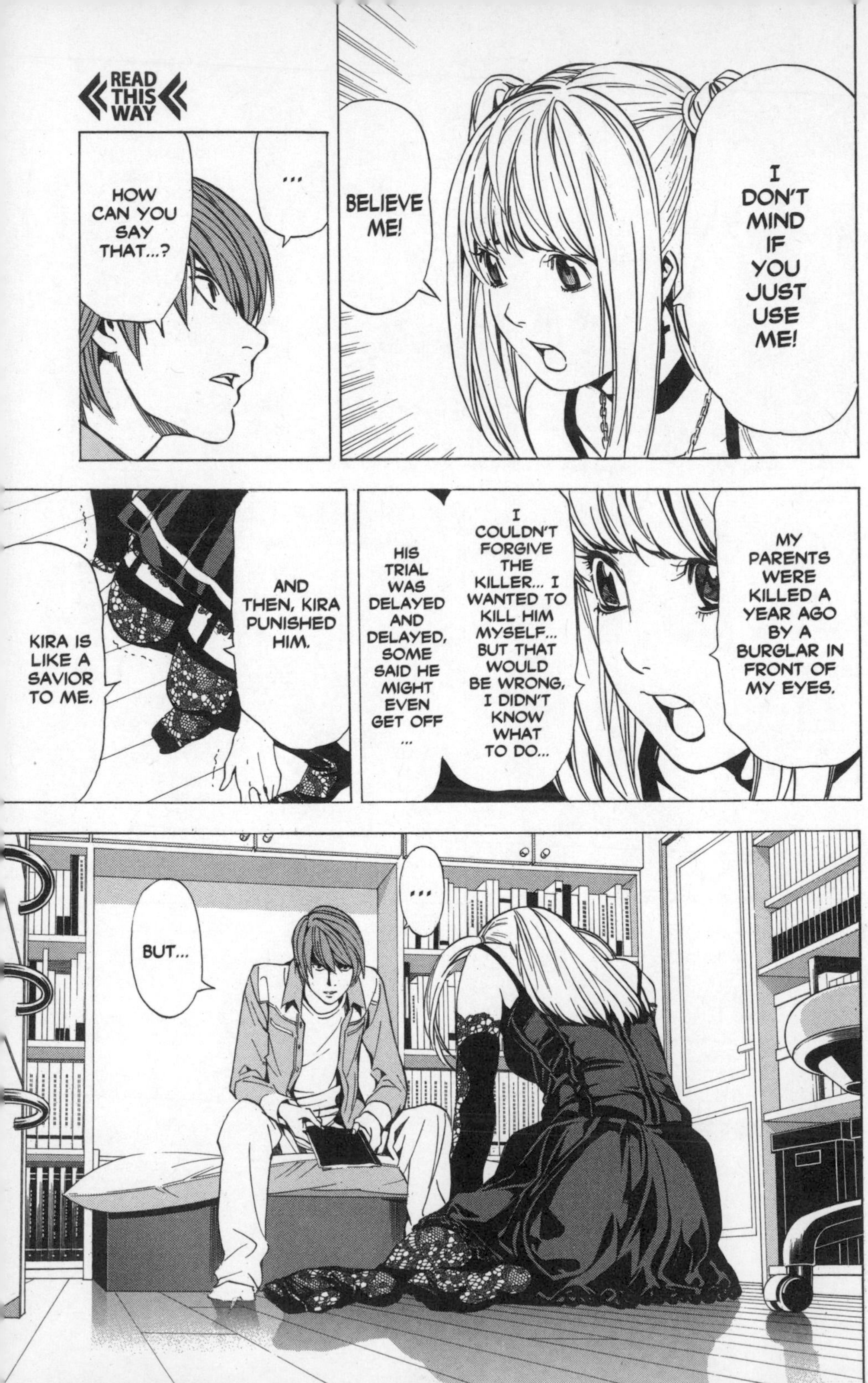
READ THIS WAY
I DON'T MIND IF YOU JUST USE ME!
BELIEVE ME!
...
HOW CAN YOU SAY THAT...?
MY PARENTS WERE KILLED A YEAR AGO BY A BURGLAR IN FRONT OF MY EYES.
I COULDN'T FORGIVE THE KILLER... I WANTED TO KILL HIM MYSELF... BUT THAT WOULD BE WRONG, I DIDN'T KNOW WHAT TO DO...
HIS TRIAL WAS DELAYED AND DELAYED, SOME SAID HE MIGHT EVEN GET OFF ...
AND THEN, KIRA PUNISHED HIM.
KIRA IS LIKE A SAVIOR TO ME.
...
BUT...

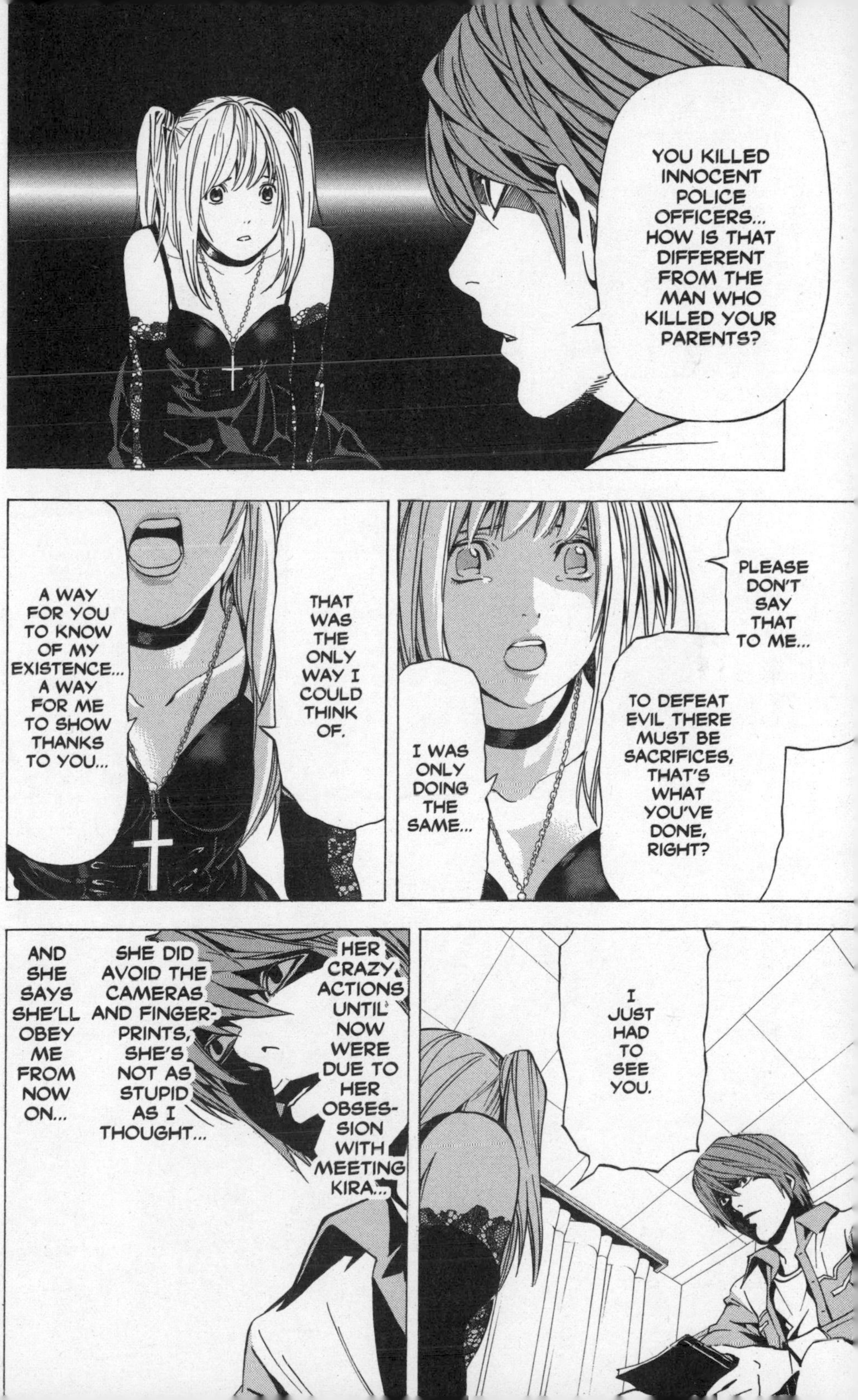
YOU KILLED INNOCENT POLICE OFFICERS... HOW IS THAT DIFFERENT FROM THE MAN WHO KILLED YOUR PARENTS?
PLEASE DON'T SAY THAT TO ME...
TO DEFEAT EVIL THERE MUST BE SACRIFICES, THAT'S WHAT YOU'VE DONE, RIGHT?
I WAS ONLY DOING THE SAME...
THAT WAS THE ONLY WAY I COULD THINK OF.
A WAY FOR YOU TO KNOW OF MY EXISTENCE... A WAY FOR ME TO SHOW THANKS TO YOU...
I JUST HAD TO SEE YOU.
HER CRAZY ACTIONS UNTIL NOW WERE DUE TO HER OBSESSION WITH MEETING KIRA...
SHE DID AVOID THE CAMERAS AND FINGERPRINTS, SHE'S NOT AS STUPID AS I THOUGHT...
AND SHE SAYS SHE'LL OBEY ME FROM NOW ON...

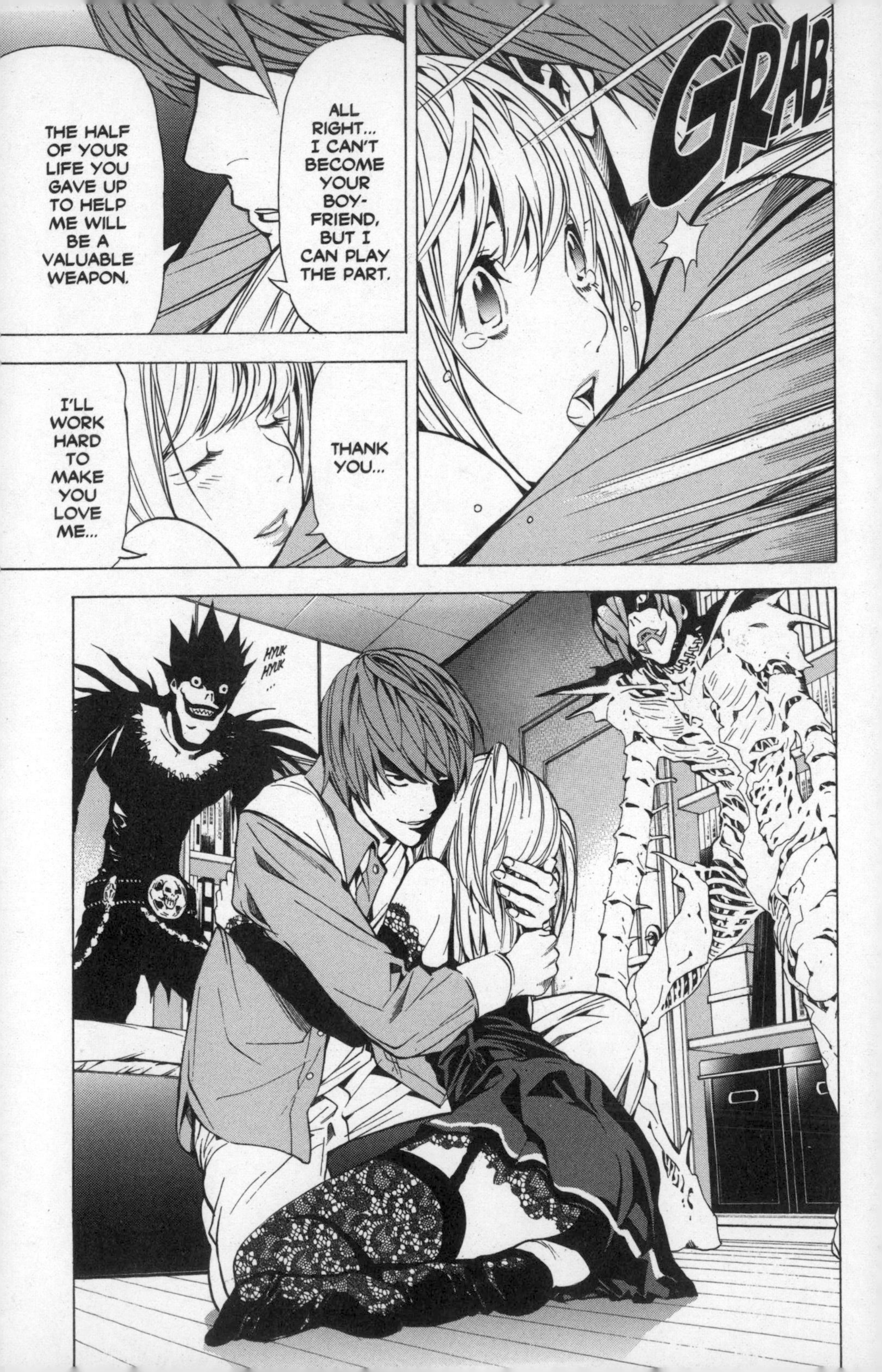
GRAB
ALL RIGHT... I CAN'T BECOME YOUR BOY-FRIEND, BUT I CAN PLAY THE PART.
THE HALF OF YOUR LIFE YOU GAVE UP TO HELP ME WILL BE A VALUABLE WEAPON.
THANK YOU...
I'LL WORK HARD TO MAKE YOU LOVE ME...
HYUK HYUK ...

DEATH NOTE
How to use it
XVN

○ It is prerequisite for the DEATH NOTE used in the human world that a living god of death makes sure that the humans in the human world use it.

人間界で使われるデスノートには、生きた死神の人間界で人間に使わせるという意思が始めになければならない。

○ It is very difficult to consider that a god of death who has possessed a human could die., but if he should die, the DEATH NOTE that he brought into the human world will not lose its power.

その後、人間に憑いた死神が死ぬ事は考えにくいが、死んだ場合、その死神が人間界に持ち込んだデスノートの効力に変化は生じない。

chapter 30 Bomb

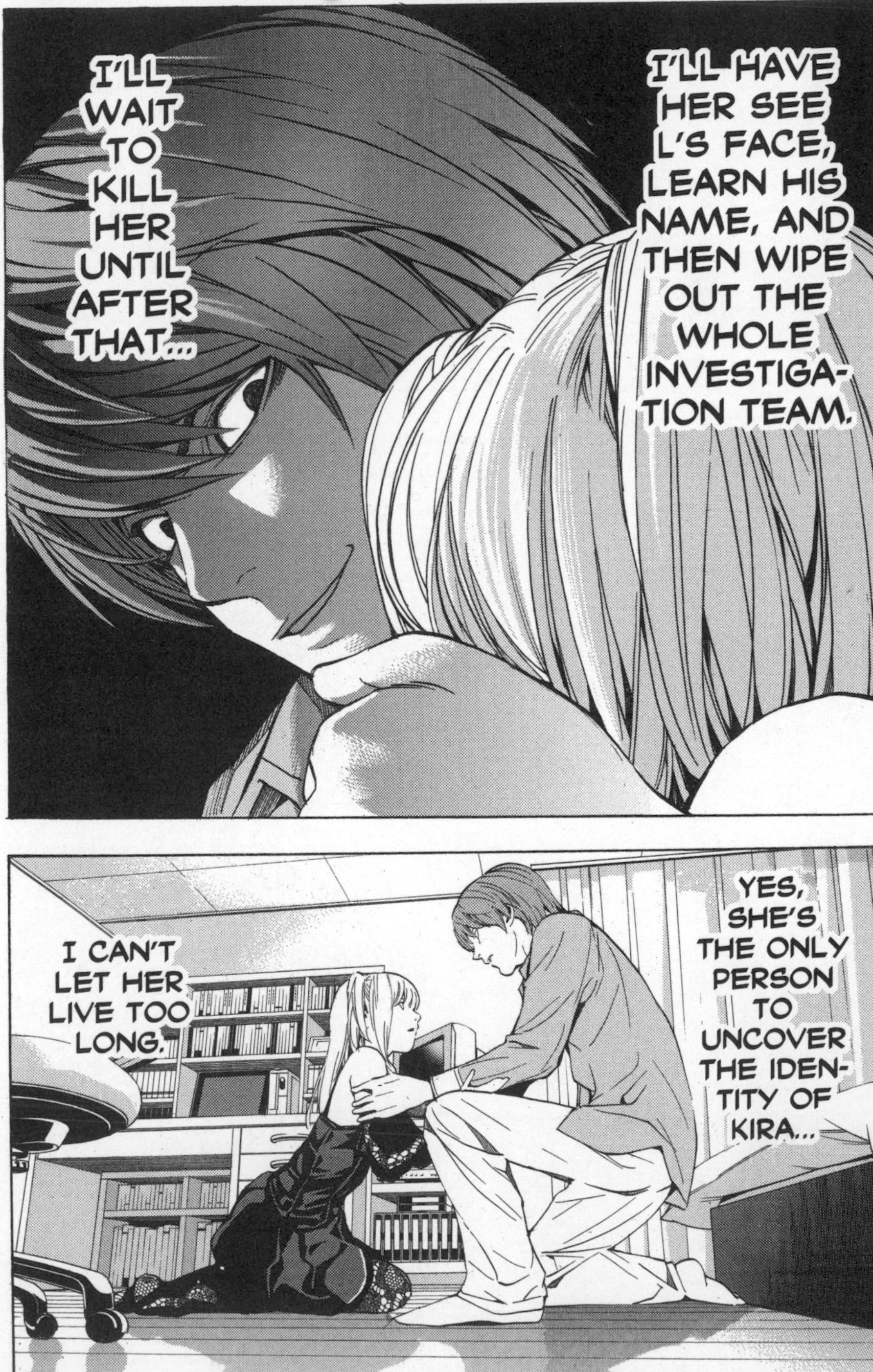
I'LL HAVE HER SEE L'S FACE, LEARN HIS NAME, AND THEN WIPE OUT THE WHOLE INVESTIGA-TION TEAM.
I'LL WAIT TO KILL HER UNTIL AFTER THAT...
YES, SHE'S THE ONLY PERSON TO UNCOVER THE IDEN-TITY OF KIRA...
I CAN'T LET HER LIVE TOO LONG.

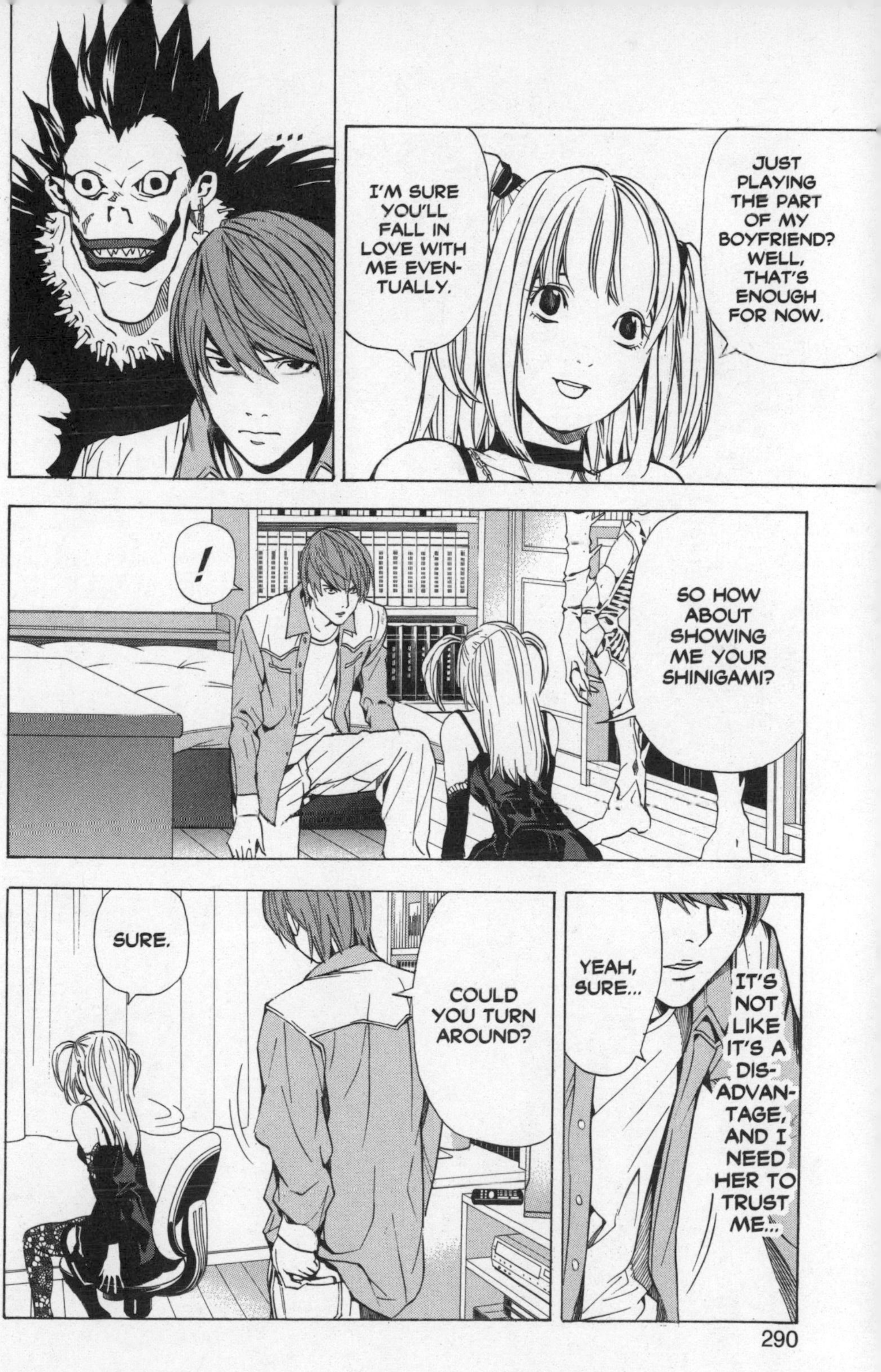
JUST PLAYING THE PART OF MY BOYFRIEND? WELL, THAT'S ENOUGH FOR NOW.
I'M SURE YOU'LL FALL IN LOVE WITH ME EVEN-TUALLY.
...
SO HOW ABOUT SHOWING ME YOUR SHINIGAMI?
!
YEAH, SURE...
IT'S NOT LIKE IT'S A DIS-ADVAN-TAGE, AND I NEED HER TO TRUST ME...
COULD YOU TURN AROUND?
SURE.

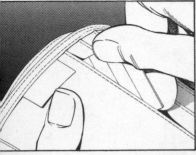

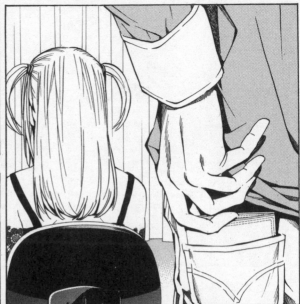

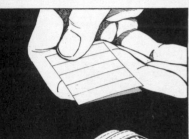

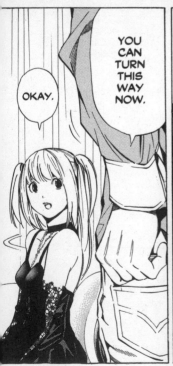

YOU CAN TURN THIS WAY NOW.

OKAY.

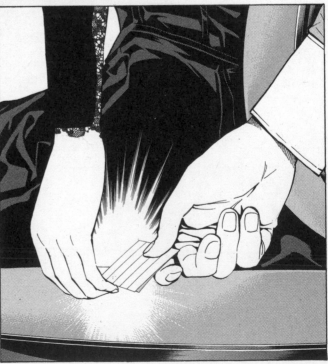

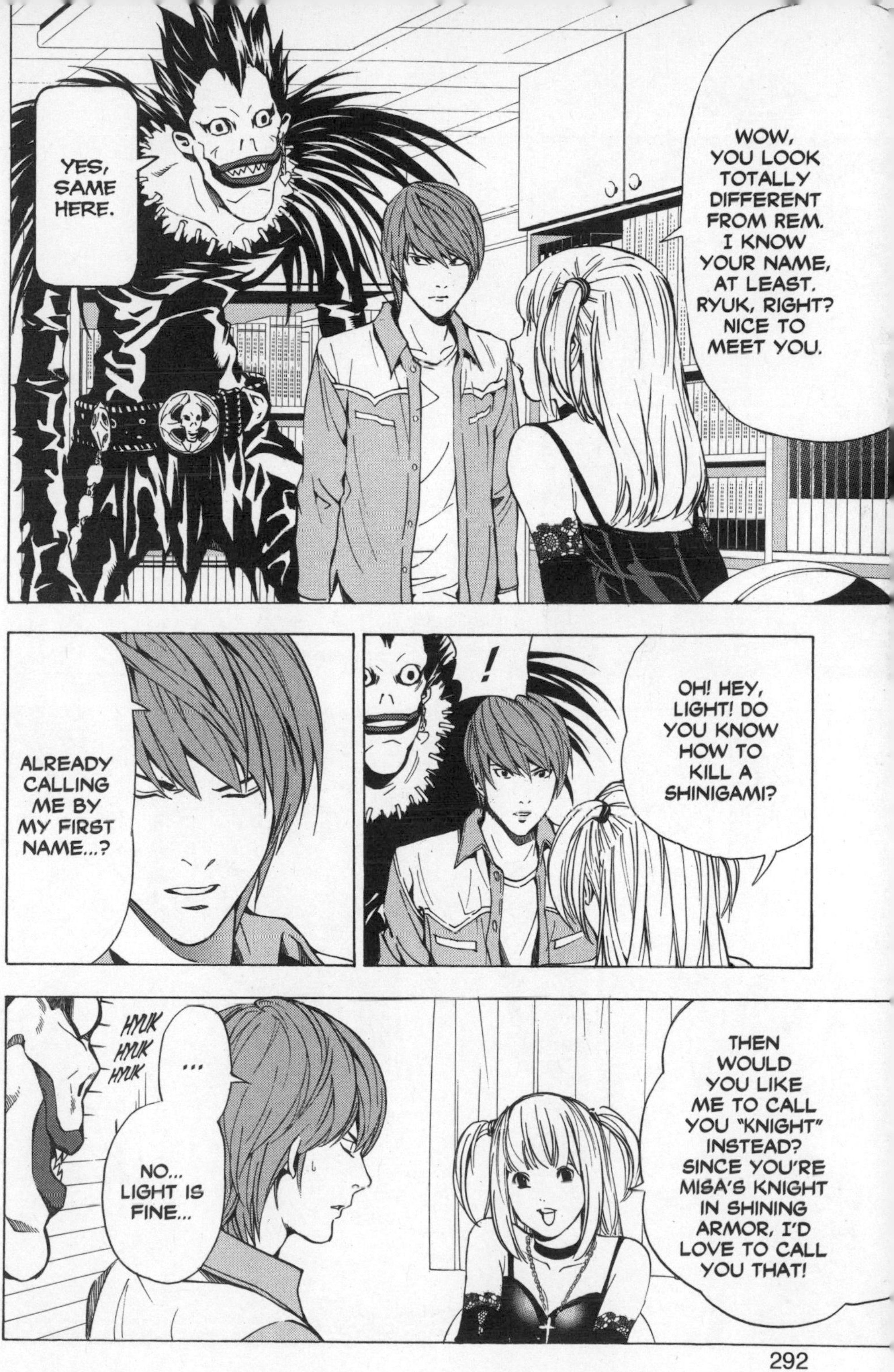
WOW, YOU LOOK TOTALLY DIFFERENT FROM REM. I KNOW YOUR NAME, AT LEAST. RYUK, RIGHT? NICE TO MEET YOU.
YES, SAME HERE.
OH! HEY, LIGHT! DO YOU KNOW HOW TO KILL A SHINIGAMI?
!
ALREADY CALLING ME BY MY FIRST NAME...?
THEN WOULD YOU LIKE ME TO CALL YOU "KNIGHT" INSTEAD? SINCE YOU'RE MISA'S KNIGHT IN SHINING ARMOR, I'D LOVE TO CALL YOU THAT!
...
HYUK HYUK HYUK
NO... LIGHT IS FINE...

READ THIS WAY

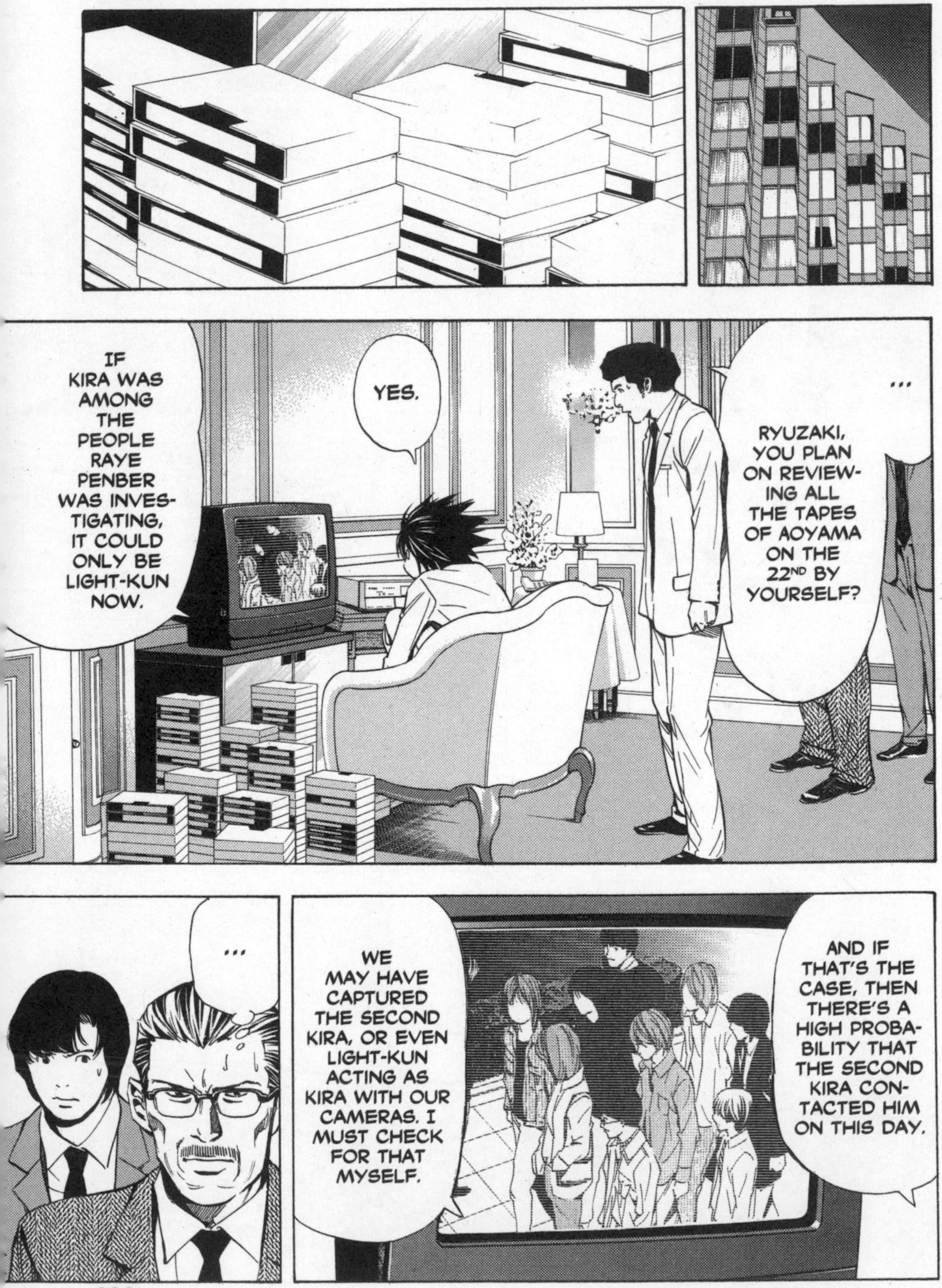
...
RYUZAKI, YOU PLAN ON REVIEWING ALL THE TAPES OF AOYAMA ON THE 22ND BY YOURSELF?
YES.
IF KIRA WAS AMONG THE PEOPLE RAYE PENBER WAS INVESTIGATING, IT COULD ONLY BE LIGHT-KUN NOW.
AND IF THAT'S THE CASE, THEN THERE'S A HIGH PROBABILITY THAT THE SECOND KIRA CONTACTED HIM ON THIS DAY.
WE MAY HAVE CAPTURED THE SECOND KIRA, OR EVEN LIGHT-KUN ACTING AS KIRA WITH OUR CAMERAS. I MUST CHECK FOR THAT MYSELF.
...

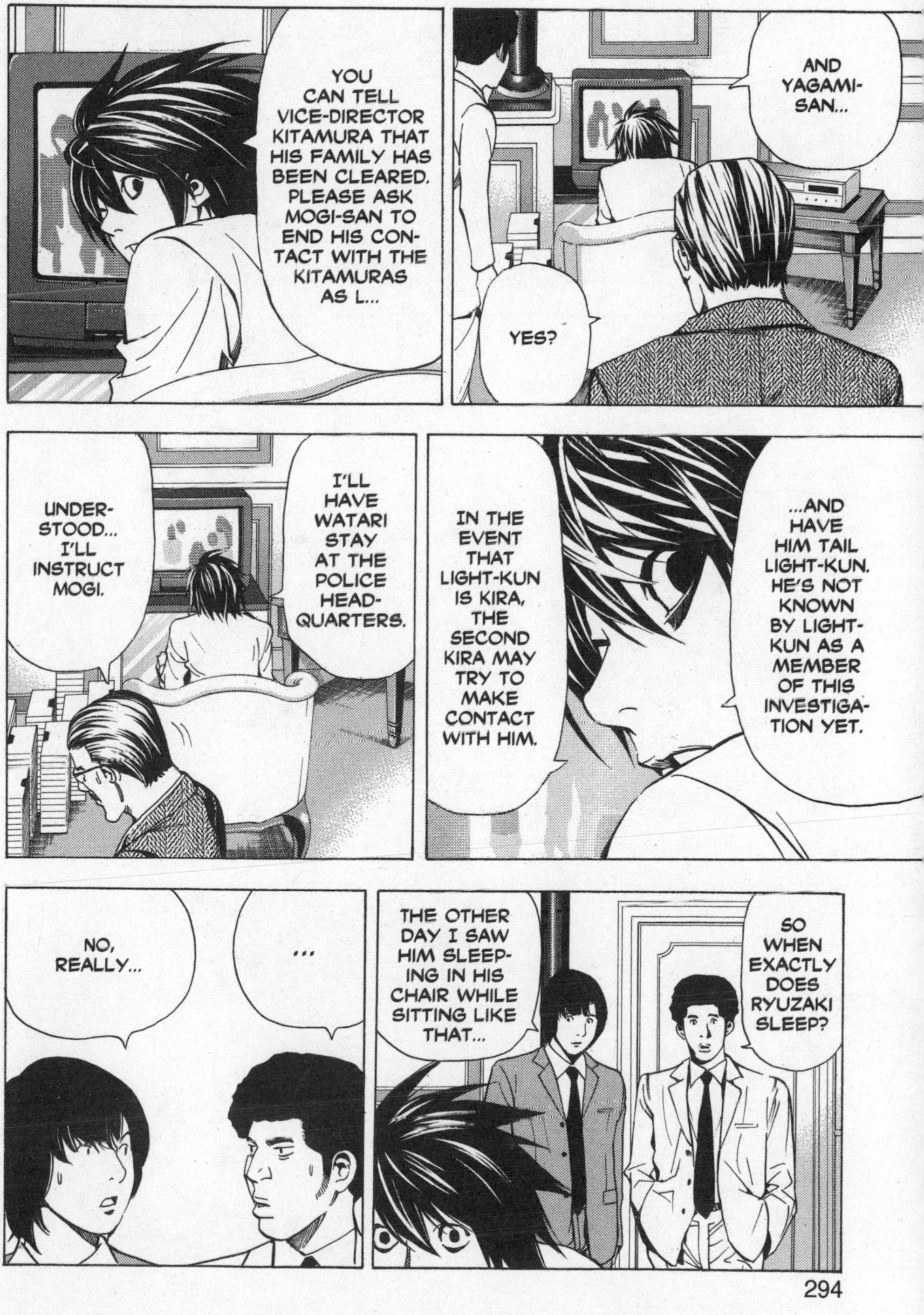
AND YAGAMI-SAN...
YES?
YOU CAN TELL VICE-DIRECTOR KITAMURA THAT HIS FAMILY HAS BEEN CLEARED. PLEASE ASK MOGI-SAN TO END HIS CONTACT WITH THE KITAMURAS AS L...
...AND HAVE HIM TAIL LIGHT-KUN. HE'S NOT KNOWN BY LIGHT-KUN AS A MEMBER OF THIS INVESTIGATION YET.
IN THE EVENT THAT LIGHT-KUN IS KIRA, THE SECOND KIRA MAY TRY TO MAKE CONTACT WITH HIM.
I'LL HAVE WATARI STAY AT THE POLICE HEADQUARTERS.
UNDERSTOOD... I'LL INSTRUCT MOGI.
SO WHEN EXACTLY DOES RYUZAKI SLEEP?
THE OTHER DAY I SAW HIM SLEEPING IN HIS CHAIR WHILE SITTING LIKE THAT...
...
NO, REALLY...

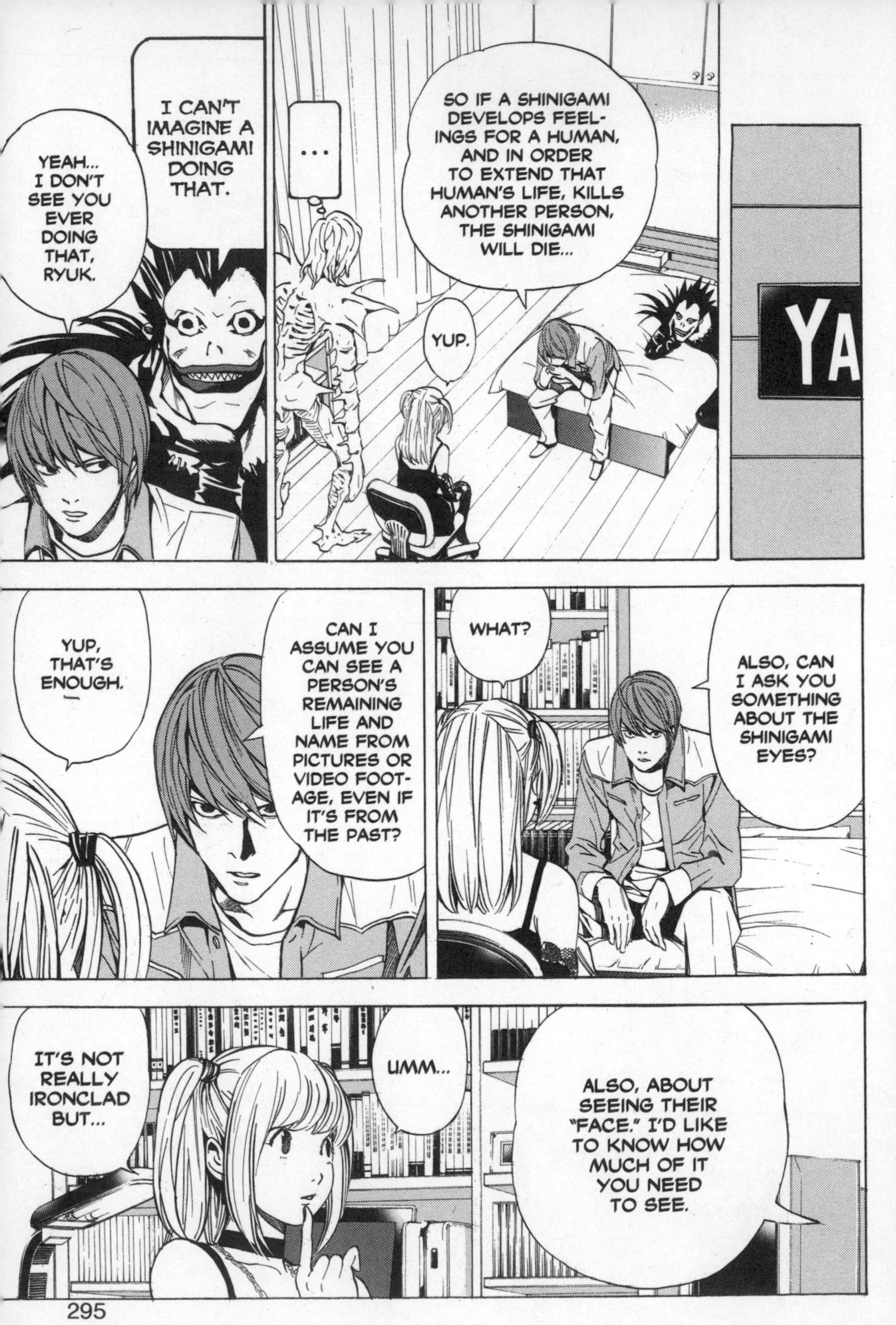
YA
SO IF A SHINIGAMI DEVELOPS FEEL-INGS FOR A HUMAN, AND IN ORDER TO EXTEND THAT HUMAN'S LIFE, KILLS ANOTHER PERSON, THE SHINIGAMI WILL DIE...
...
YUP.
I CAN'T IMAGINE A SHINIGAMI DOING THAT.
YEAH... I DON'T SEE YOU EVER DOING THAT, RYUK.
ALSO, CAN I ASK YOU SOMETHING ABOUT THE SHINIGAMI EYES?
WHAT?
CAN I ASSUME YOU CAN SEE A PERSON'S REMAINING LIFE AND NAME FROM PICTURES OR VIDEO FOOT-AGE, EVEN IF IT'S FROM THE PAST?
YUP, THAT'S ENOUGH.
ALSO, ABOUT SEEING THEIR "FACE." I'D LIKE TO KNOW HOW MUCH OF IT YOU NEED TO SEE.
UMM...
IT'S NOT REALLY IRONCLAD BUT...

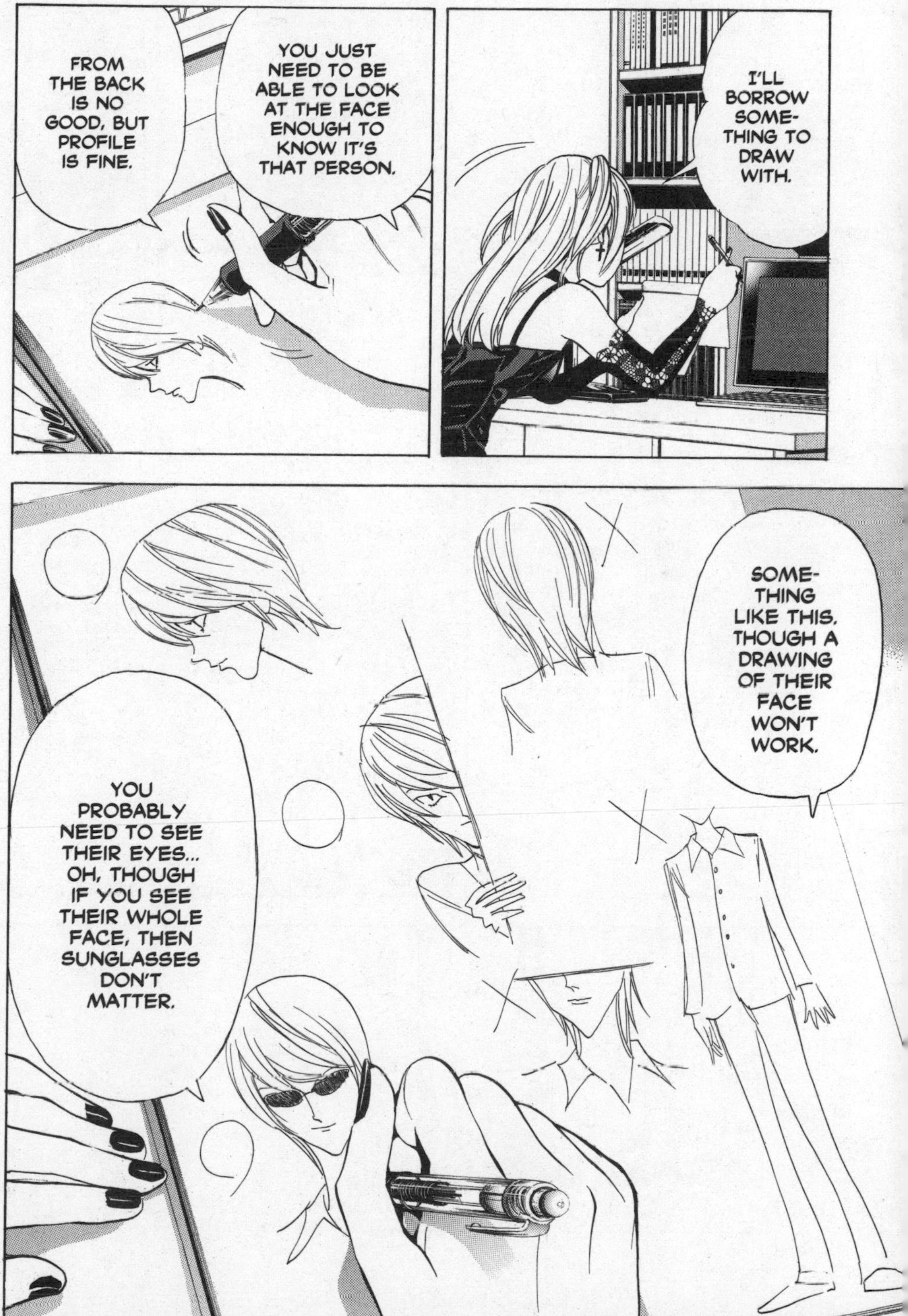
I'LL BORROW SOME-THING TO DRAW WITH.
YOU JUST NEED TO BE ABLE TO LOOK AT THE FACE ENOUGH TO KNOW IT'S THAT PERSON.
FROM THE BACK IS NO GOOD, BUT PROFILE IS FINE.
SOME-THING LIKE THIS. THOUGH A DRAWING OF THEIR FACE WON'T WORK.
YOU PROBABLY NEED TO SEE THEIR EYES... OH, THOUGH IF YOU SEE THEIR WHOLE FACE, THEN SUNGLASSES DON'T MATTER.

READ THIS WAY

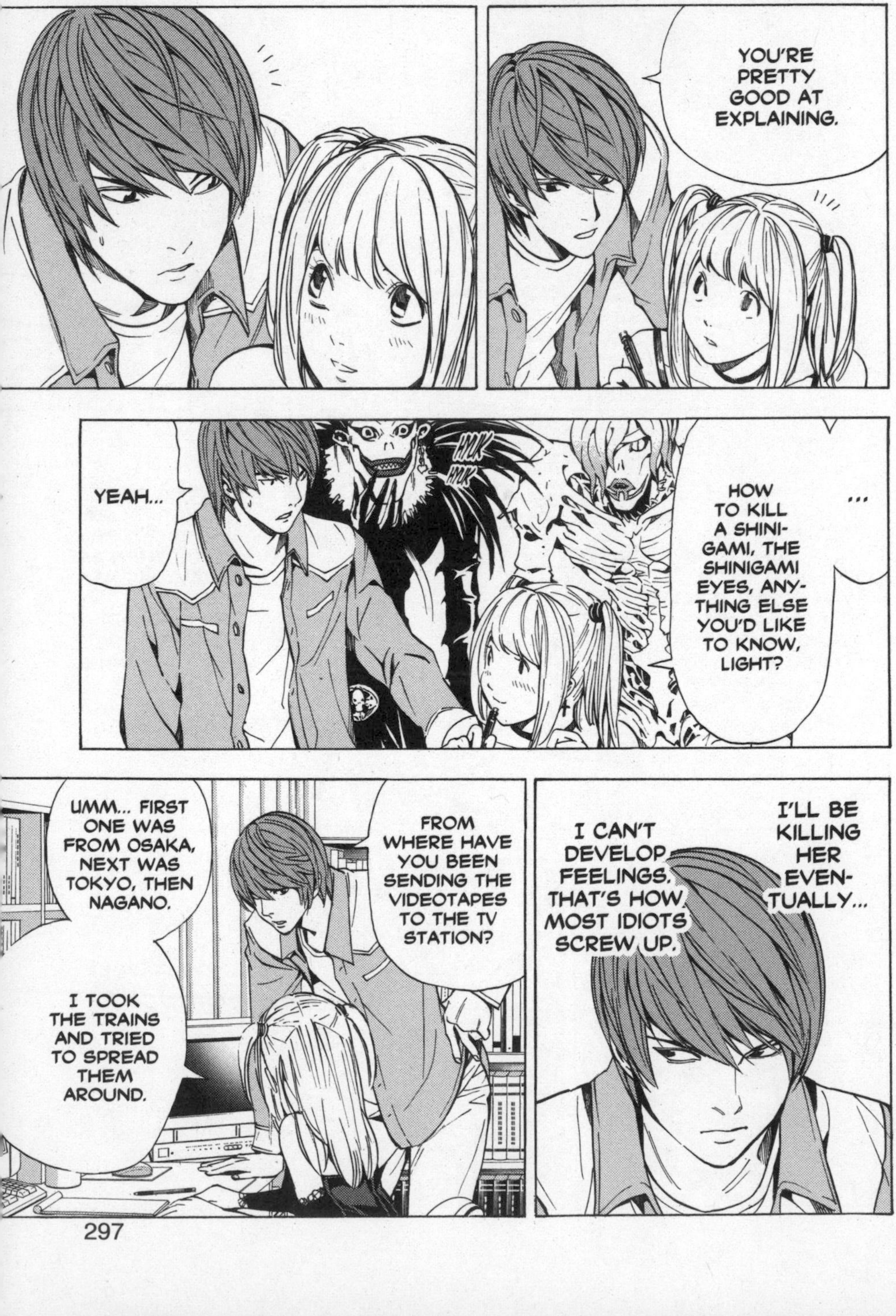
YOU'RE PRETTY GOOD AT EXPLAINING.
...
HOW TO KILL A SHINIGAMI, THE SHINIGAMI EYES, ANYTHING ELSE YOU'D LIKE TO KNOW, LIGHT?
HYUK HYUK
YEAH...
I'LL BE KILLING HER EVENTUALLY...
I CAN'T DEVELOP FEELINGS. THAT'S HOW MOST IDIOTS SCREW UP.
FROM WHERE HAVE YOU BEEN SENDING THE VIDEOTAPES TO THE TV STATION?
UMM... FIRST ONE WAS FROM OSAKA, NEXT WAS TOKYO, THEN NAGANO.
I TOOK THE TRAINS AND TRIED TO SPREAD THEM AROUND.

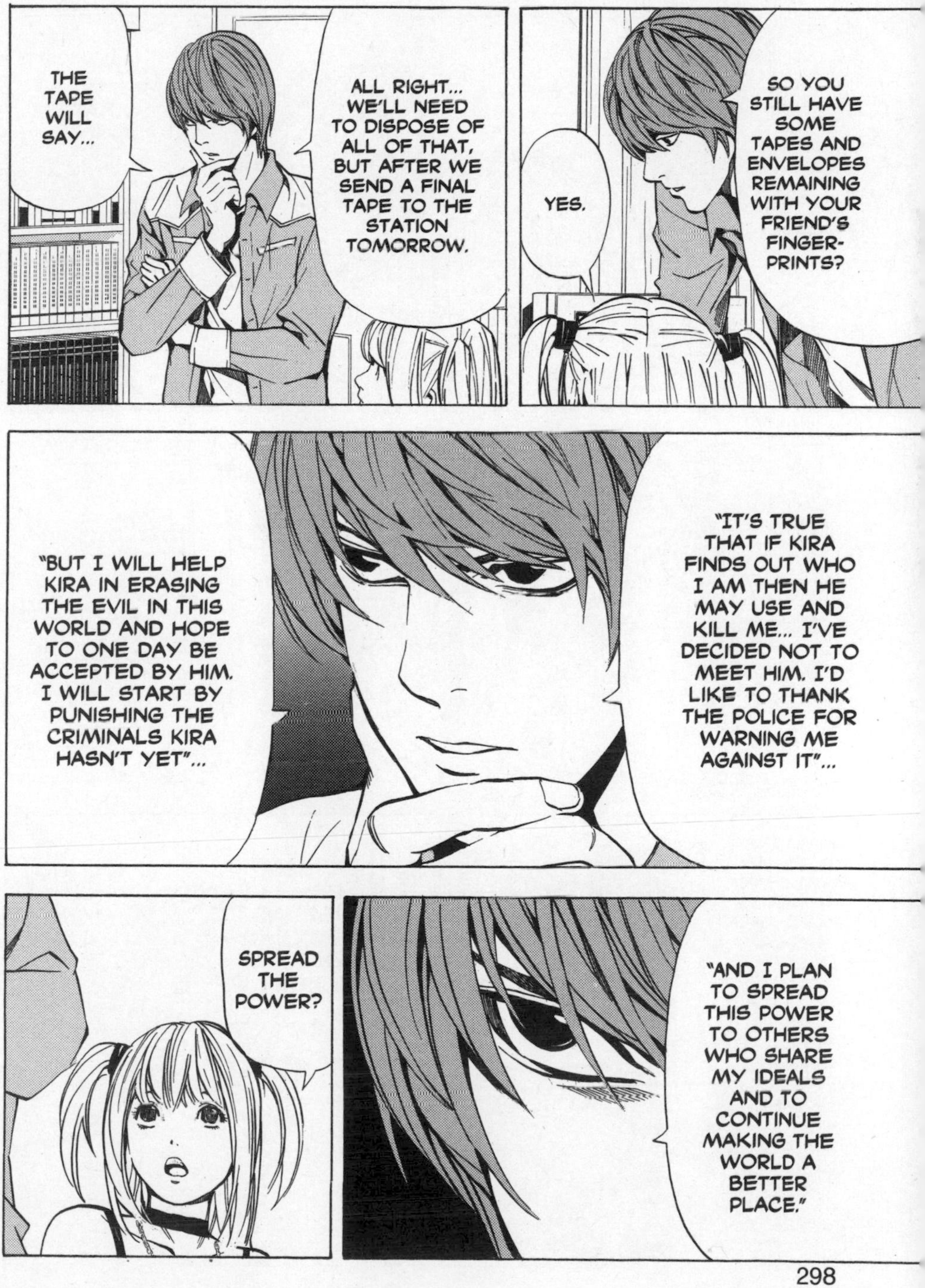
SO YOU STILL HAVE SOME TAPES AND ENVELOPES REMAINING WITH YOUR FRIEND'S FINGER-PRINTS?
YES.
ALL RIGHT... WE'LL NEED TO DISPOSE OF ALL OF THAT, BUT AFTER WE SEND A FINAL TAPE TO THE STATION TOMORROW.
THE TAPE WILL SAY...
"IT'S TRUE THAT IF KIRA FINDS OUT WHO I AM THEN HE MAY USE AND KILL ME... I'VE DECIDED NOT TO MEET HIM. I'D LIKE TO THANK THE POLICE FOR WARNING ME AGAINST IT"...
"BUT I WILL HELP KIRA IN ERASING THE EVIL IN THIS WORLD AND HOPE TO ONE DAY BE ACCEPTED BY HIM. I WILL START BY PUNISHING THE CRIMINALS KIRA HASN'T YET"...
"AND I PLAN TO SPREAD THIS POWER TO OTHERS WHO SHARE MY IDEALS AND TO CONTINUE MAKING THE WORLD A BETTER PLACE."
SPREAD THE POWER?

READ THIS WAY

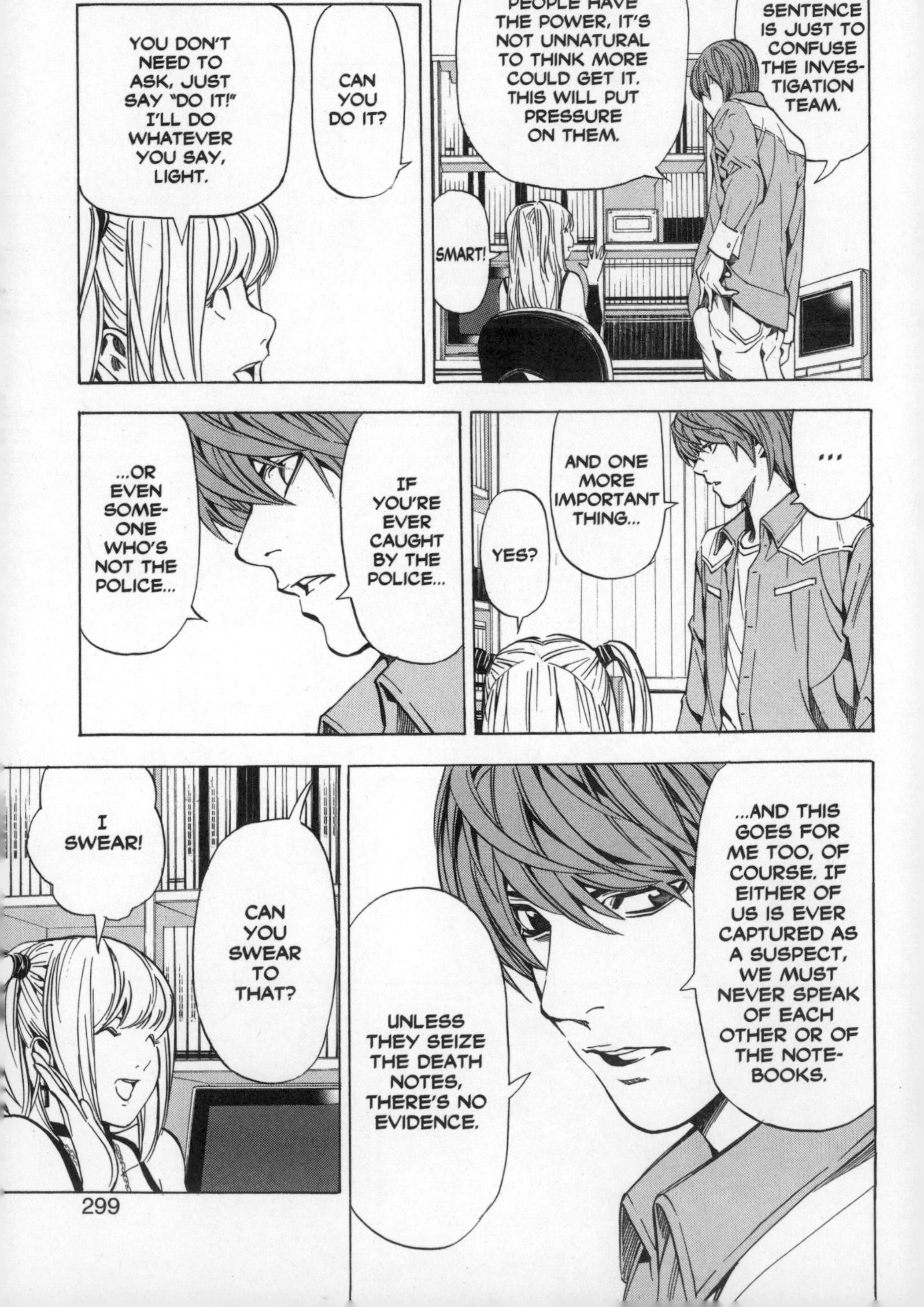
THAT SENTENCE IS JUST TO CONFUSE THE INVESTIGATION TEAM.
ALREADY TWO PEOPLE HAVE THE POWER, IT'S NOT UNNATURAL TO THINK MORE COULD GET IT. THIS WILL PUT PRESSURE ON THEM.
SMART!
CAN YOU DO IT?
YOU DON'T NEED TO ASK, JUST SAY "DO IT!" I'LL DO WHATEVER YOU SAY, LIGHT.
...
AND ONE MORE IMPORTANT THING...
YES?
IF YOU'RE EVER CAUGHT BY THE POLICE...
...OR EVEN SOMEONE WHO'S NOT THE POLICE...
...AND THIS GOES FOR ME TOO, OF COURSE. IF EITHER OF US IS EVER CAPTURED AS A SUSPECT, WE MUST NEVER SPEAK OF EACH OTHER OR OF THE NOTEBOOKS.
UNLESS THEY SEIZE THE DEATH NOTES, THERE'S NO EVIDENCE.
CAN YOU SWEAR TO THAT?
I SWEAR!

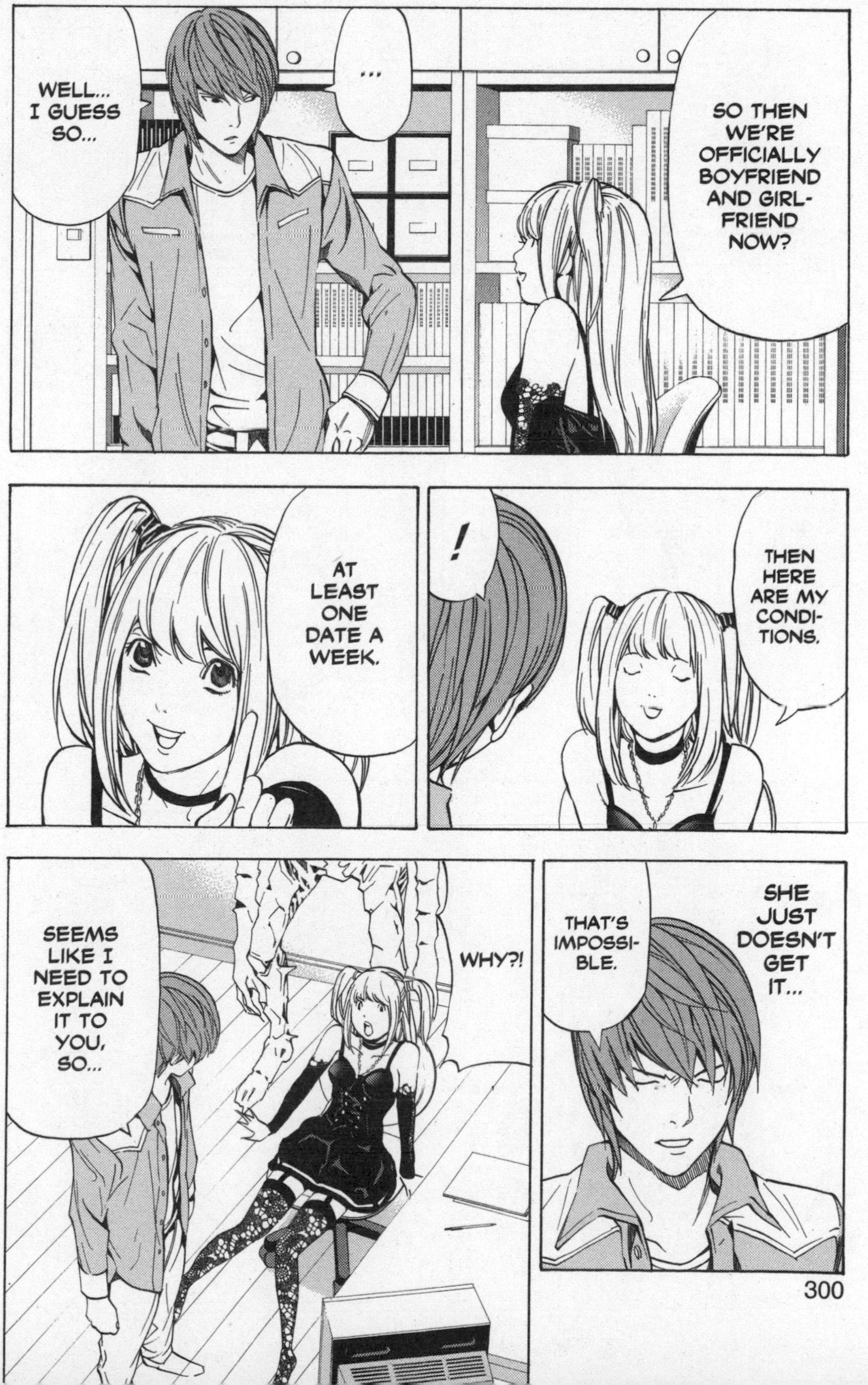
SO THEN WE'RE OFFICIALLY BOYFRIEND AND GIRL-FRIEND NOW?
...
WELL... I GUESS SO...
THEN HERE ARE MY CONDI-TIONS.
!
AT LEAST ONE DATE A WEEK.
SHE JUST DOESN'T GET IT...
THAT'S IMPOSSI-BLE.
WHY?!
SEEMS LIKE I NEED TO EXPLAIN IT TO YOU, SO...

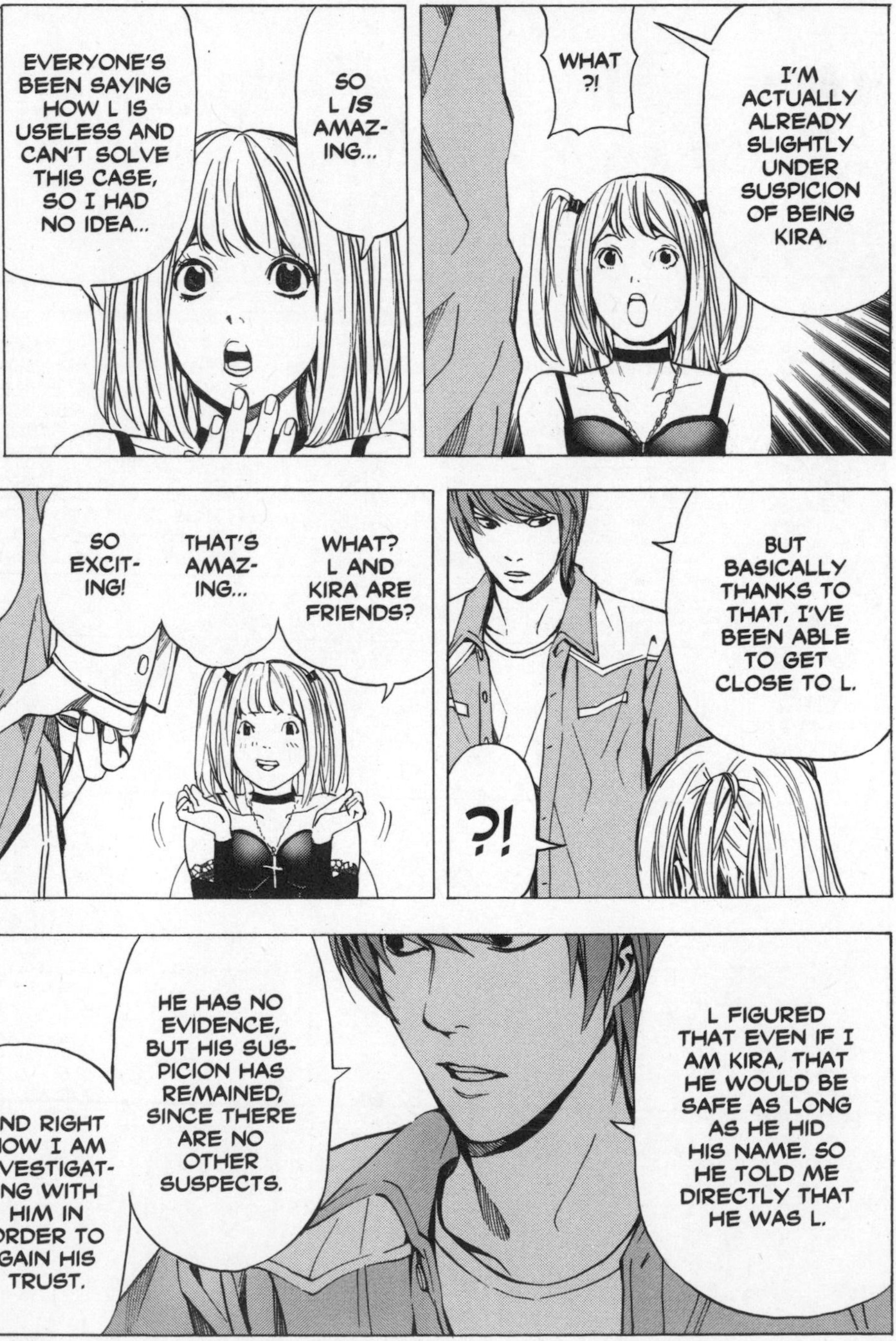
I'M ACTUALLY ALREADY SLIGHTLY UNDER SUSPICION OF BEING KIRA.
WHAT ?!
SO L *IS* AMAZING...
EVERYONE'S BEEN SAYING HOW L IS USELESS AND CAN'T SOLVE THIS CASE, SO I HAD NO IDEA...
BUT BASICALLY THANKS TO THAT, I'VE BEEN ABLE TO GET CLOSE TO L.
?!
WHAT? L AND KIRA ARE FRIENDS?
THAT'S AMAZING...
SO EXCITING!
...
L FIGURED THAT EVEN IF I AM KIRA, THAT HE WOULD BE SAFE AS LONG AS HE HID HIS NAME. SO HE TOLD ME DIRECTLY THAT HE WAS L.
HE HAS NO EVIDENCE, BUT HIS SUSPICION HAS REMAINED, SINCE THERE ARE NO OTHER SUSPECTS.
AND RIGHT NOW I AM INVESTIGATING WITH HIM IN ORDER TO GAIN HIS TRUST.

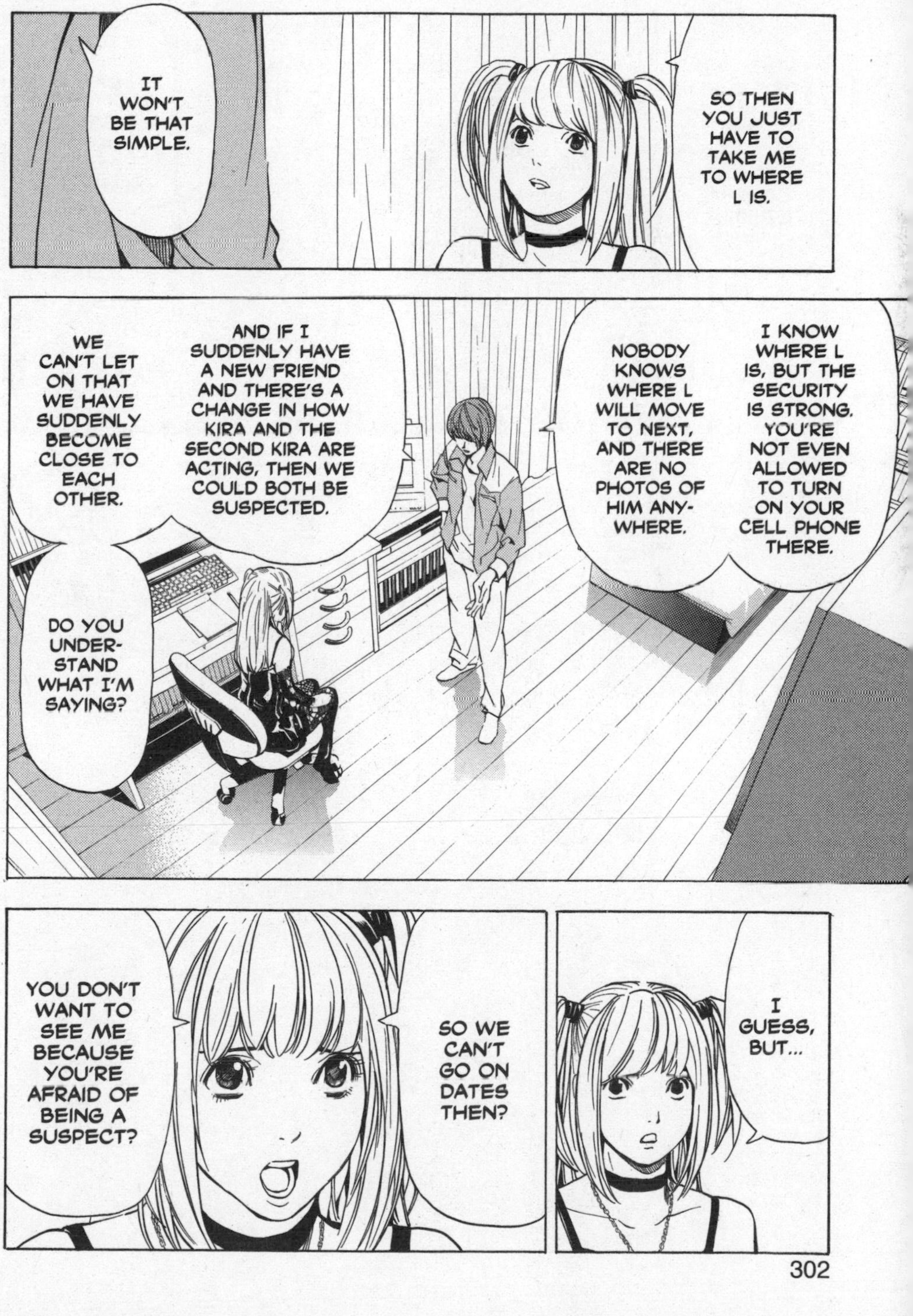
SO THEN YOU JUST HAVE TO TAKE ME TO WHERE L IS.
IT WON'T BE THAT SIMPLE.
I KNOW WHERE L IS, BUT THE SECURITY IS STRONG. YOU'RE NOT EVEN ALLOWED TO TURN ON YOUR CELL PHONE THERE.
NOBODY KNOWS WHERE L WILL MOVE TO NEXT, AND THERE ARE NO PHOTOS OF HIM ANY-WHERE.
AND IF I SUDDENLY HAVE A NEW FRIEND AND THERE'S A CHANGE IN HOW KIRA AND THE SECOND KIRA ARE ACTING, THEN WE COULD BOTH BE SUSPECTED.
WE CAN'T LET ON THAT WE HAVE SUDDENLY BECOME CLOSE TO EACH OTHER.
DO YOU UNDER-STAND WHAT I'M SAYING?
I GUESS, BUT...
SO WE CAN'T GO ON DATES THEN?
YOU DON'T WANT TO SEE ME BECAUSE YOU'RE AFRAID OF BEING A SUSPECT?

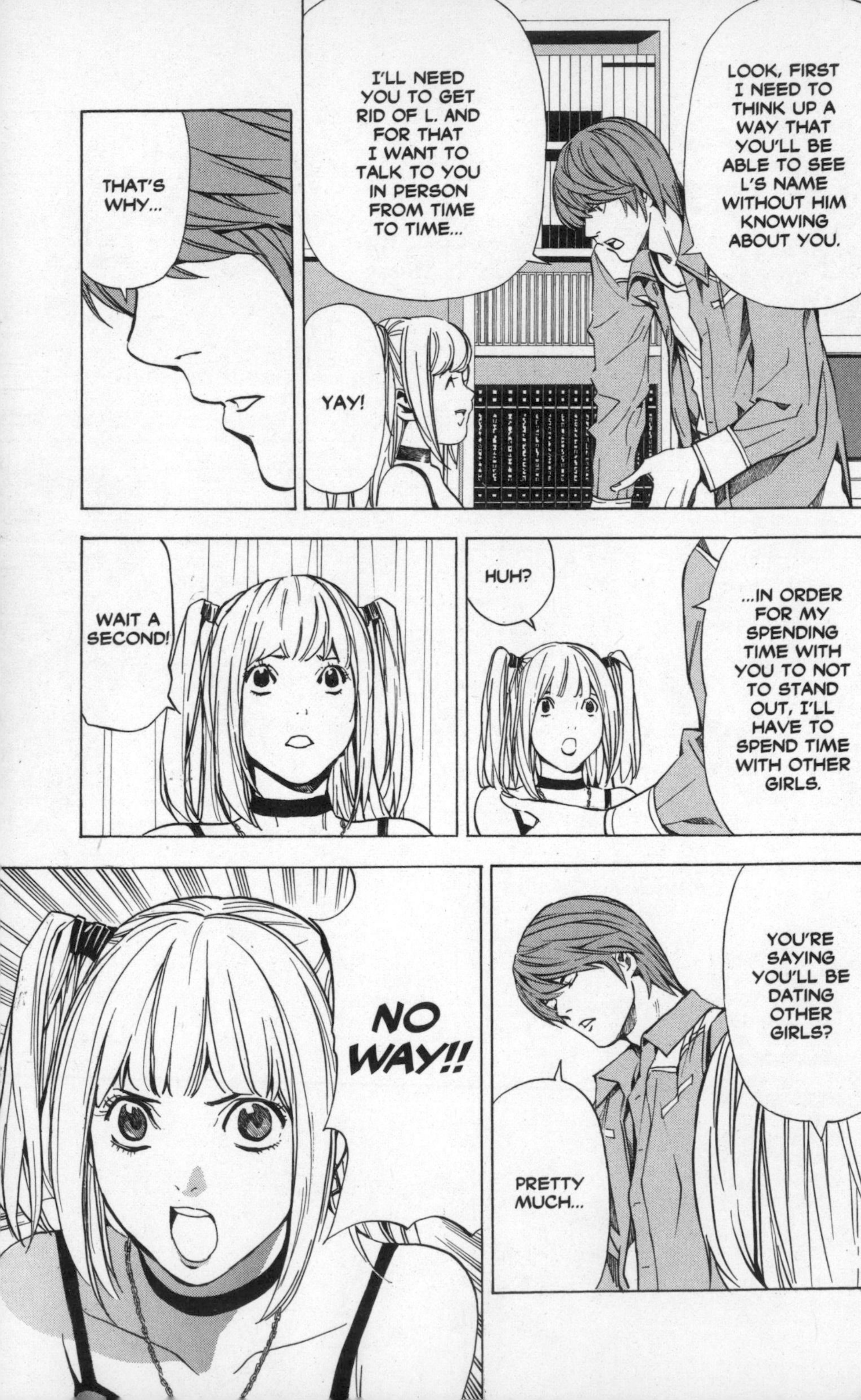
LOOK, FIRST I NEED TO THINK UP A WAY THAT YOU'LL BE ABLE TO SEE L'S NAME WITHOUT HIM KNOWING ABOUT YOU.
I'LL NEED YOU TO GET RID OF L. AND FOR THAT I WANT TO TALK TO YOU IN PERSON FROM TIME TO TIME...
YAY!
THAT'S WHY...
...IN ORDER FOR MY SPENDING TIME WITH YOU TO NOT TO STAND OUT, I'LL HAVE TO SPEND TIME WITH OTHER GIRLS.
HUH?
WAIT A SECOND!
YOU'RE SAYING YOU'LL BE DATING OTHER GIRLS?
PRETTY MUCH...
NO WAY!!

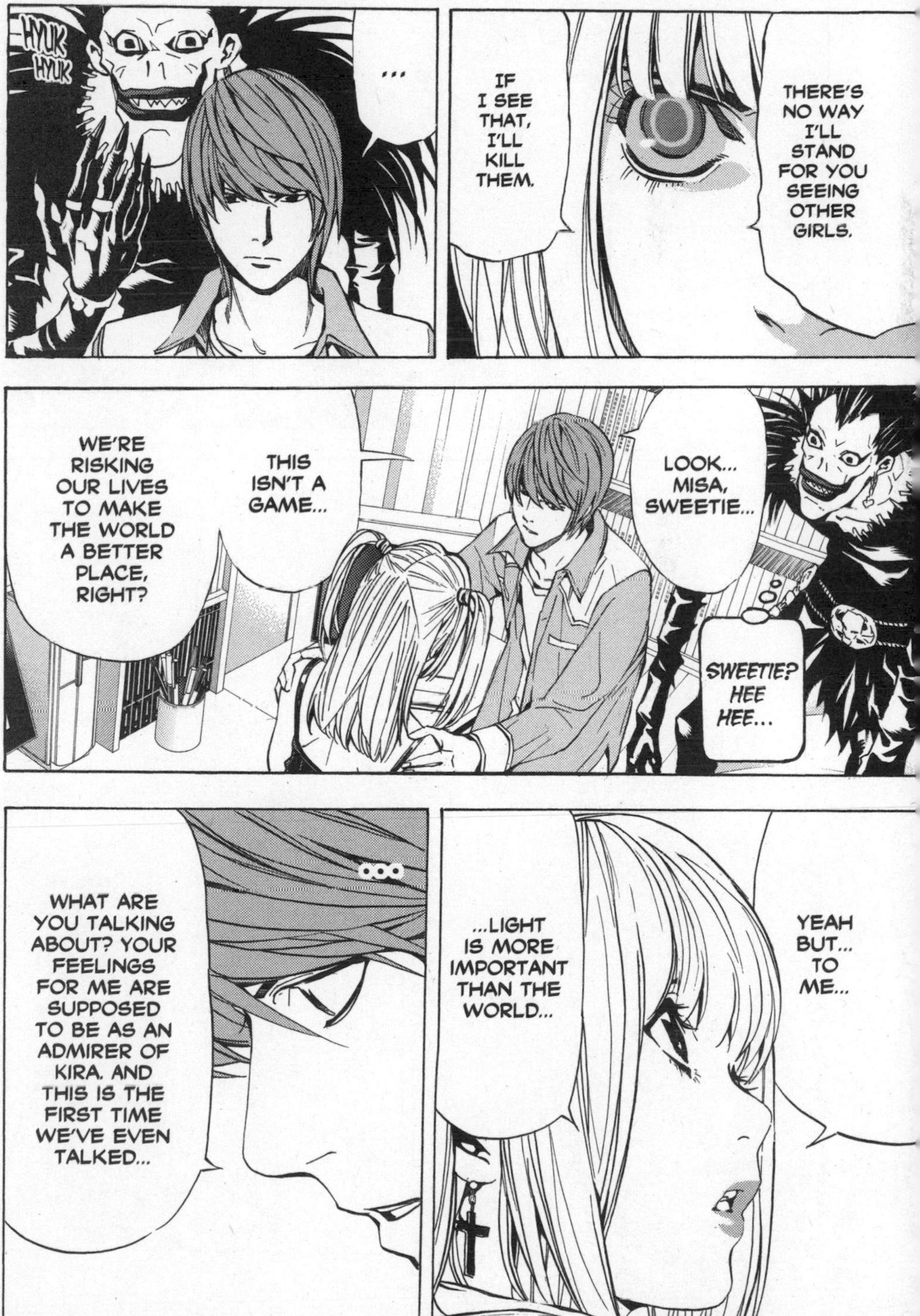
THERE'S NO WAY I'LL STAND FOR YOU SEEING OTHER GIRLS.
IF I SEE THAT, I'LL KILL THEM.
...
HYUK HYUK
LOOK... MISA, SWEETIE...
SWEETIE? HEE HEE...
THIS ISN'T A GAME...
WE'RE RISKING OUR LIVES TO MAKE THE WORLD A BETTER PLACE, RIGHT?
YEAH BUT... TO ME...
...LIGHT IS MORE IMPORTANT THAN THE WORLD...
WHAT ARE YOU TALKING ABOUT? YOUR FEELINGS FOR ME ARE SUPPOSED TO BE AS AN ADMIRER OF KIRA. AND THIS IS THE FIRST TIME WE'VE EVEN TALKED...

READ THIS WAY

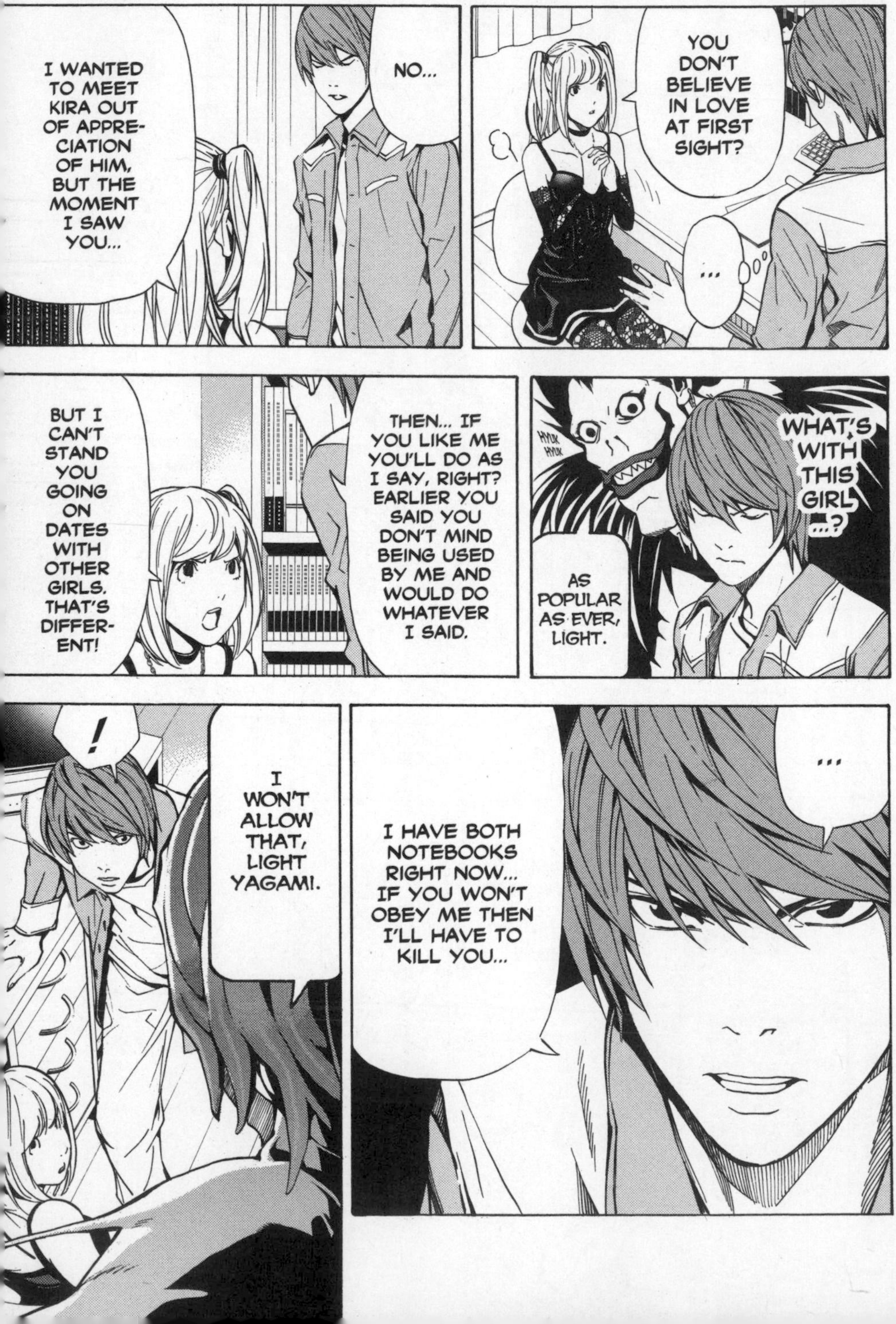
YOU DON'T BELIEVE IN LOVE AT FIRST SIGHT?
...
NO...
I WANTED TO MEET KIRA OUT OF APPRECIATION OF HIM, BUT THE MOMENT I SAW YOU...
WHAT'S WITH THIS GIRL ...?
HYUK HYUK
AS POPULAR AS EVER, LIGHT.
THEN... IF YOU LIKE ME YOU'LL DO AS I SAY, RIGHT? EARLIER YOU SAID YOU DON'T MIND BEING USED BY ME AND WOULD DO WHATEVER I SAID.
BUT I CAN'T STAND YOU GOING ON DATES WITH OTHER GIRLS. THAT'S DIFFERENT!
...
I HAVE BOTH NOTEBOOKS RIGHT NOW... IF YOU WON'T OBEY ME THEN I'LL HAVE TO KILL YOU...
!
I WON'T ALLOW THAT, LIGHT YAGAMI.

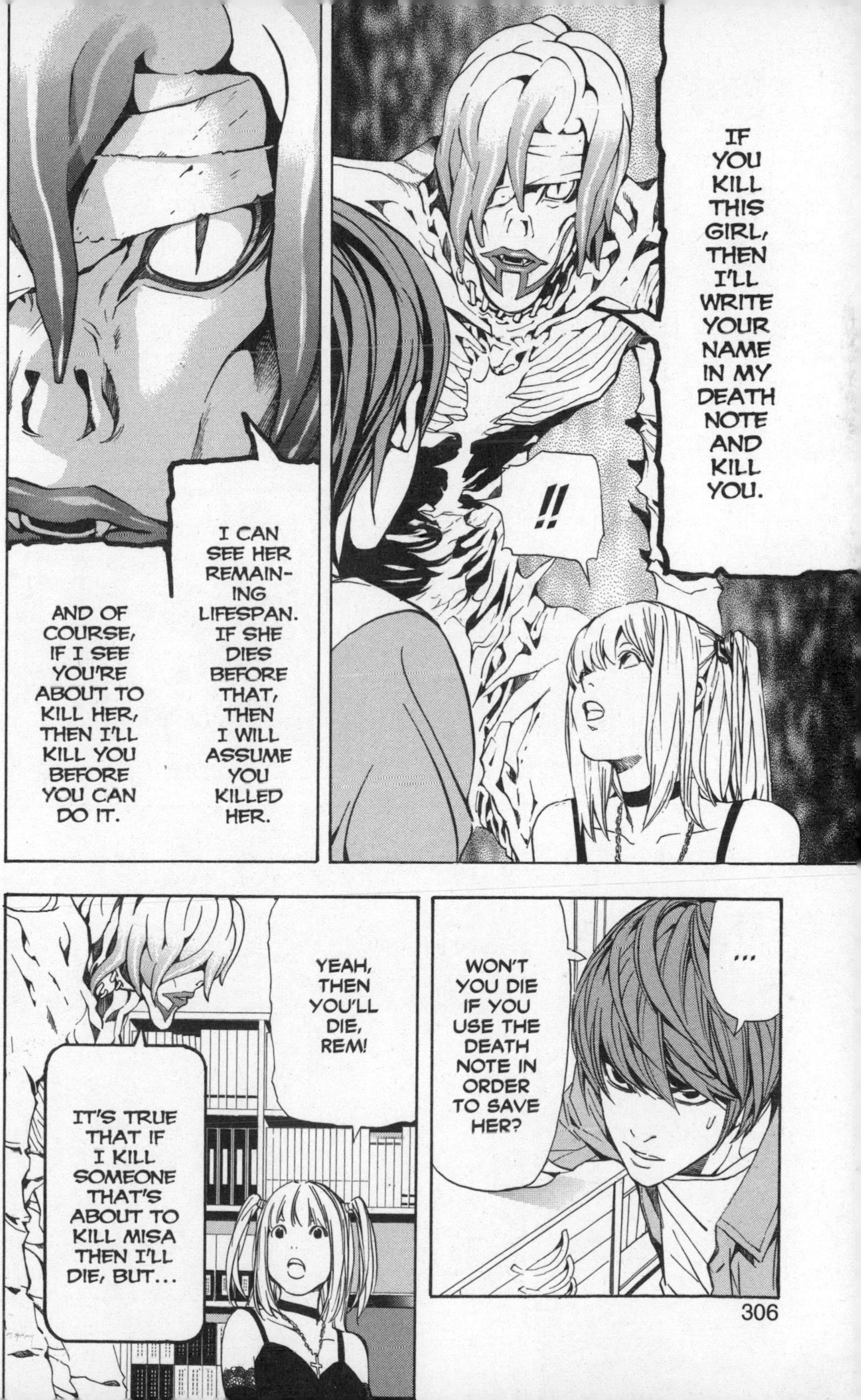
IF YOU KILL THIS GIRL, THEN I'LL WRITE YOUR NAME IN MY DEATH NOTE AND KILL YOU.
!!
I CAN SEE HER REMAINING-ING LIFESPAN. IF SHE DIES BEFORE THAT, THEN I WILL ASSUME YOU KILLED HER.
AND OF COURSE, IF I SEE YOU'RE ABOUT TO KILL HER, THEN I'LL KILL YOU BEFORE YOU CAN DO IT.
...
WON'T YOU DIE IF YOU USE THE DEATH NOTE IN ORDER TO SAVE HER?
YEAH, THEN YOU'LL DIE, REM!
IT'S TRUE THAT IF I KILL SOMEONE THAT'S ABOUT TO KILL MISA THEN I'LL DIE, BUT...

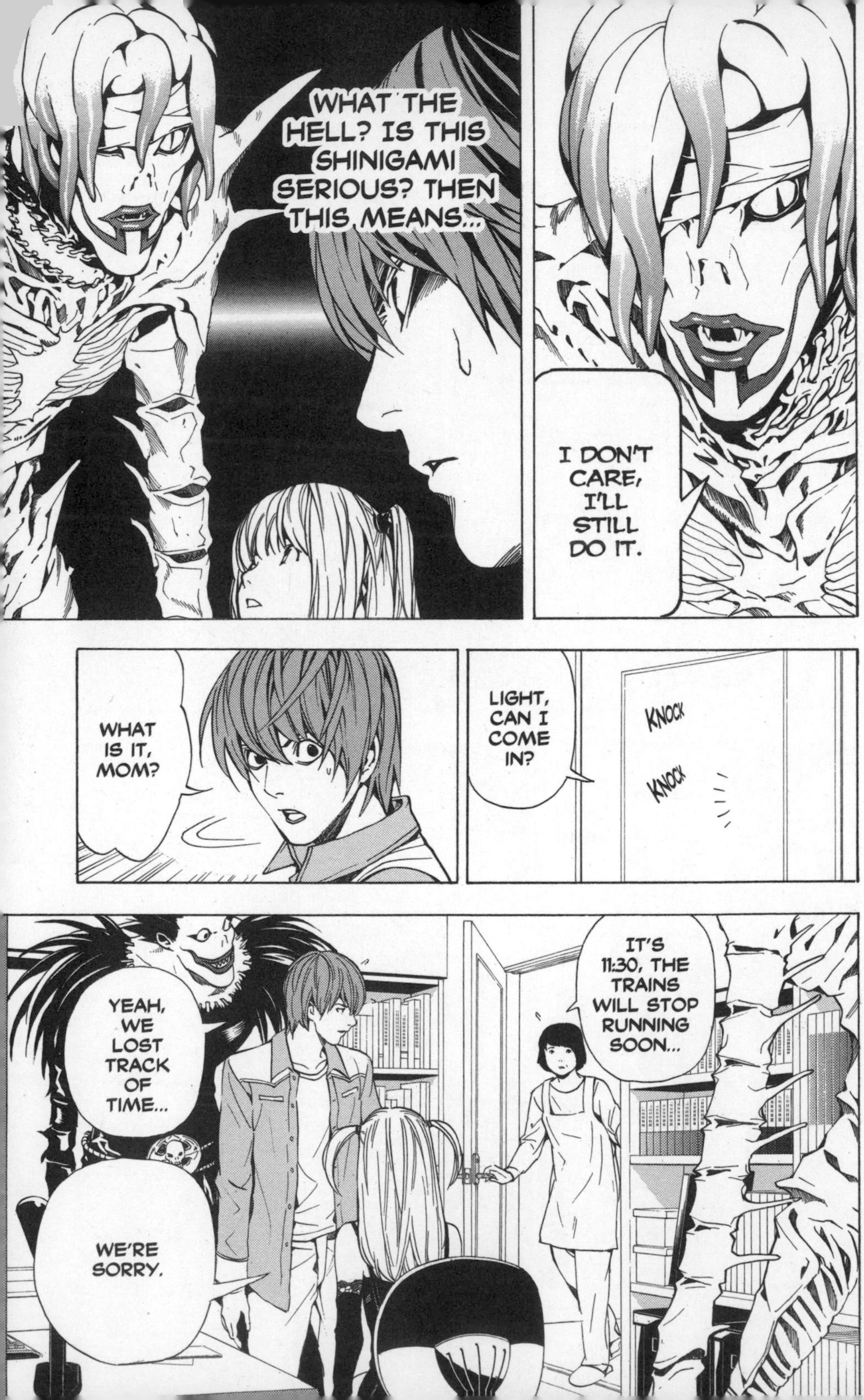
I DON'T CARE, I'LL STILL DO IT.
WHAT THE HELL? IS THIS SHINIGAMI SERIOUS? THEN THIS MEANS...
LIGHT, CAN I COME IN?
KNOCK
KNOCK
WHAT IS IT, MOM?
IT'S 11:30, THE TRAINS WILL STOP RUNNING SOON...
YEAH, WE LOST TRACK OF TIME...
WE'RE SORRY.

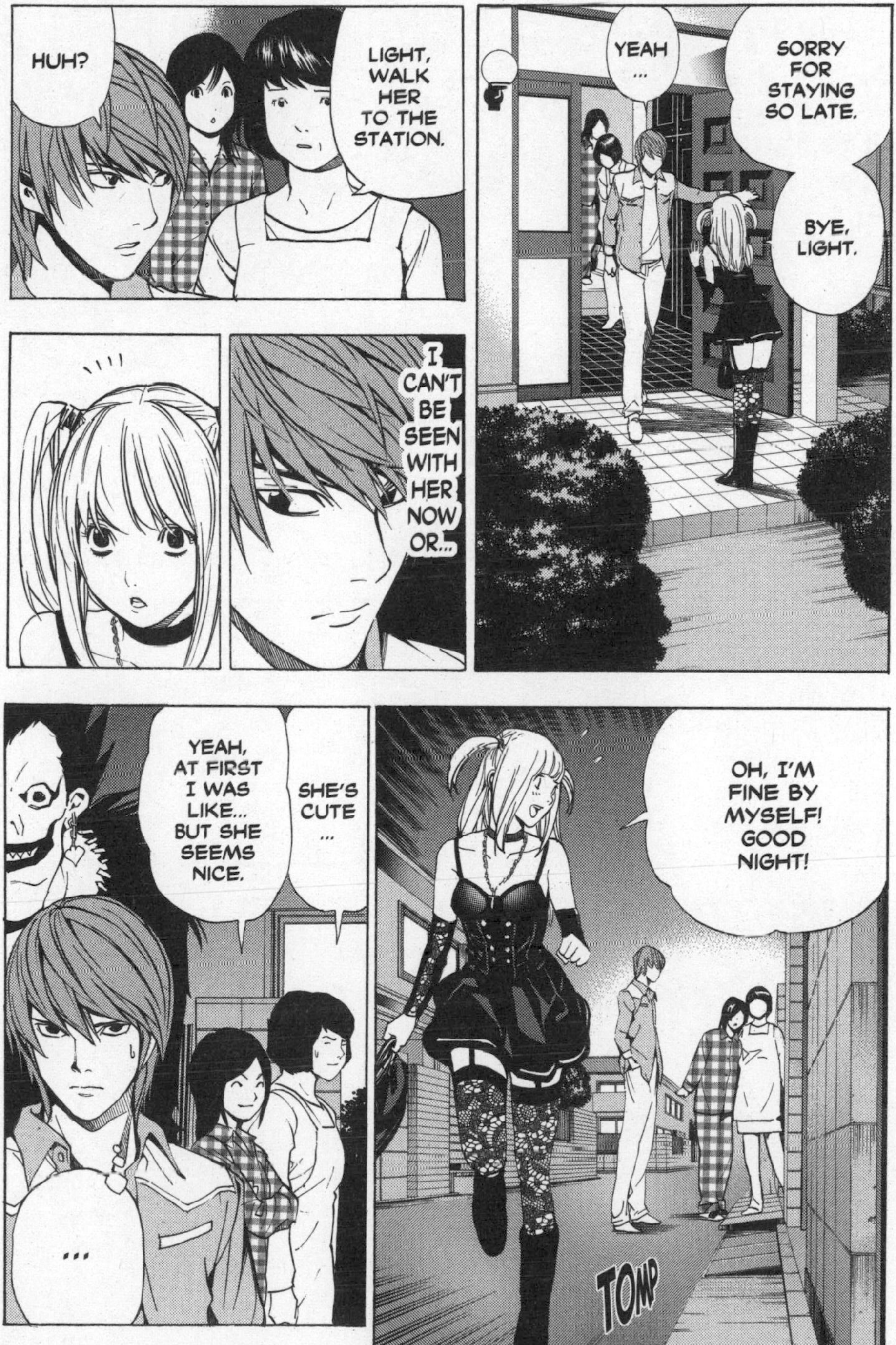
SORRY FOR STAYING SO LATE.
BYE, LIGHT.
YEAH ...
LIGHT, WALK HER TO THE STATION.
HUH?
I CAN'T BE SEEN WITH HER NOW OR...
OH, I'M FINE BY MYSELF! GOOD NIGHT!
TOMP
SHE'S CUTE ...
YEAH, AT FIRST I WAS LIKE... BUT SHE SEEMS NICE.
...

READ THIS WAY

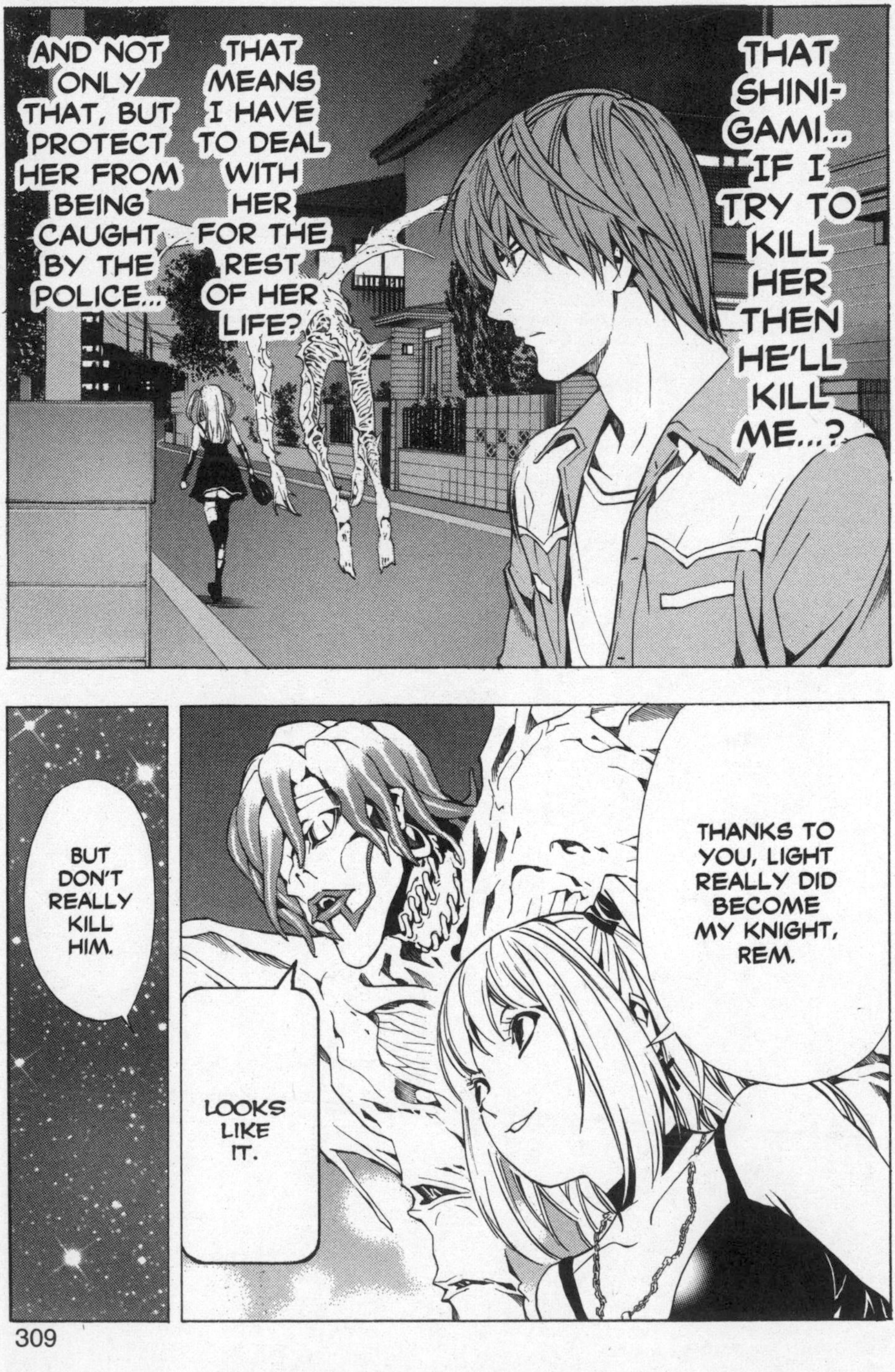
THAT SHINI-GAMI... IF I TRY TO KILL HER THEN HE'LL KILL ME...?
THAT MEANS I HAVE TO DEAL WITH HER FOR THE REST OF HER LIFE?
AND NOT ONLY THAT, BUT PROTECT HER FROM BEING CAUGHT BY THE POLICE...
THANKS TO YOU, LIGHT REALLY DID BECOME MY KNIGHT, REM.
LOOKS LIKE IT.
BUT DON'T REALLY KILL HIM.

DEATH NOTE
How to use it
XX

- In order to see the names and life spans of humans by using the eye power of the god of death, the owner must look at more than half of that person's face. When looking from top to bottom, he must look at least from the head to the nose. If he looks at only the eyes and under, he will not be able to see the person's name and life span. Also, even though some parts of the face, for example the eyes, nose or mouth are hidden, if he can basically see the whole face, he will be able to see the person's name and life span. It is still not clear how much exposure is needed to tell the name and life span, and this needs to be verified.

死神の目で人間の名前・寿命を見るには、その人間の顔の左右の半分以上を見なければならず、上下の場合は頭から鼻まで見る必要があり、目より下だけを見ても名前・寿命は見えない。また、顔の一部、目・鼻・口等が隠れていても顔全体が見えていれば、名前・寿命を見る事ができる。隠された部分が顔の何％を占めると名前・寿命が見えなくなるかは検証していくしかない。

- If above conditions are met, names and life spans can be seen through photos and pictures, no matter how old they are. But this is sometimes influenced by the vividness and size. Also, names and life spans cannot be seen by face drawings, however realistic they may be.

上記の条件をクリアーしていれば、どんなに過去の物であろうと写真や映像でも名前・寿命を見る事ができるが、写真・映像の場合はその大きさや鮮明度で見えない事がある。また、どんなに写実であろうとも顔の絵では名前や寿命は見えない。

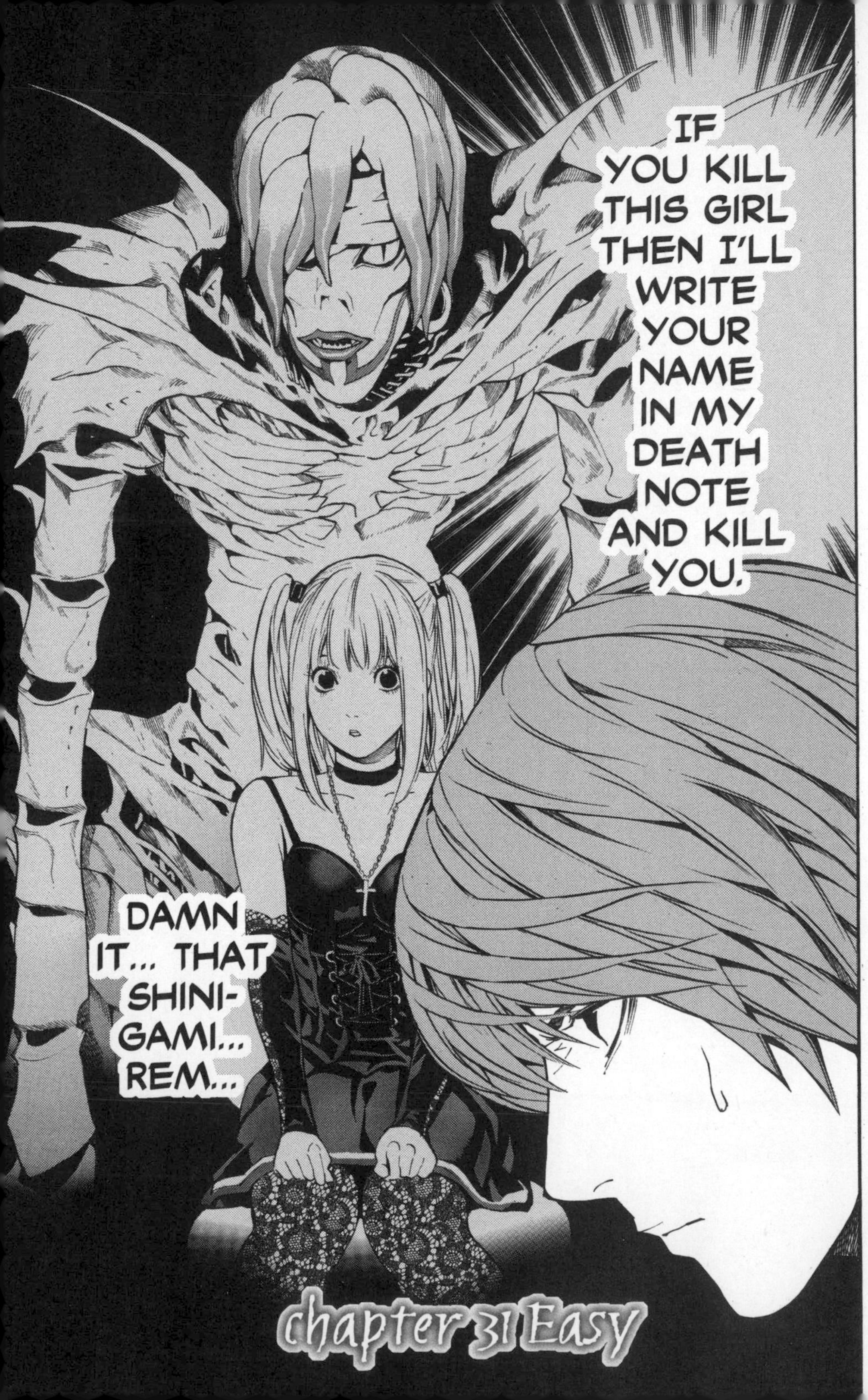
IF YOU KILL THIS GIRL THEN I'LL WRITE YOUR NAME IN MY DEATH NOTE AND KILL YOU.
DAMN IT... THAT SHINI-GAMI... REM...
chapter 31 Easy

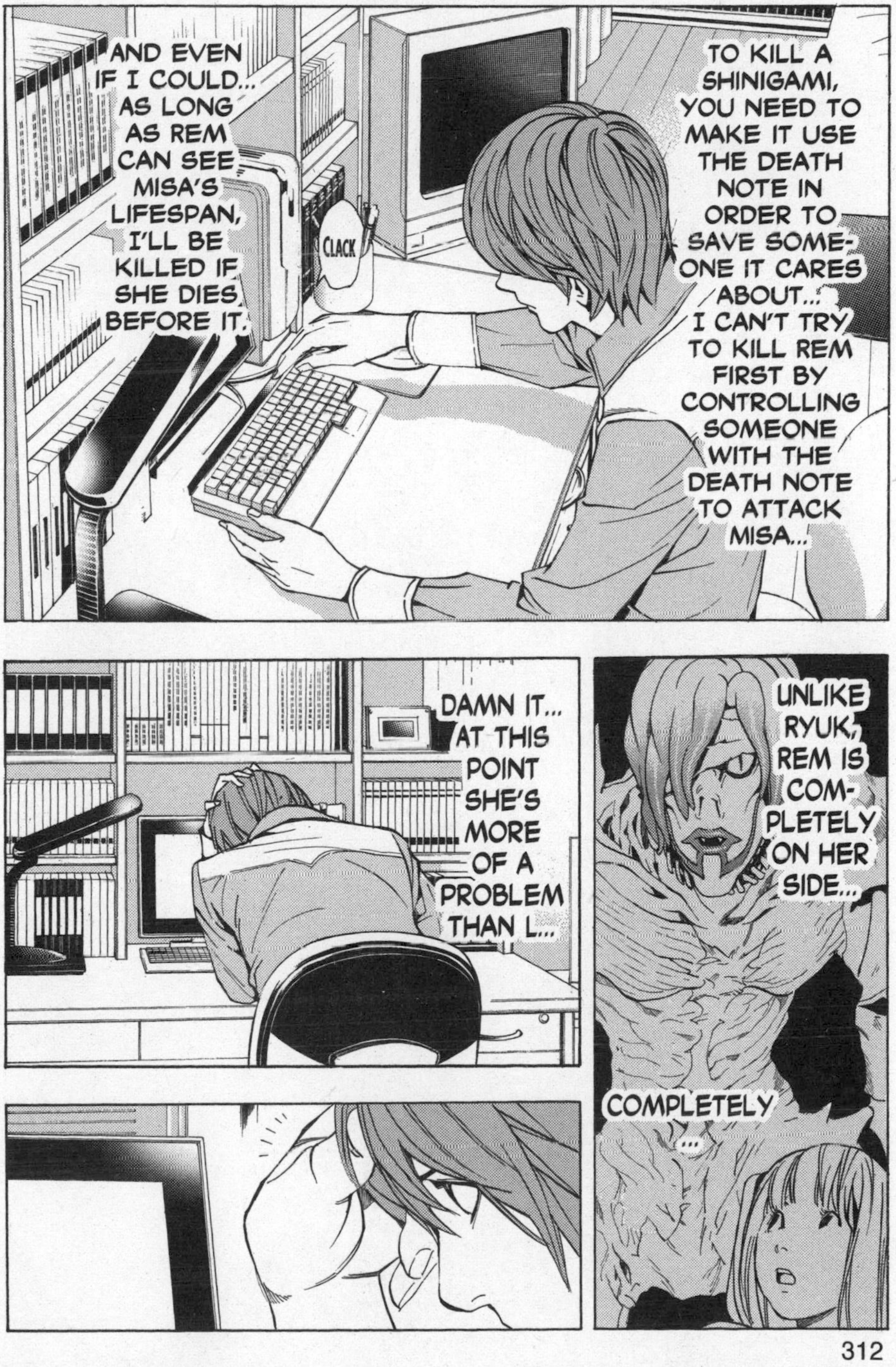
TO KILL A SHINIGAMI, YOU NEED TO MAKE IT USE THE DEATH NOTE IN ORDER TO SAVE SOME-ONE IT CARES ABOUT... I CAN'T TRY TO KILL REM FIRST BY CONTROLLING SOMEONE WITH THE DEATH NOTE TO ATTACK MISA...
AND EVEN IF I COULD... AS LONG AS REM CAN SEE MISA'S LIFESPAN, I'LL BE KILLED IF SHE DIES BEFORE IT.
CLACK
UNLIKE RYUK, REM IS COM-PLETELY ON HER SIDE...
COMPLETELY ...
DAMN IT... AT THIS POINT SHE'S MORE OF A PROBLEM THAN L...

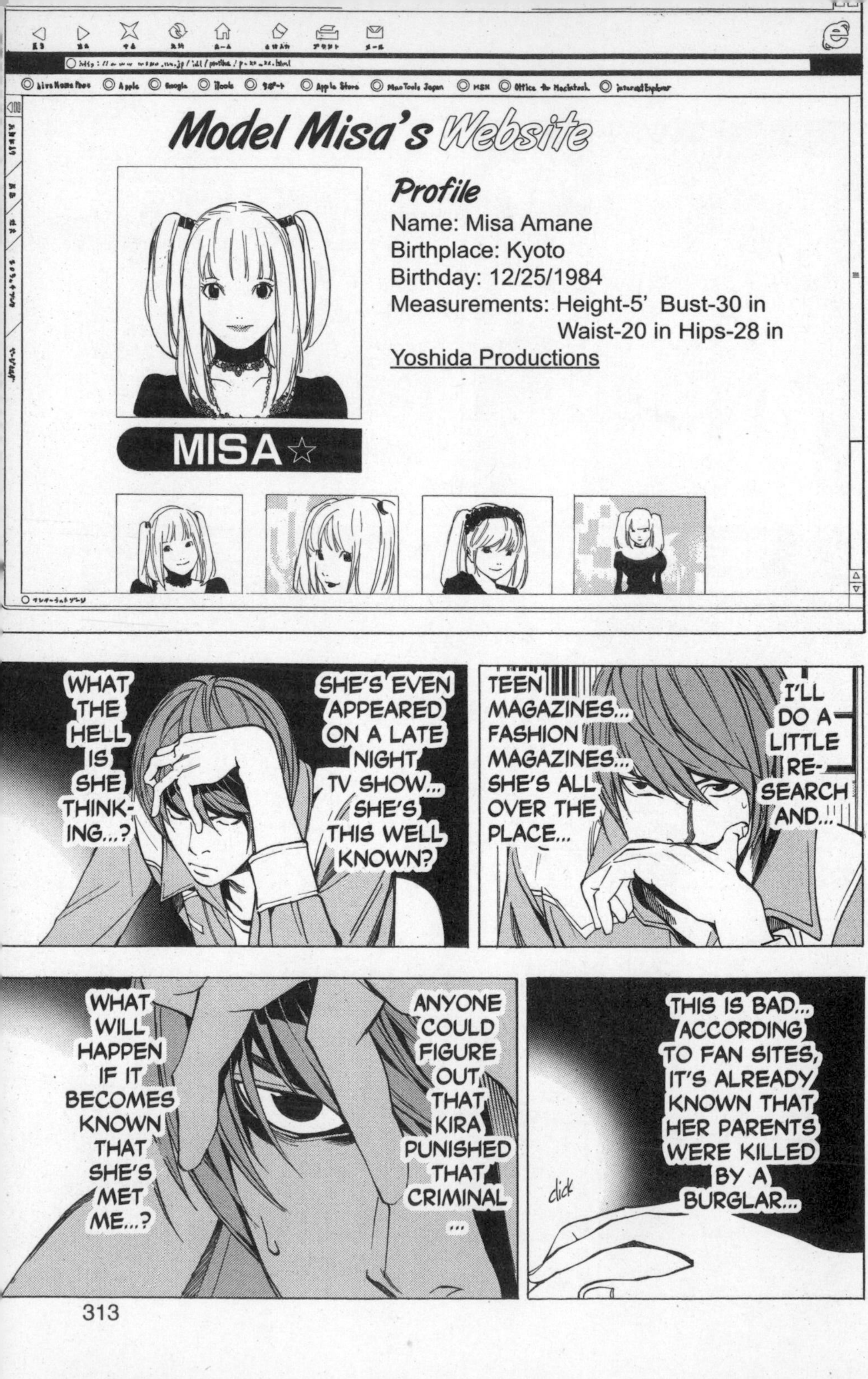
Model Misa's Website
Profile
Name: Misa Amane
Birthplace: Kyoto
Birthday: 12/25/1984
Measurements: Height-5' Bust-30 in Waist-20 in Hips-28 in
Yoshida Productions
MISA☆
I'LL DO A LITTLE RE-SEARCH AND...
TEEN MAGAZINES... FASHION MAGAZINES... SHE'S ALL OVER THE PLACE...
SHE'S EVEN APPEARED ON A LATE NIGHT TV SHOW... SHE'S THIS WELL KNOWN?
WHAT THE HELL IS SHE THINK-ING...?
THIS IS BAD... ACCORDING TO FAN SITES, IT'S ALREADY KNOWN THAT HER PARENTS WERE KILLED BY A BURGLAR...
click
ANYONE COULD FIGURE OUT THAT KIRA PUNISHED THAT CRIMINAL ...
WHAT WILL HAPPEN IF IT BECOMES KNOWN THAT SHE'S MET ME...?

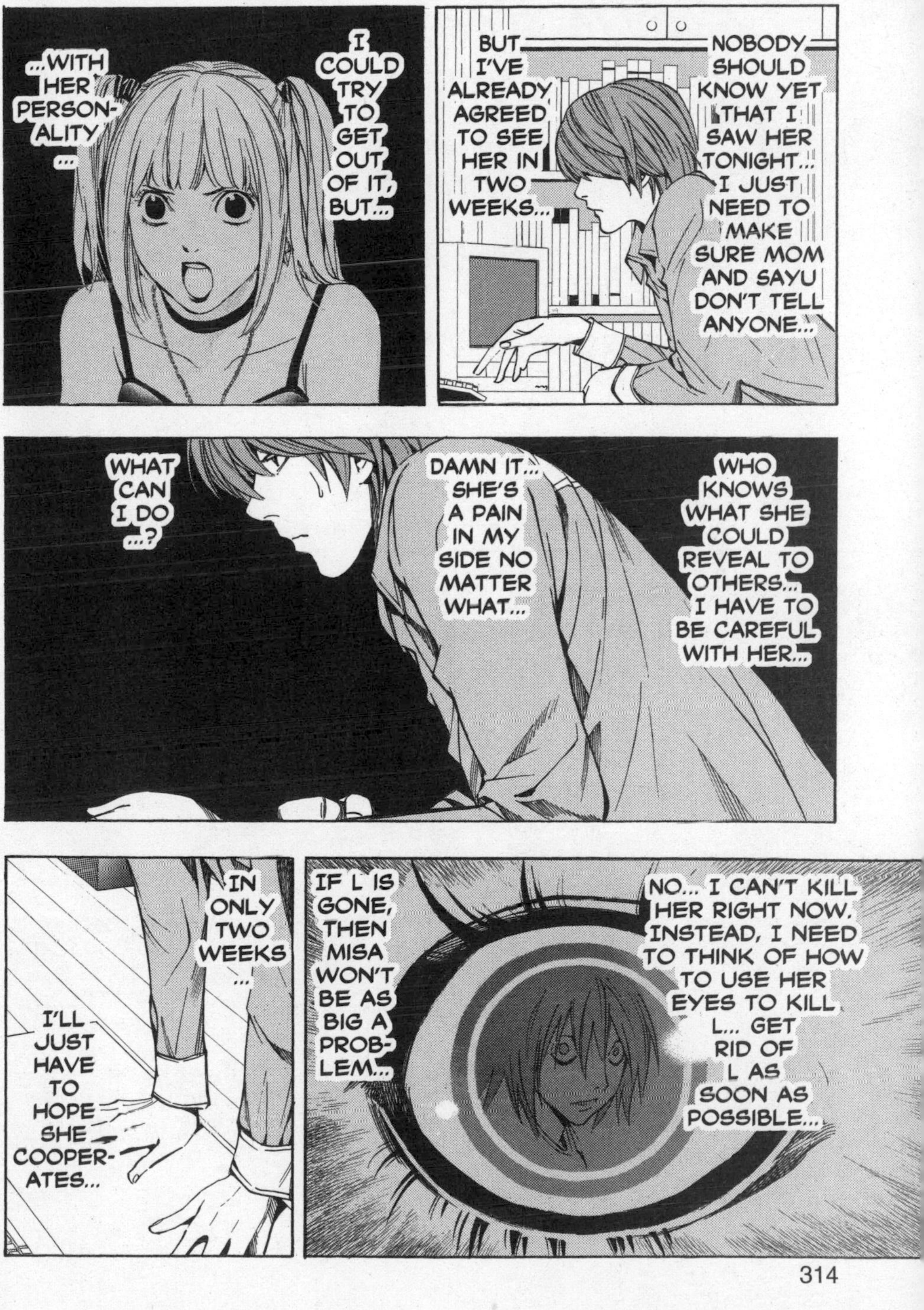
NOBODY SHOULD KNOW YET THAT I SAW HER TONIGHT... I JUST NEED TO MAKE SURE MOM AND SAYU DON'T TELL ANYONE...
BUT I'VE ALREADY AGREED TO SEE HER IN TWO WEEKS...
I COULD TRY TO GET OUT OF IT, BUT...
...WITH HER PERSON-ALITY...
WHO KNOWS WHAT SHE COULD REVEAL TO OTHERS... I HAVE TO BE CAREFUL WITH HER...
DAMN IT... SHE'S A PAIN IN MY SIDE NO MATTER WHAT...
WHAT CAN I DO...?
NO... I CAN'T KILL HER RIGHT NOW. INSTEAD, I NEED TO THINK OF HOW TO USE HER EYES TO KILL L... GET RID OF L AS SOON AS POSSIBLE...
IF L IS GONE, THEN MISA WON'T BE AS BIG A PROB-LEM...
IN ONLY TWO WEEKS...
I'LL JUST HAVE TO HOPE SHE COOPER-ATES...

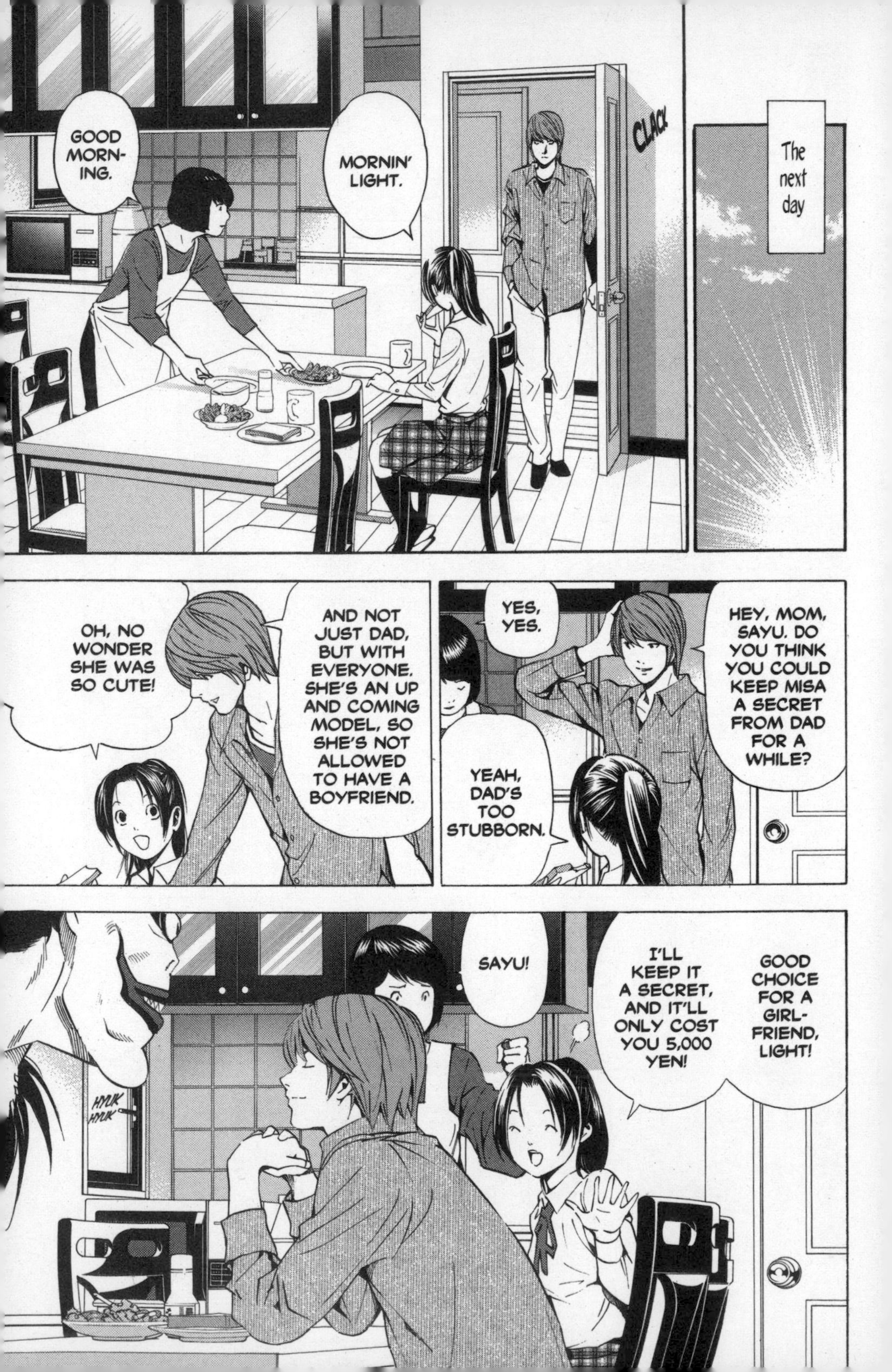
The next day
CLACK
MORNIN' LIGHT.
GOOD MORNING.
HEY, MOM, SAYU. DO YOU THINK YOU COULD KEEP MISA A SECRET FROM DAD FOR A WHILE?
YES, YES.
YEAH, DAD'S TOO STUBBORN.
AND NOT JUST DAD, BUT WITH EVERYONE. SHE'S AN UP AND COMING MODEL, SO SHE'S NOT ALLOWED TO HAVE A BOYFRIEND.
OH, NO WONDER SHE WAS SO CUTE!
GOOD CHOICE FOR A GIRLFRIEND, LIGHT!
I'LL KEEP IT A SECRET, AND IT'LL ONLY COST YOU 5,000 YEN!
SAYU!
HYUK HYUK

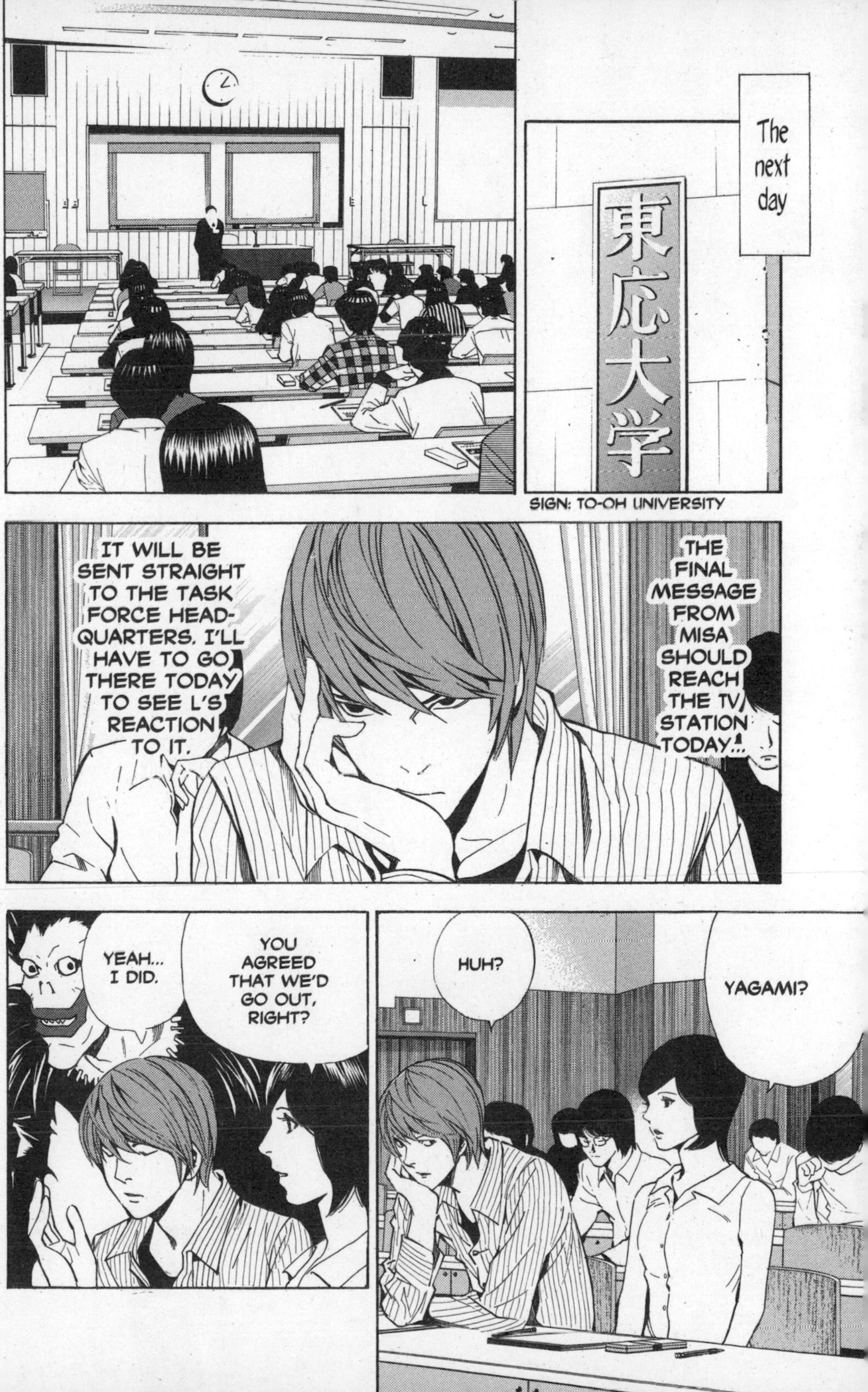
The next day
東応大学
SIGN: TO-OH UNIVERSITY
THE FINAL MESSAGE FROM MISA SHOULD REACH THE TV STATION TODAY...
IT WILL BE SENT STRAIGHT TO THE TASK FORCE HEAD-QUARTERS. I'LL HAVE TO GO THERE TODAY TO SEE L'S REACTION TO IT.
YAGAMI?
HUH?
YOU AGREED THAT WE'D GO OUT, RIGHT?
YEAH... I DID.

READ THIS WAY

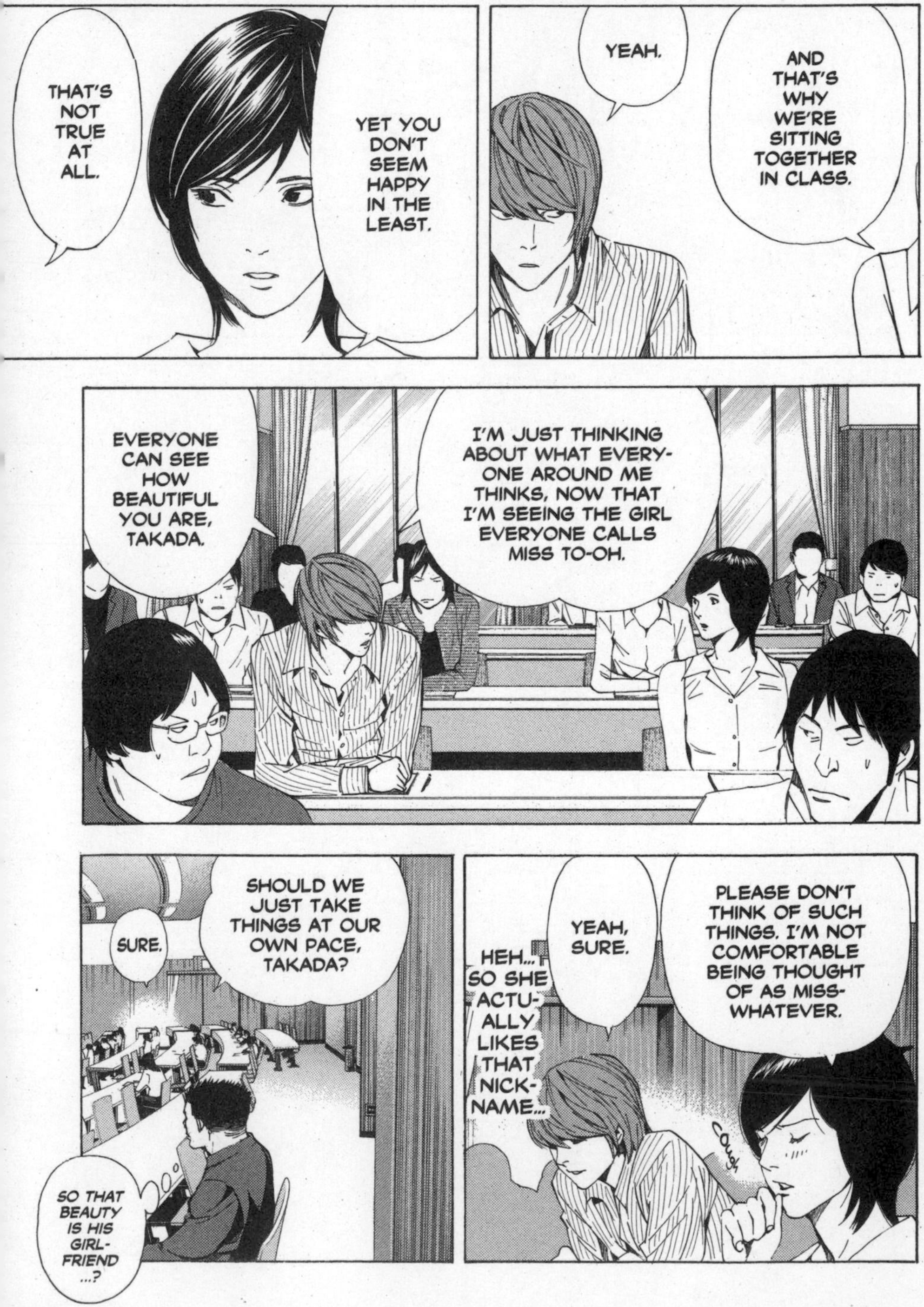
AND THAT'S WHY WE'RE SITTING TOGETHER IN CLASS.
YEAH.
YET YOU DON'T SEEM HAPPY IN THE LEAST.
THAT'S NOT TRUE AT ALL.
I'M JUST THINKING ABOUT WHAT EVERY-ONE AROUND ME THINKS, NOW THAT I'M SEEING THE GIRL EVERYONE CALLS MISS TO-OH.
EVERYONE CAN SEE HOW BEAUTIFUL YOU ARE, TAKADA.
PLEASE DON'T THINK OF SUCH THINGS. I'M NOT COMFORTABLE BEING THOUGHT OF AS MISS-WHATEVER.
YEAH, SURE.
HEH... SO SHE ACTU-ALLY LIKES THAT NICK-NAME...
COUGH
SHOULD WE JUST TAKE THINGS AT OUR OWN PACE, TAKADA?
SURE.
SO THAT BEAUTY IS HIS GIRL-FRIEND ...?

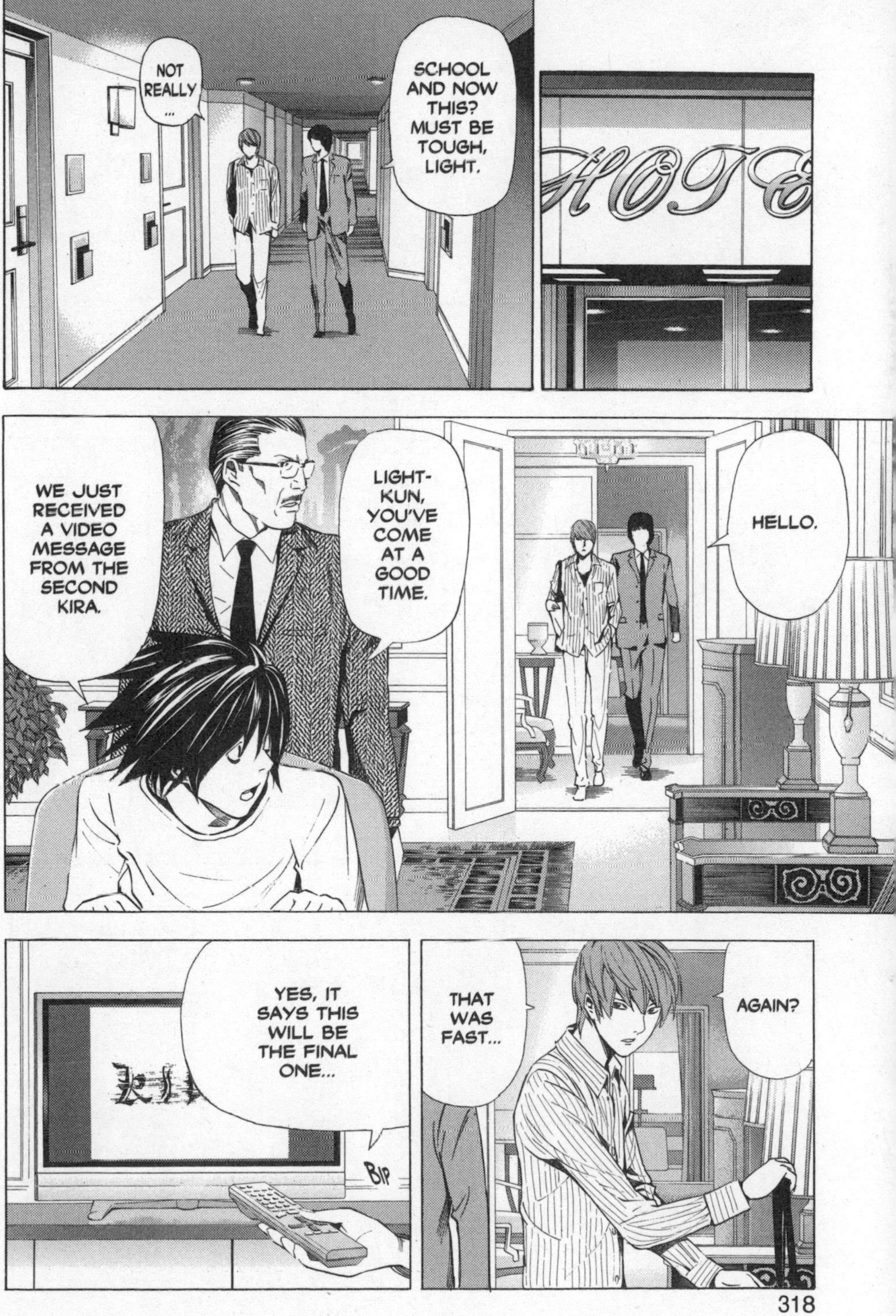
HOTE
SCHOOL AND NOW THIS? MUST BE TOUGH, LIGHT.
NOT REALLY...
HELLO.
LIGHT-KUN, YOU'VE COME AT A GOOD TIME.
WE JUST RECEIVED A VIDEO MESSAGE FROM THE SECOND KIRA.
AGAIN?
THAT WAS FAST...
YES, IT SAYS THIS WILL BE THE FINAL ONE...
BIP

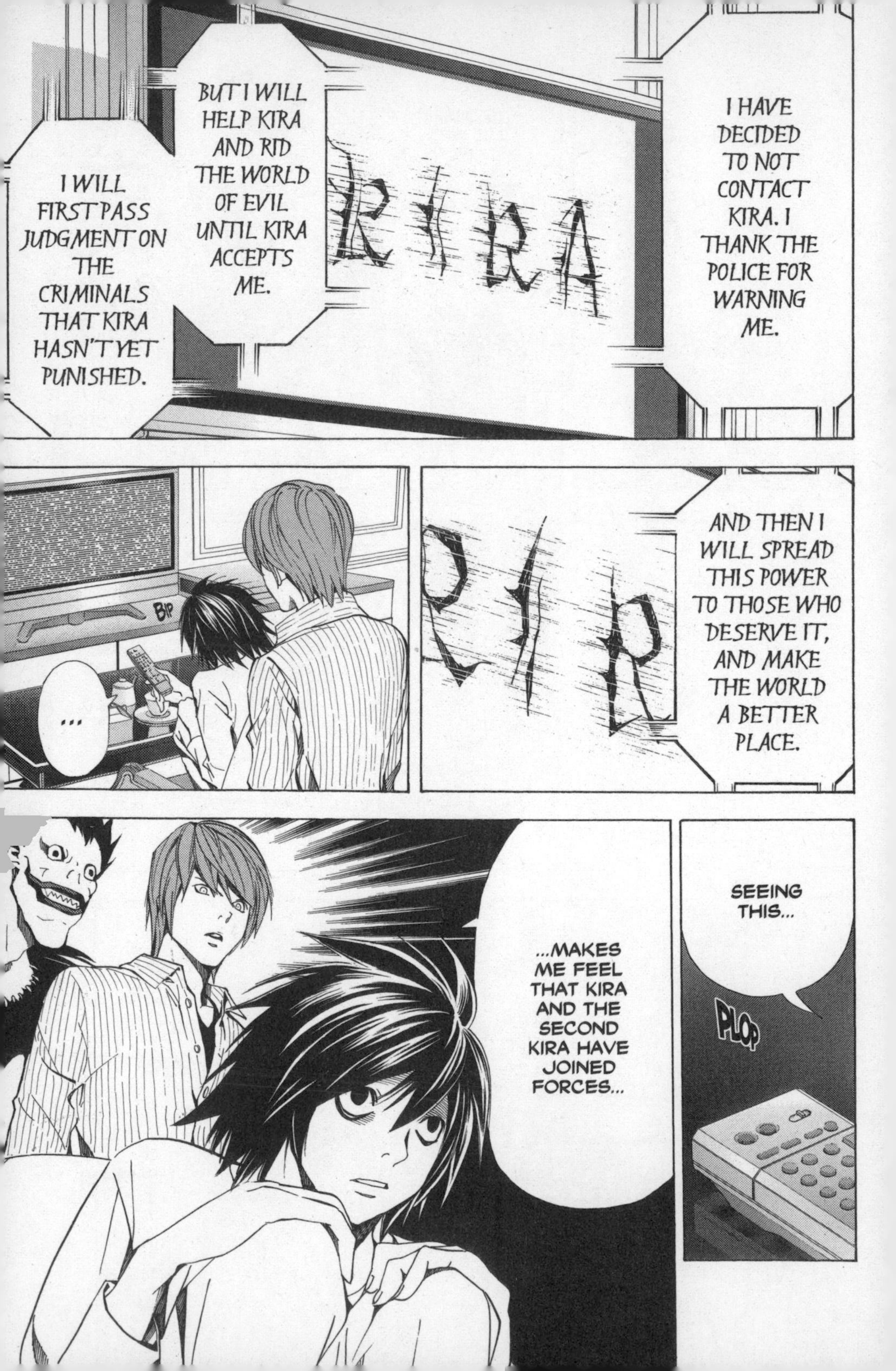
I HAVE DECIDED TO NOT CONTACT KIRA. I THANK THE POLICE FOR WARNING ME.
KIRA
BUT I WILL HELP KIRA AND RID THE WORLD OF EVIL UNTIL KIRA ACCEPTS ME.
I WILL FIRST PASS JUDGMENT ON THE CRIMINALS THAT KIRA HASN'T YET PUNISHED.
AND THEN I WILL SPREAD THIS POWER TO THOSE WHO DESERVE IT, AND MAKE THE WORLD A BETTER PLACE.
RIP
BIP
...
SEEING THIS...
PLOP
...MAKES ME FEEL THAT KIRA AND THE SECOND KIRA HAVE JOINED FORCES...

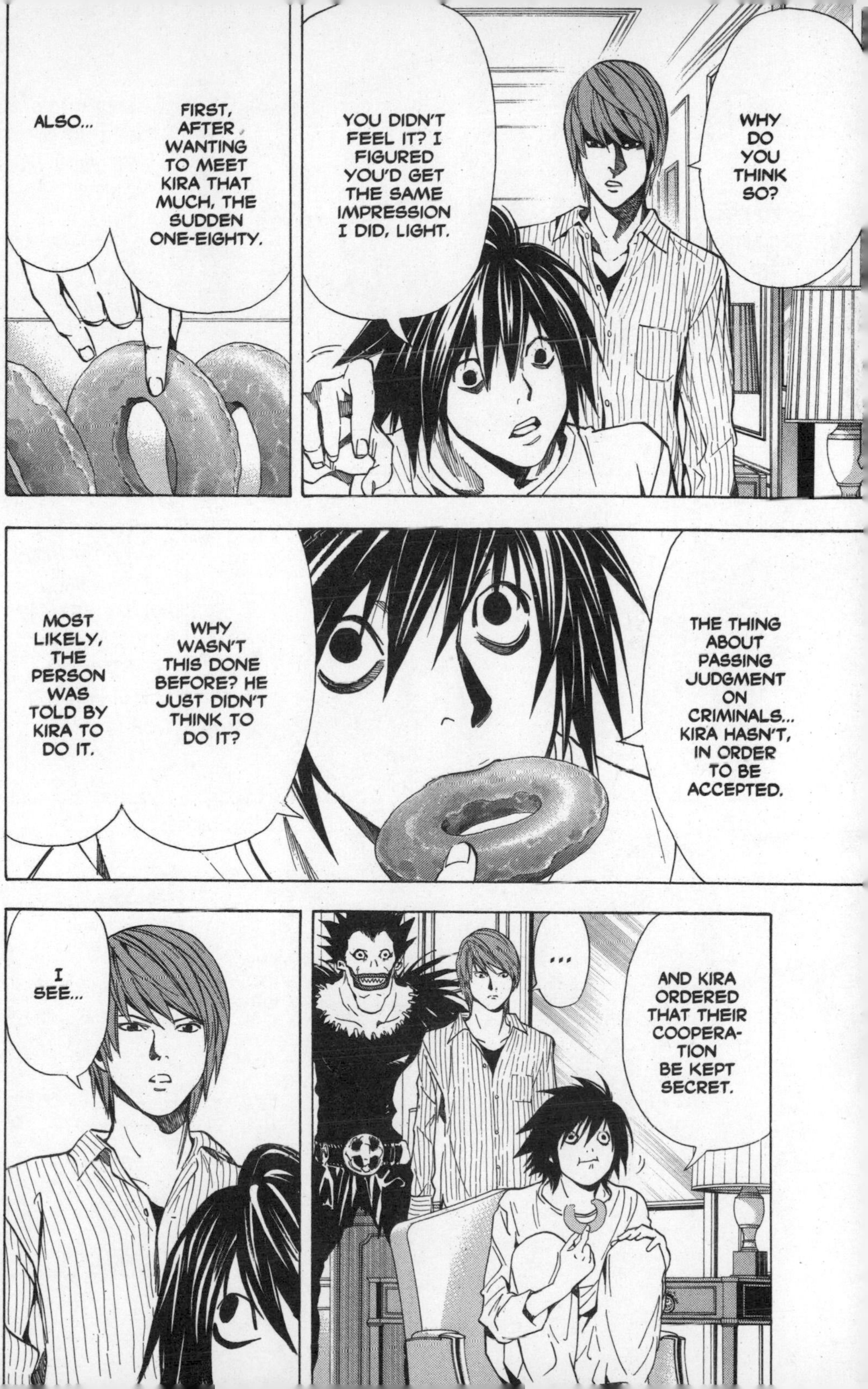
WHY DO YOU THINK SO?
YOU DIDN'T FEEL IT? I FIGURED YOU'D GET THE SAME IMPRESSION I DID, LIGHT.
FIRST, AFTER WANTING TO MEET KIRA THAT MUCH, THE SUDDEN ONE-EIGHTY.
ALSO...
THE THING ABOUT PASSING JUDGMENT ON CRIMINALS... KIRA HASN'T, IN ORDER TO BE ACCEPTED.
WHY WASN'T THIS DONE BEFORE? HE JUST DIDN'T THINK TO DO IT?
MOST LIKELY, THE PERSON WAS TOLD BY KIRA TO DO IT.
AND KIRA ORDERED THAT THEIR COOPERATION BE KEPT SECRET.
...
I SEE...

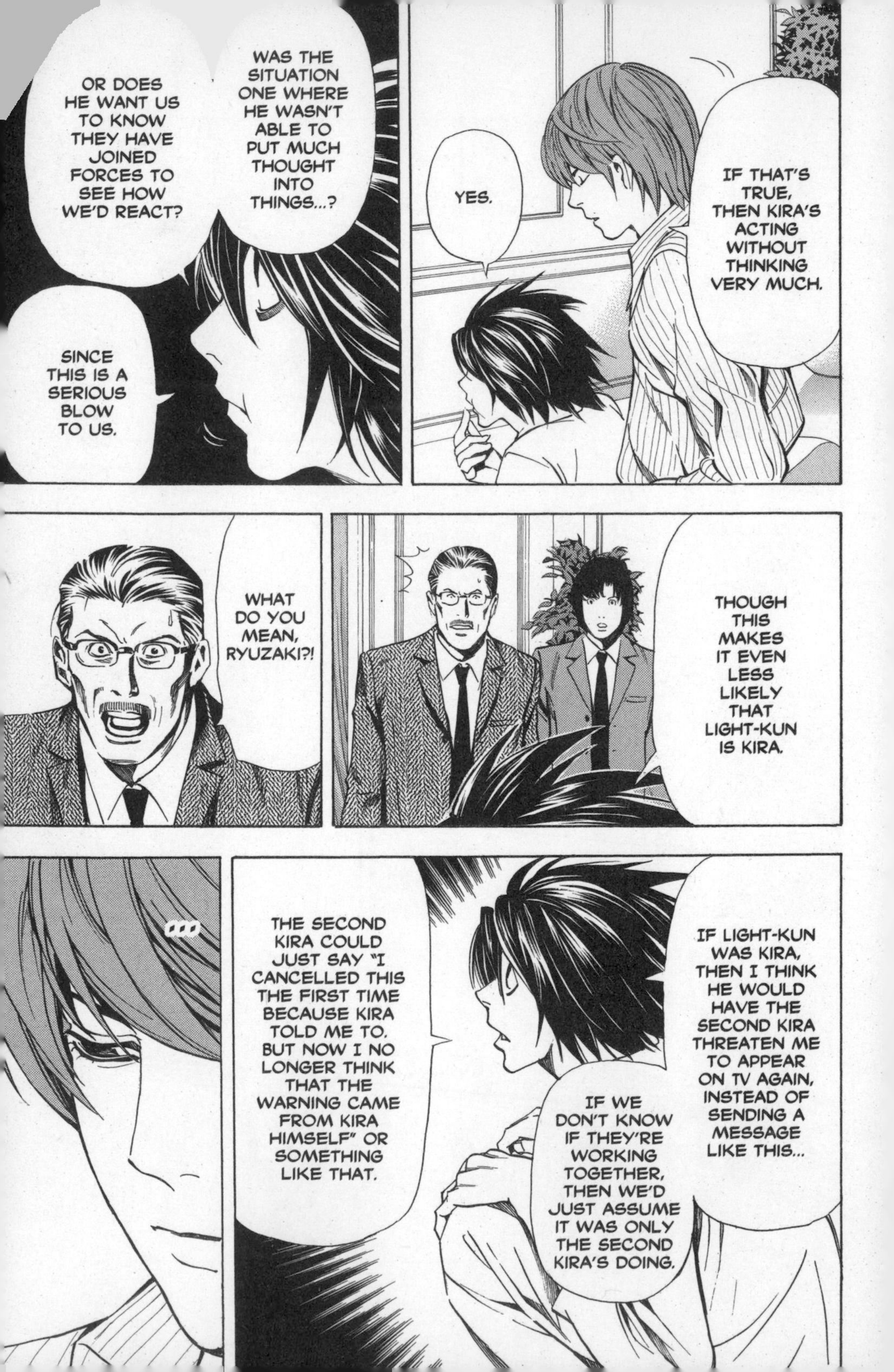
IF THAT'S TRUE, THEN KIRA'S ACTING WITHOUT THINKING VERY MUCH.
YES.
WAS THE SITUATION ONE WHERE HE WASN'T ABLE TO PUT MUCH THOUGHT INTO THINGS...?
OR DOES HE WANT US TO KNOW THEY HAVE JOINED FORCES TO SEE HOW WE'D REACT?
SINCE THIS IS A SERIOUS BLOW TO US.
THOUGH THIS MAKES IT EVEN LESS LIKELY THAT LIGHT-KUN IS KIRA.
WHAT DO YOU MEAN, RYUZAKI?!
IF LIGHT-KUN WAS KIRA, THEN I THINK HE WOULD HAVE THE SECOND KIRA THREATEN ME TO APPEAR ON TV AGAIN, INSTEAD OF SENDING A MESSAGE LIKE THIS...
IF WE DON'T KNOW IF THEY'RE WORKING TOGETHER, THEN WE'D JUST ASSUME IT WAS ONLY THE SECOND KIRA'S DOING.
THE SECOND KIRA COULD JUST SAY "I CANCELLED THIS THE FIRST TIME BECAUSE KIRA TOLD ME TO. BUT NOW I NO LONGER THINK THAT THE WARNING CAME FROM KIRA HIMSELF" OR SOMETHING LIKE THAT.
...

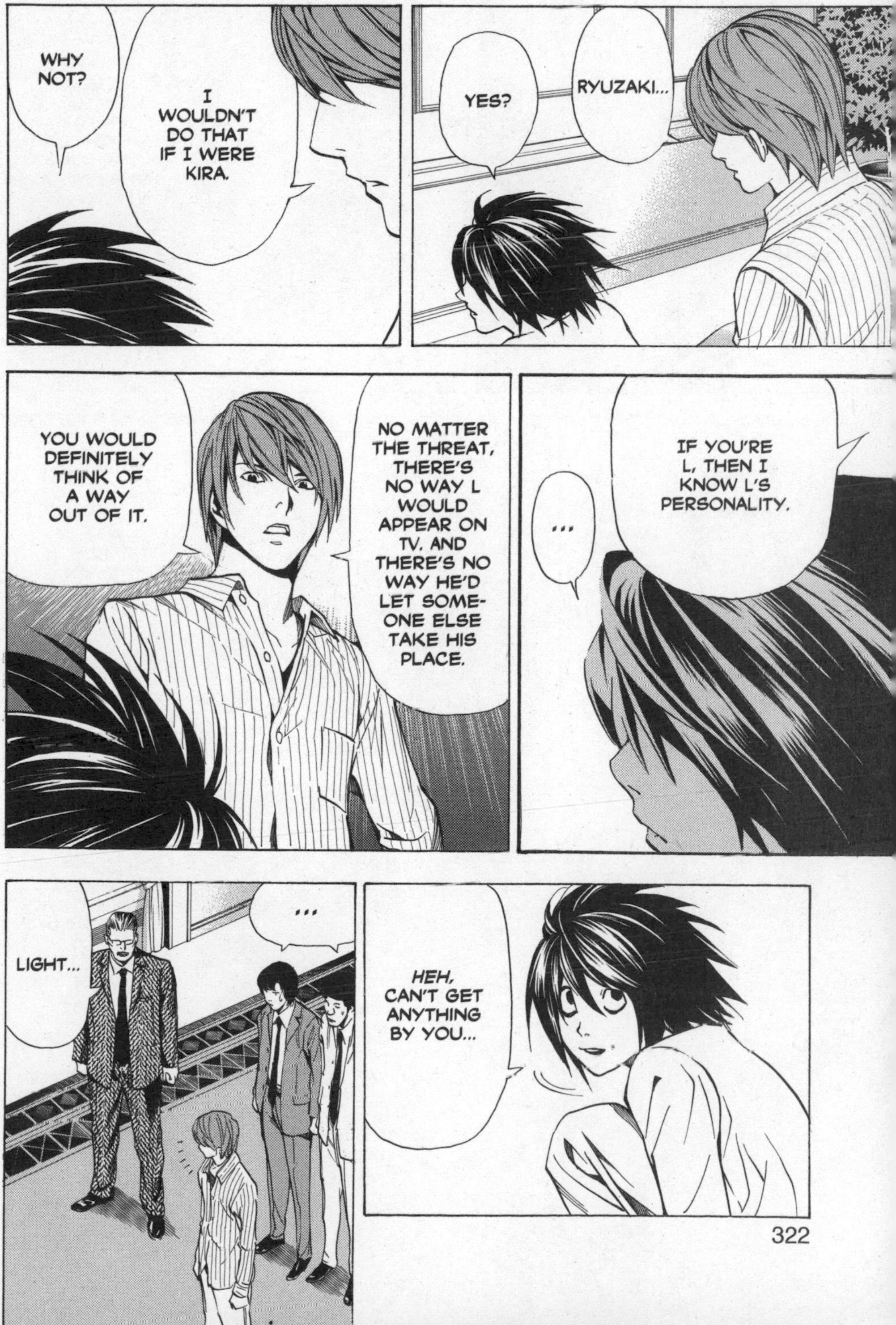
RYUZAKI...
YES?
I WOULDN'T DO THAT IF I WERE KIRA.
WHY NOT?
IF YOU'RE L, THEN I KNOW L'S PERSONALITY.
...
NO MATTER THE THREAT, THERE'S NO WAY L WOULD APPEAR ON TV. AND THERE'S NO WAY HE'D LET SOME-ONE ELSE TAKE HIS PLACE.
YOU WOULD DEFINITELY THINK OF A WAY OUT OF IT.
HEH, CAN'T GET ANYTHING BY YOU...
...
LIGHT...

READ THIS WAY

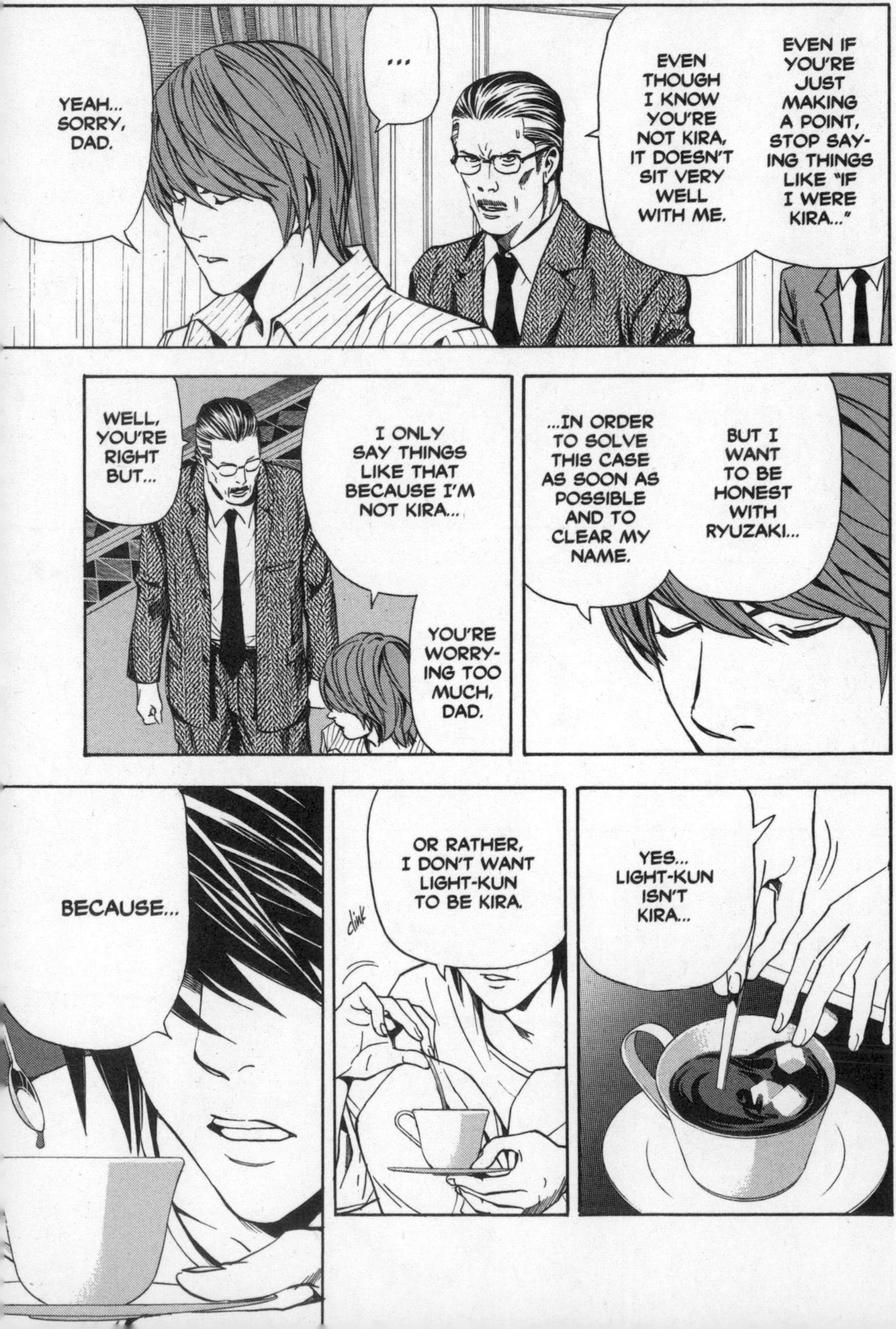
EVEN IF YOU'RE JUST MAKING A POINT, STOP SAYING THINGS LIKE "IF I WERE KIRA..."
EVEN THOUGH I KNOW YOU'RE NOT KIRA, IT DOESN'T SIT VERY WELL WITH ME.
...
YEAH... SORRY, DAD.
BUT I WANT TO BE HONEST WITH RYUZAKI...
...IN ORDER TO SOLVE THIS CASE AS SOON AS POSSIBLE AND TO CLEAR MY NAME.
I ONLY SAY THINGS LIKE THAT BECAUSE I'M NOT KIRA...
YOU'RE WORRYING TOO MUCH, DAD.
WELL, YOU'RE RIGHT BUT...
YES... LIGHT-KUN ISN'T KIRA...
OR RATHER, I DON'T WANT LIGHT-KUN TO BE KIRA.
clink
BECAUSE...

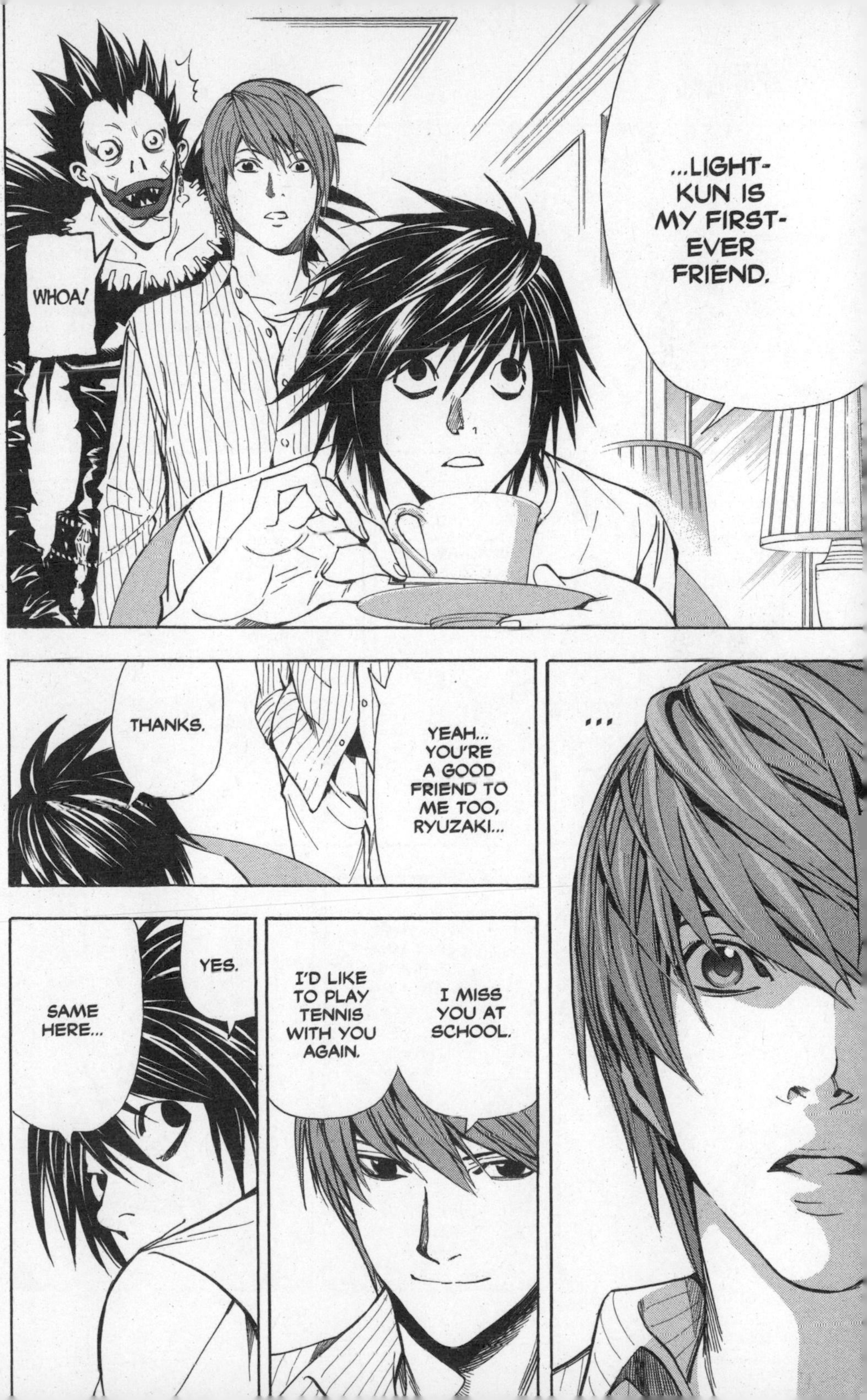
...LIGHT-KUN IS MY FIRST-EVER FRIEND.
WHOA!
...
YEAH... YOU'RE A GOOD FRIEND TO ME TOO, RYUZAKI...
THANKS.
I MISS YOU AT SCHOOL.
I'D LIKE TO PLAY TENNIS WITH YOU AGAIN.
YES.
SAME HERE...

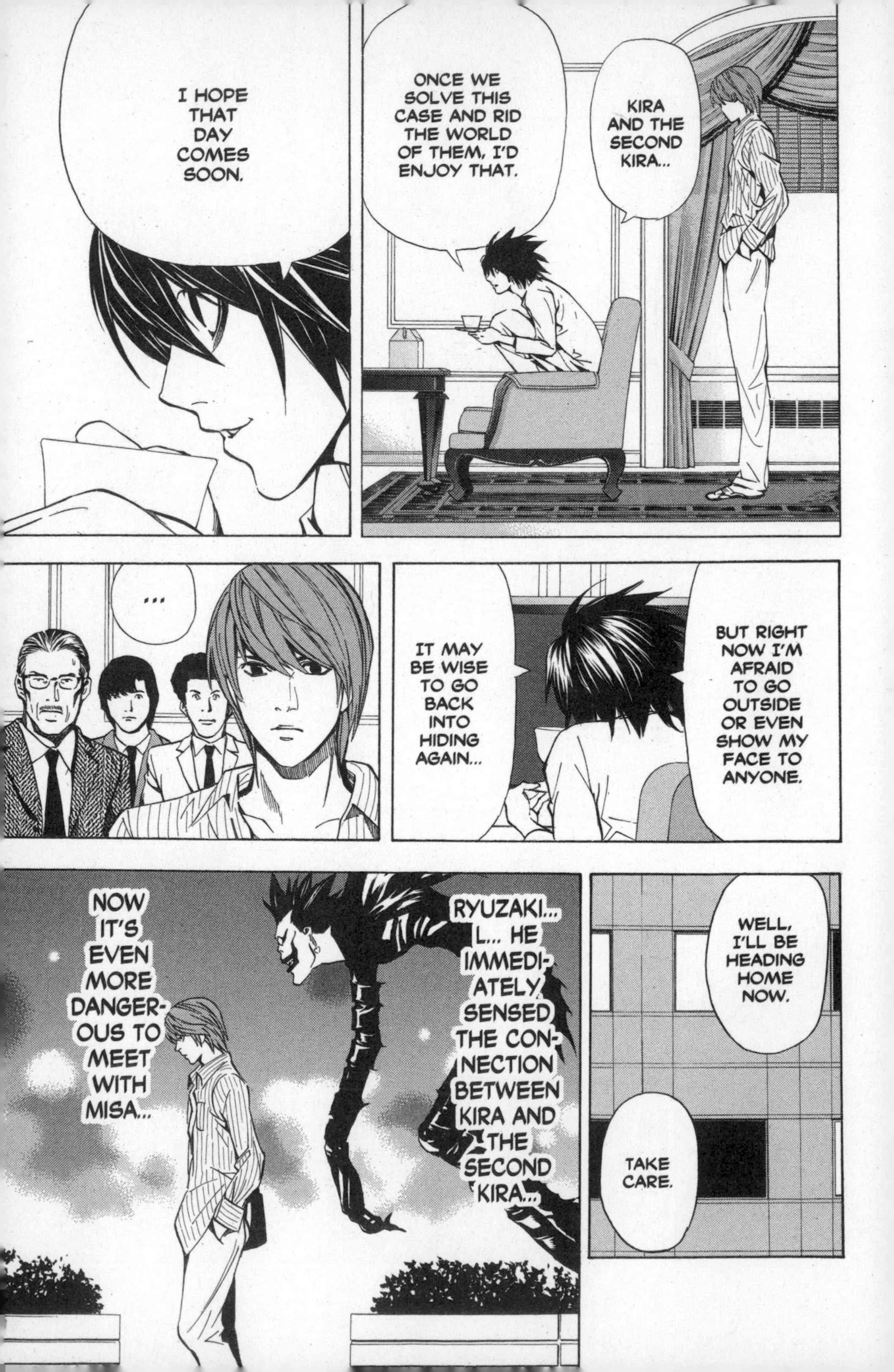
KIRA AND THE SECOND KIRA...
ONCE WE SOLVE THIS CASE AND RID THE WORLD OF THEM, I'D ENJOY THAT.
I HOPE THAT DAY COMES SOON.
BUT RIGHT NOW I'M AFRAID TO GO OUTSIDE OR EVEN SHOW MY FACE TO ANYONE.
IT MAY BE WISE TO GO BACK INTO HIDING AGAIN...
...
WELL, I'LL BE HEADING HOME NOW.
TAKE CARE.
RYUZAKI... L... HE IMMEDIATELY SENSED THE CONNECTION BETWEEN KIRA AND THE SECOND KIRA...
NOW IT'S EVEN MORE DANGEROUS TO MEET WITH MISA...

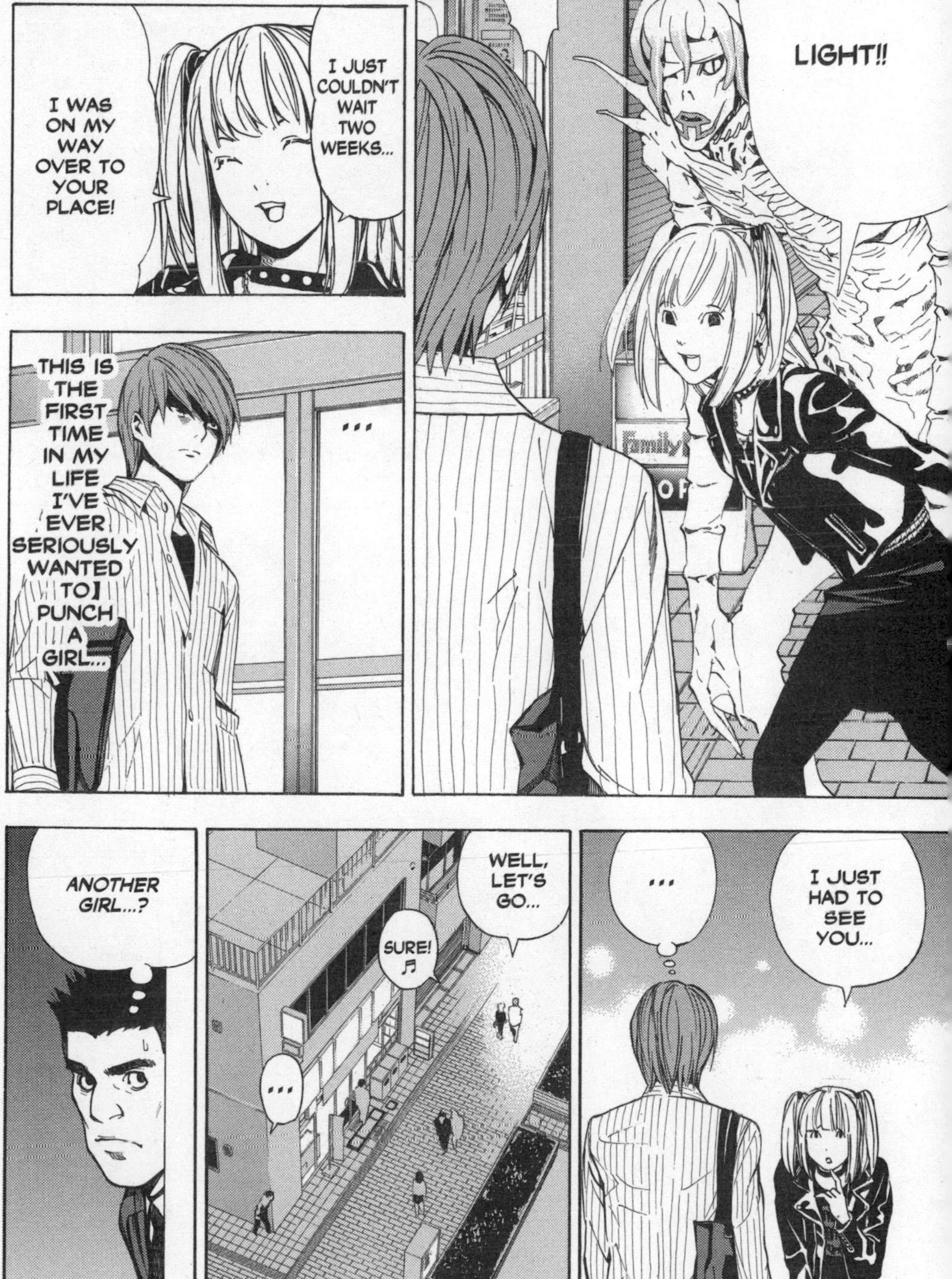
LIGHT!!
I JUST COULDN'T WAIT TWO WEEKS...
I WAS ON MY WAY OVER TO YOUR PLACE!
...
THIS IS THE FIRST TIME IN MY LIFE I'VE EVER SERIOUSLY WANTED TO PUNCH A GIRL...
I JUST HAD TO SEE YOU...
...
WELL, LET'S GO...
SURE! ♪
...
ANOTHER GIRL...?

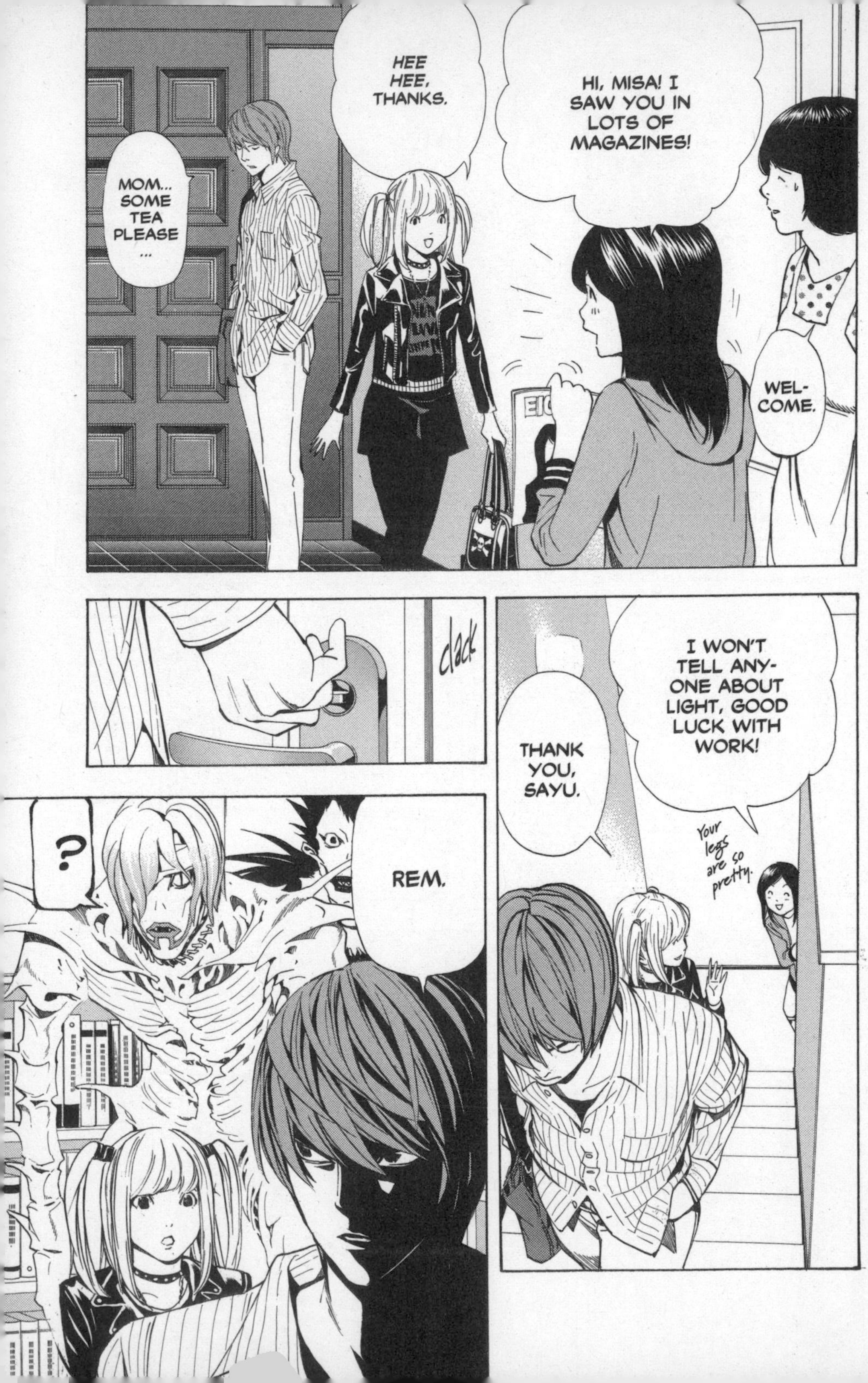
HI, MISA! I SAW YOU IN LOTS OF MAGAZINES!
WEL-COME.
HEE HEE, THANKS.
MOM... SOME TEA PLEASE ...
I WON'T TELL ANY-ONE ABOUT LIGHT, GOOD LUCK WITH WORK!
THANK YOU, SAYU.
Your legs are so pretty.
clack
REM.
?

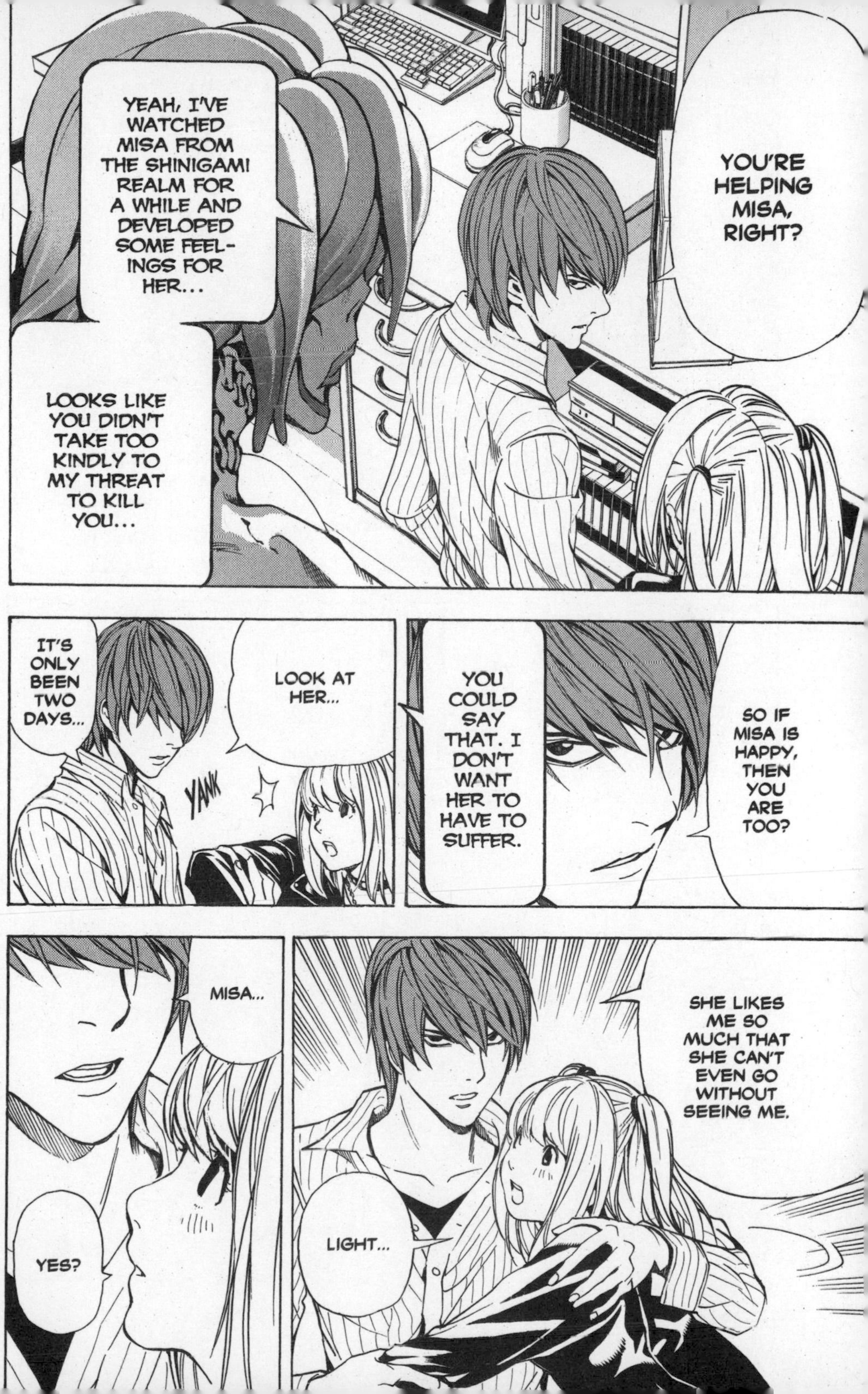
YOU'RE HELPING MISA, RIGHT?
YEAH, I'VE WATCHED MISA FROM THE SHINIGAMI REALM FOR A WHILE AND DEVELOPED SOME FEEL- INGS FOR HER...
LOOKS LIKE YOU DIDN'T TAKE TOO KINDLY TO MY THREAT TO KILL YOU...
SO IF MISA IS HAPPY, THEN YOU ARE TOO?
YOU COULD SAY THAT. I DON'T WANT HER TO HAVE TO SUFFER.
LOOK AT HER...
IT'S ONLY BEEN TWO DAYS...
YANK
SHE LIKES ME SO MUCH THAT SHE CAN'T EVEN GO WITHOUT SEEING ME.
LIGHT...
MISA...
YES?

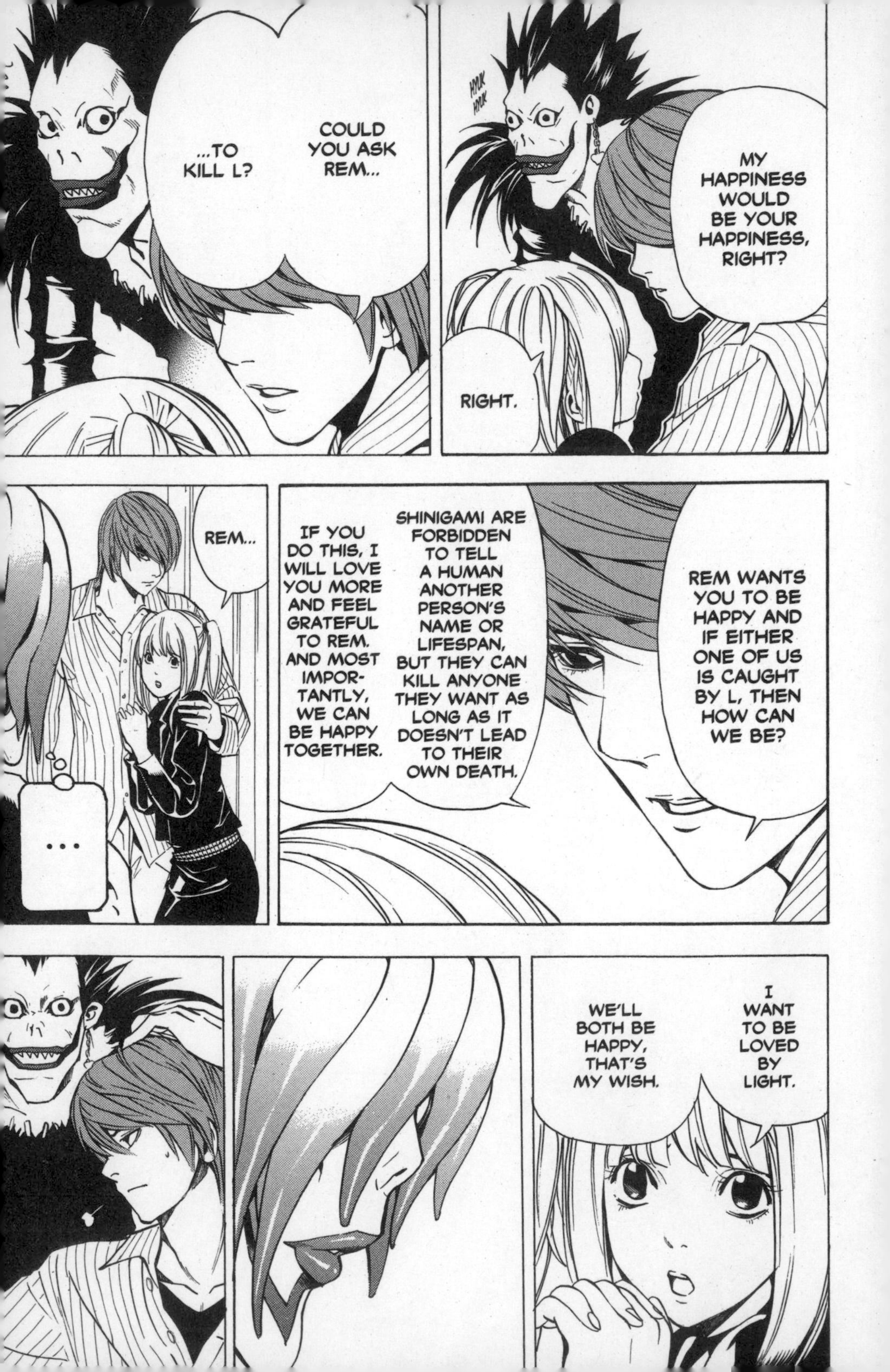
HYUK HYUK
MY HAPPINESS WOULD BE YOUR HAPPINESS, RIGHT?
RIGHT.
COULD YOU ASK REM...
...TO KILL L?
REM WANTS YOU TO BE HAPPY AND IF EITHER ONE OF US IS CAUGHT BY L, THEN HOW CAN WE BE?
SHINIGAMI ARE FORBIDDEN TO TELL A HUMAN ANOTHER PERSON'S NAME OR LIFESPAN, BUT THEY CAN KILL ANYONE THEY WANT AS LONG AS IT DOESN'T LEAD TO THEIR OWN DEATH.
IF YOU DO THIS, I WILL LOVE YOU MORE AND FEEL GRATEFUL TO REM. AND MOST IMPORTANTLY, WE CAN BE HAPPY TOGETHER.
REM...
...
I WANT TO BE LOVED BY LIGHT.
WE'LL BOTH BE HAPPY, THAT'S MY WISH.

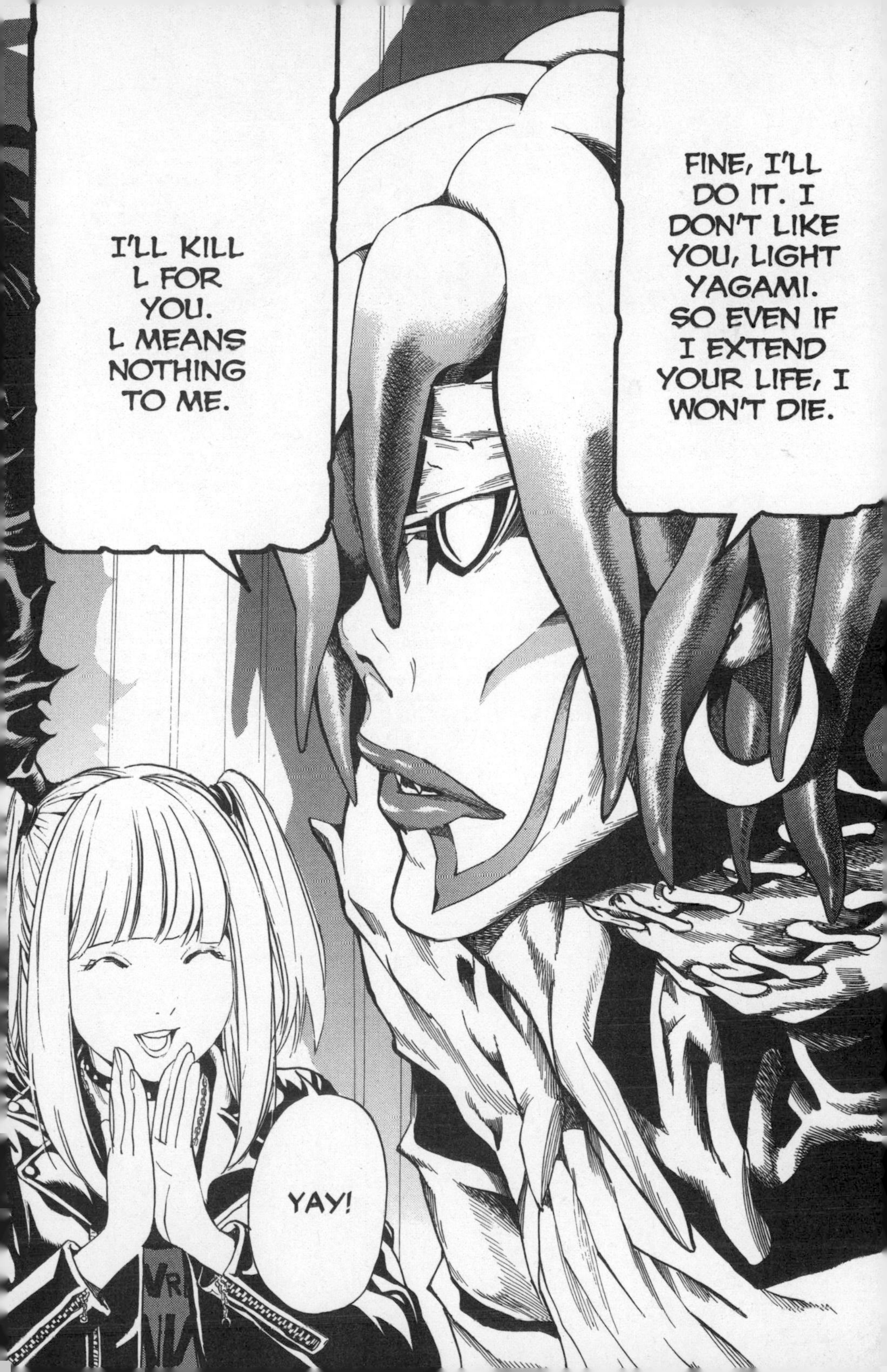
FINE, I'LL DO IT. I DON'T LIKE YOU, LIGHT YAGAMI. SO EVEN IF I EXTEND YOUR LIFE, I WON'T DIE.
I'LL KILL L FOR YOU. L MEANS NOTHING TO ME.
YAY!

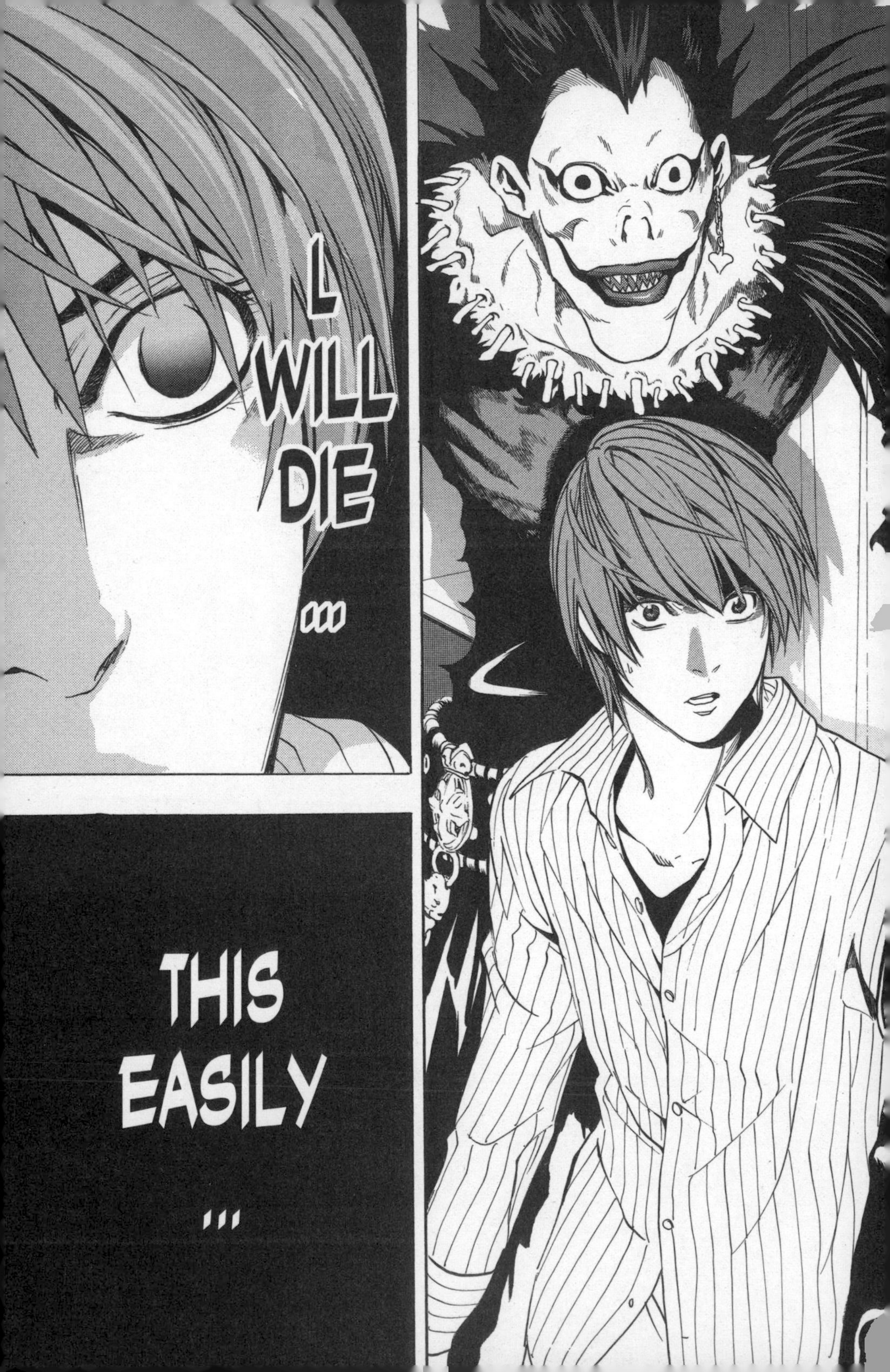
L WILL DIE ...
THIS EASILY ...

DEATH NOTE
How to Use It

○ Those with the eye power of the god of death will have

the eyesight of over 3.6 in the human measurement,

regardless of their original eyesight.

死神の目を持った人間は、元の視力に拘らず、人間界でいう
3.6以上の視力になる。

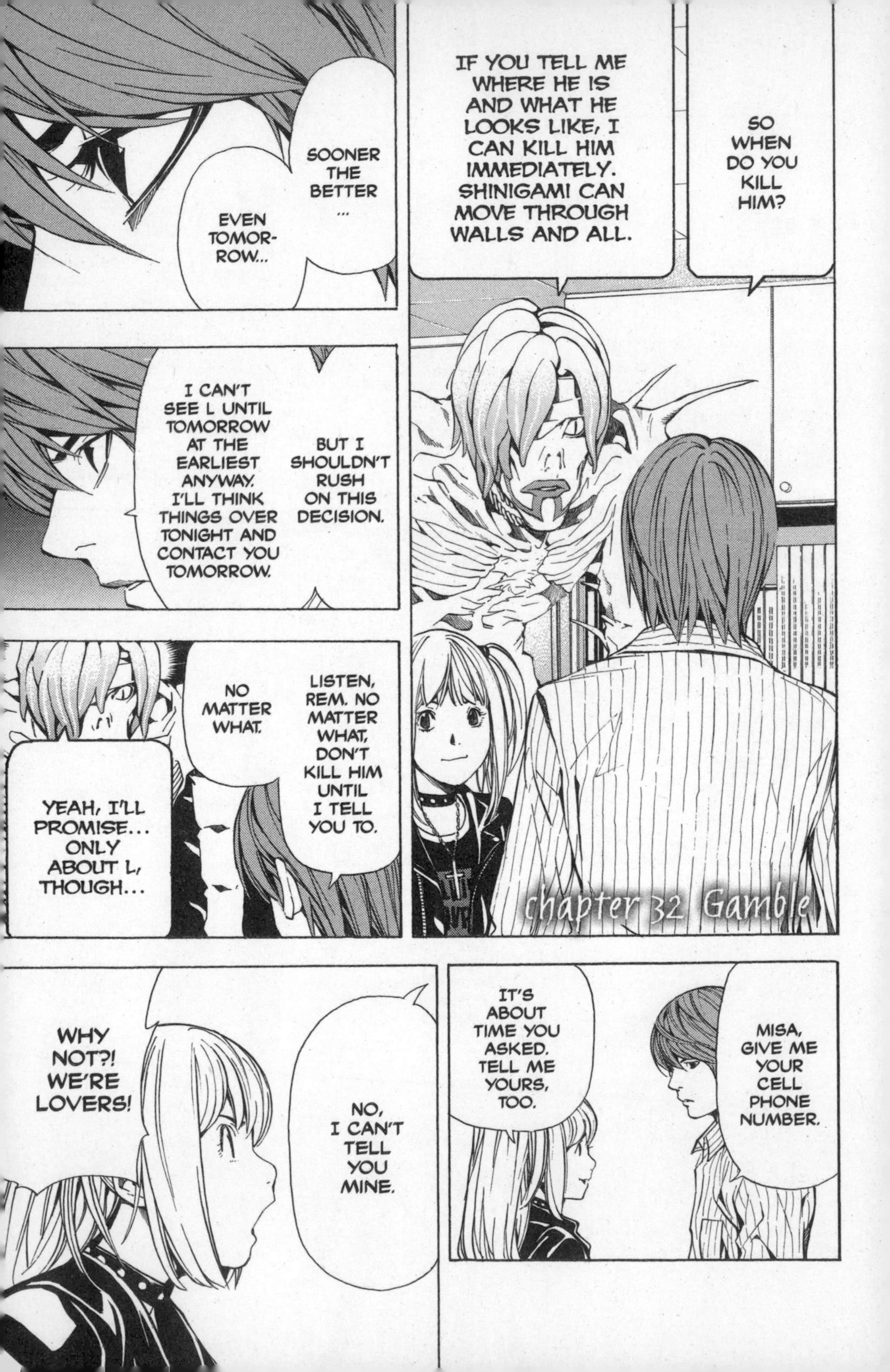
SO WHEN DO YOU KILL HIM?
IF YOU TELL ME WHERE HE IS AND WHAT HE LOOKS LIKE, I CAN KILL HIM IMMEDIATELY. SHINIGAMI CAN MOVE THROUGH WALLS AND ALL.
chapter 32 Gamble
SOONER THE BETTER ...
EVEN TOMORROW...
BUT I SHOULDN'T RUSH ON THIS DECISION.
I CAN'T SEE L UNTIL TOMORROW AT THE EARLIEST ANYWAY. I'LL THINK THINGS OVER TONIGHT AND CONTACT YOU TOMORROW.
LISTEN, REM. NO MATTER WHAT, DON'T KILL HIM UNTIL I TELL YOU TO.
NO MATTER WHAT.
YEAH, I'LL PROMISE... ONLY ABOUT L, THOUGH...
MISA, GIVE ME YOUR CELL PHONE NUMBER.
IT'S ABOUT TIME YOU ASKED. TELL ME YOURS, TOO.
NO, I CAN'T TELL YOU MINE.
WHY NOT?! WE'RE LOVERS!

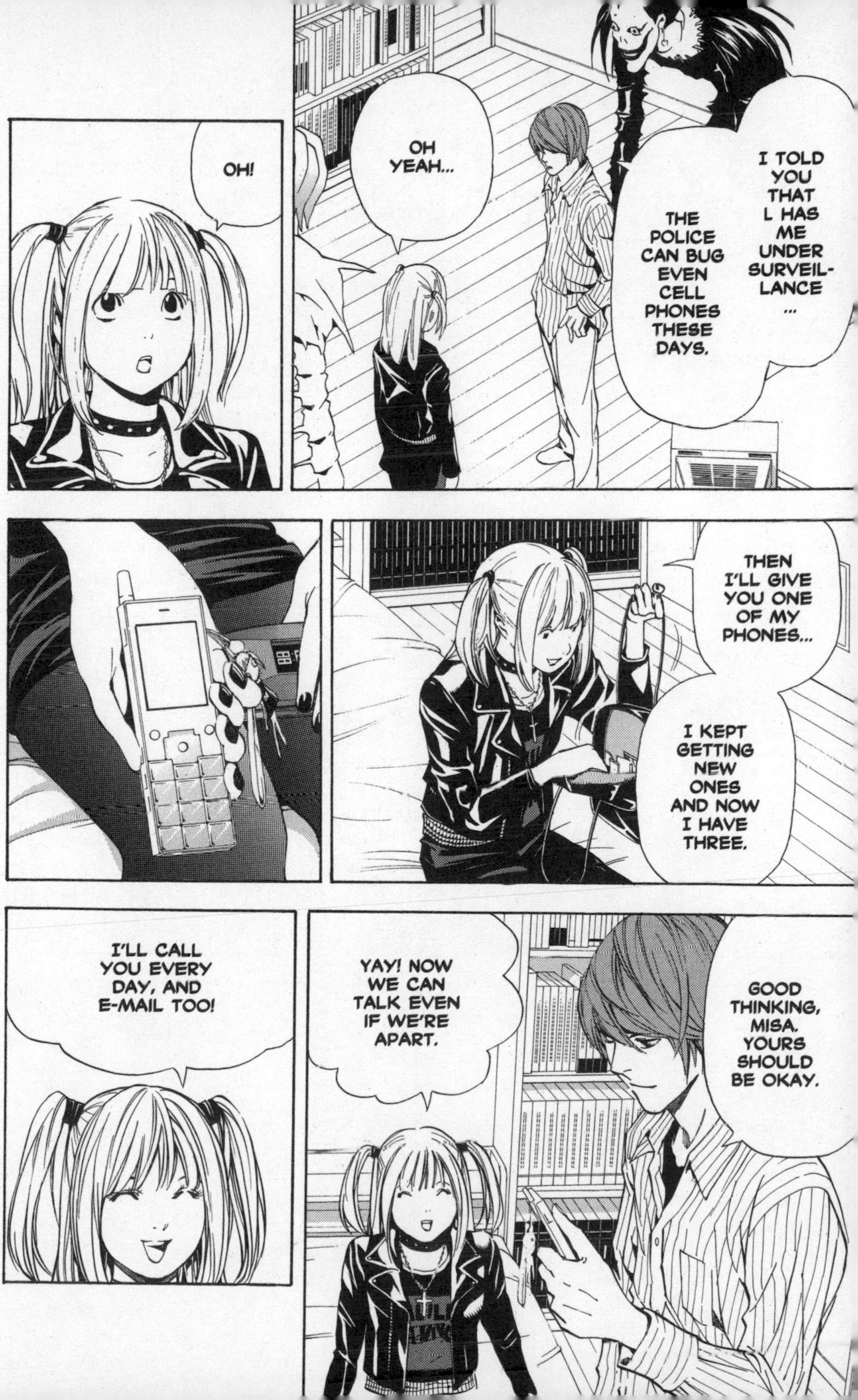
I TOLD YOU THAT L HAS ME UNDER SURVEILLANCE...
THE POLICE CAN BUG EVEN CELL PHONES THESE DAYS.
OH YEAH...
OH!
THEN I'LL GIVE YOU ONE OF MY PHONES...
I KEPT GETTING NEW ONES AND NOW I HAVE THREE.
GOOD THINKING, MISA. YOURS SHOULD BE OKAY.
YAY! NOW WE CAN TALK EVEN IF WE'RE APART.
I'LL CALL YOU EVERY DAY, AND E-MAIL TOO!

READ THIS WAY

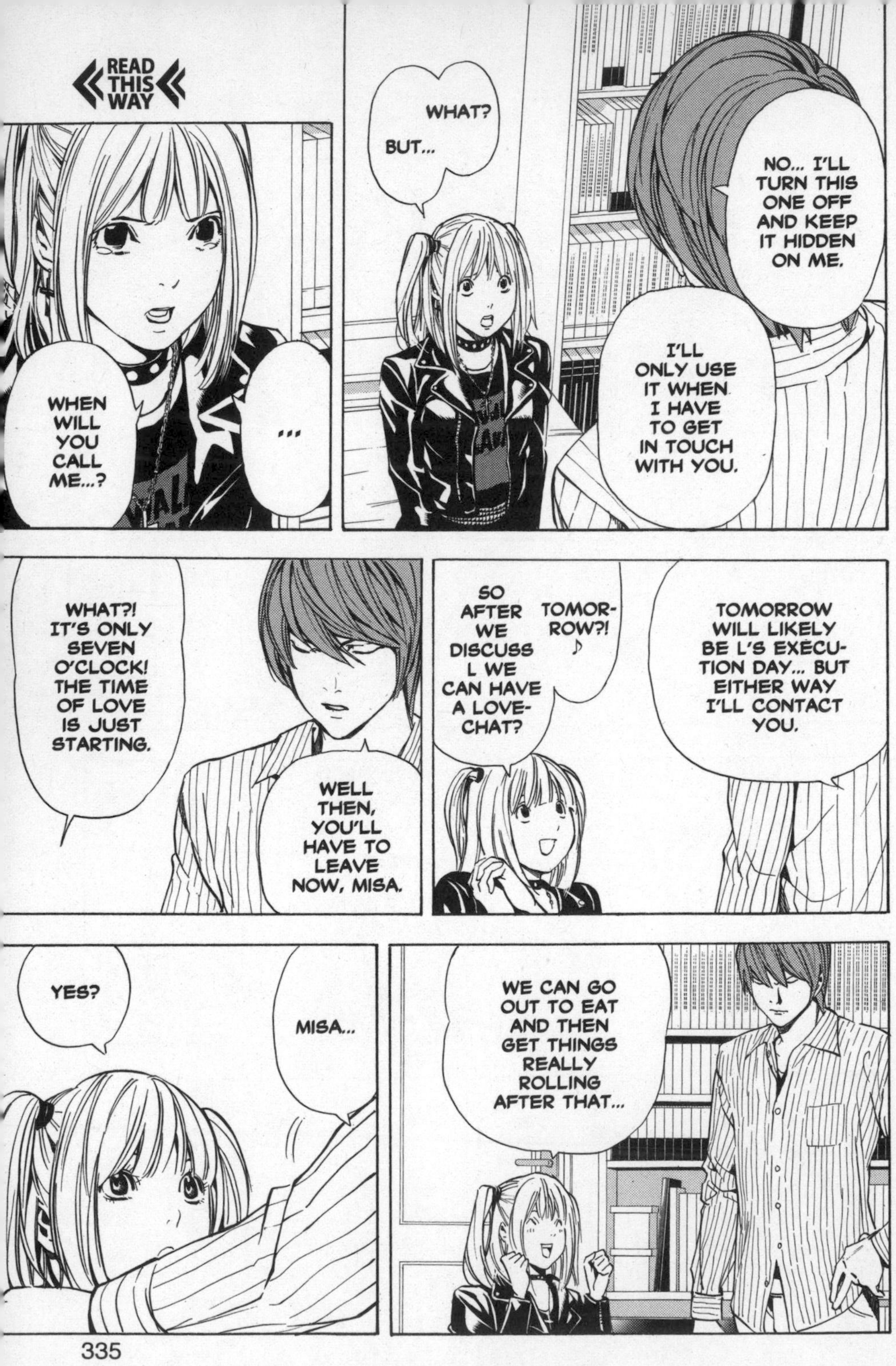

NO... I'LL TURN THIS ONE OFF AND KEEP IT HIDDEN ON ME.
I'LL ONLY USE IT WHEN I HAVE TO GET IN TOUCH WITH YOU.
WHAT? BUT...
...
WHEN WILL YOU CALL ME...?
TOMORROW WILL LIKELY BE L'S EXECUTION DAY... BUT EITHER WAY I'LL CONTACT YOU.
TOMORROW?! ♪
SO AFTER WE DISCUSS L WE CAN HAVE A LOVE-CHAT?
WELL THEN, YOU'LL HAVE TO LEAVE NOW, MISA.
WHAT?! IT'S ONLY SEVEN O'CLOCK! THE TIME OF LOVE IS JUST STARTING.
WE CAN GO OUT TO EAT AND THEN GET THINGS REALLY ROLLING AFTER THAT...
MISA...
YES?

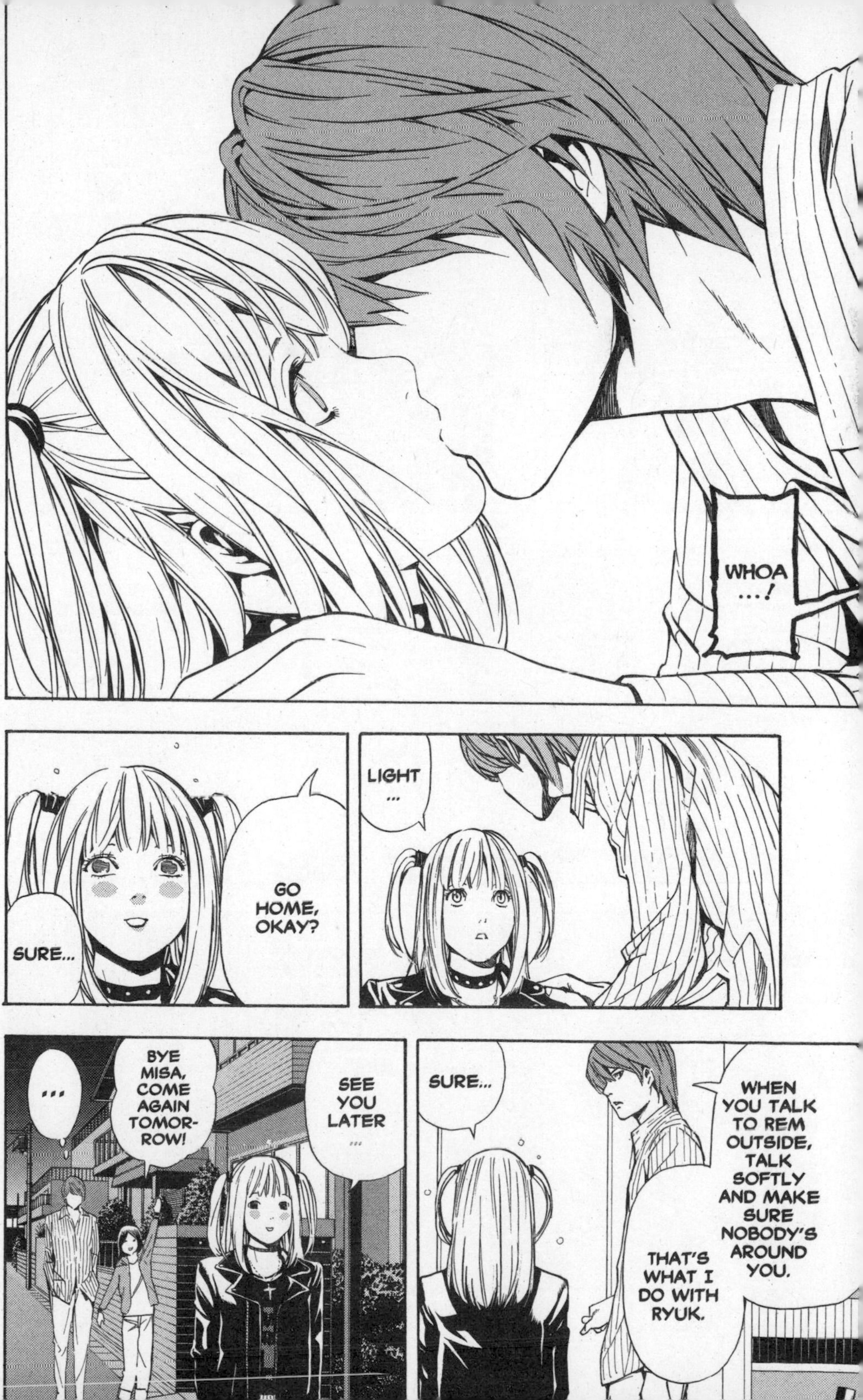
WHOA ...!
LIGHT ...
GO HOME, OKAY?
SURE...
WHEN YOU TALK TO REM OUTSIDE, TALK SOFTLY AND MAKE SURE NOBODY'S AROUND YOU.
THAT'S WHAT I DO WITH RYUK.
SURE...
SEE YOU LATER ...
BYE MISA, COME AGAIN TOMOR-ROW!
...

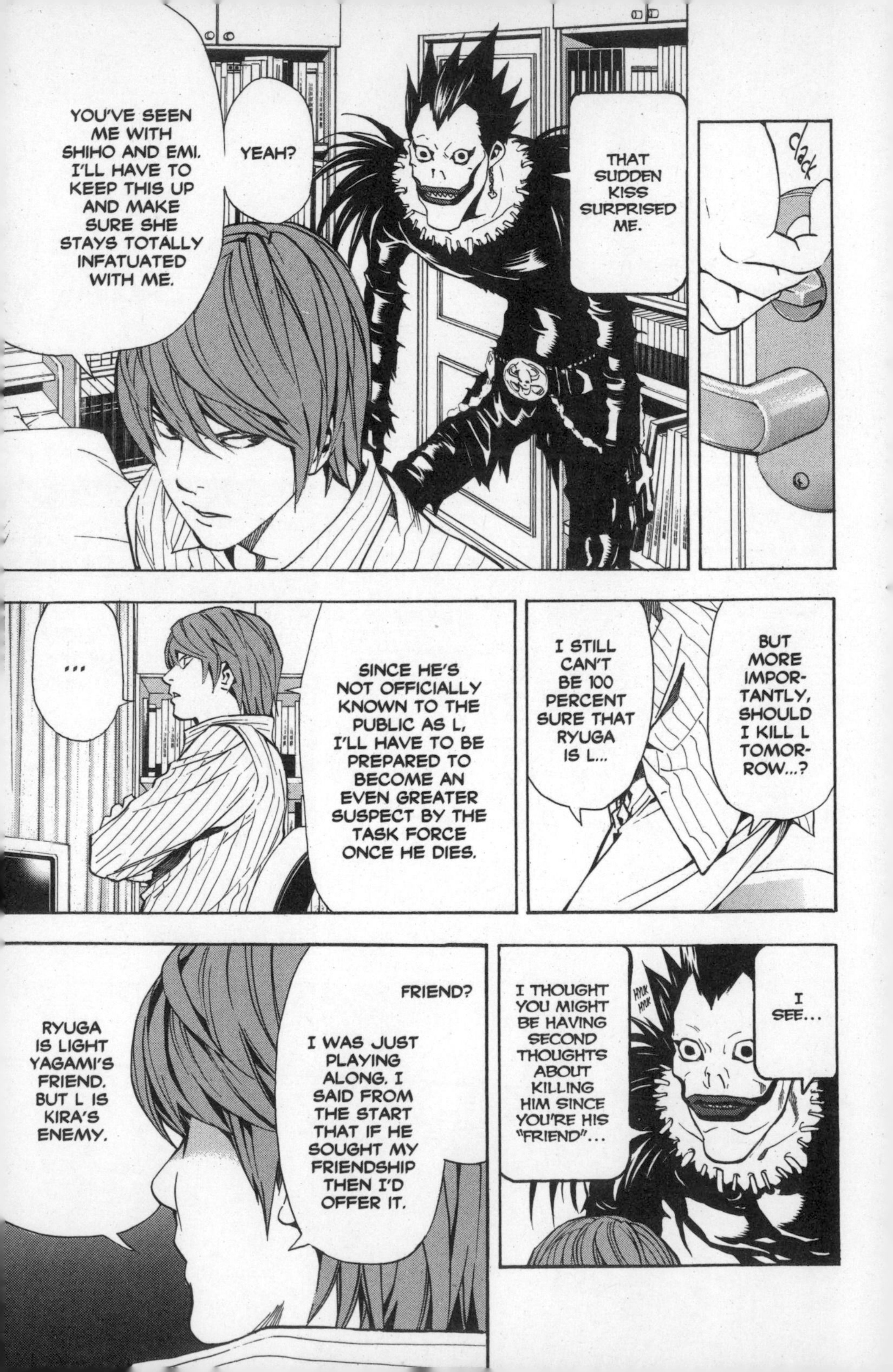
clack
THAT SUDDEN KISS SURPRISED ME.
YEAH?
YOU'VE SEEN ME WITH SHIHO AND EMI. I'LL HAVE TO KEEP THIS UP AND MAKE SURE SHE STAYS TOTALLY INFATUATED WITH ME.
BUT MORE IMPORTANTLY, SHOULD I KILL L TOMORROW...?
I STILL CAN'T BE 100 PERCENT SURE THAT RYUGA IS L...
SINCE HE'S NOT OFFICIALLY KNOWN TO THE PUBLIC AS L, I'LL HAVE TO BE PREPARED TO BECOME AN EVEN GREATER SUSPECT BY THE TASK FORCE ONCE HE DIES.
...
I SEE...
HYUK HYUK
I THOUGHT YOU MIGHT BE HAVING SECOND THOUGHTS ABOUT KILLING HIM SINCE YOU'RE HIS "FRIEND"...
FRIEND?
I WAS JUST PLAYING ALONG. I SAID FROM THE START THAT IF HE SOUGHT MY FRIENDSHIP THEN I'D OFFER IT.
RYUGA IS LIGHT YAGAMI'S FRIEND. BUT L IS KIRA'S ENEMY.

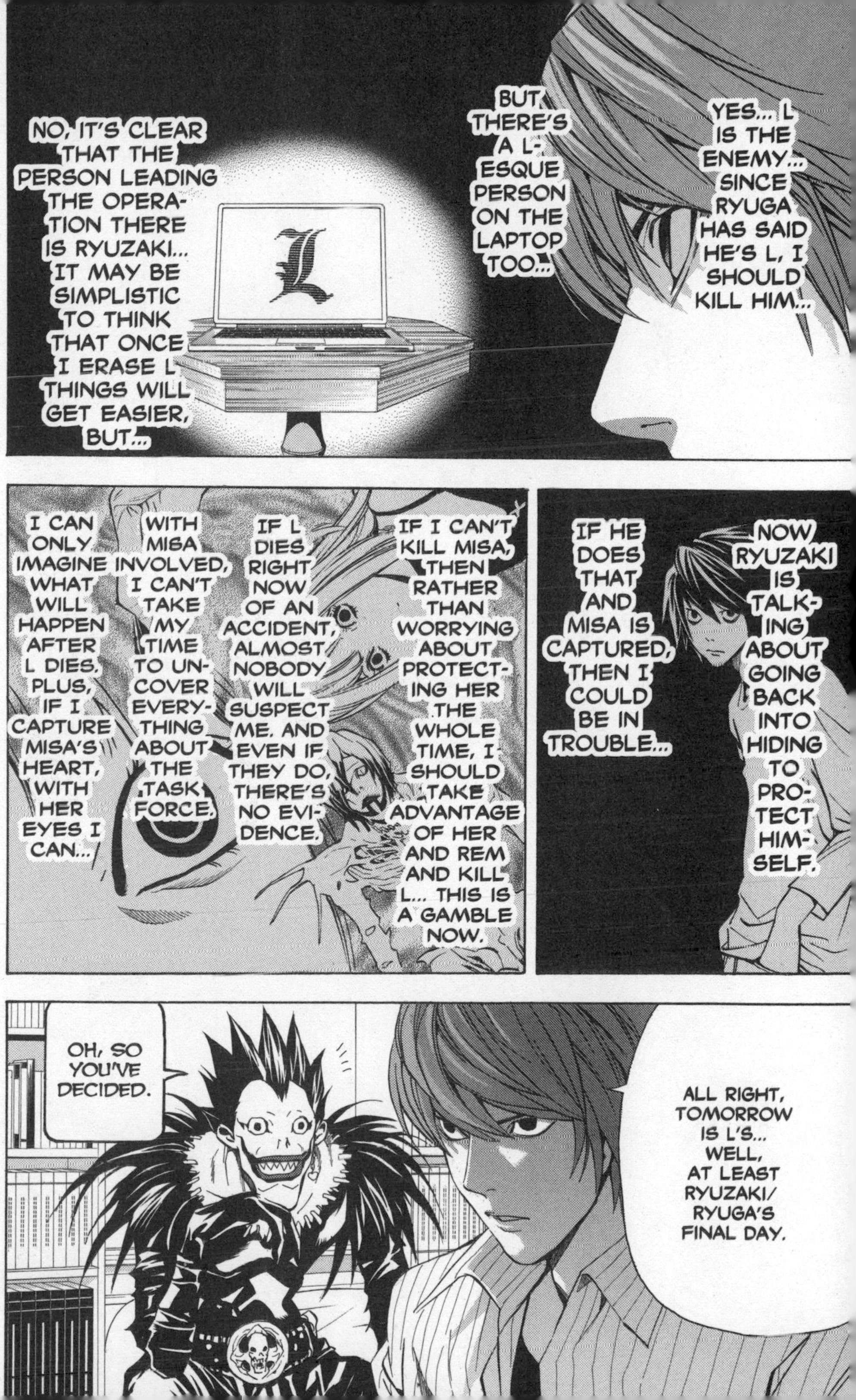
YES... L IS THE ENEMY... SINCE RYUGA HAS SAID HE'S L, I SHOULD KILL HIM...
BUT THERE'S A L-ESQUE PERSON ON THE LAPTOP TOO...
NO, IT'S CLEAR THAT THE PERSON LEADING THE OPERATION THERE IS RYUZAKI... IT MAY BE SIMPLISTIC TO THINK THAT ONCE I ERASE L THINGS WILL GET EASIER, BUT...
NOW RYUZAKI IS TALKING ABOUT GOING BACK INTO HIDING TO PROTECT HIMSELF.
IF HE DOES THAT AND MISA IS CAPTURED, THEN I COULD BE IN TROUBLE...
IF I CAN'T KILL MISA, THEN RATHER THAN WORRYING ABOUT PROTECTING HER THE WHOLE TIME, I SHOULD TAKE ADVANTAGE OF HER AND REM AND KILL L... THIS IS A GAMBLE NOW.
IF L DIES RIGHT NOW OF AN ACCIDENT, ALMOST NOBODY WILL SUSPECT ME. AND EVEN IF THEY DO, THERE'S NO EVIDENCE.
WITH MISA INVOLVED, I CAN'T TAKE MY TIME TO UNCOVER EVERYTHING ABOUT THE TASK FORCE.
I CAN ONLY IMAGINE WHAT WILL HAPPEN AFTER L DIES. PLUS, IF I CAPTURE MISA'S HEART, WITH HER EYES I CAN...
ALL RIGHT, TOMORROW IS L'S... WELL, AT LEAST RYUZAKI/RYUGA'S FINAL DAY.
OH, SO YOU'VE DECIDED.

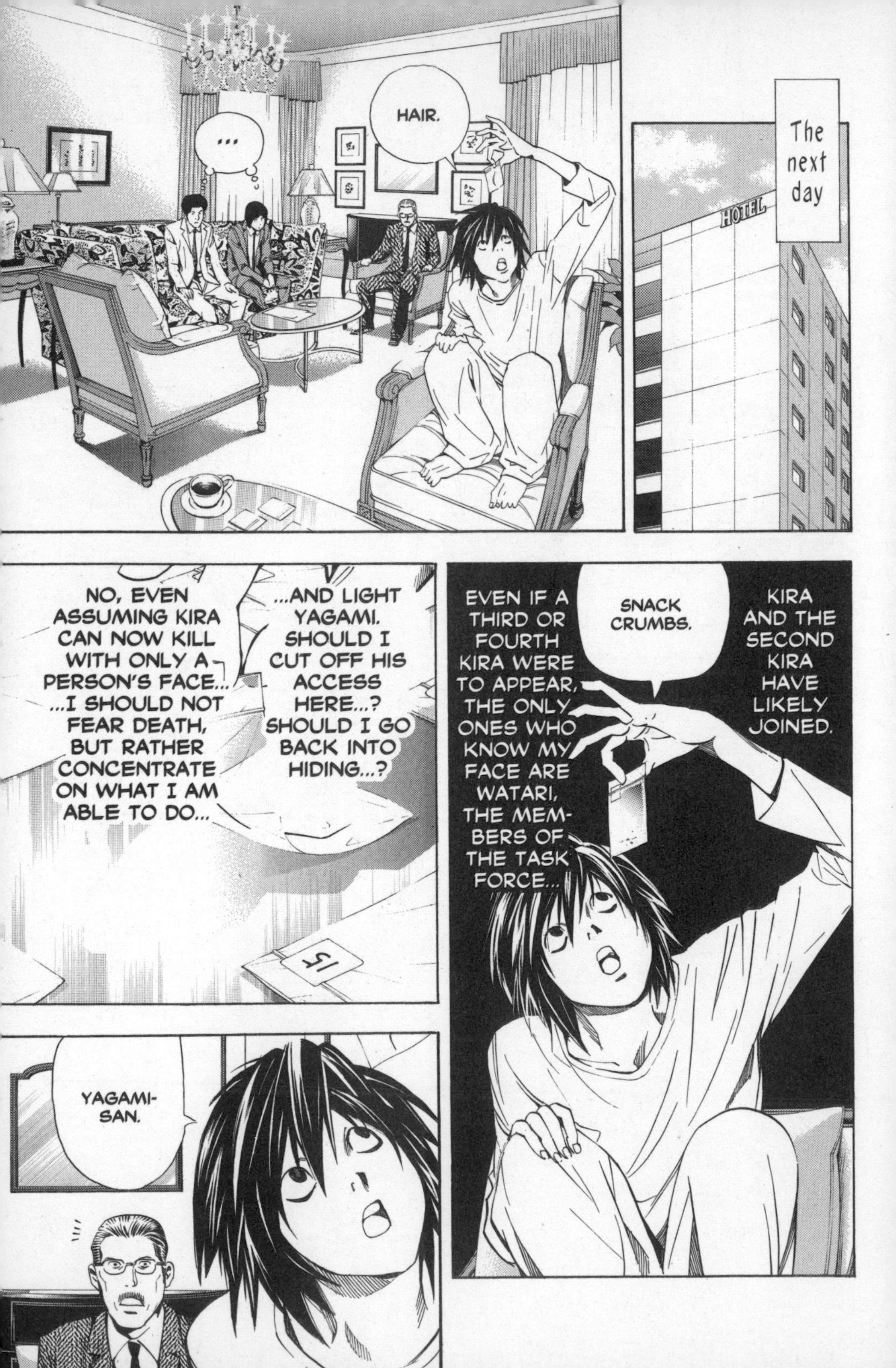
The next day
HOTEL
HAIR.
...
KIRA AND THE SECOND KIRA HAVE LIKELY JOINED.
SNACK CRUMBS.
EVEN IF A THIRD OR FOURTH KIRA WERE TO APPEAR, THE ONLY ONES WHO KNOW MY FACE ARE WATARI, THE MEMBERS OF THE TASK FORCE...
...AND LIGHT YAGAMI. SHOULD I CUT OFF HIS ACCESS HERE...? SHOULD I GO BACK INTO HIDING...?
NO, EVEN ASSUMING KIRA CAN NOW KILL WITH ONLY A PERSON'S FACE... ...I SHOULD NOT FEAR DEATH, BUT RATHER CONCENTRATE ON WHAT I AM ABLE TO DO...
YAGAMI-SAN.

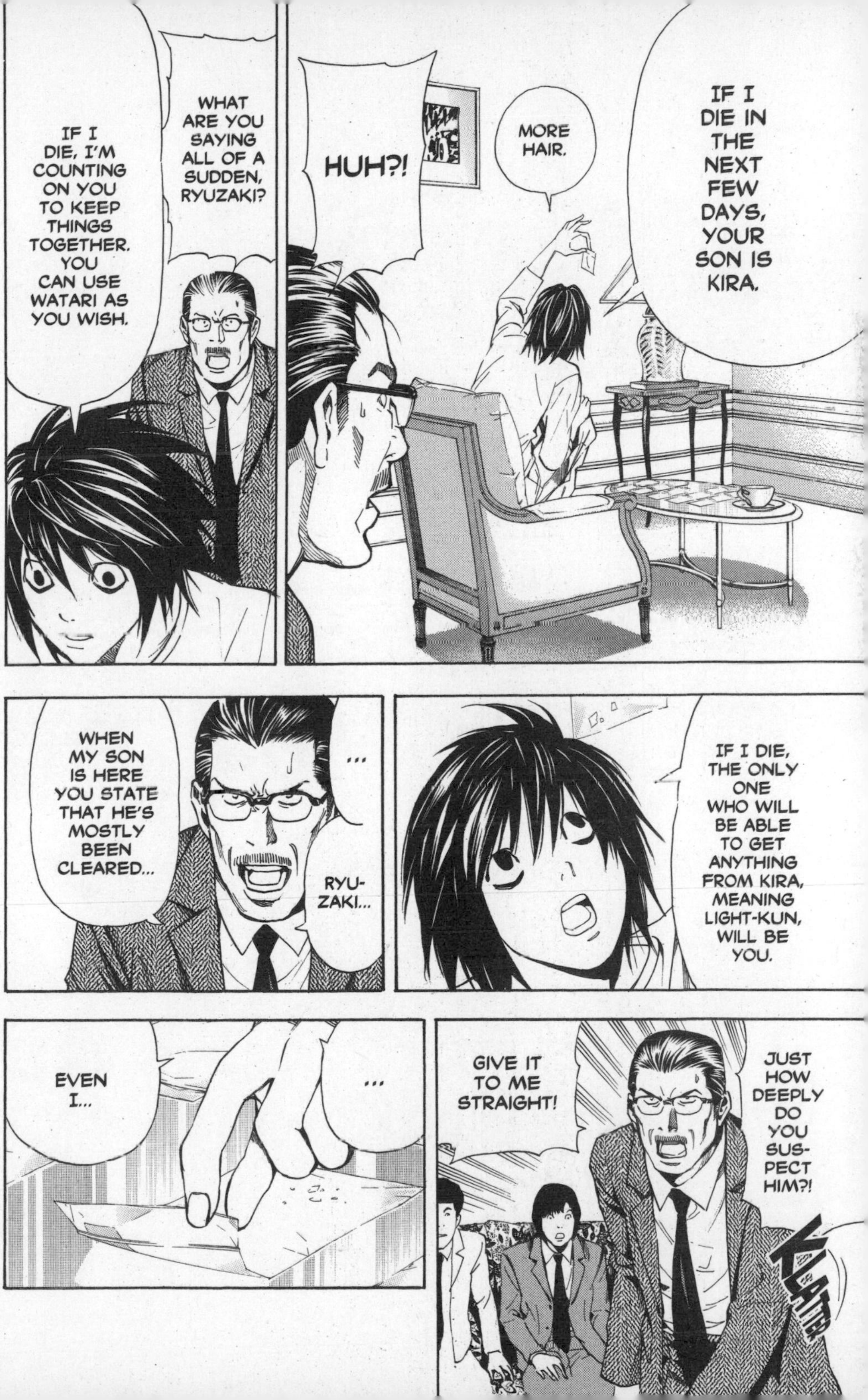
IF I DIE IN THE NEXT FEW DAYS, YOUR SON IS KIRA.
MORE HAIR.
HUH?!
WHAT ARE YOU SAYING ALL OF A SUDDEN, RYUZAKI?
IF I DIE, I'M COUNTING ON YOU TO KEEP THINGS TOGETHER. YOU CAN USE WATARI AS YOU WISH.
IF I DIE, THE ONLY ONE WHO WILL BE ABLE TO GET ANYTHING FROM KIRA, MEANING LIGHT-KUN, WILL BE YOU.
...
RYU-ZAKI...
WHEN MY SON IS HERE YOU STATE THAT HE'S MOSTLY BEEN CLEARED...
JUST HOW DEEPLY DO YOU SUS-PECT HIM?!
GIVE IT TO ME STRAIGHT!
KLATTER
...
EVEN I...

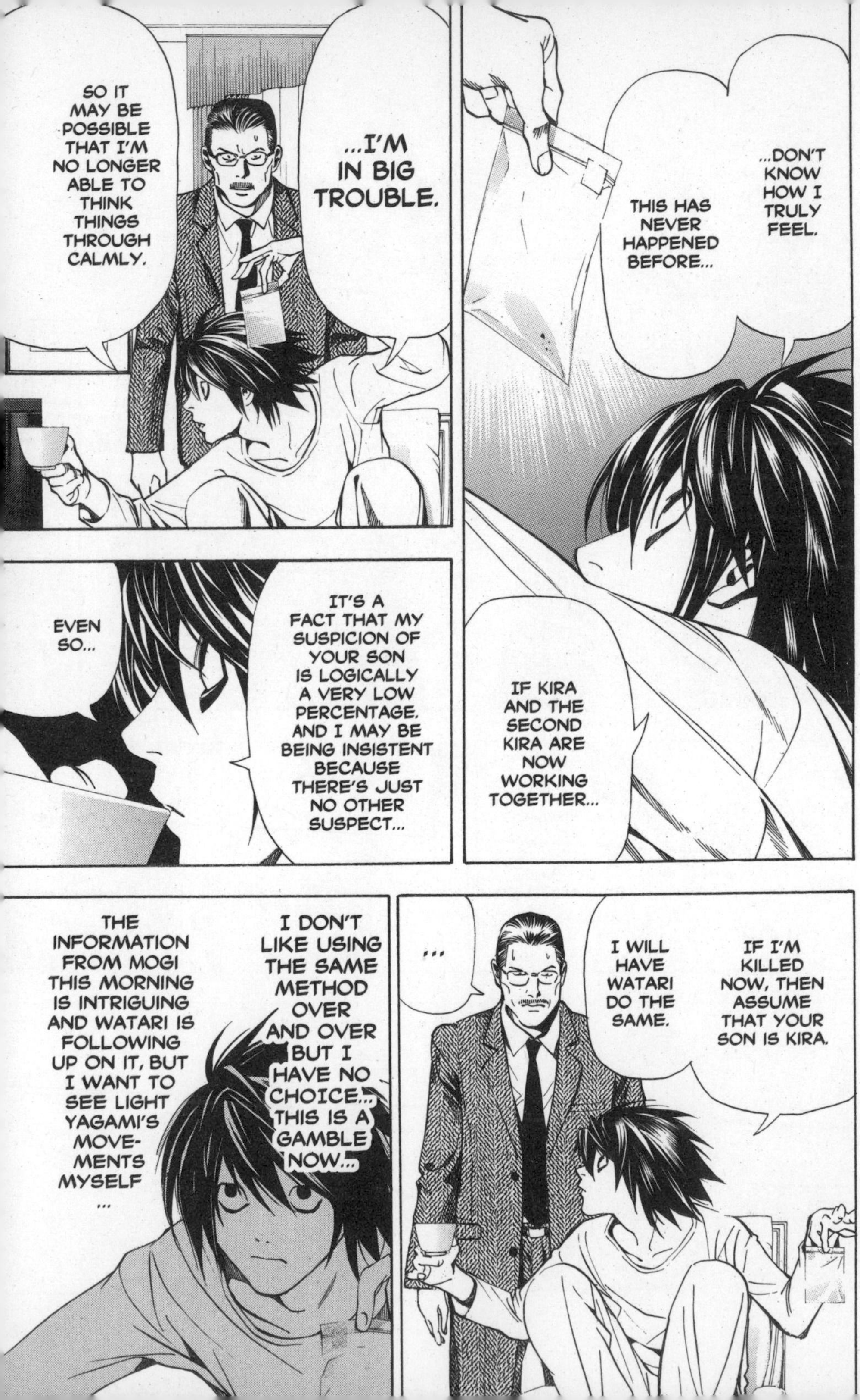
...DON'T KNOW HOW I TRULY FEEL.
THIS HAS NEVER HAPPENED BEFORE...
IF KIRA AND THE SECOND KIRA ARE NOW WORKING TOGETHER...
...I'M IN BIG TROUBLE.
SO IT MAY BE POSSIBLE THAT I'M NO LONGER ABLE TO THINK THINGS THROUGH CALMLY.
IT'S A FACT THAT MY SUSPICION OF YOUR SON IS LOGICALLY A VERY LOW PERCENTAGE. AND I MAY BE BEING INSISTENT BECAUSE THERE'S JUST NO OTHER SUSPECT...
EVEN SO...
IF I'M KILLED NOW, THEN ASSUME THAT YOUR SON IS KIRA.
I WILL HAVE WATARI DO THE SAME.
...
I DON'T LIKE USING THE SAME METHOD OVER AND OVER BUT I HAVE NO CHOICE... THIS IS A GAMBLE NOW...
THE INFORMATION FROM MOGI THIS MORNING IS INTRIGUING AND WATARI IS FOLLOWING UP ON IT, BUT I WANT TO SEE LIGHT YAGAMI'S MOVE-MENTS MYSELF ...

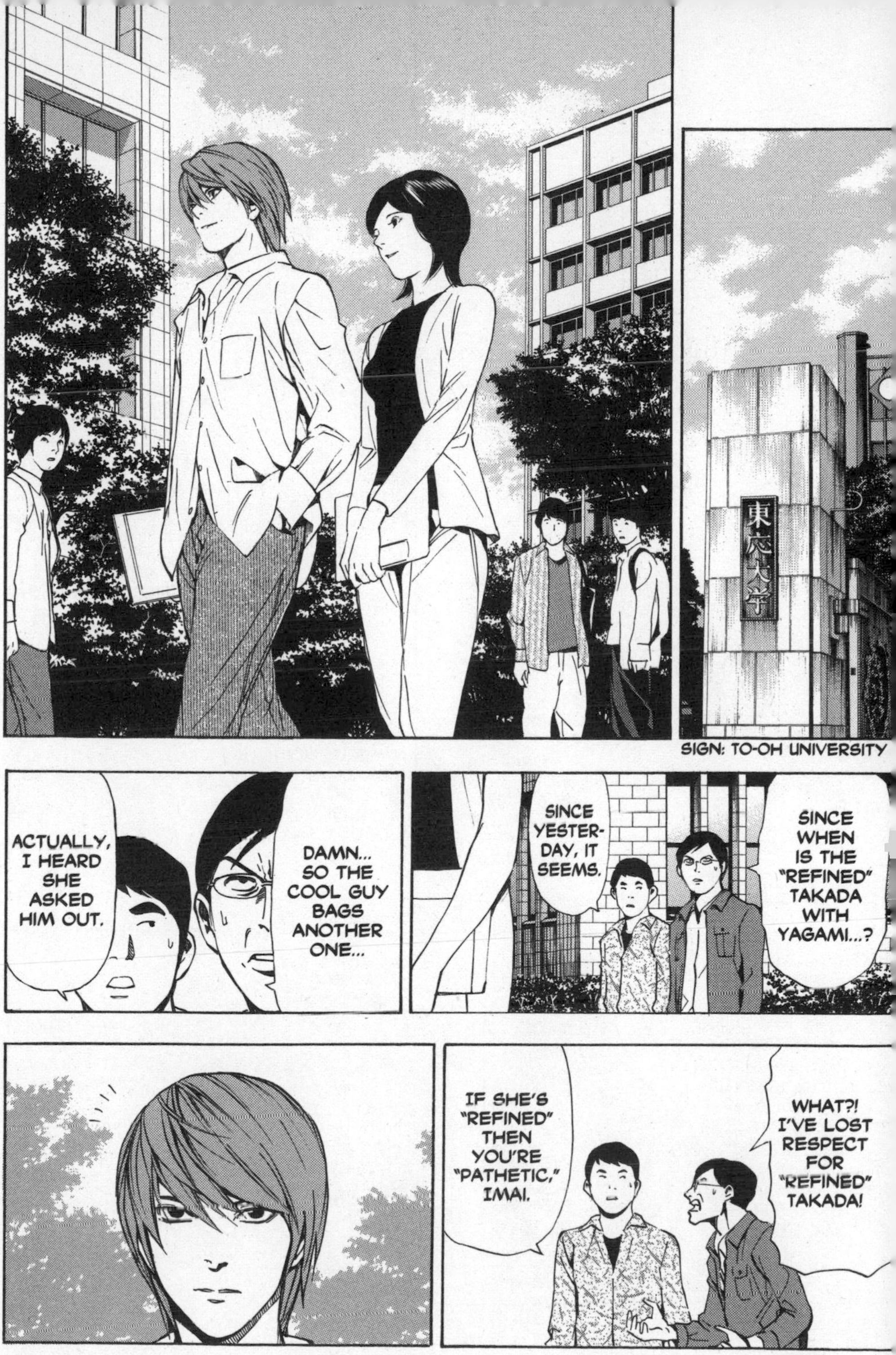
SIGN: TO-OH UNIVERSITY
SINCE WHEN IS THE "REFINED" TAKADA WITH YAGAMI...?
SINCE YESTER-DAY, IT SEEMS.
DAMN... SO THE COOL GUY BAGS ANOTHER ONE...
ACTUALLY, I HEARD SHE ASKED HIM OUT.
WHAT?! I'VE LOST RESPECT FOR "REFINED" TAKADA!
IF SHE'S "REFINED" THEN YOU'RE "PATHETIC," IMAI.

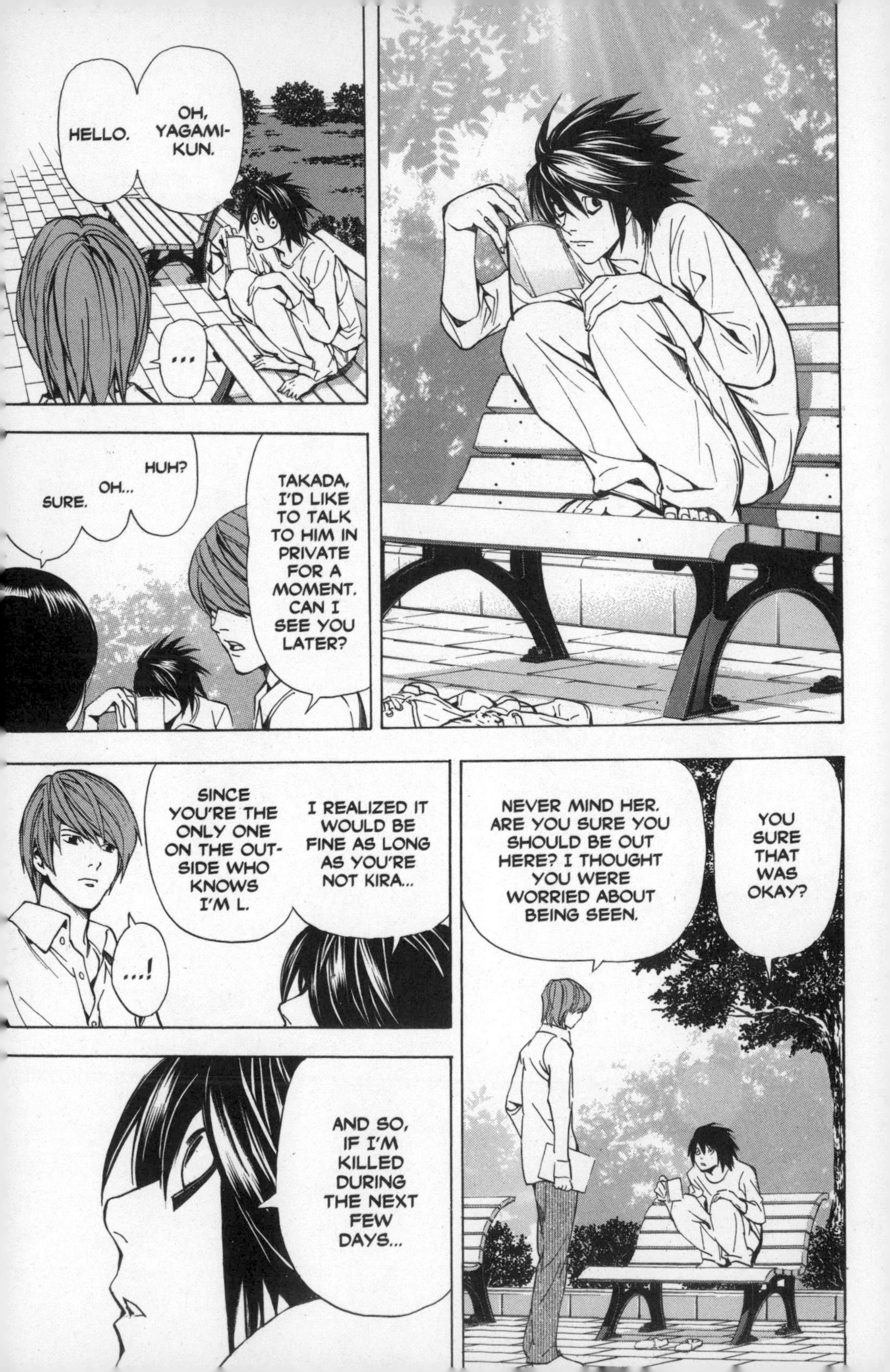
OH, YAGAMI-KUN.
HELLO.
...
TAKADA, I'D LIKE TO TALK TO HIM IN PRIVATE FOR A MOMENT. CAN I SEE YOU LATER?
HUH? OH... SURE.
YOU SURE THAT WAS OKAY?
NEVER MIND HER. ARE YOU SURE YOU SHOULD BE OUT HERE? I THOUGHT YOU WERE WORRIED ABOUT BEING SEEN.
I REALIZED IT WOULD BE FINE AS LONG AS YOU'RE NOT KIRA...
SINCE YOU'RE THE ONLY ONE ON THE OUT-SIDE WHO KNOWS I'M L.
...!
AND SO, IF I'M KILLED DURING THE NEXT FEW DAYS...

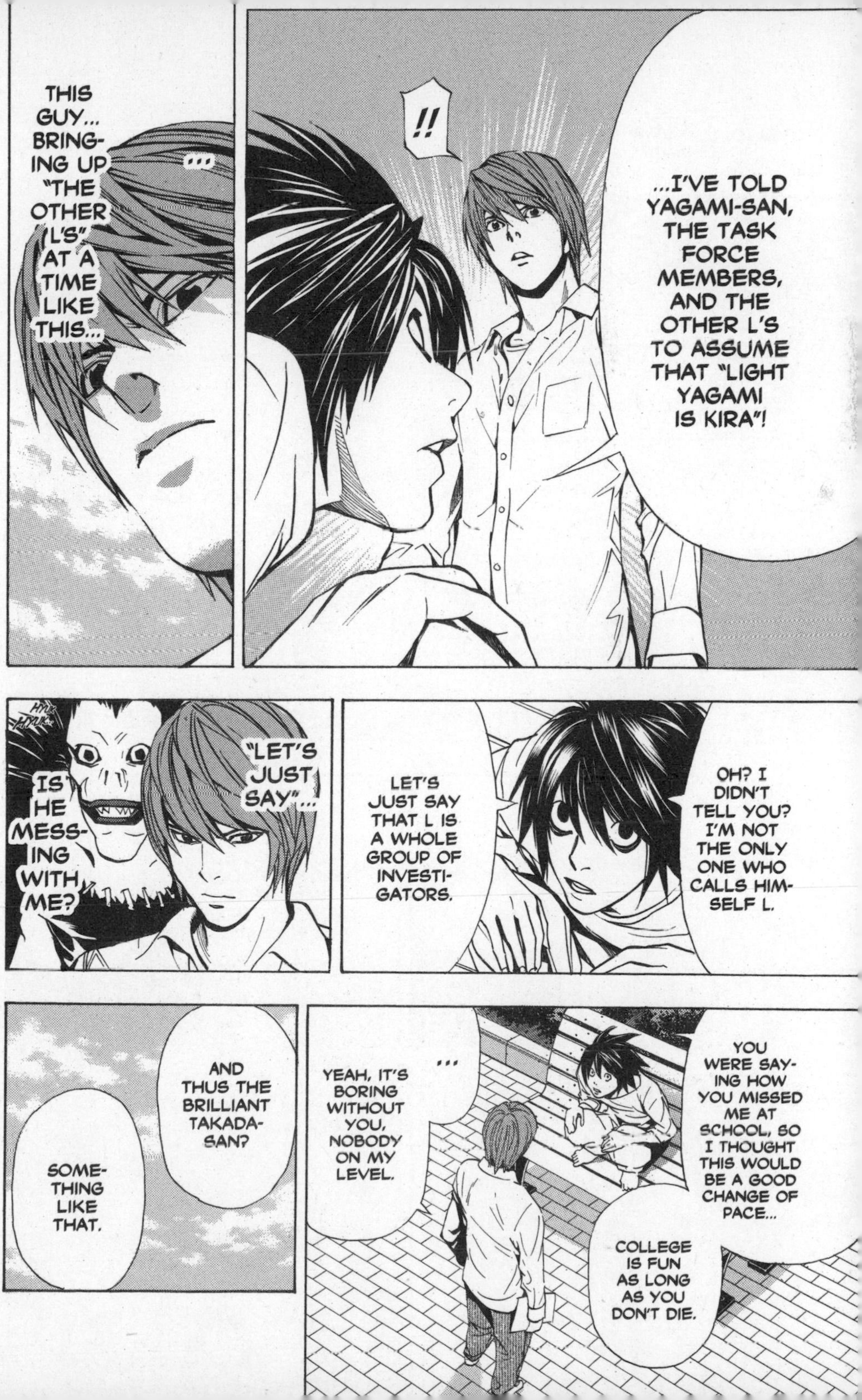
...I'VE TOLD YAGAMI-SAN, THE TASK FORCE MEMBERS, AND THE OTHER L'S TO ASSUME THAT "LIGHT YAGAMI IS KIRA"!
!!
...
THIS GUY... BRINGING UP "THE OTHER L'S" AT A TIME LIKE THIS...
OH? I DIDN'T TELL YOU? I'M NOT THE ONLY ONE WHO CALLS HIMSELF L.
LET'S JUST SAY THAT L IS A WHOLE GROUP OF INVESTIGATORS.
"LET'S JUST SAY"...
IS HE MESSING WITH ME?
HYUK HYUK
YOU WERE SAYING HOW YOU MISSED ME AT SCHOOL, SO I THOUGHT THIS WOULD BE A GOOD CHANGE OF PACE...
...
YEAH, IT'S BORING WITHOUT YOU, NOBODY ON MY LEVEL.
COLLEGE IS FUN AS LONG AS YOU DON'T DIE.
AND THUS THE BRILLIANT TAKADA-SAN?
SOMETHING LIKE THAT.

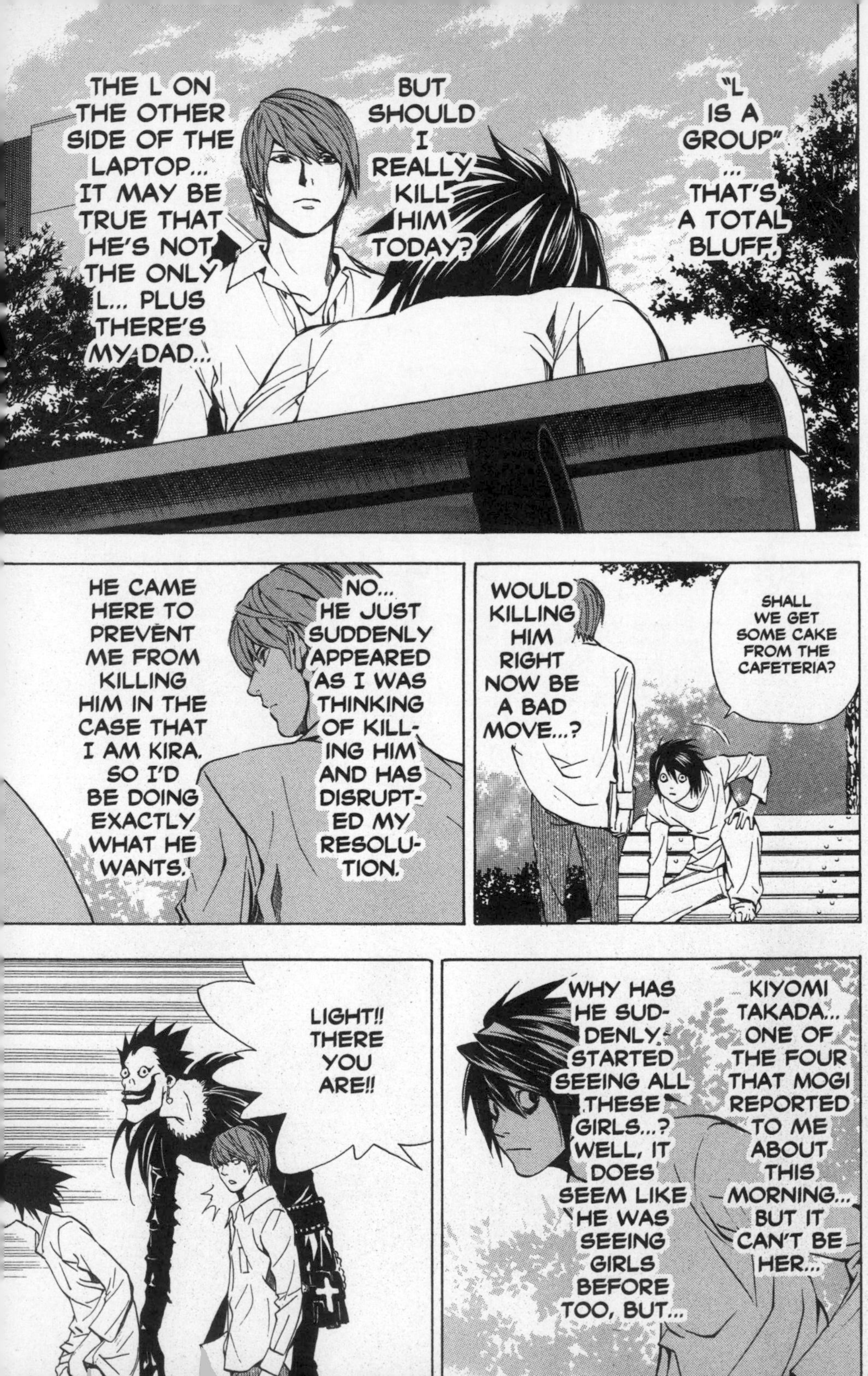
"L IS A GROUP"... THAT'S A TOTAL BLUFF.
BUT SHOULD I REALLY KILL HIM TODAY?
THE L ON THE OTHER SIDE OF THE LAPTOP... IT MAY BE TRUE THAT HE'S NOT THE ONLY L... PLUS THERE'S MY DAD...
SHALL WE GET SOME CAKE FROM THE CAFETERIA?
WOULD KILLING HIM RIGHT NOW BE A BAD MOVE...?
NO... HE JUST SUDDENLY APPEARED AS I WAS THINKING OF KILLING HIM AND HAS DISRUPTED MY RESOLUTION.
HE CAME HERE TO PREVENT ME FROM KILLING HIM IN THE CASE THAT I AM KIRA. SO I'D BE DOING EXACTLY WHAT HE WANTS.
KIYOMI TAKADA... ONE OF THE FOUR THAT MOGI REPORTED TO ME ABOUT THIS MORNING... BUT IT CAN'T BE HER...
WHY HAS HE SUDDENLY STARTED SEEING ALL THESE GIRLS...? WELL, IT DOES SEEM LIKE HE WAS SEEING GIRLS BEFORE TOO, BUT...
LIGHT!! THERE YOU ARE!!

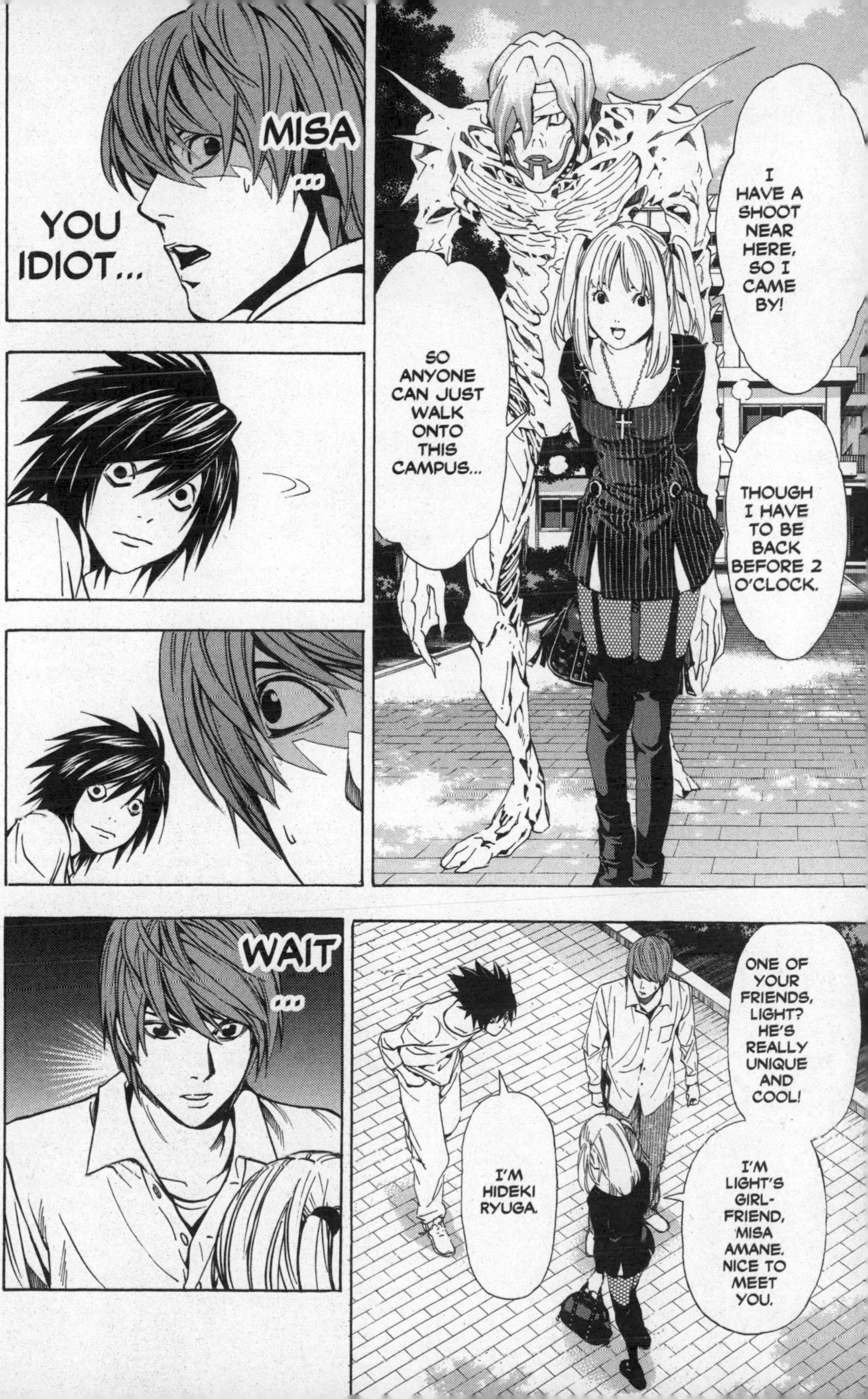
I HAVE A SHOOT NEAR HERE, SO I CAME BY!
THOUGH I HAVE TO BE BACK BEFORE 2 O'CLOCK.
SO ANYONE CAN JUST WALK ONTO THIS CAMPUS...
MISA ...
YOU IDIOT...
ONE OF YOUR FRIENDS, LIGHT? HE'S REALLY UNIQUE AND COOL!
I'M LIGHT'S GIRL-FRIEND, MISA AMANE. NICE TO MEET YOU.
I'M HIDEKI RYUGA.
WAIT ...

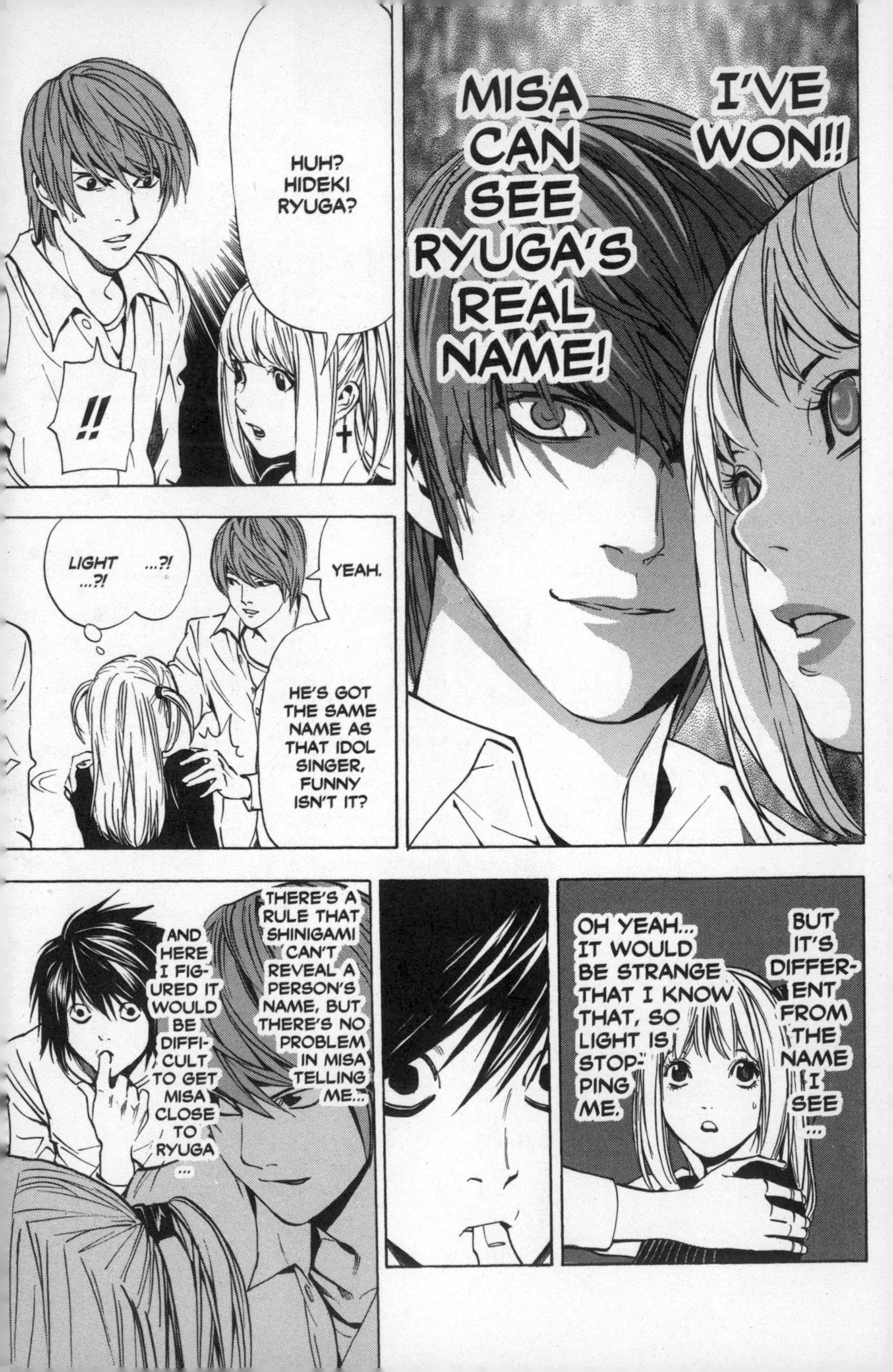
I'VE WON!!
MISA CAN SEE RYUGA'S REAL NAME!
HUH? HIDEKI RYUGA?
!!
YEAH.
HE'S GOT THE SAME NAME AS THAT IDOL SINGER, FUNNY ISN'T IT?
...?!
LIGHT ...?!
BUT IT'S DIFFERENT FROM THE NAME I SEE ...
OH YEAH... IT WOULD BE STRANGE THAT I KNOW THAT, SO LIGHT IS STOPPING ME.
THERE'S A RULE THAT SHINIGAMI CAN'T REVEAL A PERSON'S NAME, BUT THERE'S NO PROBLEM IN MISA TELLING ME...
AND HERE I FIGURED IT WOULD BE DIFFICULT TO GET MISA CLOSE TO RYUGA ...

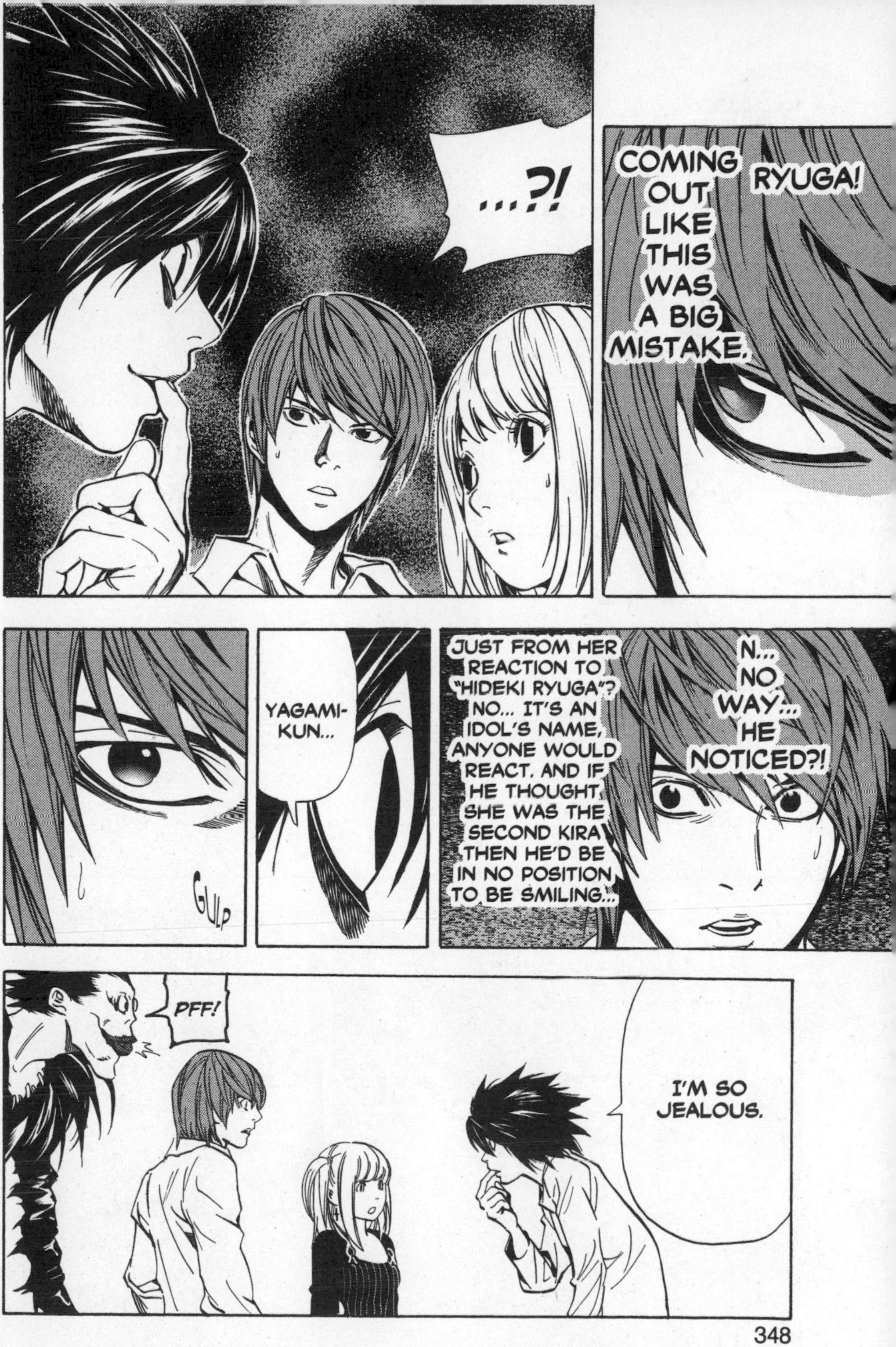
RYUGA!
COMING OUT LIKE THIS WAS A BIG MISTAKE.
...?!
N... NO WAY... HE NOTICED?!
JUST FROM HER REACTION TO "HIDEKI RYUGA"? NO... IT'S AN IDOL'S NAME, ANYONE WOULD REACT. AND IF HE THOUGHT SHE WAS THE SECOND KIRA THEN HE'D BE IN NO POSITION TO BE SMILING...
YAGAMI-KUN...
GULP
I'M SO JEALOUS.
PFF!

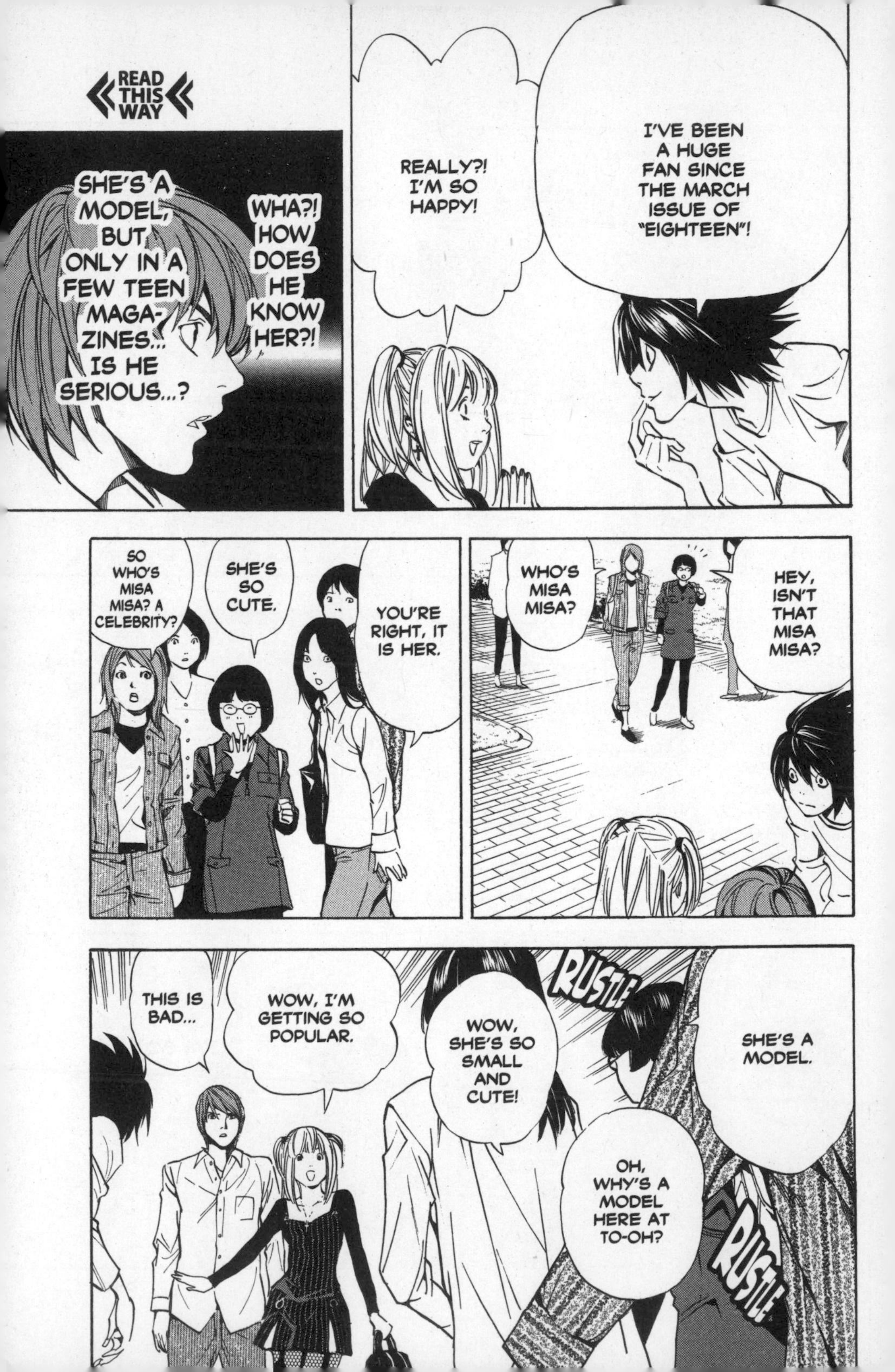
READ THIS WAY
I'VE BEEN A HUGE FAN SINCE THE MARCH ISSUE OF "EIGHTEEN"!
REALLY?! I'M SO HAPPY!
WHA?! HOW DOES HE KNOW HER?!
SHE'S A MODEL, BUT ONLY IN A FEW TEEN MAGAZINES... IS HE SERIOUS...?
HEY, ISN'T THAT MISA MISA?
WHO'S MISA MISA?
YOU'RE RIGHT, IT IS HER.
SHE'S SO CUTE.
SO WHO'S MISA MISA? A CELEBRITY?
SHE'S A MODEL.
RUSTLE
OH, WHY'S A MODEL HERE AT TO-OH?
WOW, SHE'S SO SMALL AND CUTE!
RUSTLE
WOW, I'M GETTING SO POPULAR.
THIS IS BAD...

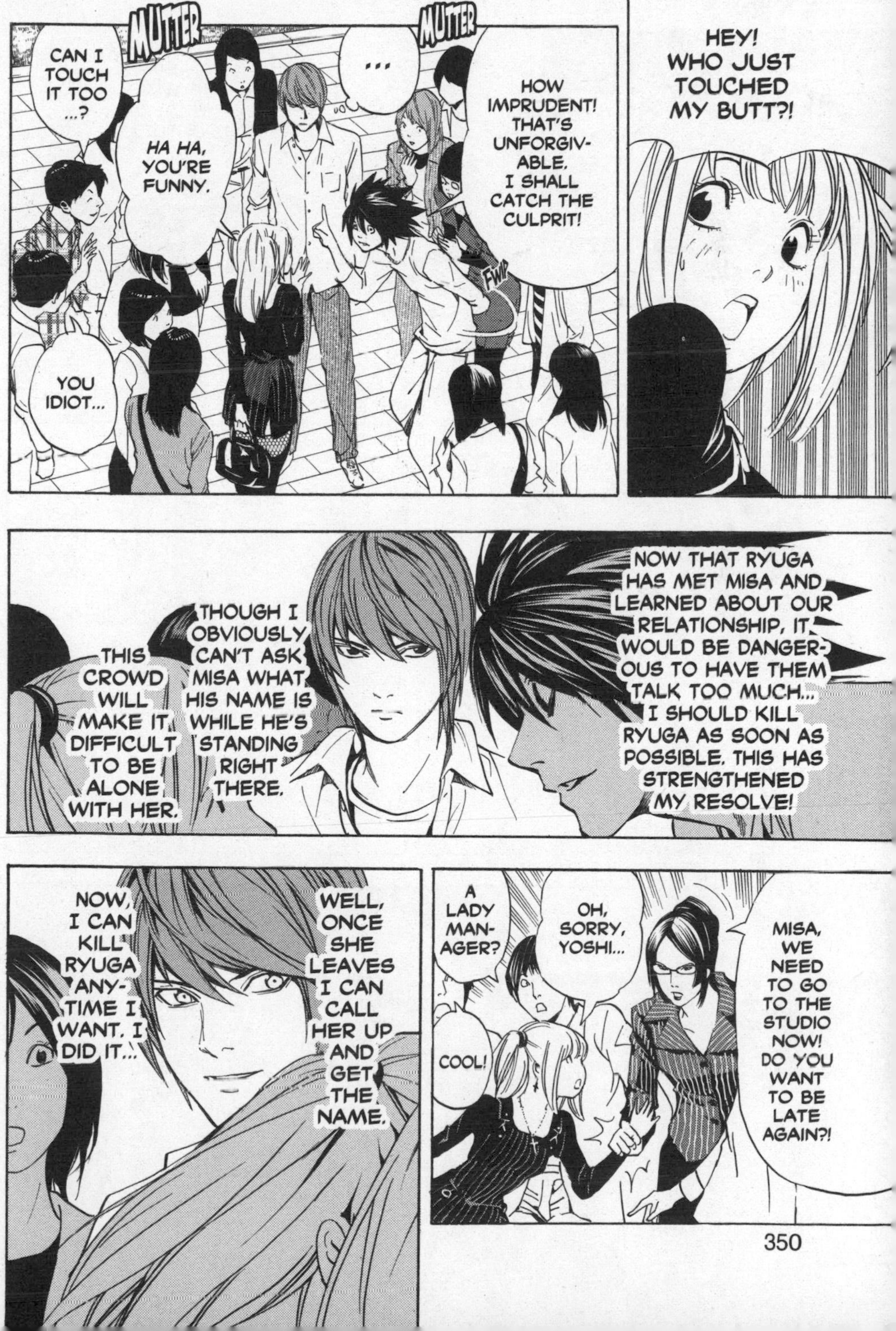
HEY! WHO JUST TOUCHED MY BUTT?!
MUTTER
HOW IMPRUDENT! THAT'S UNFORGIV-ABLE. I SHALL CATCH THE CULPRIT!
...
MUTTER
HA HA, YOU'RE FUNNY.
CAN I TOUCH IT TOO ...?
FWIP
YOU IDIOT...
NOW THAT RYUGA HAS MET MISA AND LEARNED ABOUT OUR RELATIONSHIP, IT WOULD BE DANGER-OUS TO HAVE THEM TALK TOO MUCH... I SHOULD KILL RYUGA AS SOON AS POSSIBLE. THIS HAS STRENGTHENED MY RESOLVE!
THOUGH I OBVIOUSLY CAN'T ASK MISA WHAT HIS NAME IS WHILE HE'S STANDING RIGHT THERE.
THIS CROWD WILL MAKE IT DIFFICULT TO BE ALONE WITH HER.
MISA, WE NEED TO GO TO THE STUDIO NOW! DO YOU WANT TO BE LATE AGAIN?!
OH, SORRY, YOSHI...
A LADY MAN-AGER?
COOL!
WELL, ONCE SHE LEAVES I CAN CALL HER UP AND GET THE NAME.
NOW, I CAN KILL RYUGA ANY-TIME I WANT. I DID IT...

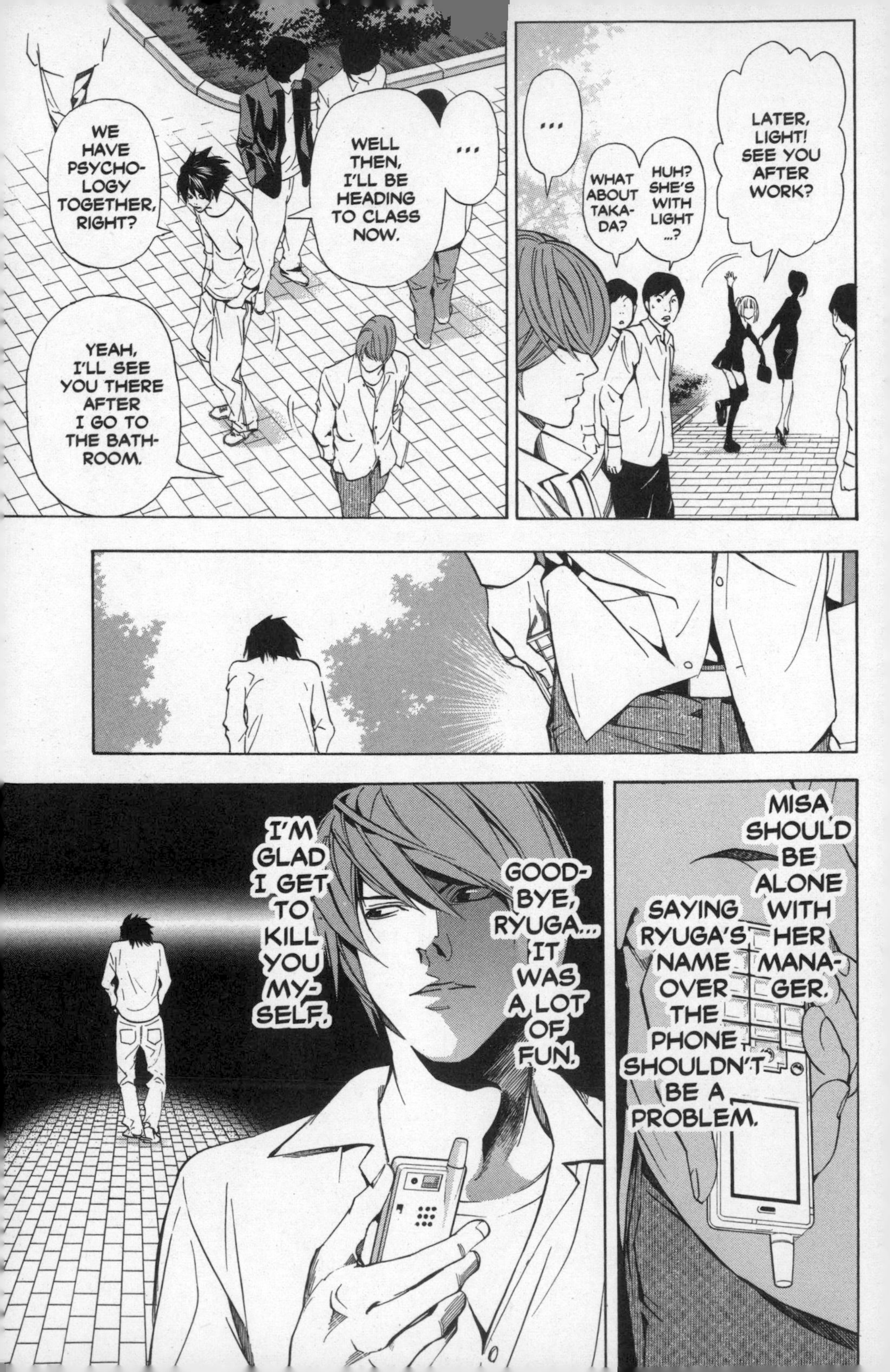
LATER, LIGHT! SEE YOU AFTER WORK?
HUH? SHE'S WITH LIGHT ...?
WHAT ABOUT TAKADA?
...
...
WELL THEN, I'LL BE HEADING TO CLASS NOW.
WE HAVE PSYCHOLOGY TOGETHER, RIGHT?
YEAH, I'LL SEE YOU THERE AFTER I GO TO THE BATHROOM.
MISA SHOULD BE ALONE WITH HER MANAGER.
SAYING RYUGA'S NAME OVER THE PHONE SHOULDN'T BE A PROBLEM.
GOOD-BYE, RYUGA... IT WAS A LOT OF FUN.
I'M GLAD I GET TO KILL YOU MYSELF.

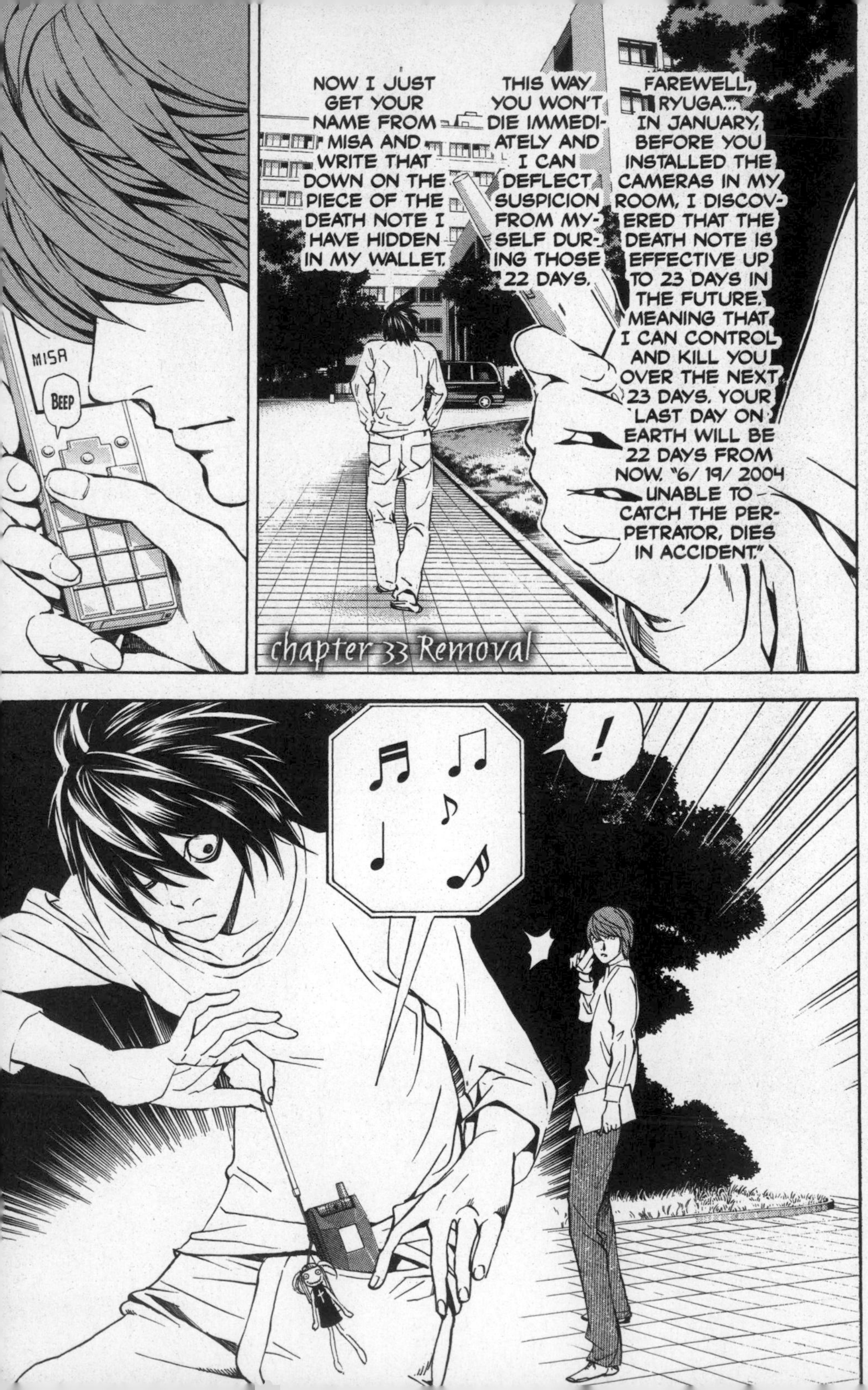
FAREWELL, RYUGA... IN JANUARY, BEFORE YOU INSTALLED THE CAMERAS IN MY ROOM, I DISCOVERED THAT THE DEATH NOTE IS EFFECTIVE UP TO 23 DAYS IN THE FUTURE. MEANING THAT I CAN CONTROL AND KILL YOU OVER THE NEXT 23 DAYS. YOUR LAST DAY ON EARTH WILL BE 22 DAYS FROM NOW. "6/ 19/ 2004 UNABLE TO CATCH THE PERPETRATOR, DIES IN ACCIDENT."
THIS WAY YOU WON'T DIE IMMEDIATELY AND I CAN DEFLECT SUSPICION FROM MYSELF DURING THOSE 22 DAYS.
NOW I JUST GET YOUR NAME FROM MISA AND WRITE THAT DOWN ON THE PIECE OF THE DEATH NOTE I HAVE HIDDEN IN MY WALLET.
chapter 33 Removal
MISA
BEEP
!

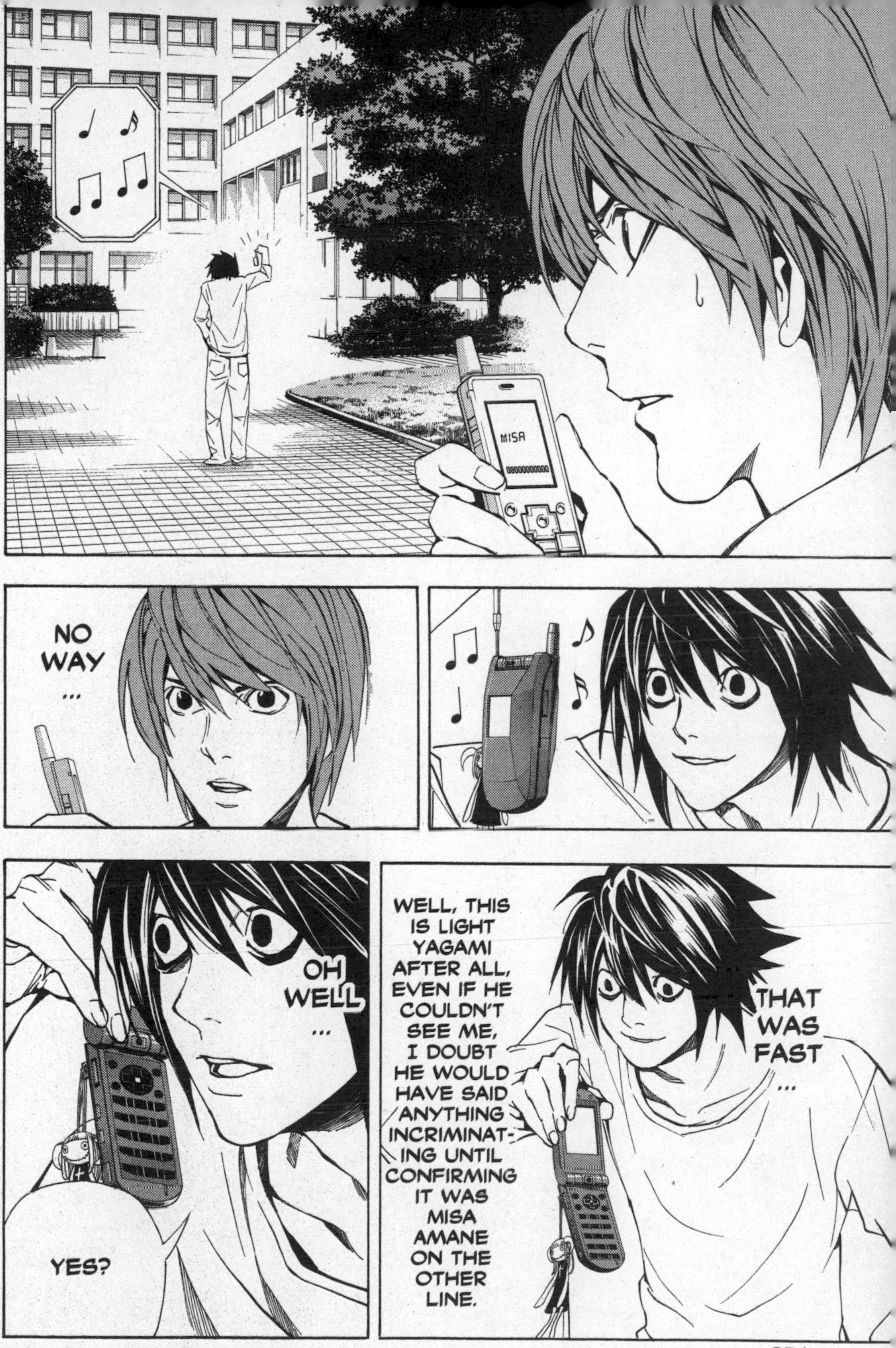
MISA
NO WAY ...
THAT WAS FAST ...
WELL, THIS IS LIGHT YAGAMI AFTER ALL, EVEN IF HE COULDN'T SEE ME, I DOUBT HE WOULD HAVE SAID ANYTHING INCRIMINATING UNTIL CONFIRMING IT WAS MISA AMANE ON THE OTHER LINE.
OH WELL ...
YES?

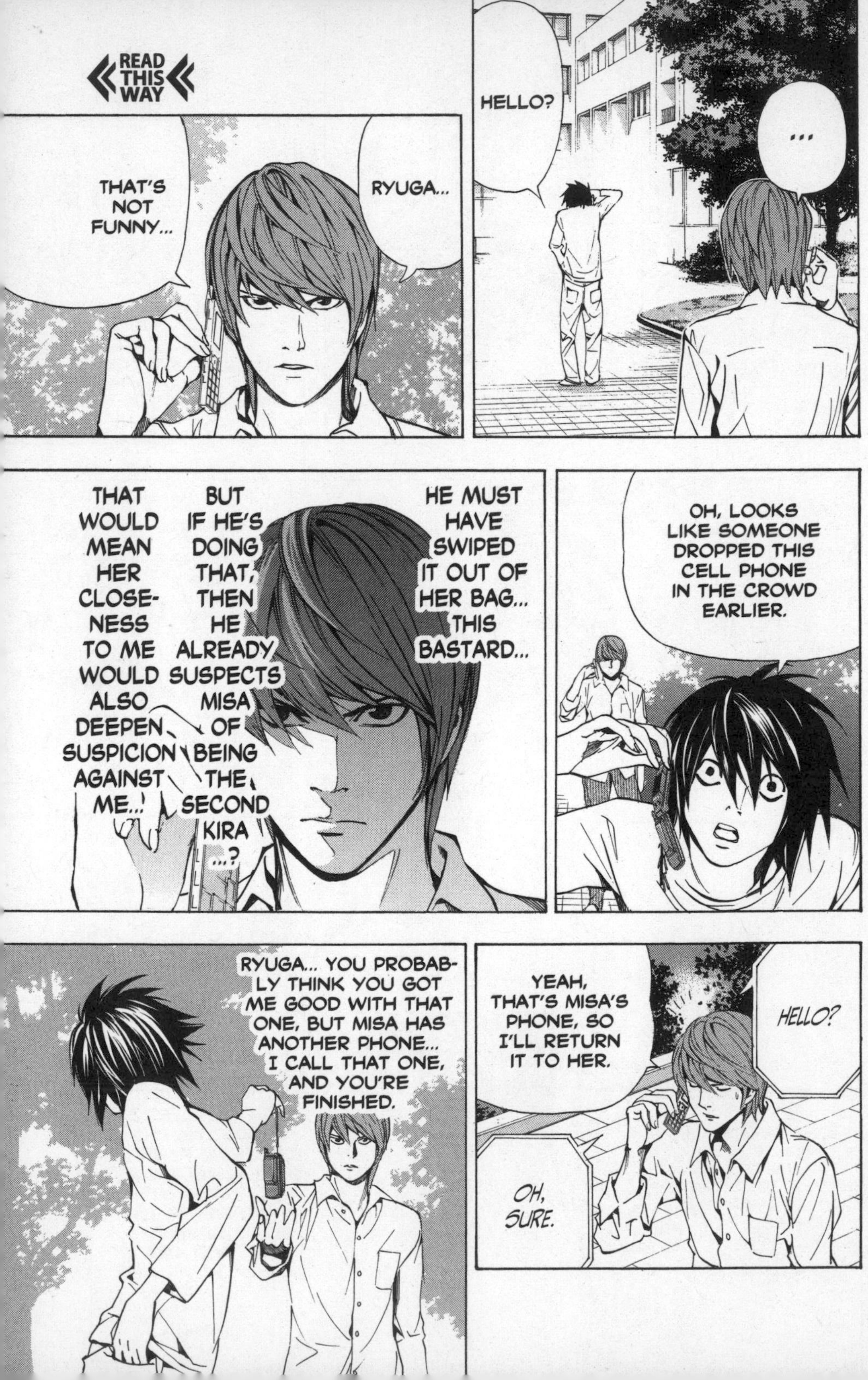
READ THIS WAY
HELLO?
...
RYUGA...
THAT'S NOT FUNNY...
OH, LOOKS LIKE SOMEONE DROPPED THIS CELL PHONE IN THE CROWD EARLIER.
HE MUST HAVE SWIPED IT OUT OF HER BAG... THIS BASTARD...
BUT IF HE'S DOING THAT, THEN HE ALREADY SUSPECTS MISA OF BEING THE SECOND KIRA ...?
THAT WOULD MEAN HER CLOSENESS TO ME WOULD ALSO DEEPEN SUSPICION AGAINST ME...
HELLO?
YEAH, THAT'S MISA'S PHONE, SO I'LL RETURN IT TO HER.
OH, SURE.
RYUGA... YOU PROBABLY THINK YOU GOT ME GOOD WITH THAT ONE, BUT MISA HAS ANOTHER PHONE... I CALL THAT ONE, AND YOU'RE FINISHED.

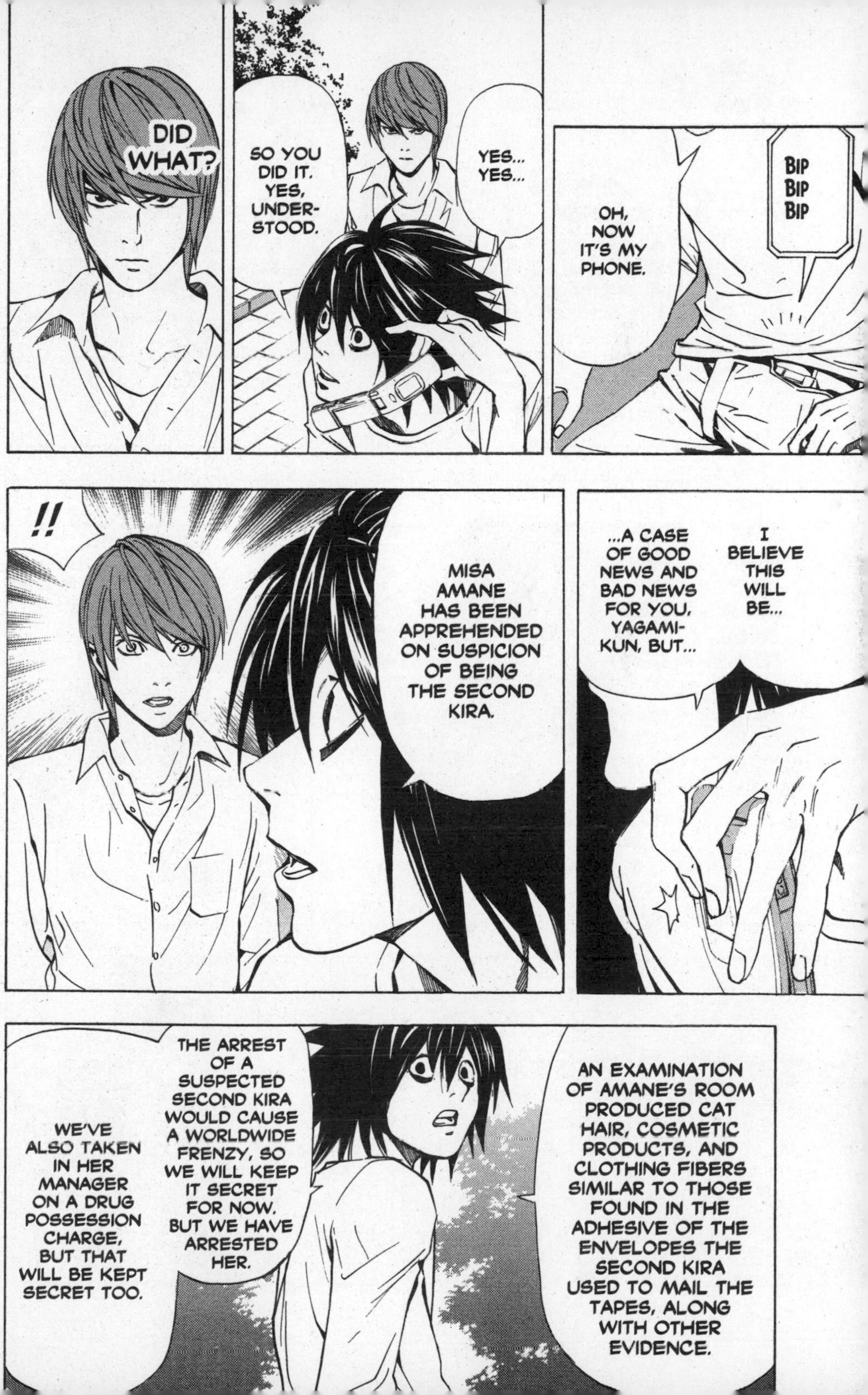
BIP BIP BIP
OH, NOW IT'S MY PHONE.
YES... YES...
SO YOU DID IT. YES, UNDERSTOOD.
DID WHAT?
I BELIEVE THIS WILL BE...
...A CASE OF GOOD NEWS AND BAD NEWS FOR YOU, YAGAMI-KUN, BUT...
MISA AMANE HAS BEEN APPREHENDED ON SUSPICION OF BEING THE SECOND KIRA.
!!
AN EXAMINATION OF AMANE'S ROOM PRODUCED CAT HAIR, COSMETIC PRODUCTS, AND CLOTHING FIBERS SIMILAR TO THOSE FOUND IN THE ADHESIVE OF THE ENVELOPES THE SECOND KIRA USED TO MAIL THE TAPES, ALONG WITH OTHER EVIDENCE.
THE ARREST OF A SUSPECTED SECOND KIRA WOULD CAUSE A WORLDWIDE FRENZY, SO WE WILL KEEP IT SECRET FOR NOW. BUT WE HAVE ARRESTED HER.
WE'VE ALSO TAKEN IN HER MANAGER ON A DRUG POSSESSION CHARGE, BUT THAT WILL BE KEPT SECRET TOO.

READ THIS WAY

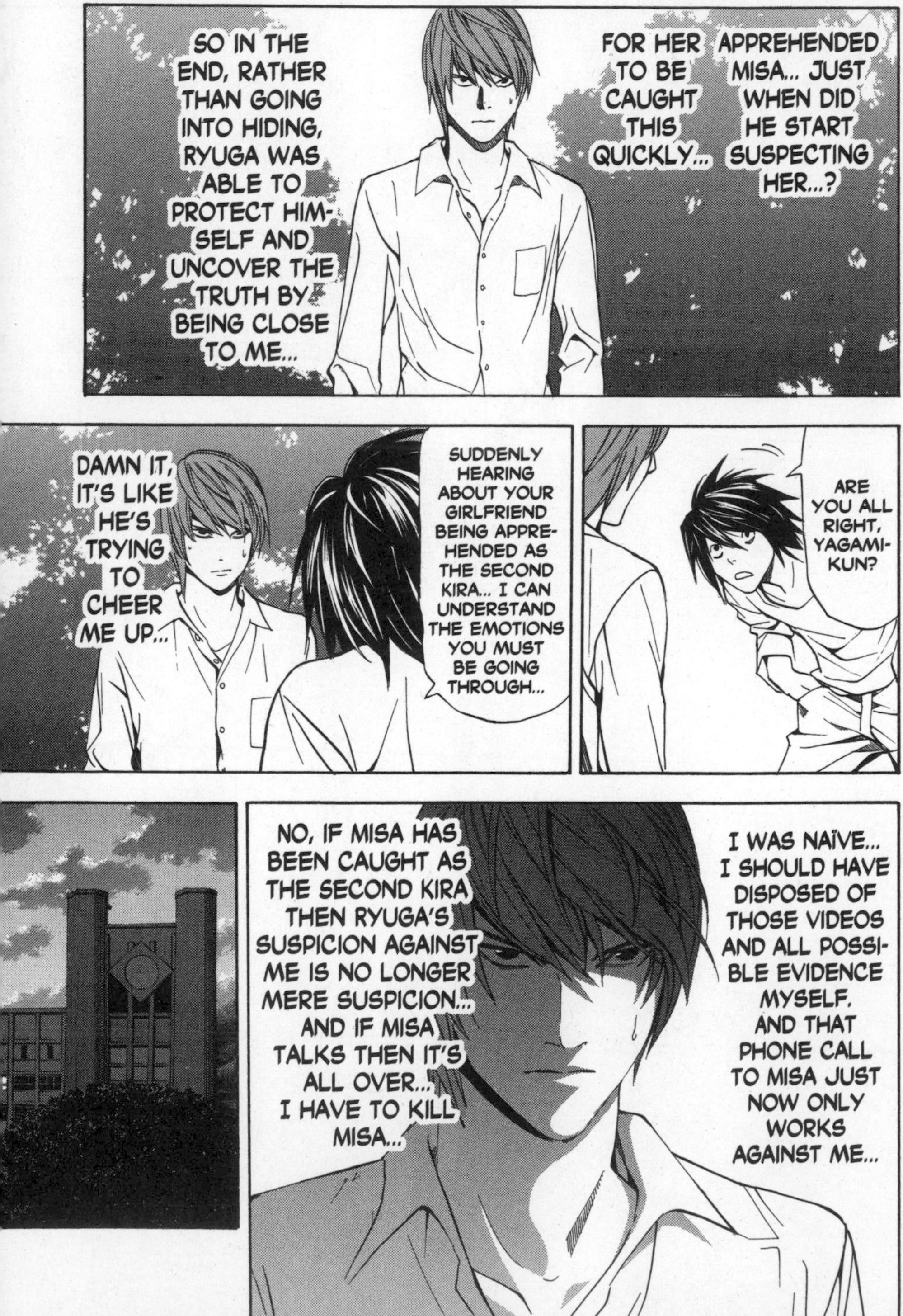
APPREHENDED MISA... JUST WHEN DID HE START SUSPECTING HER...?
FOR HER TO BE CAUGHT THIS QUICKLY...
SO IN THE END, RATHER THAN GOING INTO HIDING, RYUGA WAS ABLE TO PROTECT HIM-SELF AND UNCOVER THE TRUTH BY BEING CLOSE TO ME...
ARE YOU ALL RIGHT, YAGAMI-KUN?
SUDDENLY HEARING ABOUT YOUR GIRLFRIEND BEING APPRE-HENDED AS THE SECOND KIRA... I CAN UNDERSTAND THE EMOTIONS YOU MUST BE GOING THROUGH...
DAMN IT, IT'S LIKE HE'S TRYING TO CHEER ME UP...
I WAS NAÏVE... I SHOULD HAVE DISPOSED OF THOSE VIDEOS AND ALL POSSI-BLE EVIDENCE MYSELF. AND THAT PHONE CALL TO MISA JUST NOW ONLY WORKS AGAINST ME...
NO, IF MISA HAS BEEN CAUGHT AS THE SECOND KIRA THEN RYUGA'S SUSPICION AGAINST ME IS NO LONGER MERE SUSPICION... AND IF MISA TALKS THEN IT'S ALL OVER... I HAVE TO KILL MISA...

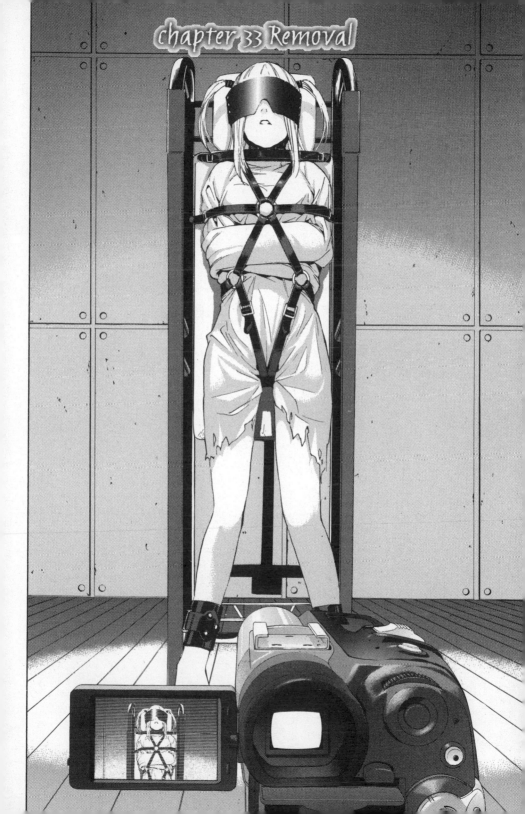

chapter 33 Removal

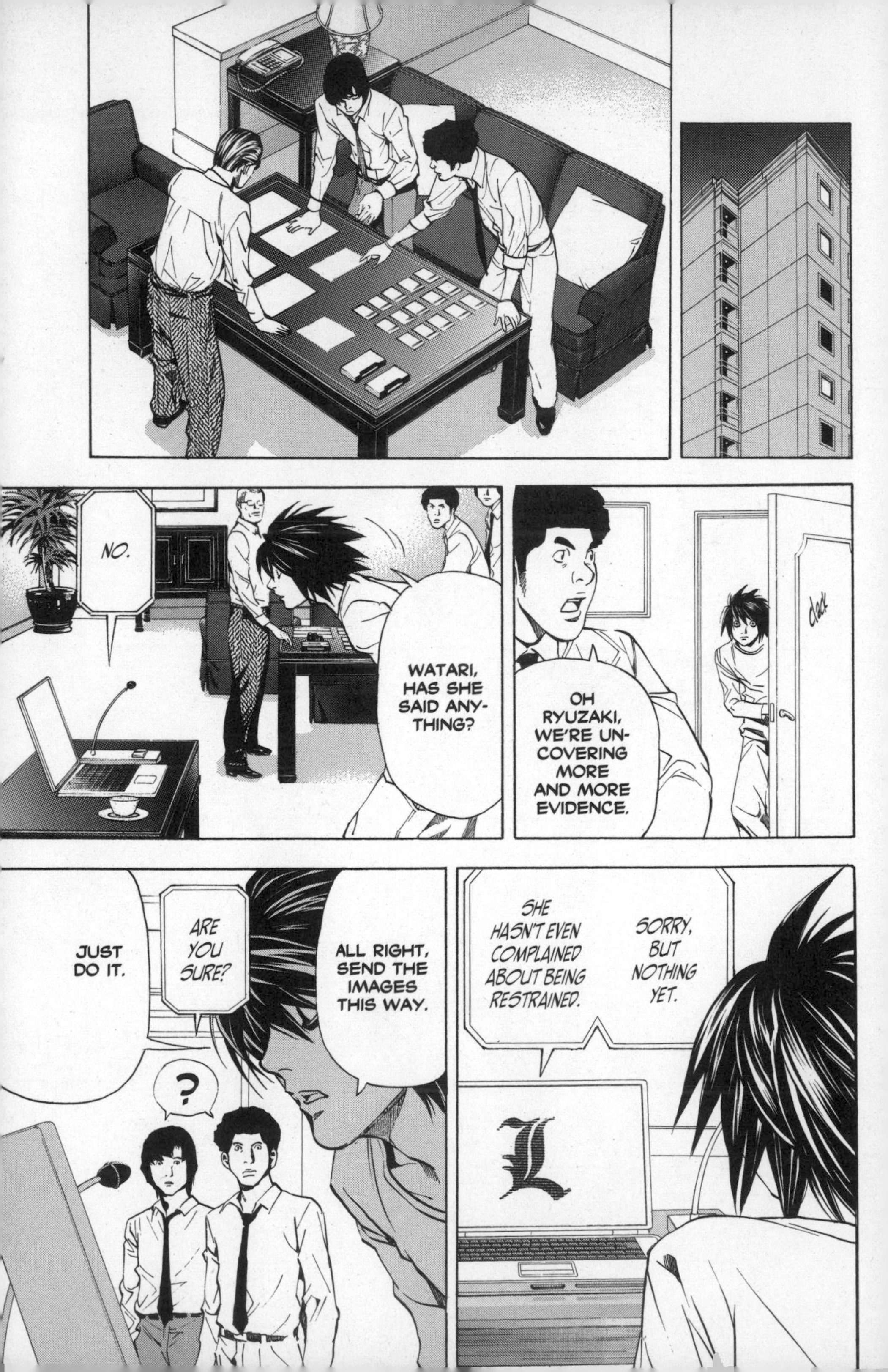
clack
OH RYUZAKI, WE'RE UN-COVERING MORE AND MORE EVIDENCE.
WATARI, HAS SHE SAID ANY-THING?
NO.
SORRY, BUT NOTHING YET.
SHE HASN'T EVEN COMPLAINED ABOUT BEING RESTRAINED.
ALL RIGHT, SEND THE IMAGES THIS WAY.
ARE YOU SURE?
JUST DO IT.
?

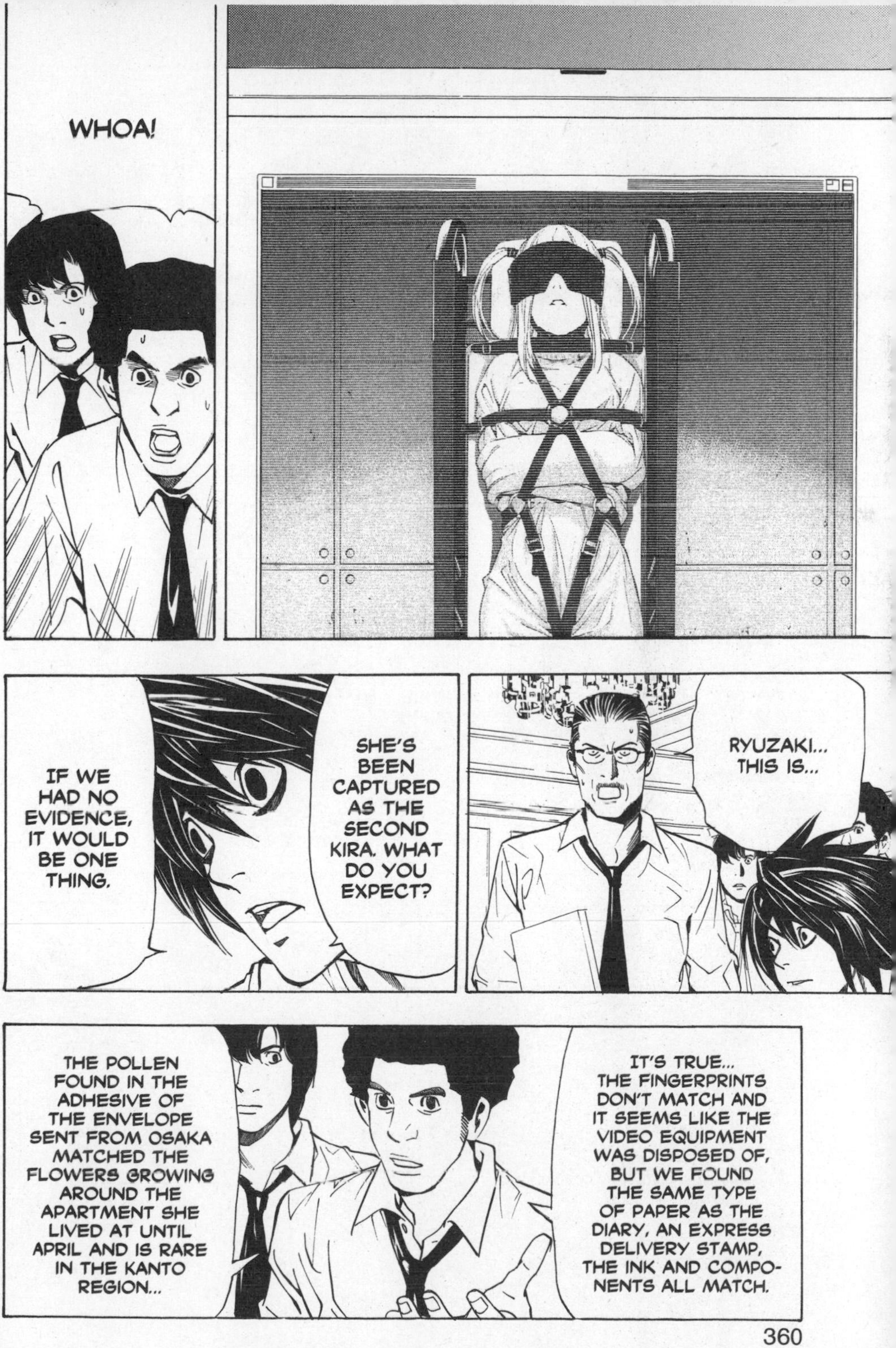
WHOA!
RYUZAKI... THIS IS...
SHE'S BEEN CAPTURED AS THE SECOND KIRA. WHAT DO YOU EXPECT?
IF WE HAD NO EVIDENCE, IT WOULD BE ONE THING.
IT'S TRUE... THE FINGERPRINTS DON'T MATCH AND IT SEEMS LIKE THE VIDEO EQUIPMENT WAS DISPOSED OF, BUT WE FOUND THE SAME TYPE OF PAPER AS THE DIARY, AN EXPRESS DELIVERY STAMP, THE INK AND COMPONENTS ALL MATCH.
THE POLLEN FOUND IN THE ADHESIVE OF THE ENVELOPE SENT FROM OSAKA MATCHED THE FLOWERS GROWING AROUND THE APARTMENT SHE LIVED AT UNTIL APRIL AND IS RARE IN THE KANTO REGION...

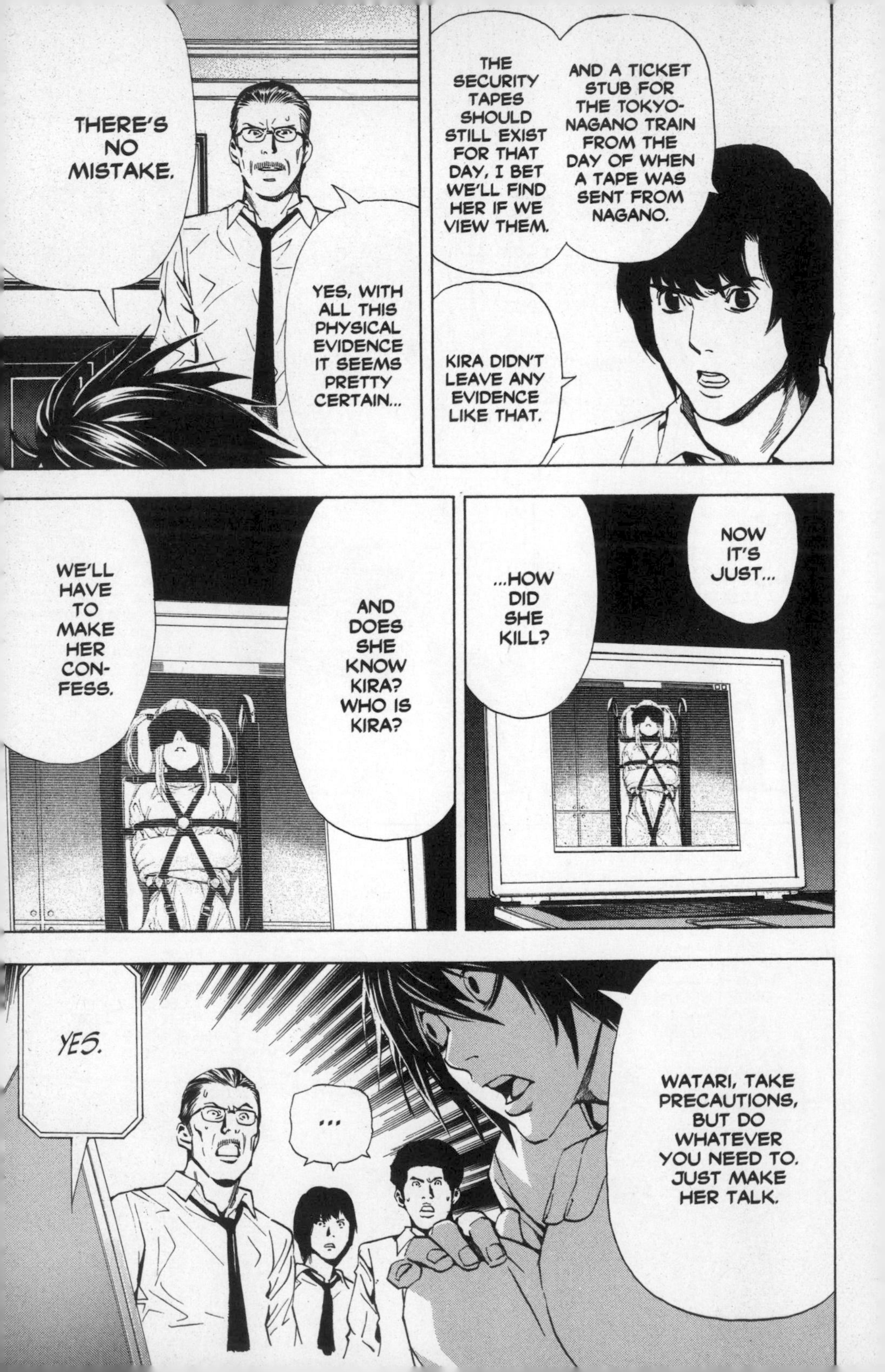
AND A TICKET STUB FOR THE TOKYO-NAGANO TRAIN FROM THE DAY OF WHEN A TAPE WAS SENT FROM NAGANO.
THE SECURITY TAPES SHOULD STILL EXIST FOR THAT DAY. I BET WE'LL FIND HER IF WE VIEW THEM.
KIRA DIDN'T LEAVE ANY EVIDENCE LIKE THAT.
THERE'S NO MISTAKE.
YES, WITH ALL THIS PHYSICAL EVIDENCE IT SEEMS PRETTY CERTAIN...
NOW IT'S JUST...
...HOW DID SHE KILL?
AND DOES SHE KNOW KIRA? WHO IS KIRA?
WE'LL HAVE TO MAKE HER CON-FESS.
WATARI, TAKE PRECAUTIONS, BUT DO WHATEVER YOU NEED TO. JUST MAKE HER TALK.
...
YES.

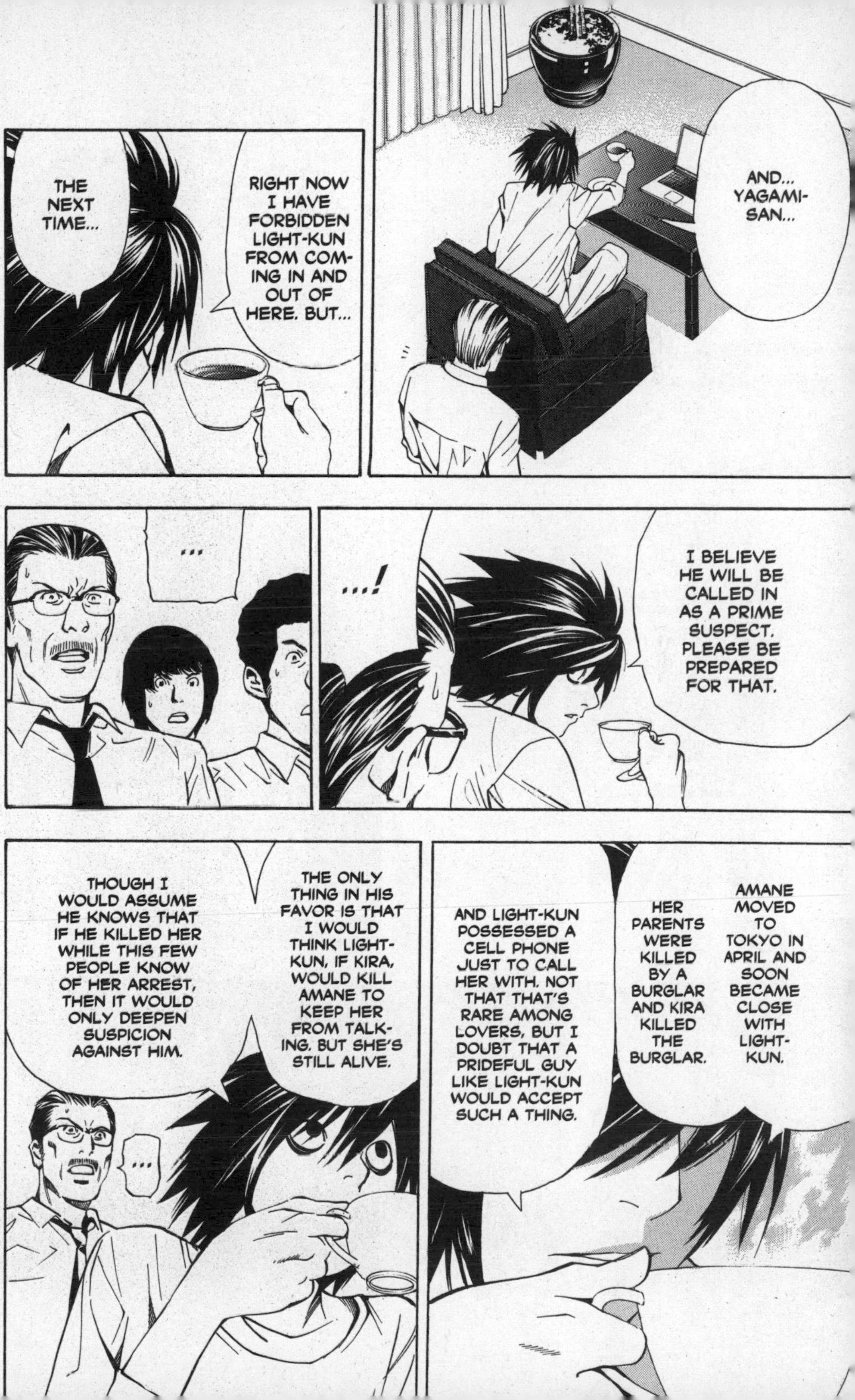
AND... YAGAMI-SAN...
RIGHT NOW I HAVE FORBIDDEN LIGHT-KUN FROM COMING IN AND OUT OF HERE. BUT...
THE NEXT TIME...
I BELIEVE HE WILL BE CALLED IN AS A PRIME SUSPECT. PLEASE BE PREPARED FOR THAT.
...!
...
AMANE MOVED TO TOKYO IN APRIL AND SOON BECAME CLOSE WITH LIGHT-KUN.
HER PARENTS WERE KILLED BY A BURGLAR AND KIRA KILLED THE BURGLAR.
AND LIGHT-KUN POSSESSED A CELL PHONE JUST TO CALL HER WITH. NOT THAT THAT'S RARE AMONG LOVERS, BUT I DOUBT THAT A PRIDEFUL GUY LIKE LIGHT-KUN WOULD ACCEPT SUCH A THING.
THE ONLY THING IN HIS FAVOR IS THAT I WOULD THINK LIGHT-KUN, IF KIRA, WOULD KILL AMANE TO KEEP HER FROM TALKING. BUT SHE'S STILL ALIVE.
THOUGH I WOULD ASSUME HE KNOWS THAT IF HE KILLED HER WHILE THIS FEW PEOPLE KNOW OF HER ARREST, THEN IT WOULD ONLY DEEPEN SUSPICION AGAINST HIM.
...

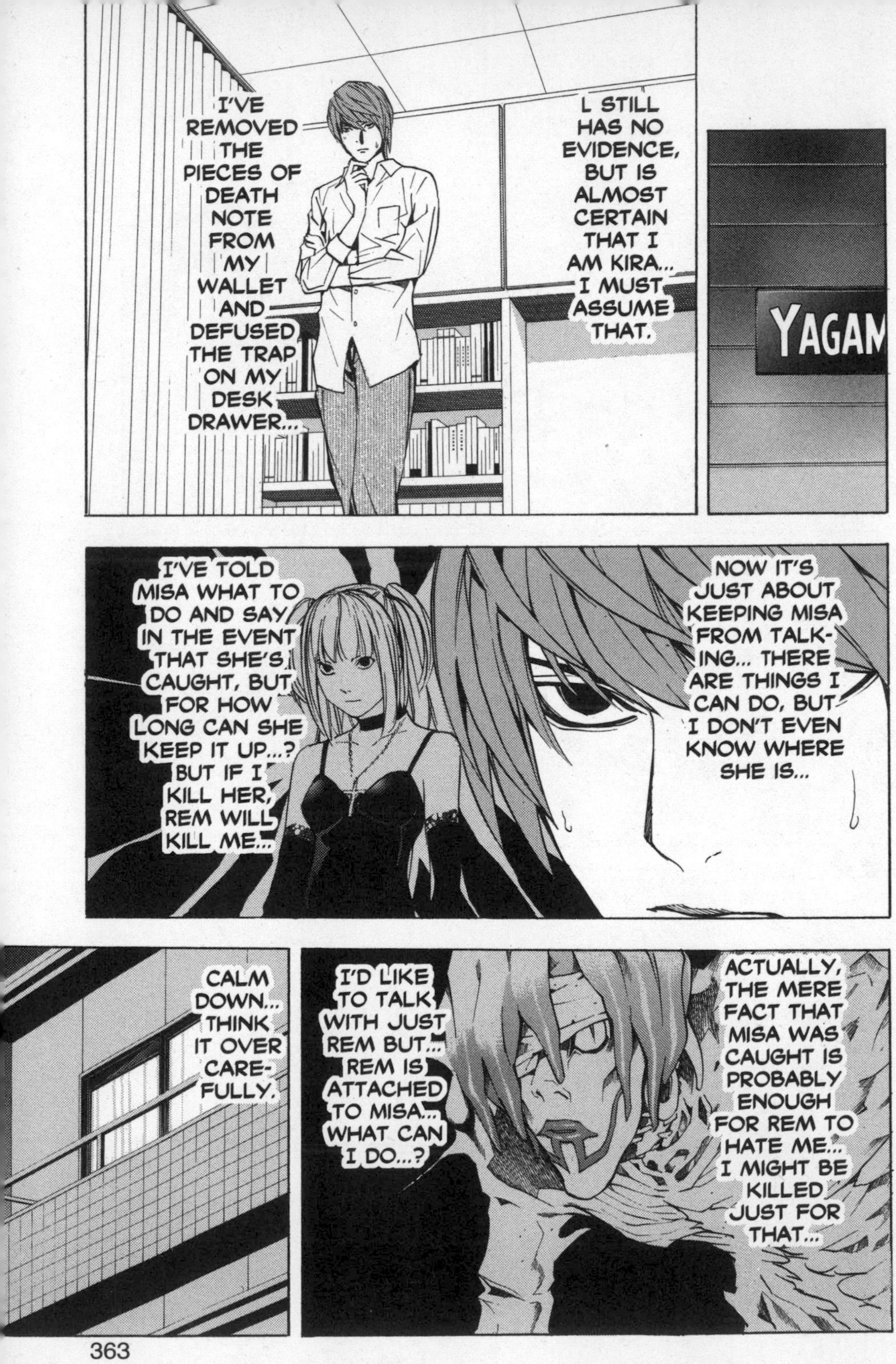
YAGAM
L STILL HAS NO EVIDENCE, BUT IS ALMOST CERTAIN THAT I AM KIRA... I MUST ASSUME THAT.
I'VE REMOVED THE PIECES OF DEATH NOTE FROM MY WALLET AND DEFUSED THE TRAP ON MY DESK DRAWER...
NOW IT'S JUST ABOUT KEEPING MISA FROM TALK-ING... THERE ARE THINGS I CAN DO, BUT I DON'T EVEN KNOW WHERE SHE IS...
I'VE TOLD MISA WHAT TO DO AND SAY IN THE EVENT THAT SHE'S CAUGHT, BUT FOR HOW LONG CAN SHE KEEP IT UP...? BUT IF I KILL HER, REM WILL KILL ME...
ACTUALLY, THE MERE FACT THAT MISA WAS CAUGHT IS PROBABLY ENOUGH FOR REM TO HATE ME... I MIGHT BE KILLED JUST FOR THAT...
I'D LIKE TO TALK WITH JUST REM BUT... REM IS ATTACHED TO MISA... WHAT CAN I DO...?
CALM DOWN... THINK IT OVER CARE-FULLY.

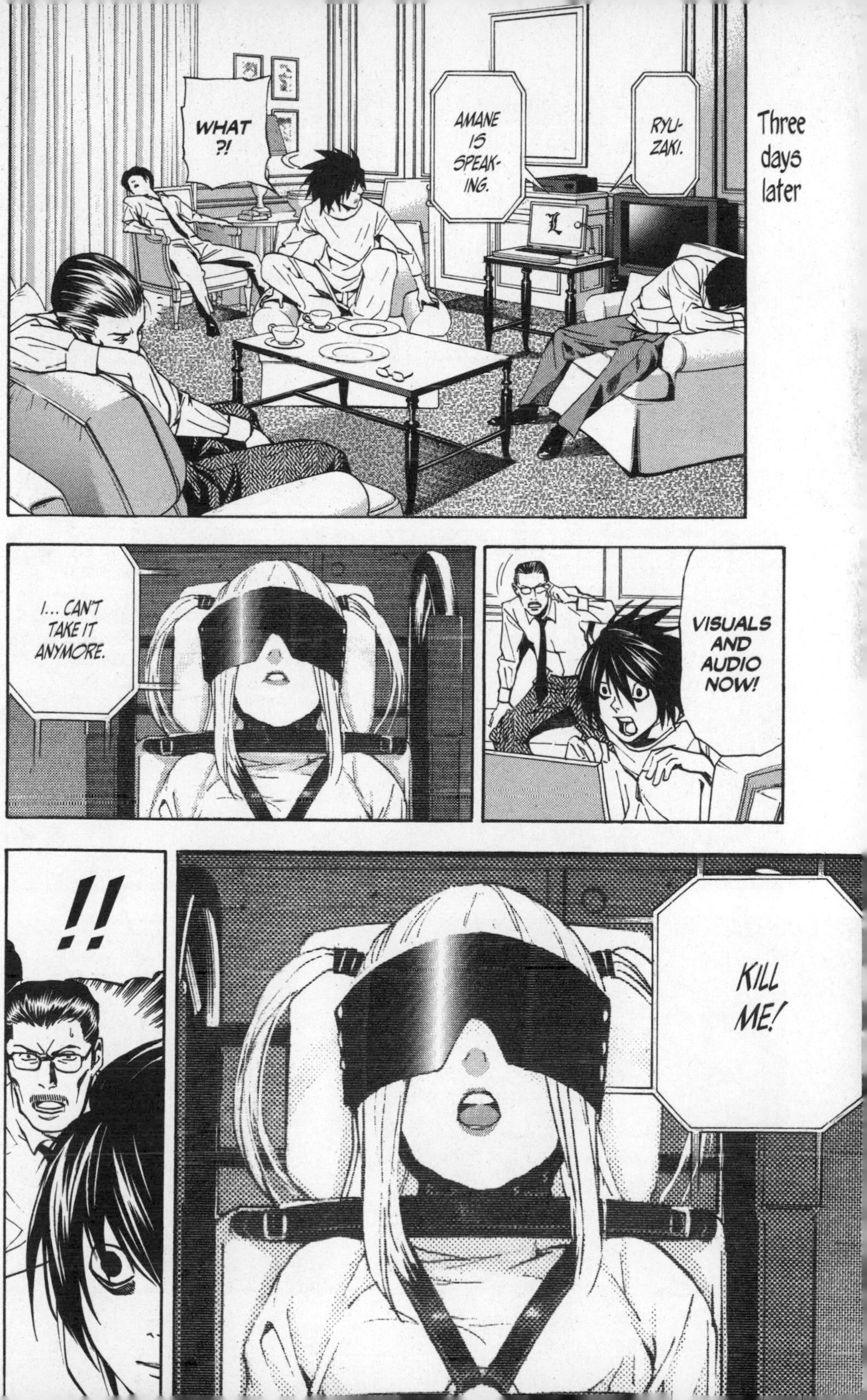
Three days later
RYU-ZAKI.
AMANE IS SPEAK-ING.
WHAT ?!
VISUALS AND AUDIO NOW!
I... CAN'T TAKE IT ANYMORE.
KILL ME!
!!

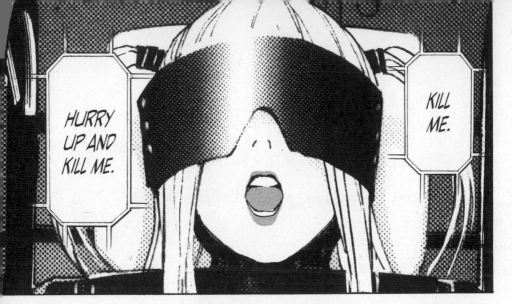

KILL ME.
HURRY UP AND KILL ME.
YOU SAID SHE HASN'T HAD WATER IN THREE DAYS, RIGHT...?
THAT'S TOO MUCH FOR A TWENTY-YEAR-OLD GIRL... SHE MUST BE AT HER LIMIT...
...
Click
MISA AMANE, CAN YOU HEAR ME?
YES...

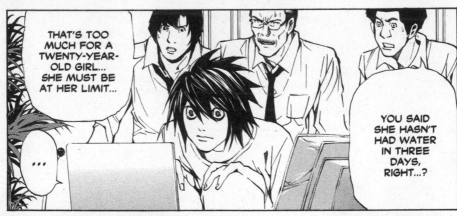

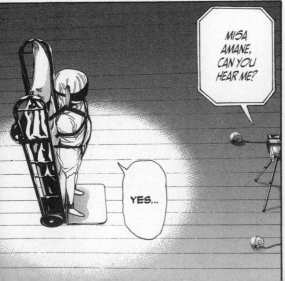

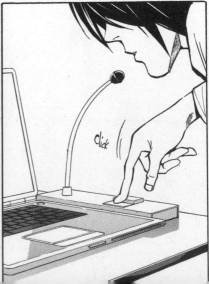

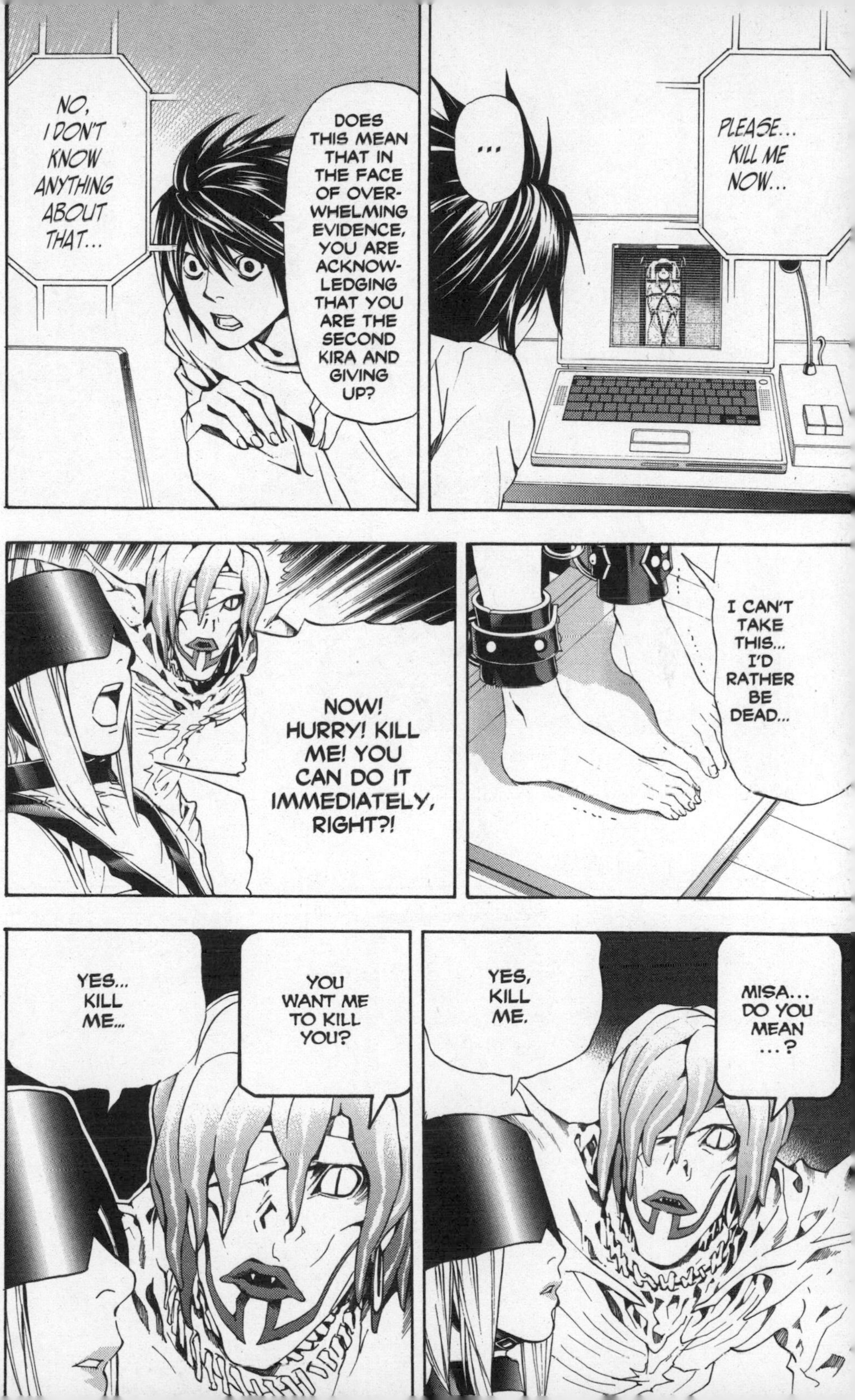
PLEASE... KILL ME NOW...
...
DOES THIS MEAN THAT IN THE FACE OF OVER-WHELMING EVIDENCE, YOU ARE ACKNOW-LEDGING THAT YOU ARE THE SECOND KIRA AND GIVING UP?
NO, I DON'T KNOW ANYTHING ABOUT THAT...
I CAN'T TAKE THIS... I'D RATHER BE DEAD...
NOW! HURRY! KILL ME! YOU CAN DO IT IMMEDIATELY, RIGHT?!
MISA... DO YOU MEAN ...?
YES, KILL ME.
YOU WANT ME TO KILL YOU?
YES... KILL ME...

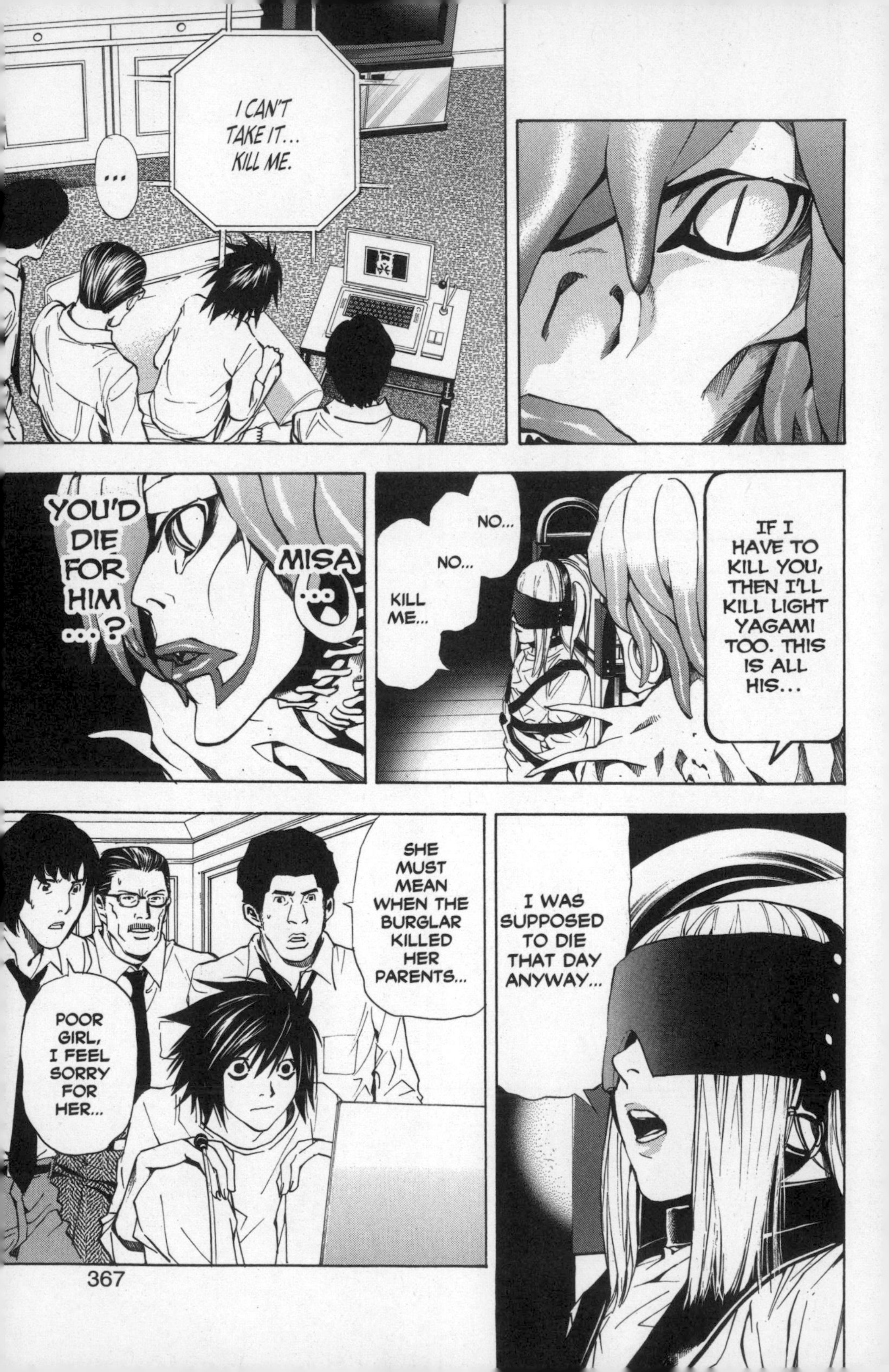
I CAN'T TAKE IT... KILL ME.
...
IF I HAVE TO KILL YOU, THEN I'LL KILL LIGHT YAGAMI TOO. THIS IS ALL HIS...
NO...
NO...
KILL ME...
MISA...
YOU'D DIE FOR HIM...?
I WAS SUPPOSED TO DIE THAT DAY ANYWAY...
SHE MUST MEAN WHEN THE BURGLAR KILLED HER PARENTS...
POOR GIRL, I FEEL SORRY FOR HER...

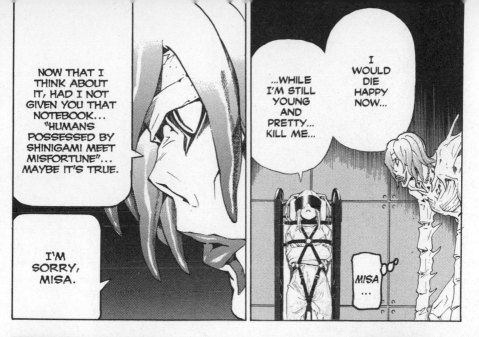

NOW THAT I THINK ABOUT IT, HAD I NOT GIVEN YOU THAT NOTEBOOK... "HUMANS POSSESSED BY SHINIGAMI MEET MISFORTUNE"... MAYBE IT'S TRUE.

I'M SORRY, MISA.

...WHILE I'M STILL YOUNG AND PRETTY... KILL ME...

I WOULD DIE HAPPY NOW...

MISA...

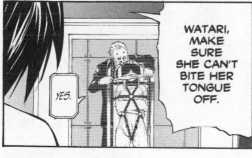

YES.

WATARI, MAKE SURE SHE CAN'T BITE HER TONGUE OFF.

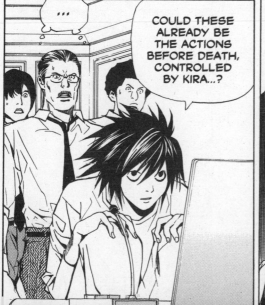

...

COULD THESE ALREADY BE THE ACTIONS BEFORE DEATH, CONTROLLED BY KIRA...?

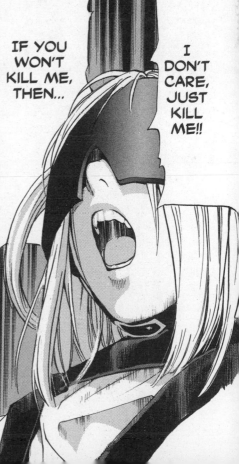

IF YOU WON'T KILL ME, THEN...

I DON'T CARE, JUST KILL ME!!

READ THIS WAY

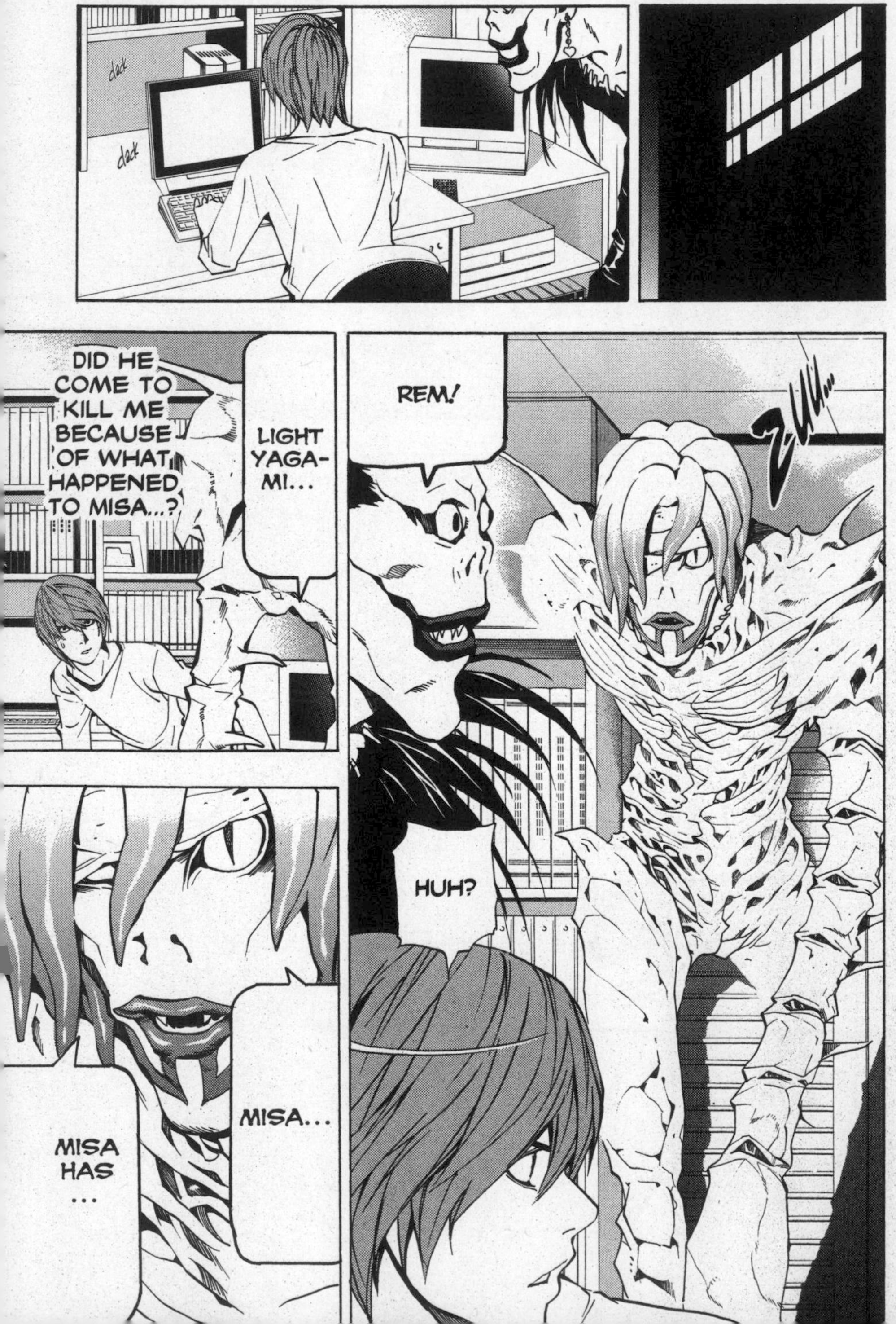
clack
clack
ZUU...
REM!
HUH?
LIGHT YAGA-MI...
DID HE COME TO KILL ME BECAUSE OF WHAT HAPPENED TO MISA...?
MISA...
MISA HAS...

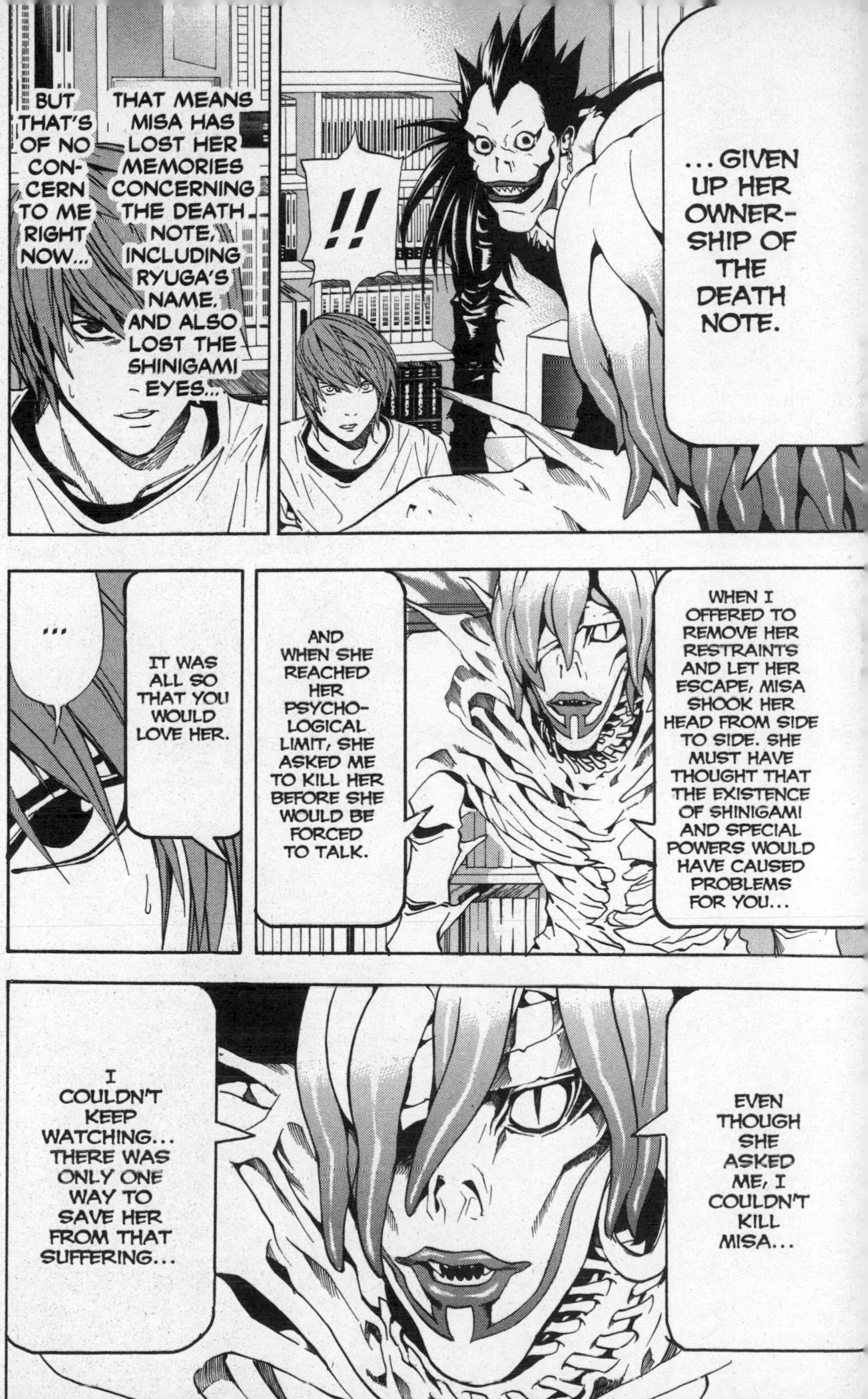

...GIVEN UP HER OWNERSHIP OF THE DEATH NOTE.
!!
THAT MEANS MISA HAS LOST HER MEMORIES CONCERNING THE DEATH NOTE, INCLUDING RYUGA'S NAME, AND ALSO LOST THE SHINIGAMI EYES...
BUT THAT'S OF NO CONCERN TO ME RIGHT NOW...
WHEN I OFFERED TO REMOVE HER RESTRAINTS AND LET HER ESCAPE, MISA SHOOK HER HEAD FROM SIDE TO SIDE. SHE MUST HAVE THOUGHT THAT THE EXISTENCE OF SHINIGAMI AND SPECIAL POWERS WOULD HAVE CAUSED PROBLEMS FOR YOU...
AND WHEN SHE REACHED HER PSYCHOLOGICAL LIMIT, SHE ASKED ME TO KILL HER BEFORE SHE WOULD BE FORCED TO TALK.
IT WAS ALL SO THAT YOU WOULD LOVE HER.
...
EVEN THOUGH SHE ASKED ME, I COULDN'T KILL MISA...
I COULDN'T KEEP WATCHING... THERE WAS ONLY ONE WAY TO SAVE HER FROM THAT SUFFERING...

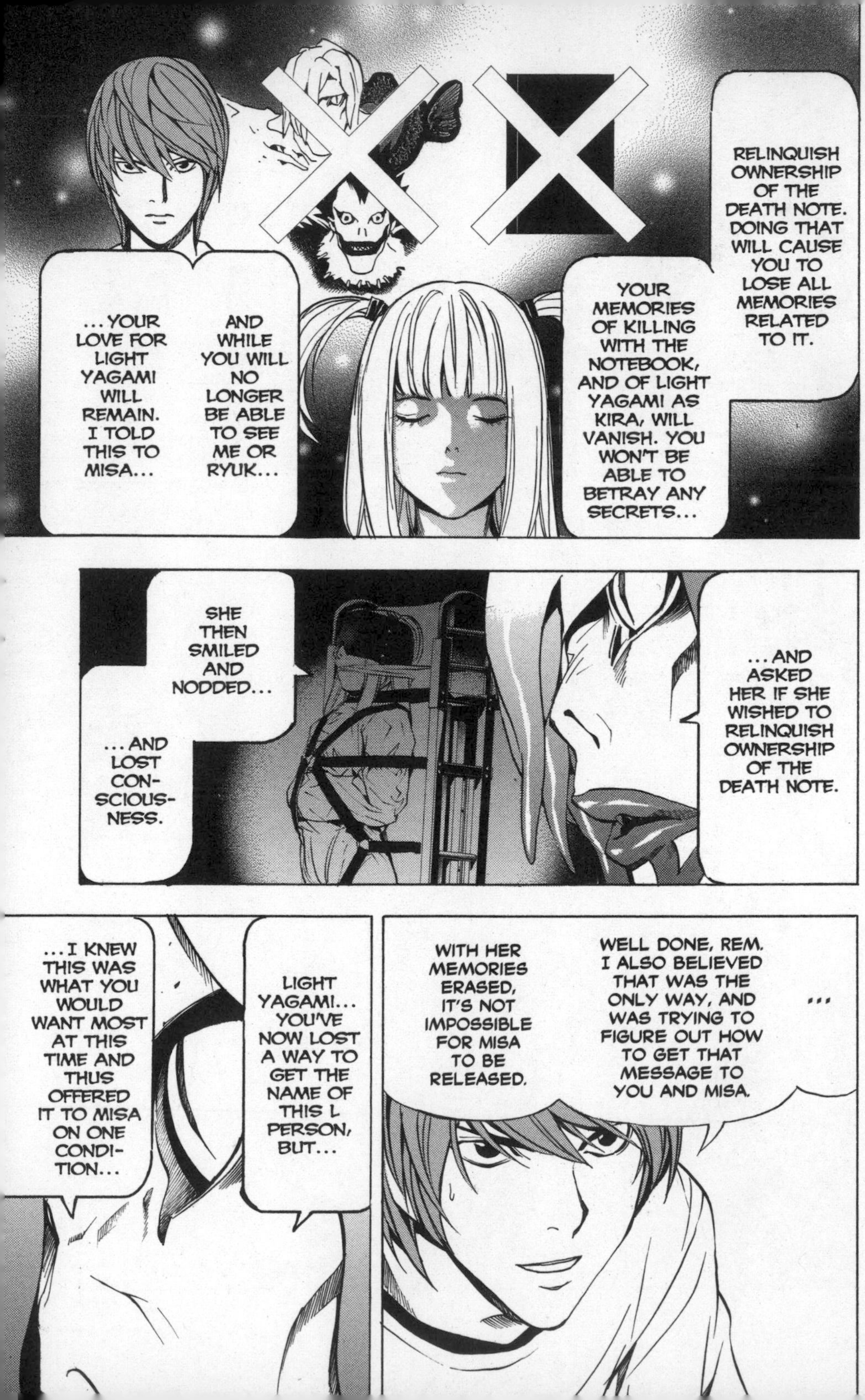

RELINQUISH OWNERSHIP OF THE DEATH NOTE. DOING THAT WILL CAUSE YOU TO LOSE ALL MEMORIES RELATED TO IT.
YOUR MEMORIES OF KILLING WITH THE NOTEBOOK, AND OF LIGHT YAGAMI AS KIRA, WILL VANISH. YOU WON'T BE ABLE TO BETRAY ANY SECRETS...
AND WHILE YOU WILL NO LONGER BE ABLE TO SEE ME OR RYUK...
...YOUR LOVE FOR LIGHT YAGAMI WILL REMAIN. I TOLD THIS TO MISA...
...AND ASKED HER IF SHE WISHED TO RELINQUISH OWNERSHIP OF THE DEATH NOTE.
SHE THEN SMILED AND NODDED...
...AND LOST CONSCIOUS-NESS.
...
WELL DONE, REM. I ALSO BELIEVED THAT WAS THE ONLY WAY, AND WAS TRYING TO FIGURE OUT HOW TO GET THAT MESSAGE TO YOU AND MISA.
WITH HER MEMORIES ERASED, IT'S NOT IMPOSSIBLE FOR MISA TO BE RELEASED.
LIGHT YAGAMI... YOU'VE NOW LOST A WAY TO GET THE NAME OF THIS L PERSON, BUT...
...I KNEW THIS WAS WHAT YOU WOULD WANT MOST AT THIS TIME AND THUS OFFERED IT TO MISA ON ONE CONDITION...

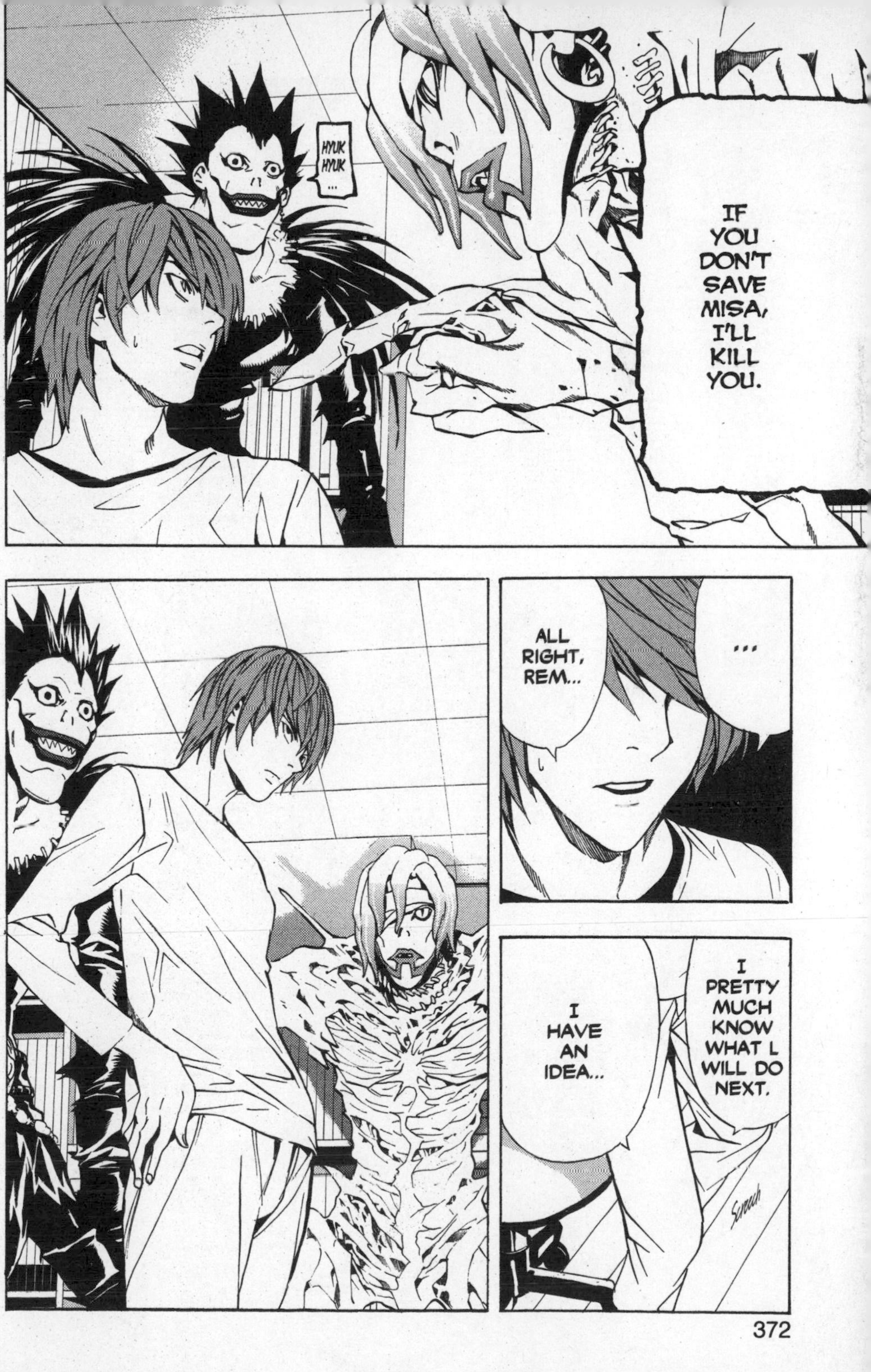
IF YOU DON'T SAVE MISA, I'LL KILL YOU.
HYUK HYUK ...
...
ALL RIGHT, REM...
I PRETTY MUCH KNOW WHAT L WILL DO NEXT.
I HAVE AN IDEA...
Screech

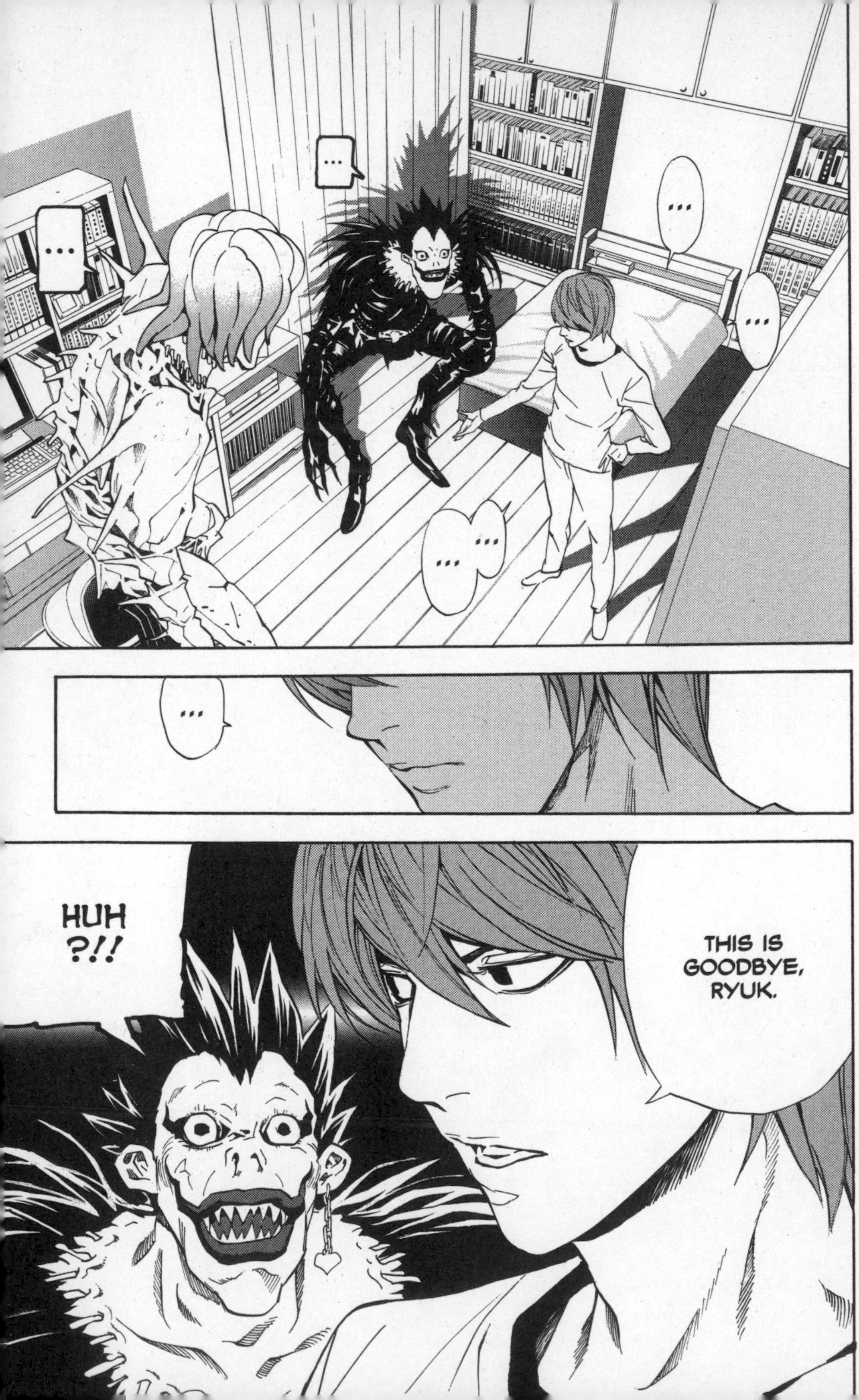
...
...
...
...
... ...
...
THIS IS GOODBYE, RYUK.
HUH ?!!

DEATH NOTE
How to use it
XXI

- the individuals who lose the ownership of the DEATH NOTE will also lose their memory of the usage of the DEATH NOTE. this does not mean that he will lose all the memory from the day he owned it to the day he loses possession, but means he will only lose the memory involving the DEATH NOTE.

デスノートの所有権を失った人間は自分がデスノートを使用した事等の記憶が一切なくなる。しかし、ノートを持ってから失うまでの全ての記憶を喪失するのではなく、自分のしてきた行動はデスノートの所有者であった事が絡まない形で残る。

chapter 34 Imprisonment

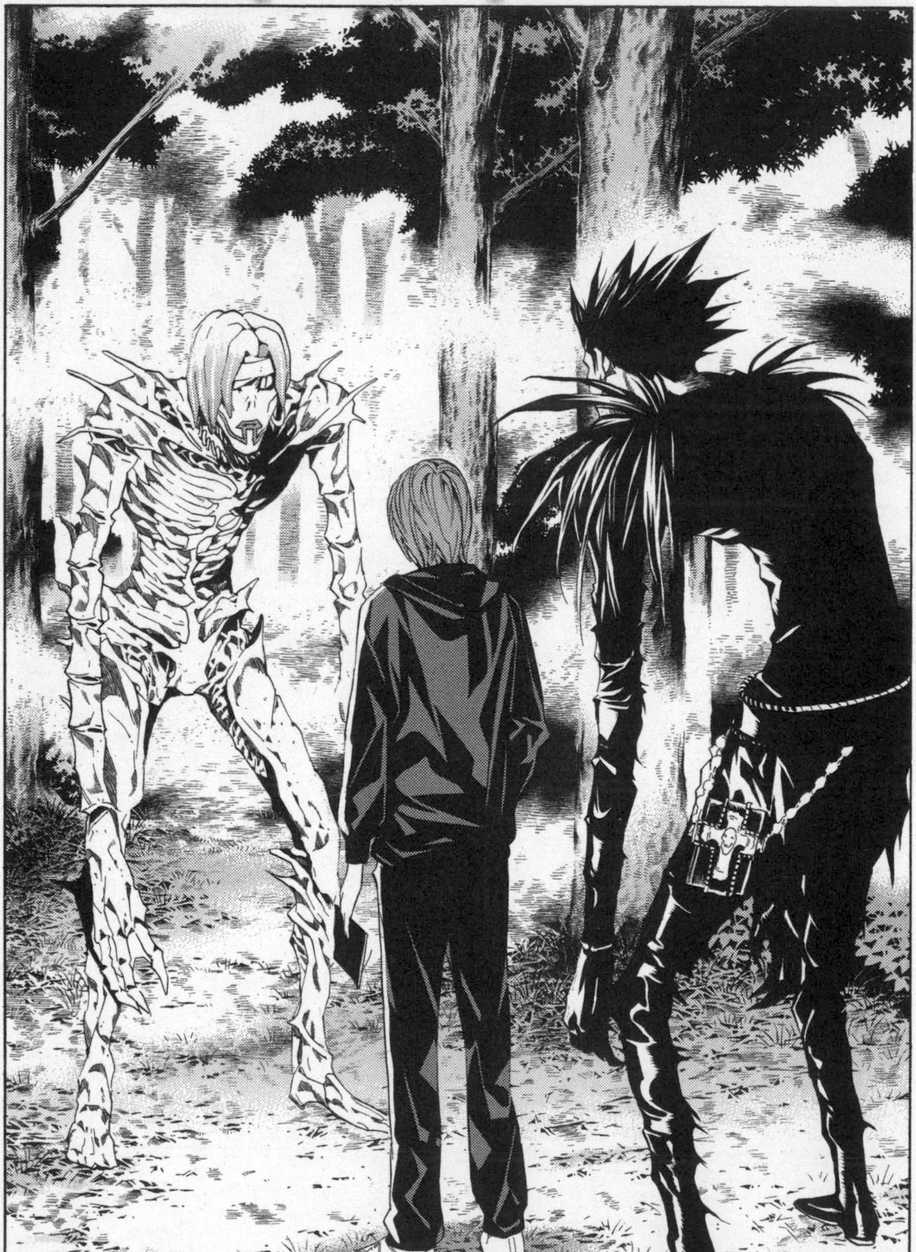

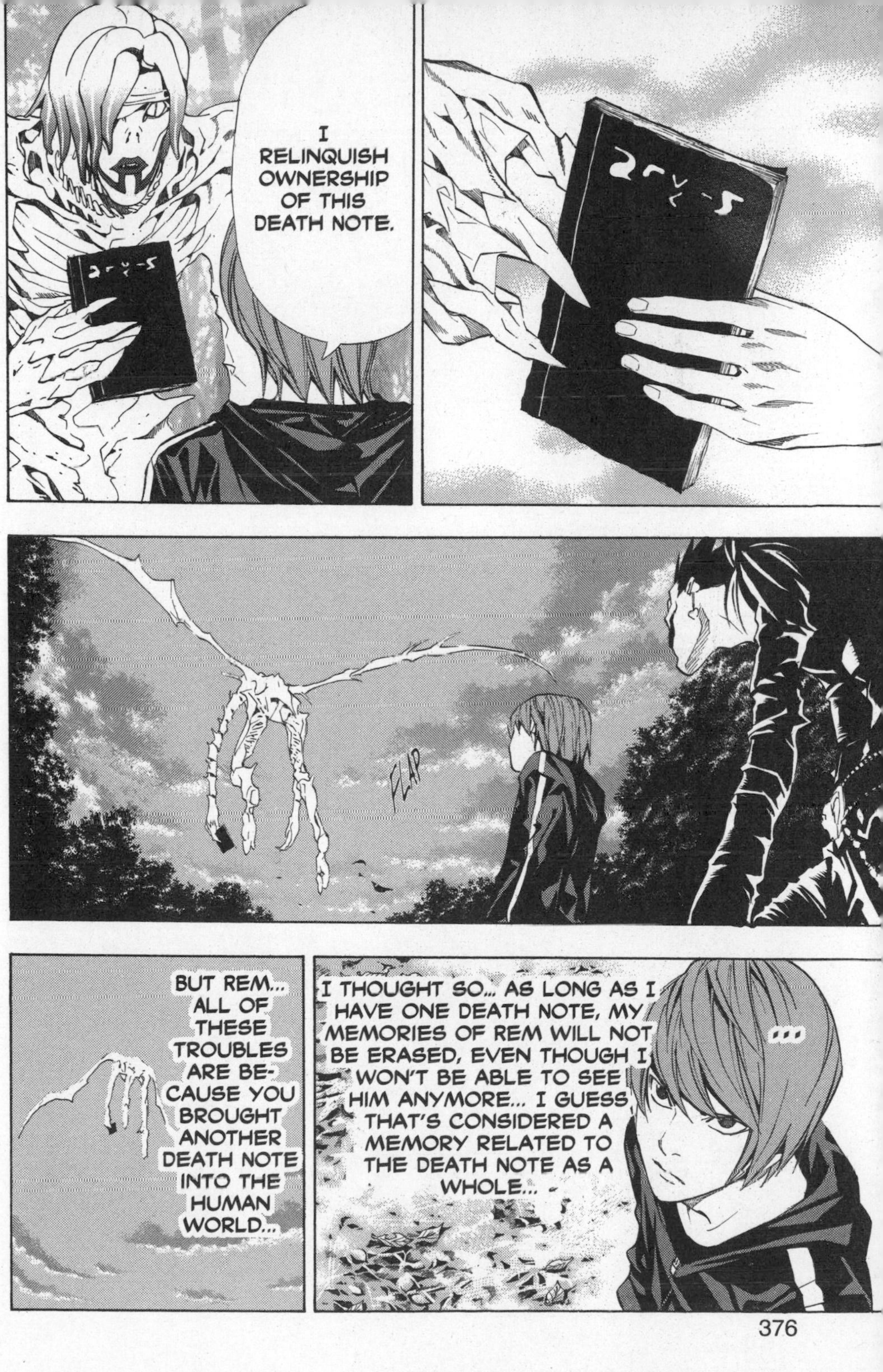
I RELINQUISH OWNERSHIP OF THIS DEATH NOTE.
FLAP
...
I THOUGHT SO... AS LONG AS I HAVE ONE DEATH NOTE, MY MEMORIES OF REM WILL NOT BE ERASED, EVEN THOUGH I WON'T BE ABLE TO SEE HIM ANYMORE... I GUESS THAT'S CONSIDERED A MEMORY RELATED TO THE DEATH NOTE AS A WHOLE...
BUT REM... ALL OF THESE TROUBLES ARE BE-CAUSE YOU BROUGHT ANOTHER DEATH NOTE INTO THE HUMAN WORLD...

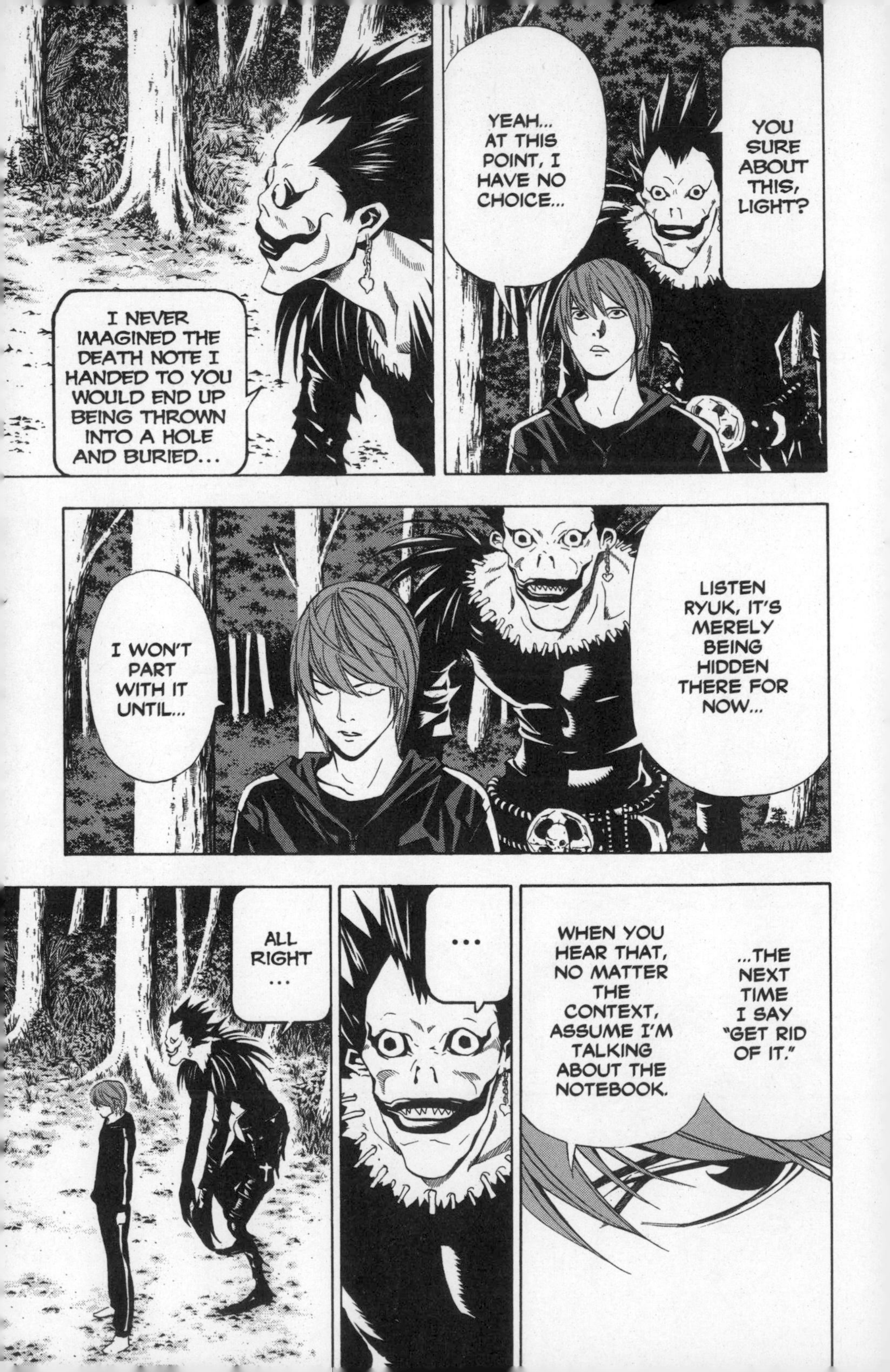
YOU SURE ABOUT THIS, LIGHT?
YEAH... AT THIS POINT, I HAVE NO CHOICE...
I NEVER IMAGINED THE DEATH NOTE I HANDED TO YOU WOULD END UP BEING THROWN INTO A HOLE AND BURIED...
LISTEN RYUK, IT'S MERELY BEING HIDDEN THERE FOR NOW...
I WON'T PART WITH IT UNTIL...
...THE NEXT TIME I SAY "GET RID OF IT."
WHEN YOU HEAR THAT, NO MATTER THE CONTEXT, ASSUME I'M TALKING ABOUT THE NOTEBOOK.
...
ALL RIGHT ...

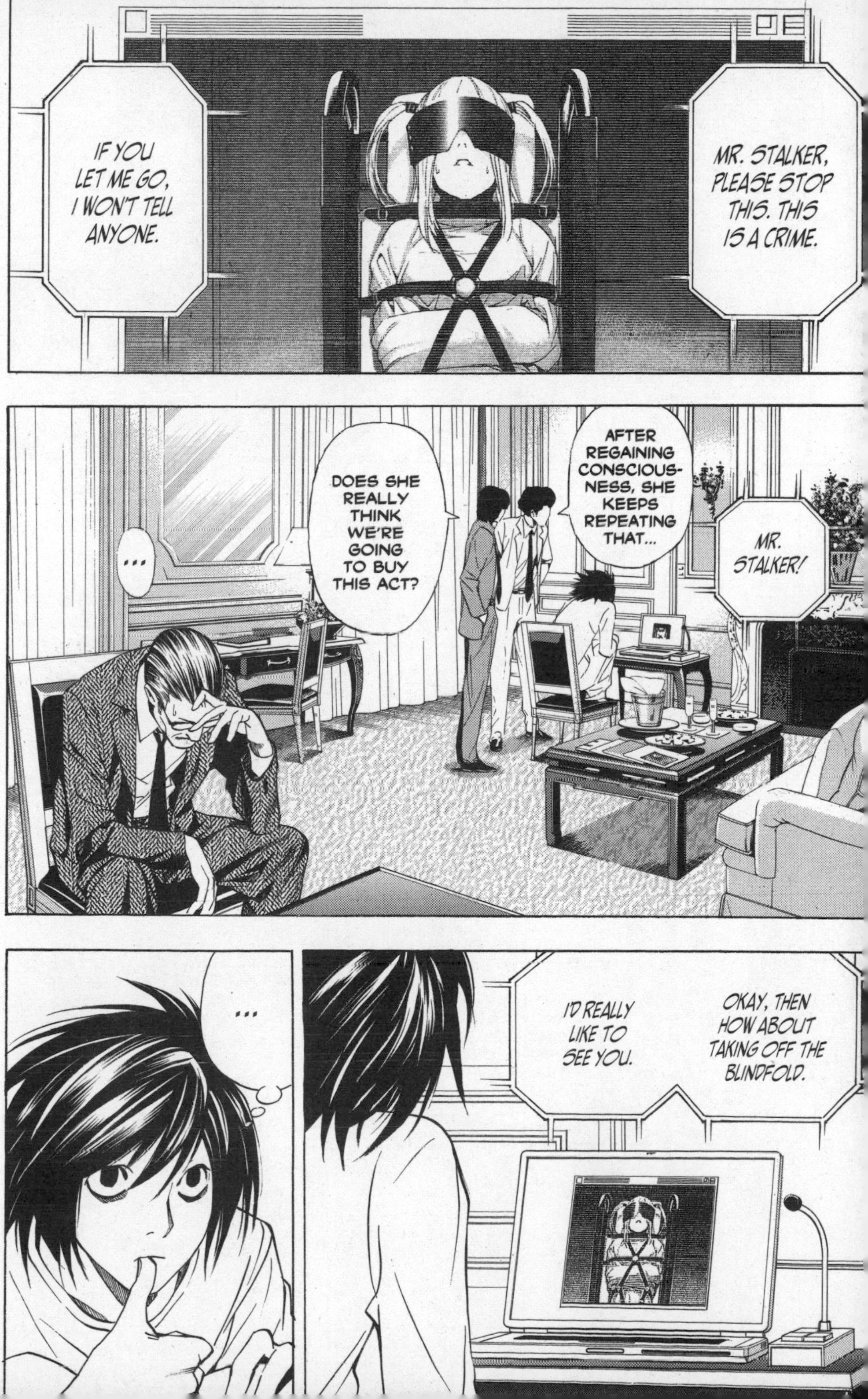
MR. STALKER, PLEASE STOP THIS. THIS IS A CRIME.
IF YOU LET ME GO, I WON'T TELL ANYONE.
MR. STALKER!
AFTER REGAINING CONSCIOUS-NESS, SHE KEEPS REPEATING THAT...
DOES SHE REALLY THINK WE'RE GOING TO BUY THIS ACT?
...
OKAY, THEN HOW ABOUT TAKING OFF THE BLINDFOLD.
I'D REALLY LIKE TO SEE YOU.
...

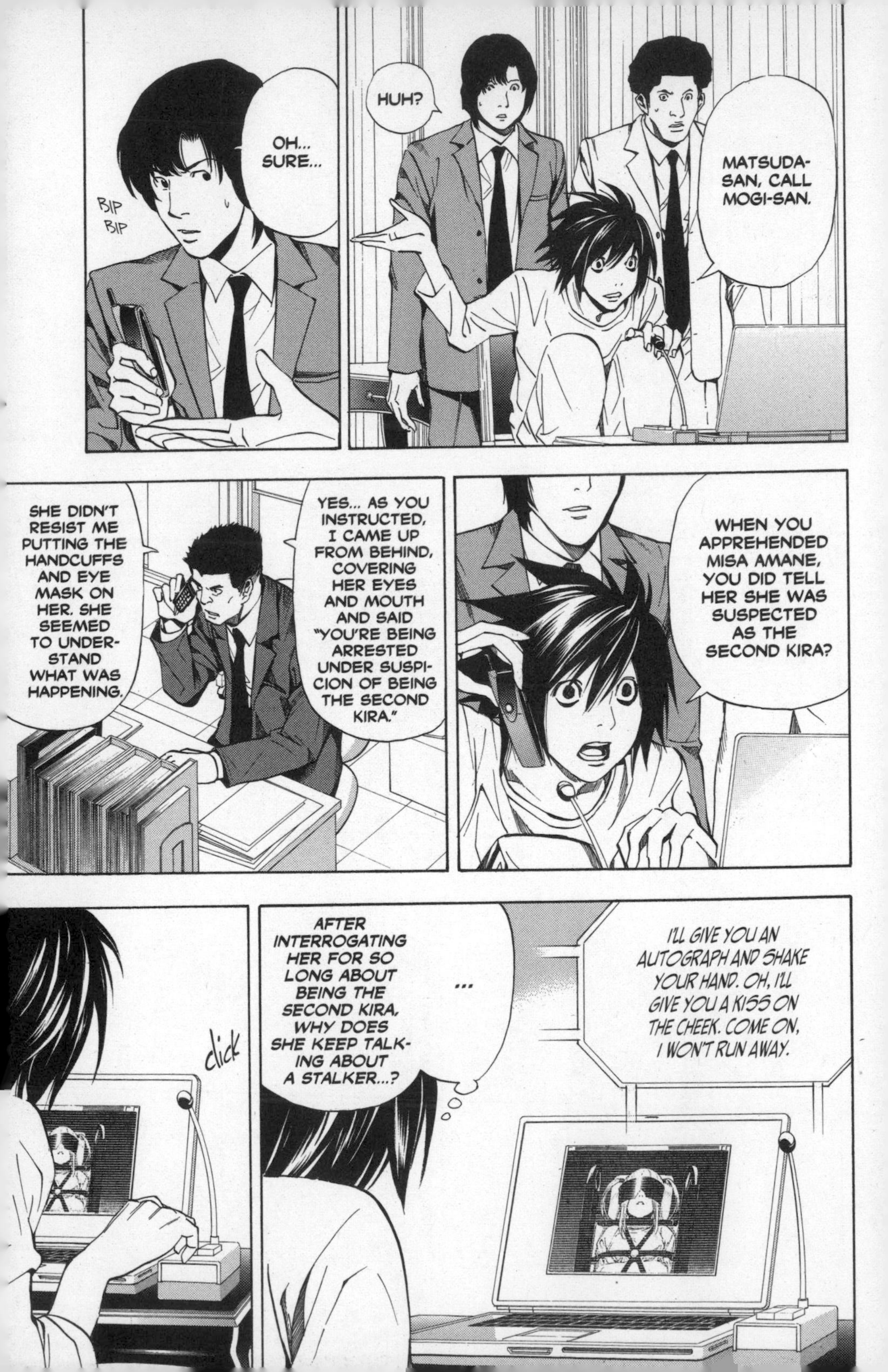
MATSUDA-SAN, CALL MOGI-SAN.
HUH?
OH... SURE...
BIP BIP
WHEN YOU APPREHENDED MISA AMANE, YOU DID TELL HER SHE WAS SUSPECTED AS THE SECOND KIRA?
YES... AS YOU INSTRUCTED, I CAME UP FROM BEHIND, COVERING HER EYES AND MOUTH AND SAID "YOU'RE BEING ARRESTED UNDER SUSPICION OF BEING THE SECOND KIRA."
SHE DIDN'T RESIST ME PUTTING THE HANDCUFFS AND EYE MASK ON HER. SHE SEEMED TO UNDERSTAND WHAT WAS HAPPENING.
I'LL GIVE YOU AN AUTOGRAPH AND SHAKE YOUR HAND. OH, I'LL GIVE YOU A KISS ON THE CHEEK. COME ON, I WON'T RUN AWAY.
...
AFTER INTERROGATING HER FOR SO LONG ABOUT BEING THE SECOND KIRA, WHY DOES SHE KEEP TALKING ABOUT A STALKER...?
click

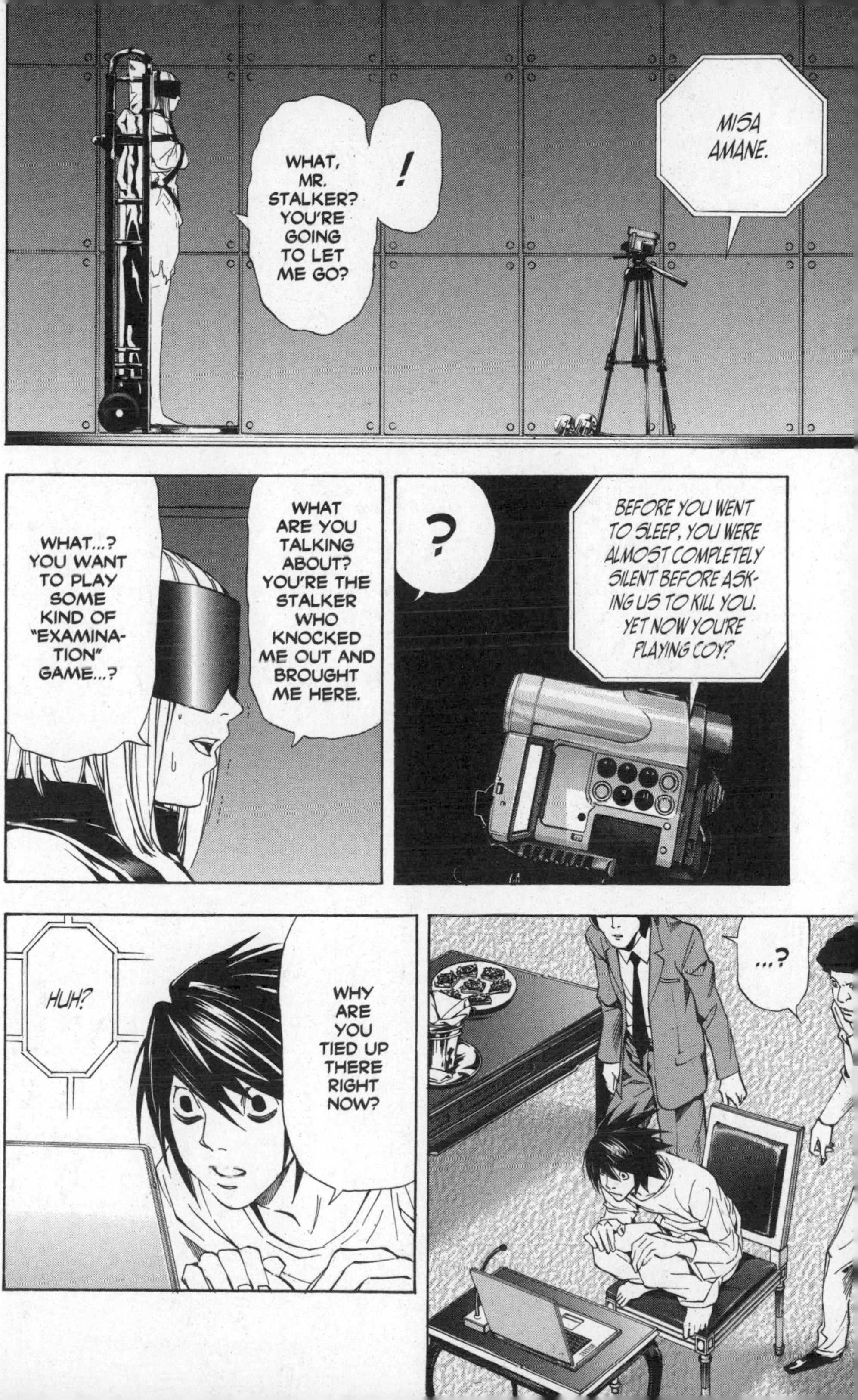
MISA AMANE.
!
WHAT, MR. STALKER? YOU'RE GOING TO LET ME GO?
BEFORE YOU WENT TO SLEEP, YOU WERE ALMOST COMPLETELY SILENT BEFORE ASKING US TO KILL YOU. YET NOW YOU'RE PLAYING COY?
?
WHAT ARE YOU TALKING ABOUT? YOU'RE THE STALKER WHO KNOCKED ME OUT AND BROUGHT ME HERE.
WHAT...? YOU WANT TO PLAY SOME KIND OF "EXAMINATION" GAME...?
...?
WHY ARE YOU TIED UP THERE RIGHT NOW?
HUH?

READ THIS WAY

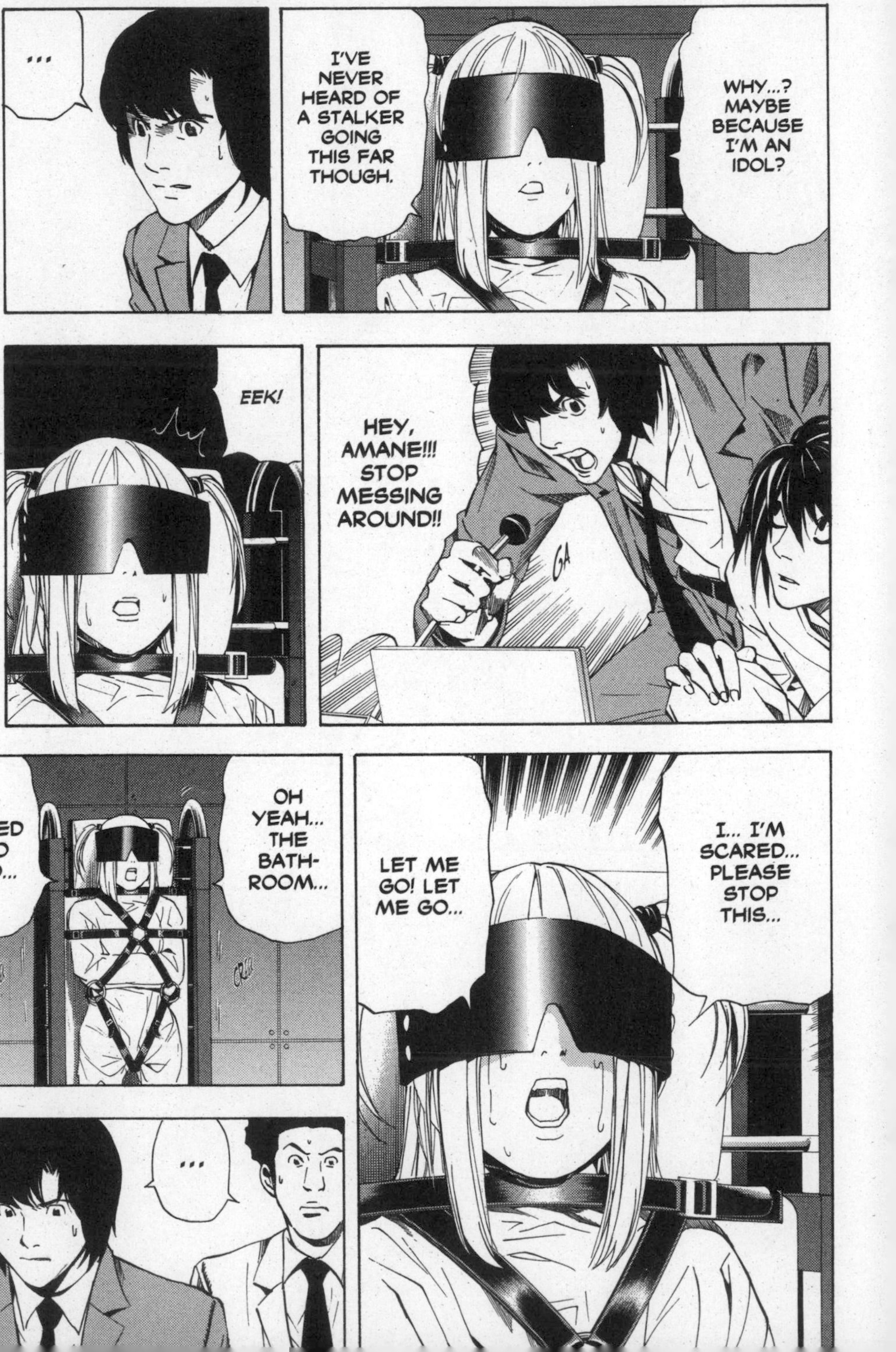

WHY...? MAYBE BECAUSE I'M AN IDOL?
I'VE NEVER HEARD OF A STALKER GOING THIS FAR THOUGH.
...
HEY, AMANE!!! STOP MESSING AROUND!!
GA
EEK!
I... I'M SCARED... PLEASE STOP THIS...
LET ME GO! LET ME GO...
OH YEAH... THE BATH-ROOM...
I NEED TO GO...
...

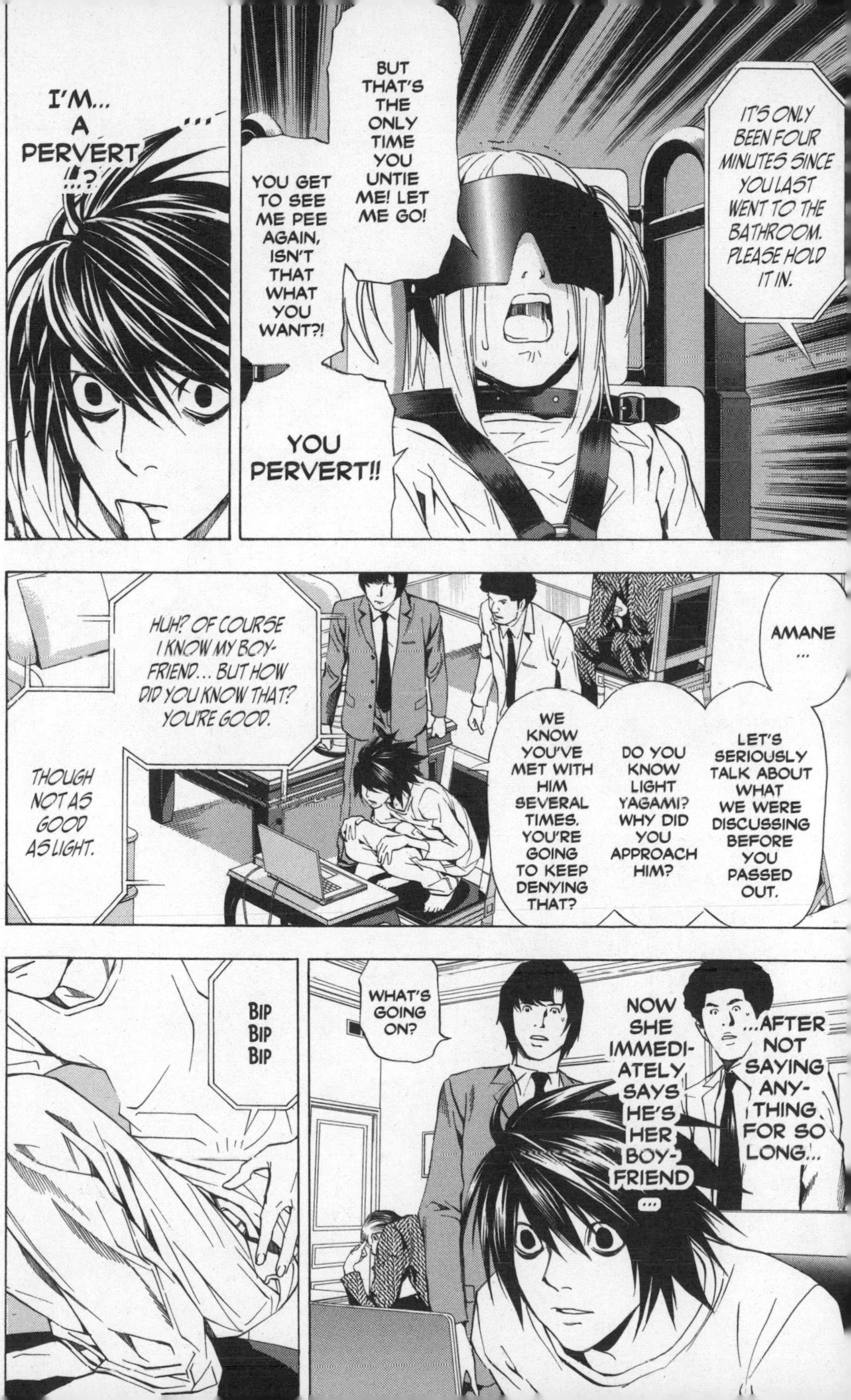
IT'S ONLY BEEN FOUR MINUTES SINCE YOU LAST WENT TO THE BATHROOM. PLEASE HOLD IT IN.
BUT THAT'S THE ONLY TIME YOU UNTIE ME! LET ME GO!
YOU GET TO SEE ME PEE AGAIN, ISN'T THAT WHAT YOU WANT?!
YOU PERVERT!!
...
I'M... A PERVERT !!...?
AMANE ...
LET'S SERIOUSLY TALK ABOUT WHAT WE WERE DISCUSSING BEFORE YOU PASSED OUT.
DO YOU KNOW LIGHT YAGAMI? WHY DID YOU APPROACH HIM?
WE KNOW YOU'VE MET WITH HIM SEVERAL TIMES. YOU'RE GOING TO KEEP DENYING THAT?
HUH? OF COURSE I KNOW MY BOY-FRIEND... BUT HOW DID YOU KNOW THAT? YOU'RE GOOD.
THOUGH NOT AS GOOD AS LIGHT.
...AFTER NOT SAYING ANY-THING FOR SO LONG...
NOW SHE IMMEDI-ATELY SAYS HE'S HER BOY-FRIEND ...
WHAT'S GOING ON?
BIP BIP BIP

READ THIS WAY

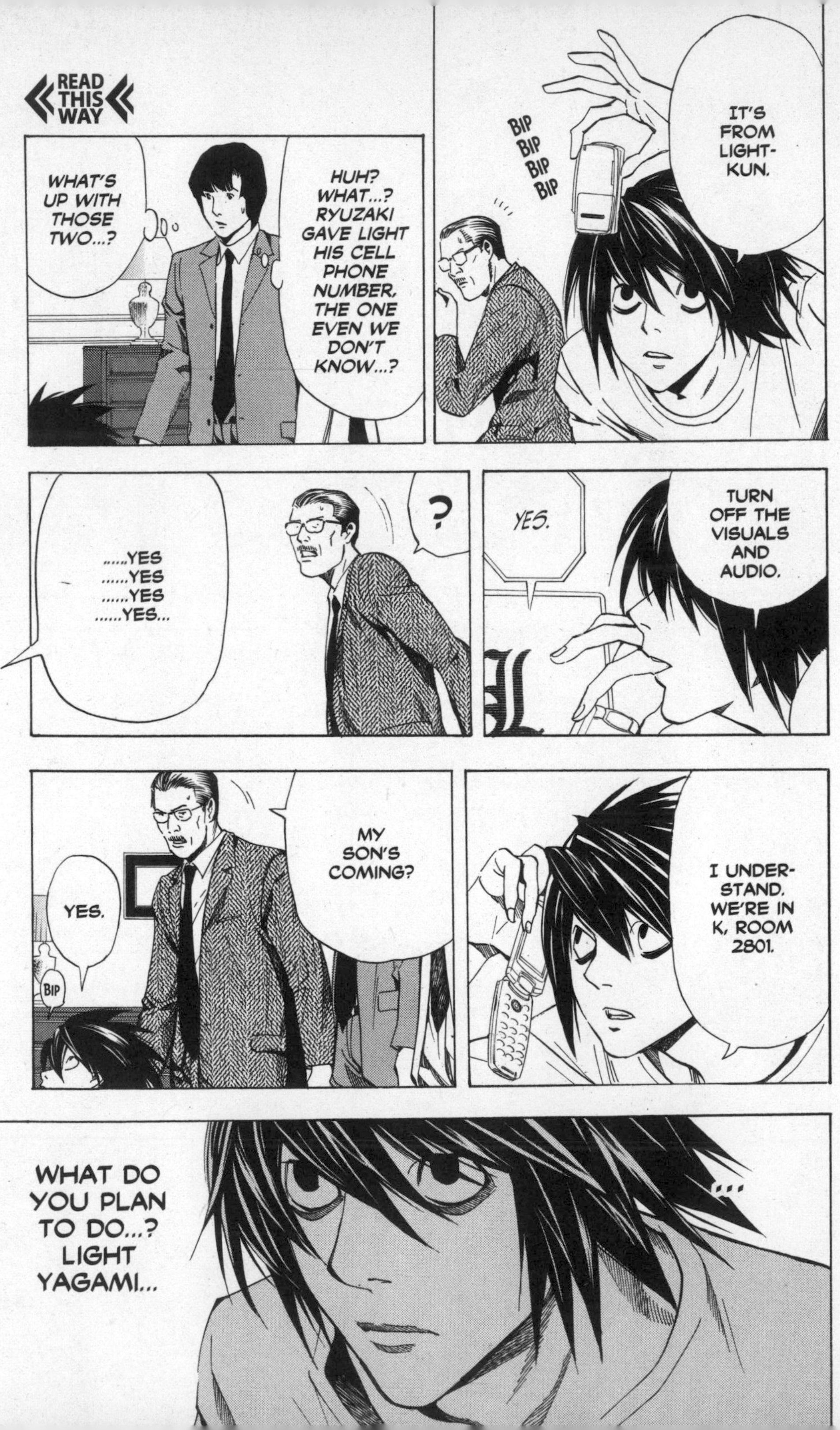
BIP BIP BIP BIP
IT'S FROM LIGHT-KUN.
HUH? WHAT...? RYUZAKI GAVE LIGHT HIS CELL PHONE NUMBER, THE ONE EVEN WE DON'T KNOW...?
WHAT'S UP WITH THOSE TWO...?
TURN OFF THE VISUALS AND AUDIO.
YES.
?
......YES ......YES ......YES ......YES...
I UNDER-STAND. WE'RE IN K, ROOM 2801.
MY SON'S COMING?
YES.
BIP
...
WHAT DO YOU PLAN TO DO...? LIGHT YAGAMI...

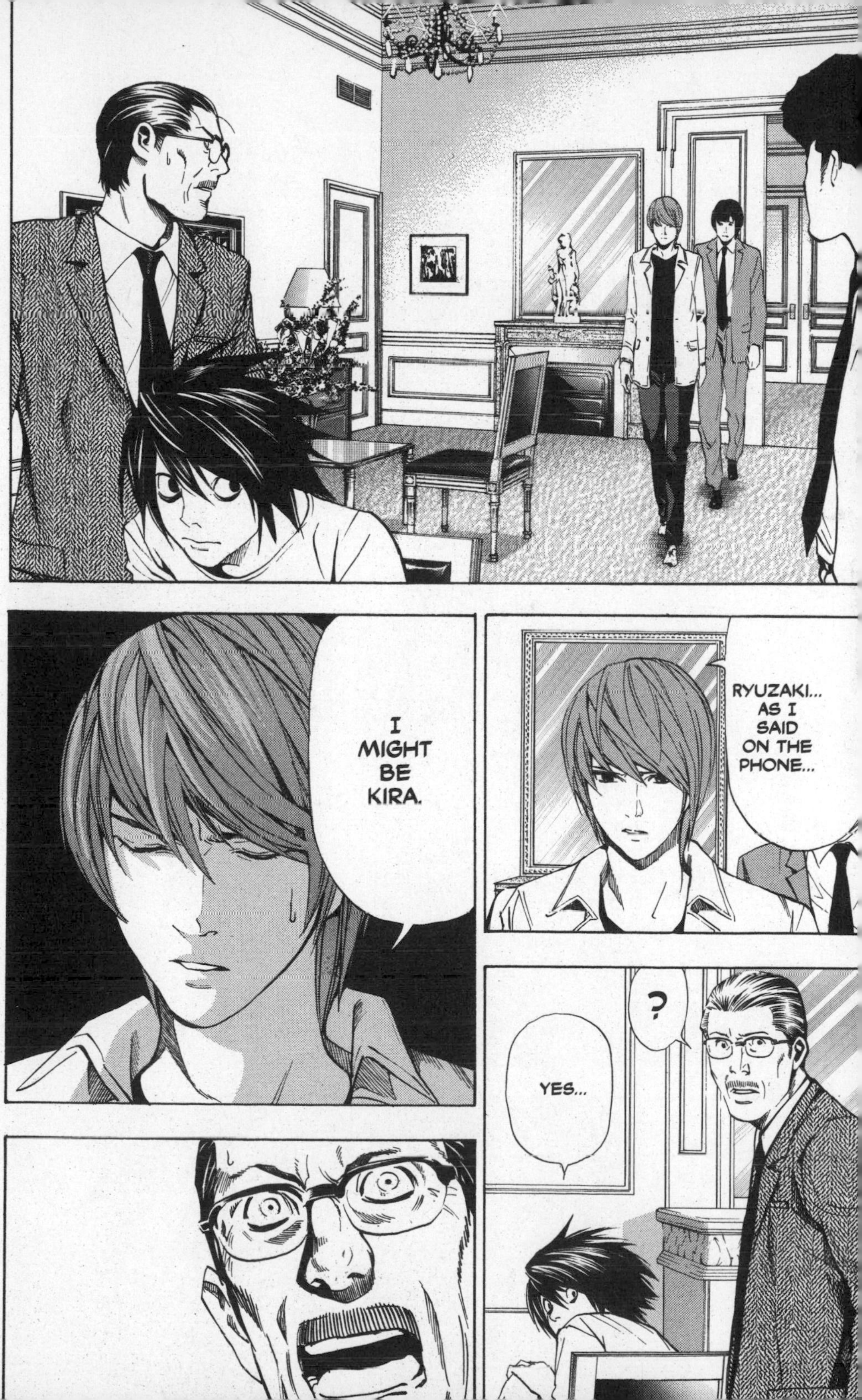
RYUZAKI... AS I SAID ON THE PHONE...
I MIGHT BE KIRA.
?
YES...

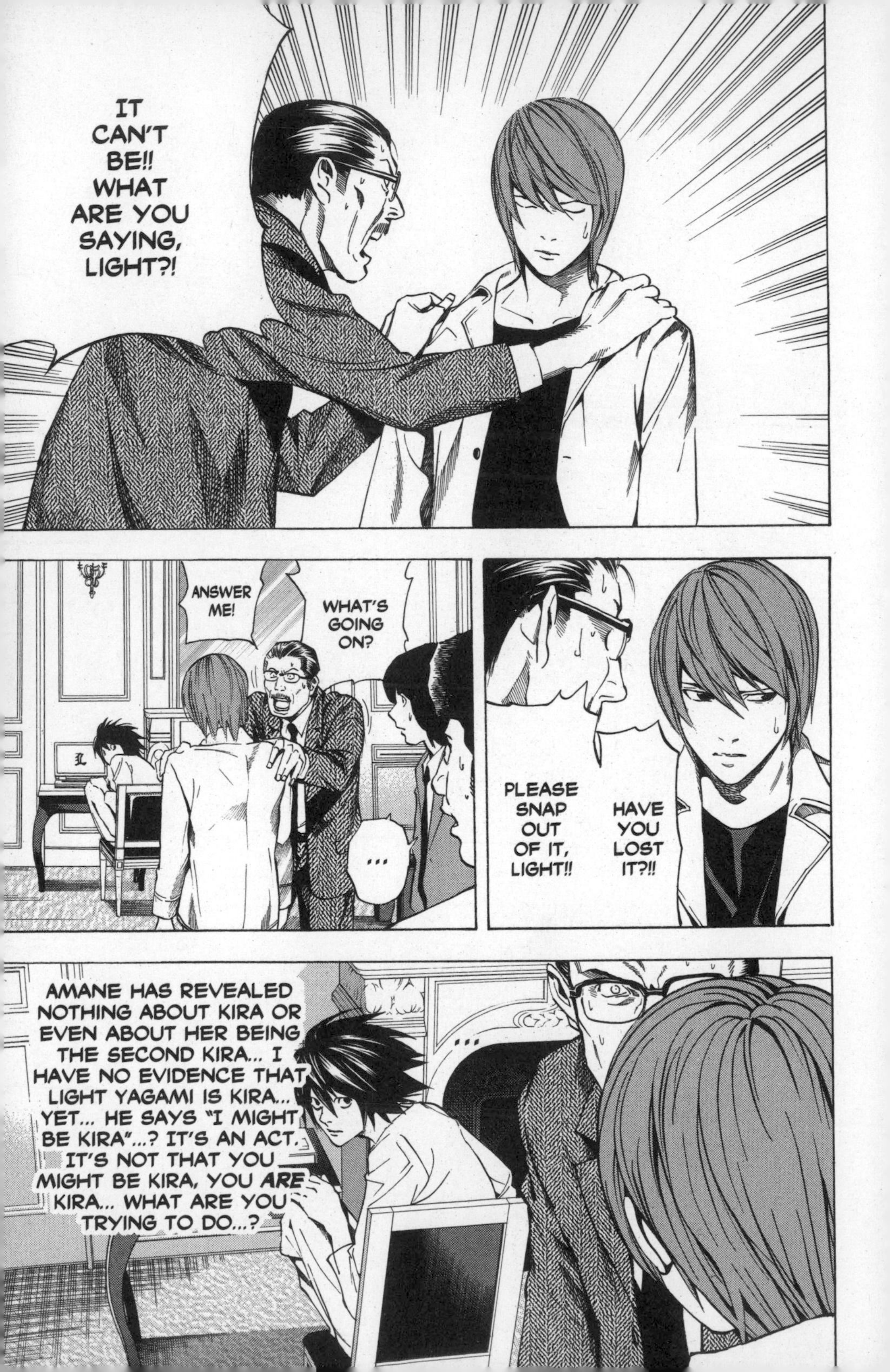
IT CAN'T BE!! WHAT ARE YOU SAYING, LIGHT?!
HAVE YOU LOST IT?!!
PLEASE SNAP OUT OF IT, LIGHT!!
WHAT'S GOING ON?
ANSWER ME!
...
...
AMANE HAS REVEALED NOTHING ABOUT KIRA OR EVEN ABOUT HER BEING THE SECOND KIRA... I HAVE NO EVIDENCE THAT LIGHT YAGAMI IS KIRA... YET... HE SAYS "I MIGHT BE KIRA"...? IT'S AN ACT. IT'S NOT THAT YOU MIGHT BE KIRA, YOU ARE KIRA... WHAT ARE YOU TRYING TO DO...?

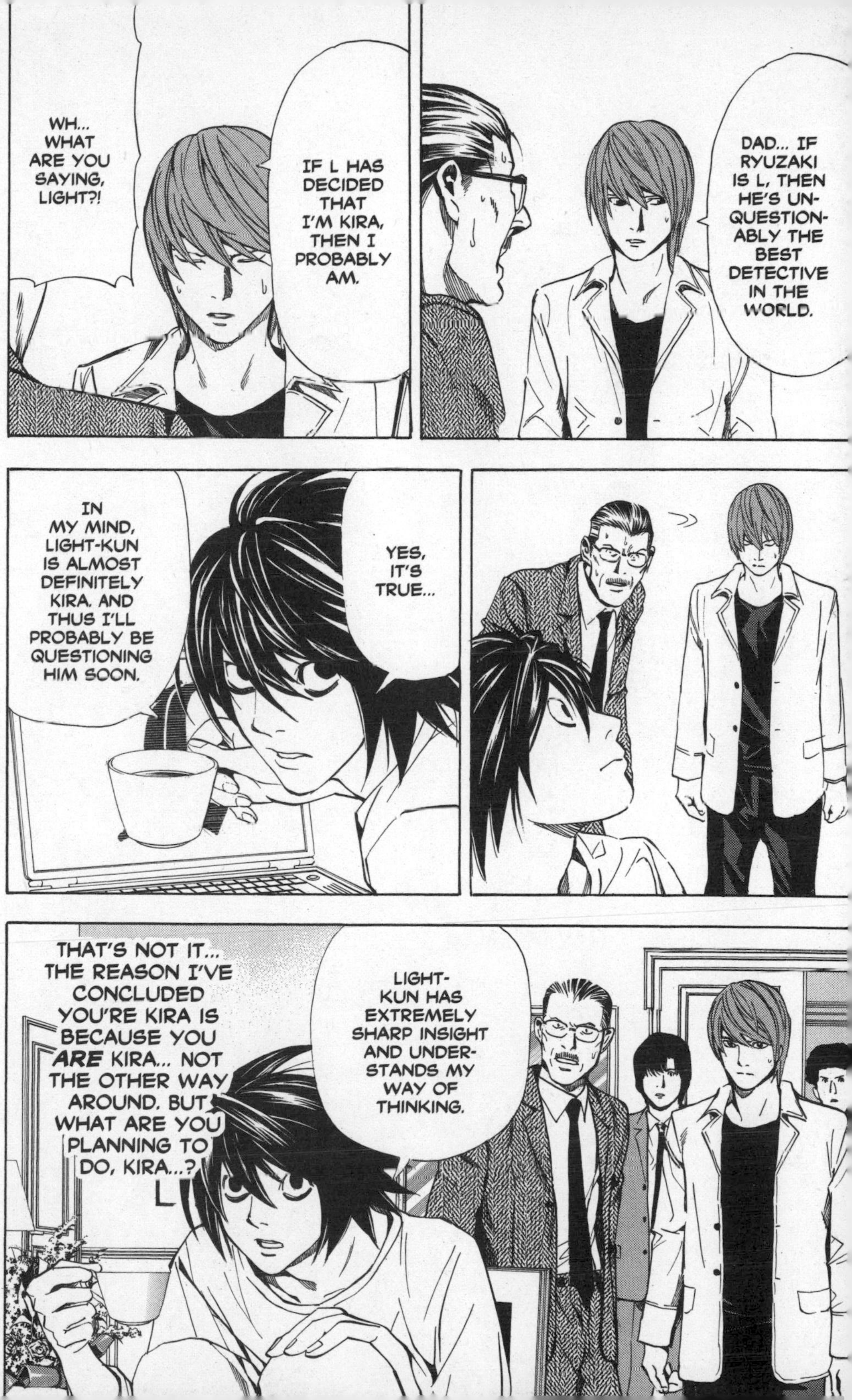
DAD... IF RYUZAKI IS L, THEN HE'S UNQUESTIONABLY THE BEST DETECTIVE IN THE WORLD.
IF L HAS DECIDED THAT I'M KIRA, THEN I PROBABLY AM.
WH... WHAT ARE YOU SAYING, LIGHT?!
YES, IT'S TRUE...
IN MY MIND, LIGHT-KUN IS ALMOST DEFINITELY KIRA. AND THUS I'LL PROBABLY BE QUESTIONING HIM SOON.
LIGHT-KUN HAS EXTREMELY SHARP INSIGHT AND UNDERSTANDS MY WAY OF THINKING.
THAT'S NOT IT... THE REASON I'VE CONCLUDED YOU'RE KIRA IS BECAUSE YOU *ARE* KIRA... NOT THE OTHER WAY AROUND. BUT WHAT ARE YOU PLANNING TO DO, KIRA...?
L

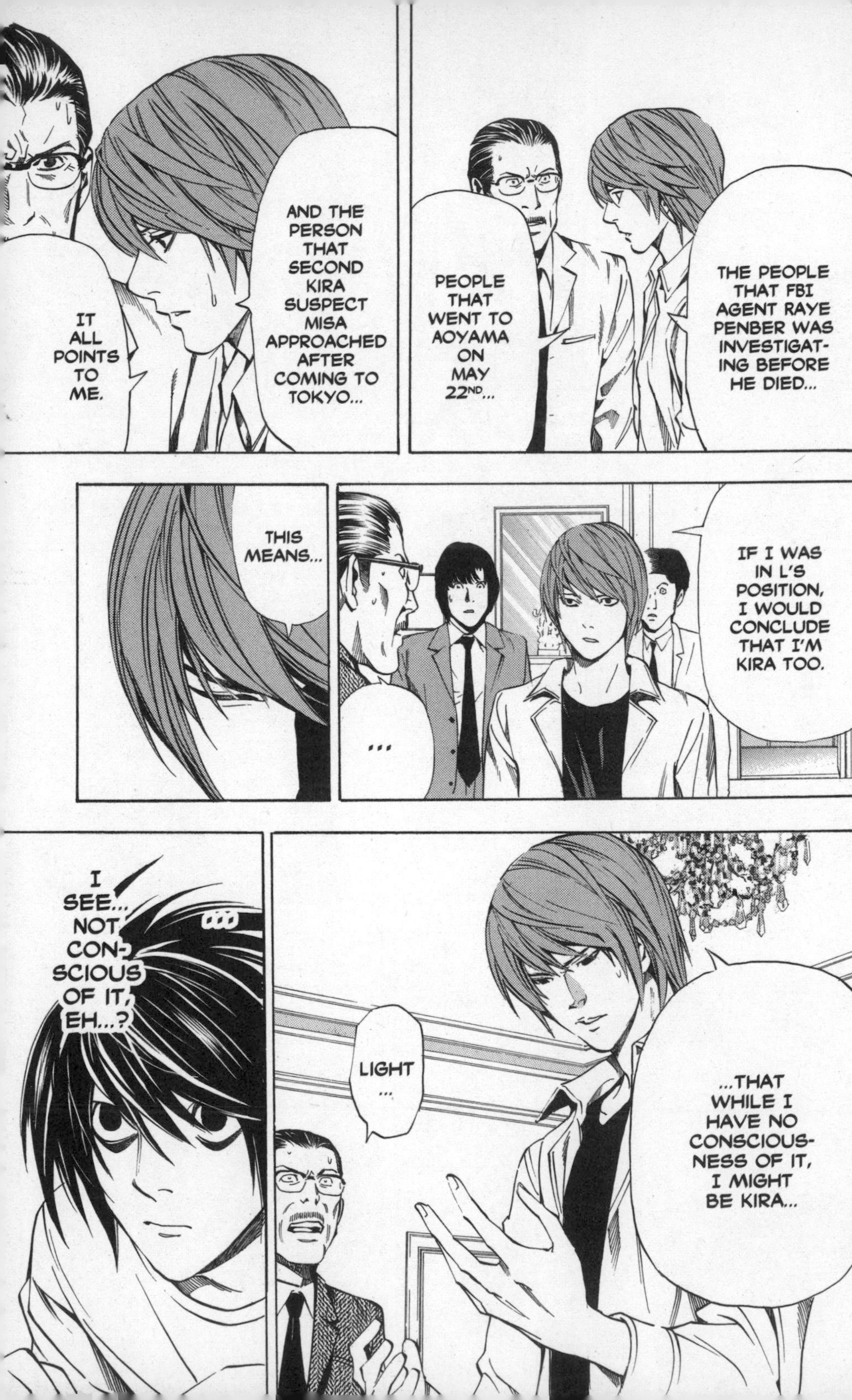
THE PEOPLE THAT FBI AGENT RAYE PENBER WAS INVESTIGATING BEFORE HE DIED...
PEOPLE THAT WENT TO AOYAMA ON MAY 22ND...
AND THE PERSON THAT SECOND KIRA SUSPECT MISA APPROACHED AFTER COMING TO TOKYO...
IT ALL POINTS TO ME.
IF I WAS IN L'S POSITION, I WOULD CONCLUDE THAT I'M KIRA TOO.
...
THIS MEANS...
...THAT WHILE I HAVE NO CONSCIOUSNESS OF IT, I MIGHT BE KIRA...
LIGHT...
I SEE... NOT CONSCIOUS OF IT, EH...?

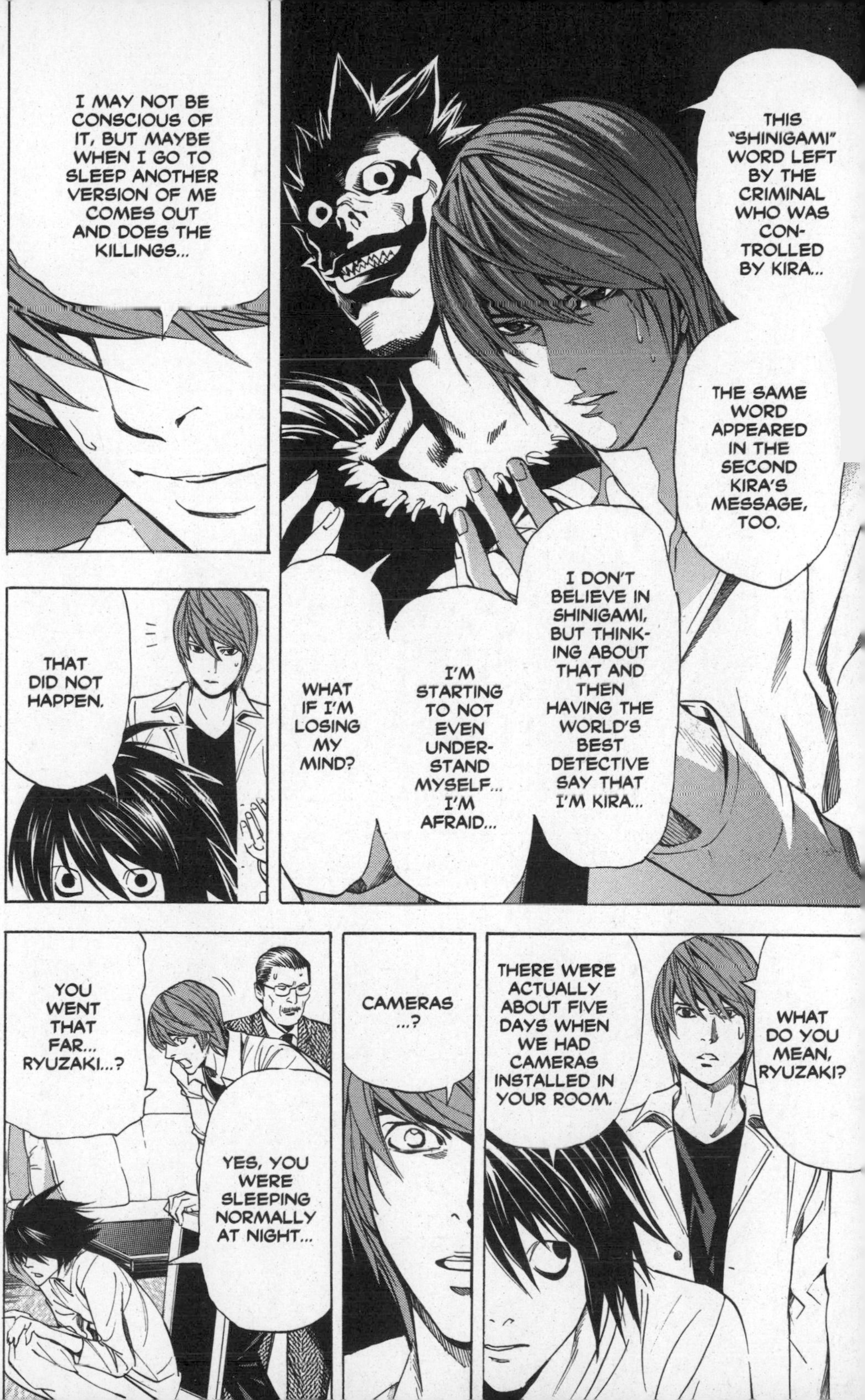

THIS "SHINIGAMI" WORD LEFT BY THE CRIMINAL WHO WAS CON-TROLLED BY KIRA...
THE SAME WORD APPEARED IN THE SECOND KIRA'S MESSAGE, TOO.
I DON'T BELIEVE IN SHINIGAMI, BUT THINK-ING ABOUT THAT AND THEN HAVING THE WORLD'S BEST DETECTIVE SAY THAT I'M KIRA...
I'M STARTING TO NOT EVEN UNDER-STAND MYSELF... I'M AFRAID...
WHAT IF I'M LOSING MY MIND?
I MAY NOT BE CONSCIOUS OF IT, BUT MAYBE WHEN I GO TO SLEEP ANOTHER VERSION OF ME COMES OUT AND DOES THE KILLINGS...
THAT DID NOT HAPPEN.
WHAT DO YOU MEAN, RYUZAKI?
THERE WERE ACTUALLY ABOUT FIVE DAYS WHEN WE HAD CAMERAS INSTALLED IN YOUR ROOM.
CAMERAS ...?
YOU WENT THAT FAR... RYUZAKI...?
YES, YOU WERE SLEEPING NORMALLY AT NIGHT...

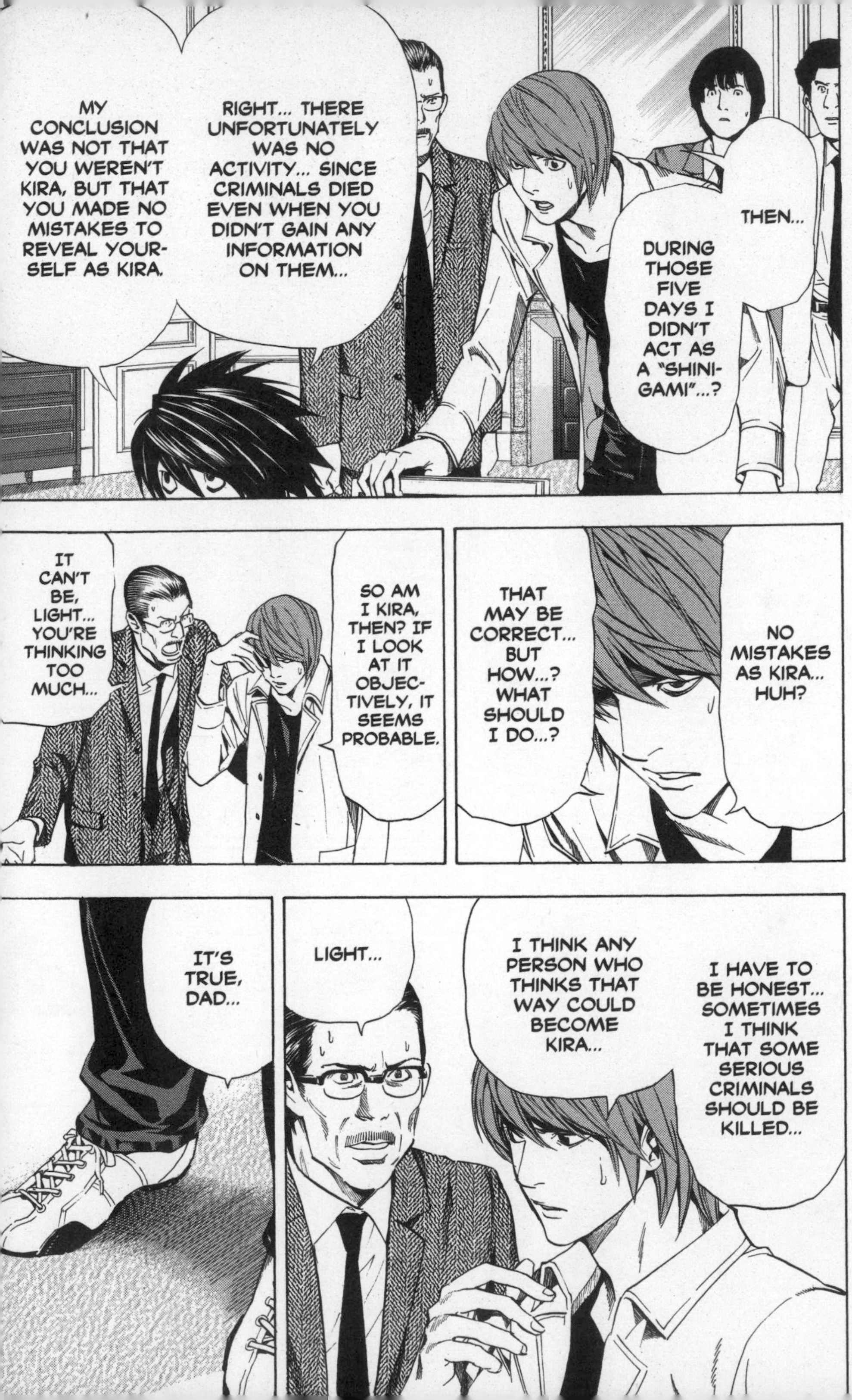
THEN...
DURING THOSE FIVE DAYS I DIDN'T ACT AS A "SHINIGAMI"...?
RIGHT... THERE UNFORTUNATELY WAS NO ACTIVITY... SINCE CRIMINALS DIED EVEN WHEN YOU DIDN'T GAIN ANY INFORMATION ON THEM...
MY CONCLUSION WAS NOT THAT YOU WEREN'T KIRA, BUT THAT YOU MADE NO MISTAKES TO REVEAL YOURSELF AS KIRA.
NO MISTAKES AS KIRA... HUH?
THAT MAY BE CORRECT... BUT HOW...? WHAT SHOULD I DO...?
SO AM I KIRA, THEN? IF I LOOK AT IT OBJECTIVELY, IT SEEMS PROBABLE.
IT CAN'T BE, LIGHT... YOU'RE THINKING TOO MUCH...
I HAVE TO BE HONEST... SOMETIMES I THINK THAT SOME SERIOUS CRIMINALS SHOULD BE KILLED...
I THINK ANY PERSON WHO THINKS THAT WAY COULD BECOME KIRA...
LIGHT...
IT'S TRUE, DAD...

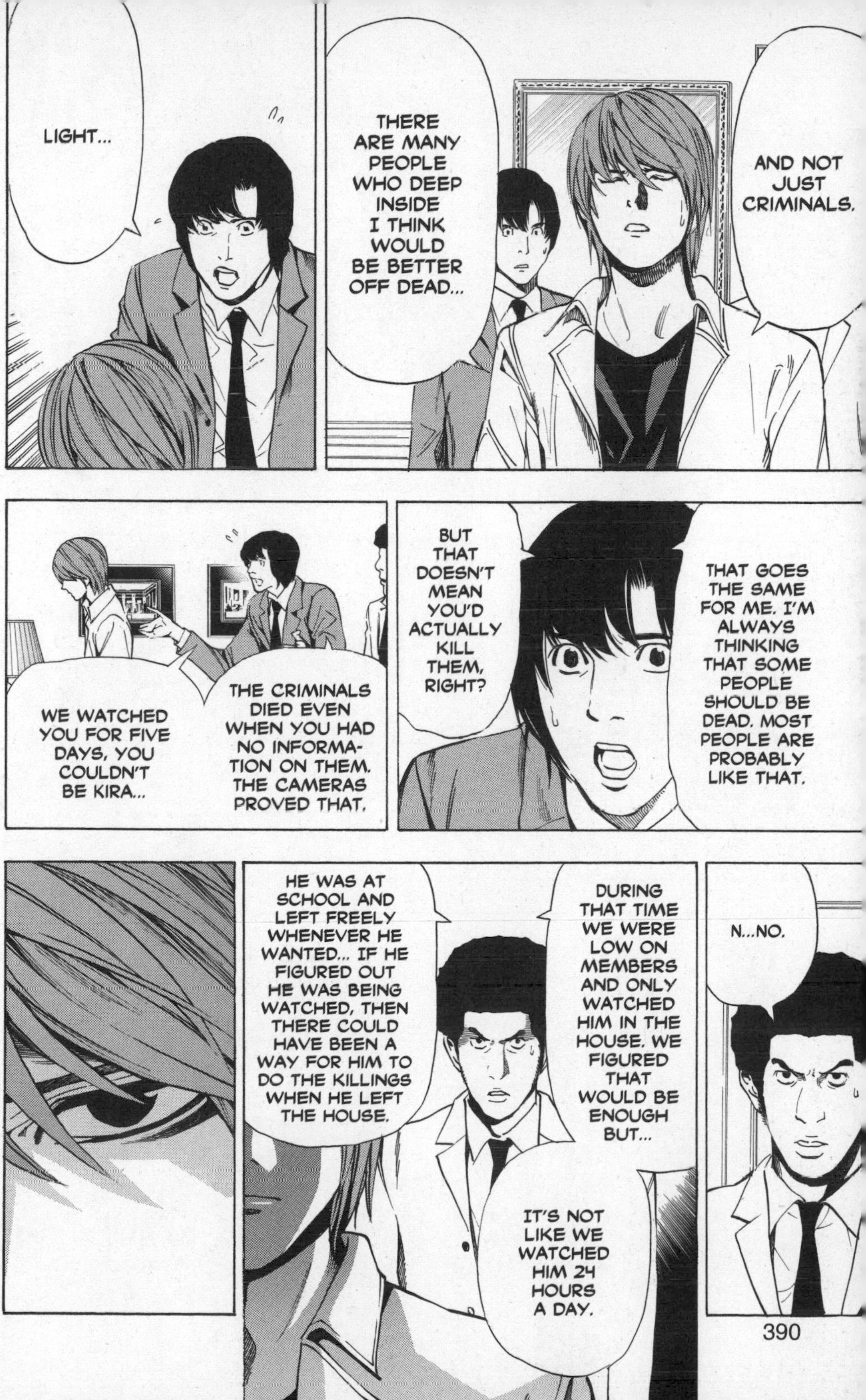
AND NOT JUST CRIMINALS.
THERE ARE MANY PEOPLE WHO DEEP INSIDE I THINK WOULD BE BETTER OFF DEAD...
LIGHT...
THAT GOES THE SAME FOR ME. I'M ALWAYS THINKING THAT SOME PEOPLE SHOULD BE DEAD. MOST PEOPLE ARE PROBABLY LIKE THAT.
BUT THAT DOESN'T MEAN YOU'D ACTUALLY KILL THEM, RIGHT?
THE CRIMINALS DIED EVEN WHEN YOU HAD NO INFORMATION ON THEM. THE CAMERAS PROVED THAT.
WE WATCHED YOU FOR FIVE DAYS, YOU COULDN'T BE KIRA...
N...NO.
DURING THAT TIME WE WERE LOW ON MEMBERS AND ONLY WATCHED HIM IN THE HOUSE. WE FIGURED THAT WOULD BE ENOUGH BUT...
IT'S NOT LIKE WE WATCHED HIM 24 HOURS A DAY.
HE WAS AT SCHOOL AND LEFT FREELY WHENEVER HE WANTED... IF HE FIGURED OUT HE WAS BEING WATCHED, THEN THERE COULD HAVE BEEN A WAY FOR HIM TO DO THE KILLINGS WHEN HE LEFT THE HOUSE.

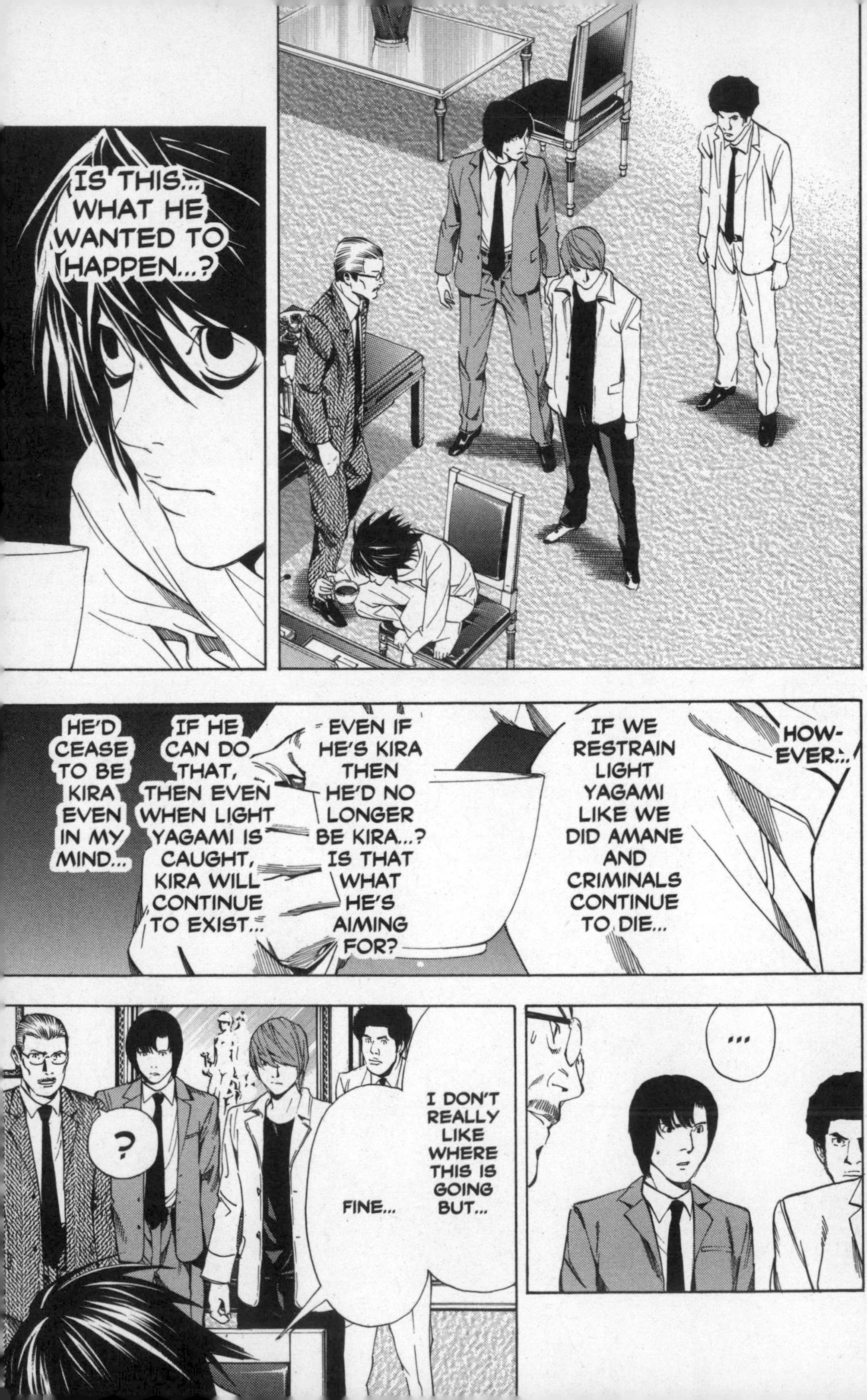
IS THIS... WHAT HE WANTED TO HAPPEN...?
HOW-EVER...
IF WE RESTRAIN LIGHT YAGAMI LIKE WE DID AMANE AND CRIMINALS CONTINUE TO DIE...
EVEN IF HE'S KIRA THEN HE'D NO LONGER BE KIRA...? IS THAT WHAT HE'S AIMING FOR?
IF HE CAN DO THAT, THEN EVEN WHEN LIGHT YAGAMI IS CAUGHT, KIRA WILL CONTINUE TO EXIST...
HE'D CEASE TO BE KIRA EVEN IN MY MIND...
...
I DON'T REALLY LIKE WHERE THIS IS GOING BUT...
FINE...
?

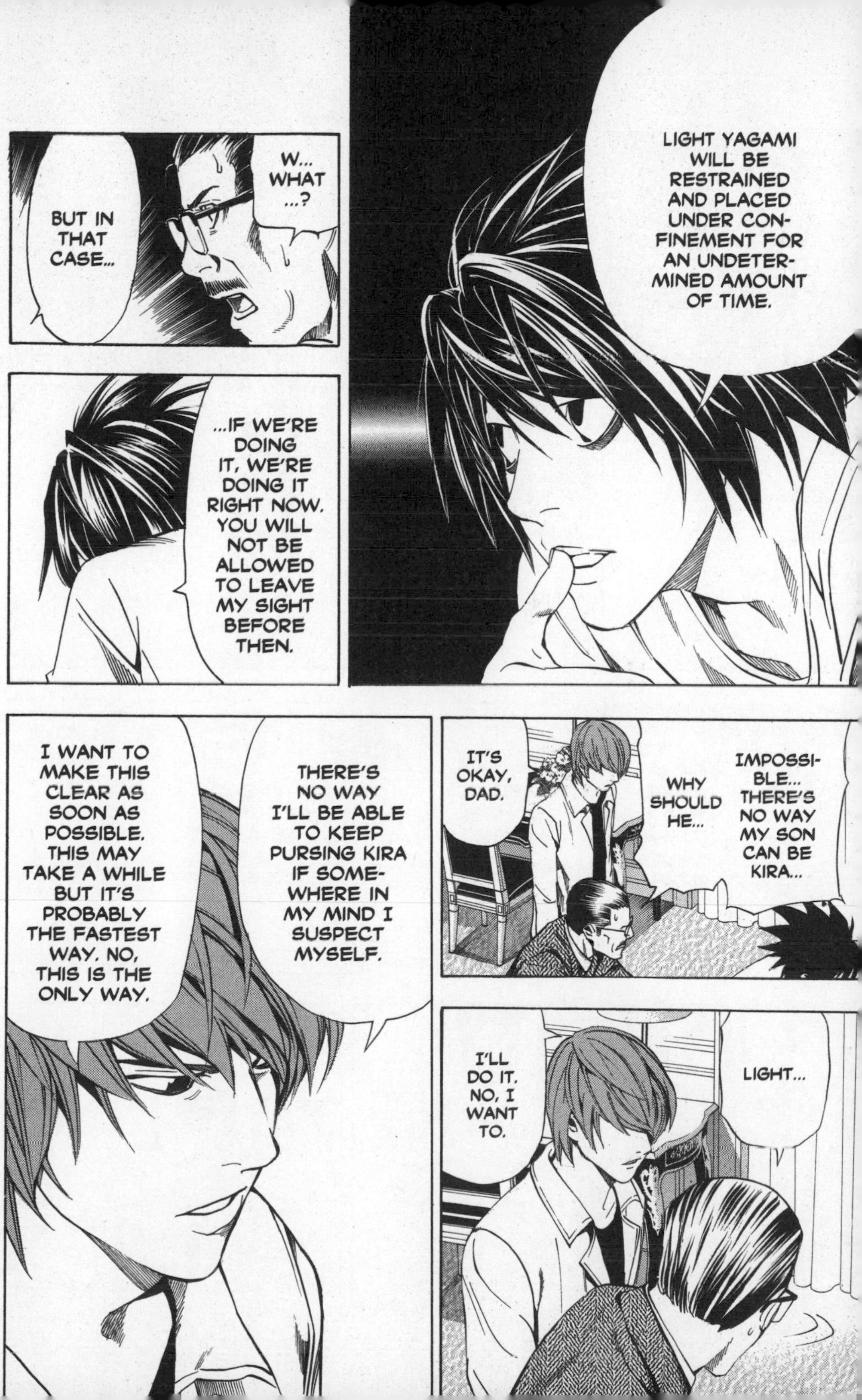
LIGHT YAGAMI WILL BE RESTRAINED AND PLACED UNDER CON-FINEMENT FOR AN UNDETER-MINED AMOUNT OF TIME.
W... WHAT ...?
BUT IN THAT CASE...
...IF WE'RE DOING IT, WE'RE DOING IT RIGHT NOW. YOU WILL NOT BE ALLOWED TO LEAVE MY SIGHT BEFORE THEN.
IMPOSSI-BLE... THERE'S NO WAY MY SON CAN BE KIRA...
WHY SHOULD HE...
IT'S OKAY, DAD.
LIGHT...
I'LL DO IT. NO, I WANT TO.
THERE'S NO WAY I'LL BE ABLE TO KEEP PURSING KIRA IF SOME-WHERE IN MY MIND I SUSPECT MYSELF.
I WANT TO MAKE THIS CLEAR AS SOON AS POSSIBLE. THIS MAY TAKE A WHILE BUT IT'S PROBABLY THE FASTEST WAY. NO, THIS IS THE ONLY WAY.

READ THIS WAY

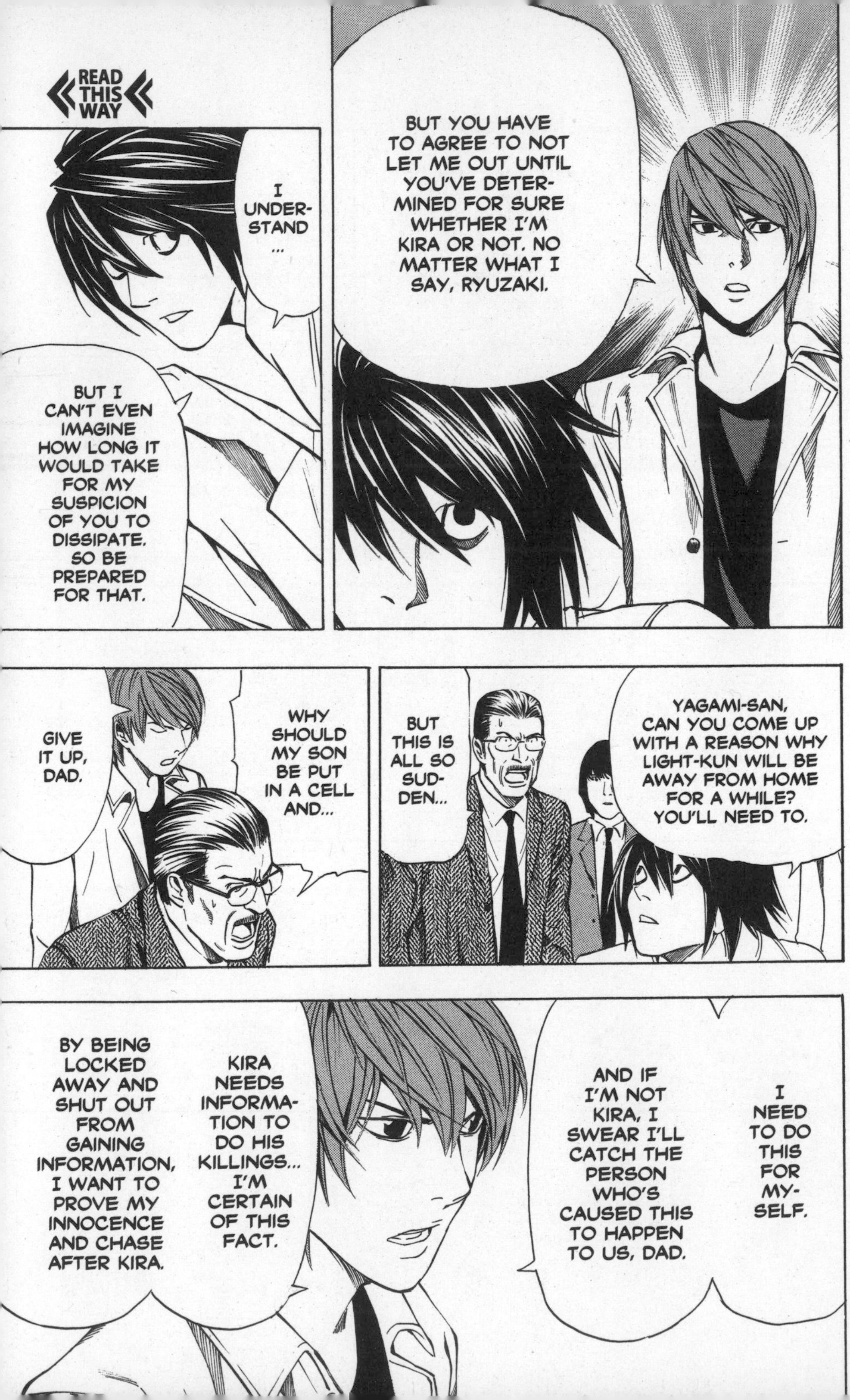
BUT YOU HAVE TO AGREE TO NOT LET ME OUT UNTIL YOU'VE DETERMINED FOR SURE WHETHER I'M KIRA OR NOT. NO MATTER WHAT I SAY, RYUZAKI.
I UNDERSTAND ...
BUT I CAN'T EVEN IMAGINE HOW LONG IT WOULD TAKE FOR MY SUSPICION OF YOU TO DISSIPATE. SO BE PREPARED FOR THAT.
YAGAMI-SAN, CAN YOU COME UP WITH A REASON WHY LIGHT-KUN WILL BE AWAY FROM HOME FOR A WHILE? YOU'LL NEED TO.
BUT THIS IS ALL SO SUDDEN...
WHY SHOULD MY SON BE PUT IN A CELL AND...
GIVE IT UP, DAD.
I NEED TO DO THIS FOR MYSELF.
AND IF I'M NOT KIRA, I SWEAR I'LL CATCH THE PERSON WHO'S CAUSED THIS TO HAPPEN TO US, DAD.
KIRA NEEDS INFORMATION TO DO HIS KILLINGS... I'M CERTAIN OF THIS FACT.
BY BEING LOCKED AWAY AND SHUT OUT FROM GAINING INFORMATION, I WANT TO PROVE MY INNOCENCE AND CHASE AFTER KIRA.

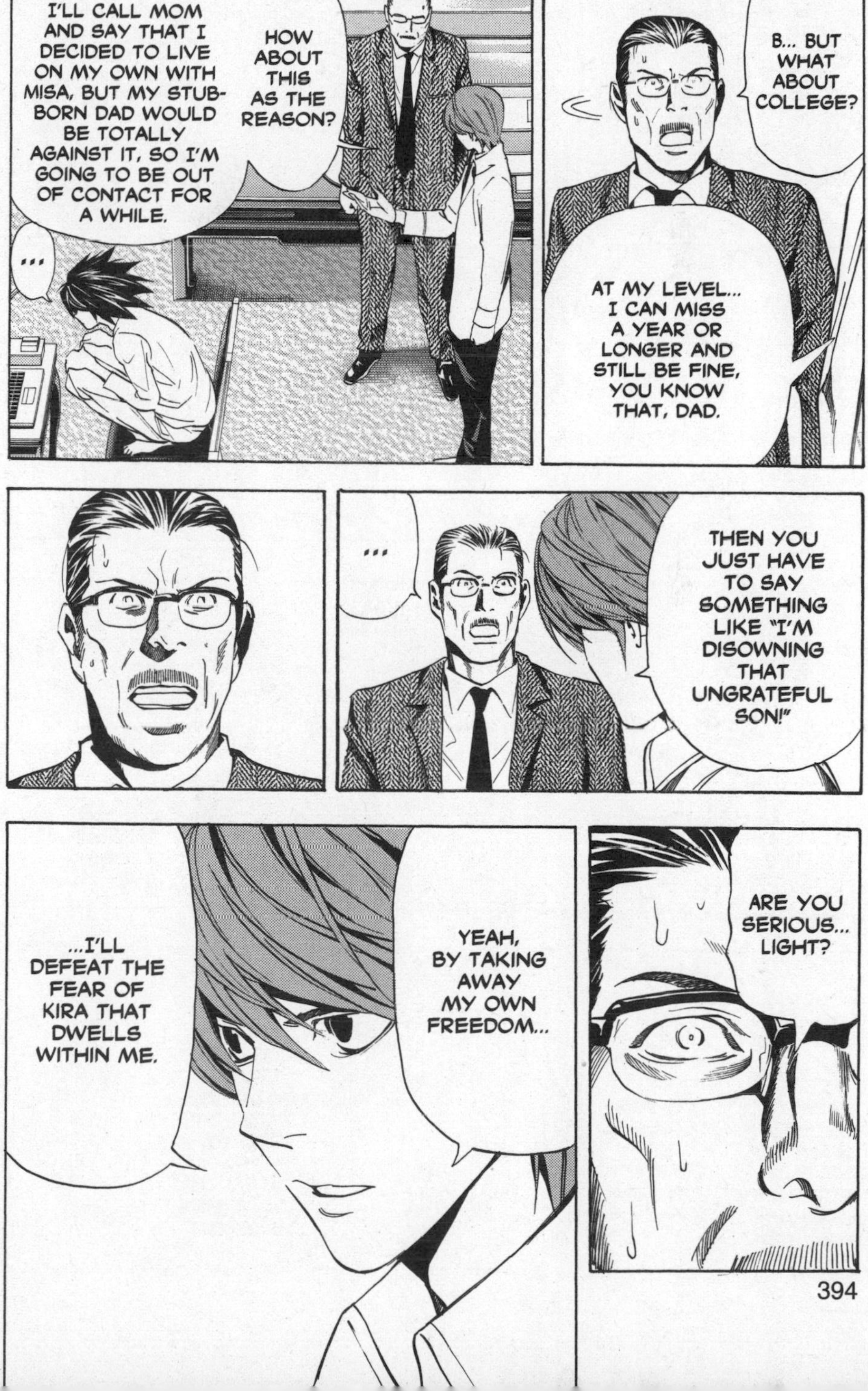
B... BUT WHAT ABOUT COLLEGE?
AT MY LEVEL... I CAN MISS A YEAR OR LONGER AND STILL BE FINE, YOU KNOW THAT, DAD.
HOW ABOUT THIS AS THE REASON?
I'LL CALL MOM AND SAY THAT I DECIDED TO LIVE ON MY OWN WITH MISA, BUT MY STUBBORN DAD WOULD BE TOTALLY AGAINST IT, SO I'M GOING TO BE OUT OF CONTACT FOR A WHILE.
...
THEN YOU JUST HAVE TO SAY SOMETHING LIKE "I'M DISOWNING THAT UNGRATEFUL SON!"
...
ARE YOU SERIOUS... LIGHT?
YEAH, BY TAKING AWAY MY OWN FREEDOM...
...I'LL DEFEAT THE FEAR OF KIRA THAT DWELLS WITHIN ME.

READ THIS WAY

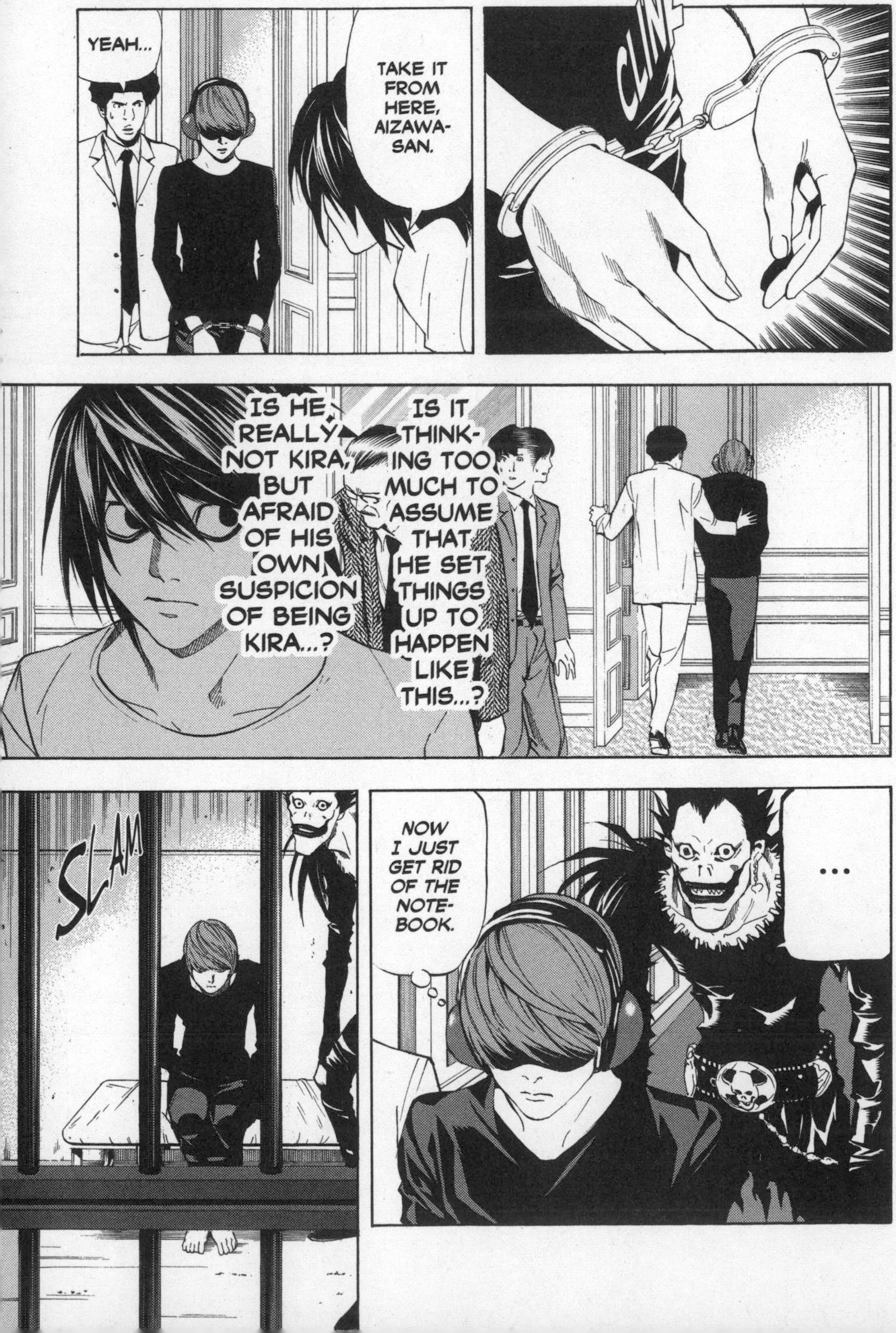
CLINK
TAKE IT FROM HERE, AIZAWA-SAN.
YEAH...
IS IT THINKING TOO MUCH TO ASSUME THAT HE SET THINGS UP TO HAPPEN LIKE THIS...?
IS HE REALLY NOT KIRA, BUT AFRAID OF HIS OWN SUSPICION OF BEING KIRA...?
...
NOW I JUST GET RID OF THE NOTEBOOK.
SLAM

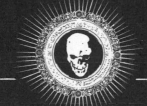

DEATH NOTE
How to use it
XXVII

○ Whenever an individual with ownership of more than

two DEATH NOTES loses possession to one of the DEATH NOTES,

he will not be able to recognize that DEATH NOTE's god of

death's appearance or voice anymore.

The god of death himself will leave, but all the memory

involving that DEATH NOTE will remain as long as he

maintains ownership of at least one other DEATH NOTE.

二冊以上のデスノートの所有権を得た人間は、一冊の所有権を失うと
その失ったノートに憑いていた死神の姿や声を認知できなくなり死神も
離れるが、一冊でも所有している限り、
関わった全てのデスノートの記憶は消えない。

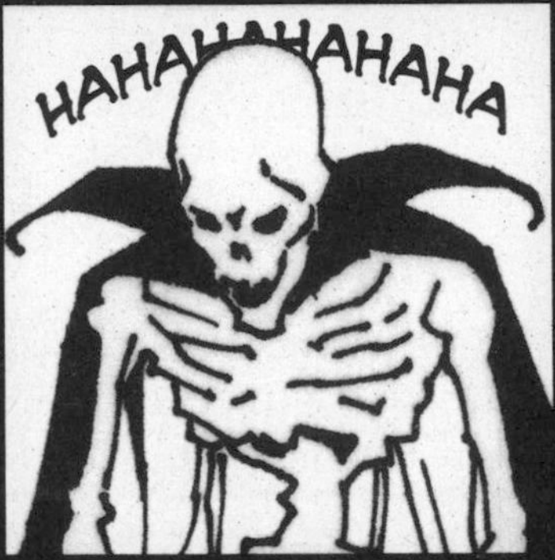
HAHAHAHAHAHA

I really loved the old TV show *Ogon Bat*. The main character was a gold skeleton with a creepy laugh, but he was a good guy! Am I the only one who'd like to see a modern remake using CGI?

-Takeshi Obata

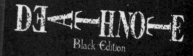
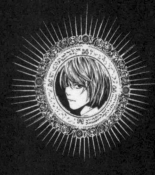
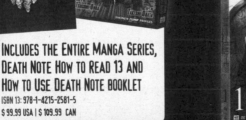
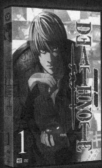
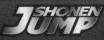

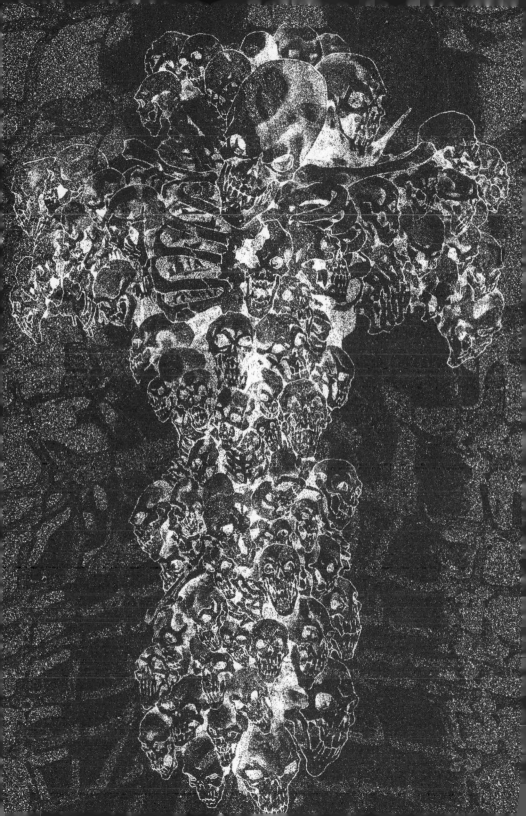

DEATH NOTE

Cover Gallery

Original Japanese Covers Volumes 1-4

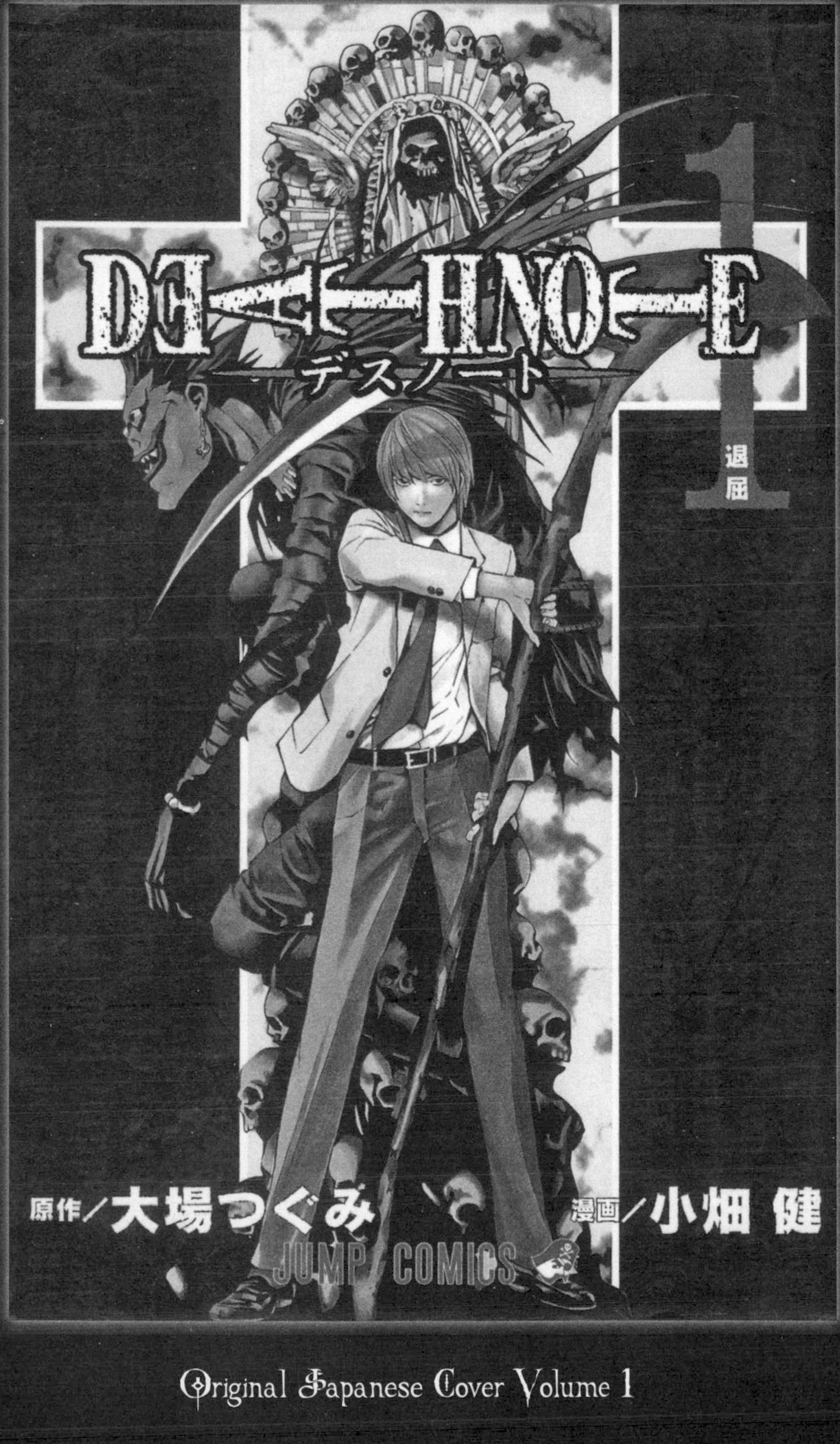
DEATH NOTE
デスノート
1
退屈
原作／大場つぐみ
漫画／小畑 健
JUMP COMICS

Original Japanese Cover Volume 1

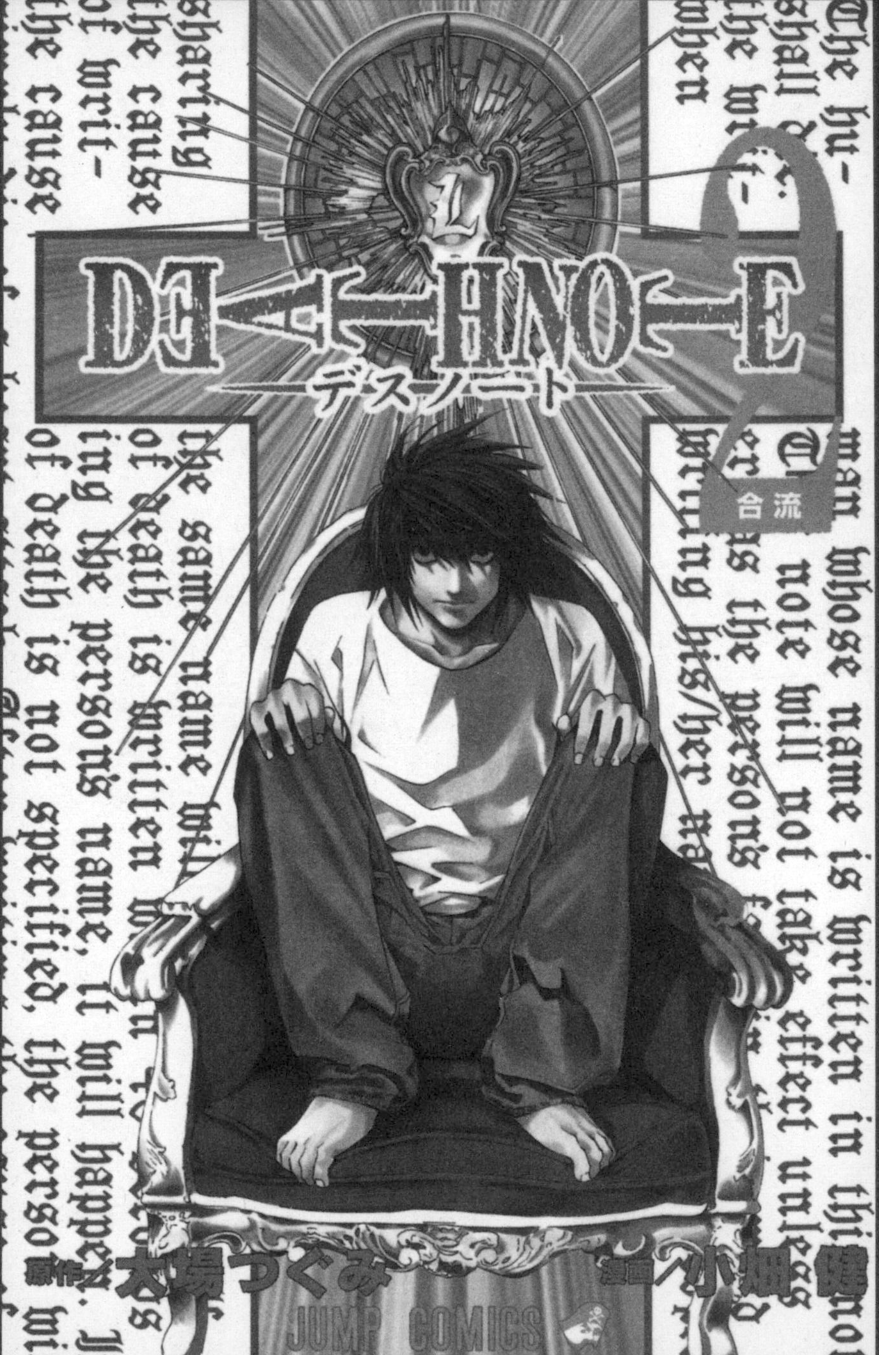
DEATH NOTE
デスノート
2
合流
原作/大場つぐみ
漫画/小畑健
JUMP COMICS

Original Japanese Cover Volume 2

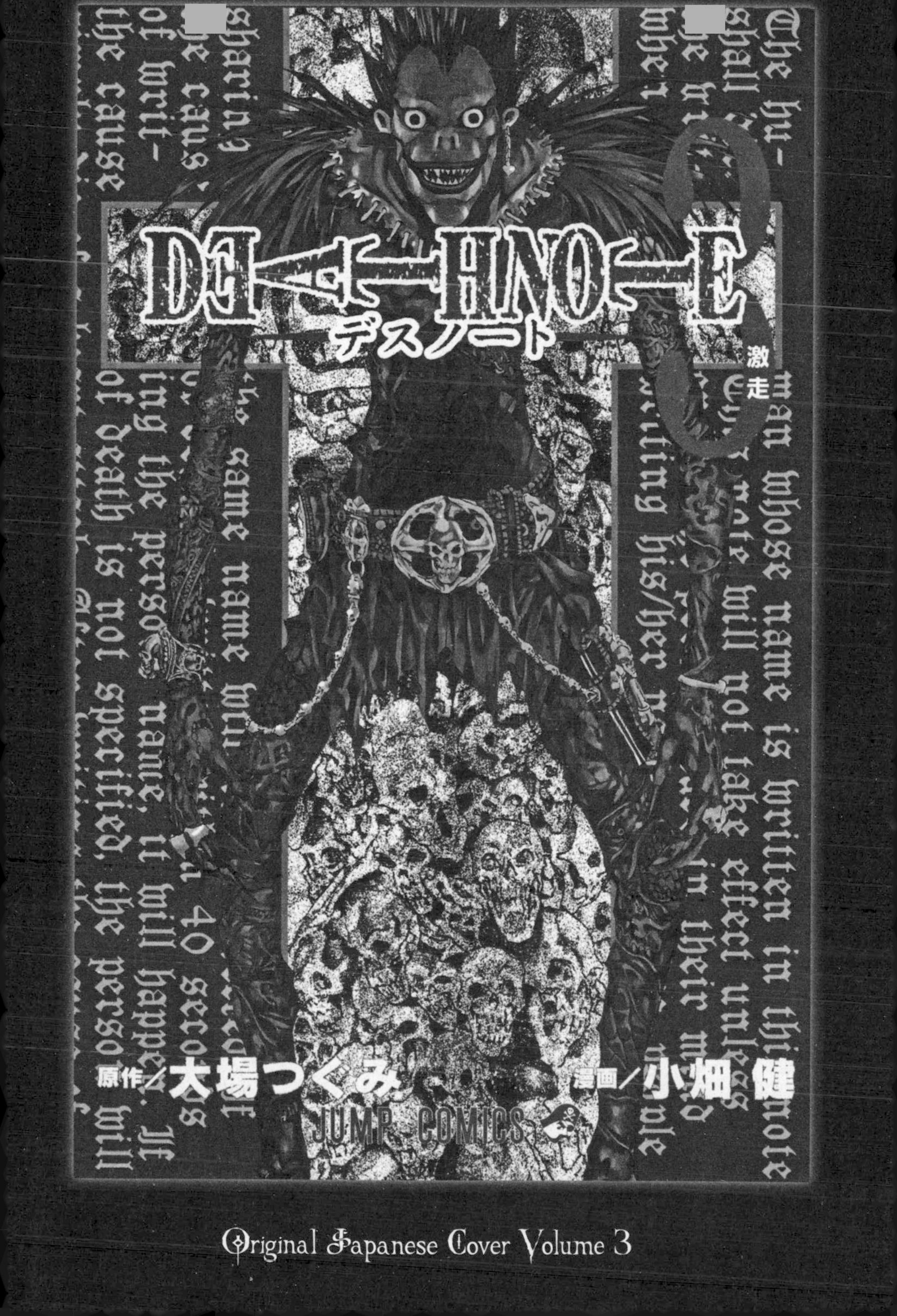
DEATH NOTE
デスノート
3
激走
原作／大場つぐみ
漫画／小畑 健
JUMP COMICS

Original Japanese Cover Volume 3

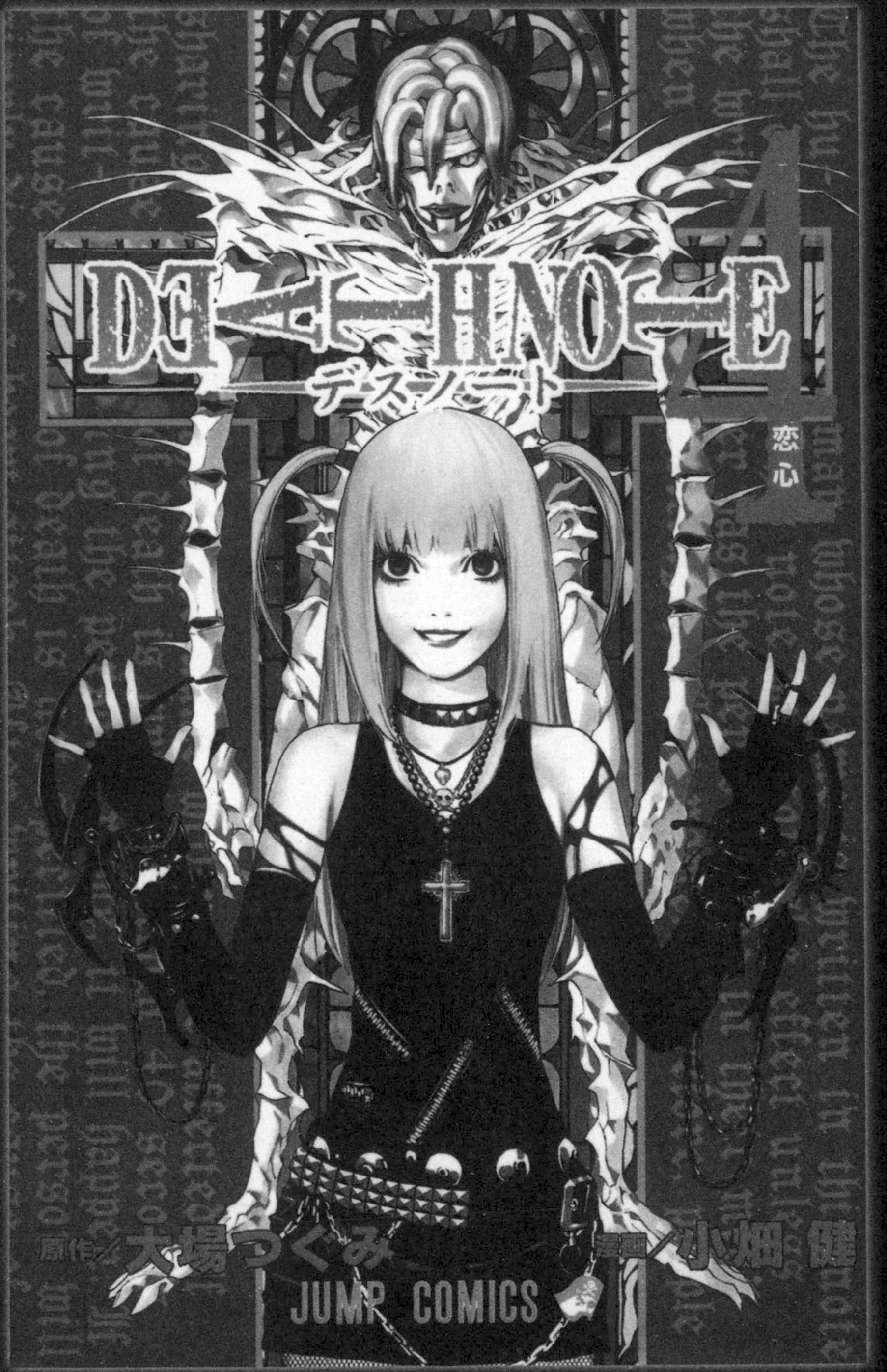
DEATH NOTE
デスノート
4
恋心
原作／大場つぐみ
漫画／小畑健
JUMP COMICS

Original Japanese Cover Volume 4